Ebla

In *Ebla*, Paolo Matthiae presents the results of 47 years of excavations at this fascinating site, providing a detailed account of Ebla's history and archaeology.

Ebla grew from a small Early Bronze Age settlement into an important trading and political centre, which endured until its final destruction in c. 1600 BC. The destruction of its royal palace c. 2300 BC was particularly significant as it preserved the city's rich archives, offering a wealth of information on its history, economy, religion, administration, and daily life. The discovery of Ebla is a pivotal moment in the history of archaeological investigations of the twentieth century, and this book is the result of all the excavation campaigns at Tell Mardikh-Ebla from 1964 until 2010, when field operations stopped due to the war in Syria.

Available for the first time in English, *Ebla* offers a complete account of one of the largest pre-classical urban centres by its discoverer, making it an essential resource for students of Ancient Near Eastern archaeology and history.

Paolo Matthiae is Emeritus Professor of Archaeology and Art History of the Ancient Near East at Sapienza University of Rome, and Fellow of the Accademia dei Lincei (Rome), the Académie des Inscriptions et Belles-Lettres (Paris), the Akademie der Wissenschaften (Vienna), the Royal Swedish Academy (Stockholm), and the Deutsches Archäologisches Institut (Berlin). From the beginning of excavations at Tell Mardikh in 1964 to the suspension of work in 2010, he was Director of the excavations at Ebla in northern Syria.

Cities of the Ancient World

Cities of the Ancient World examines the history, archaeology, and cultural significance of key cities from across the ancient world, spanning northern Europe, the Mediterranean, Africa, Asia, and the Near East. Each volume explores the life of a significant place, charting its developments from its earliest history, through the transformations it experienced under different cultures and rulers, through to its later periods. These texts offer academics, students, and the interested reader comprehensive and scholarly accounts of the life of each city.

Elis
Internal Politics and External Policy in Ancient Greece
Graeme Bourke

Aleppo
A History
Ross Burns

Palmyra
A History
Michael Sommer

Damascus
A History, 2nd edition
Ross Burns

A History of Siena
From its Origins to the Present Day
Mario Ascheri and Bradley Franco

Ebla
Archaeology and History
Paolo Matthiae

www.routledge.com/classicalstudies/series/CITYBIOS

Ebla
Archaeology and History

Paolo Matthiae

**Translated by Richard Bates,
Mattia Bilardello, and Anita Weston**

Routledge
Taylor & Francis Group

LONDON AND NEW YORK

First published 2021
by Routledge
2 Park Square, Milton Park, Abingdon, Oxon OX14 4RN

and by Routledge
52 Vanderbilt Avenue, New York, NY 10017

Routledge is an imprint of the Taylor & Francis Group, an informa business

British Library Cataloguing-in-Publication Data
A catalogue record for this book is available from the British Library

Library of Congress Cataloging-in-Publication Data
A catalog record has been requested for this book

ISBN: 978-1-138-85065-1 (hbk)
ISBN: 978-1-315-72460-7 (ebk)

Typeset in Times New Roman
by Newgen Publishing UK

Contents

Plates

Figures

Foreword

The great civilizations of the Ancient Orient which from Egypt to the Indus Valley preceded the Greek and Roman civilizations by some three millennia scattered myriad cities across a huge extension of the globe: the extraordinary phenomenon, urban, social, economic, and ideological, which since then, across all space and time, has been associated with the very idea of civilization, development, and progress. The more important urban centres produced by the great civilizations of the Ancient Orient frequently became the object of wondering admiration on the part of contemporaries and posterity, receiving both the proud appreciation of their inhabitants and the envious interest of foreign visitors.

The city as the centre of civilized living was conceived by the collective psyche as so prodigiously productive and positive that in ancient Mesopotamia it was commonly considered synonymous with civilization, and the individual historic cities were regarded as early creations of the gods believed to dwell there.

The god Enlil, head of the most ancient Sumerian pantheon, chose the location of his city, founded his celebrated sanctuary Ekur, and around it created the city of Nippur. Enki, the divine creator, had done the same at his residence in the city of Eridu. Later on, it was maintained that Babylon had been created by the god Marduk as both his divine seat and the privileged spot where, as a copy of the divine celestial palace of Esharra and the palace of the abysses of Apsu, all the gods assembled to define the destinies of mortals. The same gods, summoned by Marduk, had laboured with pikes and shovels to make bricks, and with their own hands, to the last gable-end, had created the supreme temple of Esagil.

In temples and various places in the Ancient Orient, particularly within the scope of diverse ideological perspectives, albeit rooted in a perception of a unitary world, historical cities were celebrated as places of supreme beauty. In the Ramesside Period in Egypt, Thebes (centuries later evoked, mythically, by the Homeric bards as the 'Thebes of the hundred gates', probably alluding to the innumerable monumental portals of its stunning sanctuaries) was celebrated as the unique, inimitable city where human happiness was fulfilled. Possibly in the same decades in which, in Ionia, similar echoes were reverberating of the wonders of the singular city of Amon on the Upper Nile, one of the proudest sovereigns of Assyria, Sennacherib, launching his vast programme of urban renewal at Nineveh, the chosen capital of the empire and beloved by Ishtar, and with a famous, very ancient temple at its heart, roundly proclaimed that the city was as beautiful 'as the stars in the heavenly firmament' and for centuries had been the place of urban wonders.

The immense city of Babylon was considered the centre of the universe, and almost certainly not only by the Babylonians themselves. Among its luxurious palaces and numerous temples, Nebuchadnezzar II had succeeded in completing the immense temple-tower, the Etemenanki, the near-fathomless dimensions of which had created the myth of infinite human pride, to be punished with a babel of tongues and the destruction of the tower itself. Alexander the Great had certainly not resisted its charm, and had ended his days in the palace of the great Babylonian king.

As to Jerusalem, the capital made famous, according to biblical tradition, by Solomon, the symbol of wisdom and knowledge for Hebrews, Christians, and Muslims, its ideological significance and architectural beauty earned it the Christian world's acclamation as 'the heavenly Jerusalem', inverting the oriental civilizations' paradigm of divine model and earthly replica, the city of eternal bliss granted to the just at the end of time.

Just as the construction of the city, then, was generally considered in the imaginary of the ancients as the work of the gods, since such splendid structures could only be miracles outside historical time, in the same way, the destruction of the city, as an irrefutable sign of the divine annihilating will, generated both shocked incredulity and infinite anguish. Those who had experienced similar destruction enacted it in literary works of considerable note, the so-termed "Lamentations", describing the terrible wrath of the gods at the sins of humanity, their abandonment of the guilty cities, and the devastation of all urban structures, as if by natural catastrophe, condemned to become a heap of nameless ruins, inhabited by wild animals. Celebrated examples are the intricate and touching "Lamentations" in Sumerian at the destruction of Ur and the cities of Sumer at the hands of the Elamites shortly before 2000 BC, reflecting the Mesopotamians' appalled dismay at the unimaginable events which must have been perceived as a total and irreversible crisis of civilization.

No such works are known in the vast and varied literature of the different languages of the ancient civilizations of the Ancient Orient, from Egypt and Mesopotamia to Syria and Iran. In three whole millennia, Ebla, the "City of the Throne", seat of a sovereign defined as "Star of Ebla", seems to be the only city to have received this singular honour. Its destruction forms the epic material of a long Hittite-Hurrian bilingual poem of which unfortunately only fragments are extant, discovered in 1986 at Hattusa, the capital of the Hittite empire. Composed of some ten cantos, the few extant lines of which are significant for our understanding of Hurrian language, the poem is strikingly defined as the "Chant of Release" by the actual colophons of the tablets corresponding to the single cantos, and must in all probability have been produced in the sixteenth century BC in an educated circle of eastern Hurrians settled along the upper course of the Tigris. It must have been translated into Hittite shortly afterwards, in the course of the fifteenth century BC, possibly in Hattusa itself, when the Hittites were ruled by the ambitious Tudkhaliya I, whose expeditions in Upper Syria were intended to rival the legendary feats, achieved within a very few years around 1600 BC, of the great Mursili I, conqueror of Aleppo and Babylon.

The question inevitably arises as to what induced a Hurrian poet, possibly from the still unknown holy city of Kumme, to dedicate a whole epic to the conquest of the city of Ebla, possibly by a Hurrian prince, Pizikarra, then reigning over ancient Nineveh in the heart of Assyria; or what may have urged a Hittite sovereign, a few decades on, to have the whole poem translated into the Hittite tongue, solicitously conserving the original and the translation in the library of a secondary sanctuary of the Hittite capital Hattusa until it was finally abandoned soon after 1200 BC.

We can ask ourselves whether this Hittite translation of a Hurrian epic may have caused the poem to be circulated, albeit only orally, possibly with other works of the same kind, and not only in Central Anatolia but in Asia Minor too, with the result that narrative themes, modes of exposition, stylistic expressions, and even topical episodes in these Hurrian epics became familiar among the bards of Iron Age Ionia from where Homer emerged; or whether the Hittite translation can feasibly have caused peculiarly similar themes in the history of the conquest of Ebla in the "Chant of Release" and in the legend of the siege of Troy in *The Iliad* to be transferred from an ancient Bronze Age epic of the Ancient Orient to the Iron Age founder-poem of the Western World, where gods and heroes share epic deeds, the cause of war is the sacrilegious detaining of a prince or princess in the besieged city, the gods take sides in human matters, and the advice of heroes and princes privileges orators who are 'strong in word'.

If the historical causes of the composing and writing of the "Chant of Release" on the conquest and destruction of the "City of the Throne" can plausibly be reconstructed, providing a feasible picture from which there seems to emerge, beyond all doubt, both the glory and fame of the great Syrian city and, simultaneously, its sins and sacrilege, then the extraordinary analogies between the Hurrian-Hittite epic and *The Iliad* remain among the more fascinating and evocative themes in the complex (and more intense than generally suspected) relations between the Ancient East and the archaic classical world.

What is certain is the devastating impression made on its contemporaries by the destruction of Ebla, "City of the Throne" and seat of enormous royal prestige, by a mighty and inflexible deity, for all their having witnessed the assault and conquest of cities like Aleppo and Babylon, of no less power and glory.

The city's archaeological rebirth, the subject of the present work, goes some way towards explaining its fame. At the same time, it invites reflection on its extraordinary destiny and the equally extraordinary account recorded in the "Chant of Release" by those who witnessed its disappearance from the horizon of history.

If for the ancients, appalled spectators of the eclipse as endorsed in a poetic genre whose thematic and stylistic paradigms would resurface to describe the assault and destruction of Troy, Ebla must have appeared as a prestigious centre of culture and primary political power, for the moderns, Ebla has fundamental value not simply for the reconstruction of a remote and irrevocably lost past, but also for the recovery of the far-off but no less significant roots of present-day Syria.

In fact, on the one hand, already in very ancient times, Ebla – just as Syria did subsequently in the Middle Ages and still does in modern times – represented a bridge and a means of connectivity and mediation among the most distant lands of the Orient known at that time, up to the Indus Valley, and the greatest Mediterranean civilization in the West, that is Pharaonic Egypt. On the other hand, in the second half of the third millennium BC, Ebla should have been the proof of a definitive triumph of the human race over natural asperities and diversities for those communities committed to consolidating urbanism – which flourished, at that time, only in the alluvial plains of the Nile and the Euphrates and Tigris – as a model working in every ecological situation.

In the years between 2500 and 2300 BC, for the communities of the Fertile Crescent, between Mesopotamia, Syria, and Palestine, as well as for us nowadays, Ebla was the paradigmatic example that the urban template was flexible and adaptable to the most varied and differentiated environments and that – for centuries and millennia – it would have continuously triumphed over natural harsh conditions as well as human conflicts.

Preface to the English edition

The discovery of Ebla, in upper inner Syria, covered 47 uninterrupted campaigns – between 1964 and 2010 – by the Archaeological Expedition of the Sapienza University of Rome and was only stopped by the political crisis in Syria, which led to the block on field activities. This work deeply changed our historical knowledge about the most ancient civilizations of the Ancient Near East.

Ebla, located 55 km south of Aleppo, is by far the best-known urban centre of the "Second Urbanization" of the Ancient Near East; this phenomenon took place in the central centuries of the third millennium BC and was fundamental for the history of humankind on a planetary scale. The "Second Urbanization" took place in Upper Syria and Upper Mesopotamia a few centuries after the "First Urbanization" of Lower Mesopotamia, which had taken place by the mid-fourth millennium BC. Its success led to the final accomplishment of the urban model even outside the alluvial plains of the big rivers, where the "First Urbanization" had its initial success, with the most ancient towns in Lower Mesopotamia and the most ancient territorial state of human history in the Nile Valley.

The Early Syrian Ebla of the twenty-fourth century BC – with its Royal Palace G and the famous State Archives with thousands of cuneiform texts – was the centre of a great urban culture, which was totally unknown before the Italian excavations. It was characterized by economic, social, and ideological foundations profoundly different from those of Lower Mesopotamia; it had direct relations at the highest political level with the lands of Sumer and Akkad of the Early Dynastic Period to the east and with the Egypt of the Old Kingdom to the west, and indirect relations reaching as far as distant Afghanistan.

The Old Syrian Ebla of the first half of the second millennium BC – with its palaces, temples, fortifications, quarters of private houses, its material and artistic culture – is at the origin of all the successive developments of the Middle and Neo-Syrian Periods until the eighth century BC, when the whole Syrian region was stably encompassed in the Neo-Assyrian empire and the urban structures of the region finally collapsed. The rich archaeological evidence of Old Syrian Ebla showed strong aspects of originality and continuity with the historical development of Syria in the Bronze Age; originality and continuity which were for a long time denied by modern historiography.

The author is profoundly grateful to the Cultural Authorities of the Syrian Arab Republic for their generous cooperation, and for the permanent support provided during the long years of successful excavations, which made the relationship between the Directorate General of Antiquities and Museums of Damascus and the Sapienza University of Rome an exemplary case of cooperation. The author is also extremely grateful to his colleagues Frances Pinnock and Marta D'Andrea for their fundamental and deeply appreciated help provided in the redaction of the English version of the volume.

Publishers' acknowledgements

All images are © MAIS Sapienza University of Rome, with the exception of figures 1.1–4, 1.6, 1.14, 2.1, 2.2, 3.6, 4.14, 4.15, 4.17, 8.1, 8.2, 9.2, 9.4, 10.31, 11.16, and 11.19.

1 From Tell Mardikh to Ebla
Archaeological exploration

The German excavations at Assur, begun in 1903, had inaugurated the great period of historical archaeology in the whole tormented but thrilling process of the rediscovery of the lost ancient civilizations of the Ancient Orient. Objectives and perspectives of expeditions, however, began progressively to change from those of the pioneering, fundamentally Bible-oriented archaeology of the late nineteenth century. Until then the main interest of European institutions, predominantly museums, when promoting excavations in the Near East had been to provide the great museums of Paris and London (and later of Berlin) with archaeological and epigraphic material of artistic, historical, and patrimonial importance, from the splendid Assyrian reliefs to the tablets of libraries and cuneiform archives. With the systematic approach applied to the exploration of Assur (Figure 1.1) (like that of R. Koldewey in Babylon, begun in 1899, though this presented more complex technicalities), the aims of field work became more intrinsically concerned with research and less obviously with acquiring objects.

The elements which predominantly characterized the new phase in Near Eastern archaeology, coinciding with the start of the twentieth century, comprised the desire for exhaustive knowledge of the monuments, architecture, and urban design of ancient centres, moving beyond the horizontal dimension of excavations to the deeper levels of settlements, below those of the more important, better known, and better conserved period; a heightened sensitivity towards the fundamental contexts, architectonic if not yet stratigraphic, and an unprecedented attention to the practical procedures of excavations as regards preliminary approach, observation, interpretation, and recording of finds, particularly architectural drawings.

In the interval between the First and Second World Wars, the considerable influence of the excavations of Babylon and Assur in the modern history of Near Eastern archaeology (from Mesopotamia and Anatolia to Palestine, Iran, and Syria) produced two results of particular consequence in the gradual reconstruction of the great pre-classical civilizations of the Ancient Orient, as regards both methods and results.

In the cases of Mesopotamia and Palestine, though less so in those of Anatolia and Syria, and still less as regarded Iran, the results represented

Figure 1.1 Assur, aerial view of Qal'at Shergat, with the monuments of the great Middle Assyrian centre, and the trenches of W. Andrae's excavations.

Source: By kind permission of German Expeditions at Assur.

one of historical archaeology's prime goals: the construction on an essentially taxonomic basis of a chronology of the various expressions of material culture, from architecture to ceramics, from works in bronze and coroplastic art to glyptics, through three millennia of history from the Late Chalcolithic and Proto-Urban phases of the mid- fourth millennium to the conquest of Alexander the Great in the second half of the fourth century BC.

On the other hand, the growing need to regulate the empirical aspects of excavations on the basis of explicitly stated principles and practices led to the rigorous formulation of a method for stratigraphic archaeology on the part of Sir Mortimer Wheeler and Dame Kathleen Kenyon. Based on a so-called "geological" rather than architectonic foundation, it focused on the terrain itself, the archaeological deposit on which hinged a whole inter-related system, as the vital basis for correct excavation conduct and interpretation.

This remarkably productive period in historical archaeology was also marked by a singular event for Syria, projected onto the international stage (and not simply onto specialist awareness) as a result of the discoveries of two important French missions led by Claude F.A. Schaeffer and André Parrot respectively. These began at Ugarit (Figure 1.2), on the north coast of the Levant, in 1929, and at Mari (Figure 1.3), on the middle section of the middle

Figure 1.2 Ugarit, aerial view of Ras Shamrah, with Minet el-Beydah port in the background, the Royal Palace to the left and the Acropolis to the right.

Source: By kind permission by the French Expedition at Ugarit (Ras Shamra).

Figure 1.3 Mari, aerial view of Tell Hariri, with the region of Zimri-Lim's Royal
Palace and of the Pre-Sargonic Palace in the centre.

Source: By kind permission of French Expedition at Mari (Tell Hariri).

course of the Euphrates, not far from the present-day border between Syria
and Iraq, in 1933. At the same time, conviction grew of the need for a more
sophisticated chronological classification of the material cultures. This resulted
from the substantial progress made in the same period in Mesopotamia and
Palestine since two excavations in the 1930s, most successful in data collection
on the succession of cultures – the Danish expedition to Hamah, directed by
Harald Ingholt, with the assistance of Paul J. Riis, and the United States excavation on the plain of the 'Amuq, directed by C. McEwan, with the active collaboration of a very young Robert J. Braidwood – had been unable to report
back to the scientific community with sufficient speed and documentation.

In consequence, the image of Syria to emerge from field work in the inter-
war period was primarily based on the effects of the discoveries of Ugarit
and Mari. The wealth of archaeological documentation on Ugarit (mainly
limited to the thirteenth century BC) endorsed the hypothesis that Syria was
to be considered essentially a military and commercial meeting-point (albeit
a fruitful one) for the great civilizations of Egypt, the Aegean, Mesopotamia,
and Anatolia. The equally astonishing wealth of finds from Mari – epigraphic, architectonic, and artistic – almost inevitably enforced the interpretation of the great urban centre, definitively destroyed in the early eighteenth
century BC by Hammurabi of Babylon, as the most western of the cities of

Mesopotamia, and while open to external influence, fundamentally rooted in the great Sumerian-Akkadian tradition of Babylonia.

Despite the discoveries of Neo-Syrian monumental art from the early centuries of the first millennium BC (frequently mis-defined as Neo-Hittite or Syro-Hittite) on the part principally of Felix von Luschan, Leonard C. Woolley, and Max von Oppenheim in the ancient centres of Samal, Karkemish, and Guzana, and, in the 1930s, the findings of the French in Ugarit and Mari, the art and architecture of the Syrian Bronze Age seemed to deserve Ernest Renan's (in)famous, vivid, and caustic definition of Iron Age Phoenician culture after his disappointing exploration of the great Phoenician centres in 1860: the only originality of that culture was its total lack of originality.

An invitation to revisit this summary but seemingly inevitable judgment came with the 1955 publication of findings from the 1936 and 1949 excavations of ancient Alalakh on the plain of Antioch at Tell Atshanah by one of the greatest archaeologists of the twentieth century, Sir Leonard Woolley, also responsible for the previous, sensational discovery of Ur in Sumer. Following the new historical lines of Ancient Near Eastern archaeology, he worked systematically, both in terms of horizontal exposure, gathering as much data as possible on the most significant settlements from Middle Bronze II in the eighteenth and seventeenth centuries BC and Late Bronze I, particularly in the fifteenth century BC, and on the vertical, his in-depth excavation bringing to light a notable succession of important temple constructions from at least the period running from the nineteenth to the thirteenth century BC. For the first time in the archaeological exploration of Syria, it was thus possible to recover relevant documentation, principally of the architecture and glyptics, ranging, with reasonable certainty, from the central phases of Middle Bronze to the end of the Late Bronze Period, from what was defined as the "forgotten kingdom" of Alalakh, a vassal princedom of Aleppo at the peak of its splendour. While serious chronological errors had invalidated the dating attributed by the excavator to the deeper levels of Alalakh XVIII–VIII, Woolley's dating of the more recent levels, particularly Alalakh VII, were basically sound, and today are placed between c. 1725 and 1600 BC, with Alalakh IV dated between approximately 1500 and 1400 BC.

However, even before verifying the definitive results of the excavations, the importance of the Alalakh findings for a critical revision of long-rooted negative historiographic judgments on Syria was quickly apparent to Henri Frankfort, the great Dutch archaeologist who in the 1920s had already with great acumen perceived the enormous potential for a more systematic archaeological exploration of the Syrian area aimed in particular at a number of crucial historical problems. His years of teaching in Chicago, on the other hand, lay behind his wish to lead his memorable excavations in central Mesopotamia, in the area flanking the River Diyalah.

It was Frankfort, shortly before his untimely death in 1954, who recognized that the palaces of Alalakh VII and IV constituted the evidence for a hitherto unsuspected continuity in Syria's architectonic tradition for at least a millennium, from 1750 or shortly afterwards to the years around 720 BC, when the majority of Syria's Aramaic principalities succumbed to Assyria, which reduced them to imperial provinces. Shortly afterwards U. Moortgat-Correns, E. Strommenger, E. Porada, and H.J. Kantor, in diverse ways and accents, called attention to the great originality and high standard of the court glyptics from the engravers' workshops which for the first time were defined as Old Syrian, after which I worked to identify, define, and demonstrate the originality of all artistic productions of Middle Bronze I–II Syria and their substantial continuity throughout Late Bronze I–II down to the upheavals giving rise to the Iron Age in the early decades of the twelfth century BC.

It was, then, this scenario of new and unexpected historical issues inaugurated by Woolley's findings at Alalakh, the vassal kingdom of the great Yamkhad kings, centre-stage protagonists of the history of Syria and beyond in the years of Shamshi-Addu I of Assyria and of Hammurabi of Babylon, which prompted two fascinating research paths within the framework of a developed stage of historical archaeology.

This would, on the one hand, allow a critical reconsideration based on a long-overdue acknowledgement of continuity and originality in the cultural, religious, and artistic traditions of Syria in the second and first millennia BC down to the Hellenistic era; and on the other, would strengthen attempts to locate the most ancient historical roots of the Old Syrian culture in the third millennium BC through systematic and targeted excavations to verify the breadth and depth of this newly discovered originality in the Old Syrian world; lastly, it would substantiate the elements and characteristics of a continuity which in different and more complex forms than those of the Mesopotamian world seemed also to have penetrated the Middle Syrian phases of the Late Bronze Period and the Neo-Syrian phase of the Iron Age.

Much of this fervour of critical thought and new perspectives, typical of the 1960s, lies behind the Sapienza University of Rome approach to the systematic excavations at Tell Mardikh, in Inner Syria, west of the Euphrates and some distance south of Aleppo, opposite one of the passes through the compact mountain chain which extends the Lebanese mountains to the north and opens the route to the Mediterranean. Strategically located at the beginning of this Mediterranean road which led to ancient Ugarit, Tell Mardikh constituted an exceptionally important centre, not least on account of its geographical location, being comparable to Aleppo, to the north, with respect to the valley of Antioch; to Qatna, to the south, with respect to Tripoli and the Plain of Akkar on the Mediterranean coast; and to Damascus, further south, with respect to the ports of Beruta, present-day Beirut, and the very ancient town of Byblos (Figure 1.4).

Like Aleppo, a city of unrivalled continuity and for more than four millennia a fundamental point along the various commercial routes, the ancient city hidden below the hill of Tell Mardikh (Figure 1.5) must have benefited from its position midway between the broad course of the Euphrates and the narrow coastal plain of the Mediterranean on the east–west route;

Figure 1.4 Byblos, aerial view of Gebeyl, with the Phoenician ports, and the Crusaders' Castle.

Source: Public Domain.

Figure 1.5 Ebla, view of Tell Mardikh from the north, with the Acropolis emerging to
the left, behind the ramparts of the Old Syrian fortification.

and equally from its central position on the fertile plateau of central-inland
Syria termed Bilad ash-Sham by the Arabs, between the Oasis of Damascus
to the south and the passes of the Taurus providing access to Anatolia in the
north on the south–north route.

The name of Ebla disappeared from ancient sources around 1200 BC,
at the end of the Bronze Age, to re-emerge in the late nineteenth century,
after some 30 centuries of oblivion, when sporadic mentions were detected
in important cuneiform texts; these were early second millennium BC copies
of original inscriptions from the powerful Semitic Akkadian dynasty from
somewhere between the late twenty-fourth and twenty-third centuries, when
these powerful sovereigns, in agreement with the clergy of the most venerated
temples of Sumer, imposed their rule in southern Mesopotamia. In one of
the most ancient of these triumphal inscriptions, the dynasty's founder, the
great Sargon of Akkad (c. 2340–2284 BC), states that on one or possibly
more expeditions to the West he had sacrificed to the god Dagan as lord of
the region in the most important sanctuary of Tuttul on the Euphrates; had
subjugated the cities of Mari, Yarmuti, and Ebla, and had reached the Forest
of Cedars and the Mountain of Silver, possibly the Amanus and Taurus
respectively. Some decades later, the nephew and third successor to Sargon,
Naram-Sin of Akkad (c. 2259–2222 BC), similarly lauds a further extensive
undertaking in the Upper Country, the regions of the Upper Euphrates and
Upper Syria:

Never since the founding of humankind has king among kings ever taken Armanum and Ebla ... Nergal opened the way for Naram-Sin the powerful, and gave him Armanum and Ebla: he then offered the Amanus, the Mount of Cedars, and the Greater Sea. Due to the weapon of Dagan, exalting his kingship, Naram-Sin the powerful did conquer Armanum and Ebla and from the banks of the Euphrates to Ulisum, did smite the peoples whom Dagan delivered to his hand, and these carried the basket of Aba, his god, and held within his dominions the Amanus and the Mount of Cedars.

The above, very ancient data, with a few more which seemed to indicate Ebla's proximity to Urshu, a town in Upper Syria seemingly located by an important Hittite text on Hattusili I's expeditions in Syria between Alalakh, in the Antioch region, and the Hittite capital Hattusa in Central Anatolia, all caused Ebla for many years to be sought in the extensive territory to the west, north, or east of Aleppo. According to early proposals, then (by P. Jensen, J. Lewy, S. Langdon, S. Smith, and B. Maisler), the city conquered by Sargon should be in the region of the Amanus Mountains or on the plateau of Antioch, while others opted for an area further north, near Mardin (B. Landsberger and E. Dhorme) or the region between Birecik and Gaziantep (M. Falkner); there were, however, those (E. Unger and W.F. Albright) who located it on the Balikh or the confluence of the Balikh and the Euphrates, and identified it with present-day Tell Bi'a, in actual fact the ancient Tuttul (Figure 1.6).

Figure 1.6 Tuttul, aerial view of Tell Bi'a, with the mediaeval city of Raqqah and the Euphrates in the background.

Source: By kind permission of German Expedition at Tuttul (Tell Bi'a).

What all scholars had omitted to perceive in the relatively few references to the city in the ancient sources was the importance of the association between Ebla and Aleppo, attested both in ritual Hurrite textual fragments found in Hattusa and in the long Theban list of Asian cities conquered by Thutmose III, engraved on one of the pylons of the great Temple of Amon in Karnak, ancient Thebes.

Thus when, in 1964, the Sapienza University of Rome's archaeological mission started excavating at Tell Mardikh, just under 60 km south of Aleppo, few would have predicted that the almost 60 hectares of settlement would turn out to be precisely the great Syrian city triumphantly taken by Sargon and Naram-Sin of Akkad, politically and commercially linked with Gudea of Lagash and Shulgi, Amar-Suen, and Shu-Sin of Ur, which in all probability had been besieged and finally conquered by the Hittite armies of Hattusili I and Mursili I, and over whose ruins the victorious army of Thutmose III of Egypt was to march decades later (Figure 1.7).

Although one of the most extensive pre-classical settlements in Syria, Tell Mardikh (Figure 1.8) had almost completely escaped the notice of twentieth-century scholars. W.F. Albright, on one of his journeys from Jerusalem to Iraq, had passed very close to it in the late 1920s; H. Ingholt had visited it while directing the excavations at Hamah in the 1930s, but had failed to

Figure 1.7 Karnak, Amon-Ra's Temple, detail of the cartouche with the name of Ebla in Egyptian hieroglyphs, among Thutmose III's conquests on the seventh pylon, 15th century BC.

Figure 1.8 Ebla, aerial view of Tell Mardikh from the north-west, with the Old Syrian ramparts.

mention it; A. Moortgat and B. Hrouda, on the other hand, had been there in the late 1950s and had marked it on a map of the major archaeological centres in Syria.

The present writer first went there in July 1962 after seeing in the Aleppo Museum the remains of a basalt basin engraved on three sides (Figure 1.9), accidentally found on the tell a few years previously, salvaged by the Syrian archaeologists and erroneously catalogued as of the early first millennium BC. The realization of its actually being circa 1,000 years older considerably increased its interest, making a visit to its place of discovery more than apposite. The following year Rome University (as it was then called) was invited by the Directorate General of Antiquities and Museums of Damascus to begin excavating the site, making a second visit necessary both to obtain further information and to complete the official procedures regarding the permit to excavate.

Three fundamental elements determined Rome University's choice of Tell Mardikh as a base for what it hoped would be a systematic archaeological exploration: the site's size and the particular morphological configuration of its 56 hectares, and the clearly-marked topography in the circle of the ramparts, in the large ring-shaped Lower Town and in the central Acropolis; the prevalent presence over the whole tell of ceramic fragments mainly dating from between the beginning of Early Bronze IVA (c. 2400 BC) and late Middle

Figure 1.9 The carved double basin discovered in the Lower City of Tell Mardikh, before the beginning of the Italian excavations; main face, 19th century BC.

Bronze II (c. 1600 BC), with later material only on the Acropolis, where there should have been only recent strata of any consistency; and the important find of what then was the only carved basin, datable to around 1900 BC, attesting unquestionably to royal commissions of some note, executed by workshops of extremely high standards.

The present-day morphology of the Tell Mardikh site is representative of the large fortified urban settlements of the Bronze Age. While not particularly common in inland Syria, they are well known in Upper Mesopotamia, and certainly usual in historical sites that over the years have not been subject to major stratifications profoundly altering the urban conformation of the last great ancient city. This is the typology of a settlement with an approximately central Acropolis marked by a hill, small but higher than the rest of the tell, a large ring-shaped Lower Town completely surrounding the Acropolis, and a well-defined and sharply-raised peripheral ridge which almost continuously separates the ancient city from the surrounding countryside.

This characteristic and very evident three-part division of the present-day shape of the hill concealing the ancient ruins obviously depends on the conformation of the urban space in part realized in previous settlements, but above all in the last great centre. The three topographical areas still clearly visible correspond, from the inside outwards, in the great city of the classical Old Syrian Period finally destroyed in the years around 1600 BC, to the fortified Citadel of the great royal public buildings; the Lower Town comprising the majority of the other public buildings, secular and religious, with the areas of private houses; and the massive Ramparts which would have surrounded the whole urban centre. The three-part division, as mentioned above, is well-known in a series of urban centres of the Bronze Age in Upper Mesopotamia, the so-termed "Kranzhügeln" ("crown-shaped hills") gener- ally covering non-secondary settlements of the second half of the third mil- lennium BC in north-east Syria; it is also familiar in inland Syria in minor but important sites from the second half of the same period such as Al-Rawda and Tell Sheyrat. In western Syria, on the other hand, even taking into account urban centres contemporary to Ebla in the first half of the second millennium BC, the morphology is quadrangular and less pronounced on the site of the ancient Citadel, as in the cases of the great tell of Mishrifeh, over ancient Qatna, near Homs. And while the "Kranzhügeln" of Upper Mesopotamia are circular and very regular, Tell Mardikh has a singular ellipsoidal conform- ation with a number of slight depressions peculiar to this site which must have been the deliberate result of careful planning.

When the Italian Archaeological Mission in Syria began excavating at Tell Mardikh (Figure 1.10), the first year's soundings were carried out through circumscribed trenches on the west side of the Acropolis (Area D), in two adjacent areas of the Lower Town South-West (Areas B and C), and on the slope of the more pronounced of the passages to the south-west which opened onto the high embankments encircling the centre and in which there was probably a city gate (Area A).

From these initial soundings there began to emerge, from the second cam- paign onwards, a number of important monuments of the great city from the early second millennium BC: the Temple of Ishtar (Area D) on the Citadel, the Temple of Rashap (Area B) in the Lower Town South-West, and the Damascus Gate (Area A). The very regular pace of the excavations of the first decade, up to 1973, identified and brought to light, sometimes only partially, a number of other important buildings from the same Old Syrian Period, between 2000 and 1600 BC: the Temple of Shapash/Shamash (Area N) in the Lower Town North; the Sanctuary of the Royal Deified Ancestors (Sector B South), and above all, albeit in a very small part, the Royal Palace E (Area E) and the East-South-East Fortress (Area N) on the eastern walls.

The second decade of excavations began with the identification, in 1974, of the Royal Palace G (Area G) from the mature Early Syrian Period (between 2400 and 2300 BC) on the south-west slopes of the Acropolis, and were par- ticularly marked by the great discovery in 1975 (completed in 1976) of the celebrated Royal Archives. In the same decade, while different sectors of the extensive complex of the Royal Palace G were being explored, from the Administrative Quarter to the Southern Quarter, and to the South and West Units of the Central Complex, the systematic exploration began of the great public buildings of the successive classical Old Syrian Ebla in the Lower Town West, including the locating and excavating of the extensive Western Palace (Area Q) and three important but partially looted tombs in the Royal Necropolis beneath.

In the third decade of systematic exploration, since 1984, a circumscribed sector of Building G2 (Sector G South) was excavated, on the southern slopes

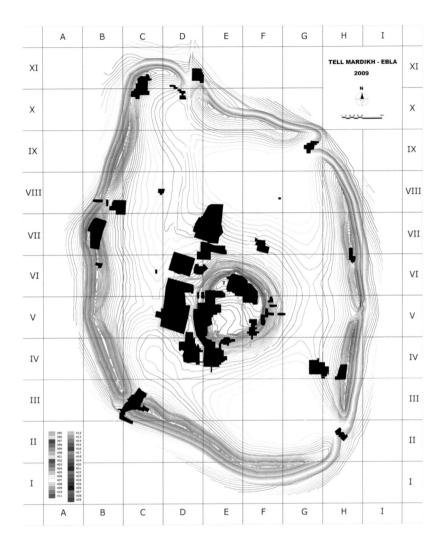

Figure 1.10 Tell Mardikh, topographic plan with the areas excavated up to 2009.

of the Acropolis. This decade also yielded the majority of the important Old Syrian monuments of the Lower Town: the Northern Palace (Sector P North: Figure 1.11), the Sacred Area of Ishtar and Temple P2 (Sector P Centre), the Cult Terrace of the Lions (Sector P South), and the Archaic Palace (Sector P North), predecessor of the Northern Palace, while the location of at least one royal tomb from the great period of the Archives was found, totally ransacked, on the Acropolis (Sector G West).

Excavations in the fourth decade concentrated particularly on the ramparts of the archaic and classical Old Syrian city, investigating the Western and

Figure 1.11 Ebla, ruins of the Northern Palace of the Old Syrian period, with the Acropolis in the background, from the north, 18th–17th century BC.

Northern Forts (Areas V and AA respectively: Figure 1.12), the Euphrates and the Aleppo Gates (Areas BB and DD respectively), and outlying residential areas (Area Z), some of them close to the Citadel (Sector B East). Further research on the Lower Town, in the fifth decade of excavations, produced a series of important extensions to the excavating of Royal Palace G, the discovery of the Southern Palace (Area FF: Figure 1.13), the salvaging of an entire quarter of very well-preserved private houses (Sector B East) from the classical Old Syrian Period and, above all, from 2004 onwards, the locating of the great Temple of the Rock (mature Early Syrian, Area HH) in the South-East Lower Town, with the first well-preserved remains of the late Early Syrian city of the last centuries of the third millennium BC. Renewed excavations on the Acropolis, which characterize the second half of the fifth decade of the archaeological investigations at the site, have led to a noteworthy result: that is, the discovery of the Red Temple (Area D) in the western sector of the central mound.

The systematic exploration of Tell Mardikh, which began in 1964, had by 1968, with the discovery of the basalt torso of the statue of Ibbit-Lim, king of Ebla, sanctioned the identification of the site with ancient Ebla. Shortly afterwards, in 1975, the discovery of the Royal Archives revealed a mass of data on the most ancient history not only of Ebla but of a large swathe of Syria. These early years, then, produced a clear time-line for Ebla throughout almost a millennium of history, from the mid-third to the mid-second millennium BC. After the still obscure centuries producing the first urban settlements in Mesopotamia, to which that of the virtually unknown Mardikh

Figure 1.12 Ebla, ruins of the Western Fort of the Old Syrian Period, on the top of the rampart of the fortifications, from the south, 18th–17th century BC.

Figure 1.13 Ebla, general view of the Southern Palace of the Old Syrian Period, from the north-east, 18th–17th century BC.

I, of the Protohistoric Period (c. 3500–3000 BC) belongs, the real urban development of Ebla must date to the Early Dynastic Period I–III of Mesopotamia, during the centuries of the Old Kingdom of Egypt, in the still obscure phase of Mardikh IIA (c. 2900–2400 BC), corresponding to the archaic Early Syrian Period (Early Bronze I–III).

The first great flourishing of Ebla came about during Mardikh IIB1, the age of the Royal Archives (c. 2400–2300 BC), the mature Early Syrian Period (Early Bronze IVA), corresponding to the last decades of the Early Dynastic IIIB Period and to the early years of the Akkad Dynasty in southern Mesopotamia, when Egypt was ruled by the first pharaohs of the VI Dynasty of the Old Kingdom. After the massive destruction of the first Ebla, very probably at the hands of the great Sargon of Akkad (Figure 1.14), the birth of the second city, of Mardikh IIB2 (c. 2300–2000 BC), in the late Early Syrian Period (Early Bronze IVB) took place in the years in which Mesopotamia was governed by the Akkad Dynasty, the II Dynasty of Lagash, and the Ur III Dynasty and when Egypt was the scene of severe social unrest in the First

Figure 1.14 Detail of the Stele of Sargon of Akkad, with the king's figure, from Susa, 24th century BC.

Source: By kind permission of the Louvre Museum.

Intermediate Period; this ended with the ascent of the XI Theban Dynasty, founder of the Middle Kingdom.

The second Ebla was equally violently destroyed, possibly some time before the end of the late Early Syrian Period, while the restored settlement of the third great Ebla of Mardikh IIIA (c. 2000–1800 BC), in the archaic Old Syrian Period (Middle Bronze I) retained its importance through the successive classical Old Syrian Period (Middle Bronze II) of Mardikh IIIB (c. 1800–1600 BC), throughout the four centuries dominated in Mesopotamia by the Dynasties of Isin, Larsa, and Babylon, and in Egypt by the glorious XII Dynasty of the Middle Kingdom and the decadent dynasties which followed, which were finally conquered by the Asiatic Hyksos.

The destruction of the third Ebla towards 1600 BC marked the end of the last great city. This was followed by the modest rural settlements of Mardikh IVA and IVB (c. 1600–1200 BC) in the Middle Syrian Period (Late Bronze I and II), through the centuries of conflicts and power balances among the empires of Mittani, of Egypt of Dynasties XVIII and XIX of the New Kingdom, of the Hittites of the imperial age, and of the Assyrians of the great Middle Assyrian monarchy.

When the Bronze Age ended the memory of Ebla was probably lost. The small village of Mardikh VA-C (1200–535 BC) remained, in a considerably circumscribed area of the previous great urban settlement, during the centuries of the Neo-Syrian Period I–III in the Iron Age, through which Luwian and Aramaic Syrian princes almost uninterruptedly – but vainly – attempted to contrast first the expansionism of the Assyrian Empire and then later, for a few decades, that of Babylon. The two last settlements, that of Mardikh VIA–B (c. 535–55 BC) in the Persian-Hellenistic Period, which oversaw a rural rebirth, and that of Mardikh VIIA–B (c. 55 BC–600 AD) in the Roman-Byzantine Era, when a minor monastic community of stylites settled in the constantly ransacked ruins, end the long history of the decadence of the immense expanse of ruins of one of the most glorious cities of the Ancient Orient.

For a few weeks only, in late 1098 AD, it provided shelter to the detachments of one of the two great expeditionary forces of the First Crusade, led by Godefroy de Bouillon, on the road to Jerusalem.

2 Ebla and early urbanization in Syria

In the somewhat complex urbanization process of western Asia taking place soon after the middle of the fourth millennium BC – when the conditions for its first basic developments were being determined in Lower Mesopotamia and Elam on the one hand, and, in parallel, in the Nile Valley on the other – in the highly diversified scenario, not least in terms of ecological conditions, of the extensive area between the coasts of the Levant and the Valley of the Indus subject to the phenomenon, the urban models that eventually emerged vary considerably in form and in time sequence, according, of course, to the specific environmental and historic conditions of the different regions. If the debate remains animated as to the most significant stimuli behind the urbanization process, together with the probability that very different stimuli contributed to its implementation, in a complex whole in which primary and secondary motivations can easily be interchanged by modern theories and criticism, there is, however, no doubt that the places where urbanization and the formation of the State were first completely and lastingly realized are those of the great alluvial valleys of Egypt and Greater Mesopotamia, where conditions allowed for floodwater irrigation, though probably with water basins and not yet with extensive canal systems.

This soon assumed the nature of intensive agriculture, characterized by an abundance of produce allowing for the surplus to be gradually administered by specially constituted privileged classes; the redistribution of this surplus through different processes; specialized trade practices, and the gradual division of society into classes. Cultural elements of particular intellectual significance would have developed in this profound revolution of the means of production and the organization of society: the invention of writing on a symbolic level, monumental architecture and artistic expression at the level of urban planning, and the general shape of the city.

These are the elements to emerge forcefully in the centres of so-termed "primary urbanization" in Lower Mesopotamia during the period of early "State formation". The clearest case in point is Uruk, rightly defined as the first city in history on account of its extraordinary importance and the fundamental role it played in the shaping of the first urban civilization (Figure 2.1). Here, during the long centuries of the Late Uruk Period (between 3400 and 3000 BC)

Figure 2.1 Uruk, ruins of the White Temple in the region of Anu's Ziqqurat,
    Protohistorical Period, 32nd–31st century BC.

Source: Public Domain.

and the phases of Uruk V and IV, the splendid structures of an extraordinary
monumental centre were raised and renewed, with imposing buildings, almost
certainly public, in the so-called area of the Eanna inside a vast urban settlement which most probably covered some 250 hectares. No stratigraphically
reliable finds exist regarding the oldest written documents found at Uruk, but
the numerous celebrated economics texts from the city, the oldest examples of
human script, in all likelihood belong to this period. However, to the various
phases of Uruk IV in particular, continued in part in Uruk III (defined in the
stratigraphic succession of Uruk as the Jemdet Nasr Period, from the name
of a northern settlement in Babylonia) belong numerous specimens of the artistic and material culture of Lower Mesopotamia to which, with the founding
of the first cities in history, we owe the creation of a complex economic-social
system which precisely on account of its structure needed to extend its limits
beyond Lower Mesopotamia, where it had originated.

Indeed, during Middle Uruk (between c. 3600 and c. 3400 BC), then more
extensively during Late Uruk, up to around 3000 BC, all the representative
elements of the Uruk culture were already established in a number of new
settlements: certainly those on the middle course of the Euphrates, from
Habubah Kebirah/Kannas to Jebel Aruda and Tell Sheykh Hassan; and
according to some scholars, also on the Middle Tigris, with characteristics

possibly comparable to Nineveh. These have actually been defined as colonies of Uruk in Upper Mesopotamia, characterized by the presence of exclusively southern cultural elements, while in a series of other centres slightly further to the north, the elements of Uruk culture mix with local cultures generally defined as Late Chalcolithic III (corresponding to the Middle Uruk Period) and IV (corresponding to Late Uruk). The reasons leading Uruk settlers to the area of Lake Assad on the upper course of the Middle Euphrates are still under debate, although a number of hypotheses have been advanced; namely, that they were outposts created to protect the storage of raw materials essential to Uruk culture – for example, certain types of wood and metal, from copper to silver and perhaps tin, though this specific area of the Euphrates was not particularly close to the areas providing such materials; that they were settlements organized to control long-distance commercial routes towards the Mediterranean, given that in this area the westward routes leading to the ports of Ugarit in the north and Byblos to the south, whence the Delta could quickly be reached (and where recently, in Buto, evidence both of North Syrian Protohistoric ceramics and characteristically Uruk-like clay cones have been found) no longer followed the course of the river; or that they were places where defectors or refugees from Uruk, ejected from their homeland for social revolt connected with the relatively over-rapid urbanization, had transferred the mother culture, dawning institutions, and in general all the elements of urban civilization recently established at Uruk and in Sumer.

To the main question as to whether the Uruk colonies on the Euphrates were behind the urbanization in the northern regions, from east to west, in Upper Mesopotamia and in inland and coastal Syria, configuring a direct derivation of North Mesopotamian and North Syrian urbanization from the primary example of Protohistoric Lower Mesopotamia, it is seemingly possible to reply in the negative for at least two significant reasons. On the one hand, Uruk's colonial settlements were abandoned and disappeared suddenly and inexplicably, in a relatively advanced phase of Late Uruk, leaving no direct heirs; on the other hand, neither in Upper Mesopotamia nor in Upper Syria, even at the end of the Late Uruk phase or immediately afterwards, was there any manifestation of widespread urbanization with features of the recent, relatively intense presence of Uruk settlers even in a limited area of the Middle Euphrates.

This consideration apart, there were certainly highly complex social structures in settlements of generally modest dimensions prefiguring actual urban formations in the phases of the Late Chalcolithic Period (II–III). Some of these, in the first half of the fourth millennium BC, preceded the intrusive presence in the south of the colonies of Middle and Late Uruk. As yet sporadic, they stretched over an extensive geographical area from the eastern Taurus in Arslantepe and the piedmont Taurus in Hacinebi through to the upper basin of the Khabur to Tell Brak and Tell Hamukar in Upper Mesopotamia, the Iraqi Jezirah on the Upper Tigris, to Tell Hawa and Tepe Gawra. Although the topographical data for such a remote epoch are as yet

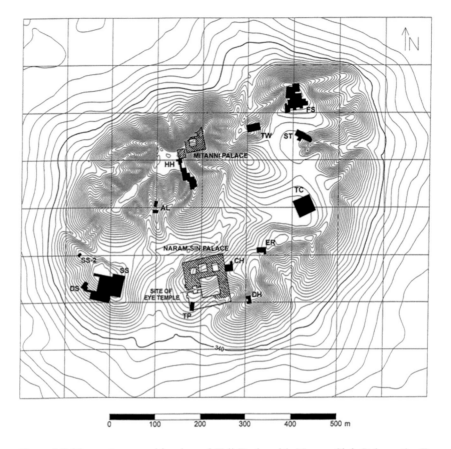

Figure 2.2 Nagar, topographic plan of Tell Brak, with Naram-Sin's Palace, the Eye
        Temple, and the Temple and Palace of the Mittanian Period.
Source: Courtesy of Augusta McMahon.

insufficiently reliable, estimates given for Tell Brak (Figure 2.2), called Nagar
in the last half of the third millennium BC, suggest an area of at least 45
hectares, which could have reached some 100 hectares of urban development,
while Hamukar is thought to have plausibly been just over 100 hectares and
Hawa slightly less than half of this.

    On the other hand, within what is sometimes called the Late Local
Chalcolithic (to indicate developments which differ regionally from the Taurus
to the Jezirah, but in origins and formation are not connected with Sumer)
rare examples of monumental architecture are found which would seem to
have developed independently of the culture of Uruk. One such example is
the celebrated Eye Temple in Tell Brak, the characteristic tripartite structure
of the final phase of which was undoubtedly inspired by the famous public

buildings of Uruk, traditionally regarded as temples but today for the most part considered as multi-purpose (including religious) public assembly halls. However, considering both that various planimetric elements of the Eye Temple, such as the cruciform central body and the tripartite division of part of a lateral wing, seem to be taken from a local tradition and, above all, that the three more obscure previous phases, called the White, Grey, and Red Eye Temples, present decidedly local features such as the numerous limestone figurines of the so-called "eye idols", it seems very probable that the famous temple had grown from a local cultural environment, parallel to but independent of the development of ancient Uruk, to which only later, after the middle of the fourth millennium BC, would elements have been added deriving from the southern influence of colonies on the Euphrates and possibly the Tigris.

What is certain is that, outside the large centres which may have had significant political, economic, and commercial relations with the Uruk colonies and the centres of Protohistorical Sumer, both in the Upper Khabur region, in minor centres like Leylan, Kashkashuk, Kuran, and Nustell, and in the Middle Khabur region, in Bderi, Umm Qseyr, Ziyadeh, and other such settlements, materials from the south are found datable to Middle and Late Uruk, thereby simply marking a frequency of contact.

The situation is the same in western Syria, although materials from the Uruk culture are considerably more scarce, while the development of local cultures is both more continuous and more homogeneous. These are attested by the numerous items of "Chaff-Faced Simple Ware", so-called on account of the amount of straw on its surface, of the 'Amuq F phase, parallel with Late Chalcolithic IV and V. Interestingly, a number of the well-known "Bevelled-Rim Bowls", the very simple and rather crude oblique-sided goblets generally found in large quantities on Uruk sites, and almost certainly connected with some wide-spread mechanism of food production or distribution, were found precisely in this period, in some cases outside their natural context, both in the 'Amuq sites on the north coast, in Ebla itself, and in Hamah; that is, in inland Northern and Central Syria. However, while at Hamah, as in the 'Amuq plain, levels of the second half of the fourth millennium BC have been excavated, whence these pots probably came, at Ebla, no sector of Tell Mardikh has been excavated to such a depth and antiquity. Despite this, the presence, however rare, of these very specific pots in areas used to produce the bricks of Royal Palace G, from the second half of the third millennium BC, demonstrates beyond all doubt, on the one hand, that some settlement, provisionally named Mardikh I, was active at least in the Late Chalcolithic IV–V; and on the other, that it shared at least some of the characteristics of the centres of western Syrian local culture with contacts with the Middle and Late Uruk Sumerian world.

The occasional presence of these Urukite bowls in the 'Amuq, at Hamah, and at Ebla is all the more indicative in that there has been no trace of them in surveys in either the Sajur basin, at Lake Jabbul, at the river Quweyq, or in the rest of the 'Amuq plain, or on the Mediterranean coast. In addition, their anomalous presence in Ebla should be considered along with the sporadic fragments of the local "Chaff-Faced Ware" and the discovery of a number of seals of a relatively common type, with the usual double-sloped reverse and image of a goat-like figure, a human figure holding up non-identifiable objects on each side, and an arachnid with four legs and double claws: elements which confirm beyond all possible doubt that some settlement of local culture from at least Late Chalcolithic IV but possibly even III (towards the mid-fourth millennium BC) was present on the Ebla site, and that in the phase of Mardikh I or a little later this entered into contact with the Uruk areas of the Middle Euphrates which, while not unusual, was far from frequent in Syria in the regions to the west of the great river.

The situation outlined above clearly demonstrates that, on the one hand, the first phase of urbanization in Uruk, with elements of its culture, extended far north along the Euphrates certainly and the Tigris possibly; and on the other, that phenomena of increasing social complexity and of administrative centralization developed in Upper Mesopotamia, from Hamukar to Hawa and Brak, at least in a number of centres still relatively unknown to us and which, while possessing nothing of the culture of Uruk, but conversely having a marked local character, seemed however to have constituted to all effects urban phenomena of the type which developed in the country of Sumer.

The Uruk colonies disappeared from the Middle Euphrates area, possibly in the years immediately preceding 3000 BC, during the last century of the fourth millennium BC. During the first centuries of the third millennium, in Lower Mesopotamia, in different areas to the south of Baghdad, urban culture was becoming stabilized, gradually extending in the Early Dynastic Period through complex and varied phases of urban development and the occupation of territories, and following different lines of continuity; in Upper Mesopotamia, on the other hand, as in western inland Syria, the local pressure towards increasing social complexity neither intensified nor spread. Thus, while in Sumer, the centre of Uruk rapidly expanded to an impressive 400 hectares (and more, in some opinions) – despite having putatively entered a period of crisis at the end of the Uruk Period (that of Jemdet Nasr, when the centres of Habubah Kebirah and Gebel Aruda were already abandoned) – and the city walls traditionally attributed to Gilgamesh were erected, in the extensive northern areas, where relations with Sumer and Akkad seemed to have continued uninterruptedly, processes of acute regionalization were soon under way, producing firmly structured and increasingly characterized regional identities.

However, if isolated and certainly rare centres such as Tell Hamukar to the east and Tell Brak in central Upper Mesopotamia were evolving forms of (as yet undocumented) autonomous urban settlements in the ancient phases of the archaic Early Syrian Period, approximately corresponding to the Early Dynastic I and II Periods of southern Mesopotamia, when Babylonia was developing autonomous urban centres which gradually took control of relatively extensive regions, producing both wars and hegemonies given the widely-spread competition among the various centres, the process of urbanization in the northern areas certainly seems not to have seen homogeneous, extensive, and decisive developments.

This only occurred at the end of the phase of strong regionalization in Early Bronze I–II, during Early Bronze III, in parallel or with temporal mismatches which were probably more apparent than real, both in Upper Mesopotamia and in Upper Syria. There is indeed no doubt whatsoever that a number of centres in the eastern regions all took on the structure of large urban centres in the period from shortly before 2600 to 2400 BC: Urkish, present-day Tell Mozan; Shekhna, on the site of Tell Leylan; Nagar, in the Tell Brak which had already undergone previous important developments; Tell Khuera, to the west of the Balikh, and, further west, Tell Sweyhat, which some consider to be the Burman mentioned in the Ebla Archives; Tell Banat/Tell Bazi, possibly equivalent to the Armi of the Ebla texts and the Armanum of Naram-Sin; and Tuttul, present-day Tell Bi'a on the Euphrates, near mediaeval Raqqa.

It was very likely only at this point, or certainly not much before 2600 BC, that Ebla too developed into a proto-urban settlement, which, however, cannot have much exceeded 10 hectares. Tradition attributes a long period of development to the city of Ebla, local memory recording a lengthy succession of royal predecessors of the historical names listed in the Archives; not only their names have been handed down but their place of burial – principally Binash and Taribu, two minor sites close to Ebla corresponding almost certainly to present-day Benash and Atareb, where at the time of the Archives ceremonies were held as cult worship of the deified royal ancestors.

Although still rare, given the superimposition of the very extensive monumental Early and Old Syrian cities, consistent evidence exists of the urban settlement of Ebla's Early Bronze III Period, corresponding to the Mardikh IIA phase and probably datable to 2600–2500 BC. This came to light on the southern slopes of the Acropolis, in sections of structures immediately beneath peripheral sectors of the Royal Palace G of the great city of the Royal Archives. Although relatively circumscribed, the 15 or so rooms of Building G2 (Figure 2.3) are extremely significant, excavated for some 30 m from west to east and to a width of no more than 10 m on the south–north axis in the South Sector of Area G. The ruins probably belong to a peripheral area of an old Early Syrian royal complex which possibly extended over a not inconsiderable part of the southern side of the Acropolis: in fact, this area includes several minor rooms, slightly over 4 m in length, but also wide rectangular rooms, 9 x 4 m in size, and apparently is a mud brick unit, including three rows of rooms. In support of this, remains were found of a number of rectangular spaces around a courtyard which would seem to be granaries, implying that this was the food storage area of the Sector G South complex 20 or so metres to the east, in the Area CC, again on the slopes of the Acropolis but to the south-east, at exactly the same height (Figure 2.4).

If this hypothesis holds, then the ruins could be decentralized areas of a complex the palatine nature of which is attested by both its extension and its topographic position; both buildings seem to penetrate north towards the

Figure 2.3 Ebla, Area G South, ruins of Building G2 of the archaic Early Syrian Period, on the south slope of the Acropolis, from the east, 26th–25th century BC.

Figure 2.4 Ebla, Area CC, storage rooms for cereals, probably belonging to Building G2, from the north-west, 26th–25th century BC.

centre of the Acropolis hill in a good state of conservation. To the east the ruins seem to have been abandoned after a bad fire. The pottery of Building G2 is characterized by a modest percentage of the typical Red-Black Burnished Ware, a variant of the famous Khirbet Kerak Ware of the Palestinian area, albeit probably of Caucasian provenance, and by well-attested correspondence with the phases of 'Amuq H and Hamah K in forms which, on the one hand, produce relatively frequent exemplars of characteristic hemispherical bowls with decorated rims, and on the other, announce the chalice-shaped typologies of Early Bronze IVA.

Within the context of the astonishing developments to emerge from the site between the end of Early Bronze III and Early Bronze IVA, this as yet tentative evidence of Early Bronze III architecture from Ebla undoubtedly indicates increasing social complexity, the beginning of a highly hierarchical organization, centrally stored agricultural surplus, and probably marked economic differentials. While the evidence is hardly abundant even as regards landscape archaeology, some of the data to be inferred from surveys in the basins of the minor rivers in the area to the west of the Euphrates provide evaluative elements which seem significantly to endorse the findings beginning to emerge from the excavations of Tell Mardikh in what might be defined as the pre-palatial phases.

In fact, in the basins of the Orontes to the west, the Quweyq in the centre, and the Sajur, as well as in Lake Jabbul in the east, there was an extremely high increase in settlements during Early Bronze I–III, in some cases tripling in number; while between Early Bronze III and Early Bronze IVA there is no evidence of further increases, settlement numbers remaining stable, while a small but significant number increase in extension. The two phenomena are easily explained. First, Early Bronze I–II saw a multiplication of villages with continuously increasing control over and agricultural and pastoral exploitation of territory which far exceeded earlier patterns, no doubt on account of increased demographics. Later, between Early Bronze III and Early Bronze IVA, throughout Upper Syria, again due to demographics (though not exclusively so), there emerged a greater population concentration in a number of privileged settlements, during a time-span of a few decades, which quickly assumed not only the size of cities but the characteristics as well: considerable social complexity, a centralized administrative hierarchy, and growing economic differentials, all belonging to advanced proto-urban phenomena.

The real question concerns why – when the ascertained and consolidated presence of the Uruk colonies failed to develop urban phenomena from the local culture of the Late Chalcolithic, both in Upper Mesopotamia and in Upper Syria, in the last centuries of the fourth millennium BC – secondary urbanization did however come about some time later, when the colonies had been gone for some centuries and the model of primary urbanization was no longer physically present, as it were, in the regions of new urbanization.

The answer is not easy, but two points are clear enough. On the one hand, in the early phases of Early Bronze (I–II), territorial control of agricultural and pastoral activities in the northern areas was still too fragmentary and discontinuous for the southern Mesopotamian model to be adopted, although this could be considered as having already been resolved during Early Bronze III. On the other hand, contacts with Lower Mesopotamia in this last phase and in Early Bronze IVA were so close and closely documented, input from Sumerian-Akkadian culture so substantial, beginning with writing, and economic integration with Sumer and Akkad so clear and consolidated that the secondary urbanization of Upper Mesopotamia and Upper Syria must have been structurally functional to the now well-established primary urbanization of Lower Mesopotamia.

Various hypotheses have been advanced as to the precise historical reasons for the flourishing of secondary urbanization in Upper Mesopotamia and Upper Syria between 2600 and 2400 BC: autonomous development of local societies devoid of either political or economic connections with the southern Mesopotamian world; northern societies' participation in the very intense and lucrative inter-regional trade, or aggressive reactions, even open war, on the part of north Mesopotamian and north Syrian societies. In actual fact, it is certain that the considerable developments in secondary urbanization necessarily had their basis in the local agricultural and pastoral economy, everywhere substantial enough to perform territorial controls over a relatively large area, which implied integrated sheep and goats, and cattle breeding. It is equally certain, however, that two factors must have entered into the equation here both continuously and sporadically: on the one hand, international trade, both occasional and in terms of constant supplies to southern cities of the goods and fundamental raw materials available in the northern regions; and on the other, military campaigns organized by the southern cities in all likelihood as much to guarantee these supplies as to acquire land for themselves.

All this implies that the establishing of secondary urbanization in Upper Mesopotamia and Upper Syria was probably the product of a number of concomitant reasons rather than one alone. Current theses, it has to be added, consider that whatever reason – local development, international commerce, or inter-regional wars – was behind the extensive northern development, the northern elite groups would have emulated the southern Mesopotamian models in order to legitimate, reinforce, and magnify their own power, although it seems more feasible that, without wishing to minimize substantial structural differences between southern and northern societies and systems of production, much more than simple emulation was involved in the consideration of the now acclaimed state organization of Sumer and Akkad. It is a fact that government administration methods and procedures practised in the mature Early Syrian Ebla of Mardikh IIB1, at the time of the Royal Archives, were clearly derived from those invented and experimented on some decades previously in the Kish area.

The very significant second urbanization which began after 2700 and ended before 2400 BC was basically a substantially unitary process regarding the northern regions of Mesopotamia and Syria south of the Taurus, from the Tigris to the Mediterranean which, at the same time, had undergone different phases and rates of development in the single regions. It was certainly not, however, either a completely separate and independent phenomenon or directly and univocally deriving from the more ancient, initial urbanization of Lower Mesopotamia. The establishing of the new social, economic, ideological, architectural, and territorial system in the cities of Sumer and Akkad at the end of the fourth millennium BC must have set in motion a series of secondary processes, initially slow in transforming the economic and social systems of the geographical areas with which the first southern cities established occasional contact or lasting relations, given both the material needs of the new states and political structures and the probably extensive awareness of the new urban structures which must have spread rapidly in vast surrounding regions of the Ancient Orient.

Even in regions such as Upper Mesopotamia and Upper Syria, the development possibilities of which were not determined within the terms of the intensive agriculture of the alluvial valley of Lower Mesopotamia, the population increase allowed the cultivation of extensive territories while the potential for the integration of agriculture and animal herding was increasingly evident, and awareness grew of the exceptional opportunities offered by control over sought-after raw materials such as wood, stone, and metals. Once these basic preconditions had been implemented at a local level, contacts and relations with southern Mesopotamia, which would have increased significantly through trade and of course wars, certainly induced a number of elite groups in Upper Mesopotamia and Upper Syria to take the initiative to transfer essential skills to these northern regions. These would have encompassed above all administration and urban planning, but also advanced material technologies, allowing urbanization to take lasting root in Sumer and to spread almost immediately to the nearby country of Akkad.

In the context outlined above it is likely that incipient proto-urban forms began to develop, of considerable social complexity, hierarchically organized and economically differentiated, to which the remains from the southern slopes of the Acropolis belong. This may already have happened during Early Bronze III, in the central and late phases of Mardikh IIA, certainly before 2500 BC, during the more recent reigns of the numerous predecessors of the great sovereigns of the age of the Royal Archives, still vividly remembered in mature Early Syrian Ebla. It was only in the last reigns before the three documented in such detail in the Archives (possibly between 2450 and 2350 BC) that the organizational foundations were laid for the splendid mature Early Syrian Ebla of Mardikh IIB1.

3 Ebla, Mari, Akkad
From city-states to empire

In its far from brief history, traceable for the best part of a millennium despite long periods of silence in the written sources, Ebla underwent three serious phases of destruction across the centuries, marking its development, changes, and traditions. The first one we know of with certainty is that which, towards 2300 BC, ended the glorious mature Early Syrian Period, at the end of Early Bronze IVA (Mardikh IIB1), corresponding to the great early Ebla of the age of the Royal Archives. The second occurred in the last decades of the Mardikh IIB2 settlement, ending the still relatively obscure late Early Syrian Period; that is, around 2000 BC, during the transition from Early Bronze IVB to Middle Bronze I. The third was the city's final destruction, after which Mardikh IIIB's settlement was abandoned, never again to be an urban centre. This took place in the reduced span of years towards 1600 BC, at the end of the new and last great flourishing of the classical Old Syrian Period, at the end of Middle Bronze II.

The first great Ebla of the Royal Archives age would seem to have been achieved in a relatively short period. The result was a city of almost 60 hectares by around 2400 BC, along the lines of other great urban centres in Upper Mesopotamia: Shekhna, present-day Tell Leylan; Nagar, now Tell Brak; and Urkish, modern Tell Mozan. In all these important sites urban development was swift and sudden, around or shortly before the middle of the third millennium BC. The Ebla of the Archives period was in all likelihood developed over a large area in a few years, and although it is obviously impossible to identify the author of the city walls whose pattern was followed by the planners of the third Ebla at the beginning of the second millennium BC, it is not to be excluded that it was one of the immediate predecessors of Igrish-Khalab, the most ancient of the sovereigns documented in the Archives – Ishar-Malik, Kun-Damu, and Adub-Damu. No evidence exists pointing to one rather than another.

Certainly, the long tradition of Ebla monarchs – 23 before Igrish-Khalab, their memories so alive in the city that several were named in the fundamental ritual of the renewal of kingship – would imply a more gradual process of urbanization. There is no doubt, however, that the cult of sovereigns buried in the mausoleums of the small town of Binash, possibly the birthplace of the Ebla royal family, in no way excludes the profound, possibly gradual, but relatively short metamorphosis, shortly before early Mardikh IIB1, of its social and economic structures which was to lead to a conspicuous settlement expansion, a highly-centralized administration, and more extensive (and expanding) territorial control.

The reigns of the three Ebla sovereigns whose documents were kept in the Royal Archives, Igrish-Khalab, Irkab-Damu, and Ishar-Damu, were respectively of over 5 years, approximately under 10, and over 30 (perhaps 36): a total of some 50 years. Written documents of all these years were present in the Administrative Quarter at the time of destruction. According to city government praxis the king was assisted by a high-ranking dignitary (his post hereditary like that of the monarch) whose exact title is not known – possibly "Superintendent of the Saza", probably the general designation of the palace's central administration – but who was certainly some sort of palace prefect or grand vizier.

At the time of Igrish-Khalab, the function may have been accomplished by more than one eminent figure, while during the reign of Irkab-Damu, Arrulum officiated exclusively. For a very short period, between the death of Irkab-Damu and Arrulum to the coronation of the last sovereign, Ishar-Damu, the vizierate was held for almost 18 years by Ibrium, a figure of great prestige (Figure 3.1). He was succeeded by his son Ibbi-Zikir, another energetic figure who continued to serve under Ishar-Damu, holding the position

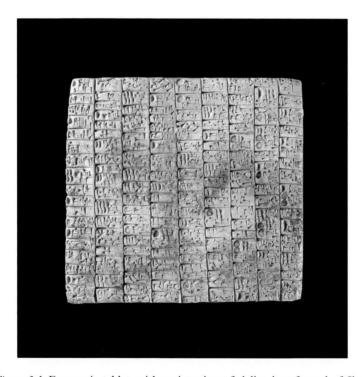

Figure 3.1 Economic tablet, with registration of deliveries of wool of Ibrium's time (TM.75.G.1319), clay, from the Archive L.2769, 24th century BC.

for several years – certainly more than 15. In the last years before the city's destruction he designated his son Dubukhu-Adda to succeed him. The son, in his turn, would have served under the heir to the throne Prince Irak-Damu, son of Ishar-Damu, who was certainly still reigning at the time of the appalling destruction which put an end, albeit temporarily, to the existence of the city and its political power.

If the city's name of Ebla was beyond doubt, the expression *Ebla wa Saza*, "Ebla and Saza", is slightly opaque. It appears frequently in the Archives and designates, physically and institutionally, the state structure of the city and the local government exercised there. However, although a convincing interpretation is difficult in that, despite the numerous extant documents (in which, however, protocol formulae of the chancery never appear), no indication of royal ideology is ever given, it is perhaps safe to say that this striking hendiadys linking the names of the city and palace and their physical reality is enacting a significant semantic shift connected if not determined by the city's new political relevance.

It is indeed probable that the place-name Ebla gradually assumed a wider topographical and geographical application, indicating not only the main city but also the territory it ruled or administered in different forms and ways, just as it is equally feasible that Saza, a Sumerian term which in Lower Mesopotamia probably indicated the seat of government, both concretely and figuratively, became the term to designate the government of the new Ebla state, striking to its contemporaries in the perhaps revolutionary centralized nature of its structure.

The fact that the name of the city was used by its chancery in this way may explain the use of the place-name Ebla for the whole region in the Mesopotamian world, decades and centuries later, by the chanceries of Naram-Sin of Akkad and Gudea of Lagash. Here it seems to apply to the region once dominated by Ebla in the Archives age, rather than the city of Ebla itself.

While the Ebla texts offer no light, of course, on the political history of the years preceding the three sovereigns known from the Archives, an important letter from Enna-Dagan (Figure 3.2), a king of Mari, to an anonymous king of Ebla, very feasibly Igrish-Khalab, lists a number of important conquests by his predecessors in the northern and western regions; this was clearly to intimidate the Ebla king, whose expansionist ambitions had probably begun to be noticed. Enna-Dagan states that it was Anubu of Mari who first looked northwards, then his two successors Saumu and Ishtup-Ishar conquered Raak, in the same region, plus Emar on the Euphrates on the site of the mediaeval Meskene.

The height of Mari's military expansionism was under Iblul-Il, also known from votive inscriptions in temples from the metropolis of the Middle Euphrates, who seems to have conquered the entire northern Khabur area before advancing as far as Khashshuwan, probably in the hilly region at the foot of the Amanus range. It was probably in consequence of various Mari monarchs' exploits northwards and westwards that Ebla seems to have paid a

Figure 3.2 Tablet with the letter of Enna-Dagan of Mari to the king of Ebla (TM.75.G.2367), clay, from the Archive L.2769, 24th century BC.

not inconsiderable annual tribute to Mari (tens of kilos of silver and gold) possibly until as late as the central years of Irkab-Damu's reign, to avoid ending up in the expansionist sights of the great city on the Euphrates. Possibly as late as Irkab-Damu's reign, then, Enna-Dagan was flaunting his triumphs and claiming if not subjection, certainly cautious deference from Ebla.

Among the wars waged by Ebla (reconstructed on the basis of information provided by the economic texts of the Royal Archives, however frequent, sporadic, fragmentary, or indirect), one of the most ancient but also most significant must be that against Abarsal. This was a city of some importance, possibly to the east of the Euphrates, which had brokered an important treaty with Ebla whereby an unequivocal series of manipulative clauses put Ebla in a position of clear advantage (Plate VI).

The victorious campaign seems to have been conducted by Ibrium, when Arrulum was vizier, in the early years of Irkab-Damu's reign, and probably explains the origin of the gradual advance of the limit of the Ebla and Mari spheres of influence along the line of the Euphrates, in the Tuttul region south of Emar, near mediaeval Raqqa. It is, indeed, a fact that Abarsal was mentioned ever more infrequently in the Archives, as if of considerably less importance, and, more significantly, that in a series of cases, allied cities or vassal states of Ebla's sent their princes or prestigious representatives to Tuttul to swear fealty to Ebla, probably in the large sanctuary of the god Dagan, whose prestige was enormous throughout the Middle Euphrates Valley.

No doubt exists that at this point, in various but generally direct ways, Ebla ruled over important centres of the Euphrates such as Karkemish in the north and Emar in the south, extending its hegemony to the Balikh area east of the Euphrates, and south-east as far as Tuttul. To the south, in Central Syria, ancient Hamat (present-day Hamah) was certainly part of its direct dominions, which most probably extended further south, whereas it is difficult to say whether westwards they exceeded what was probably the natural limit formed by the barrier of Jebel Ansariyah, the northern extension of the Lebanon mountains, including the fertile plains of Ghab and possibly 'Amuq, crossed from south to north by the Orontes.

In the second half of Irkab-Damu's reign, some 40 years before the first great Ebla was destroyed, the greatest powers in Upper Syria and Upper Mesopotamia must have been Ebla in the Aleppo region, Nagar (present-day Tell Brak) in the Khabur region, and Mari on the middle course of the Euphrates. If, as seems proven, Ebla's dominions stretched as far as the Balikh and Tuttul, Nagar faced the city on its eastern confines, and Mari on its south-east. In both the northern and eastern regions, there were probably relatively important cities whose relations with Ebla varied. One such seems to have been the Armi of the Ebla Archives, possibly the Armanum of the royal inscriptions of Naram-Sin of Akkad, which must have been in the north. An intriguing suggestion proposes locating it on the place of the modern sites of Tell Banat and Tell Bazi, where a city of some 40 hectares existed from the mature Early Syrian Period, while the location of Haddu, a far from insignificant city apparently long contested by Ebla and Mari, remains a total enigma.

As documented by the Royal Archives, Ebla also held intense diplomatic relations with important urban centres at some distance, such as the enigmatic Khamazi, a city possibly north-east of Assyria, beyond the Tigris, which appears in the "Sumerian King List" as one of the cities which, despite its decentralized location, for a brief period achieved supremacy over Babylonia, and above all Kish, the metropolis of Akkad in northern Lower Mesopotamia. A copy of a letter in the Ebla Archives sent to Khamazi by a very high-ranking Ebla dignitary speaks in terms of fraternal friendship between the two cities, while numerous administrative documents mention not infrequent relations between Ebla and Kish at even higher levels, and visits exchanged between kings, queens, and princes.

Ebla's diplomatic relations were considerably more extensive, including countries at considerable distances, although in these cases the evidence is to be found not in the Archives but in archaeological finds in the ruins of the Royal Palace. The most surprising and, however, most solid are those with the Egypt of the great pharaohs of the Old Kingdom, documented in the numerous Egyptian stone bowls of royal provenance, two of which bear the inscription of two important sovereigns of the IV and VI Dynasty.

The lid of a cylindrical alabaster vessel with the hieroglyphic titles used in the first part of the reign of Pepy I (Plate V), the third pharaoh of the VI Dynasty, certainly bespeaks the exchange of gifts in Ishar-Damu's time, while the numerous fragments of a sophisticated four-spouted diorite lamp preserve in hieroglyphics two of the official names of the great Chefren, who built the second pyramid of Gizah (Figure 3.3). Pepy I's lid represents the oldest synchronism linking Egypt, Syria, and Mesopotamia, and attests that Sargon of Akkad, Ishar-Damu of Ebla, and Pepy I of Egypt were contemporaries. At the same time, it bears witness to the cordial relations between Memphis and Ebla shortly before the city was destroyed, while Chefren's lamp, extraordinary in being the first finding in Asia of an object belonging to the great pharaoh, exception made for Byblos alone, is equally astonishing given that he lived just under 200 years before the destruction of Ebla.

If it was Chefren himself who sent the lamp to Ebla, this would indicate beyond a shadow of a doubt, improbable as this is, that Ebla was already famous and powerful several decades before Igrish-Khalab. Yet there exist only two alternative, less audacious possibilities. Either the lamp was sent to Ebla by a successive pharaoh, possibly Pepy I, which is far from impossible (while remaining strange), or it came to Ebla as the result of the sacking of a third city where Chefren had originally sent it: in this case the sacked city could only

Figure 3.3 Pharaonic diorite lamp, bearing a hieroglyphic inscription with Chefren's name, from the Royal Palace G, 26th century BC.

have been Byblos, the one Asian city where conspicuous numbers of important Egyptian objects were found belonging to pharaohs of the Old Kingdom.

Further astonishing proof of Ebla's relation, direct or indirect, with extremely remote countries is the exceptional discovery of some 40 kilos of rough lapis lazuli in the Royal Palace. The beautiful, intensely blue stone was the most sought-after semi-precious stone in the Ancient East (and in Sumerian and Akkadian connoted purity and splendour), to the extent that the hair and beards of the gods were said to be made of it. It was found only in the mountains of Badakhshan in Afghanistan (and possibly in remote regions of eastern Iran), close to the country the Sumerians called Aratta, from which they claimed to procure the stone. It arrived in Mesopotamia from Aratta via one of two long caravan routes, negotiating the desolate wastes of the Iranian deserts and finally reaching Ebla either from the south, through centres of Lower Mesopotamia such as Ur, Kish, and then Mari, or from the north through cities like Khamazi, Nineveh, and Nagar. Ebla very probably had the royal monopoly of long-distance trade in lapis lazuli, routing it through ports like Byblos to the courts of the pharaohs of the Old Kingdom, where it was greatly appreciated. They also traded it for perfumes and essences conveyed in precisely the diorite and alabaster vessels found in such quantities so many centuries later in the rooms of the Royal Palace, but also (perhaps especially) for the abundant gold from Nubian mines at least partly controlled by the political power of Memphis.

After re-establishing some sort of balance between Mari and Ebla later in Irkab-Damu's reign (Figure 3.4), thereby apparently reversing the situation in Ebla's favour after the damage done by Iblul-Il of Mari's western exploits, from the start of Ishar-Damu's reign, Ibrium began to wage very successful wars in precisely the northern lands where Mari had held sway some time earlier. The wars were against Armi, and therefore Khalsum: Armi, against which Ibrium fought with his son Bigama (who then disappears from the documents) was defeated but never fell, while Khalsum was defeated and victoriously taken by Ibrium and Ibbi-Zikir, thereafter associated with the vizierate. Ebla's interest in this period was clearly centred on Armi, arguably the most important city in the region. It would almost certainly have put up a fight, while other centres such as Adabig, Luatum, Kakmium, Iridum (later Irrite), and Karkemish offered support to Ebla while not always maintaining the alliance. Indeed, immediately afterwards Ibrium launched an expedition against Kakmium, which had probably rebelled, in the shifting context of alliances and wars in which Nagar seems to have been in constant conflict with Armi, and was hence the natural ally of Ebla.

Ebla politics seem to have taken a decidedly bellicose turn from the beginning of Ibbi-Zikir's vizierate (Figure 3.5), in the second half of Ishar-Damu's reign, when almost every year he personally conducted some military campaign, only very rarely replaced by the sovereign. For the first six years these were against cities in the northern regions, very probably allies of Armi, which, however, was left in peace, while conquered cities included Agagallish,

Figure 3.4 Economic tablet with the registration of incomes and outputs of silver and gold (TM.75.G.1353), clay, from the Archive L.2769, 24th century BC.

almost certainly the Igagallish of Hattusili I's inscriptions and of the "Chant of Release", narrating Ebla's final fall in 1600 BC. Between the seventh and tenth year of Ibbi-Zikir's vizierate he turned his attentions southwards in a series of campaigns against centres in the kingdom of Ibal, seemingly a federation of cities possibly in the region of Homs and Selimiyah.

After his tenth year in power, Ibbi-Zikir appears to have arranged the marriage of Ishar-Damu's daughter, Tagrish-Damu, with the king of Nagar's son, and an alliance with Kish, thereby placing a stranglehold on Mari which was exploited by the very able Ebla general, possibly in the thirteenth year of the vizierate. The campaign was impeccably organized from both a diplomatic and a military perspective, obtaining the support, as explicitly stated in the documents, of numerous allied cities, from Manuwat and Nirar to Kablul through their messengers, from Raak, Burman, Garmu, Iritum, and Kakmium through the kings themselves, and then from Kharran and Urshaum (later called Urshum), through their Elders. A number of interesting details emerge: in Tuttul, Ibbi-Zikir received messengers from Kish, the powerful southern city, assuring its support; Haddu behaved likewise, despite all Mari's insistence on Ebla's unreliability, but most curious of all, two dignitaries from

Figure 3.5 Economic tablet with a yearly account of goods, of Ibbi-Zikir's time (TM.75.G.2070), clay, from the Archive L.2769, 24th century BC.

Kish and one from Nagar brought Ibbi-Zikir reinforcement contingents for the final battle with their common rival.

The conflict ended with a victorious battle at Terqa, now Tell Asharah, only 50 km north of the metropolis of the Euphrates; a document notes that it was Dubukhu-Malik who brought 'the news that Mari was defeated' to Ebla. For reasons which obviously fail to emerge from the economic texts, however, Ibbi-Zikir took no advantage from the victory. While Ishar-Damu sent gifts to his victorious general and to the allied kings of Nagar, Haddu, and Kish, and a brother of the king of Kish, Bushushum, went in person to encounter the vizier of Ebla, Ibbi-Zikir decided to to seal the peace with his newly defeated rival. This was translated into an immediate alliance with Mari while that with Kish was reinforced by giving its king another daughter of Ishar-Damu, Keshdut, in marriage.

Against all the expectations or predictions of the canny and fortunate Ibbi-Zikir, however, no more than three years later events took an unexpected turn, and brought about the ruin of the Ebla of Ishar-Damu, probably then at the height of his political and economic fortunes. Ibbi-Zikir had clearly failed to judge the clever personality of Sargon of Akkad (Figure 3.6), who in those very years was conceiving an enormously ambitious and revolutionary political design. This was founded, moreover, on a new and definitive military reform consisting in a stable professional army which, with a core of 5,600

Figure 3.6 The so-called head of Sargon of Akkad (M.11331), copper, from Nineveh, 23rd century BC.
Source: National Museum of Iraq.

men, as he himself notes in his inscriptions, would accompany the sovereign wherever he went. Although of course no data emerge from the Ebla Royal Archives as to the impending catastrophe about to befall the city, three basic facts are known. First, Sargon himself, in an important votive inscription in the famous Temple Ekur of Enlil at Nippur in Sumer, notes that the god Dagan of Tuttul gave him possession of Mari, Yarmuti, and Ebla. Second, recent archaeological documentation to emerge from Mari implies that very few years probably passed between the destruction of Ebla and that of Mari itself since the names of two kings in the city are known and are successors to the last ones cited in texts in the Ebla Archives. Third, the fact that a year name of Sargon's is conserved which mentions the conquest of Mari but not of Ebla indicates that the two cities were destroyed in two different campaigns, although mentioned together in the triumphal inscription at Nippur, since both cities were in the west. It was very probably Ibbi-Zikir's reckless but successful anti-Mari campaign which induced Sargon to intervene, unexpectedly undoing the seemingly renewed Ebla–Kish alliance and taking advantage of Mari's inability to control the Euphrates route. Related to this is a singular passage in an administrative text in the Ebla Archives which seems to contain a veiled allusion to Sargon. The text, from the last years before Ebla was destroyed, speaks of 'the king of Kish and his son, Ishkunnunu of Kish', which is incomprehensible unless we interpret the title of 'king of Kish', a normative designation for the Great King, as Sargon, who was probably already governing in Akkad, and infer that one of his sons, called Ishkunnunu, had been given a position of office and resided in Kish. The passage is inexplicable if applied to a traditional king of Kish residing in his city, with a son also designated lord of Kish, while it is completely feasible if alluding to a sovereign who, while adopting the title of king of Kish, resided in his new capital of Akkad and had left the government of Kish to his son, who thus appeared as the city governor.

The ambitions of Ishar-Damu and Ibbi-Zikir regarding Ebla belong most probably to years when there seem to have evolved parallel political trends which might be termed proto-imperial, on account of both the wide horizons of influence beyond the circumscribed and homogeneous geographical areas, and the complexity of the administrative systems implemented on a scale unprecedented in the traditional Early Dynastic horizons of Mesopotamia. The reasons for this phenomenon are in part elusive, but may lie in the need for economic development of the most powerful cities with a vast territorial control as regards supplies and raw materials in considerably more extensive geographical contexts, both in Lower Mesopotamia with Lugalzagesi of Uruk and in Upper Syria with Ishar-Damu of Ebla, and possibly in Upper Mesopotamia too, with the contemporary lord of Nagar. In different but parallel ways, Lugalzagesi of Uruk and Ishar-Damu of Ebla may have attempted to set up imperial structures of government, pushing to control much vaster areas, in addition to extensive but circumscribed territories like Lower Mesopotamia, in Lugalzagesi's case, and Upper Syria in Ishar-Damu's: areas yielding resources to be accessed with all the direct bargaining power of unmediated political dominion; that is, proto-imperial in conception. It took Sargon's genius to equip these ambitions with political, military, and ideological structures consonant with the scope of the project, while it was his good fortune to have successors with similar talents, able to preserve his structures of empire for several decades.

The situation in Upper Syria proved particularly volatile, and only a few years after defeating Ebla, Sargon besieged and destroyed Mari in the wake of the at least partial military success on the part of the new lord of the city, documented in the recent findings there. Yarmuti met the same fate; the town still eludes precise location but may possibly lie on the Mediterranean coast, which would explain why in his inscriptions, Sargon the 'Great King' boasts he had ruled from the Lower to the Upper Sea, namely from the Arabian/Persian Gulf to the Mediterranean Sea.

As the Royal Archives make clear, once Mari had been defeated, only Nagar remained in Upper Mesopotamia, probably weakened by the long conflict with Armi, and Nagar was certainly defeated by a king of Akkad before Naram-Sin built his palace-arsenal (which is more of a fortified warehouse than a provincial imperial residence). With Nagar removed from the fray, of the cities which had wielded significant political power as important, though not primary, rivals of Ebla itself, there remained Armi – or Armanum, almost certainly an alternative name – alone. With the devastation of Armi/ Armanum in Naram-Sin's era there ends the project of imperial dominion possibly prefigured at Uruk and Ebla, but executed relentlessly and with success only by Sargon and his successors.

When on more than one occasion Naram-Sin, boasting of his victory over 'Armanum and Ebla', mentions defeating Rish-Adad of Armanum (with no mention of any king of Ebla) and brags of having annihilated Armanum's mighty defences, he is alluding explicitly not to the conquest of Ebla, already put to pitiless sword some decades before by his grandfather Sargon, but to the conquest of the city, Armi, which had inherited the political mantle in Upper Syria, possibly ruling over a large part of the territory which, before Sargon, Ebla itself had long dominated.

4 The Royal Palace in the age of the Archives

Space and function

No archaeological evidence of any substance exists as to the times, means, propulsions, or resistance regarding the gradual development, in the decades before 2400 BC, of the archaic Early Syrian (Early Bronze III) settlement into the mature Early Syrian city of the age of the Archives. Although this is serious as regards the topography of the urban settlement, some limited elements have emerged of the structures preceding the building of Royal Palace G (Figure 4.1) at the far western side of the Acropolis. In the area immediately to the south-east of the façade of the later Temple of Ishtar, below the two floors of Royal Palace G, fragmentary remains were found of three successive phases of a building, the so-called Building G5, probably part of the palace residence preceding the construction of the large royal complex of the mature Early Syrian Period.

The remains of this period, archaeologically defined as Early Bronze IVA, are considerably relevant, though limited to three complexes of varying significance but certain date, and to fragments of the great city ramparts which could, however, equally belong to the late Early Syrian Period: the Royal Palace G (Area G), once the royal residence and the headquarters of central administration, which covered a large part of the Acropolis; the Temple of the Rock (Area HH), one of the city's most important sanctuaries, in the south-east area of the Lower Town; and Building P4 (area P), discovered at the north-west base of the Acropolis, which would have been part of a service complex for either the palace or the temple. Comparing the (relatively scarce) historical data inferred from the Archives with the archaeological data from the excavations, only one relatively certain element emerges regarding the protagonists and history of the destruction of the Early Bronze IVA city; namely, that the last king of Ebla recorded there is Ishar-Damu, Irkab-Damu's son, assisted in government by the powerful and experienced vizier Ibbi-Zikir. The latter had overseen state affairs for several years with the collaboration of the previous vizier, and had for some time trained his own son, Dubukhu-Adda, in the same role.

There is no explicit mention of either Sargon or his new capital Akkad in the extant Archives (one of the Ebla texts possibly alludes to him) while frequent mention is made of Kish, to whose last IV Dynasty king the founder of the Akkad Dynasty was "cup-bearer", according to Mesopotamian tradition.

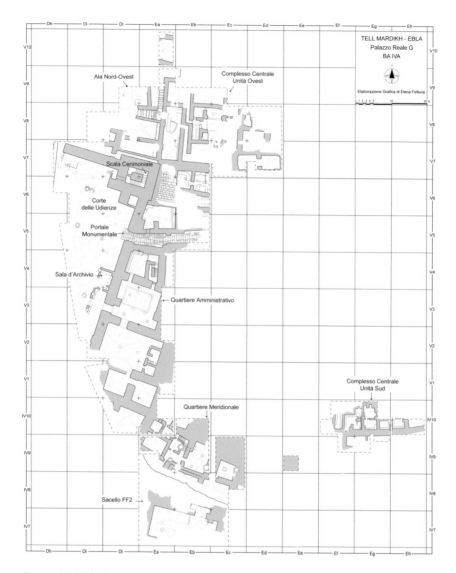

Figure 4.1 Ebla, Royal Palace G, schematic plan with the indication of the sectors and quarters of the Early Syrian palace complex, 24th century BC.

However, as seen above, several clues, both historical-artistic or from the material culture on the one hand, and epigraphic and palaeographic on the other, all point to Sargon of Akkad as responsible for the destruction of the mature Early Syrian Ebla, as indeed he himself had proclaimed in one of his victory inscriptions. It is also very likely that only shortly before Sargon's triumphal expedition (the success of which, he notes, was due to the god

Dagan of Tuttul), a series of Egyptian gifts arrived in Ebla which included a precious alabaster vase, the lid of which carried a hieroglyphic inscription with the titling from the first part of the reign of Pepy I, the third pharaoh of the VI Dynasty of Egypt, whose reign of some 50 years was approximately as long as Sargon's own. It is far from easy of course, within such a time-span, to date precisely the important expedition to the west which not only led Sargon to crush the power of Ebla but also to lead his army as far as the Taurus and the Amanus ranges. A substantial later tradition, however, reflected both in the so-called "historical omens" collections of oracular formulae based on hepatoscopy and in the chronicles of the Babylonian priesthood, put the celebrated expedition in the third or eleventh year of his reign; that is, at the beginning rather than the end of his 56-year rule.

If, then, it would seem to be certain, on the one hand, that Sargon of Akkad was responsible for destroying mature Early Syrian Ebla, and on the other, that Sargon of Akkad, Pepy I of Egypt, and Ishar-Damu of Ebla were contemporaries, it is far more difficult to determine by how many years the completion of the architectural components of Royal Palace G and Building P4 of Ebla's Lower Town predate the destruction. One feasible hypothesis is that they were built at the time of Ebla's first king whose (relatively few) texts were still kept in the Archives; namely, the Igrish-Khalab who preceded Irkab-Damu on the throne. Since the reigns of Igrish-Khalab, Irkab-Damu, and Ishar-Damu probably cover no more than 50 years and since, as seen above, Sargon probably defeated Mari and Ebla, albeit possibly in separate campaigns, but still within the early years of his reign, then in terms of absolute chronology it is wholly feasible that the largest architectural complexes in the mature Early Syrian Ebla were built between 2370 BC and 2350 BC, and that Ebla was defeated by Sargon shortly before 2300 BC.

The ruins from the mature Early Syrian Period of the Archives have a different significance, their extension and monumental size varying considerably; they also belong to very different if very important sectors of the ancient settlement. The most peripheral was most certainly part of the Archives-era fortification. Part of a short stretch of a massive mud bricks (identical in dimensions – 0.60 m by 0.40 m – to those of the Royal Palace G) town wall (Figure 4.2), was included and sealed within the huge ramparts of the successive archaic Old Syrian Period. A massive defensive wall more than 6 m wide, still standing at a height of 3 m in the north-west area of the rampart, it probably followed the same course of the ruined wall where, a few centuries later (early Middle Bronze I), the great twentieth-century BC ramparts were erected. This recent discovery is of enormous significance topographically and in terms of urban planning since it reveals that the twenty-fourth century BC city of the Archives was as extensive as the urban centre of the twentieth century BC, already covering a surface of more than 50 hectares.

The complex of architectural structures, dating almost certainly from Early Bronze IVA, includes the Royal Palace G, the Temple of the Rock, and a series

Figure 4.2 Ebla, Area AA, a segment of the mud brick wall of the fortification of the Early Syrian town, below the Old Syrian rampart, from the north, 24th century BC.

of small rooms forming Building P4, constructed at the north-west foot of the Acropolis, in part on a small terraced area of the slope (Figure 4.3). Building P4 includes a number of probably multifunctional rooms: the evidence found indicates food preparation, the storage of various goods, and some handicraft activity. The making of flour is attested in several rooms by the frequent presence of benches with basalt grindstones, while nearby workshops were certainly used to cut stones and shells both for the inlay work of wall-panels mainly for palace use, and for small animal statuettes of which, however, no remains have been found in the ruins of Royal Palace G. Large numbers of various inlays, not always homogeneous, in a narrow room of Building P4 would imply that these were components waiting to be mounted into finished panels, rather than the remains of destroyed or scattered panels mounted in the same room.

On the other hand, the two well-preserved and almost identical fragments of animal figures, possibly bulls, in a small room in Building P4, which must have belonged to a series of figurines, probably of deities, would imply that the area was a workshop for work of some complexity, possibly intended for cult purposes. The discovered part of Building P4 was certainly a production and storage area of both foodstuffs and handicraft items, all serving the needs of the palace and possibly the temples. Equally certain is the architectural

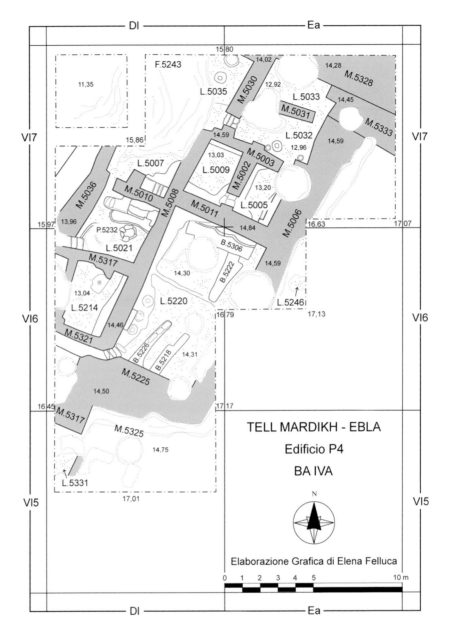

Figure 4.3 Ebla, Area P, schematic plan of the Early Syrian Building P4, in the Lower City North-West, 24th century BC.

standard of the complex, considerably inferior to the monumental and harmoniously planned structures of both the administrative and ceremonial quarters of the Royal Palace G on the Acropolis and the imposing temple structures, such as the Temple of the Rock, which came to light in the southeast part of the Lower Town. The mud bricks, almost always a single row only, the cramped, variously interconnected rooms, the unlevelled difference in floors, the many small stairways and raised inner spaces, the over-exploitation of every available space, the near-absolute lack of linear planning, and the hive-like layout of the rooms set Building P4 apart from the linear, quasi-theatrical, airy monumentality of the great public works, whether sacred or secular, which clearly characterized the architecture of Ebla at its peak.

It would seem likely that the architecture of Building P4, so unlike that of the Royal Palace, or the Temple of the Rock, reflects the domestic norm of Early Bronze IVA of which, however, to date we have no remains of any significant size. What is problematic is the relation of Building P4 to the public architecture of the great city of the period of the Early Syrian Archives. Two equally plausible possibilities present themselves. On the one hand, the building may well have been a peripheral annex of the Royal Palace, serving the palace craftsmen; on the other, we cannot exclude its belonging to the workshops of a cult area, the cult buildings of which are as yet undiscovered, below the large Sacred Area of Ishtar, of the archaic and classical Old Syrian Period. However, while there exists evidence in support of both hypotheses, no other would seem in any way likely.

By far the most important architectural structures from Ebla's mature Early Syrian Period (and one of the most significant of all Syrian architecture, in the absolute) is the Royal Palace G. This must have been an extraordinarily extensive and articulated complex of government buildings. Impressive if limited remains have been found, in a good state of preservation, in particular from public, administrative, and ceremonial areas with a number of secondary sectors which were either storage or residential areas. Royal Palace G must have included many possibly independent structures which extended over a large part of the area which is today beneath the Acropolis of Tell Mardikh, reaching the foot of the small hill formed by the various more ancient settlements possibly over a natural rock protrusion.

In all, the Royal Palace G probably extended over 20,000 to 30,000 square metres if, as evidenced in the south-western region of the base of the Acropolis, its peripheral areas reached in one direction almost as far as the outskirts of the Lower Town, while the extraordinary area of palace blocks excavated so far covers just over 4,700 square metres, so presumably between 17% and 23% of the total surface area. Almost all the areas uncovered, in a good state of preservation, as stated above, are on the slopes of the Acropolis of Tell Mardikh, for two basic reasons: the area was never subject to more than sporadic superimpositions of later settlements, and it proved a particularly protected location. In fact, where the excavations extended both to the top of the Acropolis and to the base of the hill, the levelled terrain and repeated superimpositions of successive constructions have at best considerably flattened the ruins of the Early Syrian palace, but have in most cases caused the ruins to be completely swept away.

Unless, then, terracing and multi-levels have created protection for the ruins of the large palace complex, or superimpositions of buildings without deep stone foundations have spared the more ancient ruins, further extensive areas of the Royal Palace G in equally good condition are unlikely to be found anywhere, with the possible exception of the slopes of the Acropolis, beyond the south-west region excavated so far. There are, however, hopes that the slopes of the central hill of Tell Mardikh may yield limited but well-preserved remains of peripheral areas, like those brought to light so far, some of them possibly with considerable elevations. Indeed, what is particularly significant about the ruins of the Royal Palace G, apart from the extreme functional relevance of the sections discovered so far, is the impressive elevation of many of their features, which for long stretches reach as high as 7.10 m and no lower than 4.50 m and 2.50 m.

Since the known sectors of the mature Early Syrian Royal Palace G are considerably peripheral (compared with the topographically central cores), it is not even hypothetically possible to attempt to reconstruct the general conformation of the structures articulating the entire monumental complex. What is certain, however, is that the Royal Palace G included an extensive and possibly composite group of structures constituting the Central Complex, the individual architectural units and functional areas of which were located almost exclusively on the top of the Acropolis. These included the residential and service areas, the latter probably comprising storage and workshop areas of the very large palace complex. This Central Complex must have been quite considerably damaged, and only small portions of two peripheral sectors have been found, one to the south and the other to the west: the West Unit (Figure 4.4), on the western edge of the Acropolis, south of what already in the mature Early Syrian Period of the Archives must have been an important cult area, later concealed by the construction of the large Temple of Ishtar in Area D, from the archaic Old Syrian Period of the early second millennium BC; and the South Unit, the remains of which, discovered in the upper region of the southern slopes of the hill, have been cut away by the erosion of the Acropolis slopes.

The West Unit was devoted to food production and included areas of varied dimensions and collocation, since the ground of the Acropolis probably already sloped from north to south, and had been adjusted by means of a series of shallow terraces. The most important of these terraces separated a northern sector, higher as quota, and decommissioned to make room for the Red Temple, from a southern lower sector remained in function until the sargonic destruction. This meant that the westernmost areas were independent rather than intercommunicating, their doors all presumably arranged along a south–north ramp; the doors to these rooms must have been on the west side. Some evidence of this, found in many of these areas, north of the great Monumental Staircase, is provided by the well-preserved low clay benches of various forms, many with basalt grindstones still in place with their pestles, and irregular basins at the foot of the blocks, clearly to collect the ground

Figure 4.4 Ebla, Royal Palace G, the razed structures of the West Unit of the Early Syrian Central Complex, from the east, 24th century BC.

Figure 4.5 Ebla, Royal Palace G, benches with grinding stones in place for grinding cereals in room L.3926, from the west, 24th century BC.

flour (Figure 4.5). The various foodstuffs were then most probably stored in the South Unit, the rooms of which were generally small, although the many pots of different types and dimensions found there indicate that at least in part the rooms were also ceramics deposits.

The West and South Units of the Central Complex were clearly service areas, located on the periphery of the presumably extensive residential quarters of the important area, which the texts call 'Saza'. If these were indeed of the dimensions implied by the size of the Acropolis, it may be inferred that they were inhabited not only by the king and queen and household but also, possibly in the last years of Mardikh IIB1, by some of the higher palace dignitaries such as the vizier Ibbi-Zikir and his son Dubukhu-Adda.

On the western slope of the Acropolis, immediately to the west and below the West Unit (therefore to the north of the large Court of Audience) is a sector comprising only two rooms facing south and a sharply angled stairway to the north. On the floor of the southernmost of the two were found the first tablets of the Royal Archives, while the other contained the relatively well-preserved remains of at least two splendid items of furniture, a wooden throne and table, carved with a number of figurative elements. This room was reached by a sharply angled stairway apparently descending from the (possibly) cult area of the Acropolis where the Red Temple was built in the last years of the mature Early Syrian city; the stairway may well have led into as yet unidentified rooms of the West Unit of the Central Complex near the edge of the Acropolis.

It is likely that the Central Complex of the mature Early Syrian Royal Palace G extended over a large part of the Acropolis, on terraces descending from north to south, and that its peripheral quarters were built against terraced walls, partly collapsed, as in the South Unit, which corrected and regularized the contours of the central hill of the whole urban settlement. It probably had only one monumental entrance on the south-western slopes of the Acropolis itself. While secondary entrances to the upper quarters of the Royal Palace G, on other sides of the hill, cannot be excluded, the entrance to the Central Complex was most definitely the Monumental Gateway which, with its long basalt stairway stretching more than 22 m to the southern summit of the Acropolis, compensated a difference in level of some 7 m (Figure 4.6), while revealing a slight misalignment the function of which is not clear. If the stairway was an open entrance, it may have separated, to the north and south, two large and completely independent sets of buildings: the northern set which, from south to north, included the Kitchens of the Court of Audience and the Ceremonial Staircase, four ramps of stairs enclosed in a steep rectangular tower in the north-east corner of the Court of Audience; and the more extensive southern set, including the rooms, inner court, Throne Room, and Treasury of the Administrative Quarter. There are no conclusive indications as to whether the Monumental Gateway (Figure 4.7) was covered or otherwise, but the whole eastern prospect of the Court of Audience would certainly have appeared more architecturally integrated had it had a single façade onto which the gate to the stairway opened. One element in favour of this possible reconstruction is the fact that both sides of the jambs of the

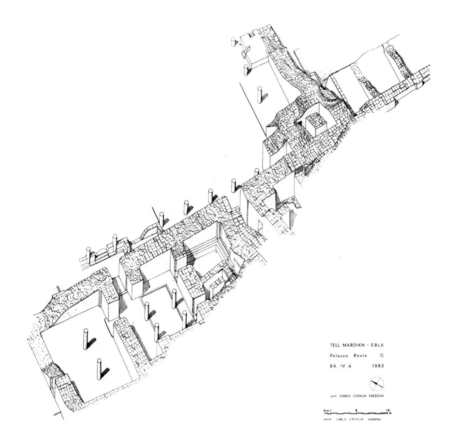

TELL MARDIKH - EBLA

Palazzo Reale   G

BA IV A   1983

arch CARLO CATALDI TASSONI

0 m 1   5   10

arch CARLO CATALDI TASSONI

Figure 4.6 Ebla, Royal Palace G, detailed isometric view of the Administrative Quarter and of the Court of Audience, from the east, 24th century BC.

Monumental Gateway reveal indentations indicative of shutters framed by a recess, one plausible hypothesis being that the stairway was covered only in the lower part before it narrowed somewhat irregularly, forming the exit from the covered section towards the upper part of the stairs.

The Monumental Gateway led into the upper quarters of the Royal Palace G from the Court of Audience, the latter being a structure of considerable architectural but also logistic and functional purpose. It undoubtedly was the palace's main gathering and reception area, but in terms of layout equally served as the hub linking the living quarters of the general community and the residential quarters of the king and his court, while also accommodating the Kitchen for the preparation of guest drinks on the northern side and the offices of the royal chancery and the store-rooms of the Treasury on the southern side.

All sides of the Court of Audience probably had the porticoes which are partially extant only on the north and east sides (nothing remains of

Figure 4.7 Ebla, Royal Palace G, the Monumental Gateway of the entrance to the
upper quarters of the Central Complex, from the west, 24th century BC.

the other two sides, destroyed by the superimposition of the successive Old
Syrian city): the dais for the throne was probably midway down the northern side (Figure 4.8). This would certainly have been where the king and
his dignitaries received princes, messengers, and foreign merchants, organized

Figure 4.8 Ebla, Royal Palace G, the royal dais below the northern porch of the Court of Audience, from the east, 24th century BC.

caravans and foreign expeditions, and received various palace administrators for most of the year, when weather conditions permitted the partial exposure. The Court's peripheral position, with respect to the rest of Royal Palace G, whereby the king could receive anyone coming from outside the city on the palace doorstep, as it were, obviously makes it ideally suited to its functions. This organically conceived functionality of the Court is equally attested by both the double access to the upper quarters of the palace, allowing access to the city's political authorities, and the proximity between the Court and the Administrative Quarter, where the records of transactions made in the Court were transcribed and filed.

The Ceremonial Staircase, enclosed inside the large rectangular tower at the north-eastern corner of the Court of Audience, was private, and lavishly inlaid with mother-of-pearl floral decorations on each step (Figure 4.9). It was almost certainly reserved for the king and his highest dignitaries, and connected the north porch with the royal dais and residential quarters of the Acropolis, providing the king with private access to the palace complex. A further Court–Central Complex connection was of course the Monumental Gateway; this would certainly have been public, used by functionaries not belonging to the king's entourage.

On the north side of the Gateway was the entrance to the small Court Kitchen, clearly a service area strictly providing for the Court of Audience, and containing about a dozen fire-places in a good state of preservation (Figure 4.10). That it was not intended for the preparation of palace meals is

Figure 4.9 Ebla, Royal Palace G, detail of the steps with the impression of mother-of-pearl inlays in floral patterns, Ceremonial Staircase, from the west, 24th century BC.

clear both on account of its position at the side of the Monumental Gateway, which would have been non-normative and impracticably far from any dining area, and the lack of any trace of animal flesh or cereals, while it contained plentiful evidence of powdered herbs used in infusions which would have been served to guests.

On the other hand, the fact that the rooms of the Royal Archives, for the temporary or permanent preservation of the cuneiform tablets, are in two areas below the eastern porch of the Court of Audience (L.2769 and L.2712) and in another area, in the north sector of the Administrative Quarter (L.2764) – that is, midway between the documented place of the royal dais on the northern side (L.2715) of the same Court and the presumed site of a second dais against the southern wall of the Throne Room (L.2866) – sanctions the idea that the frequent distribution of foodstuffs, seeds, materials, and goods mentioned in the Archives must have taken place and therefore been recorded by the administration scribes, precisely in the Court of Audience, and in the Throne Room. There was probably no substantial difference in function between the two rooms, the smaller and indoor Throne Room probably simply replacing the larger and more open Court of Audience in inclement weather, or for smaller or more private meetings.

The Court of Audience of the Royal Palace was a particularly monumental construction of singular originality. In the first place, the collapse of the Court's perimeter walls, particularly those on the eastern side, has revealed that the elevation of the porched side must have been no less than 13 m, and

Figure 4.10 Ebla, Royal Palace G, the fire-places in room L.2890 of the Royal Kitchen in the north side of the Monumental Gateway, from the west, 24th century BC.

probably between 13 and 15 m, particularly since the width was a considerable 2.80 m, with the height of the northern elevation being the same. If, then, the porches extended on the no longer extant western and southern sides, it would be plausible to imagine that the elevation of all sides would have been similar and thus unified.

In the second place, the northern and eastern porches must have been of a considerable height, given that there is no trace of the juncture of the roofing supported by the columns on the faces of the sides of the structure up to approximately 7.10 m, at least near the tower of the Ceremonial Staircase. The porches were in fact probably surmounted by lower open loggias and would thus have been some 7 or 8 m high and the loggias some 5 or 6 m.

In the third place, the presence of the antae as starting points for the column lines emerging from the perimeter walls of the tower of the Ceremonial Staircase would imply that similar solutions had been adopted at the other ends of the porches, creating scenic wings which, in relation to the corner towers, would have increased the theatrical aspect of an already elaborate space, etched by the shadows of the columns on the uninterrupted glow of the white plaster.

Behind the Court of Audience, and immediately to the north of the northern side, where the dais of the throne stood, was a small cluster of rooms denominated as the Northern Quarter, including a long, narrow west–east corridor, which ran behind the north porch and led to a number of rather large rooms facing south–north. This sector, at a height significantly lower than both the Western Unit of the Central Complex and the intermediate North-West Wing (not communicating with the Court of Audience) was probably approached only through a small door immediately to the west of the royal dais of the Court's north porch. It would have served to store the goods received in the audiences held in the Court (it was in one of these rooms that the excellently preserved remains were found of the splendid miniature statuettes in gold, silver, jasper, steatite, and wood, probably belonging to a precious royal standard).

The whole spatial ensemble of this Court of Audience must have been of considerable theatricality, its monumental lines and size communicating a sensation of grandeur which is virtually unparalleled in the contemporary Early Dynastic architecture of the world of Lower and Upper Mesopotamia.

A similar sense of spatial grandeur, albeit on a very different, much reduced and compressed scale, is found in the Administrative Quarter of the Royal Palace, almost certainly the heart of what the Royal Archives define as the Saza, while it is very likely that the Throne Room area, with the adjacent rooms for the storage of precious materials, was the sector of the palace called in the text 'House of Wool', undoubtedly corresponding to the Treasury. If it is certain that 'Saza' designated all the architectural spaces on, or at the foot of the Acropolis, including cult buildings, it cannot be excluded that 'House of Wool' referred to not only the Throne Room complex but the whole of the Administrative Quarter.

This quarter was the main reception area of the whole palace complex. Situated around a small porched inner courtyard (Figure 4.11), it included two rooms on the north side, one of which, via a four-ramp staircase, giving access to the upper floor, and a larger hall on the south side, the Throne Room. Both the spatial layout and the various finds bespeak the particular significance of this functionally fundamental sector of the Royal Palace. In the small inner courtyard was found the greatest concentration of elements of inlay from the celebratory wall panels, the remarkable fragments of two heads in steatite, representing a king and queen, and the majority of the diorite and alabaster vases of Egyptian manufacture sent to Ebla from Memphis, mostly at the time of the VI Dynasty of Egypt. In addition, the large rooms opening to the south, behind the Throne Room, yielded several remains of miniature images in steatite, lapis lazuli, and gold, besides a large quantity of blocks of raw lapis lazuli, all proof that it was these sectors of the Royal Palace which held the greatest concentration of precious goods from far-off countries and sophisticated figurative works from the royal workshops.

The Administrative Quarter was a much-reduced scale replica of the basic elements of the monumental plan of the Court of Audience, the small inner courtyard L.2913, with its ground-floor porch and open gallery on the upper floor accessed by the four-ramp staircase of the northern set of rooms, clearly reproducing something of the Court's spaciousness. A number of other elements, both spatial and functional, while to an extent concealed by the considerable difference in scale between the Court of Audience and the Administrative

Figure 4.11 Ebla, Royal Palace G, the courtyard L.2913, inside the Administrative Quarter, from the north, 24th century BC.

Quarter, endorse the idea of a deliberate equivalence when planning the two reception areas of the palace. The stairway of the north sector (Figure 4.12), for example, must, like the Ceremonial Staircase, have had the dual function of a private corridor for the king and his dignitaries from the residential quarters of the Central Complex to the Throne Room, and a route to the inner open gallery. Similarly, the royal dais, which would have stood against the south wall of the Throne Room, was intended to show the enthroned sovereign between and behind the two columns of the large room, a replica of the arrangement in the northern porch of the great Court. Thus in both cases, immediately to the side of the royal dais, perfectly symmetrically but in inverse proportions, there opened the door which accessed the store-rooms to the north of the Court of Audience, denominated the Northern Quarter, and the two large rooms of the royal stores to the south of the Throne Room (Figure 4.13).

The sophisticated design of both the Court of Audience and the Administrative Quarter, with a number of far from secondary elements coordinating and corresponding between the two, are obviously the product of an architectural culture of considerable maturity, able to contemplate both

Figure 4.12 Ebla, Royal Palace G, detail of the first ramp of the staircase to the north
of courtyard L.2913 in the Administrative Quarter, from the south, 24th
century BC.

grandiose and highly theatrical spaces and refined, small-scale, restrainedly
effective solutions. The mature Early Syrian Ebla of the age of the Archives
clearly had architects capable of incorporating existing architectural styles
and features into their creation of spaces, in order to meet both functional
needs and their clients' desire to exalt the ideology of kingship. What is more
difficult is pinpointing the location of a similar architectural culture which the
Eblaites might have shared.

Recent excavations, however, have suggested that a feasible geographical area might include not only inland Upper Syria but centres of Upper
Mesopotamia too, possibly configuring a mature Early Syrian architectural
culture, the temporal roots of which are as yet uncertain, with at least elements of unity probably including inland central-northern Syria from the
Taurus to the Homs region, but extending to western Upper Mesopotamia
between the Euphrates and the Balikh area, although probably not as far as
the Khabur. The contemporary Royal Palace of Tell Khuera (Figure 4.14), for
instance, while on a much smaller scale than Ebla's grandiose equivalent, has
a layout of its reception rooms which is clearly similar to those of Ebla. It also
seems to have been a relatively limited, but compact and organic architectural

Figure 4.13 Ebla, Royal Palace G, room L.2984 of the southern annexes of the Throne Room in the Administrative Quarter, from the south-east, 24th century BC.

complex, like the royal palaces of Mesopotamia of the Early Dynastic II–III Period and a number of government buildings of the archaic and classical Old Syrian Period. The central core of this palace building, in what was one of the most important centres of political power in the Balikh area in the age of the Ebla Archives, includes a small hall, its entrance to the east, consisting only of two large rectangular side rooms: a smaller one to the north and a larger to the south with a dais on its shorter side. This latter area would appear almost certainly to be a longitudinal Court of Audience with a bent-axis entrance. The bent-axis entrance certainly re-enacts a feature of the cult architecture of Early Dynastic Mesopotamia, but the general layout of the central hall, with two groups of rooms to either side, one of them the Throne Room, is identical to the design of the Administrative Quarter of Ebla's Royal Palace, although the dimensions of the reception room, while considerable, would seem to be about one third smaller than those of Royal Palace G's Throne Room.

As in the case of Tell Khuera, there are hints that even at Tuttul the architectural pattern of the palatine building did not have secondary relations to the concept present in the Royal Palace G of Ebla. The excavated area is somewhat limited in scale, offering only a moderately extensive fragment of what would have been the contemporary palace complex of Tuttul, present-day Tell Bi'a, on the Euphrates, midway between Karkemish and Mari. However, here too, in this important city, diplomatically and administratively connected with both Ebla and Nagar, a small, porched courtyard, similar to that of the Ebla Administrative Quarter, divided on opposite sides

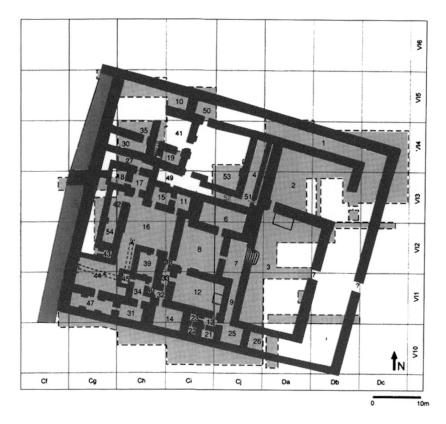

Figure 4.14 Tell Khuera, Royal Palace, schematic plan, 24th century BC.
Source: Courtesy of Jan-Waalke Meyer.

a considerably more spacious area which was certainly a reception room (most likely similar in size to the Throne Room in Ebla) and a less extensive room; differently from Ebla, much smaller areas were arranged along a third side. The arrangement, then, of a small courtyard, porched or otherwise, flanked on at least two sides by two rooms, one large and rectangular, designated as an audience hall and in fact functioning as a throne room, while still non-standardized as regards position and axis, would seem to have been a common layout formula which, adopted in Tuttul and Tell Khuera, in Ebla found its most organic and harmonious realization, and reached monumental proportions, with a graceful dialogue between open and closed spaces, in the admirable Court of Audience. The layout is far from prevalent in the great tradition of Old Syrian palace architecture, not only as regards Ebla, but finds possible echoes in the repeated use of columns in original Middle Syrian palace complexes such as the Royal Palace in Ugarit (Figure 4.15), and re-emerges (at least according to currently available documentation) in

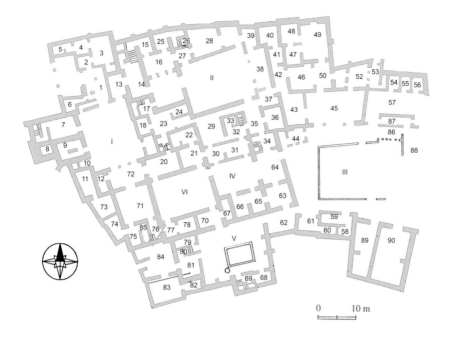

Figure 4.15 Ugarit, Royal Palace, schematic plan, 14th–13th century BC.
Source: Courtesy of Valérie Matoïan.

one of the palace areas of the Aramaic Neo-Syrian citadel of Hamat (ninth–eighth century BC), thus revealing unexpected elements of continuity in the architectural tradition of Syria from the late third to the first centuries of the first millennium BC.

Regarding the more outlying sector of Ebla's Royal Palace G – the Southern Quarter – it is difficult to be categorical in attributing functions to areas. It is likely, however, that at least the northern premises of the quarter, close to both the rooms of what has very plausibly been designated the Treasury, and the massive retaining structures at the foot of the Acropolis, had a residential function, possibly for some high-ranking official of the palace administration. Extremely original and as yet unsurpassed is the Hall of Painted Plaster (Figure 4.16) which, without its relatively narrow partition wall, would be a large rectangular space some 20 m in length. In the westernmost part stood a central column base, while in the eastern part it featured three large latitudinal niches, creating an extraordinary spatial effect, compounded by the equally original geometrical motif, seemingly painted on the plaster in a large, multiple niche, not far above ground level. Since the dire plundering, near-fatal fire, and levelling of the ruins have almost totally deprived this extraordinary hall of any contextual element, other than a large inlaid rosette, it is difficult

Figure 4.16 Ebla, Area FF, schematic plan of the Hall of Painted Plaster (Shrine FF2), 24th century BC.

to posit any specific function; it is, however, possible that such a spatially and aesthetically sophisticated chamber had a cult function.

Although the individual units of the Royal Palace G seem to have often used very skilful technical and spatial connections (e.g. the high terracing and ample courtyards) to unify elements, which must have given the entire complex a far more organic aspect than would be expected from the fragmentary ruins which have come down to us, the Saza complex in Ebla was undoubtedly composed of areas which were spatially autonomous, typologically original, and functionally specific, probably so as to make extensions easily viable; at the same time, no independence seems conceived for it within the perimeter limits, precisely to allow integration within a larger unit. Such a planning mode is unlike any in contemporary Mesopotamia of the Early Dynastic IIIA–B Period, where palace complexes, while difficult to analyse in their spatial and functional aspects, as is the case of Kish (Figure 4.17) and Eridu, are generally large, organically planned constructions characterized by geometrically consistent perimeters subdivided into sectors and not, conversely, aggregates of composite additions to pre-existing cores. On the other hand, even though palace structures in the following Old and Middle Syrian Periods seem to have been conceived on unitary principles, in the Mesopotamian fashion, albeit with typically Syrian spatial formulae, it is known for certain that in the later Neo-Syrian Period, in the Iron Age centuries, the residential and administrative complexes of the Luwian and Aramaic principalities were very different from their large Mesopotamian counterparts, being modulated through the multiplying and juxtaposing of buildings, similar in type and spatial arrangement but probably different in function – the so-called *khilani.*

Historically considered, then, it would appear that in the spatial and typological complexity of Royal Palace G in Ebla lie the early roots of a typically Syrian way of conceiving palace structures, not as compact and separate blocks but as articulated aggregates of buildings which in these beginnings seem not to bespeak the replication of any prior canonized model, and which

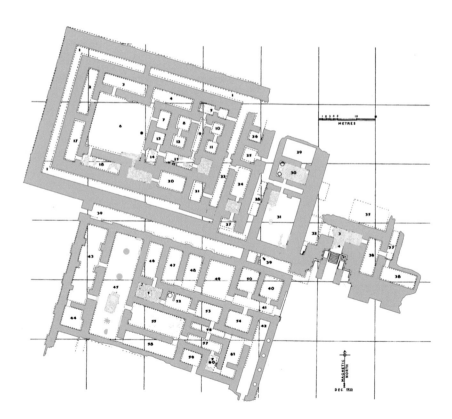

Figure 4.17 Kish, Royal Palace of Tell Ingharra A, schematic plan, 25th–24th century BC.

are not isolated from the urban context, but rather closely inter-related with it through monumental "hubs": points of articulation intended to avoid disjunctions in the urban layout. The multiple buildings and their adaptability to pre-existing man-made structures thus emerge as characteristic elements of the mature Early Syrian architectural culture, in the planning of palace complexes which apply these principles (at least in the case of Ebla) to offer varied and original solutions, with a keen sensibility as to different functional needs, but also an ability to represent the ideology of an ambitious proto-imperial power through the use of aspects of monumentality and refined spatiality.

In the following Old and Middle Syrian Periods, throughout the various contexts of the Syrian area, canonized and functionally specialized spatial typologies gradually became established; the same process had occurred with cult architecture in the same mature and late Early Syrian Period. Subsequently, in the Neo-Syrian Period of the early first millennium BC, the principles of multiple constructions and their adaptation to any pre-existing feature were to produce various very successful monumental solutions, above all in Tell Taynat and Samal, but also in Karkemish, Guzana, and Hamat, particularly as regarded palace architecture: solutions bearing the hallmark of a long and ancient tradition nourished by external influences ingeniously re-elaborated.

5 Early Syrian religion, the Red Temple, and the Temple of the Rock

Before the Ebla Royal Archives were discovered, little data were available upon which to frame an understanding of religion in Syria over the long course of the third millennium BC. Whatever data were available could only be derived indirectly, and from sources of peripheral provenance. With the exception of scant evidence available from the far-eastern periphery of the Syrian world (derived, inevitably, from the findings at Early Dynastic Mari, on the Middle Euphrates), or from the further western periphery (documented in the Early Bronze II–III Byblos), all other data (amounting to very little) came from Mesopotamian sources, such as Sargon of Akkad's mention that the largest place of worship in the region of the Euphrates was the temple of the god Dagan, at Tuttul. In the near absence of documentary evidence from remotest antiquity, our notions regarding religious cults in Syria in the third millennium BC and its pantheon were merely conjectural and had to be rather boldly inferred from far later documentation.

The finding of the Ebla Archives, however, have enabled us to form a picture of religious phenomena at Ebla and in vast regions of Syria in the third quarter of the third millennium BC; considering the remoteness of the period under investigation, the picture is remarkably comprehensive. The archives contain very many detailed financial accounts detailing the monthly administration of official cults at the city's temples by high-ranking authorities in the kingdom (Figure 5.1), and other texts shed light on the cults, divinities, and temples of several other cities, while the study of the onomastics in the Archives' texts, frequently revealing the origin of the people mentioned in the texts from certain Syrian cities, allows insights into the nature of popular religion.

The Archive inscriptions provide sufficient material for a clear representation of worship and beliefs in Ebla and Syria. At the time of the city's full development, the general features of its complex polytheistic system can be understood to have been shared by the north Syrian region (possibly extending to the north Mesopotamian region), with only minor exceptions; furthermore, there are strong elements of continuity with what we know of developments in the Syrian world in the subsequent centuries. While there undoubtedly were religious institutions of a local nature at a number of other cities, which were

Figure 5.1 Tablet with a list of monthly offerings to the deities of the Eblaite pantheon (TM.75.G.2238), clay, from the Archive L.2769, 24th century BC.

especially attached to certain divinities and at some variance with Eblaite cults, the elements that prevail over an extensive geographic expanse display clear traits of consistency and uniformity. As for chronological continuity, although the perpetuation of the cult of a small number of highly significant deities is not testified in later times, these have to be seen as exceptions within a general framework of continuity.

Two further aspects of religion in Early Syrian Ebla have to be mentioned. First there is the problem of the role played by a number of deities of the coeval Mesopotamian pantheon (worshipped in the Sumerian cities of southern Babylonia particularly). With regard to actual Eblaite religious practice it is probable that those deities were known, and possibly also venerated, only by a restricted elite, within select circles of society, and at court. Second, the nature of the documents at hand (essentially, financial and administrative records) prevents us from fully perceiving the developments of religious phenomena in the Early Syrian Period. To give one obvious example, while such deities as Hadad and Ishtar were patently present and had already acquired a certain relevance, they were not as yet quite so prominent in the dynastic cult and in popular devotion as they would be, as we know, around the turn of the second millennium BC.

At the head of the Eblaite pantheon in the era of the Archives was the god Kura, who is also the most perplexing divinity to appear in the written documents of the third quarter of the third millennium BC. It was long believed that Kura had at some point vanished, perhaps after the destruction of Ebla at the hands of Sargon, and not only from the city over which he had presided and the dynasty which he had protected, but also from the Syrian region at large, unlike other gods and goddesses of the pantheon.

The reading of this divine name as Kura is conventional: in fact, the second syllable has only one reading, whereas the first one may be read in different ways; thus, the name may be read differently as concerns the first syllable. In whichever way we read the first syllable, it seems impossible to recognize this name in any deity of the following religious history of Syria in the second and first millennia BC.

The numerous occurrences of his name in the Archives enable us to infer that the otherwise obscure Kura (coupled with Barama, his consort) was a god who certainly enjoyed paternal (and possibly celestial) attributions; he was patron god of the city, and resided in the main temple at Saza, where he received offerings more copious than all the other gods, and was worshipped by the king, other dignitaries, and foreign princes in a crucial oath-swearing ceremony with offerings and the ritual use of ointments. Although none of the interpretations and etymologies adduced to account for his name are persuasive, and arguments in favour of a Hurrian origin are unconvincing, it is possible that the god did not differ much from the (also rather ill-defined) type of Dagan of Tuttul, but had paternal and celestial attributions akin to those which, in Syria, were to belong to El in the pantheon of Ugarit in the Middle Syrian and possibly even Old Syrian Period.

The name of Kura was invoked first in the king's verdicts, before both Utu (Sumerian form for the Semitic Sun-god Shamash) and Adda (the great Storm-god), who in the Mesopotamian tradition likewise were guarantors of legal procedures and of curses; two temples closely associated with kingship were erected to him. The first temple stands close to the city walls and the Gate of Kura and was the site at which, at the start of the lengthy celebrations for the renewal of kingship (illustrated in the Archives' "Ritual of Kingship": Figure 5.2), the queen would enter the city after waiting for sunrise in the fields outside the city walls. The second temple stands within the Saza, the central palatine administrative complex, where the elaborate ritual of kingship concluded with the enthronement of the royal couple at the end of a pilgrimage to the shrines of their deified ancestors. Kura and Barama, the supreme divine couple, were celestial archetypes of the earthly royal couple, and it is with their archetype that the new king and new queen came to be identified after a three-week-long progress involving rites and pilgrimages (conspicuous among which were those in homage of the deceased, and thus deified, kings and queens).

It is also likely that Kura is to be identified with the 'god of the king', a term that appears quite frequently in Eblaite texts. This would signify that he

Figure 5.2 Tablet with the first redaction of the "Ritual of Kingship" (TM.5.G.1823), clay, from the Archive L.2769, 24th century BC.

was overtly regarded as the dynastic godhead and protector of the long line of city lords, whose last descendent was overthrown by Sargon of Akkad.

A recent plausible proposal is to identify this same, very ancient Eblaite deity with a god of fertility of the fields, typologically not too distant from the archaic Dagan. This god was known in the first centuries of the first millennium BC in Phoenician milieus, but he was also venerated in imperial Assyria, and was used in north-western Semitic personal names.

This god, known as Kurra, was perhaps also attested in the second millennium BC. In the third millennium BC he might have been the lord of the gods, dispenser of natural fertility, and ruler of the sweet water of the abyss. As such he was probably venerated in the central inner regions of Syria, and Ebla might have been his main cult place, whereas other deities, with similar characteristics, Dagan in the Euphrates Valley and El on the Mediterranean coast, had similar functions in the other regions of Syria, to the east and west. The tragic fate of Ebla, at the end of the mature Early Syrian Period might have led to an eclipse for this god, once so highly revered, whereas Dagan and El suffered from this fate only in a very limited way and in more recent times.

After Kura, one of Ebla's most venerated deities was Ishkhara (Figure 5.3), a goddess of fertility and love whose strong links to the earth element were signified by the scorpion, her animal emblem; Ishkhara was also a patron of kingship, and has structural features closely resembling the Semitic goddess Ishtar (appearing in later Old Babylonian and Hittite sources, and customarily believed to originate in the Hurrite tradition). Adda, the great Storm-god, was similarly celebrated in the pantheon, in the second millennium BC occupying the most renowned place of worship in the citadel of Aleppo, and under

Figure 5.3, a & b Ushra-Samu's cylinder seal, and impression with the goddess Ishkhara's figure (TM.07.G.200), limestone and gold, from room L.9583 of the Northern Quarter, 24th century BC.

the equivalent guise of Hadad, as well as under the epithet of Baal "Lord", became the protagonist of the Ugaritic cycle. Most importantly, there was also the mysterious Nidabal or Adabal (the reading of the name is uncertain) venerated at Ebla and numerous other Syrian cities; he too vanished, under this denomination, from later documentation, although the likeliest interpretation for him is as a god of rainfall, morphologically not unlike Adda.

While the interpretation of Nidabal (or Adabal) as a Moon deity is to be rejected, since it rested on a false analogy with Ugaritic documentation, the plausible reading of the name as Adabal would suggest a composite name – *Ada'-Ba'al* – featuring the common Semitic epithet for "Lord"(*ba'l*) and a verb form from a stem that carries the meaning of "knowing" (*yada'*). A hitherto unknown name for a divinity would thus emerge from the second half of the third millennium BC which is linguistically and structurally comparable with the canonical Itur-Mer and Yakrub-El from Mari in the first half of the second millennium BC.

Another highly revered god with important functions in the Eblaite pantheon is Rashap, a chthonic warrior-god, purveyor of epidemics and death, traditionally associated with the Mesopotamian god Nergal and probably venerated as god of the Underworld, feared and revered throughout the second millennium BC in inland and coastal Syria, and then featuring later still, in the first millennium BC, as an awe-inspiring fire spirit of the ether in Aramaic, Phoenician, and even Hebrew cults.

Among the less frequently occurring names of gods who nonetheless had a temple at Saza, the very heart of Ebla, and were certainly prominent in the divine hierarchy in the age of the Archives are Ashtar, Ashtabil, Gamish, and Shamash or Shapash.

Ashtar, or Ishtar, was most certainly the equivalent of the Sumerian goddess Inanna in Ebla too. Celestial and chthonic aspects combined in her, as she was at once assimilated with Venus, the 'morning and evening star', but was also a goddess of fertility and love, and so tempestuous and violent in temperament as to be known in Ebla by the epithet 'lioness', with reference to her iconic animal. It is probable that already in the third quarter of the third millennium BC, the Eblaite Ishtar was both goddess of fertility and war, with a typical conjunction within the same character of rule over love and violence; the same would later occur in Syria and in Mesopotamia, where the celestial Inanna was rather similarly represented.

With a name possibly related to the form Ashtabi-El reconstructed in Mari, Ashtabil is, in his turn, a fearful warrior-god who appears to have had some importance in the domain of state and dynastic rites; his cult was possibly circumscribed, affecting a limited sphere of influence. The divine features of Gamish also appear to have been similar; judging from references to him in the Archives he was highly revered in Ebla and in the northern region, where the city of Karkemish stood, named after him. While his features are not easily defined, he was almost certainly a warrior-god with analogies with Nergal, and was to survive into the first millennium BC as the national god of the country of Moab, in the Transjordanian region, under the equivalent form of Kemosh.

Based on primarily onomastic evidence, the Sun-god whose name consistently appears as Utu in the Ebla Archives (following the Sumerian ideographic form) is likely to represent a goddess of the type of the Ugaritic Shapash, as in almost all of the Syro-Palestinian area, rather than a god akin to Shamash, belonging to the Mesopotamian area. As in all of the ancient eastern Semitic world, in Ebla too this astral deity would have been invested with the crucial functions of patron of justice and equity in the social, economic, and political domains: such attributions descended from the widespread conception that the sun, as all-seer (given its primary position in the universe) and all-discloser (in its habitual cosmic journey), was the divine power which could rigorously and infallibly discern good from evil.

Among the numerous minor gods of the Eblaite pantheon are the divinized personifications of the insignia of kingship (such as Agu, or the Agu – respectively the royal crown and the king's and queen's crowns paired, featuring quite prominently in the "Ritual of Kingship") as well as the deified forms of natural elements, such as rivers and mountains. Instances of these are Two Balikh (in fact the left affluent of the Euphrates, identified as a dual form in several Mesopotamian sources on account of the presence of an underground counterpart of the visible course), or Ammarig, a mountain reported in later Hittite texts as standing in the land of Mukish and quite certainly the seat of a Storm-god in the region of Antioch.

With regard to several of the cities in the region of Ebla and of the north Mesopotamian area, the Ebla Archives quite commonly refer to the 'god of the city' with no further specification. While in the instance of the city of Tuttul, at least, there is no doubt that the presiding god would have been Dagan, fully established as its chief divinity from at least the age of Sargon of Akkad, in the majority of other cases they were probably Storm-gods; that is, localized embodiments of Adda/Hadad.

A phenomenon that is widely attested in the Ebla personal names and other areas of Upper Syria and has to be identified as a feature of archaic religion, on the one hand, and on the other as a common feature in the western Semitic area is the widespread presence (reflected by numerous occurrences in Royal Archive documents) of divine entities who stand for personifications of tribal bonds of kinship. Damu is an eminent instance, to be interpreted in all likelihood as "blood" (understood as the founding element upon which kinship rests), while the clan itself had its divine counterpart in Lim, and possibly also in Kamu, less frequently attested (possibly to be interpreted in the tribal sense of "lineage").

The remarkable status enjoyed by such divinities, who presided over the cornerstones of the social structure but had no related import on the cosmic or natural plane, stands out vividly in Early Syrian Ebla. Not only was their importance, in general, frequently reflected in the composition of the hundreds of names cited in the Archive texts, but more particularly it was manifested in the names of royalty (where they appeared in repeating patterns), not least in the more recent segment of the two dozen or so kings who were deified upon death; it was, finally, further documented by the importance attributed to the institutionalized cult of the deified royal ancestors in the years immediately preceding Sargon's destruction of the city, in rites where the ancestors were referred to as 'the gods of the kings who reside in Taribu' – one of the two sites, with Binash, of the royal cenotaphs and mausoleums. These elements allow us to assess the importance attributed to the divinities that symbolized tribal and family bonds down to the mature Early Syrian Ebla. Worshipped in popular religion as well as in the elitist cults of the court, these divinities almost certainly originated in the pre-urban period and were instrumental in the gradual process that led to permanent settlement.

The archaic features of the religious system in the mature Early Syrian Ebla are further suggested by Kura's and Ishkhara's prominence in the city. This bespeaks a state of affairs which bears structural analogies with the prominence of Dagan at Tuttul and in the Euphrates Valley, a situation clearly preceding the full establishment of gods like Adda/Hadad and Ashtar/Ishtar in Upper Syria and Upper Mesopotamia. The age of the Archives (c. 2300 BC) appears to be the age in which Kura still survives as the unrivalled lord of the city's pantheon, while at the same time Adda and Nidabal/Adabal (within Ebla itself) together with several other Storm-gods in other centres of Upper Syria appear to be gaining in prominence; in parallel, there also appears to be a tendency for more archaic female deities, such as Ishkhara, to converge towards and merge with divinities who were to enjoy almost exclusive affirmation only a few centuries later, such as Ishtar.

It appears that towards the beginning of the second millennium BC, Ishtar came to be known among certain influential Mesopotamian priestly orders (such as that of Assur) as the 'Ishtar of Ebla', and is to be regarded as the forebear of Astarte (present across the entire Syro-Palestinian area in the first millennium BC) as well as the Atargatis of the Classical Period, whose name was probably a conflation of Astarte and Anat, and who came to enjoy such popularity and importance, not only in the East but in Rome too, as to be universally known in Imperial Age sources as the "Syrian Goddess".

The existence of an elitist sphere of religious cult in mature Early Syrian Ebla can be inferred without doubt from the presence of a small number of Sumerian hymns among the literary texts held at the Royal Archives (Figure 5.4); protagonists of these are some of the greatest gods in the pantheon of southern Mesopotamia, such as Enlil, the great god of Nippur; Enki, the Creator-god of Eridu; and Utu, the Sun-god of Larsa and Sippar. It is less plausible that the texts were held at the Archives for didactic purposes alone; what is more credible is that the gods of these literary compositions were objects of worship, however restricted, among the circle of court members in frequent contact with the greater cities of Akkad and Sumer, thereby absorbing elements of the culture.

Figure 5.4 Tablet with a literary text in Sumerian (TM.75.G.2658+), clay, from the
Archive L.2769, 24th century BC.

Although it is beyond doubt that such elitist devotions excluded even the
mid-ranking officials of the palatine administration, the large number of
incantations in the Semitic language preserved in the Archives refer to myths
which on the other hand were common heritage. They usually feature as protagonist the Storm-god Adda/Hadad, who even in this remote age was probably a god of the more ancient Semitic peoples of northern Syria. There is
then the issue of a common (though not quite unitary) literary culture among
the peoples of Kish and Ebla: the question is raised by the presence of a
Semitic hymn in the Ebla Archives which is taken to be the most ancient literary composition in any Semitic language to survive in writing; celebrating
the god Shamash, a parallel version of the hymn has been found at Abu
Salabikh, in the country of Akkad. It is, however, unlikely that the regions of
Kish and Ebla shared common religious elements of any relevance.

On the plane of popular religion in Early Syrian Ebla, a wealth of information (though yet to be studied in detail) is certainly encoded in personal names
from both Ebla and Syrian cities whose inhabitants are frequently cited by
name in the Archives' texts. It is certainly of some interest that certain gods
were not the object of particular veneration in the official cults (since they are

seldom mentioned in the monthly accounts of offerings presented by state dignitaries) while their names were commonly embedded in personal names, although the reasons for such popularity may vary significantly case by case. Then theophoric names are not always easily explained, particularly when the embedded elements are city names (as occurs with Aleppo, Nagar, or Mari): the reference in these instances is probably to a celebrated sanctuary in the city or its vicinity.

The high frequency in names of the element Il/Ilum (which simply means "god") can be easily accounted for whether the term designated a particular and unspecified god or alluded generically to some divine power and thereby to the divine world *tout court*. A similar logic seems to apply to Be, a Sumerian ideogram which, like the Semitic Baʻl, simply and generically means "lord" – a designation that patently applies to any god.

Typical of Semitic onomastics in general (and thus also Eblaic ones in particular) is the use of adjectives that refer to divine attributes, which reflects in the relative frequency of such epithets as Gamal "benevolent", Dashilu "prosperous", Danu " powerful", Ishar "just", Mudu "wise", Naim "propitious", and Damigu " good". A class of elements widely represented in personal names in the Archives is exemplified by Zikir (strictly limited to individuals from Ebla, and never occurring as the name of a divinity in any of the cults) and Malik (with regional circulation: widely attested in Ebla and largely popular in the entire north Syrian region). Though in different senses, both appear to be instances of theophoric names referring to the semantics of highly valued ethical principles and ideals: Zikir is certainly related to a stem signifying "to name", "to mention", "to recall" and thus probably points to a term akin to "fame" or "prestige"; the interpretation of Malik, on the other hand, is doubtful over the whole Semitic area, though it may designate a divinized function derived from a very common stem that possibly had the specific meaning of "behaving in kingly fashion".

Compared with the wealth and variety of written documents (however schematic) regarding the religious domain in mature Early Syrian Ebla, providing information on more than 40 distinct deities, archaeological evidence is far more limited (though valuable) and consists in the remains of what probably were the two most important temples (from the ideological and monumental point of view) not only of Ebla, but of the entire Syrian region in the age of the Royal Archives. These are the Temple of the Rock, at the southeastern extreme of the Lower Town, close to where the Steppe Gate would be erected in the ramparts of the later Early Syrian city (Figure 5.5) and the Red Temple, erected on the western edge of the Acropolis and close to the Royal Palace to the north.

The Temple of the Rock (Plate IV) was an imposing, albeit peculiar, devotional building of the mature Early Syrian Period; it featured a façade with projecting antae, a latitudinal cella, and a vestibule of the same size as the cella, and, judging by the considerable depth of its outer walls (6 m), may have risen to over 15 m. It faced east and lay close to the Early Syrian rampart,

Figure 5.5 Ebla, Temple of the Rock, view of the cult building, from the south, 24th
century BC.

which, in this area as also in the western segment of the city fortifications,
constituted the core of the mighty Early Syrian ramparts.

It is of especial relevance that the latitudinal cella mirrored by an identical
vestibule are spatial features wholly foreign to the tradition of the third Ebla
of the Early Syrian period. Likewise, the eastern orientation of the temple
and its peculiar positioning, somewhat compressed against the city walls and
with the full extent of the Early Syrian Lower Town at its back, lying west, are
unusual features when compared with the canons of orientation and loftiness
that characterize later Early Syrian temples. Furthermore, the Temple of the
Rock was erected on a slight peripheral rise of the limestone hill upon which
the as yet almost wholly unknown archaic Early Syrian city was founded,
and after which, on the grounds of plausible Semitic etymology, the city was
named. The toponym "Ebla" occurs, in fact, both in Palestine and Arabia as
the term for a low limestone hill.

The bedrock at the site that was chosen for the imposing temple of the
mature Early Syrian Period was not levelled: irregularities and cavities in the
rock, to be found in the cella and vestibule floor, were left fully visible and
incorporated within the covered area of the sanctuary, as though they bore
some special significance to its builders. In particular, the cella was erected
in a spot marked by a broad ellipsoid cavity that is still perfectly visible, with
three wells burrowing into the depths of the rock to the subjacent aquifer
(Figure 5.6). These wells were probably once springs which carried special

Figure 5.6 Ebla, Temple of the Rock, the cella L.9190, with the oval opening and the three wells, from the south, 24th century BC.

historical or mythical significance, presumably as residence to some powerful god presiding over subterranean fresh waters, and as the primaeval site of the city's foundation.

We are induced to believe, then, that precise reasons (ritual in nature but not easily identified – though certainly related to the physical, historical, or mythical significance of the rock) determined that the Temple of the Rock be erected at such a peculiar spot on the urban plan, flanking the city walls and in the vicinity of one of the city gates; what we can guess is that these reasons were attached to the irregularities and cavities in the limestone surface, which were not only carefully preserved but indeed made the object of religious reverence, determining the position of the temple's cella. The site for the sanctuary must have been chosen with regard to the physical nature of the place (due to the presence of fresh water springs), to its historical significance (as site of the original settlement), and to its mythical association with the residence of a great god in the abyss below.

Although there are no other instances in Syrian archaeology of a temple with a cella opening onto a cavity communicating with underground waters, the short Imperial Age treatise *De Dea Syra* (attributed to Lucian of Samosata) discussing the great, most revered sanctuary of Atargatis at Hierapolis in Syria provides valuable comparative evidence: there too the cella stood upon a cavity, and the founding of the temple was related to the legend of Deucalion and Pyrrha in the Greek version of the Flood myth.

While dedicated to a goddess of the Ishtar/Astarte type of the Roman Age, the Hierapolis sanctuary must have originally been connected with an ancient local deity of the type of the great Enki of Eridu, the Mesopotamian lord of the abyss and of fresh waters, as can be inferred from the peculiarity of the underlying cavity and the attribution of its foundation to Deucalion.

From all of this cross-evidence we are able to infer that in the age of the Archives, the Temple of the Rock was dedicated to the great Kura, chief god of the Eblaite pantheon. The Middle Syrian mythological texts from Ugarit, in the second half of the second millennium BC, explicitly and repeatedly state that El, chief god of the Ugaritic pantheon, resided 'at the source of the rivers, in the midst of the course of the two oceans' (like the Mesopotamian god Enki), while in Old Syrian glyptics from the first half of the second millennium BC, El was usually portrayed with the same attributes as Enki, bearing overflowing pots of water, or with subterranean waters flowing from his figure.

As mentioned previously, the Eblaite god Kura may be regarded as an archaic analogue of El, distinguished by chthonic rather than celestial features: this aspect is clearly specified in the Ugaritic texts which place El's residence 'at the source of the rivers and oceans', which in turn reads as an allusion to his rule over subterranean waters, on the one hand, and on the other to his residing in the depths of the abyss – exactly like the god Enki of Eridu. If Eblaite Kura was, like Ugaritic El, the lord of fresh waters and resided in the abyss, then it is quite reasonable to infer that his first place of worship was the Temple of the Rock at the south-eastern periphery of the Lower Town of Ebla. It is very likely that at Ebla as in the land of Sumer, it was believed that every urban centre was raised after the foundation of the main sanctuary by the polyadic god. Therefore, it is likewise plausible that it was held that the Temple of the Rock had been erected by the very same god Kura as his own residence or as a gateway to his mythical seat in the oceans.

Clear textual indications of the decentralized topographic location of one of the two Kura temples at Ebla supporting this interpretation are found in highly significant passages from the "Ritual of Kingship", a crucial text in the Royal Archives recovered in three parallel versions. The ritual prescribes the series of liturgical acts the royal couple had to perform in the course of an important religious ceremonial which some believe to relate to the royal nuptials, and others, more plausibly, to a three-week-long ritual for the renovation of kingship, centred of course around the king and queen. The first act in the ritual is the queen's entrance into the city at the Temple of Kura, by the city walls and Kura Gate; the description indicates that the queen had to await sunrise in the fields outside the city. There followed a long series of ritual acts performed by the king and queen together in the course of a prolonged pilgrimage to several sites in the environs of Ebla, to the burial grounds of the ancient deified kings; at the close of the ritual, the royal couple entered the Temple of Kura within Saza, the palatine area of government in the Early Syrian city.

The texts inform us that in the age of the Royal Archives there were two temples devoted to the great patron god Kura: one, decentralized, stood by the walls and the gate that bore the god's name; the other, in a central position, stood within the site of political power, the Saza. The two sanctuaries certainly bore special significance since both were connected to crucial stages in the ritual of kingship, at the beginning and end respectively: the temple connected with the Kura Gate, where the long ritual began, had been built to face east since ritual prescribed that the ceremony of the renovation of kingship should start at dawn with the queen's entrance into the city and the temple, just as the temple was lit by the rays of the rising sun.

There is every reason to believe that the Temple of the Rock which stood by the Steppe Gate of the Early Syrian city (certainly to be identified with the Early Syrian gate described as the Kura Gate in the Archives text) was the first of the two temples devoted to Kura, and that the ritual of kingship began at this shrine (ending much later at the second Temple of Kura within the Saza on the Acropolis). This explanation at once accounts for the east-facing orientation of the Temple of the Rock and for the narrowness of the doorway between vestibule and cella (Figure 5.7), just 1.40 m wide in a wall 5.60 m thick. Within the imposing temple walls, the door stood as a monumental slit endowed with special symbolic significance, as it was the gateway for the early

Figure 5.7 Ebla, Temple of the Rock, the door to the cella L.9190, with traces of the destruction, from the west, 24th century BC.

rays of light that, as outlined above, marked the queen's entrance into the city. The strong links between Kura's Temple of the Rock and royalty suggest that the temple and its underlying rock further bore some mythical-historical connection to each other, referable to both the foundation of the city and the divine consecration of kingship in archaic Early Syrian Ebla.

The finding of the Temple of the Rock and its identification with the first of Kura's two sanctuaries in the "Ritual of Kingship", combined with the recent finding of the Red Temple on the Acropolis (by the Royal Palace and clearly within the Saza), is of tremendous significance in the interpretation of the historical and religious mapping of the city. It was believed that the second temple was located below the imposing Ishtar's Temple on the Citadel of the later Old Syrian city, which is the well-known cult building of Area D, on the west edge of the Acropolis (Plate I).

This imposing building of the third Ebla was erected (probably during the first decades of the second millennium BC) over a large mud brick platform, similar to those used for the Early Syrian Royal Palace G. A small sounding made in its cella during the first decade of excavations brought to light the remains of a cult building of the last centuries of the third millennium BC. The temple which – immediately after the Old Syrian city (corresponding to the last and final Ebla) had been refounded – became the dynastic sanctuary of the great Ishtar, patron goddess of the city, had probably been built over the ruins of Kura's Temple of the Saza. In fact, the texts of the Royal Archives state that it stood very close to the buildings of the great mature Early Syrian palace.

Soundings made in 2008 all around the Old Syrian temple of Ishtar and inside its cella, antecella, and vestibule, allowed us to bring to light the basic elements of the plan of the building called the Red Temple for the dark red colour of its bricks (Figure 5.8).

This second, very important mature Early Syrian cult building was erected after the north sector of the West Unit of the Central Complex of Royal Palace G had been deactivated and razed. This took place in an advanced phase of Early Bronze IVA, during Ishar-Damu's reign. Later on, the temple was destroyed at the same time as the whole settlement of the age of the Royal Archives, at the end of Early Bronze IVA.

Regarding its structure, the Red Temple had very thick walls, a deep vestibule, and a slightly longer than large cella: it appeared as a single cella structure with antae and had strong similarities with the Temple of the Rock for its typology, size, and proportions. The moderately broad cella found in the Temple of the Rock (featuring as an alternative to the moderately long cella in the Red Temple) might either represent an archaic spatial feature of Eblaite architecture belonging to the Early Syrian Period which was soon discontinued; or suggest that, during the mature Early Syrian Period, a canonical architectural template had not yet been established. In the time of the Archives, the cella was probably usually square in plan, and it could be either larger (probably in earlier times) or longer (perhaps prevalently later), whereas the later Old Syrian tradition privileged the long cella.

Figure 5.8 Ebla, Red Temple, the ruins of the Early Syrian cult building below the cella of the Old Syrian Ishtar's Temple of the Acropolis, from the east, 24th and 18th–17th century BC.

The Red Temple featured some spatial refinement: at all four corners of the building there were low buttresses, approximately 0.20–0.30 m thick, looking like corner towers. Two columns formed a porch in the vestibule (Figure 5.9), and four columns divided the cella, creating a larger central nave and two narrower side naves. The bases of the two columns of the vestibule, and two out of four columns in the cella were found still in place: they were massive, slightly bulging limestone cylinders. Large fragments of the bases of the two back columns of the cella were re-employed in the foundations of the later Ishtar's Temple while other fragments were found scattered in the cult area. Three steps of beautiful limestone slabs accurately worked created a short entrance staircase to the vestibule porch, as large as the façade of the building. The Red Temple (Temple D2) of the western sector of the Acropolis (Figure 5.10), with its sophisticated architectural structure, overlooked, from the north, the imposing ceremonial wings of the Royal Palace G, and has certainly to be identified with Kura's Temple in the Saza, where the solemn entrance of the king and queen took place, after they had been consecrated again by the long ritual, honouring the deified royal ancestors. At the same time as the king and queen, the cult statues of Kura and Barama also entered the temple, concluding the complex ritual of the renewal of kingship, as described in the "Ritual of Kingship".

This cult building was probably erected at the climax of the success of Ebla's political power, shortly before the terrible destruction by Sargon, in a

Figure 5.9 Ebla, Red Temple, detail of the two columns in the vestibule of the Early Syrian building, in the sounding in the antecella of Ishtar's Temple of the Acropolis, from the north-west, 24th and 18th–17th century BC.

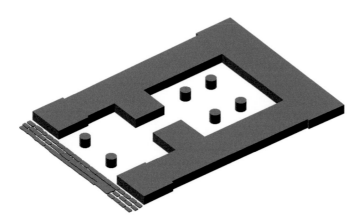

Figure 5.10 Ebla, Red Temple, schematic isometric view of the mature Early Syrian cult building, 24th century BC.

year when the economic texts of the Royal Archives register the delivery of a very relevant, and definitely peculiar amount of silver for Kura's Temple. It was certainly planned to be the dynastic sanctuary of the powerful Early Syrian lords of Ebla. It is not astonishing, therefore, that the dynastic temple of the archaic Old Syrian Period, dedicated to the goddess Ishtar, new patron deity of the Eblaite dynasty, was built over its ruins.

The Temple of the Rock of the first Ebla is extremely important from the historical, religious, and ideological points of view, but it is also very important for the typological and spatial characteristics of its architectural concept. The temple is marked by three architectural aspects: its type with antae in the façade, the latitudinal plan of the cella, and the vestibule and cella having the same proportion and size. The presence of the antae will be a characteristic of the whole history of cult architecture of Syria until the Iron Age. The two other aspects are clearly very ancient features of the Eblaite architectural tradition of the Early Syrian Period, which had no following in the later Old Syrian Period.

The temple plan with projecting antae thus appears to have been a constant (though not exclusive) feature of Syrian religious architecture. While there are variations on the basic design, it nonetheless has parallels in both the Palestine of Early Bronze II–III and Upper Mesopotamia in the central part of the third millennium BC. The broad cella, on the other hand, was discontinued in later architecture at Ebla, but is a constant feature of Palestinian temples in the archaic urban architecture of the third millennium BC (regardless of differences in the plan of the vestibule): it may then be regarded as an archaic feature of the more ancient architectural traditions in the archaic Early Syrian world of the mid (if not early) third millennium BC. Although not yet backed by archaeological findings, this early tradition found a parallel in contemporary Palestinian religious architecture, which had by then established its canon, but was also more modest in scale. Whereas the temple type with same-sized cella and vestibule entailed a considerably deep vestibule, the model was abandoned over the subsequent decades, leading to the short vestibule of all Early Syrian temples; the cella, conversely, was later made deeper, resulting in an elongated shape.

With its structural affinities with the Temple of the Rock, the Red Temple testifies to the unity of the architectural culture of the mature Early Syrian cult architecture, given the presence of the antae, the approximately square plan of the cella, and the very deep vestibule. It also presents the possible beginning of the tradition, probably not yet canonical, of the longitudinal cella, which will become longer in the late Early Syrian period in temples that are not palatial and dynastic, as appears in the cult buildings erected in those years over the ruins of the Temple of the Rock.

The only other known temple from inland Syria that might have been founded at the close of the mature Early Syrian Period in the land the Royal Archives call Ibal (south of Ebla, in the region east of Hamah and of Homs) has recently been discovered at al-Rawda, and supports this hypothesis.

Compared to the Temple of the Rock (which is also far more monumental in scale), this temple has an approximately square cella and shallow vestibule, and matches the religious architecture documented by the temples that began to be built in succession upon the ruins of the Temple of the Rock from the late Early Syrian Period.

In the domains of religion and ideology, as well as architecture, it appears that the foundations for subsequent traditions were laid in the mature Early Syrian Period. While the cult of the deified royal ancestors had already been developed to a high degree of sophistication (and remained a feature of religiosity in Syria for centuries, throughout the Bronze Age at least), other phenomena were incipient, but already attested. The divinities related to fertility were already frequently evoked, as in the instance of Hadad, documented not just at Ebla but elsewhere in Syria, and Ishtar, the 'Lioness', who was already an important goddess of fertility and war. Neither Hadad nor Ishtar, however, had yet fully acquired the status and significance that would distinguish them in the following centuries.

Ishkhara and Ishtar, and possibly also Kura and Hadad, must certainly have been the object of complex processes of syncretism which eventually promoted Ishtar and Hadad to the position of prominence and universalism that made them popular gods in large sectors of the Roman world down to the onset of Late Antiquity. Similarly, the architectural models developed in mature Early Syrian Ebla in the third quarter of the third millennium BC were to initiate a long-standing tradition, at least as regards religious architecture. The proportions and spatial layout involved in the original model were re-elaborated in the course of architectural history in Syria and Palestine beyond even the age of Solomon, king of Israel, in the tenth century BC, when, according to biblical tradition, he built the legendary First Temple of Jerusalem. Although the building was destroyed in the sixth century BC, its legacy survived as an influence in Western architecture down to the Renaissance and Baroque period.

6 The State Archives

Economy, culture, and society

Ebla entered the history and legend of Near Eastern archaeology with the discovery of numerous cuneiform tablets in the State Archives housed in the Administrative Quarter of Royal Palace G. This was mainly on account of the extraordinary dimensions of the find, the great age of the texts, the official nature of the documents, and their location outside the Mesopotamian area. Discovered for the most part in 1975, the texts total more than 17,050 inventory items, including just under 2,000 whole or nearly whole tablets, while the large number of fragments would indicate an original total of between 4,000 and 5,000 tablets, a number which has obviously more than quadrupled with the destruction of over half the documents when the palace complex was destroyed.

The dating of the Ebla texts to between 2350 and 2300 BC is exceptional as regards antiquity outside the Mesopotamian area where, conversely, the first cuneiform texts belong to the late fourth millennium BC. Before the discovery of the Ebla texts, no cores of cuneiform tablets of any substance were known outside Babylonia, Elam, and Assyria before the second half of the twentieth century BC. More external questions of dates and numbers apart, their truly exceptional importance lies in their representing an ample but also cohesive section, basically left intact at the time the city was destroyed, of the central archives of a powerful and politically significant kingdom from the third quarter of the third millennium BC which at the moment of destruction was about to play a decidedly proto-imperial role. This particular point can only be fully evaluated by considering two facts which reveal the unique aspects of the epigraphic find at Ebla. First, these texts and their records cover almost 50 years of the administration of the kingdom, a particularly long period for document conservation. Second, in the Sumerian and Akkadian world of Lower Mesopotamia, throughout the whole third millennium BC, while many substantial cores of archives survive, mainly from important temple complexes (Lagash, for example, but also Ur and Nippur), the only texts in any way comparable in political importance to those of Ebla are all much smaller and more heterogeneous groups, produced by the central administrations of the kingdoms of Sumer and Akkad.

The tablets of the Archives were found, almost intact, in rooms of the Administrative Quarter or of the Court of Audience of the Royal Palace G, rooms the functions of which are not difficult to imagine (Figure 6.1). The greatest concentration was in the large Archive L.2769 (c. 14,750 inventory numbers; Plates II–III, 1), where they were found on collapsed wooden shelves (Figure 6.2, Figure 6.3) almost certainly on the east, north, and west walls of the room (Figure 6.7, Plate III, 2); this was the only area of the palace certainly devoted to their permanent conservation; it was equally certainly the main palace Archive. The room containing the second largest number of fragments was the Small Archive L.2712 (c. 900), where the texts were stored on two shelves on the north and west walls (Figure 14.5). The room was probably a temporary deposit for the tablets, and also contained various weights and vessels. The third room, also possibly a temporary storage, was the trapezoidal store-room L.2764 (c. 535), where the texts had probably been stored on mud brick benches with carved wooden shutters. A fourth room, curious in terms of its function but also producing a significant number of finds, was the vestibule L.2875 (c. 655), in which the tablets were placed on two low mud brick benches built in front of the door to the Great Archive (Figure 6.4). Since benches are unquestionably places to sit, and fragments of bone styli and a steatite eraser had been found in the same room, clearly a transit area, it can be presumed that documents would have been written, selected, and classified before being stored definitively in the main Archives.

A much smaller number of fragments (c. 90) was found in the destroyed level of the inner court L.2913, where, however, they probably ended up during the plundering and the fire, having been stored elsewhere. Only a small number of tablets – some 15 texts – were discovered in 2004 in the three small rooms built against the east wall of the Throne Room L.2866, consisting of a single row of mud bricks like the Great Archive of the eastern porch of the Court of Audience (Figure 6.6). It is certain that these documents of the terminal years of life of the city, all represented by short texts which register delivery of metals often in small amounts, had been only temporarily deposited in those warehouses, before they were brought to the place of their permanent storage, which probably was the Great Archive L.2769 nearby. Some 40 texts and three well-preserved tablets were found on the floor of two other rooms, L.2586 in the North-West Wing north of the northern side of the Court of Audience, and L.3462 in the Southern Quarter respectively, undoubtedly for reasons of consultation and not preservation. Lastly, the same Court of Audience (L.2752) produced a find of some 25 tablets in front of the eastern porch, in correspondence with the Monumental Gateway. These were almost all large, and had been left at floor level on two wooden planks which would have formed a sort of tray to carry them (Figure 6.5). Some of these tablets are strangely incomplete, and must have been abandoned either by servants, intent on disposing of deteriorated texts at the moment the palace was attacked, or by plunderers removing archive documents at the first signs of the fire. Integration of data deducible from the texts of the Royal Archives, over

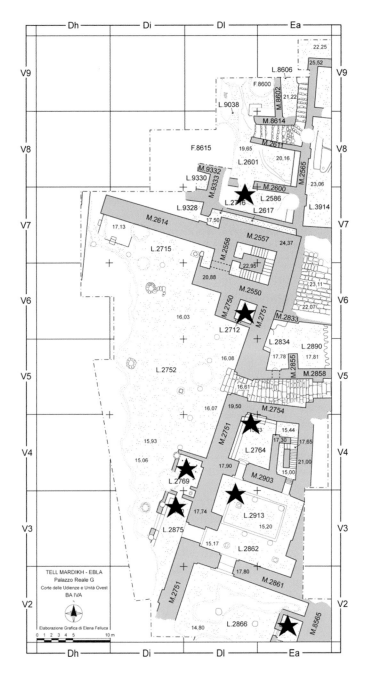

Figure 6.1 Ebla, Royal Palace G, schematic plan of the Administrative Quarter, with indication of the main finding places of tablets, 24th century BC.

Figure 6.2 Ebla, Royal Palace G, detail of the tablets in place against the east wall of the Archive L.2769, in the Administrative Quarter, from the west, 24th century BC.

Figure 6.3 Ebla, Royal Palace G, tablets in place on the floor, against the north wall of the Archive L.2769, from the south, 24th century BC.

Figure 6.4 Ebla, Royal Palace G, tablets in place before the benches in the vestibule L.2875 of the Administrative Quarter, from the east, 24th century BC.

Figure 6.5 Ebla, Royal Palace G, tablets in place on wooden boards in the Court of Audience L.2752, before the Monumental Gateway, from the south, 24th century BC.

Figure 6.6 Ebla, Royal Palace G, the small room L.8778, against the east wall of the Throne Room L.2866, from the north-west, 24th century BC.

Figure 6.7 Ebla, Royal Palace G, reconstruction of the Archive L.2769, with the placement of the tablets on the shelves, 24th century BC.

three-quarters of which are accounts, furnishing combined and controlled information when read in conjunction with the archaeological documentation of Royal Palace G (seriously sacked, but still preserving remains of materials bespeaking commercial relations with very distant countries) allows a reconstruction of the foundations of the city's economy in a period corresponding to the last decades of the Early Dynastic III Period of the Mesopotamian world, and a relatively early phase of the VI Egyptian Dynasty.

The written documents, however, while supplying a store of information of primary importance are not of course guaranteed to cover all aspects of the mature Early Syrian city's economy. Other groups of as yet undiscovered archives must have existed in the palace, as attested by the very few texts from the Southern Quarter regarding aspects of the administration of agriculture and the timber trade, while other sectors of the economy, while important, were in all probability not recorded with the precision and thoroughness of the texts in the Royal Archives, as seems to have been the case with supplies of precious materials such as lapis lazuli.

Fundamental information from the finance-related texts of the archives, then, was supplemented by data from archaeological findings. On the one hand, the archives produced several very specific classes of invaluable documents, reconstructing the palace economy: monthly statements of textiles, clothing, and metal objects, etc., obviously produced and distributed under royal control; or monthly records of incoming supplies of gold and silver, obtained through the king, the city lords, and from allied or vassal cities. On the other hand, archaeological finds in the Royal Palace such as the numerous blocks and fragments of lapis lazuli (some 42 kilos in all) from as far away as Afghanistan or, in the inner court of the Administrative Quarter, the large numbers of Egyptian diorite and alabaster bowls produced by the pharaonic workshops constitute extraordinarily positive contributions to the reconstruction of the economic base for Ebla's success, above all in the last years of the great mature Early Syrian city.

It is this convergence of documentary elements which gives a convincing picture of the unusual complexity of Ebla's economy at the time of the Archives, determined by supplementary factors at different levels creating a particularly flourishing situation, accentuated by a series of ever higher peaks, until the terrible destruction which seems to have appeared with no forewarning. The base of Ebla's economy at that period was undoubtedly its extensive agriculture, in an area where the average yearly rainfall, just over 250 cubic millimetres, allowed not only the cultivation of cereals, but typically Mediterranean arboriculture, such as olives and grapes: as the Archives (Figure 6.8) and palaeobotanical evidence attest, considerable quantities of wine and oil were produced, especially in the karst plateau of inland Syria extending west of Ebla, to the north and the south, flourishing in the increased rainfall and the particular hill formations.

This sound base for the agricultural economy, centred on the Mediterranean triad of wheat, olives, and grapes, was complemented nutritionally by pulses

Figure 6.8 Administrative tablet dealing with land allotments (TM.75.G.1768), clay, 24th century BC.

in particular, providing secondary protein. To this should be added the enormous climatic advantages allowing productive agriculture and livestock farming, the latter rich and diversified both on the city's outskirts and even more in the area under the city's direct political control. The hilly regions with increasing proportions of rainfall, extending west of Ebla, provided rich pasture for considerable herds of cattle, while the gradually drier lands stretching from the east of the city through the vast steppes of the outer areas of the Syrian-Arabic Desert were ideal for the transhumance of vast herds of sheep and goats.

The Archives texts document very explicitly both the husbandry practices and, even more, their capillary control under the administration of the central chancery. This would clearly have been supplemented by a series of smaller peripheral centres providing partial analytical data regarding different parts of the territory; these would then have been elaborated and integrated into the comprehensive, synthetic accounts drawn up by the central administration and still available, in considerable numbers, in the Royal Archives. In a manner not unjustifiably deemed astonishing, these record herds of several thousands of various kinds of oxen and cows and tens of thousands of sheep and goats. Such numbers, recorded by the Saza central administration, must, of course, refer to herds and flocks dispersed over huge areas and not simply within the immediate outskirts of the city, where they would have been a menace to agriculture. They also record both a considerable extension, not local but regional, of territory under the direct control of the administration, and the probable existence of a wide-spread if not quite capillary existence of smaller administrative centres and the frequent presence of central administration scribes over the whole area.

There was also a third level of integration, however, besides that of agriculture and animal farming. This was less fundamental than the other two for the early stages of the state economy's development, but an essential contribution to the extraordinary progress which made of Ebla not merely an important regional centre with considerable local control, but a political power with extensive international relations and proto-imperial ambitions. This level regarded controlling the supply of basic raw materials, fundamental on the level not only of subsistence but for the development of sophisticated technologies possible, according to criteria of advanced specialization and mass production, only through the unabated dominance of urban culture. This began to be established first in the alluvial regions of Lower Mesopotamia, characterized by the irrigation practices of intensive farming as far back as the late fourth millennium BC and then, from almost the mid-third millennium BC, in the areas of Upper Mesopotamia and inland Syria, where the necessity of dry farming called exclusively for extensive farming over vast areas.

Control of this kind (which of course could be exercised indirectly, with the collaboration of minor potentates politically connected with Ebla) in a more schematic form concerned timber, especially cedar, present in the Lebanon mountains and in those of the northwards extension of the western ridge running parallel to the Mediterranean coast; silver, present in the Amanus Mountains north-west of Ebla, a virtual hinge between the south–north chains of Syria and the west–east chains of Anatolia; and copper, rich deposits of which lay in the long Taurus chain, closing off the tablelands of Syria to the north and separating it from the Anatolian plateau.

Cedar provided an extremely strong and resistant timber, in lengths unimaginable in other tree species. It was highly appreciated in both Egypt and Mesopotamia, and from the early third millennium BC at the latest, it was transported into the alluvial valleys of the Nile, the Tigris, and the Euphrates, areas completely lacking in straight and resistant high-stem trees. The wood fast became an essential asset in the monumental architecture of the urban civilizations spreading across both Egypt and Lower Mesopotamia.

Silver, on the other hand, acted as a benchmark for the value and price of all goods in the urban civilizations of western Asia, from Babylonia to Elam, and from Upper Mesopotamia to inland Syria, where in an archaic era wool had once been used. Copper, with tin, was obviously the basic component in the alloy comprising bronze, and was present in a far higher percentage than tin (less readily available), according to a ratio, which tended to stabilize towards the late third millennium BC, of nine parts to one, as attested both in several accounts in the Ebla Archives and empirically in contemporary bronze tools discovered in Ebla's Royal Palace. In metallurgy, bronze, of course, represented the great innovation at the beginnings of urban civilization, as eloquently revealed in archaeological documentation of the many workshops for bronze working recently discovered in Early Dynastic Mari. Its importance is immediately obvious in the development of metallurgical high technology in the historical phase of urban civilization's consolidation, which took place over much of the third millennium BC in several areas of western Asia.

Direct or indirect control of timber, silver, and copper supplies, in the decades around the mid-third millennium BC, meant being able to condition, for better or for worse, the development of the great urban centres which had developed in the previous centuries across the whole of Lower Mesopotamia, by assisting or impeding the supply. This placed Ebla in a position of strength on the international scene and opened up ambitious interventionist possibilities for interfering drastically in the economy and politics of major potentates in what was the Sumerian-Akkadian world of the Early Dynastic III Period of Lower Mesopotamia, the uncontested driving force behind urban civilization.

Moreover, Ebla's extraordinary economic-political centrality, determined in the course of the twenty-fourth century BC by a skilful exploitation of a privileged geographical and environmental situation, was further strengthened in those same decades by the city's assumed function in long-distance trade in precious stones. These were also very important in terms of prestige, and considered to indicate the highest possible level in urban society. The unprecedented quantities of blocks of raw lapis lazuli in the Royal Palace of Ebla (which, having escaped the notice of Sargon's plundering army, must have been only part, and possibly a small one, of the amount originally present in the Administrative Quarter) is impressive proof of Ebla's role in the long-distance lapis trade between Afghanistan (almost certainly the mythical land of Aratta, which according to Sumerian texts had large quarries of the stone) and Egypt, where the pharaohs of the Old Kingdom were among the admirers of what was considered the most precious stone known to humanity.

To play such a central role in long-distance trade, Ebla took advantage of its geographic and strategic position. On the one hand, it stood midway between the Euphrates, marking the caravan route by river and land from Lower Mesopotamia, where by means of two itineraries, to the north and south respectively, crossing the desert areas of Iran, the lapis lazuli arrived from far-off Badakhshan, and the Mediterranean, the ports of which were in constant contact with the Nile Delta, either Byblos or possibly Ugarit. On the other hand, the city also had the advantage of facing one of the rare passes which still today provide a means of crossing the compact and steep if not high mountain chain which extends the Lebanon ridge to the north.

While a part of the lapis lazuli arriving in Ebla through Iran and Mesopotamia was retained for use in the palace workshops, to create works in situ in the great centre (numerous fragments of which have been found), the majority was probably exported to the court of Memphis. In exchange, the pharaohs of the Old Kingdom sent precious diorite and alabaster vases, containing essences and perfumes, many of which have been found in the ruins of the Administrative Quarter of Royal Palace G. They also, however, sent considerable quantities of gold, which in the later third millennium BC arrived in abundance from Nubia, dubbed the 'land of gold' by the Egyptians. If, indeed, the powerful pharaohs of the V and VI Dynasty sent only a modest part of their Nubian gold, of which they probably procured regular supplies, it is not surprising that the monthly entries for gold and silver in the Ebla Royal Archives accounts mention large quantities of silver and considerable amounts of gold as monthly entries in the Palace Treasury.

If the basis of Early Syrian Ebla's economic development would seem, then, largely comprehensible, as is its close relationship with the Mesopotamian world, it is still no small matter to list the components of the Early Syrian culture of the Archives age which are foreign to the culture of Lower Mesopotamia; and conversely to define the ways in which this Upper Syrian culture shares in the unquestionable unity characterizing every cultural aspect of Sumer and Akkad in the third quarter of the third millennium BC, the period of the mature Early Syrian Ebla's zenith. There is no doubt that in basic aspects of the structuring of the administration, rather than specific elements of the political institutions, – as regards, for example, its mind-set and the basic lines of communication in the wider sense – Early Syrian Ebla would seem to have taken essential and characterizing elements from the Early Dynastic world of Lower Mesopotamia, which must, however, have been adapted to a somewhat different tradition and local history. It was, of course, a tradition with which the Syrian Protohistoric society of the Uruk Period would have come into close contact in past centuries, and with which relations had never been completely severed even in the initial and central phases of the Early Dynastic Period, in the early third millennium BC.

As regards the institutions, the fact that the Ebla Archives used the Sumerian term *en*, "lord", the most ancient Mesopotamian royal title which possibly dates from the Protohistoric Period, to designate the holder of the royal office would seem to suggest a complete correspondence between the Sumerian and Eblaite idea of kingship, although it was more probably a choice made by the Ebla chancery since the term was used to describe this particular office in the foreign language of the administration, Sumerian. This seems confirmed by the fact that the Eblaic reading of the Sumerian logogram *en* in the local Semitic language was *malikum*, which in all the western Semitic languages means "king" and not *bēlum*, "lord", as it was in Akkadian, the Semitic language of southern Mesopotamia.

In reality, this scribal correspondence in Ebla between the Sumerian *en* and the Eblaic *malikum* signals that despite appearances, kingship in Ebla did not actually correspond to the function of high priest and spouse of the city goddess, which was certainly part of the Sumerian concept of *en* and of the ideology of kingship not only in Uruk, but probably in all the Protohistorical urban centres of Lower Mesopotamia. Consequently, the Eblaic use of *malikum* for "king" clearly indicates that the use of the logogram "e n" for the sovereign was merely a scribal invention, not implying correspondence between the royal institution of Uruk and the other urban settlements in Lower Mesopotamia and that of Ebla and the other contemporary cities of Upper Syria and Upper Mesopotamia governed by a leader equally designated *en*.

Moreover, the Sumerian term *lugal*, initially accompanied by, and alternating with *ensi*, and then consistently alone, probably meant "king" from the central phases of the Early Dynastic Period of Lower Mesopotamia onwards, and in the Ebla chancery was never used to designate the "sovereign", but rather a number of very high-ranking officials with important government roles (of which however there is no clear trace in the institutions of contemporary cities in the Mesopotamian world): further indication that the institutional reality of Sumer and Akkad on one hand, and of Ebla and the other urban centres of Upper Syria on the other, are distinct and only partially analogous.

The closer analogy probably lay in some sacredness of the figure of the *en/malikum* in Ebla and in other Early Syrian centres, which was certainly true for the *en/bēlum* in Uruk and other Protohistorical centres of Sumer. The problem remains as to why the Ebla chancery used the archaic Sumerian term "e n" for "sovereign" and not the more current term *lugal*, by then (the period of the Ebla Archives) in common use in Lower Mesopotamia. Since in the southern Mesopotamian area only Uruk continued to use *en* to designate the sovereign (till the end of the Early Dynastic III Period, when the Archives texts were written), it could be inferred that relations between Ebla and Uruk were strong in that period. This is nowhere indicated in the Archives, however, where mention is never made of Uruk while, conversely, the presence in Ebla of scribes from Kish and Mari is most definitely noted.

The influence in mature Early Syrian Ebla of writing and administrative procedures from the Kish region, and therefore from the country of Akkad in general, and from what has been defined as the "Kish culture" in particular, might explain many particularities of the Archives texts. A plausible hypothesis, then, explaining their use of the logogram *en* for "king" in Ebla is that it looks back to a relatively ancient tradition, when the term was still used in southern Mesopotamia to indicate the head of the urban community. This would have been probably no later than the Early Dynastic II Period and possibly around 2700–2600 BC, which indeed seems to have been the time of the first complete urban developments in Upper Mesopotamia and possibly Upper Syria.

An institutional idiosyncrasy, typical of Ebla of the Archives period, is the peculiar duality at the highest levels of state organization, observed nowhere else in the Mesopotamian world. All the contemporary kings of Ebla, in every government action, not least administrative and military, appear to have worked in conjunction with a high-ranking figure from the central government, a post covered in the Archives decades by Arrulum, Ibrium, and Ibbi-Zikir in succession (Figure 6.9). This very high official may hypothetically have been defined as *lugal Saza*, "great man of the Saza", indicating the supreme head of the administrative complex, or in Sumerian, precisely, the "Saza".

To give some idea of the complexity and range of this figure's responsibilities, second only to the king, Eblaite scholars have by convention used the term "vizier". A series of administrative texts present him first and foremost as the head of the *lugal*, the "Lords" of the Saza administrative system who were part-managers of various sectors of the administration (Figure 6.10) and part-governors of urban and rural centres under Ebla's jurisdiction. Particularly in the central and final phases of the Archives it emerges clearly that this function, which possibly only became hereditary, like the monarchy, from this moment on, acquired its full authority through the great prestige first of Ibrium (Figure 6.11) and then of Ibbi-Zikir; the latter personally led

Figure 6.9 Economic tablet, registering deliveries of gold and silver by Ibbi-Zikir (TM.75.G.1998), clay, 24th century BC.

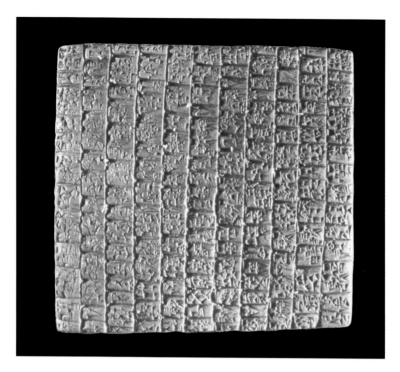

Figure 6.10 Economic tablet, with a monthly account of deliveries of textiles (TM.75.G.1345), clay, 24th century BC.

a series of important military campaigns for Ebla, apparently all victorious, against far-off and powerful kingdoms such as Mari, as described in Chapter 3 (pp. 32–40).

The vizier's increasing importance in Ebla's last years, before its destruction by Sargon, is also demonstrated by the fact that relations between the family of Ishar-Damu, the last king of Ebla documented in the Archives, and that of Ibbi-Zikir, the last vizier, became much closer with the marriage of two of their offspring. In this seemingly asymmetrical royalty–vizierate diarchy, possibly in existence in Ebla for years, but which assumed strength during Irkab-Damu's and Ishar-Damu's reigns, and the corresponding vizierates of Ibrium (Figure 6.12) and Ibbi-Zikir, it is feasible to infer that royalty was characterized by some aspects of sacredness and the vizierate by administrative aspects in the broadest sense.

The fact that the ritual of the renewal of kingship invested both king and queen, and that the long rites celebrated in Ebla and in the burial places of their royal ancestors ended in Kura's Temple in the Saza, where the royal couple assumed a role which was an earthly reproduction of its heavenly counterpart between Kura and his companion goddess, seems sufficient proof of the

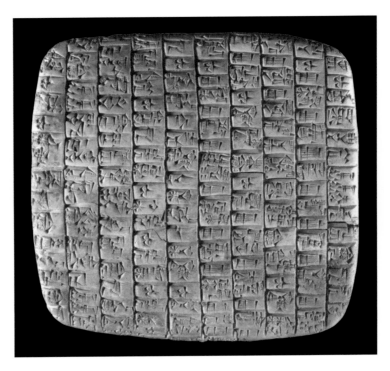

Figure 6.11 Administrative tablet with royal decisions concerning Ibrium's family possessions (TM.75.G.1444), clay, 24th century BC.

sacredness of Ebla's monarchy, confirmed by the many sacrifices offered to the deceased kings throughout the ritual. It seems very likely that at this period, too, the royal dead were considered as taking their place among the gods, archaeological evidence in Ebla and epigraphic documentation in Ugarit showing this to have been the case in the following Old and Middle Syrian periods.

The institution of the vizierate, on the other hand, would have been a purely secular function, defined by the evolution of the complex administrative structure, the head of which would have had to assume an increasingly consequential role given the wide range of responsibilities regarding economy, citizenry, and military society, all documented in the Archives (Figure 6.14). This emerges particularly clearly from, on the one hand, the accounts recording entries of gold and silver in the Palace in the name of the vizier, the Lords, and the allied or subject cities; and on the other, from the administrative texts containing reports that the vizier received or instructions he sent his functionaries on a variety of subjects. This considerable increase in the vizier's functions – as head of administration at the time Ebla was considerably increasing its power base (that is, the last years of the Archives period, when it extended its not inconsiderable territorial control to proto-imperial

Figure 6.12 Economic tablet with a yearly account of goods of Ibrium's time (TM.75.G.2031), clay, 24th century BC.

horizons, with parallel, unprecedented power assigned to the role of military leader) – very feasibly led to a substantial imbalance between the two functions of monarchy and vizierate. It is also possible that, albeit in different ways, this imbalance among civic institutional functions was taking place in the same period in Lower Mesopotamia, as may be inferred from the Lagash crisis during Urukagina's reign, and possibly in Uruk, where Lugalzagesi would not have been untouched by proto-imperial ambitions, before his defeat by Sargon. If compared to similar crises possibly experienced in the south, at Lagash, Kish, and Uruk, and in the north, at Mari, Ebla, and Nagar, it is probable that only Sargon's genius would have been able to create new administrative institutions to govern vast territories conquered by the force of weapons, to elaborate an ideology commensurate with the new situation while based on time-honoured conceptions, and to amplify the scale of administrative structures to meet the empire's unprecedented dimensions.

Similar imbalances and contradictions seem to have emerged in other aspects of Ebla's institutions in the Archives era. One such is the co-existence in government (Figure 6.13) of the *lugal*, the Lords, and the *abba*, the Elders, literally the "Fathers". The latter comprised a large group of figures of evident

Figure 6.13 Administrative tablet of rations for the Palace personnel (TM.75.G.1655), clay, 24th century BC.

standing, quoted in the Archives as both individuals and something resembling a college. Beyond almost all shadow of doubt these represented the city's aristocracy, which seems to have maintained its central role of representation but also possibly of government which it had occupied from past times, before sedentary life became the norm and when tribal and family roots still carried exceptional weight: a significance it must gradually have lost as urban society became structured into classes and trades.

While the Archives give no indication of any contrasts between the *lugal* and the *abba*, the former were almost certainly the result of the articulation of government at an urban level and therefore a relatively recent innovation. This does not exclude the probability that many of them were, at least initially, Elders of particular prestige and ability; while the *abba* members were a throwback to an archaic social structure clearly maintaining a foothold through blood, rather than acquiring position through meritocratic abilities suited to the new demands of urban life. This co-presence of Lords and Elders is documented in the archives not only of Ebla but of numerous urban settlements, although, possibly through a relative provincial backwardness and the very recent character of other urban organizations, the *abba* are

Figure 6.14 Administrative tablet with royal decisions about land belonging to Tisha-
Lim (TM.75.G.2396), clay, 24th century BC.

mentioned much more frequently than the *lugal* outside Ebla (in the city, as
in any urban centre of growing complexity, the role of the Lords was, on the
contrary, in continuous expansion).

A complex but illuminating problem regarding the Ebla of the Archives
age which has to be addressed is the type of written and specifically literary
culture attested by the chancery documents at the time of the destruction
perpetrated in the years between the Early Dynastic IIIB Period and the age
of the Akkadian Dynasty in terms of Mesopotamian chronology.

First, while there are clues (for example, the use of the sumerogram "e
n" to designate the local *malikum*, the sovereign of Ebla) that the chancery's
written culture dates back to some decades before Igrish-Khalab, the first king
recorded in the Archives in contemporary documents, the presence in Ebla of
authoritative scripts by scholars from Kish and Mari attests quite definitely
that the written culture with which Ebla was in contact was that of Akkad;
further proof of this are various forms of current administrative procedures
in Ebla, which are those of the region of Kish and not of Sumer, the southernmost region of Ur and Uruk. These two factors, plus the unusual but very
clear Eblaic use of the important Sumerian term *lugal*, point to the strong

influence of written Sumerian culture during the Early Dynastic II Period, probably between 2700 and 2600 BC, the years in which, significantly, the first consistent phenomena began to appear of the development of secondary urban civilization in Upper Mesopotamia and possibly in Upper Syria too.

The establishment of a written Sumerian culture in Ebla almost certainly belongs to a second wave of influence in the decades when early urban phenomena were undergoing consolidation, not least in Upper Syria – the decades of the Ebla Archives, thus between 2400 and 2300 BC, and not before the Early Dynastic IIIB Period. This affirmation of Lower Mesopotamian written culture could be considered part of a more general process of expansion – cultural, rather than political or even less military – of the Akkadian culture beside and beyond the middle course of the Tigris to the east and the Euphrates to the west. It should be viewed within the cultural and political predominance of the period in Lower Mesopotamia, not least that of Kish, repeatedly recorded in the Ebla Archives before the political affirmation of Sargon, initially a prominent dignitary of the Kish sovereign according to a reliable tradition.

Second, the conspicuous presence of several different drafts of what are virtually monolingual Sumerian lexicons (Plate VII, I) in the main Archive of Ebla's Royal Palace G, listing the various semantic fields, from the natural world to crafts and trades, clearly indicates that the Ebla chancery had systematically equipped itself with the factual and didactic instruments to master not only the language of administration of the urban Sumerian-Akkadian world, but that of daily and intellectual life, considerably beyond any requirements of palace administration. If these Sumerian lexicons, an ordered and reasonably complete classification which undoubtedly also presents an epistemological account of the Early Dynastic world of Lower Mesopotamia, are undoubtedly copies of lexicons drawn up in the major scribal centres of the Early Dynastic III Period, from Uruk to Kish, it is equally beyond doubt that, conversely, the four major (if partially incomplete) Sumerian-Eblaic bilingual editions (Figure 6.15) still extant are not copies of works compiled in the chanceries of Kish, Mari, or any other centre of Akkad or the Middle Euphrates, but the original result of a careful, complex, and erudite work of elaboration and translation by expert Eblaite scribes.

The fact that these scribes possessed the sophisticated palaeographic and philological knowledge to draw up such precise editions of what are in fact the first bilingual dictionaries in human history, comprising the quantitatively substantial sum of more than 1,500 lemmas, attests to their being, beyond all doubt, masters of the art of writing on a par with the most learned scholars in the main centres of Sumer and Akkad. A number of them are known from the colophons of the tablets themselves: Tira-Il, for example, who in one colophon compiled a whole list of Eblaite scribes; Enna-Il, the author of one of the most detailed lexicons; Azi, well-known as the prolific scribe of several literary texts; and Iraz-Il, author of the Eblaite copy of the important list of names and professions.

Figure 6.15 Bilingual lexical tablet, with the second group of lemmas of the canonical list (TM.75.G.1774), clay, 24th century BC.

The presence in Ebla of different copies of the monolingual lexicons in very interesting variations (Figure 6.16), some of them in phonetic Sumerian script rather than the traditional logographic, implies that they were compiled as help in the reading of lemmas for non-Sumerian scribes: the local scribes, for example, who must have comprised the majority of the authors of the extant texts, while only very rarely, seemingly, were Sumerian lexical tablets imported directly from the scribal centres of Sumer or Akkad.

On a more general level, of course, the presence of the Sumerian-Eblaic bilingual lexicons in Ebla, and their great antiquity (the most ancient bilingual texts in the cuneiform world, which over the next centuries was to produce even more complex multilingual texts) can be explained by the fact that Ebla is the most ancient urban centre known to us to have developed in an environment speaking a different language, where Sumerian had no role whatsoever, but which widely and sophisticatedly had used the cuneiform script invented in the late fourth millennium BC in Lower Mesopotamia as a means of expressing the Sumerian language.

Third, it is particularly interesting that the Palace Archives of the mature Early Syrian Ebla contained a number of literary texts, such as hymns and incantations (Plate VII, 2) which were obviously unrelated to administrative

Figure 6.16 Sumerian lexical tablet, from originals of Shuruppak (TM.75.G.2515), clay, 24th century BC.

or governmental matters. Some of these texts, basic in importance if few in number, are written in Sumerian, others in Semitic. The major literary texts, at least three but possibly all of which were produced by Eblaite scribes in the city itself, as their colophons attest, are a Sumerian composition mentioning the god Amaushumgal and the country of Aratta, kept in two copies, and two very notable compositions in Semitic. The first of the Semitic texts, also known from a copy from Abu Salabikh, a Lower Mesopotamian centre close to Nippur, has as protagonist the Sun-god Shamash (Figure 6.17), invoked as a radiant torch of heaven, who stirs up 'soldiers from foreign lands' and is patron of merchants in far-off countries; it also lists various other gods including Enlil, Sin, Ea, and the Anunna, and mythical places such as the Apsu. The second text, found only in Ebla and dedicated to the goddess Nisaba, first-born of the great Enlil, also cites Anir, Ea, Ishtar, and Nanibgal among the gods; Sumer, Subar, and Tilmun among the countries, and among the cities Eresh, the centre of the cult of Nisaba in Lower Mesopotamia.

Several copies of incantations were found in the Ebla palace chancery, including various versions in both Sumerian and Semitic. The genre seems to have been prevalent in the third millennium BC, from Lower Mesopotamia to Egypt, where a considerable number are found in the ritual pharaonic

Figure 6.17 Literary tablet, with a Semitic hymn for the god Shamash (TM.75.G.2421), clay, 24th century BC.

collections of the famous Pyramid Texts. Part at least of the Egyptian group seems to have been produced in Ebla and redacted in the same local language of the administrative texts, the lexicons, and the place-names of the city and its environs. It is impossible to know for certain why Sumerian and Semitic literary texts were preserved in the Palace Archives though they may have served didactically, as exercises for the (extremely expert) chancery scribes.

The literary texts in Sumerian were certainly composed in Sumer, despite no copies having been found in Lower Mesopotamia, where however a number of incantations came to light in the city of Shuruppak. The situation is more complicated as regards the Semitic texts, although the hymns to Shamash and Nisaba probably belonged to the culture of Kish, as did a part of the incantations, whereas a part was composed at Ebla. For a general evaluation of the literary culture in palace circles in Ebla, these presences and differences in provenance point, however, to the scholars of the Archives age Ebla having had a thorough knowledge (almost certainly more extensive than the texts discovered so far) of the holy writings of Lower Mesopotamia, both the Sumerian world centred on Nippur and the Akkadian circles centred on Kish.

It should also be noted that, while the unexpected but far from incongruous presence in the Ebla central Archives of Sumerian and Semitic literary texts of no pertinence to the administration is significant, on the other hand, it is very probable that more convenient centres, such as Ebla's major sanctuaries, contained a greater number and variety of religious texts, in that these would have constituted temple libraries, as certainly was the case across the Sumerian-Akkadian world in the same decades. What should be stressed, however, as being more important for an assessment of the unquestionably complex culture of the mature Early Syrian Ebla, is that some time before the reign of Ishar-Damu, the last king, the palace circles of the royal chancery seem to have developed a literary finesse and originality which was undoubtedly the result of a far from superficial or fragmentary familiarity with the culture and literary tradition of contemporary Lower Mesopotamia.

This is also evidenced in the various elaborate and frequently sophisticated chancery documents produced by the city scribes, not least the Treaty between Ebla and Abarsal (Plate VI), the administrative reports exchanged between the vizier and other officials, and the palace verdicts on legal questions, all of which indicate both a tradition of some standing and, above all, logical and formal skills in organizing clauses, formulas, and argumentation, clearly the result of a considerable and systematic elaboration of writing, conceptually and stylistically.

A further fact to consider is the existence of some very peculiar historiographic elaborations by Ebla authors of political events and episodes which seem based on historical reality but are presented as fictional narrative not devoid of ambiguity and paradox. One such is the account of the exploits of Igga-Lim of Ibal, which took place after the death of Irkab-Damu of Ebla, or that concerning Shuwamawabar of Mari on the relations between Ebla, Mari, and Addu (Figure 6.18). Of peculiar originality, they present rhetorically sophisticated accounts, interpretations, and appraisals of events evincing both a historical rationale and fictional elaboration: something between a chancery report and a historical novel.

When attempting to reconstruct the scribal and literary culture of Early Syrian Ebla, it seems clear that the basic southern Mesopotamian influence of the Kish region had to be adapted to local linguistic and cultural features, obvious examples being the incantations, political and diplomatic reports, treatises, verdicts, and other less common genres. In the same way, any reconstruction of at least the main characteristics of Ebla society must be predicated on an identification of the aspects which are essentially and specifically Early Syrian, concealed by the Sumerian terminology of the late Early Dynastic administrative procedures current in the Ebla chancery.

It is still extremely difficult to give an overview of the mature Early Syrian society in Ebla. Notwithstanding the considerable amount of already published administrative and accounts texts, only now is a systematic study going ahead of the prosopography, and synthesized evaluations are produced for whole sections of the administration which only individually can provide a generally valid comprehensive reconstruction. At the same time, the final publication of several types of administrative texts recording the distribution of food rations among dignitaries, functionaries, and staff of the Royal Palace, fundamental in

Figure 6.18 Historical-literary tablet, with the tale of the mission of Shuwamawabar of Mari to Haddu (TM.75.G.2561), clay, 24th century BC.

relation to the primary issue of the structure of mature Early Syrian society has allowed researchers to trace, in general terms, at least some of its basic features.

The expression 'Saza and Ebla', used throughout the administrative texts, which, as said above, must refer to the palace complex of the city of Ebla generally ('Saza') and to the urban and, probably, extra-urban territory ('Ebla'), most probably indicates a bipartition which is also administrative, since each of the two entities must have had a large staff of its own with operational roles. In the various very different documents recording food rations, prevalently though not exclusively delivered on a monthly basis, the most significant structure in terms of amounts allocated was the 'House of the King', which certainly meant the administrative unit including not only the extended family of the sovereign, but also a conspicuous number of the House staff.

If the unit's very denomination bespeaks the model of aristocratic society then prevalent, the texts demonstrate that this same model extended to other prominent family groups of the time. The texts of the so-termed Small Archive, which seem to date from only the last three years of Ebla's life before its destruction by Sargon, also list as rations recipients the 'House of

Dubukhu-Adda', vizier Ibbi-Zikir's son, the 'House of Kharani', the 'House of Azimu' and several others, including other important members of the palace administration. It is difficult to quantify the recipients in the 'House of the King' but an average of rations for more than 200 people has been calculated, though undoubtedly some totals include several hundred workers; this presumably means that the staff of the 'House of the King' were also spread over other urban and rural centres probably in the Ebla vicinity. It has been noted that although the exact household composition of the 'House of the King' is not known (for example, members' degree of kinship with the king), the female staff of the palace are listed separately under the denomination 'Women of the King', which also included a considerable number of servants and assistants and was recorded under a separate account.

The 'House of the King' group must also have included a large number of kin, domestic staff, and occasional guests, but although the female administrative unit was separate, the 'Mother of the King' may also have come under the king's household, since she had a number of important public functions and is nowhere mentioned as a specific recipient of rations, either singly or as head of her own staff.

Interestingly, in these texts recording rations, the king is often grouped with the Elders who, then, must have had close and stable links with him, both in Ebla and other cities with which there was frequent contact. Their numbers are not easy to establish, even in Ebla itself, and the fact that they vary between 35 and 48 in no way indicates that the higher figure truly represents their presence in the capital, contradictory indications pointing to them having been considerably more numerous in the last years of the Archives. On the one hand, it is obvious that when the 'House of the King' receives rations for a diplomatic journey to another city, a number of Elders accompany him (who could however be family members only); on the other hand, mention is made both of a 'House of the Elders' and of 'Women of the Elders', in some texts amounting to some tens of inhabitants.

The female staff of the palace, as has been noted, had separate accounts, kept by at least two administrative units continually mentioned both as regards the 'Women of the King' and the 'Young Women of the King', the first group obtaining larger rations. From the clear recurrence of names, it is certain that a number of women moved from the second into the first unit, though it is impossible, of course, to say what change of state occasioned this: age, cooptation, or marriage.

What is also certain is that the 'Women of the King' included not just his wives but other female figures, including his sons' daughters and wives. While canonically the first mentioned is always the queen in the accounts regarding the 'Women of the King', in the texts of the Small Archive, covering the city's last years of life, two other female figures, immediately following the *maliktum* (queen), receive the same rations, double that of the other women. Hierarchical principles of allocation also apply to other women, although with no apparent reason. Speaking generally, but probably accurately, the

'Women of the King' were likely to have comprised a considerable body, mainly though not exclusively the wives, daughters, sons' wives, and other relatives of the king, resident in the palace and possessing their own internal hierarchy; their staff would include a further not inconsiderable number of women working as servants, wet-nurses, cooks, spinners, and weavers. Whether the residence of the 'Women of the King' was separate from that of the king and his 'House' remains an open question, but this seems likely given the unit's separate accounts, like those of the 'Young Women of the King', who on average received half the rations of the 'Women of the King'.

Of the male staff directly employed by the palace and receiving rations from the central administration, their exact work and status is rarely given, unlike that of the women. We know that the latter were employed in the kitchens, in all domestic duties within the palace complex, and in small-scale production of, for example, weaving and spinning, while the women defined as being 'gone outside the city' were probably agricultural labourers, working in the fields outside the city gates.

The number of female workers amounted to several hundred, indicating textile mills on a considerable scale; this is endorsed by the great quantity of textiles distributed by the palace administration and recorded in the monthly accounts.

Male workers seem to have been particularly active in the domestic and social spheres controlled by the palace: namely, the several hundred smiths registered in the Archives and similar numbers of joiners and carpenters, with hosts of barbers, doctors, singers, scribes, and judges, who are not, however, included as such in the rations records, probably because they were included in the individual administrative units going under the name of the head of one of the extended family groups, the greatest of which was the 'House of the King'.

All personnel were apparently organized in groups, headed by officials, and sub-divided into teams. The functionaries divided into two groups, the first employing three types of superintendents (*ib – ib, a – am, ú – a*) overseeing personnel in the palace complex, while the second included officials responsible (*ugula*) for male labourers employed in outside work and sub-divided into "houses" or "districts", in their turn composed of teams of some 20 or so workers. Several categories of male staff, frequently denominated by their function and generally listed under the 'House of the King', are messengers, merchants, and groups of people from Armi: this city clearly had a special relationship with Ebla above all in the last years of the city's life, when a number of Armi subjects most probably resided there and had ceremonial or religious roles.

The mature Early Syrian Ebla's social structures were, we knew, extremely sophisticated, and the required degree of specialization in work and production would necessarily have been on a par. The palace administration seems to have met these civic requirements as efficiently as the military powers of early Ebla rose to the considerable challenges in their own field, not least the victorious Mari expedition (where an equally sophisticated diplomacy seems to have played its part).

But it was the military organization as revolutionized by the genius of Sargon, founder of the Akkad Dynasty, which remained unparalleled as opposed to that of mature Early Syrian Ebla, whose traditional social structure, devoid of advanced techniques in either armaments or military skills, could ultimately do little against the invincible war-machine of Akkad's professional army.

7 Artistic expressions and material culture in the mature Early Syrian Period

Despite being thoroughly sacked and then set on fire by Sargon of Akkad's army, the Royal Palace G produced much fragmentary yet significant evidence of various forms of artistic expression in the age of the Archives and allowed a reconstruction of many central aspects of the city's figurative culture, albeit occasionally tentative. Evidence of material culture, on the other hand, is extensive, not least as regards pottery, and the condition of finds in the Royal Palace G has in more than one case allowed the relative dating of the remains of different kinds of decoration and furnishings in the palace complex.

The objects found in the Royal Palace G can be grouped according to type, technique, and function, besides, of course, their artistic quality. In taking these categories into account, their homogeneity with or independence from the figurative culture of southern Mesopotamia of the last Early Dynastic and the first Old Akkadian Periods has a specific interest for a historical judgment of mature Early Syrian culture.

Wall panels would seem to have been the most common type of artistic product from the Royal Palace, judging from the sheer quantity of finds. While probably considerably varied in terms of technique, they were almost always made of different materials, and each had clearly defined uses, subsumed however under the final function of commemorating royal power and the city administration. Two types of panel seem to have been most common in the palace complex. The oldest was composed of a wooden base comprising a series of juxtaposed flat planks, with carved spaces to accommodate relatively large but flat figurative marble engraved inlays, each one representing an autonomous scene and together forming superimposed, horizontal friezes (Plate X). The panels were often of considerable dimensions and attached to the walls, and were probably made of only wood and marble (Figure 7.1).

The second type, almost certainly more recent and probably a development of the earlier kind, also had a wooden base, but here the front of the wooden planks, rather than being flat, was carved, reproducing part of the figurative elements of the compositions in relief, like the naked parts of the human figures, which were covered with gold foil, while the images were completed by relief inlays applied to the wooden base – in shell or limestone for clothing, and in lapis lazuli or steatite for beards and hair.

Figure 7.1 Inlay of the "Standard of Ebla", with an Eblaite warrior carrying felled heads of enemies (TM.88.G.256–257), marble, reused in the floor of L.4436 in the Central Complex of the Royal Palace G, 24th century BC.

The major differences between more archaic and more recent types, then, were two-fold. First, there was no relief in the earlier kind (Figure 7.2), while in the second type all figures were more or less in high relief (Figure 7.22); and second, where in the former the only colour contrast lay between the generally creamy colour of the marble and the brown of the wood, the latter were vividly polychrome in the contrast between the brown background and the gold, limestone, lapis lazuli, and steatite, to which was occasionally added a red stone to represent the tawny coat of the rare figures of lions.

The subjects of these wall panels, both flat and in relief, are in some cases impossible to reconstruct but may have related to various rituals. Frequently, though not exclusively, however, they were scenes of triumph after battles, lion hunts, and slaughter, or scenes portraying the administrative structure, generally involving parades of officials and functionaries. As to the origins of the celebratory panels in Ebla's Royal Palace G, these are certainly to be looked for in the influence of artefacts from the palace and temple workshops of Mesopotamia of the Early Dynastic II and III periods. At the same time, while there are certainly very close analogies between large figurative inlaid panels

Figure 7.2 Inlay with a walking human-headed bull (TM.76.G.519), limestone, from the hall of the Administrative Quarter L.2866, 24th century BC.

with registers produced in Kish, Mari, and Ur, and the archaic Eblaite panels, it is equally certain that the more recent relief panels on wood, decorated with gold and polychrome stones, are typically Eblaite in production.

The heads and busts of men and women (Plate IX, 1–3) are a second type of artefact, very rare in the Royal Palace G and only extant in a seriously fragmented state. These, like the more recent type of panels, were composed of different precious materials, from a wooden core covered in gold leaf, to steatite, lapis lazuli, and limestone. While the function of the wall panels is relatively clear, that of the heads, probably of important personages of the realm, is more difficult to guess with any certainty, since the hypothesis of their being votive works is to be excluded, and though theoretically they may be royal ancestors, any proof, either textual or archaeological, is almost impossible to adduce.

These Ebla artefacts in the round, human heads or busts composed of a variety of materials, can only belong to a specific, mature Early Syrian development with its roots in the southern Mesopotamian culture of the Protohistoric age – possibly in the workshops of Uruk – from which it extended, spatially and temporally, into other important southern centres such as Ur and Girsu, and even into the northern regions both along the Tigris to Assur and Nineveh, and along the Euphrates to Mari.

A third, very peculiar and somewhat enigmatic artistic typology includes significant if dismembered statuettes of various materials, again in the round but in miniature (Figure 7.3). These must have included mythical images, such as human-headed bulls and bull-men (Plate XIII), but also human figures: kings, queens, and possibly officials (Plate XII, 1). Exceptionally refined

Figure 7.3 Hair-dresses from miniature statues (TM.04.G.824 + 835 + 888), steatite and lapis lazuli, from L.2982 of the Administrative Quarter, 24th
century BC.

materials were used, including wood for the inner cores, steatite and lapis lazuli
for beards and hair, steatite again for clothing, marble for all the naked parts
of some figures, gold for particularly refined cloaks (Figure 7.4), jasper for cult
vases, and silver or gold for the naked parts of human bodies. While in general
it cannot be excluded that the statuettes were used in small, plastic groups,
belonging to specific fixed elements of decor (Plate XII, 2) (for example, elements of particularly precious furniture or refined musical instruments), there
is certain evidence that at least in one case some of the images were assembled
to compose scenes in ceremonial court insignia. These were standards, usually carried by high-ranking officials in processions, as documented in the
representation on the steles of the sovereigns of the Lagash, Akkad, and Ur
III dynasties.

A fourth type of artistic production, undoubtedly an important element
in the furnishings of the palace, are figurative works in wood which, unlike
the previous three categories, have a subordinate rather than autonomous
function in a specific arrangement of decor (Figure 7.5): wooden furniture –
tables, chairs, cabinets – possessing their own specificity but in which all the
figurative carved elements, rather than being secondary or purely ornamental,
were emphasized for their own independent value, whether in relief or in
the round.

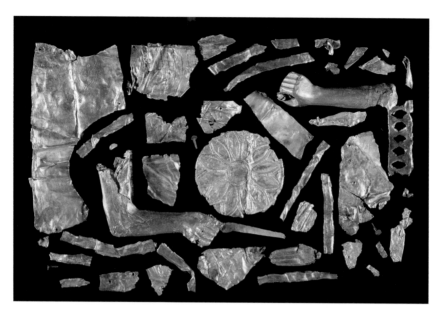

Figure 7.4 Revetment foils from miniature statues and from panels, gold, from L.2982 in the Administrative Quarter, 24th century BC.

Figure 7.5 Arm rest of a throne with bulls and lions carved in the round (TM.74.G.1019–1026), wood and mother-of-pearl, from L.2601 in the North-West Wing, 24th century BC.

Given the great fragility and perishable quality of the charred wood, remains of wooden carving which had decorated the precious furniture of the Royal Palace G are of course extremely rare, but significantly, mention is still made of gifts of precious furniture from Ebla, around the mid-twenty-first century BC in Neo-Sumerian sources of the Ur III Dynasty under Amar-Suen and Shu-Sin. This implies, on the one hand, that unlike Lower Mesopotamia, where wooden furniture decorated with figurative elements was unusual, Upper Syria must have had a long and consolidated tradition of wood-carving; and, on the other, that Sumer continued greatly to appreciate the late Early Syrian carved furniture, even more than a century after Sargon's destruction of Ebla.

Figurative inlaid panels in wood and marble (Figure 7.6); figurative relief panels in wood, gold, and semi-precious stones; heads and busts in the round in wood, gold, and steatite or lapis lazuli; miniature statuary in wood, marble, gold, silver, and jasper, and furniture inlaid with open-work scenes in relief and in the round were all, then, produced in the palace workshops of Ebla and destined to decorate principally the reception rooms of the Royal Palace G. These must not only have had their origins in very different artistic traditions, but must also have had different functions and purposes while still appearing, in the age of the Royal Archives, as parts of the unified figurative high culture in the mature Early Syrian Ebla.

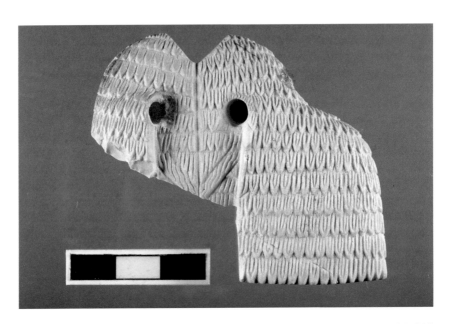

Figure 7.6 Inlay with a seated female figure with *kaunakés* cloak (TM.04.B.888), marble, 24th century BC.

The basic inspiration in some of the most significant of these productions, such as the narrative panels in wood and marble, or the heads in the round in various precious materials, has its roots in the figurative culture of southern Mesopotamia of the Early Dynastic III Period, from both northern centres such as Kish and most definitely Mari, and southern centres such as Ur and possibly Lagash, Uruk, and Nippur. This would also apply to the significant palace glyptics of the Royal Archives age, and points to the adoption not only of the cuneiform of Kish's scribal tradition, but of handicraft techniques and expressive trends of Lower Mesopotamia in the formative decades of the mature Early Syrian Ebla's artistic culture, possibly as early as the years which correspond to the Early Dynastic IIIA Period, immediately before and around 2500 BC, and certainly in the first half of Early Dynastic IIIB, approximately a century later. The process would have been aided, of course, by the very probable presence of palace craftsmen sent to Ebla from Kish and Mari, in parallel with the Archives-documented presence of scribes from the same two cities.

These various influences initially produced works which were probably strongly dependent on oriental models but which increasingly began to show marks of technical and iconographic re-elaboration which ultimately transformed the original artistic output and saw the emergence of an Early Syrian artistic sensibility. Greater difficulty is encountered, however, in historically evaluating the numerous remains of the mature Early Syrian Royal Palace G's artistic production at the time of its sacking by Sargon of Akkad. This is due, on the one hand, to the highly fragmentary nature of the majority of the works and, on the other, to their being attested only at Ebla, whereby it is impossible to locate them within any cultural framework documented as being homogeneous and of proven origin.

Only in a small number of cases (not however insignificant) is it possible to reconstruct some aspects at least of the original structure of the works from the Royal Palace G. The majority of them would seem to have had the function of celebrating various feats or the apparatus of government. The first objective is illustrated in one of the major works from the age of one of the last sovereigns before the Archives period, probably Igrish-Khalab; limited but far from negligible remains were recovered, since they had been reutilized as floor decoration in the doorway to a small room in the West Unit of the Central Complex.

This was originally a large wall panel, some 3 m high (Plate X), comprising a series of juxtaposed vertical wooden boards, into the front of which was set a series of marble open-work inlays, between 12 and 16 cm high, each representing a battle scene or mythical beings, and originally arranged in 12 superimposed horizontal registers, separated by a narrow geometric frieze of lozenges, formed of triangular tesserae, also of marble.

Such a precise reconstruction of this exceptional panel is due to one whole vertical wooden board having been reused, in the last refurbishing of the room in the Central Complex, sunk into a cavity in the threshold floor. The

Figure 7.7 Inlay from the "Standard of Ebla", with an Eblaite warrior dragging a
defeated enemy (TM.88.G.191), marble, re-employed in the floor of L.4436
of the Central Complex of the Royal Palace G, 24th century BC.

board was placed in the cavity face-down, without removing the inlays on the
front; they were thus preserved, as the cavity in the floor presented, in perfect
order and separated from the lozenge partitions, a whole, if narrow, vertical
section of all the registers originally appearing on the panel's front.

The ten upper registers present alternating scenes of military triumphs and
one recurring mythological image, while the two lower both, unusually, show
military scenes (Figure 7.7). The first of these showed sequences in which an
Eblaite soldier held up the severed enemy's heads, pierced a captured enemy
(Plate XI) or pushed forward a bound prisoner, or carried plundered loot;
while the second type of scene always depicted a front-facing lion-headed
eagle, its wings spread as if gliding on the backs of two human-headed bulls
moving in opposite directions. The same type of motif was almost certainly
not repeated for the length (unknown) of the panel, however, insofar as in
one of the three floor cavities where three wooden boards were reused, a
completely different marble inlay decoration was found, depicting a deeply-
grooved skirt, most likely belonging to a composite figure, a characteristic
of the second, more recent type of panel comprising a wooden inlaid base
covered in gold for the naked parts of the body and using various stones for
the clothing, much larger in dimension than the complete scenes of inlays
(Figure 7.8).

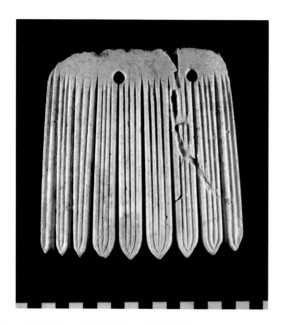

Figure 7.8 Inlay with the large king's skirt of the "Standard of Ebla" (TM.88.G.520), marble, 24th century BC.

The obvious deduction is that the whole panel presented on one side a much larger figure, almost certainly of a king, at least three times taller than all the other human figures and worked in relief in limestone, gold, and lapis lazuli, towards whom advanced processions of Eblaite soldiers with prisoners and war trophies, in registers alternating with others where the lion-headed eagle was depicted. Since all the inlaid panels with soldiers present them turned in the same direction, the panel was clearly meant to depict the return of a military expedition with Ebla's victorious soldiers presenting the spoils of war to their triumphant sovereign, represented on a scale consonant with his hierarchical position, and also to imply that the victory had been assured by the will and protection of a great deity, depicted according to the well-established norms of the iconographic patrimony of the Early Dynastic III Period of Lower Mesopotamia, where Imdugud, the lion-headed eagle, is one of the shapes of gods of the type of Ningirsu of Lagash, and certainly also of Ninurta and Nergal. Given that by the time of the Early Syrian world, as almost certainly later in Syria, the Mesopotamian Nergal was considered the equivalent of Rashap, the Syrian god of war and death, it is very probable that in the art of the palace of Ebla, the image of the lion-headed eagle had been adopted to represent their own local war god.

The panel depicting a mature Early Syrian Ebla's triumph has also been defined as the Ebla Standard, on account of the structural (but not typological) analogy with the famous Ur Standard, found intact in one of the tombs of the slightly more ancient Royal Cemetery of Ur; this too celebrates, on two sides, a military victory in a specific item of furnishing. It has also been compared with the so-called Mari Standard, which, while reduced to fragments, may well have been similar in both typology and theme, albeit on a smaller scale. Compared with both of them, however, the Ebla Standard presents two original features as to technical structure and iconographic conception: the co-existence of relief in different materials and of inlays and the pattern of the representation with the triumphal scene and images of the god under whose auspices the military venture was concluded are equally peculiarly Eblaite.

It is probably true, however, that, albeit in a different art form – that of victory steles to be dedicated in the temples – it was Early Dynastic Mesopotamian works of military celebrations which inspired the representation of the sovereign (in a hierarchical different size) with his warriors, arranged in registers which alternated the image of the king and the pantheon deities juxtaposed with earthly warriors. Both these representational criteria appear in the famous Vultures Stele of Eannatum of Lagash, and must at least in part have been applied in a second victory stele, an important if small fragment of which was discovered at Tell Halawa, in Upper Mesopotamia, and in which expressive features of Sumerian-Akkadian Lower Mesopotamia have been transposed into north Mesopotamian milieus.

If, though, the Ebla Standard clearly belongs to an Early Dynastic artistic genre of southern Mesopotamia, which has produced a number of very similar works in typological, iconographic, and thematic terms, it is equally true that these were re-elaborated by Ebla's palace workshops in a very recognizable style emerging, in particular, in bolder and less stereotyped compositions and a freer and more dynamic design conception.

It is these characteristics of particular elegance of composition, already present as the basic inspiration in more ancient works, previous to the final reconstruction of the Royal Palace G, which re-emerge in the extremely fragmentary inlaid panels of the last decades of the mature Early Syrian Ebla's life, which may be ascribed to the reigns of the last two kings of the Archives era, Irkab-Damu and Ishar-Damu (Figure 7.9).

As regards theme, it is significant that lion or leopard hunts also appear in a number of scattered fragments of marble inlay, technically identical to those of the "Ebla Standard" celebrating a military victory (Figure 7.10). This ancient subject, bound up with the specific competences and prerogatives of Mesopotamian monarchy and already documented in a Protohistoric stele from Uruk, in Lower Mesopotamia, in the years around 3000 BC, was, then, also present in Early Syrian inlaid work, celebrating the king and, in his conquest of wild animals, symbolically demonstrating his commitment to primaeval order over the constant resurgence, in historical and mythical time, of the forces of Chaos.

If, then, military and hunting triumphs, the prerogative of the mature Early Syrian kingship of Ebla, were the possibly exclusive subjects of the archaic type of flat wall panels and standards in wood and inlays, the subjects

Figure 7.9 Inlays of cloaks, skirts, and hair-dresses of officials' figures from composite wall panels, limestone, steatite, from the Administrative Quarter, 24th century BC.

Figure 7.10, a & b Fragments of inlaid panels with a scene of a hunt of a leopard (TM.04.G.777 + 550), marble, from the Court L.2752, 24th century BC.

of the more recent relief and inlaid panels would possibly have been more differentiated, and certainly less easily identifiable, given the greater dispersion and dislocation of the extant remains. The considerable quantity of inlays discovered mainly in the Administrative Quarter, which in at least three different dimensions, and in limestone or shell, present the skirts, belts, cloaks, and turbans of high-ranking members of the Ebla court (Figure 7.9), some of them certainly kings, would imply that the most recurrent subject of the panels was processions of officials received, welcomed, or rather headed by the king.

The repeated presence in the inlays of woollen turbans (Figure 7.11), always depicted frontally and in high relief and characterized by a padded "brim", slightly raised above the forehead and with a tuft on one side, would point to this being the typical headwear of the Ebla kings in the mature Early Syrian Period. Indeed, given the mode of representation and the contexts, one of these frontal figures could be nothing other than the king of Ebla himself. He appears both in the scenes of the palace glyptic, wearing a pleated woollen skirt or a cloak, and a turban of this kind, beside a woman with long, loose hair, and in one of the wooden inlaid panels, with an axe clutched to his chest.

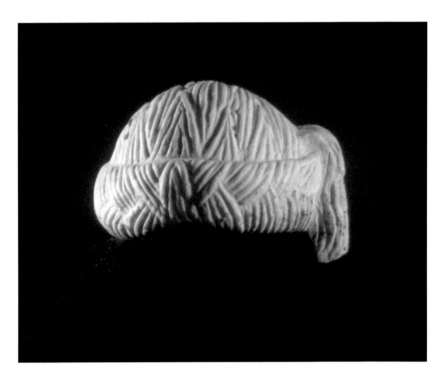

Figure 7.11 Eblaite royal tiara from a composite miniature statue (TM.89.G.268), marble, from L.2890, in the Court's Kitchen, 24th century BC.

The aim of these panels, depicting rows of relatively undifferentiated dignitaries, probably smaller than the figure of the sovereign, was almost certainly to parade the efficiency of the Saza administration in its representative seat of civic government and exalt Ebla's political power by marshalling what were in all likelihood the Lords and Elders of the kingdom. A beautiful piece of inlay presenting a seated female figure with a pleated woollen mantle (Figure 7.6) may be the core of a portrait of an Eblaite queen from the Archives age, in whose texts the queen is often given a position of considerable importance.

If the celebration of the government structure was probably the most prominent and most frequently depicted theme on the walls of the Administrative Quarter, it was certainly not the only one, though it is difficult to identify the precise subject of other panels, produced by the same technique and in all probability used to decorate the rooms of Royal Palace G. The inlays discovered range from the remains of relief figures of naked prisoners, their arms tied behind their backs, obviously implying that the more recent typology of panel continued to present standards in celebration of military triumphs, to walking human-headed bulls (Figure 7.2), which could equally be parts of mythological images of the war god, as in the older standards, and figures of grazing sheep and goats with no easily plausible context.

Other highly refined images of excellent workmanship, like the leopard, his head front-facing in the round (Figure 7.22), or the lion in similar pose, may have been inserted into representations which while not seemingly of combat may have structural affinities with the well-known friezes of the contemporary late Early Dynastic glyptics of Lower Mesopotamia and the cylinder seals of high-ranking Ebla dignitaries known through numerous impressions on clay sealings, again in Royal Palace G.

To return momentarily to text typologies in the Archives (problems of reconstruction and interpretation duly taken into account), there is no doubt that the panels in high relief in a certain sense correspond to the accounts and records registering the entries of gold and silver into the palace predominantly through the king and the Lords. While the exact nature of this correspondence is difficult to define, it cannot be excluded that the scenes with the Lords and Elders were intended precisely to depict specific operations performed in the Court of Audience and in the Administrative Quarter of the Saza, just as, in more general terms, it is clear that they represented an evocative general celebration of the structure of the city's Early Syrian government.

In the same way, works of the type of the "Ebla Standard" and other lessknown (and possibly less monumental) but almost certainly documented successors in the city's last years, all celebrating military triumphs, find a correspondence in what could be defined chancery literature, in letters such as those of Enna-Dagan of Mari to the king of Ebla dealing with his military exploits, but equally in the peculiar reports and accounts of a political, diplomatic, and military nature, between literary narration and administrative report, such as those regarding the undertakings of Igga-Lim of Ibal or those of Shuwamawabar of Mari concerning relations between Ebla, Mari, and Addu.

In comparison with the celebrations of military and political undertakings and those of government and administration in the different types of wall panels in the palace, the themes treated in the beautiful wood-carving of the ceremonial court furniture are considerably different. The retrieval of these highly fragile specimens of palace craftsmanship in the mature Early Syrian Ebla is little short of miraculous; at the same time, any contextual reconstruction of the images is impossible, not least taking into account that the very nature of the work meant they were not organized into organically developed scenes. What is known for certain is that among the retrieved images predominate figures of the court on the one hand, all front-facing, from the king in full majesty, with his royal insignia (Figure 7.12) and possibly his warrior's helmet, an item also known from the inlaid panels, to one or possibly more long-haired girls and women, among whom it might be possible to recognize the queen (Figure 7.13a, Figure 7.13b), and, on the other, scenes of war and myth, both probably strictly connected with the idea of kingship.

In the latter sphere, great significance was accorded the traditionally royal motif of the naked hero clasping and stabbing a standing lion (Figure 7.15), a paradigm which is recurrent in the Old Syrian figurative culture and is attested in Ishtar's Stele, surviving into the Neo-Assyrian and Achaemenid world in celebration of imperial kingship. Equally important, in the sphere of war, was the theme of two warriors stabbing each other (Figure 7.16) – an image alien to the Early Dynastic figurative culture of Lower Mesopotamia but completely in keeping with the new concept of war and its topical moments, soon to be represented in the victory steles of Sargon of Akkad's successors.

Images of superb naturalism, which must have been the predecessors of the later, quite extraordinary tradition of Syrian ivory-carving, down to the masterpieces of the Iron Age, enhanced by the open-work technique, leading to representations almost in the round, depict both figures of bulls and lions and scenes of wild animals attacking cattle, sheep, and goats (Figures 7.14 and 7.17), in forms which are arrestingly free of the conventional stylemes which were so prevalent in contemporary Early Dynastic glyptics in the Sumerian-Akkadian world, and equally arrestingly rich in plastic modulation of a formal sophistication bespeaking considerable development over time.

In terms of meaning and function, it is difficult to find a single theme in the figures and scenes of the wood-carving on palace furniture. If it is true, however, that front-facing male figures are to be interpreted as different images of the king in his many prerogatives, and the female counterparts as representations of the queen in her court and cult functions, then the images as a whole are in different ways alluding to the ideology of kingship, as a basic institution overseeing both the balance of the forces of nature, preventing their slide towards chaos, and the events of man, curbing the slide towards evil. From this perspective, the king with his turban, axe, and cloak is presented as the civic institution guaranteeing natural order, while with his plated helmet

Figure 7.12 Inlay with front-facing figure of an Eblaite king, wearing tiara and cloak, and holding an axe (TM.74.G.1000), wood, from L.2601 in the North-West Wing, 24th century BC.

he appears as the military institution ensuring social order. The queen, with her different hair-styles and in ways which, while difficult to be precise, are assured by her central role in the "Ritual of Kingship", assists the king in keeping universal order, most clearly in the sphere of fertility of course.

The scenes depicting the royal hero slaying the lion and wild beasts attacking domestic animals variously illustrate the royal function in the natural order, while the warriors stabbing each other probably stand for the contrasts involved in maintaining order in the human world. Certainly, this

Figure 7.13a Inlay with front-facing figure of an Eblaite queen (TM.74.G.1016), wood, from L.2601 in the North-West Wing, 24th century BC.

Figure 7.13b Fragmentary head of a female figure (TM.74.G.675), wood, from L.2601 in the North-West Wing, 24th century BC.

Figure 7.14 Inlay with a lion attacking a bovine (TM.74.G.1012–1015), wood, from L.2601 in the North-West Wing, 24th century BC.

Figure 7.15 Inlay with a hero stabbing a standing lion (TM.74.G.1007–1009), wood, from L.2601 in the North-West Wing, 24th century BC.

Figure 7.16 Inlay with warriors stabbing each other (TM.74.G.1011), wood, from L.2601 in the North-West Wing, 24th century BC.

Figure 7.17 Inlay with a lion tearing a goat to pieces (TM.74.G.1010), wood, from L.2601 in the North-West Wing, 24th century BC.

fragment of the warriors is violently expressing a typically Early Syrian way of illustrating the fraught issue of social and human order from a viewpoint which is alien to Early Dynastic Mesopotamian ideology, but which is vigorously pointing forwards to that which will prevail only a few years later in Mesopotamia too, in the second Akkad generation, among the masters of the workshops of the imperial school of the new lords of the universe.

It is, of course, completely obvious that the decoration of the official furniture of the Royal Palace G should represent relatively explicitly yet subtly the ideology of Early Syrian kingship, belonging as it probably did to a sumptuous state decor for official purposes, but equally logical that the subjects of the glyptics of palace functionaries (known for the most part from clay sealings [Figure 7.18] for the jars and caskets stored in the warehouses of the Northern Quarter) should also hint at a divine, heroic, and regal world foregrounding the function of kingship.

In the case of glyptics, however, it is the genre itself which must have conditioned the expressive code, in that the compositional schemes of those in the Ebla palace of Mardikh IIB1 most certainly depend in their entirety on the late Early Dynastic iconographic patterns of Lower Mesopotamia,

Figure 7.18 Sealing with cylinder seal impressions (TM.75.G.588), clay, from L.2716 in the Northern Quarter, 24th century BC.

particularly on those attested at Kish in the Early Dynastic IIIB Period. These follow the well-known pattern (Figure 7.20) of a chain of mythical and heroic beings fighting wild and domesticated animals variously humanized in their structure or simply in their behaviour, in the so-called contest scenes between mainly lions, bulls, or buffaloes, bull-men, and heroes, all standing erect in rows seemingly forming one uninterrupted frieze.

Although only two of the 15 or so seals, the figural content of which has been (sometimes partially) reconstructed, carry inscriptions – that is, those belonging to two functionaries, Rei-Naim and Ibdula, mentioned in the Archives texts – those sealing palace goods were undoubtedly the property of central officials of the Saza administration. In all these palace seals (Figure 7.19), which were only a part of early Ebla's glyptic production and represented only the exclusive tastes of the town elite, the friezes are often framed at the top and bottom in an arrow design or, more rarely, with a succession of human, animal, or mythical heads. Although the variants must have been numerous (Figure 7.21), as in the classical Mesopotamian glyptics of the Early Dynastic IIIB Period, all these friezes depicted human, animal, and mythical figures characterized by an almost vertical rather than

Figure 7.19 Sealing with cylinder seal impressions (TM.75.G.614), clay, from L.2716 in the Northern Quarter, 24th century BC.

Figure 7.20 Reconstruction of four seals documented by the sealing discovered in room L.2716 of the Northern Quarter, 24th century BC.

oblique position, preventing any partial superimposition of figures as often happened in the older Early Dynastic phases. This verticality of the mature Early Syrian Ebla's glyptics of the most elevated style is found again in Lower Mesopotamia, especially in the "Lugalanda style" from the important Sumerian centre of Lagash, in the years immediately prior to the advent of Sargon of Akkad.

The number of figures in the Ebla friezes goes from a minimum of four to a (rare) maximum of nine, while the single groups have a minimum of two and a maximum of four figures, and in some cases five. And while figures of bulls, lions, and bull-men, in the attitudes canonized by the Early Dynastic production of the Mesopotamian world – the bull-men in the typical Mesopotamian formation of lower-body bull, bust human, and face human but with bull's horns and ears – are frequent in these friezes, completely alien to the Sumerian-Akkadian sphere is the far from rare front-facing figure of a goddess (Figure 5.3) generally dominating two lions, one at either side of her and facing each other. This figure is characterized by a tiara with horizontal horns, wider at the base, with a possible three-part central vertical element and a skirt of two counterpoised series of wide overlapping flounces turned upwards and outwards. The goddess is clearly an important deity of wild animals, and is represented in the act of grasping the two lions by the neck or raising a bull by one of its front hooves and catching the hind paw of a lion,

Figure 7.21 Sealing with cylinder seal impressions (TM.75.G.630), clay, from L.2716
    in the Northern Quarter, 24th century BC.

turning it upside down. The forerunner of a long, widespread, and popular
iconographic tradition in the Syrian and Aegean world, the Mistress of Wild
Animals is almost certainly also a fertility goddess who protects domestic
animals and keeps wild animals at bay or under control.

This was very plausibly the mature Early Syrian iconography of Ishkhara,
which in the Royal Archives seems to have played a determining role in the
official cult of the contemporary Ebla's dynasty, as confirmed by the recent
discovery in one of the Northern Quarter rooms of a beautiful inscribed
seal (Figure 5.3) belonging to the third dignitary, Ushra-Samu, known to us
from the Archives. The seal still retains part of its gold-leaf casing, and the
goddess appears in the customary frieze of figures together with the scorpion,
the well-known symbol of Ishkhara surviving into the later Mesopotamian
iconographic tradition.

A number of other images, equally alien to the world of Lower
Mesopotamia, are connected with the innovative appearance of such a typically Eblaite image in a context inspired and profoundly marked by the influence of Early Dynastic Sumerian-Akkadian iconography. Two in particular
among these are two human figures, one male, one female, front-facing, the

man wearing the turban of the kings of Early Syrian Ebla, the woman with her hair loose on her shoulders. A third image which would seem to be Eblaite in inspiration is an original re-elaboration of the bull-man – that is, a cow-woman – clearly depending from the popular Sumerian-Akkadian creation. Lastly, a variant of Mesopotamian prototypes is certainly represented by the naked, kneeling hero, with flowing beard and hair, but with two peculiar horizontal curls on his forehead and a stylized plaited belt around his waist, who in an Atlas position bears on his shoulders a peculiar round symbol with four faces, two leonine and two possibly human.

The two human figures, one with a tiara, the other with flowing hair, are without doubt the royal couple who, in life or from the afterlife (the point is unclear) assist the great goddess Ishkhara in taming wild beasts and protecting domestic animals, as their positions within the frieze compositions clearly show. Equally beyond doubt would be the naturalness of creating the woman-cow counterpart to the bull-man in a milieu where a great goddess of nature dominates and the king and queen share an equal role in controlling all forces of nature, wild and domestic. The male–female principles, clearly effective precisely through the association at the level of kingship, are thus mirrored in the mythical world among the followers of the great goddess.

One singular ideological aspect yet to be fully explored is represented by the bearded and curly-haired Atlas figure. His plaited belt, an abbreviated symbol of the fresh waters of the abyss, and kneeling position, the four-part world seemingly on his shoulders, bespeak an original Early Syrian elaboration of the well-known figure of the bearded, curly-haired mythical Mesopotamian hero known in later Mesopotamian texts as Lakhmu, originally certainly a follower of Enki of Eridu, the great divine creator of the Sumerian world of the gods. If, as discussed in Chapter 5 (pp. 67–68, 77–82), various elements seem to indicate that the great Kura was a divinity not unlike El in the belief-systems of coastal Syria, but also like Lower Mesopotamian Enki, lord of the waters of the abyss, then this Eblaite Atlas-hero supporting the globe most plausibly belongs to the divine sphere of the head of the pantheon, Kura.

Put in very general terms, it would seem certain that the mature Early Syrian friezes of the Ebla palace glyptics express the idea that the world of nature, dominated by a great goddess, exists within a delicate balance between opposing elements; that the Ebla king and queen are proactive protagonists in this scheme, and that this delicate and unstable state of things applies to the entire universe, in all its four parts. Once more, this Eblaite concept of the four-part division, evidently well-established throughout palace circles responsible for royal ideology, must almost certainly have been the influence behind Naram-Sin of Akkad's creation, only a few years later, of the title of "king of the four regions (of the earth)" to signify explicitly a universal kingship. A further possibility to consider is that the presence of this four-part symbol on the mature Early Syrian Eblaite seals (Figure 7.18, Figure 7.20) may have been implying an inclination towards universal dominion in palace politics in the years of Ishar-Damu of Ebla, which in actual fact, through the energetic personality of Ibbi-Zikir, materialized into a policy which it is difficult not to define as proto-imperial.

In ways comparable with those of the parallel literary experiences known from the (rare) hymns in honour of the gods, from the myths of the incantations, and from the chancery of the mature Early Syrian Ebla's narrative compilations, palace glyptics also express a profound Early Syrian conceptual and ideological re-elaboration of Early Dynastic Mesopotamian themes, here prevalently connected with kingship in figurative terms, albeit within forms typical of contemporary Sumerian-Akkadian Mesopotamia. The Early Syrian milieus in Ebla were able to adapt the well- established Early Dynastic stylemes and iconographic and compositional formulae of Mesopotamia, and to enact concepts and ideals representative of their own world, creating new images on an iconological level and at the level of style fusing forms and syntactic connections to a new and extraordinarily mature sensibility. The robust plasticity of the Ebla palace friezes is evident in the lions' vibrantly modelled sinuous bodies and thick manes, and in the traditional fleece costumes, subtly diversified although stylized overall. This is conjugated with a predilection for tense, firm lines evidenced in the agile tracing of the nervous hoofs of the bulls, shading off into the stout, massive bodies.

In both the glyptics and the wood-carving, elements of this kind bespeak a mature and systematic study of nature deriving from considerable experience which probably – given the lack of any documentation to date – goes as far back as the archaic Early Syrian period and which places the productions of the Royal Palace G workshops of the various artistic genres exemplified in relatively homogeneous situations, at the high point of a considerable, conscious investigation into high-level research.

Examples of the exceptional quality of the Early Syrian Ebla's palace workshops' output in the years around 2350 BC, in all its various and technically demanding accomplishments, are the two beautiful hair-dresses, again one male, one female, formed of several plaques of steatite worked separately and then mounted on a wooden core (now lost), and completed. The faces were probably carved in the wood, in the round, and possibly covered in gold or silver leaf according to repeated mentions in the administrative texts of the Archives. The male hair-dress (Plate IX, 1–3) was a considerably complex mass of curls ending in small plaits falling over the forehead: undoubtedly a ceremonial and certainly royal arrangement, as indicated by the female head's very simply coiffed long loose hair, the typical image of the queen as represented in glyptic scenes.

The heads may have belonged to statues of a royal couple, possibly in wood and near to life size, placed at the entrance to the Throne Room, where indeed the pieces of steatite scattered in the sacking were found. They may also, however, have been simply busts of a king and queen, the Archives texts citing the presence of gold-plated royal heads, possibly one male and one female, in the "House of Wool", which, as discussed in Chapter 4 (see pp. 50–51

Figure 7.22 Small figure of standing leopard (TM.77.G.260), limestone, from the court L.2913 of the Administrative Quarter, 24th century BC.

and 56), must have been the palace Treasury, somewhere in this area of the Administrative Quarter.

The state of preservation of the two heads does not, of course, allow a confident aesthetic judgment, and it is difficult even to imagine how the hair, particularly the male's, would have been arranged in the upper central part. However quite clearly only extreme mastery and an admirable concept of final unity would have produced, from steatite plaques of different shapes and sizes, making symmetry a hazardous calculation, the superbly articulate and organic plastic whole, devoid of all schematism, as is particularly clear in the nape of the head where the absence of the mass of hair reveals the body structure.

If, as is likely, the rest of the two statues or heads was indeed carved in wood, a board bearing the remains of two heads carved in relief and discovered in the Trapezoidal Archive of the Administrative Quarter gives some idea of the contemporary Ebla wood-carvers' skills.

The not infrequent remains of very accurately made miniature wigs and turbans in the round, mainly in the rooms of the Administrative Quarter, would imply that a composite, small-scale statuary of different materials was common in Royal Palace G. Its functions are not clear but must obviously have been connected with palace furnishings of a purely secular nature. The recent spectacular find, in the Northern Quarter, of two exceptionally fine miniature female statues – one standing, made in wood, marble, steatite, gold, and jasper; and one seated, of wood, silver, steatite, and jasper, with a small incense burner in bronze – has led to the conclusion that the three elements were in all probability the components of a miniature sculpture forming the upper part of a ceremonial standard (Figure 7.23). It represents a queen standing in adoration (Plate XV) before a statue of a seated dead queen, possibly deified (Plate XVI); a number of clues point to the adoring queen as being Tabur-Damu, wife of the last king, Ishar-Damu, and the dead queen as being the powerful queen-mother Dusigu, wife of the previous king, Irkab-Damu.

To return momentarily to glyptic production, documentation brought to light in the levels of the mature Early Syrian Ebla have revealed that these founding years of Syria's artistic tradition produced a centre–periphery thematic dichotomy. If the clay seals of the palace attest to the vitality of its possibly recent glyptic tradition of the highest level, with a strongly ideological bent, centred on symbols of kingship and power, a number of storage jars

Figure 7.23 Reconstruction of Tabur-Damu's standard, with the queen facing a funerary statue of the queen-mother Dusigu, wood, gold, silver, bronze, steatite, limestone, jasper, from L.9583 of the Northern Quarter, 24th century BC.

bear the impression (obviously made before firing the jars) of cylinder seals of a decidedly different, popular thematic nature.

These seals are for the most part relatively large and may have been of wood or bone, with predominantly geometric or floral themes; the rare human figure tends to be schematized and stylized, and represented among tools and weapons, clearly continuing a long village tradition inspired by the agricultural world of products now arriving at the palace through an updated system of redistribution. Sharing very little with the glyptic traditions of Early Dynastic Lower Mesopotamia, they seem to belong to the contemporary glyptics partly of coastal Syria and partly of Upper Mesopotamia, albeit with features of their own: a rustic expressionism at some remove from the problematic of the palace workshops inspired by royal commissions.

Although no connections seem to exist among the different trends in seal production, the fact that there was already a high versus popular stylistic divide in Syria in the late third millennium BC is of great interest. As the figurative history of the Syrian world develops, regional trends and formal tastes from popular, rural environments are seen to influence even the expressive trends of palace workshops in the various urban centres, injecting a language of popular immediacy into a higher stylistic register.

As concerns material culture, the pottery of the mature Early Syrian Period was collected in the Royal Palace G, in its different sectors, and in Building P4, which was certainly related to an important temple, or to the palace itself. It is thus of a particularly high quality compared with the common productions of other contemporary centres of inner Syria. The pottery horizon of Early Bronze IVA Ebla is, therefore, extremely significant for and representative of the culture called, since the first half of the twentieth century, the "Caliciform Culture" of inner Syria and of the Orontes Valley.

The name of this ceramic culture comes from the conventional name given to the most frequent shape of the small-sized Common Ware, the so-called "Hamah goblets", which derive their name from the archaeological contexts where they were first found, during the Danish excavations at Hamah. The goblets (Figure 7.24) are elegant chalices of small to medium size, with a slightly bulging body, tapering to the small, flat, or ring-shaped base. Ring-shaped bases are slightly profiled, with a kind of button in the centre. The clay is usually whitish, light yellow, or green, or very light brown; the walls are very thin and the vases are worked on the wheel and usually well fired, sometimes producing a metallic sound. The smaller goblets have a flat outer surface and natural rim, whereas the numerous medium-size goblets have a tubular shape, sensibly tapering towards the base, and a slightly narrower mouth. Their rim is usually slightly swollen to the outside and they feature a very typical decoration of the outer surface, with very regular horizontal waves, from which they have been defined as "Corrugated Ware". These Ebla goblets were also made in a well-purified and highly fired ware, mostly brown or dark grey-green in colour, and corrugated: when touched, these vases make a metallic sound, and for this reason have been called "Metallic Ware".

Figure 7.24 Table ware from different rooms of the Royal Palace G, clay, 24th century BC.

In the horizon of the Royal Palace G of Ebla, these goblets are very frequent, but other types of goblet are also attested, with the same shape, but featuring a monochrome black paint, with very regular thin spared bands, which are the oldest type among the Hamah painted goblets. On the other hand, the typical goblets with painted bands of different height, and with spared wavy lines, with black or red paint, are totally absent in Mardikh IIB1, whereas they were found at Ebla in the later horizon of Mardikh IIB2.

In the same class of pottery there are also miniature goblets (Figure 7.25), small open bowls with oblique walls and slightly pointed rims, and, most of all, a type of open bowl, of different sizes, nearly semi-globular, with a typically thickened rim, sometimes swollen on the outside. Some bowls of this type are quite typical: they have a ridge below the rim and occasionally the same shape is used for tripod bowls; more seldom they have a long tubular spout. Rarer types include a kind of small bottle, with rounded body, high neck, and cylindrical oblique spout, and a small juglet, with rounded body, out-turned rim, and short tubular spout.

The monochrome Painted Ware, including other shapes for the goblets, was more widespread in the later Mardikh IIB2 period. Two types, however, were prevalent in the Archives age although possibly only in the refined palace contexts; namely, two small bottles with a red-violet painted decoration in groups of horizontal bands on the body and neck: one type is an egg-shaped bottle with short neck and rim slightly swollen on the outside, and the other type is a bottle with an almost round body, relatively high neck, and slightly everted rim, swollen on the outside.

Figure 7.25 Table ware from different rooms of the Royal Palace G, clay, 24th century BC.

Among the relatively rare painted vases were black-painted juglets with trefoil mouth, sometimes featuring the pattern of an eye on the lip, and the body having an oval rather than round section; they bear a decoration on the shoulder in a horizontal band, with metopes, and chains of triangles, filled with a net of lines, from which wavy lines go down to the base, with a very characteristic plaited pattern. The ware of these juglets is very light in colour, and the black paint sometimes diluted; the vases were probably, therefore, a luxury product possibly appearing outside the palace contexts of Ebla, albeit in very few specimens.

In the medium-sized vessels of the same Common Ware the surfaces are treated in various ways, following traditions known in workshops widespread in other centres of the same period. The most frequent type is a slender jar, with a large flat base, an almost tubular body, slightly and gradually expanding towards the mouth, marked shoulder, relatively long neck, and short everted rim, rounded or slightly squared on the outside. This type of jar was probably used to carry oil or wine, and sometimes features a surface decoration usually called "Smeared Wash", with irregular, horizontal, very light bands, mostly creamy yellow or very light green in colour.

Shorter jars have also been found, with a round bulging body, rather large flat base (a common element), short neck, and everted rounded rim: their ware is light brown, well fired, making a metallic sound, like the corrugated goblets and the ribbed bowls. These medium-sized vases were hand-made, as appears from the typical irregularities of the inner surface; the neck and rim, on the other hand, were applied on the slow wheel.

Medium or medium-to-large pots were used for different kinds of goods storage. One type was apparently specially made at Ebla. This was a tall jar with a large flat base, of a porous, relatively unpurified, and only lightly fired ware, greyish, pinkish, or light brown in colour, and covered by an irregular whitish or light green wash. Almost without a neck, it had an everted rim with the outer face marked by a very typical triple groove.

Other jars, equally tall and large in size, were probably used for cereals: their ware was reddish and well fired, or a purified light yellow, medium fired, with a straight, natural, slightly everted rim. Other jars were shorter and larger, in light brown or very light greyish-green ware, well fired, the swollen, rounded rim starting directly from the shoulder, and ending with a more or less pointed tip at the external lower sector of the rim.

The Cooking Ware pots were dark brown or greyish-black in colour, often with scorch marks, and include small, egg-shaped cooking pots with the rim swollen on the outside and the typical "hole-mouth" opening, but rather large, almost round cooking pots were also found, the function of which is certain as some of them were found in place on the fire-places in the Kitchen of the Court of Audience. These large cooking pots are very representative: their ware is thick in micaceous grit, their outer surface is frequently marked by thickly packed, regular, horizontal incised lines, and they feature a slightly everted, natural rim, with a lightly swollen, rounded edge.

The pottery horizon of Mardikh IIB1 is very homogeneous, and well documented: it certainly corresponds well, in the southern region, to the levels of Hamah J8–6, which are the three oldest levels of the Caliciform Culture of the Orontes Valley, and, in the northern region, to the probably advanced phases of 'Amuq I in the Antioch Plain, whereas in the Euphrates Valley the most significant parallel is to be found in Selenkahyah 3. These certain correspondences create an adequate chronological frame, although it is certain that the strongest homogeneity in the ceramic culture – ecologically homogeneous too – is more fully accomplished in the region of inner Syria, between the Taurus Mountains to the north, the Euphrates Valley to the east, and the Jebel Ansariyah to the west, with its northern and southern borders in the regions north of Aleppo and south of Homs; in this region Ebla was in a central position, both geographically and culturally speaking.

As regards its ceramic culture, the region features very strong elements of unity in all the vessel shapes, with one possible exception only; namely, the presence in the 'Amuq area of the typical Red-Black Burnished Ware, a variant of the so-called Khirbet Kerak Ware, certainly of eastern Anatolian origin and widespread in the Palestinian region, where it probably arrived through coastal routes, excluding an inland diffusion.

It is very clear from the material culture both that this cultural unity pivoted on the strongly dynamic role of Ebla, and that it did not reach, to the north-east, over the border of the Euphrates, where sites in the region such as those of the ancient centres of Karkemish and Tuttul, near modern Jerablus and Raqqah, feature peripheral characteristics as compared with the central region, albeit in a frame of basic homogeneity. Such is the situation also to the south-west, in the sites in the southern Orontes Valley, from the Ghab to the Ruj, which are very close to the central area represented by Ebla.

In some sites in the Euphrates Valley, and just to the east, in the Balikh Valley, which were under the political control of Ebla, at least during the last decades of the Royal Archives age, the correspondences are relatively limited, and it would seem very clear that the centre of a different cultural unit was more to the east, in the region of Nagar, where Tell Khuera was probably the pivotal centre. Much in the same way, to the west, limited correspondences are to be found in the coastal region, where perhaps Ugarit played a central role in a region probably extending to the south, at least to the Akkar Plain, or even as far as Byblos.

With regard to the development of the material culture of the region, Ebla was clearly the pivot of a coherent cultural complex which had its origins in Early Bronze III and was successful in Early Bronze IVA, and this was independent even of the predominant political role Ebla played for several decades, and from its ambitions to a proto-imperial predominance.

Notwithstanding the catastrophic destruction of Mardikh IIB1, which put an end to Ebla's leading role in the cultural sphere and its hegemony in the economic and political spheres, the material culture of the inner Syrian region, from the Orontes Valley to the steppe of the Syro-Arabic Desert, faced no drawbacks and failures but continued to flourish, albeit only in a number of urban centres which had not suffered from the crisis of the main centre, guaranteeing a continuity which, for some decades at least, Ebla was no longer capable of keeping.

8 The crisis in the Early Syrian world and the archaic Old Syrian renaissance

The marks of the terrible destruction by Sargon, that put an end to the great and powerful mature Early Syrian city of the Royal Archives can be seen everywhere in the urban settlement of Mardikh IIB1. After the devastating fire that probably led to the scattering of the surviving population of the city, there was probably no rapid or gradual reconstruction in Ebla. Although there are no documents to suggest that one or another of Sargon's two immediate successors – Rimush and Manishtushu – carried out new expeditions in Syria, the crushing defeat, which certainly meant the complete collapse of the city's structure of government, probably excluded the possibility of any political recovery in the short term. In some limited parts of the ruins of the palatine structures of the city there are some poor adaptations no later than the late Early Syrian Period of Mardikh IIB2, although most of the surfaces of Royal Palace G so far brought to light bear no trace of reoccupation in the decades following the destruction.

These data indicate that extensive areas of the great mature Early Syrian settlement were abandoned, and only a small part of the population remained there or returned. A few decades after Ishar-Damu's defeat, Naram-Sin of Akkad recorded his victory over Armanum and Ebla (Figure 8.1) in the triumphant votive inscriptions dedicated in the main sanctuaries of Lower Mesopotamia, claiming that no one 'since the foundation of humankind' had ever succeeded in the feat that had led to the conquest of Armanum and the defeat of its king Rish-Adad. By this, he probably meant to indicate to his subjects in Sumer and Akkad that his triumph had taken place in the land of Ebla, which was certainly well known in Lower Mesopotamia, as a result of Sargon's recent exploit. It is significant that Naram-Sin cites the king of Armanum by name and makes no mention of a king of Ebla. His chancery may have used the name of Ebla to indicate the region where Armanum was to be found, which may have been little known to Akkad as it had only recently risen to a position of political prominence. Alternatively, the king of Armanum, which, as we have said, certainly corresponds to the oft-cited Armi in the texts of the Royal Archives, really had explicitly assumed the title of "king of Armanum and Ebla" to indicate his having taken Ebla's place in the domination of the region.

Figure 8.1 Votive lamp of Naram-Sin of Akkad, recalling the victory over Armanum and Ebla (MAH 0.710), green marble, 23rd century BC.

Source: Musées Royaux d'Art et d'Histoire, by kind permission of Eric Gubel.

As the Armanum of Naram-Sin and the Armi of the Royal Archives must have been the same city, the recent suggestion that this important centre should be located on the site of Tell Bazi/Tell Banat on the Euphrates, south of Karkemish, seems wholly reasonable. Its area was around 40 hectares and it must have had a powerful, triple fortification, partly brought to light in Tell Bazi, which seems to correspond well with some of the main descriptive features of the royal inscription of Naram-Sin. In addition, the use of the name of Ebla to indicate not only the capital city, but also the territory it controlled, seems to have been foreshadowed by the frequency with which even the royal chancery of Ebla used the expression "Saza and Ebla", apparently to indicate the extent of the city's dominion.

A similar broad use of the name of Ebla reappears a few decades later in a royal votive inscription of Gudea of Lagash (Figure 8.2), an important Sumerian prince of Lower Mesopotamia. Recalling distant countries of the east and west, from which he had received materials for building the famous Enninu temple for the main god of Lagash, Ningirsu, he mentions the fine wood 'from the city of Urshu and the plateau of Ebla', where Ebla was clearly just a geographical indication as to Urshu's whereabouts for the Sumerians in distant Lagash. Gudea's reference suggests, however, that Urshu, which is often mentioned in the texts of Ebla's Royal Archives under the equivalent form Urshaum, succeeded Armanum in regional hegemony over the land of Ebla, showing that in Gudea's time, in the last decades of the twenty-second century BC, Ebla had still not recovered any significant political power or autonomy.

Urshu is usually located north of Aleppo and west of the Euphrates, between the present Syrian–Turkish border and the Taurus Mountains,

Figure 8.2 Gudea of Lagash's Statue B, with the inscription recalling the timber coming from the Ebla region (AO 2), diorite, from Telloh, 22nd century BC.

Source: By kind permission of the Louvre Museum.

though an alternative view has it that it may have been much closer to Ebla, south of Aleppo. Either way, it seems certain that first Armi/Armanum, until the time of Naram-Sin of Akkad, and then Urshu, until the start of the III Dynasty of Ur, took over Ebla's political legacy, controlling part, at least, of the territory that Ebla had ruled. During the later reigns of the Neo-Sumerian sovereigns Shulgi, Amar-Suen, and Shu-Sin, who succeeded the founder of the III Dynasty, Ur-Namma, to the throne of Ur, Ebla probably recovered a significant political role: in fact, messengers and merchants from the city often visited the Sumerian metropolis at that time, bringing precious textiles and fine furniture to the powerful lords of Ur. The mention of Ebla in the inscriptions of Naram-Sin and Gudea seems like the chancery's attempt to make clear where Armanum and Urshu were on the map. Nevertheless, the Neo-Sumerian administration meticulously recorded the presence of "men of Ebla" (repeatedly mentioned by name) at the court of Ur, and this strongly indicates trade and direct political contact between the Ur of the III Dynasty and Ebla in the first half of the twenty-first century BC.

What does archaeology reveal about the second Ebla, contemporary with Naram-Sin, Gudea, and Shulgi? Actually, despite repeated attempts to reach the remains of the city that had succeeded the first Ebla of the Royal Archives, beneath the levels of the third archaic Old Syrian Ebla, until very recently most of the traces of this settlement from the last centuries of the third millennium BC were incomplete, to say the least. There are, however, scattered ceramic fragments from the period, strongly concentrated on the slopes of the massive ramparts, built at the outset of the archaic Old Syrian Period, suggesting that the remains of the second Ebla were razed and removed as material for these ramparts very early in the second millennium BC, when the third Ebla was rebuilt.

This is certainly why there are abundant ceramic fragments of Early Bronze IVB on the slopes of the ramparts and almost none in the Lower Town, and it is significant that the terrain containing those fragments in the ramparts themselves always seems full of architectural debris and ashes from what must have been a violent destruction. We must infer that the second Ebla of the late Early Syrian Period was also badly destroyed and its ruins removed at the beginning of the archaic Old Syrian Period, and massed up to build along the line of the ancient walled fortification the mighty earthen-work ramparts that surrounded the third Ebla in the early second millennium BC.

These signs, indicating the presence of a relatively important settlement in Early Bronze IVB over the abandoned ruins of the mature Early Syrian city of Early Bronze IVA, are confirmed by new data that have recently emerged, shedding further light on the second Ebla of the age of the II Dynasty of Lagash and the III Dynasty of Ur. For the first time, well-preserved remains of the late Early Syrian city have been found over the imposing ruins of the Temple of the Rock of the great city of the Royal Archives, and in some areas to the north and east. Early on in the late Early Syrian Period what seem to be merely private houses (Figure 8.3) appeared at the foot of the ruins of the Temple of the Rock and against its outer walls. Against some parts of the thick towering walls of the Temple of the Rock, some humble structures were also built to contain the imposing ruins of the older temple and, a little later, the remarkable Temple HH4, which was soon flanked to the north by the smaller Temple HH5.

The houses north and east of the great sanctuary were not razed or removed in the large-scale urban reorganization involved in re-founding the third Ebla simply because they were protected by their closeness to the great ruin. The remains of the two temples alongside, which were relatively exposed, were razed but did not disappear, perhaps out of traditional respect for the remains of sacred buildings. Indeed, shortly after the reconstruction of the archaic Old Syrian Period, two later and quite significant new temples of the third and last Ebla were built on them. It seems likely that Temple HH4 and Temple HH5 were raised in a central phase in the historical development of the late Early Syrian Period, quite close in time to Shulgi's age.

Figure 8.3 Ebla, Area HH, remains of late Early Syrian private houses, at the feet of the ruins of the Temple of the Rock, from the north, 22nd–21st century BC.

It is certain that the ruins of the grand complex of Royal Palace G of the age of the Archives were abandoned, without any attempt to rebuild them, at least in the fairly significant, monumental area of the Administrative Quarter, either immediately after the destruction by Sargon of Akkad or later. However, after some time had passed, new buildings rose up in the wide urban area, which must also have included quite extensive ruins. These buildings were significant in size, and also for their function, revealing the rebirth of a political power of some importance, which corresponds to the evidence of the administrative documents of the III Dynasty of Ur around 2050 BC. This political and religious rebirth is clear from the archaeological evidence. The political aspect can be seen in the certainly incomplete attempt to build a royal residence in the Archaic Palace (Figure 8.4), which has been partially brought to light in the Lower Town North (Sector P North), beneath the ruins of the royal Northern Palace of the later classical Old Syrian city. The religious aspect is evident in the attempt to revive an important centre of worship on the very site of the ancient Temple of the Rock on the eastern periphery of the Lower Town (Area HH), and perhaps, too, on the Acropolis (Area D), in the heart of the mature Early Syrian Saza, where Kura's Temple stood.

The striking succession of cult buildings on the site of the Temple of the Rock indicates the powerful cultural continuity between the first and second Ebla in the basic sphere of religious beliefs too, something which is also

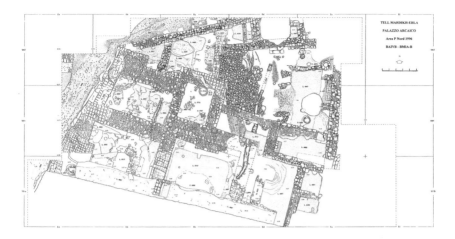

Figure 8.4 Ebla, Archaic Palace, detailed plan of the late Early Syrian building, and of the archaic Old Syrian additions, 21st and 20th–19th century BC.

obvious from material culture. It also indicates the developments in architectural culture between the years that saw the fall of the great mature Early Syrian city and the less glorious late Early Syrian Period. Temples HH4 and HH5 (Figure 8.5) show that in the important sphere of architectural culture, there was both continuity with the Early Syrian age of the Archives, but also a change in planning and spatial sensibility, compared with that recently lost glorious period.

The continuity is evident from the fact that, like the previous Temple of the Rock, Temple HH4 also has an axial structure and an *in antis* façade. It differs, however, as the broad cella of that older sanctuary became a long cella in Temple HH4, and the vestibule was now much shorter than the cella. The transition in temple typology from broad to long cella happened in Ebla, then, during the late Early Syrian Period, and seems to have been a development in architectural culture in inner Syria towards the end of the third millennium BC. The influences may have come from Upper Mesopotamia, where temple architecture, at least in Tell Halawa A, Tell Khuera, and Tell Qara Quzaq, had already adopted the long-cella typology in the age of Ebla's Archives.

This development in temple typology in Ebla's architectural culture is all the more important as the form of the cella in cult architecture, particularly in the defining features of the entrance being axial or transversal and the longitudinal or latitudinal development of the cella, is one of the most characteristic architectural features in the Syro-Palestinian world in the Bronze Age. Thus, in Palestine in Early Bronze II–III, the usual temple type consists of axial entrance and wide cella, and we have now discovered that this was so in Upper Syria, too, at least in Early Bronze IV, although the two traditions differed in where they placed the antae on the façade and in the spatial proportions.

Figure 8.5 Ebla, ruins of Temples HH4 and HH5 of the late Early Syrian period; in
the background to the right, the ruins of the Temple of the Rock, from the
north-east, 22nd–21st century BC.

Ebla may have been depopulated immediately after the destruction of
Mardikh IIB1 and may now have been slowly reviving demographically, politically, and culturally. This was the period of the political domination of
Upper Syria, first by Armi/Armanum and then by Urshaum/Urshum, from
the age of Naram-Sin of Akkad in the mid-twenty-third century BC to the
time of Gudea of Lagash in the second half of the twenty-second century
BC. During this time, despite the strong demographic, political, and cultural
crisis, Ebla stood fully involved in architectural and material culture and in
other developments of high urban culture, in which it had played a leading
role until the terrible destruction brought by Sargon of Akkad.

It is in the sphere of ceramic culture that the continuity of development
from the mature Early Syrian culture is clear in Ebla, too, in a context that
links it with various other centres in Upper Syria, from the region of Hamah
in the south to Antioch in the north, and the Euphrates Valley to the east.
Chronologically, Mardikh IIB1 clearly corresponds very closely to Hamah
J6 and, more generally, to 'Amuq I and Selenkahiyah in its earlier phase. The
developments of Mardikh IIB2, which are also broadly similar to 'Amuq J
and Selenkahiyah in its later phase, again correspond perfectly with those
later revealed by Hamah J5-1. Recently, the data emerging from the excavation of Area HH of Ebla, on the ruins of the great Temple of the Rock, where
a good stratification of deposits of Early Bronze IVB has been certified for
the first time, provide still more detailed, extended, and certain information

than in Hamah. What is so far available shows a general convergence between Mardikh IIB2 and Hamah J5-1, indicating clear lines of generally parallel developments in inner Syria, at least from Aleppo to Hamah.

While remaining rigorously part of the Caliciform tradition that developed during the late period of the mature Early Syrian culture, some innovations in pottery are clear from the early period of Mardikh IIB2. There were mono-chrome goblets painted black or, more rarely, red, decorated with horizontal bands, often with fine horizontal combings on the broader bands, variously grouped on the upper part of the vessel, almost always with bell-shaped or modelled bases, but no longer flat or in the shape of flattened rings, as in the previous period corresponding to the age of the Archives (Figure 8.6). At the same time, another type of monochrome painted pottery began to establish itself, painted pink or pinkish-brown, usually somewhat diluted, applied in fine horizontal bands on the neck or the high shoulder of middle-sized jars, with a typically out-turned, rounded rim. Another very typical, widespread innov-ation from the early years of Mardikh IIB2 is that of open bowls, with the rim profiled on the outside. This kind of bowl was very common, sometimes painted on the inner or outer rim with one or two high bands painted black or red, often wiped off in wavy motifs by means of a stick's incisions. However,

Figure 8.6 Late Early Syrian painted pottery of the Caliciform horizon, retrieved in a pit of the cella L.9190 of the Temple of the Rock, 23rd century BC.

the older periods of Mardikh IIB2 show very typical forms of Mardikh IIB1 persisting, though not the same care in the consistency and firing.

The central period of Early Bronze IVB saw the widespread production of painted goblets with the usual decoration and shape of the base, but definitely larger than usual: in these goblets, painted red more often than black, the shape becomes markedly spheroid in the upper part of the vases and the wavy decorations become more frequent. Later on, in Mardikh IIB2, however, the painted goblets become less frequent, less varied in decoration and smaller, while some previously unknown types appear, particularly in medium-small and small specimens. A very characteristic type is the bowl with straight slanting sides and vertical rim outside, marked by two or three distinct horizontal grooves, unknown in painted specimens.

The gradual decline in painted pottery seems a general characteristic of the final phases of Early Bronze IVB, both in the variety of decorations and in the quantity produced. There are even quite a few examples of goblets that have the same form as in previous periods, but without any painted decoration or, in its place, a series of almost unvaried thin parallel grooves made on the wheel, which provide a very simplified form of the same decoration that was previously made on bands of black or red paint. A kind of Cooking Ware, absent in the palace assemblages of Mardikh IIB1, gradually spread in the early phases of Mardikh IIB2, and, later on, became more and more common. In fact, there were again the so-called "hole-mouth" spheroid or oval cooking pots with thickened rim, but they were flanked by many large bowls with quite an open shape, slanting side, and rim typically folded back and thickened on the outside, and frequently a rough external surface.

How far did the reconstructed late Early Syrian city of Mardikh IIB2 actually extend? It is hard to say as its remains were razed and often removed, but traces have been identified in the central area of the North-West Lower Town, and around the piled-up ruins of the great Temple of the Rock of the Archives age in the South-East Lower Town there were built what seem to have been private houses. These not seriously damaged, precisely because they were built next to the former sanctuary, and were protected by the cult building. It seems, then, that the new city extended relatively far inside the walls of the earlier one, but it is also likely that the urban pattern was quite loose-knit, probably concentrated around certain outcrops such as Temples HH4 and HH5 in the area of the old Temple of the Rock, and the site of the Archaic Palace in the north of the Lower Town.

The Archaic Palace in Sector P North (Figure 8.7) is the most significant and most obviously original building that has come down to us from the late Early Syrian city, although it certainly belongs to the last decades of Mardikh IIB2 and was not completed, at least so far as the original ambitious project goes. Although it has been impossible to excavate more than the northern sector of the building, as the remains of the central and southern area lie below the later Intermediate Palace and Northern Palace respectively of the archaic and classical Old Syrian city, the Archaic Palace, with its unusual

Figure 8.7 Ebla, Archaic Palace, the ruins of the north-west sector of the original late Early Syrian building, from the north-west, 21st century BC.

trapezoidal structure and its buttressed northern façade, seems particularly original. In terms of the internal subdivision of spaces there are two long rooms in the western sector, which were probably to be repeated symmetrically in the eastern sector, where they were never built, and a large central room with a dais against the northern back wall, probably with wooden panelling on the walls, which would have been the Audience Hall. As a result, the building seems strangely like a work that is part of a solid tradition, planned according to canonical principles that, nevertheless, are not to be found anywhere in the Royal Palace G of the previous period. The only obvious similarity with the buildings of the previous mature Early Syrian Period are the very thick walls (up to 2.80 m), as in the palace of the age of the Archives, with low stone bases, using large slabs and blocks laid out with gaps, which were common in the Early Syrian Temple of the Rock, but completely unusual in later Old Syrian architecture.

It is, however, certain that both the late Early Syrian temples, built over the Temple of the Rock, and the Archaic Palace, which was planned, if not as the real royal palace, then certainly as a ceremonial palace, like its Old Syrian successor, have a dignity and coherence that show it was a period only apparently in decline. Indeed, it is very probable that the two temples of Area HH and the palace of Area P, built in an advanced phase of the late Early Syrian Period, reflect a time of cultural, political, and commercial rebirth for Ebla, which might have followed the period of Urshu's predominance, corresponding to Gudea of Lagash's reign. In the years immediately following, the economic texts of the central years of the III Dynasty of Ur record messengers and merchants from Ebla at the courts of Shulgi, Amar-Suen, and Shu-Sin, bringing precious furniture and textiles for the powerful lords of Ur, which suggests Ebla was enjoying a new flourishing, not long before a new and terrible destruction.

One piece of archaeological evidence of the contribution of long-distance trade to this brief rebirth might be the finding in Temple HH4 of a magnificent long pearl of carnelian, bi-conical in form, typical of the productions of the Indus Valley. Art work in Ebla in the late phases of Mardikh IIB2 was of high quality and carried on the tradition of the previous mature Early Syrian Period, as is confirmed by the discovery in Temple HH4 of some excellently produced eyes of steatite and limestone, probably belonging to votive images from the temple and, in one particularly large example, to a cult statue.

Clear traces of the terrible destruction of the late Early Syrian city can be found in the ash and ceramic materials in the ruins piled up in various sectors of the mighty ramparts built in the archaic Old Syrian Period. This disaster hit the city not long after the erection of Temples HH4 and HH5, in the south-east region of the Lower Town, and when the Archaic Palace was still under construction. Indeed, the whole eastern sector of the building was never completed according to the original plan, but was altered significantly after the destruction, when it was readapted to the urgent needs of the new lords of the third Ebla, who were involved in the huge task of rebuilding the new urban centre in the early twentieth century BC.

Until a few years ago, it was generally assumed that the destruction of the second Ebla in the last years of the twenty-first century BC had also finally ended the late Early Syrian culture of Mardikh IIB2. Now, however, it seems we must recognize that it probably took place only shortly before the end of the culture of Early Bronze IVB. In fact, in the area of private houses built around the ruins of the Temple of the Rock of the mature Early Syrian Period, it seems there are poor traces of an attempt at reconstructing the buildings by people who were still producing the same pottery as in the last years of Early Bronze IVB. These attempts at reoccupation did not last long, and there appears to have been a marked weakening in the sense of cultural continuity with the glorious phase of the age of the Archives, as refuse pits were excavated on the walls of the ancient, venerated Temple of the Rock, which may have been demolished but were still visible. After the new destruction that put an end to the second Ebla, a much larger population who knew techniques in pottery using different procedures from the traditional ones took possession of the territory of the old urban area.

As we have already said, we do not really know who was responsible for the destruction of the second Ebla. However, if there are historical grounds for thinking that messengers and merchants from Ebla at the court of the great sovereigns of the III Dynasty of Ur came from the city in a late phase of Mardikh IIB2, then it follows that in the reign of Ibbi-Sin, the last, unfortunate king of that dynasty of Ur, Ebla was no longer able to send representatives there, in the very years when the Amorites from the west and the Elamites from the east were putting ultimately fatal military pressure on Ur. We should also remember that in a fragment of an inscription, it was Shu-Sin of Ur who seems to have celebrated an expedition to the west, during which, in a particularly damaged context, Ebla seems to be mentioned along with Mari and Tuttul.

It is clear, then, that an extremely plausible and interesting hypothesis, though so far totally unproven, might be that a strong parallel existed between the events of those years in Upper Syria and those that overturned the world of Lower Mesopotamia.

First, the destruction of the second Ebla might have happened in the period –no more than a few decades – between 2025 and the earliest years of the twentieth century BC, when a text on economic matters by Ishbi-Erra, first sovereign of the I Dynasty of Isin, once again mentions new peoples of Mari and Ebla.

Second, if the second Ebla was not destroyed by Shu-Sin himself, it might have fallen victim to one of the frequent attacks carried out, according to Neo-Sumerian sources, by the Amorites in that period against the western provinces of the dominion of the III Dynasty of Ur, and that might very well have impacted on the urban centres of Upper Syria too.

Third, if Ebla did capitulate to an attack by a powerful Amorite prince at the head of a large army in the very years when the sovereigns of the III Dynasty of Ur had built a huge wall in the desert against these incursions, this might explain why the material culture in the third Ebla, particularly in pottery, shows, alongside elements of continuity, clear signs of a break.

The most recent data indicate that the destruction of the second Ebla of the late Early Syrian Period was immediately followed by a short-lived attempt, by some of its former inhabitants, to rebuild at least some sectors of the devastated city. It is therefore not unlikely that a substantial force of Amorites attacked, conquered, and devastated the city shortly after 2025 BC, probably around 2000 BC, when the Elamites succeeded in taking Ur, which had been weakened by constant internal turmoil, and then retired, perhaps with a view to further sieges and raids on other large late Early Syrian urban centres. In just a few years, the entire late Early Syrian political system of Upper Syria was being turned upside down by the Amorite forays and the attempts to reconstruct the ancient cities by small, impoverished groups of inhabitants failed. At the same time, a few powerful Amorite princes with a significant following of men decided to re-found at least some of the cities that had been destroyed, particularly those that had had a more glorious past and greater political and economic power.

It was a similar situation to that of the Amorite princes in this period who, in Lower Mesopotamia, founded, first, the I Dynasty of Isin, and, shortly after, the Dynasty of Larsa, trying at once to assume control of the glorious city of Ur and setting about rebuilding the magnificent city that had been devastated by the Elamites, proclaiming themselves its heirs. In the same way, an ambitious Amorite chief who had large numbers of men at his command returned to the ruins of Ebla, determined to rebuild it and quickly restore its political dominance.

It must certainly have been an Amorite prince of great prestige and determination whose aim was the rebirth of the ancient glory of Ebla. The daring enterprise seems to have been guided by two lines of policy that were only apparently in conflict with each other, but that might explain why he succeeded in recreating the social cohesion that determined the success of the initiative. The new lords of the city wanted to explicitly affirm continuity with the mature Early Syrian culture of the first Ebla, repeatedly and consistently including in the very names of the new sovereigns the names of Lim and Damu, the dynastic gods of the greatest kings of the most glorious period of the old city. They also did everything they could to ensure that the polyadic divinity of the re-founded Old Syrian city was Ishtar, probably through a syncretism with the chthonic Ishkhara. The heavenly Ishtar was already worshipped assiduously, particularly in royal circles of the city in the mature Early Syrian Period, and was a most venerated patron of the main groups of Amorite nobles who made up the core of the new rulers.

So far, we cannot be certain that it was the enlightened sagacity of just one or two intellectually and politically distinguished figures who managed to complete the complex, ambitious plan for the rebirth of the third Ebla in the course of a few years. It is certain, however, that a few decades after its destruction, Ebla managed to reassume a central, dominating role in inner Syria, which effectively restored the glories of the older, more splendid city.

9 From Ebla to Yamkhad

The territorial states of the Amorite Age

It is probable that the major centres of the great urban culture of the mature and late Early Syrian Period in inner Syria were repeatedly destroyed over the years, now one, now another city being affected, either as a result of regional wars, when the damage was probably not particularly serious, or of external interventions when, much more often, there could be deliberately radical devastation. However, even the most serious destructions, like that affecting Ebla around 2300 BC, at the end of Mardikh IIB1, which put an end to the flourishing city of the Royal Archives age, and was brought about by a powerful, organized external intervention, by what would soon prove to be an irresistible political force, did not in any way lead to the collapse of the culture of Upper Syria. On the contrary, under the guidance of other centres, it continued to prosper, even allowing Ebla itself durable revivals, when the city continued to participate in the unified culture of the region, even though it had lost its political, and probably cultural, primacy.

We are almost completely in the dark as to who was responsible for the destruction of the second Ebla around 2000 BC, towards the end of the late Early Syrian Period, but this time there was a definite break in cultural development. Though some forms of continuity that should not be underestimated have been observed, this break is striking in all aspects of material culture, particularly in pottery, metalwork, and building techniques, as well as, very probably, in artistic expression and architectural concepts.

In traditional archaeological terms this break is expressed in the transition from the great phase of Early Bronze IVA–B to the new period of Middle Bronze I. If the traditional Middle Chronologies of Mesopotamia and Egypt are correct, it took place just when the Amorite princes seized power in Lower Mesopotamia, founding important dynasties such as those of Isin and Larsa, and, a few decades later, Babylon, Uruk, and Eshnunna, to name only the most significant. At the same time in Egypt, after the XI Theban Dynasty had re-founded the pharaohs' power, initiating the Middle Kingdom, the glorious XII Dynasty, which also originated in Thebes, established itself, providing a powerful thrust to the new unified state of the Nile Valley.

It was the firm intention of the sovereigns of Isin and Larsa to draw on the great Mesopotamian tradition most recently represented, throughout the twenty-first century BC, by the important III Dynasty of Ur, which had seen a powerful, branching organization of government include much of unified Mesopotamia, in a highly centralized state, sub-divided into provinces ruled by central officials of the efficient Neo-Sumerian monarchy. Nevertheless, despite the many wars they fought, the Amorite princes did not succeed in recreating a unified kingdom and, above all, they were unable to maintain international, commercial, and political relations with powers outside the southern Mesopotamian world, while the prestigious kings of Ur had kept up constant relations from Syria to Iran. This is certainly why the sources of the archaic Old Babylonian Period, unlike the administrative texts of the III Dynasty of Ur, no longer mention Ebla at all, and it disappears from the texts of Lower Mesopotamia in this period. The oldest mention of Ebla in the second millennium (almost certainly in the early twentieth century BC), seems to be in an important royal inscription engraved on the basalt votive statue of the king of Ebla Ibbit-Lim, son of Igrish-Kheb. Its discovery in Ebla in 1968 made it possible to say with certainty that Tell Mardikh was the ancient Ebla, the city long searched for by archaeologists between southern Turkey and northern Syria (Figure 9.1).

Various information of great interest appears in this inscription: first of all, the king calls himself *meki* of Ebla, using an enigmatic title that is almost certainly a dialect form of *malikum*, meaning "king" in all the western Semitic languages; second, the dating of the dedication of the statue is provided in a peculiar fashion by the formula 'the eighth year since Ishtar revealed herself in Ebla', which must indicate an event of exceptional importance in the city's religious history, and might even be Ishtar's assumption as polyadic goddess of the city; third, the statue was dedicated in Ishtar's sanctuary, in order to celebrate the introduction into the temple of an important cult fitting, a 'basin', which was probably the kind of double basin found in at least one specimen in every Old Syrian temple so far discovered.

A few years later, the royal title of *meki* was again used in the inscription of a king of Ebla, Ib-Damu, appearing in a seal reused (Figure 9.2) in the level of *kārum* II in Kanesh, the present-day Kültepe in Central Anatolia, where very many Old Assyrian texts have been found (as they have, to a lesser extent, in other trading colonies of Assyria) from between the late twentieth and early nineteenth centuries BC. And it is in the same period that a Meki of Qedem is mentioned in a famous Egyptian literary text, probably written at that time, the "Tale of Sinuhe", which tells of the peregrinations in Asia of a high Egyptian official of the pharaoh's court, who fled Egypt on Amenemhat I's death, just before the possibly turbulent reign of his successor Senwosret I. If Qedem might indicate an undefined region of Central Syria, unless it alludes to the east in general, Meki in the tale must have been assumed as a personal name, while knowing that it was a possibly widely used royal title in Syria that meant only "king", just as in Egypt the title "pharaoh", deriving

Figure 9.1 Inscribed torso of Ibbit-Lim of Ebla's archaic Old Syrian votive statue (TM.68.G.61), basalt, from the south-west sector of the Acropolis, 20th century BC.

from the Egyptian royal epithet *pr'3* "Large house", was commonly used to refer to the lord of Egypt without mention of his actual name.

Decades later, in the royal correspondence of Mari, at the time of Shamshi-Addu I of Assyria, around 1800 BC, the probably local, and now ancient, title of *mekum/meki* was used to designate the kings of Upper Syria. Very probably, this was the traditional Eblaic pronunciation of the title *malikum*, which was certainly not used only for the kings of Ebla, but also for other sovereigns of Upper Syria, understandably regarded in both Egypt and Mesopotamia as a characteristic royal title in those regions.

As it is certain that he reigned in the early years of the twentieth century BC, as the archaic language of his inscription contains particular analogies with the Old Assyrian texts of Cappadocia, and the epigraphy of his statue is very close to the texts of the late third millennium in Mesopotamia, Ibbit-Lim must have been an important sovereign of early Old Syrian Ebla. As is suggested by the dating formula, it must have been he who introduced the cult of Ishtar at Ebla, or, rather, by virtue of a syncretism with the chthonic Ishkhara, made of the heavenly Ishtar, who was already worshipped at the

Figure 9.2 Drawing of two impressions on tablets of a cylinder seal reused and re-
incised, originally the property of king Ib-Damu of Ebla, clay, from
Kanish, 21st–19th century BC.

Source: By kind permission of Beatrice Teissier.

time of the Royal Archives, one of the major deities of the ancient city, the
real polyadic goddess of the revived Ebla. To have given her name to eight
years of his reign, the event of Ishtar's appearance in Ebla must have been
considered extraordinary by Ibbit-Lim, who probably also made patroness of
the dynasty the goddess who for centuries, even after the final destruction of
the city, was still called *Eblaitu* – "The Eblaite one" (Figure 9.3).

It is very likely that, during the archaic and classical Old Syrian Periods,
Ebla was the most important cult centre of the great Syrian goddess of love,
fertility, and war, who enjoyed extraordinary popularity down to the time of
the Roman Empire, both in her austere form as lady of universal fertility,
and in her licentious, seductive aspect as goddess of love, by which she was
identified with the planet Venus, "the star of evening and of morning", which
was the first to appear at dusk and the last to disappear at dawn in the starry
heavens of the night.

In the archaic Old Syrian Period, then, as well as Ibbit-Lim and his father
Igrish-Kheb, who probably reigned shortly before 1950 BC, at least one other

Figure 9.3 Upper register of the main face of Ishtar's Stele, with the goddess's Old Syrian image (TM.67.E.224 + 85.E.85 + 85.G.350), basalt, from Shrine G3, 19th century BC.

sovereign of Ebla, Ib-Damu, who lived around 1900 BC, is known from the seal inscription preserved in the impressions of Kanesh II. The names of these kings are of great interest, as they show strong continuity with the names of the glorious mature Early Syrian dynasty of the age of the Archives: in fact, Lim and Damu were gods who frequently appeared in the names of the Ebla dynasty, which was swept away by Sargon of Akkad, while Kheb may be an abbreviation of Khebat, the great goddess of Aleppo, companion of Hadad, and the verbal form *igrish* of the oldest of these sovereigns is actually identical with that of an important king of the Archives age, Igrish-Khalab.

Whoever was responsible for the destruction of the city at the end of Early Bronze IVB around 2000 BC, and whatever the context of that event (as with what happened at almost the same time in Lower Mesopotamia, the Amorites might have had a hand in it), it is likely that those who rebuilt Ebla were princes of the same stock or, at least, the same linguistic group as the mature and, perhaps, late Early Syrian kings of Early Bronze IVA and, perhaps, IVB. Alternatively, Amorite princes wanting to continue the glorious history of the first Ebla of the Royal Archives, took names that displayed this continuity, just as in Isin and Larsa, the Amorite chiefs who founded the new dynasties competed to reconstruct the devastated Ur, which Ishbi-Erra of Isin had helped to ruin.

Though there is no written evidence of how substantial the political power of Ebla was in the archaic Old Syrian Period, during Middle Bronze I, it is very likely that, as is suggested by the monumental extent of the settlement of Mardikh IIIA, the rebuilt third Ebla was the dominant power of Upper Syria south of the Taurus Mountains at least as far as the region of Hamah. The very mention of Ebla in the Old Assyrian texts of Cappadocia shows that for the rich merchants of Assur, who did not go directly from Assyria to Central Anatolia, but had commercial interests south of the Taurus Mountains, it was Ebla that was the main political, commercial, and cultural presence in those regions.

We should therefore imagine that, in the Upper Syria of the archaic Old Syrian Period, Ebla was what Isin and Larsa, despite their occasional rivalry, were in the archaic Old Babylonian Period for Lower Mesopotamia. In remarkably similar ways these situations of regional political hegemony were ended in just a few years by Yarim-Lim I of Aleppo (Figure 9.4), who gave the kingdom of Yamkhad lasting supremacy in Upper Syria, and, shortly after, by Hammurabi of Babylon, who made his kingdom the dominant power in Lower Mesopotamia.

Some scholars claim that the irresistible rise of Yarim-Lim I of Yamkhad might have been the result of a prestigious military victory over the powerful

Figure 9.4 Aleppo, Citadel, view of the cella of Hadad's Temple, with the archaic Neo-Syrian carved orthostats, from the south, 9th–8th century BC.

Source: By permission of Syro-German Expedition at Aleppo Citadel.

figure of Shamshi-Addu I of Assyria, the creator of an extensive but short-lived empire in Upper Mesopotamia in the years of the rise to political and diplomatic power of the great Hammurabi's Babylon. This happened around 1780 BC, during the transition from Middle Bronze I to Middle Bronze II, and does not seem to have caused any destruction of Ebla, which probably recognized the emergence of the new power without suffering attack.

Though there is no doubt that, after Yarim-Lim I's feat, the kings of Aleppo were considered "Great Kings" for a long time, throughout the classical Old Syrian Period, not only in the region, it is probable that Ebla, as the major political power in the previous two centuries, became a loyal ally and vassal of the kings of Aleppo, becoming fully part of their power system.

This situation of organized and integrated involvement in a system of regional alliances, that was perhaps little different from that which Ebla itself had ably managed in the mature Early Syrian Period and that was now centred on Aleppo, seems to be eloquently indicated by the marriage, around 1650 BC, of a princess of Ebla with the son of king Ammitakum of Alalakh, who belonged to a royal family that descended from a lesser branch of the lords of Yamkhad. It is certain, however, that Ebla remained a powerful and prestigious urban centre, able, to give just one eloquent example, to handle important international relations independently of its powerful neighbours of Yamkhad.

In fact, probably around 1750/1725 BC, Ebla was being ruled by the same Immeya whose name appears both, without any title, on the rim of a silver platter in the Tomb of the Lord of the Goats (Figure 9.5), and as the recipient of a letter sent to a sovereign that was found in the area of the private houses of Area B of the South-West Lower Town. If they were not two different kings with the same dynastic name, which we certainly cannot rule

Figure 9.5 Immeya of Ebla's silver platter (TM.78.Q.497), from the Tomb of the Lord of the Goats, 18th century BC.

out, it is clear that Immeya of Ebla, shortly before 1750 BC, had received from Egypt a royal ceremonial club/mace in ivory, silver, and gold inscribed with the name of a pharaoh in hieroglyphics. The gift came from a pharaoh of Asian origin, Hotepibra Harnejheryotef, who, somewhat unusually for an Egyptian pharaoh, described himself as the "Son of the Asiatic" (Plates XXX–XXXI, 1–4).

There must have been another sovereign of Ebla after Immeya, whose name has survived in incomplete form as Hammu…, who appears as the lord of a functionary who owned a cylinder seal, whose impression has been left on a sealing discovered in the East-South-East Fortress on the eastern ramparts (Figure 9.6). It is interesting that both these names of kings of Ebla, the second of which was probably Hammurabi, are not just Semitic but, plausibly, Amorite, as Immeya was certainly a diminutive. A third royal name of Ebla for the classical Old Syrian Period, that has been handed down from findings in excavations, is that of Indilimma (Figure 9.7), previously read as Indilimgur, which has survived both in the dating formula of a legal document discovered in the Western Palace, and in the inscription of a beautiful dynastic seal (preserved in various seal impressions on jars' shoulders) of a prince who claimed to be his son. As the jars with the impressions of Indilimma's son were found in contexts of the destruction of the city at the end of Middle Bronze II, this prince was very probably the heir to the throne nominated by Indilimma, but who probably never succeeded him, due to the destruction of the classical Old Syrian city. If things went like that, it is clear that Indilimma must have been the last king, who had to suffer the terrible destruction that finally wiped out the third Ebla.

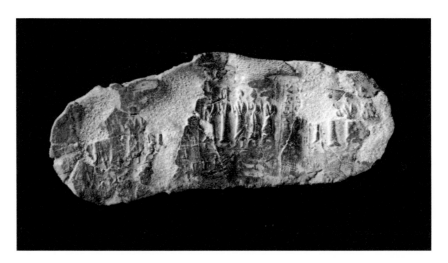

Figure 9.6 Sealing with cylinder seal impression of an official of Hammu[rabi] of Ebla (TM.71.M.343), clay, from the East-South-East Fortress, 18th century BC.

Figure 9.7 Impression on a jar of the seal of Indilimma of Ebla's son (TM.79.BQ:126/
1), clay, from the Western Palace, 17th century BC.

The great Old Syrian city of these last years of Middle Bronze II is
also mentioned in the fragments of a couple of ritual Hurrian texts from
Boghazköy, as well as Aleppo, showing how close the two centres were, both
geographically and culturally, and also in a Hittite text that probably refers
to the feats of one of the two great Old Hittite kings, Hattusili I or Mursili
I, who carried out a series of military campaigns in Syria in the late seventeenth century BC. The two major historical texts that have passed down
the Syrian feats of Hattusili I suggest that he attempted in vain to bring
down Aleppo, which may have been saved by support from a not clearly
defined Hurrian king, who was certainly an important sovereign in the
Hurrian world. Hattusili conquered at least two important vassal cities of
Yamkhad, Alalakh and Urshu, weakening Aleppo's power in the very heart
of its dominions.

The archaeological chronology for the settlement of Mardikh IIIB now
makes it certain that Ebla was destroyed at the time of the expeditions into
Upper Syria by Hattusili I and Mursili I, and that, if Hattusili I had conquered
the city, this feat, too, would have been mentioned along with those concerning
Alalakh and Urshu in his texts. In addition, as it seems that the Mardikh IIIB
pottery is slightly later than that of Alalakh VII, whose destruction is now
unanimously identified with that mentioned in the texts of Hattusili I, it is
very probable that his great successor Mursili I was responsible for taking and
destroying the third Ebla.

This hypothesis, which is not opposed by any serious archaeological arguments, is now supported by a series of deductions that can be made from the exceptional bilingual epic of the "Chant of Release" (Figure 9.8), originally written in Hurrian, fragments of which have come down to us in the two versions, Hurrian and Hittite, that were retrieved in 1983 and 1985 in two minor sanctuaries of the Upper City of Hattusa, where they had been preserved until the abandonment of the city early in the twelfth century BC. This epic, which is unique in the extensive literature of the Ancient Orient, narrates in mythical-historical tones the destruction of Ebla, and was very probably written down in eastern Hurrian during the sixteenth century BC, and translated into Hittite, certainly in Hattusa, almost certainly in the fifteenth century BC, given the presence of clearly Middle-Hittite expressions, perhaps in the time of Tudkhaliya I, whose ambition was to return to the splendours of Mursili I, as he showed by trying to conquer Aleppo again. There is therefore no doubt that if the "Chant of Release" was of Hurrian origin, it must have wished to celebrate a memorable feat that was probably carried out by the Hurrians, and, if it was translated into Hittite in Hattusa, it must have celebrated feats that the Hittites felt were part of their own history.

Given the striking chronological closeness of the fall of Ebla with the drafting of the Hurrian-Hittite poem, it is very likely that what it tells of had strong historical foundations, and it seems probable that Ebla was conquered

Figure 9.8 Tablet of the Hurrian-Hittite "Chant of Release", clay, from Boghazköy, 16th–15th century BC.

Source: By kind permission of Jürgen Seeher.

by Hurrians allied with Hittites, and, more precisely, by a Hurrian king allied with Mursili I, whose feats Tudkhaliya I wanted to repeat.

It only survives in fragments, but the "Chant of Release", the second part of which is almost completely lost, includes repeated interventions of great gods in the conquest of Ebla: Teshub, of the eastern Hurrian city of Kumme in the Upper Tigris valley; the goddess of the Underworld Allani; and Ishkhara, who, as we have seen, was one of the greatest deities of Ebla at the time of the Royal Archives. According to the poetical narrative, Teshub of Kumme threatened the king of Ebla, called Meki of Ebla from the Eblaic title for king, with annihilating the city, breaking the 'inner wall' and the 'outer wall' like a fragile pot, letting it fall into the 'moat' that surrounded it, if Ebla did not at once free the prince of the city of Igagallish, who was being sacrilegiously held prisoner in Ebla.

Following this serious threat, Meki of Ebla asked his princely allies for their opinion and, though he was personally in favour of giving in to the threat of the god Teshub, the assembly was convinced by the reckless advice of a figure described as 'powerful of speech'. And so Meki had to tell the furious Teshub that Ebla refused to release the prince. The few other narrative elements that can be reconstructed include a kind of party in the Underworld organized by the goddess Allani, in which a drunken Teshub risks being seduced by the cunning Allani, who may have tried to dissuade Teshub from carrying out his threats against the proud city that opposed his desires.

Something of great importance that has not been sufficiently considered is that, apart from some sententious passages difficult to place in the context of the complex general narrative scheme, the introduction, most of which has fortunately survived, mentions as the subject of the epic, apart from the name of Ebla, only those of the three gods Teshub, Allani, and Ishkhara, and that of Pizikarra of Nineveh, an unknown, possibly Hurrian lord of the town on the Tigris, which was not far from Kumme, though we do not know its exact location. As Pizikarra of Nineveh is the only mortal whom the poet claims in the introduction to want to celebrate along with the gods, it is very likely that, alongside the divine protagonist Teshub, it was Pizikarra of Nineveh who was, according to the "Chant of Release", the mortal protagonist of the taking of Ebla. It seems clear, then, that we must infer that Pizikarra of Nineveh was the real conqueror of Ebla, to whom, in the mythical-historical vision of the poet, Teshub of Kumme, a Storm-god who was lord of a celebrated sanctuary not far from Nineveh, gave the task of punishing the proud city for rebelling against the will of the gods.

The historical elements that can be deduced from this poetic tale seem coherent. On the one hand, the cause of the war was the illegitimate and perhaps sacrilegious detention of a prince of the unidentified city of Igagallish, which cannot have been far from Ebla. This unleashed the gods' wrath, and the author of the destruction desired by the god Teshub of Kumme was Pizikarra of Nineveh, who must have had ties with the Hittites, if the poem was translated and preserved in Hattusa. Now, since the historical texts of

Hattusili I indicate that Igagallish, which was clearly allied with Aleppo, was conquered by Hattusili I, it seems obvious that, perhaps on this sovereign's death or at the beginning of Mursili I's reign, Aleppo and Ebla probably retook various cities that had passed to the Hittites, including Igagallish, probably through cruelties or sacrilege that might have unleashed the gods' wrath. It is hard to know why, in the poem, the god Teshub of distant Kumme should have sponsored the unfortunate cause of the citizens, and perhaps of the lord of Igagallish, but it seems clear that, while at the time of Hattusili I, the Hurrians seem to have been mainly allies of Aleppo, at the time of his successor, Mursili I, many of them probably moved over to the Hittites, following a policy of at least partially overturning the alliances, which began to be effected, we know from contemporary accounts, by Hattusili I himself, and were clearly successfully concluded by his successor Mursili I.

The extraordinary similarities, thematic and otherwise, between the "Chant of Release" and *The Iliad* in the narrative of the wars against Ebla and against Troy – from the very same cause for the siege, in the illegitimate holding of a prince or princess, to the involvement in the battles of gods and princes perhaps on both sides of besiegers and besieged; from the prolonged discussions in assemblies of princes to debate questions that are the exclusive province of the sovereign, to the presence in the assemblies of rousing speakers whose oratory is used against the opinion of the king himself; from the banquets of the gods called in relation to human affairs that involve the divine world itself, to the precise formula of the introduction and the epithets used for the heroic protagonists – all this may be difficult to explain in detail, but seems to suggest unsuspected relations between Hurrian poetry and Homer, no less deep and substantial than those already brought out between the Hurrian world and Hesiod.

If, as seems very probable, Pizikarra of Nineveh really was the conqueror of Ebla at the time of Mursili I and, therefore, powerful eastern Hurrian princes supported the great Old Hittite king in his final attack on Aleppo and its allies in Upper Syria, and if, as has been reasonably conjectured, Babylon maintained traditional good relations with Aleppo, we might think that a broad strategic alliance set up by Mursili I was the reason for the somewhat enigmatic and peculiar victorious raid he made against Babylon, followed by a hasty retreat and the immediate taking of power by the Kassites. This farsighted alliance may have involved Hittites of Anatolia, Hurrians from the Upper Tigris, and Kassites of the Zagros Mountains in devastating Aleppo, Babylon, and their allies in Upper Syria, and Upper and Lower Mesopotamia, overturning the whole power system that had lasted for little less than two centuries along much of the arc of the Fertile Crescent.

On the one hand, the alliance between Hittites and eastern Hurrians in Upper Syria would explain Mursili I's success against Aleppo and Ebla, when Hattusili I had failed; and, on the other, a previous alliance between Hittites and Kassites would explain the triumphant incursion against Babylon without any advantages resulting for Hattusa, because there was probably a pact that the Kassites would take power there. It is certain, however, that, though Mursili I's sensational military successes in the few years of his reign long resounded in the memory of the Hittite world, they did not have positive consequences for Hattusa's power, while they opened the way in southern Mesopotamia to the lasting affirmation of the Kassite dynasty in Babylon and the empire of Mittani in northern Mesopotamia, which soon extended from Assyria to the Mediterranean and in which the Hurrians played an important role.

In a critical situation of an altered balance of power between the major powers of Mesopotamia, Anatolia, and Syria, partly induced, with some probability, by a microclimatic crisis in the years leading up to 1600 BC, which might have caused persistent drought for some time with resulting famines and regression in urban life, centres that were once practically impregnable like Aleppo and Ebla probably became particularly vulnerable as a result of a significant demographic fall.

As a result of this situation of clearly perceivable crisis, some political and military powers had remained intact, partly due to their different geographical position, like Hattusa in Central Anatolia, but also those of the eastern Hurrians and the Kassites of the Zagros Mountains, who are sometimes, significantly, described in modern historiography as "Mountain Peoples". They cynically decided to take advantage of the difficulties of the rich cities in the Fertile Crescent, launching a coordinated mortal attack against the wealthiest of them. From this attack, celebrated by a Hurrian bard in poetic tones that did not conceal the historical reality, Ebla was unable to recover.

10 Town planning and architecture in the Old Syrian city

After the second Ebla of the late Early Syrian Period had been destroyed, towards the end of Early Bronze IVB around 2000 BC, the inhabitants of the destroyed city may have returned among the ruins of the settlement very shortly after it had been devastated by fire. As in the case of the previous, equally terrible destruction of the first Ebla in the Archives age, when its remains may not have been reconstructed, there are some very limited adaptations of shelters of some kind, just as various rubbish pits, with pottery remains from an occupation in the final phase of the late Early Syrian Period, have been found over the traces of the second destruction of Ebla, particularly in the area of the venerated Temple of the Rock from the mature Early Syrian Period.

The rebuilding that began the new city of the early Old Syrian Period, in the years immediately after 2000 BC, was certainly a great feat of town planning, its size, organization, and probably timing designed by a new political authority with clear ideas and a clear strategy, supported by a population of significant size. The structure of the great urban settlement that was conceived, which was certainly started in early Middle Bronze I (probably between 2000 and 1950 BC) seems to have been conditioned by badly deteriorated remains surviving from Early Bronze IVA and IVB, and also to have been the result of a clear city plan that had to accommodate them (Figure 10.1). What the new form of the city did have to partly adapt itself to were essentially the remains of the massive mud brick town wall of the great city of the age of the Royal Archives and, in the central area of the settlement, the mostly buried ruins of the Royal Palace G of the same period. These were located on quite high ground on the top and slopes of the small hill that had been created by the overlapping of the older pre- and proto-urban settlements, on the outskirts of the area to be rebuilt.

The solution to the problem of incorporating these remains in the project was fairly simple and straightforward, but above all seems to have been adopted consistently as soon as the reconstruction of the urban centre began.

On the one hand, the new, imposing, fortified wall was planned and built as a single whole, using the newly developed technique of the high, thick ramparts that in just a few decades were to become a characteristic of cities, first in Syria and then in Palestine. It was decided to follow the line of the

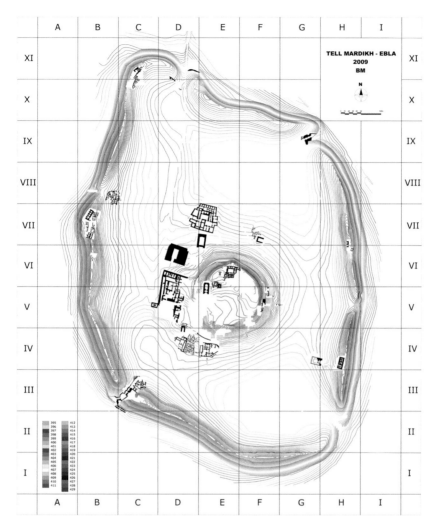

Figure 10.1 Ebla, schematic plan of the archaeological site, with the architectural remains of the Old Syrian city, 18th–17th century BC.

ancient ruined mud brick wall of the Early Syrian city, which would then form the core, against, around, and above which the mounds of earth of the ramparts would be piled up.

On the other hand, the more or less central, uneven hillock, formed by the overlapping of the former levels of the settlement and the remains of the often massive mud brick structures of the Palace of the Archives age, naturally became the Citadel of the new city centre (Plate XVI, 1), where the main public, secular, and religious buildings of the new political power were erected. It was protected by a second fortified wall using the same technique, but with the ramparts replaced by the natural steep slopes of the hill, to which were added stone and mud brick walls at the base and summit.

There remained the question of what to do with the remains of the late Early Syrian city, which were probably scattered across various areas, if not everywhere, in the extensive ring-shaped area between the foot of the Citadel and the ramparts. It was decided to demolish and remove them, which would provide some of the enormous amount of earth needed to build up the mighty fortification of the outer wall.

The possibility that, after the destruction of the city of Early Bronze IVB, a period of time went by in which the settlement of Middle Bronze I grew without being protected by walls should not be ruled out. This could not have lasted long, as the terrain from within the settlement that was used to build the ramparts contains plenty of pottery from Early Bronze IVB and, to a lesser extent, from an earlier period, but there are no fragments from Middle Bronze I. We must suppose that, when the wall was built, the remains of the Early Syrian city were still on the surface throughout the city, whereas there was no time for materials of Middle Bronze I to accumulate anywhere.

This means that the rampart (Figure 10.2) must have been built at the beginning of Middle Bronze I by an already established political authority that could call on notable human resources. Very probably, the decision to raise the huge rampart was taken by the founder of the dynasty himself, who

Figure 10.2 Ebla, Area Z, the western rampart of the Old Syrian city, with the remains of the stone scarp of the inner wall, from the north-east, 20th century BC.

took control of the late Early Syrian city that had been destroyed, and who seems to have been responsible for a vigorous renovation programme.

In the same period, immediately after 2000 BC, in politically similar situations in Lower Mesopotamia caused by the Elamite destruction of Ur, the capital of the great Neo-Sumerian flourishing of the III Dynasty of Ur in the twenty-first century BC, both the founder of the Dynasty of Isin, Ishbi-Erra, and that of the Dynasty of Larsa, Gungunum, named the twelfth and twenty-first year of their reigns, respectively, after the building of the city wall of their capitals. A century later, in the first years of his reign, around 1895 BC, Sumuabum, the founder of the I Dynasty of Babylon, boasted of building the 'great wall of Babylon', which was probably completed 20 years later in the fifth year of the reign of his successor Sumula-El.

The archaeological evidence of Ebla clearly shows that the reconstruction of the great ramparts dates from the beginning of Middle Bronze I, and the historical comparison with Lower Mesopotamia shows that building city walls was normal in the early second millennium BC, and was a founding political act of the political power of a new dynasty, both for its essential defensive function and for its powerful symbolic value. It may therefore be that it was Ibbit-Lim who was responsible for building those walls: he was the son of Igrish-Kheb, and his votive inscription allowed us to identify Tell Mardikh with Ebla. Alternatively, one of his immediate predecessors, if he was not the founder of the new dynasty, made his capital on the site of the older glorious Early Syrian city, so suggestive for the wealth of its historical associations and for the perhaps still striking remains of its ancient power.

In the inscription on Ibbit-Lim's statue, the language of which clearly places it between the end of the Neo-Sumerian and the early Old Babylonian Period, having affinities with the oldest Old Assyrian texts, the king of Ebla recalls that, eight years after 'the goddess Ishtar had appeared at Ebla', a basin and a statue of hers were brought into the Temple of Ishtar. This religious event was clearly regarded as fundamental in the history of the kingdom, and can only be interpreted as Ibbit-Lim's adoption of the cult of the great goddess as a polyadic cult in Ebla, and as the act by which Ishtar became the patron of Ebla's royal family. That this was so is shown both by the fact that, perhaps since Ibbit-Lim's time, the largest sanctuary in the Citadel of Ebla, which was certainly dynastic (the so-called Temple D), was dedicated to Ishtar. Equally significant is the fact that cylinder seals probably related to Ebla milieus, which survive from their impressions, mainly from the decades around 1900 BC, often bear the image of Ishtar beside the figure of a sovereign, who, in at least one case, was certainly the king of Ebla.

Since, as is explicitly stated in his votive inscription, it was Ibbit-Lim who introduced the polyadic and dynastic cult of Ishtar to Ebla, this theologically revolutionary act was very probably the work of a strong personality, who may also have been the founder of the city's new political power, which was sealed by the symbolic founding act of building the great city wall.

Once again, in the more traditionalist circles of the new capitals of the Amorite dynasties of contemporary Lower Mesopotamia, the introduction of new divine simulacra and the nomination of the high priests and priestesses in the polyadic sanctuaries preceded or accompanied the act of building the walls, both at Isin and Larsa. It is therefore probable that, not unlike the new lords of Babylonia of the same period, Ibbit-Lim's role had both a theological and political dimension. In building Temple D on the Acropolis, where the Royal Palace E had also to be built, he introduced Ishtar's cult to the city with whose name she would be linked for centuries, and also raised the extraordinary rampart with a perimeter of almost 3 kilometres. If, however, Ibbit-Lim was not the founder of the new dynasty of Ebla, as is however also suggested by the fact that his father Igrish-Kheb was not indicated as king of Ebla, the rebirth of the city must have been the work of an immediate predecessor of whom we know nothing.

It is absolutely certain that, despite some minor evidence of continuity, the art work of the new third Old Syrian Ebla, in early Middle Bronze I, marks a clear break with that of the mature and late Early Syrian culture of Early Bronze IVA and IVB, which are basically a unit. However, the new rulers, who greatly wished to rebuild the city that had twice been destroyed, very probably wanted, for ideological reasons, some clear references to the glorious Early Syrian dynasty of the age of the Archives. This programmatic position, which clearly emerges from the very names of the new sovereigns of the city, which are Eblaite and not Amorite, both in their verbal forms and in the names of the gods evoked, is also clear from the town-planning programme, which seems to have been inspired by an idea of a genuine renaissance of the Early Syrian city. Indeed, it carefully followed not only the course of the walls of the venerated ancient city, but meticulously respected almost everywhere the cult places, erecting new temples on the very sites of the ancient sanctuaries and, for the most part, even followed the placing of the main public buildings, particularly in the case of the Royal Palace E of the Acropolis, and, still more so, in that of the Northern Palace.

From the start, the new form of the early Old Syrian city was organized into three clearly distinct sectors that even today are evident in the disposition of the hill system, which conceals the ruins of the old centre and reflects precisely the form of the city at the time of its final destruction in the classical Old Syrian Period around 1600 BC. This pattern involved, first of all, the fortified Citadel at the centre of the settlement, extending for no more than 2 hectares of ground, and containing the new Royal Palace E, the royal residence and seat of the central palatine administration, and, along with some other possibly minor sacred places, the dynastic sanctuary of the polyadic goddess, Ishtar; second, a large ring-shaped urban area of no less than 45 hectares, the Lower Town, in which a ring of public, sacred, and secular buildings at the foot of the Acropolis gradually gave way to the residential areas that reached the base of the external fortifications; and, third, the outer circle of massive ramparts, occupying 10 or so hectares, where cemeteries were located on the inner slopes in various areas, particularly to the south, and where, later, arsenals, fortresses, and watch-towers were built on the summit, to supplement the city's defensive system. As we have indicated, priority was certainly given to building the outer walls of the city and to at least preparing the inner walls, while the only sacred place built in this early period was probably Ishtar's dynastic Temple on the western edge of the Citadel.

The building of the outer fortifications, with their perimeter of around 2,800 m, was probably the absolute priority of the new lords of Ebla. We can get an idea of this huge enterprise if we consider that they were constructed using a method widespread throughout Syria and Palestine in the period, by which, rather than building a sturdy wall, huge quantities of terrain, taken both from the surrounding countryside and the ruins of the city, were massed up to raise gigantic ramparts.

The thickness of the walls in early Old Syrian Ebla (Figure 10.3), which are one of the most imposing examples of the period and certainly one of the best preserved, varied between 40 and 60 m at the base, while their height was 20–23 m: even today the eastern rampart, which is perhaps the best preserved, rises steeply to a height of 22 m above the surrounding countryside. The whole rampart was originally protected externally by an almost vertical stone escarpment (Figure 10.4), probably between 4 and 6 m high, which not only stopped the massed materials from crumbling, but, above all,

Figure 10.3 Ebla, Area V, the western rampart of the Old Syrian city in the site of the Western Fort, from the north, 20th–17th century BC.

Figure 10.4 Ebla, Area A, the outer wall in big stone blocks of the southern rampart of the Old Syrian city, near Damascus Gate, from the west, 20th–17th century BC.

made any attempt by an enemy to scale the fortification almost impossible. It is uncertain whether these ramparts at Ebla and other urban centres of the period with similar structures had traditionally built walls at the top, as any remains have been lost due to their extremely exposed position. However, though it seems very improbable that a genuine wall crowned these 20-metre-high ramparts, there must have been special features, such as protection at various points of the circuit of the walls for those walking them: clear signs of the remains of these defences can be seen at the top of the south rampart and there may have been others elsewhere as well.

Although, clearly, various factors make judgment difficult, simply shifting the more or less 1.6 million cubic metres of earth from the moat or from inside the city to the perimeter of the walls would have required 5,000 men working at least 213 days, or 3,000 men working 355 days. Supposing a system of forced labour, with demanding work hours and the probability of work being suspended or seriously reduced in seasonal periods, when the labour force was required in the fields, building the ramparts alone would have needed one or two years, without considering the labour for the significant infrastructure

Figure 10.5 Ebla, Damascus Gate, the big basalt and limestone orthostats of the inner
city gate, from the south-west, 20th–17th century BC.

connected to the fortified wall, such as the city gates, the arsenals for weapons,
and the watch-towers, which were certainly one of the first defensive works
built, though probably in simpler form than those documented by the forts
and fortresses of the later classical Old Syrian Period.

It is therefore likely that, like Ishbi-Erra of Isin or Sumuabum of Babylon,
the founder of the new dynasty of Ebla – whether it was Ibbit-Lim or a predecessor – started work on the fortification of the city in the first years of his
reign, and completed it in just a few years, as happened in Babylon at the time
of the second king Sumula-El.

When the late Early Syrian city of Early Bronze IVB was destroyed,
work had already begun in the north of the Lower Town on an ambitious
and never-completed project for the Archaic Palace (Sector P North), which
may have been intended as a palace for the lords of the unlucky second Ebla
of the late phase. This means that this palatine building, located in the centre
of the northern urban quarters, was certainly finished in the very early years
of the city's new life, perhaps in haste and provisionally, but in any case so as to
have a role in the extraordinary control of the gigantic works in progress that
was necessary in what must have been the huge building site of Ebla in that
period (Figure 10.6).

Indeed, in completing the project of the Archaic Palace, leaving intact
the north-west sector of the building, with its great rectangular spaces and
the Throne Room, which must have been in the central-northern sector of

Figure 10.6 Ebla, Archaic Palace, the north-east sector of the palace with the archaic
Old Syrian refurbishing, from the south-east, 20th–19th century BC.

the building, the planners of the urban renaissance built, more modestly, the
eastern wing, which in the original project was clearly intended to be symmetrical to the already-built western one, and added an external court with a
royal dais under a canopy (Figure 10.7). Obviously, this unusual and almost
certainly temporary solution was particularly convenient at a time of intense
building work that required constant control: such a feature is unlikely to
have been separated from the need to supervise the clearing of the ruins of
the Lower Town and the building of the ramparts, which for half of the circuit were under direct observation from this vantage point of the new royal
authority. Therefore, the Archaic Palace, which was certainly intended to be
a palace in the final phase of the late Early Syrian Period, was probably the
provisional seat of the new lords of the early Old Syrian city when the main
infrastructures of the reconstructed city were being built.

The layout of the new third Ebla was conceived very rationally, following
an organic plan in which the public buildings were concentrated in
the central areas and on the fortified Citadel (Figure 10.8) itself and its
surroundings, and the private ones – the houses of functionaries, priests,
and artisans – were situated towards the outskirts of the city, up to the foot
of the imposing ramparts. In the late classical Old Syrian Period, in the

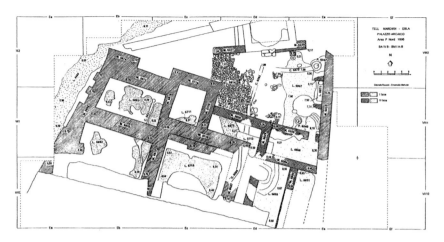

Figure 10.7 Ebla, Archaic Palace, schematic plan of the palatine building with the refections in the eastern sector, 20th century BC.

bilingual "Chant of Release", when the god Teshub of Kumme threatens to destroy the city if it does not yield to his will, a double surrounding wall is mentioned, one internal and the other external, and it is added that the god had darkly forecast that the latter would be smashed to pieces in the surrounding moat, while the urban centre would be shattered like a clay vase. This poetic description actually corresponds perfectly to the actual structure of Old Syrian Ebla, and to nothing else, as on the one hand, the inner wall in the poem is clearly the fortification of the Citadel and the outer one is the fortification of the ramparts; and on the other, we can still see to this day, everywhere around the ramparts, the circular hollow of the moat from which significant parts of the limestone and clay materials were taken that were heaped up to form the ramparts, along with the ruins of the late Early Syrian city that had been destroyed.

Some of the fundamentals of the urban structure were certainly decided from the first interventions in the early Old Syrian re-founding, establishing that the future city would have four gates, though we do not know if they were at the same points as the old gates of the mature Early Syrian period: the northern Aleppo Gate towards the western limit of the northern section of the walls; the Euphrates Gate on a north-east segment of the wall towards the great river; the Steppe Gate, facing south-east at the southern extremity of the eastern section of the fortification; and the Damascus Gate (Figure 10.5) in the south-western section of the defensive belt.

All these gates almost certainly had features that reinforced the delicate system of the entrances to the city, which may have varied from one gate to

Figure 10.8 Ebla, Area FF, the stone inner wall of the Old Syrian citadel, between the Southern Palace in the foreground, and the Acropolis in the background, from the south, 20th–19th century BC.

the other: turrets, bulwarks, and projections, particularly in the case of the Damascus Gate, which is the best preserved, but which was also intended as one of the most important from the start. Though the western side of the Damascus Gate was damaged and sacked, its original structure is well preserved: it had the classic typology of the imposing city gates of Syria and Palestine in Middle Bronze II, consisting of a long section organized in three pairs of piers that delimited two diagonal spaces, onto which opened the two passages of the double gates, whose door sockets still survive. This was the classical Syro-Palestinian system of the Old Syrian Period, familiar in a number of great urban centres in Syria, at Karkemish, Alalakh, Tell Tuqan, and Qatna: in the Damascus Gate, unusually, it combined with a second, projecting gate (Figure 10.9) two pairs of piers, and a space in the middle, outside the first gate, separated from it by a trapezoidal courtyard.

This planimetric pattern, including a projecting external gate with two pairs of piers (Figure 10.10), a trapezoidal courtyard in the middle, and an inner gate with three pairs of piers, is clearly a monumental re-elaboration of the simpler type, which was certainly due to the depth of the passage, in a city whose ramparts were 60 metres thick at the base, but which also provided a more developed and safer defensive system, with three barred passages and

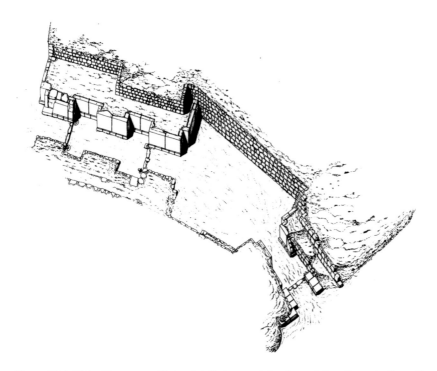

Figure 10.9 Ebla, Damascus Gate, detailed isometric view of the city gate, from the
west, 20th–17th century BC.

excellent protection for the entrances with their ramparts, which flanked the
eastern side of the entrance to the city. Although the external door of the
Euphrates Gate has been completely lost and that of the Aleppo Gate still
needs to be examined, there are strong reasons for thinking that they had the
same system, while we know little of the Steppe Gate, given its state now after
constant sacking of the stonework.

The defensive systems of these gates must have been striking. The Damascus
Gate, which had a long part of the external eastern sector of its rampart completely covered in stone, making it practically impossible to climb up, probably also had on the eastern side of the entrance an external tower that has
been almost entirely lost, and then a minor defence tower of the outer gate,
from which enemies could be kept at bay from the first entrance, and an enormous tower with an imposing stone base, as thick as the entire inner gate,
which loomed over it for the defence of the trapezoidal court from above,
should an assailing army have managed to penetrate it. The Euphrates Gate
(Figure 10.11), whose southern side is wholly lost, must have had an external
rampart and, probably, a tower on the northern side, where there are traces

Figure 10.10 Ebla, Damascus Gate, the advanced gate with the limestone orthostats inside, and the foundations of the lost orthostats outside, from the north-east, 21st–17th century BC.

both of the bases of the structure with three pairs of pillars, and the lower rows of the probable side rampart. As a modern road has been built where the Aleppo Gate once stood, we do not yet know whether there were two successive gates, an inner and an outer, and how they were structured. Their remains must in any case have been razed to the ground by repeated pillaging, but its form seems to have been not unlike that of the Damascus Gate, though less well fortified. On the eastern side of the entrance, a massive stone face, in large blocks, rather than covering the base of the rampart, protected its upper part, which seems to have been fairly large and curved (Figure 10.12), while projecting buttresses or casemates supported the external terraces in the middle, situated over the base of the rampart, at the height of which, various clues suggest, there was probably a small outer gate. On this eastern side of the gate, therefore, there was a high, curving tower instead of the massive rectangular rampart that overlooked the inner entrance in the Damascus Gate, and probably had similar functions.

If the city gates had a monumental structure with a strong horizontal development in depth, due to the great thickness of the fortified wall, with additional massive defensive features for an active response in times of siege, the whole of the outer wall was just the basic core of a complex, organized system that was architecturally integrated by the fortresses and towers along

Figure 10.11 Ebla, Euphrates Gate, the north side of the city gate, from the west, 20th–17th century BC.

Figure 10.12 Ebla, Aleppo Gate, the massive semi-circular tower on the east side of the city gate, from the north, 20th–17th century BC.

the perimeter of the ramparts, on the top and on the inner slopes, carefully designed to satisfy specific military requirements for an active strategic defence. These ranged from the need to sight the enemy to the possibility of cramming weapons in the arsenals on the walls and the need to control the whole circuit of ramparts, from top to bottom, both for ordinary maintenance and, even more, to prevent surprises in times of siege.

At least two large architectural complexes, covering a surface of more than 2,000 square metres, have been identified on the western rampart and dug out, in one case wholly. These complexes, named the Western Fort (Figure 10.13) and Northern Fort (Figure 10.14), included several structures, had various functions, such as arsenals, barracks, warehouses, workshops, and look-out towers, and were carefully situated on the top of the ramparts, partly jutting out noticeably towards the outside, mainly to ensure control of the otherwise invisible, and therefore uncontrollable, outer base of the ramparts themselves, where possible assailants might put the city at risk, particularly by excavating tunnels to penetrate the city. In other cases, when the architectural structures were designed just as arsenals and look-out posts (Figure 10.15), they simply built at the top, or on the high inner slope, what was called a "fortress" – large rectangular structures with a few rooms on the same pattern: six chambers next to a stairway that gave access to the terrace, which was the only access to the rooms, where certainly weapons were stored to be distributed at times of siege.

Figure 10.13 Ebla, Western Fort, aerial view of the fort on top of the rampart, from the west, 18th–17th century BC.

Figure 10.14 Ebla, Northern Fort, the structures on the inner slope of the rampart, with the small barracks, from the south, 18th–17th century BC.

Figure 10.15 Ebla, Western Fort, detail of the entrance to the rectangular tower of the Old Syrian complex, from the south-west, 18th–17th century BC.

Two of these structures – known as the East-South-East and the East-North-East Fortresses – have been identified and brought to light on the eastern rampart, but it is certain that there was at least a third on the southern section of the western rampart to the south of the Western Fort, while, strangely, there is no trace of these massive towers either on the north or south rampart, where the more extended fortress systems do not seem to have been designed either.

These fundamental additions to the system of outer fortifications of the Old Syrian city must have been built during the classical Old Syrian Period, perhaps after 1800 BC, but there are indications that they were preceded by similar structures, probably less organized and extensive. It is also certain that there must also have been structures like the forts and fortresses of Ebla in quite a few other cities of Syria and Palestine at the time, although very few of them have been identified and excavated – indeed, the only known example that is wholly comparable is in the Palestinian centre of Gezer, although it was recently noted that some similar remains are also probably to be found on the mighty rampart of Hazor in northern Palestine.

In the structure of the Lower Town, too, practicability and the use of the spaces between the public buildings and private residences must have been decided in a general plan, which was very probably defined from the outset of the re-foundation, while there is no doubt that the individual structures were only gradually built. Much of the western half of the Lower Town of the fully-fledged Old Syrian urban centre has been more or less completely explored, while practically nothing is known of the eastern half. Nevertheless, what has been established for the western quarters should also hold for the rest of the settlement.

It seems certain, then, that the Lower Town was run through by four large main roads, arranged more or less in radial form, which began in correspondence with the four city gates, heading, with some irregularities, towards the base of the Citadel, which was in turn surrounded, perhaps uninterruptedly, by a main ring road that ran along the foot of the inner fortification surrounding the Citadel itself. The general pattern was a series of large roads on an east–west and south–north axis that must have linked the four radial arteries, creating a sort of wide-meshed network of connections, from which in turn small lanes branched out, which might even be blind alleys and, unlike both the radial streets and those criss-crossing them, did not function as main thoroughfares, but were principally for connecting private houses, as well as, in some cases, for minor traffic.

Probably just one gate, now seriously ruined, allowed access to the Citadel crossing the inner fortification. This was in the south-western part of the high slopes of the Acropolis and was reached from a street that meandered towards the upper region of the slopes of the fortification, above and in correspondence with the inner area of the Throne Room of the great Royal Palace G of the mature Early Syrian Period and, therefore, not far from the Monumental Gateway to the inner and higher parts of the complex of Royal Palace G.

At the foot of the Citadel, before the great ring road, at irregular distances, depending partly on the presence of open spaces and, sometimes, actual squares, there began the almost uninterrupted ring of public, secular, and religious buildings that surrounded the whole base of the Citadel. To the north was the Temple of Shapash/Shamash (Area N), the Sun-god, with the entrance facing east, while to the north-north-west was the compact mass of the extensive Northern Palace (Sector P North) of around 3,500 square metres, with the entrance to the west, which may have opened onto the same radial axis of streets that descended from the Aleppo Gate. This remarkable palatine public building was certainly not residential, but must have had ceremonial purposes and was undoubtedly royal, being probably used for state functions. Immediately south of the Northern Palace began the large Cult Area of Ishtar (Area P) to the north-west of the Citadel, which included two imposing religious monuments which opened onto the Square of the Cisterns: to the north, Ishtar's Temple (Sector P Centre) with its façade facing south, and to the west the big Cult Terrace of the Lions, also called Monument P3 (Sector P South), with its main prospect facing east onto the Square of the Cisterns. This was certainly the largest cult place in the whole of Old Syrian Ebla, the public sanctuary of the great goddess who protected the city, who was the patron of the reigning dynasty, and a most popular divine figure for her associations with love and universal fertility.

The long, mighty structure of the extensive Western Palace (Area Q) began to the south of the Cult Terrace of the Lions, beyond a wide road running in the west–east direction, which connected the western quarters of the Lower Town with the base of the Citadel, not too far from where the road rising towards the gate that gave access to it began. It was certainly the largest palatine building in the Lower Town (Figure 10.16), perhaps not much smaller than Royal Palace E of the Acropolis, which extended along the great south–north axis for 115 m, more than 7,200 square metres in area and with the entrance on the southern prospect. Built on a rock ridge slightly higher than the western part of the Lower Town, its façade must have appeared slightly suspended to those entering the city from the Damascus Gate, whose radial road very probably led to monumental propylaea of some kind, impossible to reconstruct, using great masses of basalt, which were in some way to flank the road with short stairways that led to the façade of the great palatine building.

Various clues suggest that the Western Palace (Plate XVII) was the residence of the crown prince, who had particularly important functions both for administration and, even more, for the basic rituals connected with the succession to the throne and the cult of the deified royal ancestors. This remarkable building covered an extraordinarily large surface, extending for around 115 m on the great south–north axis, which must have been only a little less than that of the Royal Palace E of the Citadel, and rose on a long ridge slightly higher than the Lower Town, which it dominated with its compact mass. It certainly had two floors, probably a monumental façade with a porch opening onto the southern quarters of the city and, before it, in the south-west quadrant, there must have been monumental propylaea, that have been almost wholly lost, nothing surviving but scattered remains of the foundations in large basalt stones. Most importantly, on some of the preservation jars found in the building there was the dynastic seal of prince Maratewari, who must have been the heir to the throne of probably the last classical Old Syrian king of the city, Indilimma; also, in the area immediately north of the sector of the Audience Hall, there were, in at least two of the rooms in the building (Figure 10.17), the entrances (obviously sealed) to the funerary shafts of two hypogea of the Royal Necropolis of the last decades of the archaic Old Syrian Period and the first half of the classical Old Syrian Period.

South of the Western Palace, and south-east of the Acropolis, began what can be regarded as another important sacred region of the Lower Town, with Rashap's Temple (Sector B North) to the north, and to the south, not only the small square in front of the cult building of the god of the Underworld, but also the Sanctuary of the Deified Royal Ancestors, also known as Sanctuary B2 (Sector B South), whose access faced west towards the propylaea of the Western Palace. Immediately east of Sanctuary B2, between two roads in a north–south direction, was an area of well-preserved private houses (Sector B East), which is the only private area at the foot of the Citadel (Figure 10.18): it might have been a residential area for persons related with the clergy of the

Figure 10.16 Ebla, Western Palace, the central region of the Old Syrian royal building, from the south, 18th–17th century BC.

Figure 10.17 Ebla, Western Palace, the rooms over the hypogea of the Royal
Necropolis, from the north, 18th–17th century BC.

region sacred to the god of the Underworld, or with the administration of the palatine building, which began a little further to the east.

This public building, which is the only one that has been excavated in the southern Lower Town, to the south of the foot of the Citadel, its rear façade providing the southern prospect of the ring road at the foot of the Citadel, is the Southern Palace (Area FF), a building of striking architectural dignity, but smaller (Figure 10.19), around 1,000 square metres, than the two great royal buildings of the urban area of the Lower Town – the Northern Palace and the Western Palace. Various clues converge to suggest that this compact, almost square palatine complex (at least in its original form, though it was altered and extended in the course of time during the classical Old Syrian Period), must have been the residence of the "palace prefect", a kind of vizier, who was certainly in charge of the palatine administration in the last years of the classical Old Syrian city. Apart from the sophisticated architectural technique of the building, which closely recalls that of the royal palaces, what makes it very plausible that the Southern Palace (Plate XVIII) was the residence of this important dignitary is the presence of very unusual architectural features, like the Audience Hall, identical in structure to the halls of the king and the crown prince, and also, in particular, a most striking annex, near the entrance to the building, on the southern section of the western prospect, consisting of a long area preceded by a vestibule and divided in two by pillars and limestone basins, easily recognizable as stables (Figure 10.20).

Figure 10.18 Ebla, Sector B East, view from above of the private houses of the quarter between the Southern Palace and Sanctuary B2, from the east, 17th century BC.

Uniquely for an Old Syrian building in Ebla, fragments of preservation jars with the cuneiform inscription "palace" have been found among the pillaged ruins of the palatine building, as well as a cuneiform document comprising a list of functionaries of the city, indicating unequivocally that the building was part of the palace administration at the highest level, though probably without being a royal building. As the texts in the Royal Archives of Mari at that time refer to the high dignitary presiding over the organization of local messengers and the reception of foreign messengers as the "palace prefect", then the building's administrative function and its quasi-royal character seem certain, if we accept that the Southern Palace was the residence and office of this "palace prefect" in Ebla in the classical Old Syrian Period. This is further confirmed by the unusual presence of stables, where the foreign and local messengers' mounts were obviously kept and fed.

There was, then, an almost unbroken ring of sacred and secular buildings, all of them public, which girdled at varying distances the base of the inner fortification of the Citadel: from north to west and also to the south Shapash/Shamash's Temple, the Northern Palace, the great Temple of Ishtar, the Cult Terrace of the Lions, the Western Palace, the Temple of Rashap, the Sanctuary of the Deified Royal Ancestors, and the Southern Palace. The relationship between the Northern Palace and the Temple of Ishtar and the Cult Terrace of the Lions, which made up the Cult Area of Ishtar in the Lower

Figure 10.19 Ebla, Southern Palace, the residential and ceremonial quarters in the central-northern region of the building, from the north-east, 18th–17th century BC.

Figure 10.20 Ebla, Southern Palace, the stables for equids in the outer west sector, from the north-east, 18th–17th century BC.

Town, and between the Western Palace and the Temple of Rashap with the Sanctuary of the Deified Royal Ancestors, which made up a second Cult Area connected with funerary cults, was not just topographical, but had important ideological foundations.

In fact, the Northern Palace (Plate XVI, 1), which certainly was a kind of grand royal pavilion for receptions and audiences with the king, as is clear from its definitely non-residential structure and layout, was probably related to solemn ceremonial occasions, when a special role was played by the great polyadic goddess Ishtar. It faced towards the west, with a projecting façade towards the centre; it had no upper floor, where the residential quarters were often situated, just as there is no trace of an administrative sector, and the whole building seems to have been conceived in function of the large Audience Hall with two entrances (Figure 10.21): a public one through the western part of the long southern side, reached from the entrance to the building, clearly after waiting in one or more intermediary areas between the entrance and the Audience Hall in the western sector of the building; and a private one through the eastern part of the same southern side, which was connected mainly to two long rooms that must have been temporary waiting areas for the king and his major dignitaries.

The rooms to the north, which were connected to the two long store-rooms behind the Audience Hall on the eastern side, were very probably service rooms, organized as kitchens for preparing the large amounts of food for receptions or ceremonies presided over by the king. The three rooms on the northern side of the Audience Hall, which communicated with it alone, not only perfectly correspond, architecturally, to one of the most characteristic aspects of the typical plan for the throne rooms of the classical Old Syrian Period in Ebla and elsewhere, but are connected functionally with the Audience Hall, being clearly intended for keeping goods received by the king or to be distributed to guests during royal audiences.

Although there was no direct passage between the Northern Palace and the Sacred Area of Ishtar, we can reasonably infer that, apart from official audiences for messengers, dignitaries, and foreign princes, ceremonies were held that were in some way connected with the goddess Ishtar, who was certainly the patron of Ebla's royal family in the archaic Old Syrian Period, as we can see from Ibbit-Lim's inscription and the placing of the dynastic temple dedicated to her on the Citadel next to the Royal Palace (Area E). As the celebration of a sacred marriage between the king and a high priestess was normal in the Syria of Middle Bronze I, as in contemporary Lower Mesopotamia of the archaic Old Babylonian Period, in the period of the kings of the Dynasties of Isin and Larsa, then rites of this solemnity might well have taken place in this palatine building, given its closeness to the large sanctuary of the great goddess.

Similarly, the reason the Cult Area of Rashap, the god of the Underworld, was so close to the Western Palace lay in basic ritual aspects. When the king died, the crown prince, who dwelled in the Western Palace, had very precise

Figure 10.21 Ebla, Northern Palace, the throne room L.4038 with the round base for
the basalt tripod for incense, and the royal dais in the background, from
the west, 18th–17th century BC.

responsibilities: as we know from a Ugaritic ritual of a few centuries later,
the eldest son and daughter of the dead king were responsible for the correct
performance of the funerary rites, on which depended the deceased king
being assumed among the *rapi'uma*, the royal ancestors who had been deified and who played an essential function in protecting the city's community.
This close tie between the crown prince and the funeral rites for the deceased
king is also shown by the fact that, in the city of the archaic and classical
Old Syrian Period, the Royal Necropolis (Plate XIX) was situated under the
floors of the Western Palace, which was certainly the official residence of the
crown prince.

In addition, the Sanctuary of the Deified Royal Ancestors (Figure 10.22),
with its peripheral cellas with small altars for bronze figurines of deified kings
and its central hall with benches and dais, was certainly the place where they
performed the cult acts due to the *rapi'uma*, who had been assumed among
the gods, but also where the funerary symposia were held that were a central aspect of the cult for the *rapi'uma*. They were invoked in long rituals
containing the names of the historical and mythical ancestors of the reigning
sovereigns, which were well known in Mesopotamia and elsewhere – for
example, for the dynasty of Hammurabi of Babylon – and participated at
the funerary banquets that were solemnly held on the death of the kings. The
strong topographical relation between the palatine residence of the crown
prince, a place of royal burials, a temple of the god Rashap, and a sanctuary

Figure 10.22 Ebla, Sanctuary of the Deified Royal Ancestors, the central banquet hall, L.2124, from the north-east, 18th–17th century BC.

for the cult of the *rapi'uma*, is, then, closely connected to the basic role that was played by the crown prince in the royal funerary rites.

The large palatine structures of classical Old Syrian Ebla that we have dealt with so far, in greater or lesser detail, certainly seem to have been the most important buildings of the city that was destroyed around 1600 BC, and were certainly those with the most significant institutional functions. Of the largest of these, the Royal Palace of Area E, only a limited peripheral strip to the north, with an extensive rectangular courtyard surrounded by service rooms, has been excavated, very little compared with its original size, making any view of its overall nature impossible.

Indeed, the Royal Palace E very probably extended for much of the Acropolis, and what has been discovered so far is simply a limited rear northern section, intended for food production, as in the other two large palatine royal buildings of the Lower Town: both the extensive five-roomed North-West Wing in the Western Palace and the peripheral North Wing in the Northern Palace, with six small rooms, had a long access courtyard or a smaller courtyard and entrance corridor, and, like the North Wing of Royal Palace E, their rooms either show signs that they were used for grinding cereals, or various types of moveable or fixed ovens have been found.

Apart from the Royal Palace E, then, though the other palatine public buildings of the classical Old Syrian Ebla were apparently different in form, structure, and dimensions, they had some shared characteristics, which indicate there were architects in the city working in a deep-rooted cultural tradition, with shared principles of composition that were also applied in at least some of the major urban centres of Upper Syria. These characteristics can be summarized in the tripartite plan of the building that situates the Audience Quarter centrally, in the general layout of semi-peripheral successions of small courtyards, corridors, and rooms, and the frequent, though not exclusive, orthogonal arrangement at the perimeter wall of the peripheral rooms.

The originality of these compositional features of the Old Syrian palatine buildings is clear if we consider that in the contemporary Old Babylonian architecture the original plan for the audience halls was completely different, marked by the presence of two parallel rooms extending latitudinally; second, there is always one or more large courtyards on whose longer side the audience halls have a parallel alignment; and, third, the peripheral rooms are without exception parallel to the perimeter walls and not at right angles to them. In addition, apart from the special case of the audience halls, in any known basic plan in Old Syrian palatine buildings in Ebla that has been used for the overall organization of the spaces, it seems to have been the basic one for domestic buildings, with two long parallel rooms at the back giving onto a transversal court at the front. In contemporary Mesopotamia, by contrast, the basic scheme of domestic buildings, which was transposed into palatine architectural composition, was that of an irregular-shaped structure with a central court surrounded by rooms on the four sides.

It is a result of the prevailing, though not universal, adoption of the basic scheme of a courtyard with two long rooms at the back that the peripheral rooms in Ebla's buildings buck the trend of the classical composition of the contemporary palatine buildings in Mesopotamia, and are usually arranged at right angles and not parallel to the perimeter walls.

The most typical feature, however, of the composition of the palatine buildings in Ebla and, probably, the whole of Upper Syria, is that of the Reception Suite. It consists of a large, longitudinally extending central area, which may be a single large room or be sub-divided into two rooms by a porch of two or, at most, three columns, which separate the innermost space of the royal dais, which is usually less deep, from the more external public space, which is usually deeper, and the two side wings, that are arranged along the whole of the great central space, usually organized into three rooms on each side. This area is formally well defined, but its proportions may, nonetheless, vary considerably from one building to another. Entrance is never on the axis of the central room, which is the real Audience Hall, but corresponds to the most external of the rooms of one of the two side wings, which means that access to the great hall of the complex is always transversal. One obvious consequence of this important detail, which is true of all examples we have, is that the function of the two side wings, which are never exactly symmetrical, is very different, as the one where the entrance is, which might even be a double entrance, had the function of giving indirect access to the Audience Hall, while the other, opposite it, usually functioned as the royal storehouse.

Among the four large palaces identified so far in all three that have been completely explored – the Western Palace, the Northern Palace, and the Southern Palace – the Audience Quarter is easily recognizable, as we have said, in the central core of the structure, with only minor variations. In the Northern Palace, the central Audience Hall (L.4038) is a single unit without internal partitions, while in the Western Palace (Figure 10.23) this space (L.3038) is divided by two columns (part of the large basalt base of one of these has been found) that were between two short antae marked on the front by a niche. In the Southern Palace, in similar fashion, the rather small Audience Hall (L.8517 + L.8505) was equally divided into two separate rooms by two antae without columns, but marked in the same way by the recesses of a niche.

When, as in the Western and Southern Palaces, the Audience Hall is divided in two, normally the external vestibule is more or less square, while the Throne Room inside has a latitudinal development. As we have noted, the public entrance to the Audience Hall was never located on the axis to the dais of the throne, but the position of the entrances, numbering from one to three, may vary, although they are usually found on only one of the long sides, as the other side has rooms that are normally asymmetrical to those on the entrance side, and usually serve as store-rooms.

There was striking variety, however. In the Northern Palace, which was certainly royal, ceremonial, and without living quarters, the two entrances were placed, very functionally, on the southern side of the Audience Hall which was set west–east, with a public entrance on the western corner and a private one on the eastern corner to communicate with the larger areas reserved for the king. In the Western Palace (Figure 10.24), which also had residential functions (Plate XVI, 2) but where the crown prince's living quarters must have been on the upper floor, the public door was on the east side of the Audience Hall, set south–north, and was reached by a tortuous route that began in a vestibule (L.2943), from a portal with basalt thresholds and niche, while there does not seem to have been a private door, unless it opened onto the back wall of the Throne Room. In the Southern Palace, which was also the residence for a high-ranking non-royal administrative dignitary, the situation was more particular, in that, as well as the usual public door that opened on the south side of the vestibule of the Audience Hall, set west–east, we have evidence for both a private door communicating directly with the residential quarter (most unusually placed on the opposite north side) and a rear door that opened on the rear side of the latitudinal hall of the dais, giving onto a large rear area communicating with the kitchens and the inner store-rooms.

In all three palaces, however, access to the smaller chambers intended as store-rooms, on the opposite side to the public entrance, always opened onto the vestibule. These areas, whether two in number, as in the Western Palace, or three, as in the Northern Palace, were usually placed parallel to that side, but in the Southern Palace, because the residential quarter was also

Figure 10.23 Ebla, Western Palace, the south-west sector of the Old Syrian royal building, with the western limit, from the north, 18th–17th century BC.

Figure 10.24 Ebla, Western Palace, the central sector of the Old Syrian royal building, with the throne room L.3038, from the north-east, 18th–17th century BC.

in the northern zone, and had a layout of three parallel wings centred on the small courtyard L.8380, the two spaces set up as store-rooms were, unusually, arranged at right angles to the axis of the Audience Hall.

Although our documentation of Old Syrian Ebla is very patchy as regards the main Royal Palace E, which was undoubtedly the largest palatine building of the great city in the early second millennium BC, the structural characteristics of the palace architecture in Ebla, as they have been described so far, definitely belong to a typically Old Syrian tradition, which must have taken shape during the archaic Old Syrian Period, but which might have had its roots in the late Early Syrian Period, while there is doubt as to whether its most distinctive features were already formulated in the first great Ebla of the age of the Archives.

Palatine architecture in Old Syrian Ebla shared the same criteria of composition, though also with significant variations, as other palatine buildings of inner Syria of the period. This can be seen not only in the typology and spatial concept of the monumental city gates of the Old Syrian world, but also in the layout of the tripartite Audience Halls, in the peripheral rooms being at right angles to the perimeter walls, in the lack of large square courtyards, in the variety of the main façades, in the frequent use of columns, and in the adoption of a domestic model as the basic unit. Examples include Tell

Atshanah, ancient Alalakh, and Tilmen Hüyük, which might be the ancient Khashshum.

Defining the origins of the architectural traditions that took hold in the archaic Old Syrian Period is complex and problematic even today. While only some general features of composition, like the particular use of columns and the monumental use of porches, may date back to the mature Early Syrian Period of the first great Ebla, it is certain that specific characteristics, such as the pattern using three pairs of piers and two intermediate spaces in the city gates, and the latitudinal tripartite form of the Audience Halls, had striking precedents in Lower Mesopotamia, in the monumental centre of Ur, the capital of the powerful Neo-Sumerian empire at the time of the glorious III Dynasty. As there were fairly regular relations between Ebla and Ur in the twenty-first century BC, we cannot exclude the possibility that a renewal of at least some aspects of the architectural tradition depends on these relations with the southern Mesopotamian world.

What is certain is that, while important centres of north inner Syria, such as Ebla, Alalakh, and Tilmen Hüyük, as well as Karkemish and Tell Tuqan, and also minor cities like Tell es-Sur were part of a unified Old Syrian architectural culture, as is clear from the adoption of the widespread typology of city gates, which can also be found at Qatna, it was the architectural style of the great palatine buildings of the Old Syrian cities that may have been influenced by famous monumental examples from Mesopotamia. This altered the unity of the architectural tradition of the Syrian area in Middle Bronze I–II, which, however, seems to have been notably unitarian and well characterized, particularly as regards the concept of religious architecture. Indeed, both the remarkable Royal Palace of Qatna and the more modest Palace of Tuttul, respectively in the region of Homs and on the middle course of the Euphrates, to the south and north-east of Ebla, seem so influenced by the architecture of the monumental Royal Palace of Mari that in many respects both seem like two casts of the famous residence of the great city on the Euphrates.

While, given the city's relations with it, political and otherwise, the Mari connection may be understandable for Tuttul, whose religious architecture at the time nevertheless rigorously followed the Old Syrian tradition so well represented in Ebla, the case of Qatna is more difficult to explain. This important city in Central Syria has recently been carefully excavated, though its remains are not well preserved, and if the reconstructions of its palatine building are correct, then it seems we must admit even that architects of Mari planned such a remarkable copy of the monument of their city that it reached its greatest splendour at the time of Mari's last sovereign, Zimri-Lim, in the first part of the reign of Hammurabi of Babylon.

The unity and consistency of the architectural culture in Old Syrian Ebla, evident in the architecture both of the components of the defensive systems (ramparts, forts, arsenals, and city gates) and of the palatine buildings, emerge with still greater rigour in the religious architecture, and in this sector Ebla has some fine examples, both in the temple buildings and in other important types of monument that have not yet been documented in other urban centres of contemporary Syria.

In the canonical tradition of Ebla, the Old Syrian temples were planned following only two closely connected typologies, both of which had an axial structure with antae, a longitudinally extending cella, very thick outer walls, and stood in isolation in the city. The simpler type is the temple with a single long cella, preceded by a shallow vestibule with antae, with cella and vestibule of the same breadth and thick outer walls, almost always with the back wall thicker than the side walls. Examples would be the Temple of Ishtar in the Lower Town and the smaller Temples of Shapash/Shamash and Rashap, which were also built in the Lower Town, in the north and south-west respectively.

The more complex type is represented by the longitudinally tripartite temple, which has a shallow vestibule, followed by an antecella that is also shallow and by the traditional long cella, but maintains unaltered all the characteristics of the first type, clearly developing from a probably much earlier type. The tripartite typology is documented in Ebla both in the Temple of Ishtar on the Citadel (Figure 10.25) and in the presumed Temple of Hadad in the South-East Lower Town (Figure 10.26), two particularly important cult buildings that might have shared, along with the Temple of Ishtar in the Lower Town, a special relation with kingship, in that they are the only ones where remains of royal votive statues have been found.

The outer walls, both of the single-cella and the tripartite types, were so thick that they must all have been significantly high, clearly overlooking the panorama of the city as towers – hence, certainly, the biblical designation of the temples in Canaan as *migdal*, which is "tower" in Hebrew.

The Old Syrian temples of Ebla also have either a niche of varying depth inside the back wall of the cella, as in the Temples of Ishtar on the Citadel and in the Lower Town, or a low bench of the same width as the cella against it, as in the Temples of Shapash/Shamash and Rashap, though with varying proportions. Probably both the niche and the bench housed the divine images, in some cases enclosed in a deep niche, as in the Temple of Ishtar on the Citadel, while they were usually placed on the dais, in front of which altars and basins for holy water were placed in order to celebrate religious rites. In the Temple of Shapash/Shamash (Figure 10.27) – and nowhere else, as it was the only one where the destruction level of the end of Middle Bronze II was preserved intact without any later alteration – right in front of the bench were two basalt offering tables with a draining channel for the blood of the sacrificial victims and the remains of a limestone double basin of the kind that was certainly found in every temple in Ebla as an essential part of the furnishings.

If the spatial concept of the long-cella temple building with antae had almost certainly been a stable feature of the Old Syrian architectural culture in Ebla since the early phase of the period, both its origin in the centuries preceding the mature and late Early Syrian Periods and its spread to other urban centres in the Old Syrian world of the time raise problems.

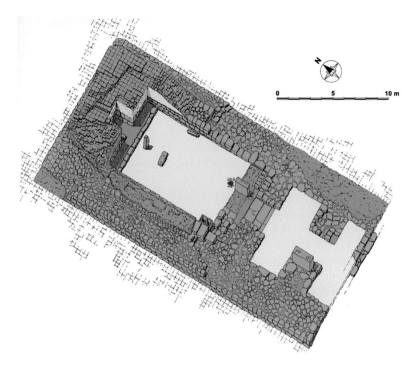

Figure 10.25 Ebla, Ishtar's Temple on the Citadel, detailed isometric view of the Old
Syrian cult building, from the south-west, 20th–17th century BC.

As regards the problem of the type's origin: until a few years ago, it was
regarded as already established also in west inner Syria in the mature Early
Syrian Period, given its presence in sites of the period in Upper Mesopotamia,
such as Tell Halawa A, Tell Khuera, and Qara Quzaq III. However, the recent
discovery in Ebla of the great Temple of the Rock from Early Bronze IVA,
and of a very similar temple at al-Rawda dating from Early Bronze IVB, which
might also have had an older phase, with latitudinal cella, shows that the situation in west inner Syria was more complex than in Upper Mesopotamia.

As for the problem of the spread of the Ebla type with longitudinal cella,
the later Middle Syrian examples, from Tell Mumbaqah to Emar, seem to
document how long-lasting this typology was (apparently the only one
attested in Old Syrian Ebla), but the presence of an extraordinarily monumental Old Syrian temple with latitudinal cella in Aleppo – the Temple of
Hadad in the Citadel of the capital of Yamkhad (but not even the façade
with antae is certain) – which seems to have been the model for the Temple
of Alalakh VII, suggests that in inner Syria in the archaic and mature Old
Syrian Periods two different traditions of religious architecture co-existed.
One, which we should perhaps regard as from Aleppo, which adopted the

Figure 10.26 Ebla, Temple of Hadad (?), the razed ruins of the cult building in Area HH (Temple HH2), from the north, 18th–17th century BC.

Figure 10.27 Ebla, Shapash/Shamash's Temple, the cella L.2500; in the background, the offering tables and the bench, from the east, 18th–17th century BC.

archaic latitudinal cella type, and the other, from Ebla, which had adopted the innovation of the longitudinal cella.

It was the recent discovery of the extraordinary sequence of temples in the south-eastern region of the Lower Town of Ebla, on the site of the monumental Temple of the Rock from the age of the Archives, that seems to have thrown light on the Old Syrian innovation of the long cella in Ebla, which was probably alien to the mature Early Syrian architectural culture of Ebla, as the Temple of the Rock had a broad cella with an equally broad vestibule. However, the latest discovery of the Red Temple of the Acropolis (Area D), which may be ascribed confidently to the last years of the mature Early Syrian Period right before the destruction of the city by Sargon of Akkad, argues in favour of the possibility that the architects of the age of the Archives were already experimenting with the model of the temple with longitudinal cella in the most challenging cult buildings.

Evidently Ebla in the age of the Archives did not share the Upper Mesopotamian architectural culture, which used the long cella, as in Tell Khuera, Tell Halawa A, and Qara Quzaq III. It may be that the formula of the broad cella and vestibule of the same size, which was extremely original, both for the Syro-Palestinian area and for the Syro-Mesopotamian one, was not limited to the Temple of the Rock for some ritual reasons that are difficult to guess, but was the norm in the religious buildings of the city of the Archives age. However, there is no doubt that the transition from the broad-cella to the long-cella type in Ebla only took place during the late Early Syrian Period, as demonstrated by the Temple of the Rock. An influence from the architectural tradition of Upper Mesopotamia, precisely at the time of Ishar-Damu, when the peaceful and military frequentation of that area by delegations sent by Ebla increased, cannot be ruled out.

As is documented by Temple HH4 on the same site as the Temple of the Rock, the innovation of the final adoption of the long-cella temple type in cult architecture became canonical in the later Early Syrian Period for monocellular cult buildings. Indeed, the plan of the late Early Syrian Temple HH4, with its long cella and fairly deep vestibule, though no longer identical in size with the cella, certainly seems the historical premise for Ebla's single-cella and tripartite types, in that the significant depth of the vestibule must have suggested the possibility of sub-dividing the space into a less deep vestibule and antecella.

On the other hand, the discovery of the late Early Syrian Temple D3, over the Red Temple (D2), with its structure with antae, tripartite scheme, and broad cella proves that, at least in Ebla's architectural tradition, the innovative adoption of the tripartite cella dates back from Early Bronze IVB.

As for the function of the temple buildings, the Temples of Shapash/Shamash and Rashap are certainly representative of the cult centres of important divinities, but have a secondary role, while Ishtar's Temples on the Citadel and in the Lower Town owe their monumental nature to the fact that Ishtar was certainly both the great goddess of the city as well as the patron of the reigning dynasty, enjoying huge popularity in the middle and lower strata of the population, and special veneration from the kings and the class of high-ranking palace officials.

The sanctuary in the Cult Area of Ishtar was the polyadic goddess's public sanctuary, but for cult ceremonies it was certainly connected to the Northern Palace, a large royal pavilion for diplomatic receptions and religious solemnities, while the Temple on the Citadel was the dynastic sanctuary, probably devoted to the cult of Ishtar as patron of the dynasty. It has been claimed that the tripartite typology of the temples in the Syro-Palestinian area is specifically connected with palatine sanctuaries because of some specific rites connected with kingship.

If the tripartite nature of the temple in the South-East Lower Town, in Area HH, seems to refute this hypothesis, its definite relation to kingship, documented by the presence of royal votive statues, like those in the two temples of Ishtar, might suggest that it too was connected to kingship, and therefore in some way regarded as a dynastic sanctuary, despite being so far from the Citadel. Now, various elements from the materials discovered in the *favissa* excavated south of the temple – such as the terracotta figurines of charioteers and the bronze images of serpents, which might allude to the god Hadad, who rode through the clouds on his chariot, and to the snake-like creature defeated by Hadad in mythical times – seem to suggest that, at least in the Old Syrian Period, the cult building of Area HH was dedicated to the great Storm-god.

If this hypothesis is correct, then the building's tripartite structure was probably linked to the definite royal connection of Hadad, which had certainly become important in Ebla itself during Middle Bronze II as a result of the prestige of Aleppo's kingship, which was under the explicit protection of the great Storm-god, and the fact that, as is shown by the dynastic seal of the Eblaite prince, son of king Indilimma, at least in the seventeenth century BC, the sovereigns of Ebla must have taken the royal ideology of Yamkhad as their model.

In the great complex of the Sacred Area of Ishtar in the Lower Town North-West, as well as the great temple to the goddess, which must have reached a notable height, given the thickness of the walls, and a series of minor buildings, whose function is difficult to identify, there was also a huge and peculiar building, in the western sector of the *temenos*, which is known as Monument P3, but which was very probably a monumental cult terrace to house the lions sacred to the great goddess.

This immense Cult Terrace of the Lions (Figure 10.28) was actually an imposing compact structure of limestone blocks enclosing an inaccessible, wide rectangular courtyard (Figure 10.29) which had no communication with the exterior. Though what remains is no higher than 1.80 m, it was probably intended to reach a height of between 15 and 20 m in the original project, which was almost certainly never completed. Its exceptional size – 52 m wide and 40 m long – makes the Cult Terrace of the Lions without parallel in the urban context of the Old Syrian city, and its upward-tapering external wall must have impressed its contemporaries as a most spectacular achievement, not very different in appearance from the *ziqqurats* of Lower Mesopotamia, whose planned dimensions were very similar and were perhaps not much higher, and usually featured at least three terraces of decreasing size.

The archaeological evidence of a cult monument consisting of a huge compact wall without any entrance, which encloses and conceals an impenetrable open-air courtyard, is most unusual. Equally strange is the fact that some rare archaic Old Syrian cylinder seals depict an extremely enigmatic cult building, rectangular in form and always featuring great blocks in alternate bands, surrounded and surmounted by two squatting lions. It therefore seems plausible that the depictions on the cylinders refer to a most unusual kind of cult building that housed the lions. In fact, in the graphic conventions in the Ancient East the rectangular outline with chess-board façade should represent a structure that had a massive, geometrically simple form, built with large blocks that were intended to be striking in their regularity. In addition, the objects, animals, or figures depicted on an architectural structure are usually interpreted as being inside the structure, signifying unequivocally that the strange building shown on the seals really did house lions.

There is some evidence suggesting that the cylinders depicting the enigmatic building with the lions had a special relation with Ebla, and it is therefore possible that on them is depicted the Cult Terrace of the Lions that was brought to light in Ebla, or a similar older building of the city. Whatever the

Figure 10.28 Ebla, Cult Terrace of the Lions, aerial view of the Old Syrian cult building, from the north, 17th century BC.

Figure 10.29 Ebla, Cult Terrace of the Lions, the court L.5050, without entrances, of the Old Syrian cult building, from the south-east, 17th century BC.

truth of the matter, it seems reasonable to suppose that the cult building with the lions on the cylinder seals reproduces a monument type of the Old Syrian world. One of the most magnificent ones has been brought to light by the excavations in Ebla, but as yet we know of no others in the Syro-Palestinian area. They were probably quite widespread, though mainly in some special cult centres.

If the two hypotheses are correct – that the seals depict an unusual cult building used to house lions, and that the type of monument shown on the seal corresponds to the Cult Terrace of the Lions in the Sacred Area of Ishtar found at Ebla – then we can infer that it must have been generally the great sanctuaries dedicated to the Syrian goddess where cult terraces were built to house the wild beasts sacred to her.

This inference is supported by two other types of particularly striking evidence, much later than the Old Syrian Period, and dating to the Iron Age and even to the age of the Roman Empire, but which might have originated in religious traditions of the more ancient Syrian world. As regards the custom of keeping live lions in temples, as late as the second century AD, the author of the famous pamphlet *De Dea Syra*, traditionally attributed to Lucian of Samosata, recalled seeing with his own eyes in one of the most famous sanctuaries of Syria at the time (the Temple of Atargatis at Hierapolis in Syria, now Membij, not far from the Euphrates in inner Syria) enclosures where lions sacred to the goddess were kept. As for the peculiar typology of the Cult Terrace of the Lions in Ebla, we should note that many biblical passages – a hundred or more – refer to a special kind of sanctuary that is presented as typical of the pre-Israelite Canaanite world, which is usually translated as "high place" – the Hebrew term is *bama'* – and which had the aspect of a cult terrace where, naturally, prayers and sacrifices were offered, and also – much less naturally – sacred prostitution was practised.

Now, if we suppose that the practice of keeping lions was not just typical of the Temple of Atargatis at Hierapolis, but was widespread in at least the main sanctuaries of the great goddess of Syria and Palestine during the Bronze Age, and particularly in the second millennium BC, and that the places where the lions were housed were generally similar in form to the Cult Terrace of the Lions in Ebla, then we might be able to explain the oddity of the biblical passages in which sacred prostitution is described as being practised on the "high places" of the Canaanite sanctuaries of Syria-Palestine. The biblical writers must have been aware that in the main Syro-Palestinian sanctuaries, dedicated to a goddess of the type of Ishtar and Astarte, two conditions often prevailed, both of them deplorable: the goddess's lions were often housed on a cult terrace, and, in a completely different type of environment, sacred prostitution was practised.

The biblical authors may have associated both practices, which were in fact common in the great sanctuaries of Ishtar/Astarte, wrongly relating the cult terraces of the goddess's lions, which were often present, with the practice of sacred prostitution. Despite this strange but not unreasonable misunderstanding by the biblical authors, their execration can be interpreted as supporting the view that, in the late Iron Age in Palestine, it was still well known that the great sanctuaries of Ishtar/Astarte contained enigmatic cult terraces, wrongly connected with sacred prostitution, but that, according to *De Dea Syra*, housed the goddess's lions.

If a great monument like the Cult Terrace of the Lions in Ebla was designed to house Ishtar's lions (and it is otherwise inexplicable, given its disconcerting typological and functional characteristics), then we should not be surprised either by its singularity or by its grandeur. While the lack of entrances in Monument P3 is explained by the need to confine the wild animals, which could clearly be lowered in cages into the courtyard from above, where there was probably equipment for sacrifices and rituals, as mentioned in the biblical passages, the extraordinarily monumental nature of the construction depends on the fact that, at least in Middle Bronze I and II, Ebla was almost certainly the largest cult centre of the great Ishtar – that Ishtar *Eblaitu* who was still remembered and venerated, several centuries after the final destruction of the Old Syrian city, in the Temple of Assur in the holy city of Assur.

The exceptionally monumental nature of the Cult Terrace of the Lions of Ishtar must have had a spectacular effect on the urban panorama of the third Ebla, probably designed, although its function was completely different, to rival visually famous architectural monuments in the contemporary cities of Mesopotamia, such as the *ziqqurats*, the famous temple towers that, as we know from the remains of those in Ur, Uruk, and Nippur, must have had similar dimensions.

Just as the Cult Terrace of the Lions of Ishtar's Sacred Area is so far a unique case in the archaeology of Syria, so another, more modest, but no less significant cult typology documented in the South-West Lower Town of the great Old Syrian centre stands alone. The structure of the Sanctuary of the Deified Royal Ancestors (Sanctuary B2) is not only, understandably, strikingly different in its sacral functions from that of the temples that were, in the ideological concept of the Old Syrian world, the gods' houses, but is most distinctive in itself, both in its plan and in its functional furnishings (Figure 10.30).

Planned as a more or less square building, with the entrance facing west – towards the world of the dead – and with one first western front sector including a large central area, probably flanked by two long side rooms, the sanctuary certainly consisted of a large hall in the centre, a third peripheral sector to the north, and a kind of south-eastern circuit that formed a fourth sector in which small square cellas alternated with long rectangular ones with the same function. Following this analysis, the function of the first entrance sector was to give access to the central area, which functioned as a vestibule for the large hall with its bench-lined walls and a dais in the centre, which must have had a particularly important significance in the general organization, and two side rooms that gave access, to the north, to the sector of the food store-rooms and, to the south, to the cult cella to the south and east.

The function of the Sanctuary of the Deified Royal Ancestors was certainly of major importance in Old Syrian religious ideology, and is explained by the co-existence in the same cult building of two features. The first is the central hall with benches and dais, intended certainly for those community symposia in honour of the royal ancestors who had been taken up among the *rapi'uma*, as they are called in the Middle Syrian royal texts of Ugarit, and who were also known in the Old Babylonian world of the I Dynasty of Babylon. The other is the peripheral cellas with the altars with antae that were particularly suitable for containing small bronze images of deified kings. These are well documented in Old Syrian bronzes, which include a number of masterpieces, like the figure of a blessing king from Qatna (Figure 10.31), who, most significantly, is crowned with the ovoid royal tiara, decorated with the multiple bull's horns typical of the divinities.

Two cult practices essential for Old Syrian society were performed, then, in the Sanctuary of the Deified Royal Ancestors, both of them supported by the food store-rooms. The peripheral cellas were the scene for the practices of the regular cult for the dead sovereigns who had been deified becoming *rapi'uma*, who provided constant protection from the hereafter to the society of the living. But there were also periodic community symposia, organized on the occasion of the death of a king, when banquets were held for the assumption of the dead sovereign among the *rapi'uma*, to which were invited, by name, all the deified ancestors who were to receive the new arrival from the world of the living into the afterlife.

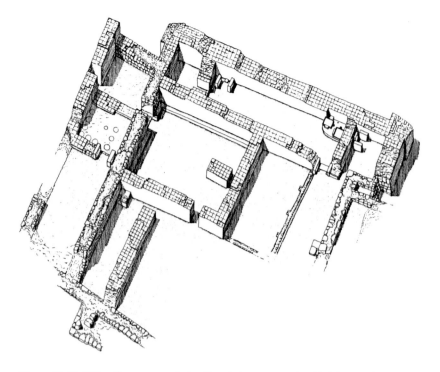

Figure 10.30 Ebla, Sanctuary of the Royal Ancestors, detailed isometric view, from the west, 18th–17th century BC.

Old Syrian architecture developed in a centre whose urban layout made up a single and coherent framework that probably goes back to a plan dating from the very earliest founding reigns of the early phase that saw the re-founding of the ancient Early Syrian city. This architectural culture was partly continuous with the previous tradition of the mature Early Syrian Period, only some aspects of which were taken up, and partly innovative, with various stimuli reworked together.

Among these stimuli, parallel and overlapping roles seem to have been played both by influences adopted in original ways, deriving from the urban culture of Neo-Sumerian Mesopotamia, contemporary with late Early Syrian Ebla, and, to a lesser extent, by innovations brought by the probably eclectic culture of the new Amorite princes, who were protagonists in the founding of the new ruling dynasties. Thus, while the three-entrance city gates in the defensive systems and the organization of the Audience Halls in the palatine complexes seem to derive from Neo-Sumerian prototypes in the Ur of the III Dynasty, the imposing ramparts of the city walls might derive from experiences of the new princes, who nevertheless respected local traditions

Figure 10.31 Statuette of a deified king, sitting on a throne (AO.3992), bronze, from Mishrifé-Qatna, 17th century BC.
Source: By kind permission of the Louvre Museum.

in architecture as in other things, and were anxious to renew the glory of the ancient powers: this would apply to Isin, Larsa, Eshnunna, and later, Babylon in relation to Ur, as probably to Ebla, Karkemish, Urshu, and perhaps Aleppo in relation to Ebla itself.

The local tradition in cult architecture seems to have been stronger: here the early and classical Old Syrian architectural traditions, in Ebla particularly, seem to have chosen to develop trends that were already established in the late Early Syrian Period, partly as a result of influences from various traditions of Upper Mesopotamia, creating an individual and coherent spatial language that unified the ancient north Mesopotamian tradition of the long-celled temples and the convergent local late Early Syrian traditions.

What is certain is that, by masterfully reworking local and different parallel traditions, the classical Old Syrian architectural culture in Ebla was able to impress a markedly unified and coherent mark on the city's centre, which, despite the serious destruction at the end of Middle Bronze II, and the total disappearance of its monuments, did not fail to exercise a lasting influence on the architectural culture of Syria, not just in the later Middle Syrian Period, but also in the Iron Age. This influence, of course, was exercised together with other cities, such as Aleppo or Karkemish, that had enjoyed the benefits of a continuity that was only temporarily and partially, but not definitively, interrupted.

Plate I Ebla, Acropolis: The Central Complex of Royal Palace G of the mature Syrian
Period and, in the background, the Ishtar's Temple of the Old Syrian Period,
from the south, 24th and 18th–17th century BC

Plate II Ebla, Royal Palace G: The cuneiform tablets in place in the Archive L.2769 of the Administrative Quarter, from the south, 24th century BC

Plate III, 1 Ebla, Royal Palace G: The Archive room L.2769 under the east porch of the Court of Audience of the Administrative Quarter, from the south, 24th century BC

Plate III, 2 Ebla, Royal Palace G: The cuneiform tablets in place against the east wall of the Archive L.2769 of the Administrative Quarter, from the west, 24th century BC

Plate IV Ebla, Area HH: The Temple of the Rock (Temple HH) in the Lower Town South-East, from the east, 24th century BC

Plate V Ebla, lid of pharaonic alabaster vessel with the cartouche of Pepy I of Egypt in hieroglyphs from court L.2913 of the Administrative Quarter, 24th century BC

Plate VI Ebla, tablet with the treaty between Ebla and Abarsal, clay (TM.75.G.2420), from the Archive L.2769, 24th century BC

Plate VII, 1 Sumerian lexical tablet with the basic canonic redaction for lexical bilingual lists (TM.75.G.2422), from the Archive L.2769, 24th century BC

Plate VII, 2 Sumerian literary tablet with incantations (TM.75.G.1772), from the Archive L.2769, 24th century BC

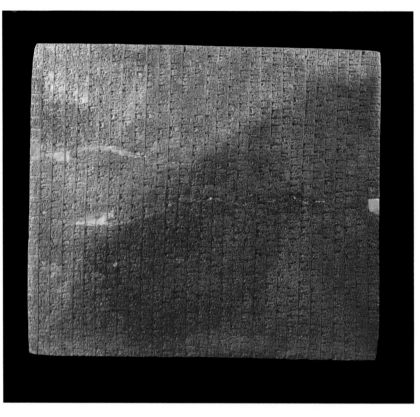

Plate VIII Economic tablet with annual account of metals at the time of Ibbi-Zikir, clay (TM.75.G.2429), from the Archive L.2769, 24th century BC

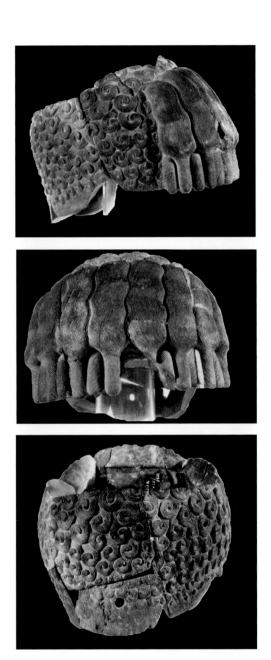

Plate IX, 1–3 Male hair-dress, steatite (TM.75.G.200), side, front, and back views, from court L.2913 of the Administrative Quarter, 24th century BC

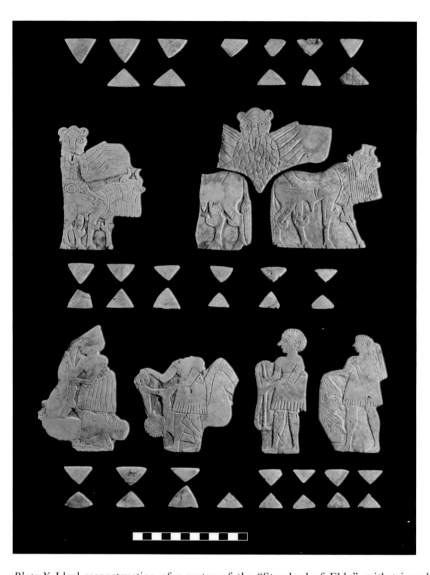

Plate X Ideal reconstruction of a sector of the "Standard of Ebla", with triumph scenes and representations of the lion-headed eagle above human-headed bulls, marble inlays, reused in the floor of L.4436 of the Central Complex of the Royal Palace G, 24th century BC

Plate XI Inlays from the "Standard of Ebla", with an Eblaite soldier piercing an enemy with the spear, marble (TM.88.G.450) reused in the floor of L.4436 of the Central Complex of the Royal Palace G, 24th century BC

Plate XII, 1 Miniature head from a panel or polymateric statuette, marble (TM.77.G.220), from the court L.2913 of the Administrative Quarter of the Royal Palace G, 24th century BC

Plate XII, 2 Miniature figurine of a crouching lion, marble (TM.778.G.320), from the court L.2913 of the Administrative Quarter of the Royal Palace G, 24th century BC

Plate XIII Polymateric statuette of a crouching human-headed bull, wood, gold, and steatite (TM.76.G.850) from the room L.2764 of the Administrative Quarter of the Royal Palace G, 24th century BC

Plate XIV Polymateric statuette of a seated queen, wood, gold, jasper, and steatite (TM.07.G.230) from the room L.9583 of the Northern Quarter of the Royal Palace G, 24th century BC

Plate XV Polymateric statuette of a standing queen, wood, silver, steatite, and jasper (TM.07.G.231) from the room L.9583 of the Northern Quarter of the Royal Palace G, 24th century BC

Plate XVI, 1 Ebla, Area P North: The remains of the late Early Syrian Archaic Palace in the foreground and of the Old Syrian Northern Palace behind them, the Acropolis is in the background, from the north, 21st, 18th–17th century BC

Plate XVI, 2 Ebla, Western Palace: The room L.3135 with 16 querns in place for grinding grains in the North-West Wing, from the south-west, 18th–17th century BC

Plate XVII Ebla, Western Palace: The North-West Wing of the classical Old Syrian building with the Acropolis in the background, from the west, 18th–17th century BC

Plate XVIII Ebla, Southern Palace: The classical Old Syrian building with the stables bottom right, from the north-west, 18th–17th century BC

Plate XIX Ebla, Royal Necropolis: Pottery in place in the Old Syrian Tomb of the Princess (Hypogeum Q.78.A), from the south, 19th–18th century BC

Plate XX Old Syrian headless statue of a standing queen, basalt (TM.88.P.628), front view, from the vestibule L.4600 of Ishtar's Temple in the Lower Town, 18th–17th century BC

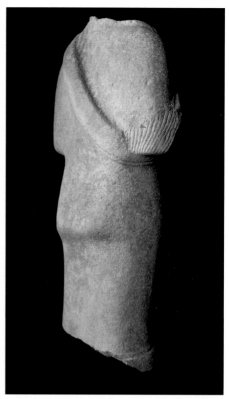

Plate XXI, 1–2 Old Syrian headless statue of a standing queen, basalt (TM.88.P.628), side and back views, from the vestibule L.4600 of Ishtar's Temple in the Lower Town, 18th–17th century BC

Plate XXII, 1–2 Old Syrian sculpted bipartite basin, marble (TM.65.D.236), front and side faces, from the cella L.202 of Ishtar's Temple on the Citadel, 19th–18th century BC

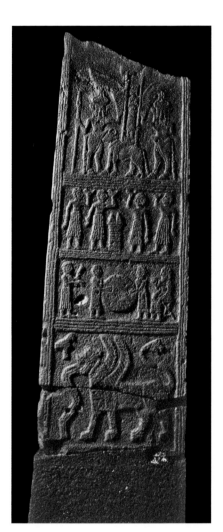

Plate XXIII, 1–2 Old Syrian Ishtar's Stele, basalt (TM.67.E.224 + 85.E.85 + 85.G.350), reused in the vestibule L.3880 of Shrine G3, 19th–18th century BC

Plate XXIV, 1–2 Old Syrian Ishtar's Obelisk, basalt (TM.06.S.1), from the south-west slopes of the Acropolis, 19th–18th century BC

Plate XXV Old Syrian head of cultic statue of Ishtar, basalt (TM.89.P.318), from the vestibule L.4600 of Ishtar's Temple in the Lower Town, 19th–18th century BC

Plate XXVI Cup in the shape of Hathoric head, glazed pottery (TM.70.B.930), from the room L.1556 of the private houses in Area B East, 17th century BC

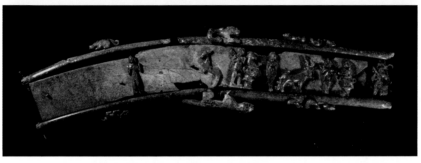

Plate XXVII, 1–2 Old Syrian talisman with representations of the funerary banquet of a king and of adoration of a human-headed bull, front and back sides, hippopotamus ivory (TM.78.Q.455), from Hypogeum C of the Tomb of the Lord of the Goats, 18th century BC

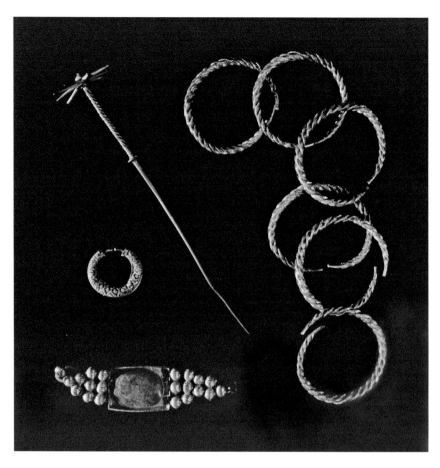

Plate XXVIII Six bracelets (TM.78.Q.370–375), a toggle-pin (TM.78.Q.369), an earring (?) (TM.78.Q.366), and a necklace with fluted mellon-shaped beads (TM.78.Q.367), gold, lapis lazuli, and amethyst, from the Hypogeum Q.78.A of the Tomb of the Princess, 19th–18th century BC

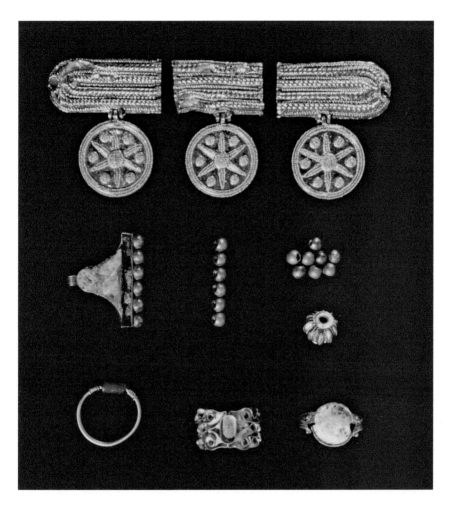

Plate XXIX Old Syrian necklace with granulation (TM.79.Q.250), elements from necklaces, beads, and earrings, in part Egyptian, from the Hypogeum Q.78.B of the Tomb of the Lord of the Goats, 18th century BC

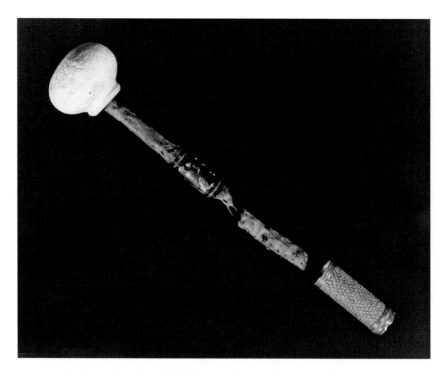

Plate XXX Egyptian ceremonial mace with cylinder with the name of pharaoh Hotepibra Harnejheryotef venerated by two cynocephali, gold, silver, ivory, marble (TM.78.Q.453 + 461 + 420), from the Hypogeum Q.78.B of the Tomb of the Lord of the Goats, 18th century BC

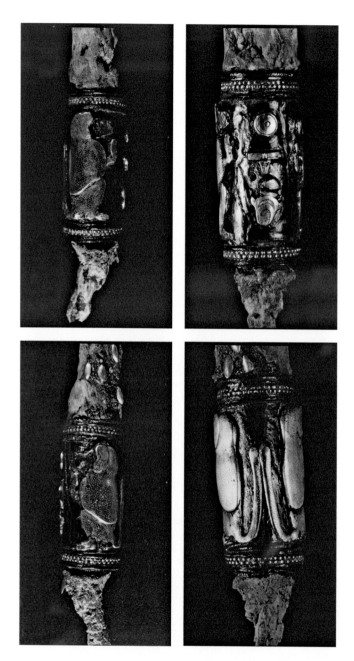

Plate XXXI, 1–4 Details of the seal with the hieroglyphic Egyptian ceremonial
mace with cylinder bearing the name of pharaoh Hotepibra
Harnejheryotef venerated by two cynocephali, gold, silver, ivory,
marble (TM.78.Q.453 + 461 + 420), from the Hypogeum Q.78.B of
the Tomb of the Lord of the Goats, 18th century BC

Plate XXXII Old Syrian head of a king with Osiriac crown, hippopotamus ivory (TM.88.P.535), from room L.4070 of the Northern Palace, 18th–17th century BC

11 Old Syrian artistic culture
Originality and continuity

The first pharaohs of the XII Dynasty were re-founding the power and political prestige of Egypt's Middle Kingdom after serious social disorders had overturned the strongly monocratic order of the Old Kingdom, and the Amorite leaders who had penetrated Lower Mesopotamia were initiating, in Isin, Larsa, and elsewhere, the dynasties that in a few decades would take total control of the territory of the countries of Sumer and Akkad, seeking to take over the heritage of the III Dynasty of Ur. At the same time, in Upper Mesopotamia, other lords, who may have been of Amorite origin, were re-founding urban centres of ancient prestige in Assur and elsewhere, along the Euphrates and towards the West and the Mediterranean, in Upper Syria, certainly in Ebla, but possibly on the coast of the Levant, too, from Ugarit to Byblos. In restoring the foundations of an urban culture that had been devastated almost everywhere, from Urshu to Hamat, they do not seem merely to have repudiated or drastically ignored the past. On the contrary, they seem to have imposed significant ideological innovations that could have been determined by the orientations of the new power groups, but they also appealed to a continuity with local traditions that was probably meant to take account of the memories of significant population groups who were part of the new status quo.

In Ebla, the cult of the new polyadic goddess Ishtar, introduced by Ibbit-Lim as a memorable event, was certainly a significant ideological innovation, while the echo of the ancient dynastic gods Lim and Damu in the names of the new sovereigns exemplifies the appeal to continuity. The title of "Star of Ebla", with which the Hurrian-Hittite "Chant of Release" designates the king of Ebla, shortly before the final destruction of the city towards 1600 BC, is certainly peculiar, but it seems to hint at Ishtar's assimilation with the planet Venus, just as the title of "Sun of Nagar", assumed a few centuries before by the kings of this important northern Mesopotamian kingdom in the Khabur region, would have been hard to detach from a special veneration for the god Shamash in Tell Brak.

It was in the name of the warlike, lascivious Ishtar, who much later would become the "Syrian Goddess" *par excellence*, that the new lords of Ebla took power, having their goddess called Ishtar *Eblaitu*, "Ishtar of Ebla", even by the most distant peoples, and they assumed the title of *meki/mekim*, a probable distortion of the local Ebla dialect, that can already be inferred from the language of the Early Syrian Royal Archives, of *maliku/malikum*, "king". On the other hand, as a symbol of Ebla's kingship, these same archaic Old Syrian kings now wore a tiara, a skull-cap, featuring a kind of peak on the forehead, which was probably simply a re-elaboration of the well-known mature Early Syrian turban of the age of the Royal Archives, also rising a little over the forehead.

Following a tradition inherited from the funerary sanctuaries built beside the pyramids of the Memphis necropolises of the Old Kingdom, the first pharaohs of the XII Egyptian Dynasty of the Middle Kingdom commissioned quite a number of royal statues that were placed in the new Middle Egyptian funerary structures, and the more ancient lords of the Dynasties of Isin, Larsa, and Babylon dedicated just as many votive statues in stone, silver, and gold in the largest temples of their cities, and in the most venerated sanctuaries of Sumer and Akkad; these were intended to "speak" to the gods, narrating to the divine world itself their deeds on the social, religious, and military plane. Although very few, fairly insignificant remains have come down to us, of the many artistic works that the first sovereigns of these Amorite dynasties of Babylonia commissioned, the formulas of the year-names of their reigns, which have been handed down in series that are almost complete for these kings, recall such things as the introduction into the sanctuaries of precious temple furnishings, such as thrones and insignia, votive statues in stone or metal, and divine images, mainly in gold or silver.

It is absolutely plausible that in Ebla, too, the first kings of the rebuilt archaic Old Syrian city were, as in contemporary Lower Mesopotamia, generous patrons of works of a similar kind with similar functions. Obviously, specific features – material, technical, typological, iconographic, or stylistic – must have characterized the objects made in Ebla, whether large statues (Figure 11.1), of which many examples have come down to us, though often seriously damaged by the fury of the conquerors of the classical Old Syrian city, or in the paraphernalia of furnishings for worship clearly adapted to the needs of temple rituals.

It is the royal inscription of Ibbit-Lim (Figure 9.1) on the (unfortunately badly preserved) bust of his votive statue, originally placed in the Temple of Ishtar on the Citadel, which shows that the statue itself had been dedicated, probably around 1950 BC or shortly before, when a ritual basin was introduced to the temple. This was certainly one of the stone basins carved on three or four faces (Figure 11.2) that are perhaps the most typical temple furnishings in Ebla, and of which we know no other examples outside Ebla.

There were various types of votive and celebratory statues, and cult and ritual furnishings that the royal workshops produced in Ebla, to satisfy patrons who were not necessarily always royal, but were at the very least members of the highest levels of the hierarchies of the palace administration and of the

Figure 11.1 Statue of an enthroned king (TM.89.P.314), basalt, from Ishtar's Temple in the Lower City, 19th–18th century BC.

priesthood: statues of the major local deities, almost certainly using various materials, covered with precious metal foils, using an ancient tradition already well documented in the administrative records of the Early Syrian Royal Archives; votive statues of the kings and queens of the city, mainly in basalt, placed, as in Mesopotamia, in the major sanctuaries, perhaps in Ebla too, to "speak" to the gods of the piety, rectitude, industry, and justice of the dedicators (Plates XX–XXI, 1–2); monumental images, sometimes in basalt, of royal predecessors who were now deities (Figure 11.3), displayed in the squares and kept in the palaces of the royal power in memory of ancient feats and to perform the basic dynastic rites; carved ritual basins (Plate XXII, 1–2), insignia of the cult with figurative elements, offertory tables with naturalistic features, placed in the temples for the ordinary and solemn rituals officiated by a sophisticated clergy, whose mythical and ritual doctrines are reflected in the decorations, always complex and articulate, and also, not infrequently, enigmatic; and steles, also usually in basalt (Plates XXIII, 1–2, XXIV, 1–2), carved on the four faces or on just one front face, with numerous divine, mythic, or ritual scenes celebrating a great divinity connected with kingship.

Figure 11.2 Side with warriors of the carved double basin discovered before the beginning of the excavations, basalt, 19th–18th century BC.

Votive statues of kings and queens have been found only in the vestibule of the Temple of Ishtar in the Lower Town (Area P), where they probably originally stood, or where they had been displaced during the sack of the city; at the foot of the Acropolis, below the Temple of Ishtar on the Citadel (Area D), where they were probably thrown after being broken to pieces during the final conquest of the city (Figure 11.4); and in the area of the presumed Hadad's Temple, in the south-east region of the Lower Town. No remains of any kind of royal statuary have been found in the area of the Temples of Shapash/ Shamash (Area N) and Rashap (Area B).

Nor has any trace been found of this type of statue in the great palatine buildings of the Acropolis, and of the Lower Town in particular, though they certainly played an important role in the official activities of the kings. This means they must have been erected only in the sanctuaries dedicated to the great goddess Ishtar, patron of the kingship of the great archaic Old Syrian city and, perhaps, to the god Hadad, who, in the last decades of the classical Old Syrian Period at least, must have assumed an important role in the protection of Ebla's kings, just as he had done for at least two centuries, and perhaps as early as the mature Early Syrian Period, for the royal family of Aleppo.

Figure 11.3 Ebla, Western Palace, carved base with two roaring lions on both sides of a figure of an enthroned Old Syrian king, basalt, in place in the Western Palace, 19th–18th century BC.

This makes it highly probable that in Old Syrian Ebla, as in the southern Mesopotamian world of the contemporary great cities that were under the dominion of the Amorite dynasties, these royal statues were dedicated in the temples with the aim of showing the gods the king's feats in various aspects of life, to obtain the necessary divine approval for his royal activities, to reassure his subjects that the king had acted in accordance with the gods' will, and to receive in exchange for his virtuous behaviour long life for the king and his dynasty.

Ideologically, then, the lords of Old Syrian Ebla shared in that peculiar and original system of communication with three protagonists – the gods' world, the kings' world, and the subjects' world – that had already developed in Early Dynastic Mesopotamia, whose citizens were only apparently disregarded passive subjects. They were actually attentive spectators, interested in the dialogue between the divine and the royal world. In it, the gods could accept or reject what the kings reported, rewarding or punishing their actions. These dedications necessarily took place in the temples, as in Mesopotamia, because the kings "spoke" to the dynastic gods who were protectors of the city, to whom they were directly responsible, while dialogue was much less frequent, and possibly non-existent, with the other gods in the pantheon.

Figure 11.4 Ebla, Ishtar's Temple in the Lower City, the votive deposit of royal statues in the vestibule L.4600, from the east, 19th–17th century BC.

Typologically, a particular feature of royal statuary in Ebla in the early and classical Old Syrian Periods is the fact that, often, if not usually (and this was certainly not so in contemporary Babylonia or Egypt), when the king dedicated a statue of himself enthroned, he seems to have accompanied it with another statue of a woman, who could only have been his queen (Figure 11.5). Remains of two pairs of royal statues from the archaic Old Syrian Period, always with the sovereign enthroned and the queen standing, have been found in the Temple of Ishtar in the Lower Town, as well as two beautiful, though badly damaged, statues of a king (Figure 11.6) and a queen (Plates XX–XXI, 1–2) from the following classical Old Syrian Period in the same posture. A fragment of a stele with the image of the Storm-god Hadad (Figure 11.7) only partly preserved, which might come from the seriously ruined sanctuary of the south-eastern quarter of the Lower Town, shows, alongside the god, and smaller, the figure of a veiled priestess, the two figures of an enthroned king and a standing queen on a dais, which could well be the reproduction of votive statues from Hadad's Temple.

However, the royal votive statues that were dedicated in the temples of Ishtar and Hadad were not necessarily representations of the enthroned king, although these were probably the most frequent, because Ibbit-Lim's statue, the only one with a dedicatory inscription, seems to have represented the king standing, and this was, chronologically, a work of the archaic Old Syrian

Figure 11.5 Fragment of statue of a standing queen (TM.89.P.313), basalt, from Ishtar's Temple in the Lower City, 19th–18th century BC.

Period. Other remains of a royal torso (Figure 11.8) holding a fenestrated axe to his chest, which were in an annex of the Temple of Ishtar on the Citadel, where Ibbit-Lim's statue originally stood, must also have been parts of a standing statue.

It is hard to say what was the specific meaning of the various typologies of the royal statues dedicated in the sanctuaries of the great gods who protected kingship, but it is certain that the statues of a king enthroned and a queen standing, without insignia or inscriptions, and the statues of kings standing with insignia or inscriptions must have had different functions and purposes in the temples. We cannot exclude the possibility that the pairs of statues of kings and queens had some relation with rites such as the sacred marriage.

Though it is certain that it was these kinds of royal statue, either enthroned or standing, with an inscription, with or without insignia, that were usually dedicated in the temples, so as to be presented to the gods, there was certainly another type of royal image, somewhat badly documented, that, rather than being erected in temples, was placed in the squares and thus exhibited to subjects in open spaces, or in royal palaces – namely, in public government buildings. These statues, unlike those that were dedicated in temples before

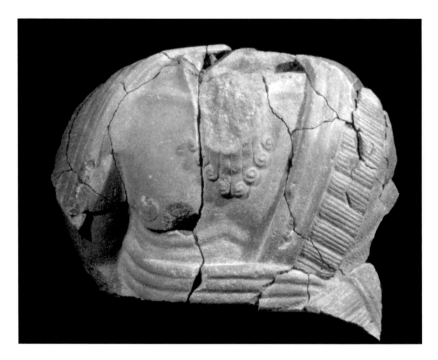

Figure 11.6 Headless bust of enthroned king (TM.88.P.500), basalt, from the vestibule L.4600 of Ishtar's Temple in the Lower City, 18th–17th century BC.

Figure 11.7 Fragment of votive stele with Hadad's figure (TM.88.S.500), basalt, from the region of the Temple of Hadad (?),18th–17th century BC.

Figure 11.8 Fragment of statue of a standing king holding a fenestrated axe (TM.75.G.728), basalt, 18th–17th century BC.

the gods so as to "speak" to them, were usually standing, and fixed on bases decorated with two figures, or four foreparts, of roaring lions (Figure 11.9).

While the statues of this second type have been almost entirely lost, two lower sections, both with sandalled feet, have been preserved, as have two bases with lions, almost complete, found in the Square of the Cisterns in the Sacred Area of Ishtar, and one particularly monumental specimen in a room of the Western Palace, adjacent to the entrance to the Tomb of the Lord of the Goats. One very important detail in the base of the statue in the Western Palace and in one of the two from the Square of the Cisterns is a royal figure in high relief seated between the two foreparts of lions. In addition, the first of these bases, under the enthroned king's image, clearly depicts a naked figure in a net, certainly a defeated enemy, over whom the sovereign stands in triumph, following an ancient Sumerian literary image that was clearly handed down to the figurative culture in Ebla in the classical Old Syrian Period.

These particular royal statues from Ebla, standing and with basalt bases with two lions, must have been non-votive images of deified dead kings, like those of two ancient kings erected many centuries later in the Neo-Syrian Period, one in Karkemish, in the square known as the "King's Gate", and one in Samal in the "Hilani J", therefore in public and palatine urban contexts, and certainly not in temples.

In the case of the base of the statue found in the room adjacent to the entrance to the Tomb of the Lord of the Goats in the Western Palace, we might suppose that the lost statue represented Immeya, who, very probably, had been buried in the hypogeum beneath. It is certain that these particular royal statues did not have the function of "speaking" to the gods, but, perhaps, of celebrating glorious dead figures, in public or palatine open spaces, although we cannot wholly exclude the possibility that they might

Figure 11.9 Base of a deified royal ancestor's statue, with roaring lions (TM.96.
P.470a+b), basalt, from the Cisterns Square, 19th–18th century BC.

receive offerings as intermediaries between the royal and divine worlds. As
to why the lion figures were usually placed alongside the small image of the
enthroned king, and were arranged as a base of the standing statue, it is
hard to provide well-grounded conjectures, but it is probably significant that
Ishtar, the lady of the lions and already explicitly described as the 'Lioness'
in the texts of the Royal Archives, was certainly the patron of early and classical Old Syrian kingship.

It seems clear, despite the fairly fragmentary state of the surviving remains,
that statuary in Old Syrian Ebla followed typologies that in some ways were
part of a complex system of communication between the divine, royal, and
human worlds, with the votive statues of living dedicators, erected only in
the temples, who reported to the gods on the feats of the kings to receive
their approval and the reward of a long personal and dynastic life; and with
the celebratory statues of the deified deceased kings placed only in the city
squares and palaces, to remind men and women of the feats of the illustrious
dead. Both could be the object of worship, although, as in Babylonia, for the
votive statues this probably only happened after the dedicator's death, while
for the celebratory statues, especially those inside the palaces, this could be

part of the regular worship of the deified royal ancestors, who had their own specific place of worship in the Sanctuary of the Deified Royal Ancestors, not far from the Royal Necropolis.

Both types of statue certainly encountered the destructive fury of the conquerors of the Old Syrian city around 1600 BC, as they may have been regarded as possessing magic powers, or simply as representing the city's royalty. The systematic and ruthless destruction of the images of the royalty of the enemy city must have been part of that magic, physical annihilation that certainly accompanied the devastation of cities when, as was certainly the case around 1600 BC, it was not a merely regional conflict to bring a city under one's own domination, but a battle between inter-regional powers, in which the goal of the war was conquest, pillage, and annihilation. It is therefore significant that the only Old Syrian statue found intact in Ebla, in the vestibule of the Temple of Ishtar in the Lower Town, is that of a non-royal figure (Figure 11.10), probably a high-ranking dignitary or a high priest, who, bareheaded, is holding in his hand a curved weapon that was probably a mark of priesthood.

Figure 11.10 Statue of sitting dignitary holding a curved weapon to his breast (TM.88.P.627), basalt, from the vestibule L.4600 of Ishtar's Temple in the Lower City, 19th–18th century BC.

The large number of remains – unfortunately often fragmentary – of votive and celebratory royal statuary in the archaic and classical Old Syrian Ebla proves that in this important city of Upper Syria what were probably palace workshops were active, producing, by order of the royal patrons, royal statues in forms, types, and quantities little different from what was normal in the temples of the main centres of southern Mesopotamia and the sanctuaries of the gods and funerary worship in Egypt.

There is a particularly remarkable discovery, even by the normal standards of Mesopotamia and Egypt, in the Temple of Ishtar in the Lower Town of Ebla. It is the remains of an almost certainly divine basalt statue (Plate XXV), which must be one of the most important cult images in the major sanctuary of the Old Syrian city. It is a female head, larger than life-size, carefully carved but not well finished, somewhat cursory particularly in the hair-dress and with a continuous furrow framing the whole face. Undoubtedly, this otherwise inexplicable furrow must have served to fix the coating of gold or silver foil that completely covered the goddess's face, following a craft tradition well known from many passages in the texts of the Archives of Early Syrian Ebla, which register quantities of the two metals that are explicitly intended for covering the faces of the gods' statues.

The great size of the image, the particular technique with the use of metal and, certainly, other stones for the lost tiara, and the very fact that, unlike all the royal votive statues, the face suffered no damage, suggest that this head is that of a large composite votive statue of Ishtar herself, and we cannot exclude the possibility that it was the major image of the goddess in her main sanctuary. This hypothesis is confirmed by the fact that some rare clay figurines from the beginning of Late Bronze I (Figure 11.11), when the city was semi-deserted, but limited activities of worship remained scattered there due to the goddess's great fame, present exactly the same hair-dress of the basalt head, with a cult band over the forehead and two braids entwined and gathered to the sides of her face. These can only have been popular reproductions of the goddess's venerated image, which the invaders may have left intact when they conquered the city around 1600 BC.

With whatever different concepts and aims, the royal votive and celebratory statues and the divine cult ones were widespread in the early centuries of the second millennium BC in every civilization of the Ancient East, from Egypt to Mesopotamia. This was not the case with the temple furnishings, which were probably typical, not so much of Old Syrian figurative culture, as of the city of Ebla. This was so for the rectangular cult double basins, decorated with relief scenes, most of them on three of the outer faces (Figure 11.12), or, much more rarely, on all four faces. Basins of this kind, of particular interest for the variety of cult representations depicted in the carvings, were usually dedicated in all the temples of the city and, indeed, in each of the temples so far discovered, there have been found remains of at least one carved cult basin, while in more than one case, there are strong indications that there were even more basins in a temple, as is practically

Figure 11.11 Stamp figurine with the image of the front-facing naked goddess (TM.88.R.624), clay, from Area R, 16th–15th century BC.

certain for the Temple of Ishtar on the Citadel and for that of Rashap in the Lower Town.

In the great majority of cases, the carved cult basins were smashed and the fragments often scattered when the Old Syrian city was destroyed, or later, in those cases when the ruins of the temples remained in view. In the Temple of Ishtar on the Citadel, however, which must have remained a place of worship even after the destruction of 1600 BC, one of the limestone basins remained in place in a corner of the cella and has come down to us intact, although partly corroded by rain. Another survived in different circumstances in the Temple of Shapash/ Shamash in the Lower Town North, which was devastated and set ablaze when the city was destroyed at the end of the classical Old Syrian Period: the basin, placed before the altar, was broken up and its pieces scattered, but one half remained in place, hidden beneath the burnt-out ruins (Figure 14.28).

The relief depictions on the carved faces of the Old Syrian cult basins are among the richest, but also most enigmatic, figurative sources for reconstructing the religious life of Syrian cities of the time. The dominant theme on the main faces of the temple basins was certainly that of a ritual banquet, which can be found both in the basin of the Temple of Ishtar on the

Figure 11.12 Side of a double cult basin with a lion-man grasping two lions (TM.65.D.226), limestone, from Ishtar's Temple on the Citadel, 19th–18th century BC.

Citadel, the best preserved one, as well as in another fragmentary specimen in Rashap's Temple in the Lower Town, but with significant variations.

On the basin of the Temple of Ishtar, in the upper register of the front face (Plate XXII, 1), on the two sides of a typical offering table with a central support ending in feet shaped as bulls' hooves, a damaged basalt example of which has been found in the Temple of Ishtar in the Lower Town, the king, wearing the typical archaic Old Syrian peaked tiara, and a bare-headed high priestess with a mass of hair falling down to her shoulders are seated. While a procession of officials carrying spears advances behind the king, and ladies with precious ceremonial vases move behind the priestess, on the lower register is depicted a flock of goats and sheep on the move, with a lion threatening them from behind, about to pounce on one of them from nearby an altar with a bird looming over it.

On the basalt basin of the Temple of Rashap, the centre of the depiction is once again a table, loaded with unleavened bread, and the king, seated and wearing the same fringed woollen cloak and the same royal tiara, raising a cup for a libation, a standing male bearded figure facing him and raising a cup. This central scene is surrounded by a crowd of bare-headed officials or soldiers, each carrying a spear and a curved weapon, advancing towards the offering table. In addition, instead of the lower register, is a line of front-facing foreparts of roaming lions on all three sides.

The theme on the basin of the Temple of Ishtar certainly hints at the banquet that followed the celebration of the sacred marriage between the king and the priestess, who would certainly have been the highest religious authority in the priesthood of the great goddess. In fact, with exactly the same iconography, this priestess's figure appears in a series of archaic Old Syrian seals, almost all of them coming from the antiques market, though one of them was discovered in one of the *favissae* of the Temple of Ishtar in the Lower Town (Figure 11.13). These seals also depict a very striking two-headed standard which, as late as the Roman Empire, may still have been kept in the most celebrated sanctuary of the goddess Atargatis at Hierapolis in Syria (now Membij), not far from the Euphrates. We cannot exclude the possibility that this remarkable cult object, probably typical of Ishtar's cult in Ebla, was kept in the Temple of Ishtar in the Lower Town, and that it had been removed during the destruction of the city around 1600 BC to another important sanctuary of the great goddess, which might have been the predecessor of the famous sanctuary where it was still worshipped at the time of Lucian of Samosata (Figure 11.16).

Although there is still no agreement as to its significance and diffusion, the rite of the sacred marriage, which is clearly alluded to both by contemporary Sumerian hymns in the early Old Babylonian Mesopotamia of the Isin and Larsa Dynasties, and in late references by classical authors, was very probably a basic aspect of Mesopotamian and Syrian religion in the first half of the second millennium BC. It took place at the beginning of the ancient oriental year in spring, and encouraged, ensured, and symbolized the rebirth of nature.

This essential cult act was closely connected with the great Ishtar, goddess of fertility in heaven and on earth, identified with the planet Venus, protector of love, as morning and evening star, who was venerated in the following centuries as Astarte, and who, at the time of the Roman Empire, with an extraordinary unbroken continuity, possibly explaining the long-lasting preservation of the sacred furnishings, was still venerated under the name of Atargatis, or, more often, with the significant title of "Syrian Goddess".

Figure 11.13 Cylinder seal impression with Ishtar's *semeion* with two heads (TM.92.P.800), hematite, from the *favissa* L.5238 of Ishtar's Temple in the Lower City, 19th–18th century BC.

The scenes depicted on the sides of the basin of the Temple of Ishtar (Plate XXII, 2) use typical figures and imaginary beings from the heritage of imagery in the Early Dynastic and Old Akkadian world of Mesopotamia, and must have alluded to mythical episodes connected with Ishtar, whose precise meaning in the Old Syrian world escapes us. Thus, the winged lion with eagle's claws and serpentine tail, who vomits streams of underground water, and the naked hero with rich curly hair and thick beard, holding a fish in one hand and the monster in the other, are figures that in Mesopotamia were connected in various ways with fertility.

The winged leonine dragon, which was certainly also used in Mesopotamia to represent the primordial demon Asakku, was just as certainly connected to the milieus of the heavenly divinities of fertility, such as Ishkur, a Rain-god, who travels the heavens in a chariot drawn by a leonine dragon. The curly-haired naked hero, named Lakhmu, was originally linked in Mesopotamia with the world of the clever Enki, the powerful creator god of Eridu, lord of the underground waters that are the source of the beneficial fertilizing rivers.

Although Lakhmu was not associated with Ishtar in Mesopotamia, it is no surprise that in the mythical re-elaborations of one of the main Syrian centres of Ishtar's cult the winged leonine dragon, creature of primaeval chaos, defeated, according to some myths, by Ninurta, but, according to others, by Ishkur, and the mythical bearded being, follower of the wise, benevolent Enki, became followers of the great goddess of fertility, so as to be both connected with the waters of the heavens and the earth. As the Old Akkadian glyptics in Mesopotamia show, the leonine dragon is the mythical being on which both a god like Ishkur and a goddess like Ishtar stand, perhaps because it was a primordial creature that had been conquered and subjugated by these gods. It is quite understandable, then, that in Syria it became a follower of Ishtar, symbolizing, not unlike Lakhmu, dominion over the fertile underground waters of the rivers and springs.

The scene with a hunter, whose arrow kills a lion attacking a bull, can be interpreted as part of the royal functions of preserving the natural order, which is threatened by wild animals, seen as aspects of the resurgent primaeval chaos, that constantly threatens humankind and the order imposed by the gods. But the scene on the other face (Figure 11.12) is much more enigmatic: a naked figure with a lion's head seizes two lions by the rear paws as if to tame them. Though the mythical, lion-headed being is itself a rather rare figure, taken from the iconographic heritage of Mesopotamia, in this case the Old Syrian re-elaboration of the image is difficult to interpret. Very probably, however, the image is once again linked to Ishtar, whose symbolic animal was the lion, which certainly made very clear the violence of this goddess, who was also mistress of war.

Already in the archaic Old Syrian Period the icons of the great Ishtar of Ebla were starting to include, alongside her more austere figure, the familiar licentious image of the goddess, exhibiting, with variations perhaps linked

Figure 11.14 Fragment of the upper part of a cult basin, with a part of the image of the front-facing winged Ishtar (TM.90.P.260a+b), basalt, from Ishtar's Temple in the Lower City, 19th–18th century BC.

to the traditions of different places of worship, the forms of unrestrained femininity – the goddess exposed in all her nudity, displaying herself with a garland in her hand, unfastening the cloak that still conceals part of her body. Despite the many attestations of the goddess's licentiousness, known above all from the Old Syrian cylinder seals, there are very few examples of her appearing with front-facing body and face and wings spreading out from her shoulders, but this was probably the official iconography of the Ishtar *Eblaitu* in its licentious form. In fact, in an extremely damaged fragment of the front face (Figure 11.14) of what must have been the cult basin of the Temple of Ishtar in the Lower Town, it is this image that appears at the centre of the scene. It is clear, then, that her image had to appear in that basin dedicated in the temple of the goddess's main Sacred Area, with various figures of acolytes and priests on either side.

It is also significant of the extent and importance of the fertility cults in Ebla that another small lower-corner fragment of the same basin (Figure 11.15) shows a small but very recognizable figure of a hierodule, also in full-frontal nudity, who must have been one of the sacred prostitutes of the great sanctuary of the goddess. One of the basalt cult basins of the Temple of Ishtar in the Lower Town, unlike all the other basins whose main front face has been preserved, usually illustrated with a ritual banquet, showed the great goddess in her licentious aspect, surrounded by the cult servants of the sanctuary.

It is particularly interesting that the naked front-facing goddess, sometimes winged, sometimes with goats in her arms, is one of the oldest known icons of the great Syrian goddess in a few rare seal impressions of the so-called Syrian style (Figure 9.2), preserved on tablets of the *kārum* II of Kültepe, ancient Kanesh, seat of the largest colony of Old Assyrian merchants in Central Anatolia. As this divine image appears in seals that are certainly in the archaic Old Syrian style, and also have iconographic features typical of the figurative tradition in Ebla at the time, including the offering table with

Figure 11.15 Lower fragment of cult basin, with figure of a front-facing naked hierodule (TM.90.P.800), basalt, from Ishtar's Temple in the Lower City, 19th–18th century BC.

central support, the royal peaked tiara, the high wickerwork conical stools, and the two-headed cult insignia, it is probable that they come from around Ebla and have maintained the iconography of some archaic Old Syrian deities typical of Ebla. Indeed, one of these seals is inscribed with the name of a king of Ebla, Ib-Damu.

It is less easy to explain the overall sense of the basic ritual act depicted on the two basins of Rashap's Temple in the Lower Town South-West, which again show a king drinking before an offering table (Figure 1.9) surrounded by armed men, with foreparts of roaring lions at the base, and on one side of the main face another standing figure of a bull-man. Although, so far as the king is concerned, the ritual act seems absolutely similar to that depicted on the basin of the Temple of Ishtar, the absence of the priestess and her replacement with a male figure, standing rather than enthroned, but who yet takes a libation like the king, rule out any relation with sacred marriage and female deities, while they suggest there may be a relation with royal cults of the afterlife.

In the first place, the Temple of Rashap was certainly the centre of worship of the god of the Underworld; second, it was in the region of the tombs of the Old Syrian Royal Necropolis; third, it seems to have been part of a structure that included the Sanctuary of the Deified Royal Ancestors; and finally, this Cult Area in the south was close to the Western Palace, which was probably the crown prince's residence. All these factors suggest that the scene on the basin reproduces one of the funeral symposia, that were certainly held on the occasion of funerary ceremonies on the king's death, which were to favour

Figure 11.16 Drawing of a cylinder seal impression on tablet with the image of Ishtar's *semeion*, clay, from Kanish, 20th–19th century BC.

Source: By kind permission of Beatrice Teissier.

his successful assumption among the *rapi'uma*, corresponding to the biblical *repha'im*, the deified royal ancestors of the late sovereign, which was essential for the future wellbeing of the community.

Various Ugaritic rites of the Middle Syrian Period, that certainly date back as religious tradition to at least the Old Syrian Period, mention these cere-monies, which were overseen by the late king's eldest son and daughter, and some Old Babylonian texts, particularly those concerning the contemporary I Dynasty of Babylon, usually known as "Hammurabi's Genealogy", list a long series of ancestors, both historical and mythical, who were invoked in these rites to participate in the symposium and receive the new arrival into the group of deified ancestors. As these rites certainly took place in the Syria of the Old Syrian Period too, and the Sanctuary of the Deified Royal Ancestors was, as we have seen, certainly the place where these rites were celebrated, the scene on the basin probably depicts the late king enthroned, the crown prince standing, and, perhaps, living officials, or the *rapi'uma* who had passed over to the other side.

There is an allusion to these funerary rites in an important and unusual funerary furnishing in hippopotamus ivory (Plate XXVII) that has come down to us almost intact, discovered in the so-called "Tomb of the Lord of the Goats" in the Royal Necropolis in the Western Palace, dating from around 1750 BC (Figure 14.40), which was almost certainly the burial place of Ebla's king Immeya, a name that appears as the owner of a silver bowl found among the funerary furnishings of the tomb. It is a beautiful talisman, unique of its kind, consisting of two series of three fine ivory plaques, held together by two pairs of sticks placed above and below; on its outer faces high-relief ivory figures were applied with ivory and bronze studs. The two series of plaques made up two figurative fields, slightly crescent-shaped, which may have been inspired by the so-called Egyptian "magic sticks" of the Middle Kingdom.

What was depicted with these figures were, on the front side, a banquet scene, and, on the rear side, an adoration scene, while on the sticks were applied figurines in the round of apotropaic animals, such as the lion and the snake. In the front scene, the protagonist of the funerary meal is a bare-headed figure, wearing a flounced woollen cloak, holding a staff, seated on a stool in front of a typical offering table with central support and bull's hooves of the kind familiar from the stone basins. Various assistants, all moving towards the seated figure and separated in some cases by a large preservation jar or by a fish, carry vases and other goods. Near the offering table are two most striking front-facing figures, completely naked, one female and the other male.

In the rear scene, the central representation is a standing bull with a front-facing human head, bearded and horned (Figure 11.17), adored by two dog-faced baboons facing each other, seated on what looks like a pot-stand. Various assistants attend the scene in this case too, at least one of whom has a fenestrated axe, and there are wild animals of the steppe, while between the bull and the dog-faced baboons appear again the two singular figures of male and female frontal nudes. On both faces, which seem to lack only very few applied elements, at the two ends opposite to those showing the banquet and the adoration are two empty spaces, as long as one plaque, as if these spaces had originally been occupied by the application of an extremely perishable material that has been completely lost and can no longer be reconstructed.

Although at least one other small magic object like this one, but with a single plaque, and with similar figurines of desert animals must have been placed in the Tomb of the Lord of the Goats, which probably complemented the meaning of the larger one, and which has deteriorated much more as a

Figure 11.17 Detail of Immeya's funerary talisman (TM.78.Q.455), hippopotamus ivory, from the Tomb of the Lord of the Goats, 18th century BC.

result of water damage, the larger of the two was probably Immeya's real funerary talisman, with the task of ensuring his successful assumption among the heavenly *rapi'uma*.

In fact, the banquet on the front face can certainly be identified as a funerary symposium for the king, who is depicted now without his tiara, the highest mark of earthly kingship, but with the staff that was perhaps symbolic of his new function as *rapi'u*, while the adoration of the human-headed bull must symbolize the effective assumption of the king – represented as a mythical being – into the sacred college of the *rapi'uma*. This last interpretation is reinforced by the fact that Old Babylonian Mesopotamian texts mention that, after his death and the performance of the funerary rites, the king galloped into the desert like a wild bull – a clear allusion to his taking possession of the desert as a desolate region of the afterlife or as a foreshadowing of the Underworld.

The two naked figures, male and female, are exceptional, in that, unlike the female nude, which was fairly common, a male frontal nude is absolutely unique in the whole of the ancient oriental iconography. They are probably to be identified with the dead king's eldest son and daughter, since a Ugaritic ritual text claims, as we have mentioned, that it was the first of the princes and the first of the princesses who were responsible for the success of the dead king's funeral. That is why they are the only two figures to appear both in the king's banquet and in the adoration of the human-headed bull, in their role as guarantors of the propitious outcome of the funerary ceremonies.

The fact that it is two dog-faced baboons that are adoring the human-headed bull, seated with their forepaws raised in prayer, and that they are two almost perfect replicas of the Egyptian dog-faced baboons who adore the sacred name of the pharaoh on Hotepibra's sceptre (Plate XXXI, 1–4), found in the very tomb of Immeya, and certainly sent as a gift by the pharaoh of Egypt Hotepibra Harnejheryotef to the king of Ebla, confirms that the bull represents the deified king. In fact, in the official Egyptian iconography, the dog-faced baboons adore the sun on the horizon, the god Ra Harakhty, otherwise the name of the pharaoh, which in Egyptian religious ideology is the god Horus and Ra's son.

If the peculiar plaques of Immeya's funerary talisman, with the striking figures applied in high relief, are a remarkable achievement for the local workshops of ivory engravers active around 1750 BC, in the classical Old Syrian Ebla of the second half of the eighteenth and the first half of the seventeenth century BC, other sophisticated ivory craftsmen were working for royal commissions.

A splendid figurine in the round of a person carrying a gazelle (Figure 11.18) as an offering is certainly a most sophisticated piece of work that probably belonged to a complex composite object that has been broken up and cannot now be reconstructed; it brings out the remarkable plastic qualities of the Ebla school, which might not have been very far from the nearly contemporary north Syrian workshops, producing exceptional figurines and caskets

Figure 11.18 Figurine of offering bearer carrying a gazelle (TM.93.P.340), hippopotamus ivory, 18th–17th century BC.

in ivory and other materials, discovered in Anatolia, from Acemhöyük to
Alaca Hüyük.

That Ebla in the classical Old Syrian Period was an important centre of
artistic craftsmanship in ivory engraving is shown by the fact that in the very
Throne Room of the Northern Palace have been found the remains of an
important figurative decoration in ivory, with the classical representation of
the Old Syrian king included in a scene very familiar in Old Syrian glyptics
of the time, in which two mirrored royal figures (Figure 11.19) are depicted at
the sides of a sacred palm or, more generally, of a sacred plant, or instead a
support culminating in a winged sun, or even of the naked goddess. Though
only one of the two royal figures (Figure 11.20) has escaped the heavy pillage
to which all public buildings were subject at the end of Middle Bronze II, the
finding of a tall stylized palm in the same place seems to guarantee that the
king's figure discovered was part of that most particular doubled royal iconography, which originated in ancient Egypt and had notable success in Asia.
This would have been because of the great prestige of the monarchy of the
Nile Valley in the milieus of the main Old Syrian courts in the early second
millennium BC. In this period, gifts to Asiatic kings from the pharaohs of the

Figure 11.19 Impression of a classical Old Syrian cylinder seal, with two mirror-like king's figures on both sides of a naked goddess (989), hematite, 18th century BC.

Source: New York, Morgan Library from Porada, 1948.

XII and XIII Dynasties were by no means uncommon, as is documented by the findings of Byblos, with splendid breast-plates that usually reproduced the doubled image of the lord of the Nile Valley as king of Upper and Lower Egypt, in mirror-like figurative schemes that must have directly inspired the stylistically significant re-elaborations of the craftsmen of the kingdoms of Syria in the early second millennium BC, which we know so far almost exclusively from glyptics.

In Egypt, the duplication of the pharaoh's figure was not only very widespread, but had a strong, clear specific reason, which Egyptians of every period were well aware of: Egypt's historical royal unity had descended from the union of two Protohistoric kingdoms of the Delta and of Upper Egypt – or, as the ancient Egyptians said, from the union of the "Two Lands". But the reasons why the Syrians adopted the figurative theme of the dual kingship and the interpretations they gave it in the Old Syrian ideological framework still seem enigmatic. Although all the examples we have of the duplication of the royal figure and his mirror-like representation in the Old Syrian world are the numerous, often very well-made, cylinder seals, and, in Ebla at least, the ivories with royal subject, it is probable that these depictions were also quite successful in monumental Old Syrian art, given that they were certainly directly inspired by the royal patrons who commissioned them.

If these images were actually also used for monumental reliefs in some important Old Syrian centres, it is easier to understand why this motif, which was highly unusual outside Egypt, was taken up many centuries later, in the

Figure 11.20 Inlay with the image of an Old Syrian king, wearing the cloak and tiara, and holding a fenestrated axe (TM.86.P.86), bone, from throne room L.4038 of the Northern Palace, 18th–17th century BC.

Neo-Assyrian world, to represent, in the most striking and official form, kingship in the Throne Room of the North-West Palace of Ashurnasirpal II, in the first half of the ninth century BC. Nor is this the only aspect of the symbolic representation of imperial Assyrian kingship that seems to have been drawn from the Old Syrian figurative tradition, as the motif of the royal seal of Assyria, with the king who heroically kills in single combat a standing lion, is clearly drawn from an ancient motif of the figurative tradition of Syria, as witnessed in Ebla itself since the mature Early Syrian Period in the wood-carvings, and then handed down to the same Old Syrian world, where it reappears in works that were certainly commissioned by royalty, such as the Stele of Ishtar.

This ivory from Ebla with the king's figures flanking the palm is a fine example of a classical iconography of the Old Syrian king, with particular attention given to the typical oval tiara, which here appears with unusual horizontal engravings, and a no less characteristic fringed cloak draped in wide wreaths. In this ivory the king probably carried a fenestrated axe, which was certainly a mark of kingship, as is confirmed by a fragment of the torso of a royal statue in basalt (Figure 11.8) coming from a shrine in front of the great Temple of Ishtar on the Citadel.

In its technique, too, the ivory of the king with the sacred palm was probably characteristic of the craftsmanship in the royal workshops. The carving on the open-work thin ivory plate with carved details, without any relief, is very probably a legacy of the marble carving in Ebla in the mature Early Syrian Period of the Archives age, a technique in which the workshops of Mardikh IIB1 produced work of the highest quality in the inlaid wall panels with an unexpected variety of subjects. It also started off a kind of production that continued in some significant urban areas of Syria and Palestine until at least the end of the Late Bronze Age, as is clearly indicated by the ivories of Tell Fekheriyah.

The same very special technique of working on thin plates was used by the sophisticated workshops of engravers in Ebla, active in that period, probably around 1700 BC, whose work shows strong Egyptian inspiration, as was also the case in what may have been just a few other north Syrian centres at the time for the production of some remarkable cylinder seals whose clearly classical Old Syrian style has a marked Egyptian influence.

A group of Egyptian-style figurative ivories, almost all of excellent quality, using the same technique, were discovered in a room that probably served as a workshop in the back of the Northern Palace. They must have been part of the decorations of bed-heads or the backs and sides of one or more thrones, which had probably been damaged and stored for restoration. In all these ivories, as well as some rarer and minor geometric motifs of Old Syrian iconography, such as the familiar braids, usually called *guilloches*, which were originally, at least, connected with fertility, there are images of typical Egyptian deities, depicted with great fidelity to their iconographic canons, from those of Hathor (Figure 11.21) with his bull's horns framing the sun's disc, to Horus (Figure 11.22) with a falcon's head, and Sobek (Figure 11.23) with a crocodile head, and the great human heads wearing the complex *atef* crown typical of the god Osiris (Plate XXXII).

Only the most general reconstruction of the contexts of these images is possible now, as the mutilated figures that have survived are too fragmentary, but it is clear that these images of Egyptian deities, some of which, like Sobek, the crocodile-god of Fayum, the extensive area of marshland that had been reclaimed by the great kings of the XII Theban Dynasty, were particularly current in the contemporary Middle Kingdom of Egypt, and were clearly made by studying carefully the precious pharaonic gifts that were to be found in Ebla, while the images on them were adopted to represent Old Syrian deities and express local religious concepts in the refined and clearly much admired artistic language of Egypt, which must have fascinated them and which enjoyed great prestige.

As we know that in Byblos in this period Hathor's iconography had been adopted to depict the great Gublite goddess, the "Lady of Byblos", a form of Ishtar/Astarte, it seems extremely plausible that Hathor's iconography

Figure 11.21 Inlay with the goddess Hathor, with the sun-disc between the horns
(TM.88.P.532), hippopotamus ivory, from L.4070 in the Northern
Palace, 18th–17th century BC.

was used to represent Ishtar in Ebla and that the heads with Osirian crowns
(Figure 11.24) were simply images of the dead sovereigns of Ebla who had
been deified. It is much more difficult and uncertain to try to identify the
divine figures hiding behind the Egyptian images of Sobek and Horus, who,
significantly, are the very ones that appear, though rarely, in the classical Old
Syrian glyptics of the period too.

The excellent quality of these ivories, like the complexity of their ideological significance, reveal how stylistically mature the workshops of the
engravers in Ebla in the classical Old Syrian Period were, managing with
remarkable versatility to re-elaborate, in a local style that was very close to its
Egyptian origins, images and forms of the Egyptian artistic culture to express
concepts and values of the Old Syrian world. One proven case of this is the
dog-faced baboons of the talisman compared with the models of Hotepibra's
pharaonic mace.

This extraordinary capacity to completely assimilate and originally re-
elaborate, at a high level, genres and forms of great foreign artistic civilizations
was one the artists of Ebla in the mature Early Syrian period had already

Figure 11.22 Inlays with figures of the god Horus with falcon head (TM.88.P.536 + 537), hippopotamus ivory, from L.4070 in the Northern Palace, 18th–17th century BC.

given brilliant proof of in relation to late Early Dynastic Mesopotamian works. They continued to do so in their treatment of Middle Egyptian artistic craftsmanship in the classical Old Syrian Period, and it seems to be a remarkably persistent gift in the palace workshops of the main centres of inner Syria from the mid-third to the mid-second millennium BC and later.

This particular talent of the Old Syrian workshops of the court may not have existed only in Ebla, but in other great urban centres of Upper Syria too. It seems to derive from a solid possession of expressive tools, firmly anchored to a local artistic vision that was highly original, allowing them to penetrate deeply into the understanding and recreation of completely different artistic forms at a high level, without misunderstandings and distortions, and with a mastery of technique so refined as not to run the risk of mechanical repetition or superficial vulgarization.

Some important works of Old Syrian plastic art in Ebla that probably date from the decades around 1800 BC are from a transitional period from the early style to the classical achievements, and may indicate that in the last years of Ebla's political supremacy, before the emergence of the kingdom of Yamkhad as the major recognized inter-regional power, the great classical Old Syrian style was forming, though Aleppo, rather than Ebla, was probably its driving force.

Figure 11.23 Inlay with the god Sobek with crocodile head (TM.88.P.538), hippopotamus ivory, from L.4070 in the Northern Palace, 18th–17th century BC.

The greatest of these works, but not the only one, is certainly the Stele
of Ishtar (Plate XXIII), which has fortunately survived in three large joining
fragments, with only the upper section lost. This was probably tapered, and
it was there, on the front face, that the main ritual scene was depicted. This
monument, which was carved on its four faces (Figure 11.25), must have been
originally erected somewhere in Ishtar's Sacred Area on the Citadel, in the
square in front of or inside the Temple of Ishtar on the western edge of the
Citadel, while, perhaps later in Middle Bronze II, not long before the final
destruction of the Old Syrian city, it was housed in a corner of the tiny vestibule of Shrine G3 in the same cult area, so that the rear face and one of the
side faces were no longer visible.

Ishtar's Stele belongs to an artistic genre that must have been quite widespread in early and classical Old Syrian Ebla, as the badly damaged remains
of a second, and a quite large fragment of a third stele of the same kind
have been retrieved on the Acropolis: these steles were probably all erected in
Ishtar's sanctuary, perhaps in the open. It is possible that all these monuments
were actually works dedicated in the dynastic Temple on the Citadel in relation to kingship, but, at least in the Stele of Ishtar, all the themes represented

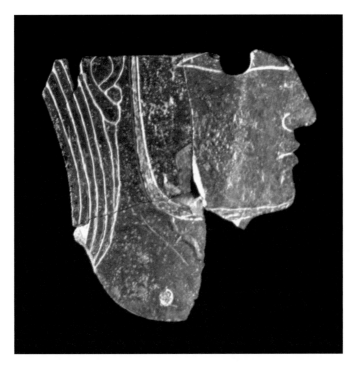

Figure 11.24 Fragment of inlay with a pharaonic head, originally wearing the *atef* crown (TM.88.P.534), hippopotamus ivory, from L.4070 in the Northern Palace, 18th–17th century BC.

in the registers of the four faces clearly refer to the celebration of kingship in relation to the goddess Ishtar, who was patron of Ebla's royal family.

In the Stele of Ishtar, the front face and the two side ones each had four registers carved in fairly low relief. This was very probably the case on the rear face, too, where because of the breakage, no trace has remained of the probable lost upper register. In addition, there were originally five, and not just four, registers on the front face, as the third register from the top was sub-divided into two superimposed scenes of equal size.

Overall, the subjects of the various panels are divine, mythical, and cultic, variously and cleverly arranged following a careful system of correspondences and echoes that we cannot fully understand, partly due to the loss of the scene of the upper front register, which probably depicted a significant cult act, whose protagonist was certainly the king who had dedicated the monument, and who does not seem to appear in any other panel. This lost scene must have been connected to the subjects of a series of others on the front face and the two side ones, but to none at the rear: they depict musicians with horns, drums, and other musical instruments in the third register sub-divided

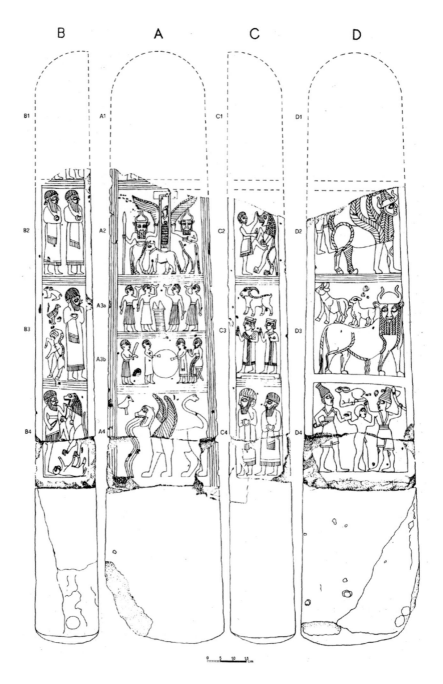

Figure 11.25 Drawing of the four faces in relief of Ishtar's Stele (TM.67.E224 + 85 + 85.G.350), basalt, from Shrine G3, 19th–18th century BC.

in two on the front face; and male and female figures of offering bearers, with bowls and other objects connected with the rite, and what are probably sacrificial animals accompanying them, portrayed in the registers on the two side faces, which are not on the same line.

There are particularly significant divine images on the second upper and the last register at the bottom of the front face, as well as in the upper registers of the rear face, while the side faces do not display this kind of scene. The most significant image in the second front register depicts Ishtar (Figure 9.3): she is shown inside a winged chapel, signifying her dominion over the heavens, between two bull-men, who are probably the guardians of the gates of heaven, flung open for the planet Venus, with which Ishtar was assimilated, as also happened in Mesopotamian iconography with Shamash, the Sun-god. The chapel placed on the back of a bull certainly hints at Ishtar's prerogative as supreme dispenser of fertility, as does the winged leonine dragon vomiting the waters of the abyss, and this dragon is, significantly, depicted in the lowest register on the front face. The same, vividly depicted mythical being appears in its canonical form as supporting a Rain-god and a great goddess, who is his companion deity, in Mesopotamian glyptics during the Dynasty of Akkad, from around 2350 BC on.

On the back of the stele are depicted two other familiar mythical beings: at the top, a tetramorphic sphinx (Figure 11.26) with a horned tiara typical of deities, a leonine body, eagle's wings, a human face, and one of her paws in the form of a bull's hoof; and, at the bottom, a man-headed bull with the usual divine tiara. If, as is likely, this peculiar series of mythical beings also had the image of a griffin at the top, there would be a perfect correspondence with the representation of mythical beings that appears in the famous contemporary "Painting of the Investiture" in the Royal Palace of Mari.

Although interpretation cannot be certain, we might think that, both in Ebla and Mari, the griffin alluded to the chaotic and hostile nature of the desert, and the man-headed bull to the ordered, beneficent nature of the cultivated earth, while the sphinx could only be an original re-elaboration of the primary symbolic value of the Egyptian prototype, hinting at kingship, whose mission was that of preserving and renewing the original divine order over the fertile and arid lands, on which the life of city communities depends.

The extraordinary and extremely rare tetramorphic form of the sphinx, symbol of kingship, which, centuries earlier, foreshadows the structure of the tetramorphic beings in the biblical vision of Ezekiel, and the symbolic beings of the Evangelists in the early Christian period, might be understood to summarize all those aspects variously shared by the man-headed bull and the griffin that allow kingship to dominate domestic and wild nature.

The subjects that, very broadly speaking, are regarded as mythical are those where, on the sides, a heroic bare-headed figure pierces a standing lion and, on the rear face, two partially specular royal images slaughter a naked, defenceless enemy with a sword and an axe. Although with our present state of knowledge we cannot give this figure a name, it is certain that

Figure 11.26 Register of the back face of Ishtar's Stele, with a tetramorphic sphinx, basalt, from Shrine G3, 19th–18th century BC.

the one killing the lion in single combat is a royal hero, as is also shown by the fact that, many centuries later, this very same motif, with the king himself in the hero's place, was the subject of the royal seal of Assyria in the Imperial Age, at least from the late eighth century to the end of the seventh century BC.

And royal figures, who represent the image of the king doubled, as we have mentioned, in a deliberately imperfect specularity, must be those that, wearing special tiaras that seem a possibly ceremonial variant of the classical Old Syrian crown of Ebla, sacrifice the unarmed enemy. The royal hero who kills the lion and the sovereign who destroys the enemy are different but conceptually symmetrical figures of kingship controlling wild nature, symbolized by the lion, and rebellious humanity, represented by the vanquished figure.

The Stele of Ishtar is, then, most certainly a work that in iconologically complex and compositionally original ways, celebrated, in the years around 1800 BC, the kingship of Ebla, placed under the patronage of Ishtar *Eblaitu*, whose monument depicts her austere iconography, just as the fragment of a basin of the Temple of Ishtar in the Lower Town was to exhibit her licentious iconography. From the time in early Middle Bronze I, when Ibbit-Lim may have introduced the cult of the great goddess as the supreme divinity of the revived archaic Old Syrian city, Ishtar must have been the patron of Ebla's kingship, but when, in the years immediately before 1780 BC, Aleppo achieved hegemony in Upper Syria under the great Yarim-Lim I, then in Ebla, too, the highest and most venerated deity of Aleppo, Hadad, lord of rainfall, probably assumed an increasingly important role, perhaps becoming in the last decades of the city's life, as in the kingdom of Yamkhad, the protector of kingship.

This ideological shift, this deviation from local tradition, and this adherence to the concept of Aleppo are eloquently witnessed by the figurative pattern (Figure 9.7) of the beautiful dynastic seal of prince Maratewari (whose difficult name was apparently Hurrian), son of that Indilimma whom various factors indicate as the last king of Old Syrian Ebla.

This well-sized cylinder seal, which has survived in various impressions discovered on large storage jars (Figure 11.27), all found in destruction levels of Mardikh IIIB, at the end of Middle Bronze II, represents the prince without a tiara, but in his royal cloak, receiving life, under the form of the Egyptian hieroglyphic sign *ankh*, from the hands of the god Hadad and of his companion Khebat, depicted in the classical form of Aleppo. This was clearly a variant of the figurative pattern of the dynastic seals of the lords of Yamkhad, familiar from the impressions on the Alalakh VII tablets. In fact, various kings of Aleppo had themselves represented on their seals, always with identifying inscriptions, facing the goddess Khebat who gives them life (Figure 11.28). With the consolidation of the kingdom of Yamkhad as a more than regional power, the concept of kingship in Ebla must have undergone a transformation in which Hadad and Khebat assumed the role that had been Ishtar's, who must have kept her widespread popularity, however, not only in Ebla, but throughout Upper Syria.

The superb dynastic seal of the last hereditary prince of the Old Syrian city, who apparently never reached the throne, as a result of the intervention in Syria of Mursili I of Hatti and Pizikarra of Nineveh, reveals the presence in Ebla of workshops of seal engravers of the highest level, as is documented by the finding of various impressions on jars deriving from a second stylistically similar seal (Figure 11.29), in this case of a high official, who appears with Hadad.

Although strangely few cylinders have been found in the levels of Mardikh IIIB, and equally few sealings with impressions of seals have been found, the glyptic findings of the archaic and classical Old Syrian Ebla show at least that some workshops of Ebla also produced in the older period, and continued to produce for some of the more recent phase, seals of very poor quality, with a linear engraving and usually just a few figures apparently in procession, almost always without divine figures and royal images. This must have been a widespread cursory output of low level, stylistically uncharacterized, that might also be called popular, and that must have been produced in a relatively extensive region from Syria to Anatolia.

Figure 11.27 Storage jar with the impression of prince Maratewari's cylinder seal on its shoulder (TM.99.Z.28/1), from the Western Residence, 17th century BC.

From at least the early classical Old Syrian Period, however, the workshops working for the temple and palace elites produced in Ebla, too, cylinders in the fine classical style (Figure 11.30) that was common to some of the major urban centres of Upper Syria, from Aleppo to Ugarit, Alalakh, Karkemish, Tuba, and perhaps many more. At first, their distinguishing feature was the sophisticated plastic patterns that were so softly blurred that they tended more and more to an excessive attention to form that has been described as baroque. We know of the seals of prince Maratewari, king Indilimma's son, and that of his high official, who may have been a palace prefect, from impressions on jars. These and the rare cylinders discovered in the residential area of the western Lower Town, or documented by a few other impressions or seals, not only were certainly the property of high palace officials, but must date from the last decades of the classical Old Syrian city. We must infer that Ebla's workshops remained loyal to the classical style without indulging in more extreme, precious baroque effects, so typical of the palace workshops of Aleppo.

Though our knowledge of the artistic work of the other large centres of Upper Syria in Middle Bronze I–II is still too fragmentary to sketch a

Figure 11.28 Detail of the impression of prince Maratewari's seal, with the head of the goddess Khebat (TM.79.Q.126/1), clay, from room L.3100 of the Western Palace, 17th century BC.

coherent account of their historical development, it is certain that, if we look at the stylistic developments of the early and classical Old Syrian Period, the workshops in the archaic Old Syrian Ebla must have had an essential role in passing on the Early Syrian figurative legacy, in developing the forms of the archaic Old Syrian style, and in laying the foundations for the magnificent creations of the classical style.

In this, the Ebla school, at court level, must have played a role not very different from that of the palace workshops in the contemporary archaic Old Babylonian centres in Mesopotamia, from Isin to Larsa and Eshnunna, so far as we can judge from the scanty documentation, compared with the Old Akkadian and Neo-Sumerian legacy, which was certainly available in the many works dedicated in the major sanctuaries in Sumer and Akkad. In Egypt, too, the many palace and temple workshops of the pharaohs of the XII Dynasty, particularly in the twentieth century BC, returned to the canons of the great statuary of the Old Kingdom, laying the foundations for the profound renewal that pervaded Egyptian statuary in the central periods of the Middle Kingdom at the time of the last sovereigns of the XII Dynasty.

Figure 11.29 Detail of the cylinder seal impression on a jar shoulder, with the god
Hadad and a high official (TM.78.Q.28/1), clay, from room L.3005 of the
Western Palace, 17th century BC.

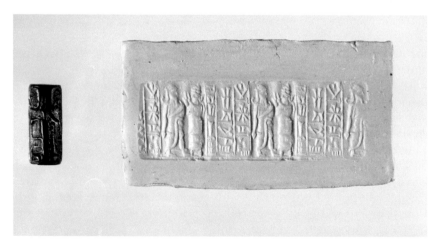

Figure 11.30 Cylinder seal with the figures of a high official and interceding goddess,
and its impression (TM.00.Z.200), hematite, from the Western Residence,
17th century BC.

It is, in fact, in the remarkable statuary of Senwosret III and Amenemhat III that there emerges a mature and surprising sensitivity to the facial expressions of the sovereigns that is strangely alien to Egyptian non-royal statuary in this period, and yet has striking affinities with the contemporary royal statuary from Mesopotamia, particularly from the Larsa and Babylon milieus. Often the works in Ebla were seriously mutilated, which means we cannot know whether their workshops shared in these innovatory stylistic currents, which seem to have spread both in Egypt and Mesopotamia from around the mid-nineteenth century BC. But, very probably, in the decades between the mid-nineteenth and the mid-eighteenth century BC, Ebla's sculptors, too, modulated the severe, somewhat rigid style of the early period with more harmonious forms in which the compact, schematic plastic masses of the older style were replaced with naturalistically conceived forms where the planes are sometimes organized with the most exquisite elegance.

Although, as yet, we have only isolated examples, a male head in limestone (Figure 11.31), discovered in the cult area of the Temple of the Rock, but, from stratigraphic evidence, dating from Middle Bronze I, is a good example of the dependence on both the Early Syrian manner and on the schematic style of the first decades of the archaic Old Syrian Period, partly for its technique, which is not unlike that typical of the workshops in the mature Early Syrian Period of the Archives age. Certainly, the reliefs of almost all the cult basins of Ebla's temples are examples of this same severe style at a more advanced stage, as is the limestone basin of the Temple of Ishtar on the Citadel, which is probably a little later than the smaller basalt basin of Rashap's Temple, and the other basalt basin that has survived only in fragments from Ishtar's sanctuary on the Citadel, which might also be the one explicitly mentioned in the votive inscription on king Ibbit-Lim's torso, which was certainly dedicated in the Temple of Ishtar.

The most recent of all the surviving cult basins probably dates from the years around 1800 BC. Only half of it survives, and it was discovered near the altar of the Temple of Shapash/Shamash in the Lower Town North. Its rear face (Figure 11.32) contains scenes of male figures ritually embracing, and on the sides, figures of front-facing protective goddesses who seem to be witnesses of a solemn event (Figure 11.33). This work, which is not one of the finest of those made in Ebla, seems to hint at the stipulation of a pact or alliance, an operation that traditionally and understandably took place under the guarantee of the Sun-god Shamash, protector of justice and equity. Its forms are less rigid and more flowing, heralding the more advanced works of the classical workshops of Ebla from around the central years of the seventeenth century BC.

A second basalt stele is very probably from this period, though from an archaic or central phase of the classical Old Syrian Period, and is carved on the four faces, like the slightly older Stele of Ishtar; two large joining fragments of this monument have recently been found by accident on the surface in the

Figure 11.31 Worshipper's head (TM.05.HH.350a+b), limestone, from the pit F.9302
in Area HH, 20th–19th (?) century BC.

south-western periphery of the Acropolis. This suggests that this monument,
which was called Ishtar's Obelisk (Plate XXIV), because of its more or less
square section, was originally standing, again like the Stele of Ishtar, in the
cult area of the Temple of Ishtar on the Citadel. Various clues indicate that
some of the reliefs of Ishtar's Obelisk were unfinished, and that only a fairly
extensive part of it has survived, badly preserved in too fragmentary a condition for any complete analysis to be possible. However, it is certain that, just
like the Stele of Ishtar, on one side, in a higher register of the main face, was
depicted the winged chapel of the great goddess, flanked by bull-men and
placed on a bull's back, and on the other, in a lower register, was a scene of
musicians, related to ritual ceremonies in honour of the goddess.

Another interesting similarity of the figurative design of the Obelisk with
that of the Stele is the presence of a register with the scene of the two Old
Syrian kings slaughtering a naked prisoner with different weapons. This
important detail confirms that all these Eblaite monuments, carved on all four
faces – whether the Stele, the Obelisk, or a third, similar monument of which

Figure 11.32 Front face of a double cult basin, with scene of officials embracing each other (TM.72.N.468), limestone, from Shapash/Shamash's Temple, 18th century BC.

little has survived – must have been connected to the cult of the great goddess as patron and protector of the city's kingship.

However, unlike the figurative pattern of the Stele, in the Obelisk, the mythical scenes of the supernatural beings and the heroic duels with the lion seem to have been replaced by a series of representations that, in various ways, display different moments of sacrifices of bulls and scenes in which officials appeared, probably presenting precious objects as a gift. It is in one of the scenes of the sacrifice of a bull (unfortunately very fragmentary) that there is the image of a figure who seems to be an acrobat jumping over the horns of a bull. This is, obviously, one of the oldest representations and certainly the only one belonging to monumental Old Syrian art, of acrobats on a bull, which were, till now, known in Syria only from rather rare cylinder seals. While the rendering of the acrobat on the Obelisk in Ebla is stylistically very far removed from the famous representations in the pictures of Knossos in Crete and Avaris in Egypt, it seems certain that the new obelisk of Ebla documents that daring acrobats on bulls were not only well known in the Syria of Middle Bronze II, but were connected to ritual sacrifices and perhaps specifically to Ishtar's cult.

Lastly, that Ebla, during a fairly advanced phase of the classical Old Syrian Period, shared in and contributed brilliantly to the stylistic renewal

Figure 11.33 Side of double cult basin with front-facing goddesses (TM.72.N.468), limestone, 18th century BC.

documented during the seventeenth century BC, particularly in the magnificent glyptic works from the kingdom of Yamkhad, is made certain by the sumptuous plasticity of the two most recent royal votive statues, male and female, found in the Temple of Ishtar in the Lower Town, which are genuine masterpieces of an art whose most innovative and successful formal inventions were certainly in Aleppo, Karkemish, Ebla, and Qatna.

12 Old Syrian material culture
Characteristics and development

Ebla was destroyed three times in the course of almost a millennium: first around 2300 BC, in the transition from Early Bronze IVA to IVB at the end of the mature Early Syrian Period; then around 2000 BC, perhaps shortly before the transition from Early Bronze IVB to Middle Bronze I, at the end of the late Early Syrian Period; and finally, around 1600 BC, when Middle Bronze II was about to give way to Late Bronze I, at the end of the classical Old Syrian Period. In the light of the evidence of the historical development of Ebla's material culture, there is no doubt that the sharpest and most striking break was that following the devastation of the second Ebla at the beginning of Middle Bronze I.

The conquest and sacking that brought an end to the great city of the Royal Archives around 2300 BC was almost certainly the work of Sargon of Akkad. It wiped out the extensive political power of a city that was using its considerable territorial control to carry out what seems to have been a proto-imperial policy, but this did not interrupt in any way the development of the mature Early Syrian culture, which continued to flourish outside Ebla, both north and south of the city. Despite the passage from Middle Bronze II to Late Bronze I, there was striking continuity in material culture in the transition, before and after the final terrible devastation of Ebla in 1600 BC by its powerful enemies, who seem to have included the Hittites of Mursili I and the Hurrians of Pizikarra of Nineveh.

By contrast, the material culture of Middle Bronze I in Syria around 2000 BC, which is the mark of the reconstructed archaic Old Syrian urban centre, was undoubtedly much more innovative as compared to that of Early Bronze IVB, with only definitely secondary signs of continuity. Not only is there no certainty about the destruction of the second Ebla, which was followed by a significant break in the development of its material culture; we do not even have any real clue as to who was involved, unlike the destruction of both the first Ebla and the third. As we have said, the only evidence is that it seems to have taken place in the same years as the disorders in Lower Mesopotamia, caused by the Amorites' migrations and territorial occupations, followed by the Elamites' invasion, which destabilized the empire of the III Dynasty of

Ur. The result was the devastation by the Elamites, not only of Ur itself, but, apparently, of all the other major cities in its mighty system.

The material culture of archaic Middle Bronze I reveals, in the phase of Mardikh IIIA, notable structural and morphological changes in the production of pottery. On the one hand, the colours and grits of the clay were strikingly different from those of the late Early Syrian workshops of Mardikh IIB2, with less variety of ceramic types and a marked standardization and uniformity of the wares. On the other, the majority of the most characteristic ceramic types of the earlier period disappeared, giving way to a series of new shapes of which only a small or very limited number can be found in the last phases of Mardikh IIB2.

In general, pottery in Middle Bronze I is much less varied and more uniform than in the final phases of Early Bronze IVB, old types disappearing and so many new types being introduced that it is clear that, morphologically, there was much innovation and little continuity.

If we assess the question on the level of craftsmanship, we must conclude that potters in archaic Middle Bronze I used clay deposits that were at least partly different, that they made mixtures of different clays, and that they used different kilns and perhaps different systems of firing. In other words, they were using completely different methods from those well known and tested in Early Bronze IVA and IVB, phases that may have introduced minor innovations and changes, but also showed evident continuity in working and production procedures.

As regards the morphological aspects, to give just a few particularly significant examples, Early Bronze IVA–B of inner Syria was notable for the small chalice-shaped vessels: so typical were they that it was often called "Caliciform Culture", for the various types and sizes of goblets, whether painted, incised, or plain. In archaic Middle Bronze I they all disappeared, as did all the types of painted small and medium-sized wares – from goblets to open bowls, bottles, and jugs – and the medium and large-sized Cooking Ware bowls, with oblique walls and out-swollen rim, the globular "hole-mouth" cooking pots, and the extremely distinctive preservation jars, whether those whose vertical rim had a flat external surface, or the more common ones with a triple-grooved rim.

By contrast, from the beginning of the archaic Old Syrian Period many new shapes of pots were created (Figure 12.1), tending to be very standardized, usually very pale, whitish, light green, tawny, or pink Common Wares. There were fairly open bowls with a rounded carination which became more and more markedly angular over time, reducing the overall height of the vessel; these were widespread in inner Syria. There were also closed, quite sharply carinated bowls with a short flaring rim, which are also often found in Syrian centres on the coast, and large open bowls, with slanting wall and a marked ridge below the strongly expanded, sometimes down-turned, rim. There were almost bi-conical carinated juglets, basically uvular, often with a rope decoration on the carination, slanting shoulders,

Figure 12.1 Archaic and classical Old Syrian pottery from the *favissae* in Ishtar's Cult
Area in the Lower City, 19th–18th century BC.

often decorated with horizontal and wavy combing, and horizontal, falling,
or slanting expanded rim. There were fairly globular and, more rarely, oval
jars with an out-turned rim moulded at the tip, so as to form a double pro-
truding edge, the so-called "double everted rim". There were uvular-shaped
jars without a neck, but with vertical rim, moulded with a slight swelling in
the central part and slightly expanded at the edge. There were, more rarely,
jugs with a fairly large globular body, a rather narrow neck, and a rim
more or less markedly swollen on the outside. There were quite globular
preservation jars, sometimes with high rounded carinations, with applied
rope decorations, and a rim that usually extended horizontally, often with
a rounded tip.

The pottery of Middle Bronze I was usually produced on the fast wheel,
unlike in Early Bronze IVB, when only the small shapes were worked at the
wheel, while medium-sized ones were hand-made, though the wheel was used
for the rim. It certainly looks like the result of standardized mass procedures,
deriving partly from the innovation of the widespread, regular use of the
fast wheel, which must have involved a drastic reduction in the number of
workshops, selective uniformity of typologies, and complete homogenization
of variations.

These same characteristics can be found in another type of clay production, widespread in Upper Syria in Middle Bronze I – that of earthenware
figurines (Figure 12.2), which were always hand-made without any use of
moulds, and which present various typologies, apparently connected with
religious worship, the functions of which are difficult to identify. In the
archaic Old Syrian Period, the most widespread type was that of a highly
stylized standing naked female, completely flat from behind, marked by
short, unnaturally thin horizontal arms, wide sometimes angular hips, a
well-marked pubic area, and, strangely emerging from a double trapezoidal
plaque, a head with pierced lobes, the forehead and nose seeming strangely
beak-like.

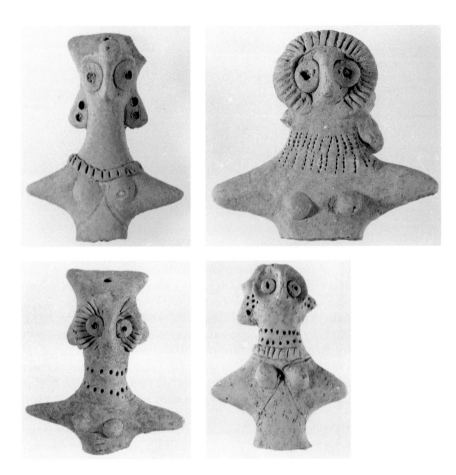

Figure 12.2, a–d Archaic Old Syrian female figurines (TM.88.R.82, TM.88. R.148, TM.88. R.122, TM.88.R.528), clay, from Area R, 20th–19th century BC.

This type of figurine (Figure 12.3) was quite widespread in inner northern Syria, from the region of Aleppo to the area of the mid-Orontes, up to Hamah and Homs. It was certainly connected to the cult of Ishtar, though it is hard to say if it was a popular representation of the goddess herself or, more probably, of the sacred prostitutes of her sanctuaries. Nor can we rule out the possibility that the type was created in Ebla and that many of those found in other centres of inner Syria were actually made in the main centre of the cult of Ishtar, namely Ebla.

Still more difficult to interpret are other kinds of widespread clay figurines, like the male images with the head terminating in a cone, or those with the face surrounded by thin parallel applications, or the three-legged monkeys, or charioteers holding insignia. The latter might be related either to deities

Figure 12.3, a & b Old Syrian female figurines of the archaic and classical phases (TM.90.G.1, TM.88.R.157), clay, from Areas G and R, 19th and 18th–17th century BC.

conceived as divine charioteers of the heavens like Hadad, the great Storm-god, or simply to the special army corps that was beginning to be used, though less widely than in the later Middle Syrian Period.

There are many, not very differentiated, figurines of quadrupeds, mainly oxen or sheep, so widespread in such different excavation contexts that it is difficult to give a single interpretation of their function. However, in the case of the female figures at least, which certainly hint at the goddess's sphere of fertility, their ubiquity clearly depended on the popularity of her cult, whether they were votive objects, as when they were placed in the *favissae* of the temples, or objects of magic value kept in the house. The quadruped figurines, however, were sometimes found in rather poor burials, and so may have substituted an animal offering for the life of the deceased in the Underworld.

Ebla was probably an important centre of metal production throughout the Old Syrian Period, some types being well documented even in the early phases, though there have not been particularly numerous findings of bronze tools and weapons. Both those found in the Tomb of the Lord of the Goats

Figure 12.4 Fenestrated axe of the so-called "duck-bill" type (TM.79.Q.343), bronze, from the Tomb of the Lord of the Goats, 18th century BC.

and the various representations on the statuary and ivories show that in Middle Bronze I there was a flourishing production of fenestrated axes in the characteristic early, broad, nearly square shape. They were widespread in the Syro-Palestinian area, even found with peculiar variants in the Iranian region, and one of the fenestrated axes in the royal tomb in Ebla may have been made in Iran. Definite examples of local production are two fine fusion moulds for this type of axe (Figure 12.5) that were discovered, in almost perfect condition, in a poor tomb, that must have been that of a Middle Bronze I craftsman, on the southern slopes of the Acropolis.

The more developed type of this kind of weapon is what is known as the duck-bill fenestrated axe (Figure 12.4). Usually thought of as being later, in its squarer form it must also have been a ceremonial emblem, as is shown by the magnificent contemporary gold specimens in the Royal Tombs of Byblos. Its length clearly exceeded its breadth, and in Ebla they seem to have been produced both in late Middle Bronze I and early Middle Bronze II, though they may no longer have been used at the end of the period. The lack of this type in the southernmost regions of Palestine, and its diffusion on the coast of the Levant as well as in the Middle Euphrates Valley, suggest that it may have been a northern variant, produced for a fairly long period. It was certainly produced for a longer period in inner Syria than on the coast of the Levant, although a representation of it in an Egyptian tomb of the nineteenth century BC is from the same period as when it was actually used, while a later one from the age of Thutmosis IV definitely seems anachronistic.

Other notable examples of typical Middle Bronze I weapons are the very elaborate, resistant spear-heads, consisting of a sharp rhomboid blade whose central midrib made it particularly strong, a collar with faceted section, ending in a ring, and a square tang ending in a hook-shaped stud, grafted onto the wooden shaft. This type of spear-head was probably created in Mesopotamia in the late third millennium BC, but there are also many less detailed and

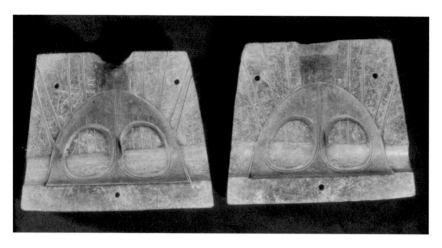

Figure 12.5 Pair of moulds for "squared" fenestrated axe (TM.84.G.30a+b),
soft-stone, 18th–17th century BC.

sophisticated examples than those of Ebla from Middle Bronze I, though a
well-preserved specimen from the Tomb of the Lord of the Goats indicates
that they were still in use in early Middle Bronze II.

Another type of well-documented, though rare, weapon in Ebla, was the
spear with its typical hollow shaft (Figure 12.6), often with a fixing ring at
the base. It was already widespread in Middle Bronze I, at least in its central phase, and was still normally in use, in the first half of Middle Bronze
II, a period to which two fine examples belong, found in the East-South-
East Fortress of Ebla's eastern fortification. Other specimens were found in
Ugarit, which may have been one of the most important production centres
of coastal Syria, and at least some of these spears certainly had a ceremonial
function. They can be seen on the carved ritual basins, held by dignitaries
performing a rite, as the tips are clearly rounded. Among the weapons used
in Ebla during the classical Old Syrian Period, there are quite a few javelin
heads and, more rarely, bronze arrowheads, which usually have the typical
central rib and short tang. The latter was an archaic feature that persisted
longer than in the spear-heads, as the hollow shaft is rarer in the small
javelin heads.

Another type is the bronze dagger with leaf-shaped blade and characteristic
concave hilt, in which a wooden or bone handle was fitted, which was usually
blocked by two pairs of wings placed at the beginning of the blade. There are
few examples of it, as it was more common in the Syro-Palestinian area in the
following Middle Syrian Period, but it seems to have been used early on in
Ebla, as it has been found in the levels of the Middle Bronze II destruction.

Many small metal objects have survived from every phase of Middle Bronze
I–II, particularly needles and hairpins, sometimes with quadrangular heads,

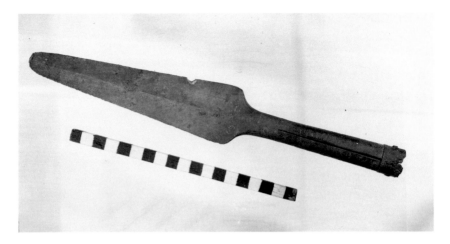

Figure 12.6 Spear-head with hollow shaft (TM.71.M.842), bronze, from L.1900 of the East-South-East Fortress, 18th–17th century BC.

but more often with a flattened end ending in a duck's head. The hairpins with a star-shaped head are probably typical of inner Upper Syria: many have been found in Alalakh and Ebla, and there is a beautiful gold specimen from the so-called "Tomb of the Princess", dating from late Middle Bronze I.

Bronze objects have been found in the tombs of the Royal Necropolis from the central part of the Old Syrian Period; they seem to be importations from the East, probably made in Iran. An example would be the four oval barrel-shaped rattles in bronze (Figure 12.7), with triangular piercings, and two hoods at the tip ending in moveable rings to hang them, and containing bronze spheres. Although this unusual type of rattle had a long history in the area of Iran, with hardly noticeable modifications in shape, we know of its existence in Iran from the early second millennium BC, and given this continuity, the specimens from Ebla were probably gifts from princes of western Iran.

Other significant remains from the tombs of the Old Syrian Royal Necropolis are the foreparts of goats (Figure 12.8) in the Tomb of the Lord of the Goats, which decorated the ends of the side pieces of thrones, and the figurines of squatting goats, which probably decorated the tops of the back of a throne (Figure 12.9). These objects, which are also of artistic interest, are unique in Syrian archaeology and very probably hinted at the god of the Underworld, Rashap, whose symbolic animal was a goat or a gazelle. It is therefore very probable that a funerary throne was buried in the Tomb of the Lord of the Goats, which was almost certainly the tomb of king Immeya, whose name appears on the rim of a silver platter, placed in the hypogeum. Being made of wood (probably covered in bronze foil), little of this throne has survived.

Figure 12.7 Barrel-shaped, open-work rattle (TM.78.Q.473), bronze, from the Tomb of the Lord of the Goats, 18th century BC.

Figure 12.8 Forepart of a goat, decorating a throne arm-rest (TM.78.Q.446), bronze, from the Tomb of the Lord of the Goats, 18th century BC.

The precious furnishings for the tombs of the Royal Necropolis, which probably all date from the mid-nineteenth century and the late eighteenth century BC, provide extraordinarily abundant and varied documentation of a particularly important sector of material culture, that of jewellery. Most of it was produced in Syria, though a small part must have come from Egyptian

Figure 12.9 Crouching goat, decorating a throne back (TM.78.Q.452), bronze, from the Tomb of the Lord of the Goats, 18th century BC.

workshops, used by the pharaohs of the late XII and, more probably, the early XIII Dynasty to send gifts to the court of the Old Syrian lords of Ebla.

The high quality of the jewellery in inner Syria, probably in the transition period from Middle Bronze I to Middle Bronze II around 1800 BC, can be seen in the gold furnishings in the Tomb of the Princess (Plate XXVIII), all in the same typical style of a north Syrian workshop in the years preceding Hammurabi's reign in Babylon. These consisted of the afore-mentioned star-shaped hairpin with twisted upper stem and disc-shaped blocking device in the middle; six "twisted rod" bracelets; a necklace with a lapis lazuli scaraboid set in the centre, enclosed by a lost decoration in *cloisonné* vitreous paste, and a remarkable ring-shaped pendant (perhaps a nose-ring; Figure 12.10), formed by two bulging plaques welded together, with an elegant granulation of lozenges and triangles.

Because of their quality, we have few points of comparison, but these jewels do resemble, in some respects, other royal works from the Levantine coast in late Middle Bronze I and southern Palestine in Middle Bronze II. The fine bracelets from Ebla (Figure 12.11), embellished with an unbroken line of minute beads in the recess between the bars, and the equally regular

Figure 12.10 Pendant or earring with granulation in a lozenge motif (TM.78.Q.366), gold, from the Tomb of the Princess, 19th–18th century BC.

close incisions on the strip edges themselves, which produces a striking glitter effect, are similar to a "twisted rod" gold bracelet from the Royal Tomb II of Byblos and to similar earrings from Ugarit, Enkomi, and Tell 'Ajjul, the site that some identify with the Hyksos stronghold of Sharuhen. The ring pendant with granulations can be compared to some large, but less sophisticated, crescent-shaped earrings from Tell 'Ajjul, also tubular in shape, with geometric granulations, usually ascribed to north Syrian workshops.

While the technique and form of the necklace's scaraboid centrepiece may have been inspired by classical Egyptian prototypes of the Middle Kingdom, the beads in this necklace, usually described as mellon-shaped due to their projecting ribs and the collars hammered flat at the ends, are of a type widespread in contemporary western Asia. They were certainly manufactured in royal workshops, from Dilbat and Larsa in Lower Mesopotamia, to Assur and Mari on the upper and middle courses of the Tigris and Euphrates.

The high level of the Eblaite jewellery is shown by the fact that this very type of fluted, melon-shaped bead is to be found in identical, sophisticated specimens in the Tomb of the Lord of the Goats, for which they used the fusion technique, as happened for some similar necklace beads of various

Figure 12.11 Bracelet with "twisted bars" (TM.78.Q.370), gold, from the Tomb of the
Princess, 19th–18th century BC.

sizes in the same tomb in a variant with elongated collars and sharp ribs, of
unique formal elegance.

There survive in the pillaged furnishings of the Lord of the Goats two larger
beads of this type (Figure 12.12). Because of the relatively marked elongation
of the collars they are often described as "spindle-shaped", and they seem to
have been fused onto a silver core. The workmanship is exceptional, and they
seem to be among the oldest specimens of pieces in hammered foil. They were
widespread in Palestine from Tell Beyt Mirsim to Tell 'Ajjul, but also in the
south at Tell Far'ah and, above all, in Megiddo, especially in the last phases of
Middle Bronze II of the southern region, certainly later than the destruction
of classical Old Syrian Ebla. It seems clear that the workshops of Ebla were
among the first to produce this kind of necklace bead, which was certainly
widespread in the whole Syro-Palestinian area. It was also one of the very few
centres (along with Byblos and Ugarit, and perhaps Aleppo and Karkemish)
that experimented with different techniques, developed types with variants,
and refined the shapes, producing pieces that would be widely imitated in the
following decades, even in small centres, particularly in the south.

Figure 12.12 Fluted melon-shaped beads, with expanded collars (TM.78.Q.438a+b), gold, from the Tomb of the Lord of the Goats, 18th century BC.

In the royal tomb of the "Lord of the Goats", various types of neck-lace must have been placed, including much rarer ones than those with fluted melon-shaped beads, which were widespread in non-royal circles too. One very peculiar and unparalleled shape is the "pseudo-barrel" bead with square section (Figure 12.13), which in the Tomb of the Lord of the Goats appears in gold, lapis lazuli, and carnelian specimens, probably alternating to striking chromatic affect. The cylindrical beads with thickened edges and the finest thread (Figure 12.14) are of great delicacy. We know of them from other similar pieces made in royal workshops, found in Royal Tomb III of Byblos and in the store-room of the Palace of Megiddo VIII. There are also examples in the royal hypogeum in Ebla, with one of the extrem-ities cut obliquely.

The Tomb of the Lord of the Goats also contains many round gold-leaf studs (Figure 12.15), with a triple series of concentric circles and four holes to allow them to be sewn on magnificent ceremonial clothes, identical to one from the same period in Kanesh, at level II of Kültepe, which was certainly exported to Anatolia from Upper Syria. They anticipated by several decades similar, though generally poorer, examples to be found in Palestine in Late Bronze I and II.

An example of the originality of the products from the workshops in Ebla is a necklace with a wide-meshed chain (Figure 12.20), which was quite common in the Syro-Palestinian area, and two acorns of rock crystal and grey-green translucent stone, with gold capsules imitating the dome of the acorn, decorated with granulation. The extraordinary sophistication of Ebla's

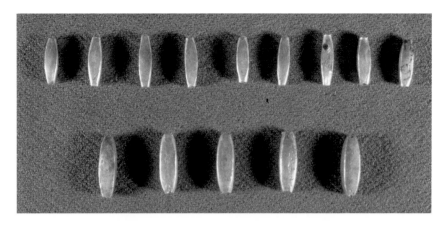

Figure 12.13 "Pseudo-barrel" beads (TM.78.Q.220 + 410), gold, from the Tomb of the Lord of the Goats, 18th century BC.

Figure 12.14 Cylindrical beads (TM.78.Q.413), gold, from the Tomb of the Lord of the Goats, 18th century BC.

Figure 12.15 Round studs, with circles in relief and four holes (TM.78.Q.411), gold, from the Tomb of the Lord of the Goats, 18th century BC.

royal jewellers is also clear from the extremely elegant variations on standard types, such as the melon-shaped golden bead in which all the edges of the ridges are decorated with the most delicate filigree. Another is the disc of gold leaf, with granulation (Figure 12.16), either merely decorative or perhaps for the handle of a stick, which is certainly comparable to some of the gold discs of the so-called "Larsa Treasure". This last set of precious objects from Lower Mesopotamia dated from the third quarter of the eighteenth century BC, making it more or less contemporary with the Tomb of the Lord of the Goats, which seems to have been for king Immeya, buried with Hotepibra's ceremonial mace, one of the many magnificent gifts he received from the pharaoh.

The Egyptian origin of this striking emblem of the pharaoh's power is certain, whereas, given the probable extended international relations of the kings of Ebla in the mid-eighteenth century BC, we can only infer that a peculiar small pendant in the form of a lapis lazuli eagle with outstretched wings (Figure 12.17), with gold clip, came from Iran. It can only be compared with an almost contemporary piece of Old Elamite jewellery.

Among the jewellery of the Tomb of the Lord of the Goats, there is a genuine masterpiece from the classical Old Syrian workshops of Ebla: the necklace with three separate pieces (Plate XXIX), each formed by an upper plaque, one rectangular in the centre and the other two with their outer limits

Figure 12.16 Disc with a decoration with granulation and *cloisonné* (TM.79.Q.200), gold and lapis lazuli, from the Tomb of the Lord of the Goats, 18th century BC.

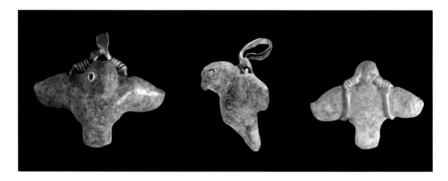

Figure 12.17 Pendant in the shape of a small eagle (TM.78.Q.387), gold and lapis lazuli, from the Tomb of the Lord of the Goats, 18th century BC.

rounded at the sides, and a disc pendant. While the plaques have four horizontal rope decorations in relief, inside which are the holes for the hanging threads, the discs have the most elegant granulated six-pointed stars in the middle, and six little globes in a triple circular frame.

This marvellous and extremely original jewel is only partly comparable to the remarkable golden necklace of Dilbat, now at the Metropolitan Museum of New York, which was certainly commissioned by royalty, and dates from around the mid-eighteenth century BC. It, too, has three disc pendants, but, instead of plaques, it has two rows of round beads. Unlike the star, as in Ebla, the discs of Dilbat have a rosette, like those of the "Larsa Treasure", but there are also striking similarities, such as the three rows of granulate framing.

Now, there is no doubt that the star in the pendants, an extremely popular motif in jewellery from Syria, Palestine, Anatolia, and Elam, is connected with Ishtar, the great goddess of the planet Venus, which is represented by the star. The rosette, too, in Lower Mesopotamia hints at Ishtar, as, according to an ancient tradition with its roots in Protohistoric Uruk, the rosette was one of the most frequent vegetation motifs symbolizing the great goddess of fertility in her various cult centres. The relation of the necklace of the Lord of the Goats and the star with Ishtar is also manifest from the contemporary clay figurines of inner Syria, depicting naked female figures, who were certainly connected with the great goddess's priesthood, wearing a necklace with three rectangular pieces above and three discs below. It is very likely, then, that the necklace of the Lord of the Goats, with the discs bearing the star motif, were a special jewel of kingship, connected to the probable function of the king of Ebla as high priest and vicar of Ishtar, under whose protection Ebla's kingship was placed, as Aleppo's was under Khebat's, the spouse of Hadad.

The very fact that the Lord of the Goats was a king explains the presence in his tomb of jewels and royal insignia of the pharaohs, which obviously only an Old Syrian king could receive as a gift and take with him to his tomb. The tomb was sacked, the stone that sealed its entrance was found out of place, and some jewels were on the entrance steps, where they must have been dropped by the robbers. This means that what has been found in the three connected hypogea of the Tomb of the Lord of the Goats is just part of its original furnishing, which remained hidden in the mud or unnoticed in the raiders' haste. That explains why a remarkable gold collar (Plate XXIX), which must have had a series of bars with spherical beads, has come down to us with just one of the two final papyrus-shaped pieces, with remains of the decoration in vitreous paste. The gold of this original necklace, as of other works of Egyptian jewellery from the same tomb, is much more reddish in colour than that of all the Old Syrian jewels in the Royal Necropolis, which are usually deep yellow.

The other works of Egyptian jewellery received by the Lord of the Goats include a gold ring (Plate XXIX), remarkable for its exquisite execution, with the motif of two lily flowers flanked by a beautiful, small, *cloisonné* scaraboid.

Figure 12.18 Egyptian ceremonial mace with a small cylinder decorated with a lozenge motif (TM.79.Q.148 + 180), gold, silver, ivory, and limestone, from the Tomb of the Cisterns, 18th century BC.

Necklaces and rings were intended as precious personal gifts between sovereigns without any specific allusion to kingship. But two extraordinary maces, each with a limestone head in the shape of a flattened pear and an ivory handle decorated with a little gold and silver cylinder must have had special symbolic value, because in reliefs this is exactly the kind of mace that frequently appears in the hands of pharaohs of the XII and XIII Dynasty during sacred ceremonies.

One of these two maces (Figure 12.18), on which the name of the pharaoh donor may never have been written, must have had an ivory handle covered in foil with inlay applied along a silver cylinder covered in gold leaf, fretted at regular intervals with lozenges. The other mace (Plate XXX) was very different: its handle, originally decorated with small gold and silver lozenges, which probably made a kind of mesh, had a silver cylinder on which two relief figures in gold had been applied of dog-faced baboons (Plate XXXI, 1–4), seated facing each other with their forepaws raised in adoration of a royal name inscribed in golden hieroglyphics.

Figure 12.19 Cylinder, possibly belonging to the handle of an Egyptian ceremonial mace, with a scale motif (TM.78.Q.420), gold, from the Tomb of the Lord of the Goats, 18th century BC.

Although one of the phonetic complements has been lost and was long ago, during restoration in Syria, replaced by an upside-down tri-litteral sign, the hieroglyphics spell out Hotepibra, which was the first name of pharaoh Harnejheryotef, perhaps the ninth of the XIII Dynasty, who reigned briefly around 1770–1760 BC, calling himself the "Son of the Asiatic". It is, however, uncertain if the tubular gold handle (Figure 12.19), with a granulated decoration in scales, which might have been the covering of the ivory handle, actually belonged to this mace.

The historical importance of the presence of this exceptional Egyptian insignia in an Old Syrian royal tomb in Ebla is huge, both in general, for the evident prestige that the lord of Ebla enjoyed among the pharaohs in the late Middle Kingdom, and in particular, for the possibility that some specific links existed between the ruling house in Ebla and the Asiatic prince who had become lord of the Nile Valley. Still more interesting, artistically and ideologically, is the fact that, in Immeya's reign, a precious Old Syrian funerary piece, indicating the deification of the king after his death, drew on the Egyptian theme of dog-faced baboons adoring the pharaoh's name. This was based on the belief that the pharaoh was the son of the Sun-god Ra, who was usually adored in Egyptian iconography by dog-faced baboons as "Sun of the eastern horizon". The side of the talisman where the king is represented shows the sovereign after the funeral banquet, as a bull with a human head, with two Egyptian dog-faced baboons at his sides in the identical attitude of adoration.

This group of objects, sent as a gift to a king of Ebla by one or more pharaohs, almost certainly of the XIII Dynasty, is an important contribution to our knowledge of both the political and artistic relations between Egypt and Syria. It can be added to the evidence we have from Egyptian and imitation-Egyptian objects in the Royal Tombs of Byblos, which were slightly older, and also from the statues – often sphinxes – sent by pharaohs of the XII Dynasty to the kings of Upper Syria. Not only breast-plates, but maces, necklaces, and rings from Egypt were brought to the court, to enrich the repertoire of Egyptian works available to the Old Syrian palace workshops, who used them as inspiration for works that imitated the Egyptian iconographic heritage with often breath-taking precision and fidelity.

In general, probably between 1850 and 1600 BC, workshops of engravers in Upper Syria produced a series of Old Syrian cylinder seals with various Egyptian-inspired features such as typically Egyptian divine figures. For example, around 1700 BC, one workshop in Ebla created strongly Egyptian-influenced ivories that must have decorated a bed or a ceremonial throne, whose remains were found, as we have seen, in the Northern Palace.

The furnishings in the tombs of the Royal Necropolis provide information on other rare palatine artefacts that indicate the variety of relations in the court of this flourishing city from the late nineteenth until well into the eighteenth century BC. A small, precious, light greyish-green *faïence* vase with a

Figure 12.20 Necklace with a pendant in the shape of two acorns (TM.78.Q.407),
gold, rock crystal, and translucent grey-greenish stone, 18th century BC.

pointed base (Figure 14.39), grooved body, and two high elliptical handles, now lost, may have been produced around 1850 BC. It was found in the Tomb of the Princess, and is comparable only with some similar contemporary specimens in rock crystal and obsidian from what is known as Serikaya's Palace in the important Anatolian centre of Acemhüyük, which some have identified with the ancient Purushkhanda. It reveals the lively trade with the world of Central Anatolia, where the Old Assyrian trade colonies were to be found in those years, and a fine alabaster vase with open shape and horizontal handles might indicate similar relations with other coastal regions of Asia Minor.

In their production of objects in *faïence*, however, the workshops in Ebla must have achieved full mastery in the last decades of the classical Old Syrian Period, as is shown by the exceptional Caliciform moulded cup with Hathor's face (Plate XXVI), discovered in one of the private houses of the South-West Lower Town. It may be compared to another contemporary fragmentary specimen from Alalakh VII, but it certainly heralds an extraordinary production of moulded clay vases with human faces, widespread in Syria and Palestine in Late Bronze I–II. True, the alabaster funerary vases for ointments, whether oval-shaped or broadening, flask-like, below, with their typical out-turned rims, are characteristic of Egypt in the late Middle Kingdom, and sometimes imitated by workshops in Syria and Palestine. But one item whose elegance is in a class of its own is the large alabaster bowl with bulging shoulder and typical pommelled lid, which must have been Egyptian workmanship of the highest quality.

By contrast, the very unusual bottles in sardonyx (Figure 12.21), limestone, and bronze, found in the hypogea of the "Lord of the Goats" and of the "Princess", may have been produced in Old Syrian workshops. Globular in shape, with banded body, high cylindrical neck, and horizontal expanded rim, they are also known from bronze specimens in the so-called "Montet Jar" deposit in Byblos, though they also have parallels in contemporary Iranian bronze works.

Another example of palatine material culture is the remarkable round weight in steatite (Figure 12.22), with geometrical decorations, surmounted by two figures in high relief of crouching lions, which was probably once part of the closing mechanism of a cult place, connected with Ishtar, lady of the lions, whose priest on earth the king of Ebla was. For the very same reason, as well as more frequently in the Tomb of the Lord of the Goats, the lion is a recurrent image in various palace tools, even in the much rarer findings in the palaces with royal functions in the Lower Town of Ebla. An example is the weight in the form of a lion in haematite, weighing 913 grams, nearly the equivalent of a double Syrian mina, whose standard value was 470 grams. As it was found in a room in the Western Palace, it must have been an official weight of the administration of the crown prince in the final period of classical Old Syrian Ebla.

Figure 12.21 Small bottle with cylindrical neck (TM.78.Q.76), sardonyx, from the Tomb of the Princess, 18th century BC.

The abundant pottery that is an important part of the furnishings of the hypogea of the Royal Necropolis dates from the last decades of Middle Bronze I and the first half of Middle Bronze II. It is eloquent testimony to the unbroken continuity of material culture between the early and classical Old Syrian Periods. The hypogea certainly belonged to people of the highest rank, whether kings or not, as in the case of the Tomb of the Princess. This explains the presence of some remarkable examples of a sophisticated monochrome painted pottery, which is usually called "North Syrian/Cilician Painted Ware" (Figure 12.23). They are jugs, sometimes small and uvular, and sometimes larger and almost globular, with a twisted handle, a lip painted with eyes, and, above all, a painted band on the shoulder in panels with thick vertical lines alternating with metopes, with highly stylized elegant figures of long-horned goats.

These jugs must all be from the same workshop and are identical with others on the antiques market and in the museums of Aleppo and Oxford, but, above all, with others known only from fragments of Alalakh X. They must date from somewhere in the middle of the period between 1900 and 1750 BC, when this kind of object seems to have been fashionable, and must have

Figure 12.22 Round counterweight with two lion figures (TM.79.Q.257), steatite, from the Tomb of the Lord of the Goats, 18th century BC.

been made in the region of Aleppo. Apart from these rare fine examples of royal commission, painted vases are infrequent during Middle Bronze II in Ebla, though some reddish-brown handleless vases, with decorative bands on the shoulder, resemble the so-called Khabur Ware, which was widespread in Upper Mesopotamia in the same decades, either imported from those eastern regions or produced in the western outreaches.

There were also developments typical of "North-Syrian/Cilician Painted Ware" during the eighteenth century BC. One example is the characteristic globular jug with narrow neck, out-turned rim, and round vertical handle, always with monochrome decorative bands with panels on the shoulder. An example of this is in the Tomb of the Lord of the Goats. Another, during the seventeenth century BC, is the large crater with the vertical twisted handles decorated in monochrome bands on the shoulder, known from some fine fragmentary specimens, which were discovered in palatine buildings of Mardikh IIIB and date from the years immediately before the final destruction of the city.

Overall, pottery in Ebla in the last decades of the classical Old Syrian Period was obviously continuous with previous productions, but some previously unknown shapes (Figure 12.24) were also made in the city's last years. These innovations can be seen mainly in the small and medium-sized shapes

Figure 12.23, a–d Jugs of the "North Syrian/Cilician Painted Ware", clay, from the
Tomb of the Princess and the Tomb of the Lord of the Goats, 19th–
18th century BC.

and in the open shapes of the usual pale whitish, pink, or greenish pottery.
In particular, there are the typical medium-sized deep bowls with wide mouth
and thickened rim on a slightly flared neck rising from a high-shouldered
body, and the thin-walled bowls with nearly globular bodies on ring-shaped
bases, and a long thin flared rim ending in a pointed tip.

Throughout Middle Bronze II large plates of dark clay, often burnished,
with a thickened rim flattened on the inside, and a disc-like or ring-like base
became more and more frequent. However, the semi-globular, medium-sized
bowl with natural rim, marked on the outside by two thin hollows, almost

Figure 12.24 Classical Old Syrian cooking pots and table ware, clay, from the private houses of Area B East, 17th century BC.

always made in whitish thin-walled clay, well purified, sometimes slightly burnished, began being produced only a few years before the destruction of Mardikh IIIB and was still being produced in the later paler ware.

The production of pottery in Ebla in the classical Old Syrian Period was part of a geographically unified area at least from the region of Aleppo, or even Karkemish, in the north as far as Homs in the south in inner Syria. However, it seems equally probable that, in the south, the level of Hamah H ended several decades before Mardikh IIIB, and, to the north, that Alalakh VII, which was almost certainly destroyed by Hattusili I, ended only a few years before the destruction of the third Ebla. On the other hand, the end of Middle Bronze IIC in Palestine, obviously quite independent of the destructions caused by Hattusili I and Mursili I, was certainly some decades later than the collapse of Old Syrian culture in the inland areas of Upper Syria.

Overall, it is certain that, as regards the material culture of Middle Bronze I–II in inner Syria, Ebla played a central role in promoting, or even in creating, a considerable number of types of the most refined jewellery, as it owned workshops – certainly related to palaces – of the highest craftsmanship, which might rival, in creativity and refinement, the royal workshops of contemporary Babylonia and Egypt. Thus far, there is no archaeological evidence for the presence in the archaic and classical Old Syrian Ebla of workshops for bronze working; yet it is likely that, for this kind of handicraft too, Ebla was one of the most active centres, with Aleppo, Ugarit, Karkemish, Qatna, and

Byblos. As regards the production of clay figurines, the workshops of Ebla were probably connected with temples, more than palaces, and were probably among the most creative as regards quality, and most active, as regards quantity, for the typologies related with Ishtar, due to the supraregional fame of the great goddess of Ebla. As for pottery production, it was probably huge as concerned the Common Ware, pale and burnished, but it is also probable that Ebla was one of the main production centres for the refined jugs and craters of the so-called "North-Syrian/Cilician Painted Ware".

13 From Ebla to Tell Mardikh
Decline of a great urban centre

Ebla never rose again after it was destroyed for the third time in the years around 1600 BC, both because the devastation was so thorough and pitiless, and because the population may already have been decreasing due to a micro-climatic crisis in the region. Despite the seriousness of the defeat, however, there were scattered and isolated archaeologically documented attempts to rebuild something from the ruins of the city that had been destroyed, sacked, and set on fire.

These attempts must have been the work of refugees, who briefly occupied some of the most important public buildings, like the Western Fort and the Southern Palace, after the invaders had beaten a hasty retreat. It is in the peripheral residential quarter of Area Z (Figure 13.1), at the foot of the western rampart, as well as in the area of the Northern Fort, that the most substantial traces of real attempts at rebuilding have been found, over the ruins of the classical Old Syrian city. These certainly date from Late Bronze I, between 1600 and 1400 BC, but the buildings remained incomplete and were clearly abandoned because of inadequate demographic and technological back-up. The temporary occupation of some of the important public buildings, like the residence of the palace prefect, or of one of the most important arsenal-forts of the city shows, on the other hand, the complete absence of any organized government and political authority in the city, devastated by the invaders' fury. The most recent excavations revealed that this phenomenon was understandably attested in whole peripheral sectors of the main palace, the Royal Palace E of the Citadel.

The first decades of the Middle Syrian Period, which certainly saw the reconstruction of major centres like Aleppo and minor cities like Alalakh in the western regions, also witnessed the failure of the cities to recover in the central-eastern region of Upper Syria, revealing, overall, a definite but fairly discreet withdrawal of the settlements further from the semi-arid area, towards the west where rainfall probably continued to allow cereals to be cultivated, which was much more difficult even a few scores of kilometres to the east. To the east, notwithstanding the presence of the lake and the marshland of the Math – formed by the Nahr Quweyq, the river of Aleppo, and

Figure 13.1 Ebla, Area Z, razed remains of re-employments and refurbishing of private houses in the Lower City West, 17th century BC.

surviving into the early twentieth century – the settlements of Middle Bronze II certainly did not revive, as we can see from the case of the most important urban centre, under modern Tell Tuqan, which was situated on the western banks of the lake.

So when, shortly after the mid-sixteenth century BC, the Egyptian army of Thutmose I marched through Upper Syria to the Euphrates, Ebla must have been a huge heap of ruins. And when, decades later, the expeditionary corps of the great Thutmose III followed a similar route, this time leaving a detailed account of the cities conquered in the famous list of more than 300 place-names in Palestine and Syria, inscribed on the Seventh Pylon of the great Temple of Amon in Karnak, the sight of the ruins left by the deadly expeditions of the Old Hittite sovereigns and their Hurrian allies cannot have been any less dismal, although some cities of the region must by then have risen again.

In drawing up the famous geographical lists of their conquests which were displayed in the great sanctuaries of Thebes, the aim of the Egyptian authorities was not so much to display to their subjects the names of prestigious, powerful cities of Asia that had been conquered, as to accumulate the place-names of cities and villages that seemed to the Egyptians to be lacking any proper form of government. Consequently, the lists put together both important and insignificant centres with little sense of geographical coherence. Accordingly, among the cities listed on the pylon of Karnak, there is no doubt that, among the once powerful centres, like Karkemish, at the time of Thutmose III still an important city, and Aleppo only slightly less so, Ebla was now a poor village of scattered dwellings of no political or cultural significance.

As a result of the failure of an initial attempt to reconstruct the city, the ruins of the third Ebla, conquered, sacked, and set on fire around 1600 BC, were not even partially removed, but completely abandoned. Particularly where there were monumental buildings, they were plundered for building materials, but they also began to be concealed by accumulations of earth that became more and more a sort of natural protection for the underlying remains. But it is certain that in the Middle Syrian Period, while important centres like Aleppo regained a leading role and minor centres like Alalakh became less significant and yet managed to remain cities, Ebla regressed to the status of a village with no more than a few rural dwellings.

Then as is only normal, when the palatine institutions disappeared and most of the Old Syrian temples were neither rebuilt nor restored, some very popular cult places of the classical Old Syrian Period were adapted and reused in poorer fashion, reduced to little more than local rural sanctuaries. That is probably how Ishtar's Temple on the Citadel became a cult place in the open (Figure 13.2), marked by two basalt standing stones and an offering table also in basalt, and how a very poor temple replaced Ishtar's great public sanctuary in the area sacred to her in the Lower Town. There was certainly religious activity there, albeit much more limited than in the classical Old Syrian Period, and this is also witnessed for the Middle Syrian Period of Late Bronze I by the deposition of simple votive objects in one of the three *favissae* that have been so far identified, which was where worshippers left all kinds of materials used on ceremonial occasions.

Actually, the name of Ebla still appears in a few written sources, though, significantly, only regional ones, even after the last great destruction that certainly ended the city's life and its political power. There are, for example, some scanty references to Ebla in Late Bronze I, in economic texts from the Archives of Alalakh IV, then capital of the small kingdom of Mukish, which was still in the orbit of Aleppo; and, in the last years of Late Bronze II, equally rare citations in the texts of Emar, in the land of Ashtata on the Syrian bank of the Euphrates, now dependent on the Hittite imperial administration.

The region south of Aleppo, between Aleppo and Hamah in inner Syria, which had been dominated by Ebla in previous centuries, was certainly called Nukhashshe in the Middle Syrian decades of the balance of power among the first empires of Mittani, Hatti, and Egypt. After the Hittite expansion to Syria by the great Suppiluliuma I, and the creation of a stable empire of Hatti in the Syrian area, dependent on the control of Karkemish, where a viceroy of Hattusa resided for Syrian affairs, it remained under the constant control of the Hittites (Figure 13.3), even during the conflicts with Egypt, which culminated in the battle of Qadesh in the region of Homs,

Figure 13.2 Ebla, Area D, the cella L.202 of Ishtar's Temple on the Citadel, with the most recent floor, the offering table, and two standing stones, 16th–15th century BC.

and the later stipulation of the famous international Hittite–Egyptian treaty between Hattusili III and Ramses II. In these same years, however, Ebla was referred to in a very different context, in relation to the greatest deity of the city and a much older tradition: a Middle Assyrian ritual discovered in the great Temple of the god Assur in Assur, the capital of Assyria, mentions among the deities still worshipped there, Ishtar *Eblaitu*, the "Ishtar of Ebla", who must still have been a goddess whose fame had spread far beyond the territory of northern Syria, many years after the city had been destroyed.

After these references, which show how the goddess of Ebla's prestige persisted over time, even in the most renowned sanctuaries of Mesopotamia, and also how the great city had declined to a small rural settlement of no political significance and perhaps very few inhabitants, the name of Ebla, in the years of transition from the Bronze Age to the Iron Age, shortly after 1200 BC, finally disappears from the ancient written sources in any kind of document.

Figure 13.3 Sealing with the impression of the stamp seal of an official of the Hittite empire (TM.07.Z.366), clay, from Area Z, 14th–13th century BC.

Even the name had very probably been forgotten in the early centuries of the Iron Age, when, as is clear from some Aramaic sources of the period, the ancient region of Ebla was called La'ash, whose oft-claimed relation with the previous Middle Syrian place-name of Nukhashshe is dubious. Just as Nukhashshe had once been a southern province of the Hittite dominion of Syria, now, despite some fluctuations in territorial control, La'ash must have been, at most, part of the Aramaic kingdom of Hazrek, the same city mentioned in the Assyrian sources as Khatarikka, and identified with what is now Tell Afis, a few kilometres north of Tell Mardikh. It may also have been part of the kingdom of Hamat for short periods, whose capital was on the same spot as the present-day Hamah.

Although the extraordinary extent of the ruins of the old city and the relatively limited areas excavated do not allow absolute certainty as to the extent of the poor rural settlements of the Iron Age, all the data converge to suggest that they covered very little territory indeed during Iron Age I (roughly between 1200 and 900 BC), limited to small areas of the Acropolis. During Iron Age II, which continued until c. 720 BC, the whole region fell under the direct administration of the Assyrian empire, whose previous sovereigns had until then carried out frequent victorious military campaigns, without establishing a province there. The extent of settlement on the Acropolis must have increased, though not markedly, and in the Lower Town, too, simple, poor structures must have been built, scattered here and there in what was now little more than open countryside.

It may be that, as part of basic territorial control by the kings of Hazrek or Hamat, some kind of fortress or watch-tower was built in this period in the western region of the Acropolis, whose eminence provided an ample view of the north Syrian region, probably as far as the southern borders of the territory, controlled, in the north, by the Aramaic principality of Bit Agushi, which, though its capital was Arpad, certainly included the city of Aleppo, its citadel, and its spectacular, ancient Temple of Hadad, with its extraordinary monuments. The Iron Age II settlement, which corresponds to the phase of Mardikh VB, may have been a poor village on the Acropolis, and scattered dwellings were built in the Lower Town, though not even reasonably well-preserved buildings have been found there, but only fragments of structures, whose building materials were clearly taken from the ruins of the classical Old Syrian city that were still visible everywhere. It is precisely this evident reusing of boulders and blocks which shows that the reason for this sporadic, uncoordinated occupation of the Lower Town in the Aramaic age must have depended almost entirely on the availability of stones ready to hand.

Very probably, there were no particular changes in the period following Iron Age III, between 720 and 535 BC, when the Persians must have been starting to establish organized territorial control of western Syria, after entering Babylon in triumph in 539 BC, with Cyrus the Great at their head, victorious over the forces of the last Neo-Babylonian sovereign Nabonidus. In the last century of Assyrian dominion and the decades in which the Neo-Babylonian empire of the Chaldean Dynasty simply assumed the legacy of the Assyrian empire in the Syro-Palestinian area (corresponding to Iron Age III), the urban system of the Luwian and Aramaic principalities finally broke up, under attack by the great sovereigns of Assyria, all forms of city life in inner Syria disappearing. The consequences for the rural settlements are difficult to assess, but between the mid-eighth and the late seventh centuries BC, the kings of Assyria frequently deported, if not masses, then at least populations of a certain size, from one region or province of the empire to another. This probably caused a crisis in the rural centres too, partially depopulating at least some areas of the empire to the advantage of others and, in particular, to the advantage of the now extensive metropolitan urban centres of Assyria, which had thus become cosmopolitan.

This may have caused a decline in population or further impoverishment of regions close to the less fertile steppe-land, and it is not unlikely that in various parts of the Syro-Palestinian area those who had previously led a sedentary life turned to pastoralism. The scantiness and uncertainty of the traces of settlements in Iron Age III in the phase of Mardikh VC may be a direct consequence of this general situation of degradation in the rural areas too, after the collapse of city life that marked the end of Iron Age II, in the years around 720 BC.

When the Persian-Greek Age began shortly after the mid-sixth century BC (corresponding to the phases of Mardikh VIA–B), the situation of the rural settlement of Tell Mardikh may have gradually changed, with some resumption of relatively organized human groups. This may have depended, first of all, on the policy of the lords of the Achaemenid Empire, fairly well known from the information in the Bible but also confirmed by other sources, of allowing, if not actually encouraging, the return of the populations deported by the Assyrians and the Babylonians to their regions of origin. As a result of this policy, though there does not seem to have been any serious renaissance of city life in inner Syria, it is very likely that in the country there was a renewed sedentarism of limited family groups, in places where previously there had been abandoned or impoverished villages of Iron Age II–III.

While a limited resumption of settlements that is still difficult to estimate in percentage terms seems to have marked the general situation in inner Syria and, in particular, the impoverished site of Mardikh VIA in the early Persian Age, the Acropolis of Tell Mardikh seems to have become increasingly rural during the fifth century BC, a trend that continued in the following century. On the north-eastern side of the Acropolis, in the highest region, a quite striking rural residence began to be built and then extended and modified. It had significant stone structures, clearly deriving from the ancient ruins that were still visible everywhere, and about 15 rooms around a central courtyard. This is what has been described as the Persian Residence of Mardikh VIA (Figure 13.4), which was a fairly long building, about 25 m by 32 m with rooms of varying size, that surrounded an elongated and slightly irregular rectangular courtyard, with a larger front entrance on the south-east side and a smaller back entrance on the northern corner.

Structurally simple as a concept, the Persian Residence might have been inspired by provincial buildings from the previous Assyrian Period, but, given the extreme simplicity of its design and a certain irregularity in its execution, it should probably be regarded as the enlargement of a domestic rural dwelling of no particular character that belongs to a cultivated Aramaic, Assyrian, or Persian architectural tradition. Three major aspects mark the archaeological context of this rural residence from the Achaemenid Period. The first was the lack of qualitatively or quantitatively significant imported materials, which shows that the settlement of Mardikh VIA was relatively isolated both from the wealthier Mediterranean coastal cities, and from the trading centres, where there were certainly Greek communities involved in trade and commerce with the western satraps of the empire. The second was the frequency of the production of clay figurines, particularly the type of terracotta figurines known as "Persian knights" (Figure 13.5) with the schematic figures of hand-modelled horses and

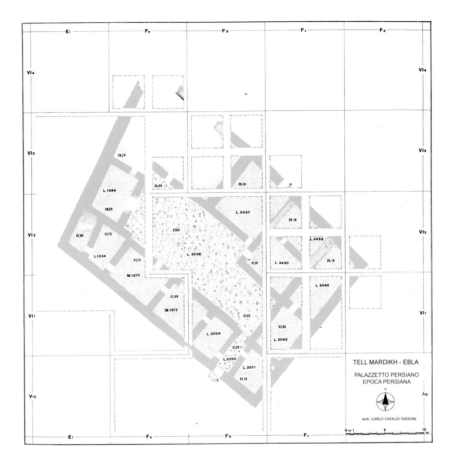

Figure 13.4 Tell Mardikh, Area E, schematic plan of the Persian Residence, in the north-east sector of the top of the Acropolis, 6th–4th century BC.

the typical bearded faces, as well as front-facing female images, naked or, more often, with ceremonial clothes and head-gear, both made from moulds, which suggests a close connection of the local rural community and Achaemenid provincial ruling groups. The third was the abundance of loom weights and other tools for spinning and weaving, which indicate the presence in the small rural settlement of textile production evidently superior to the requirements of the community itself.

If we add that one seriously argued theory regards the secondary repopulation of areas of northern Syria and the arduous rebirth of rural life in those regions in the Persian Age as depending on the creation of landed estates in the hands of Persian nobles in this period in the area west of the Euphrates, we might think that the remarkable residence of Mardikh VIA should be

Figure 13.5, a & b Figurines of "Persian horse-men" (TM.65.E.153, TM.71.E.550), clay, from Area E, 5th–4th century BC.

connected with organized farming and textiles production, in the context of an economy that exploited the resident rural populations under the responsibility of delegates of the Persian aristocracy.

In the later period of Mardikh VIB, during the decades of Greek domination after 325 BC, rustic dwellings were built that made up a small village scattered over quite a considerable part of the Acropolis up to the southern areas of the hill. It may be, then, that once the system of relatively centralized feudal exploitation in the Persian Age had been abandoned, the successors of those inhabitants managed to make the small settlement flourish for some time, in ways that were probably no different from those of rural life in the centuries of Aramaic rule that were ended by the Assyrian devastations. Before the Roman general Pompey reduced Syria to the status of a Roman province, the village of Mardikh VIB was probably abandoned (apparently during the second century BC), perhaps as part of a powerful movement of urbanization, caused by the constant foundations of new important urban centres during the government of the Seleucids, particularly, but not only, in the regions close to the Mediterranean coast.

Though no significant traces have been found so far of constructions from the Imperial Roman Age, indicating a possible hiatus in the settlement in Tell Mardikh during much of the first two centuries of the empire, in the third century AD, sporadic, but telling evidence emerges, particularly in numismatics, of human settlement of the extended area of ruins delimited by the prominence of the imposing ramparts. Very probably, between the fourth and the seventh centuries AD, in a clearly defined area of the huge field of ruins at the western foot of the Acropolis, a small community of Byzantine Christian eremites was established there who tried to follow St Simeon Stylite's spectacular and fascinating example of rigorous asceticism in the fifth century AD, which he had practised only a few kilometres further west, as is shown in a crudely engraved stone, found lying in Tell Mardikh, with the schematic image of a monk ascending a column.

Some features typical of the poor stylite hermitages in the region, such as a well connected with a tank, as well as fragments of paving and the remains of scattered low columns suggest that it was a very small community of eremites who had established themselves, as often happened, among ancient ruins. These fragmentary, poorly preserved surface remains surmount an unusual base about 3 m high, entirely built with blocks openly plundered from the surrounding ruins of the Western Palace, above the ruins of the far eastern sector of that building, which had been razed to the ground. The choice of place for the hermitage in the extensive area of the ruins of the old urban centre must have been suggested by the presence in the immediate vicinity of the tombs of the Royal Necropolis of Middle Bronze I–II. Indeed, while one of the tombs was found completely emptied and without any trace of the pillaging, fragments of tiles and a few shards from the Byzantine period were found in another that had also been badly despoiled, indicating that the rich hypogea of the early and classical Old Syrian Necropolis were certainly pillaged and reused quite often in this period.

After the Arab conquest of Syria by Khalid ibn al-Walid, with the decisive defeat of the Byzantine army in the pitched battle of Yarmuk in 636 AD, under the caliphate of Omar, the Christian hermitage was probably abandoned in the space of a few years, and in the same area of Tell Mardikh, in a place as yet unidentified, or perhaps outside the area of the former settlement, a place of Islamic worship was built. This must certainly have been the source of the fine squared blocks that have been found, dating from the ninth or tenth century AD, some with schematic Arabic inscriptions in Kufic characters in praise of Allah. A number of them were removed and reused in a wall (Figure 13.6) that barred the entrance to the ancient Damascus Gate of the great classical Old Syrian centre, which was clearly still partly visible at the time the structure was built, with the aim of impeding access to the tell from the south-west.

Now, if we consider that using blocks with religious inscriptions in Arabic (Figure 13.7) in a wall is clearly a secondary use for them, and that in several cases that use was at odds with the sense of the writing, thus clearly indicating that those who built the barrier in which they were used cannot have been Muslims, it is reasonable to wonder who exactly was responsible for the slapdash closure of the entrance to the South-West Gate of the ancient city, which had been destroyed in the seventeenth century BC.

A plausible answer to this seemingly difficult problem may be found in the sources for the Crusades, which are unanimous that a significant expeditionary

Figure 13.6 Tell Mardikh, Area A, the closure of the Islamic Period through the Damascus Gate towards the west rampart, from the west, 9th–10th century AD.

force in the First Crusade stopped for a few weeks in the very region of Tell Mardikh, between September and December 1098. After the small centre of al-Bara fell into their hands in September 1098, a force of Crusaders had decided to head for Jerusalem from Antioch via inner Syria, unlike the main expedition, which followed the coastal route. They stopped between al-Bara and the important city of Ma'arret an-Nu'man, about 20 kilometres south of Tell Mardikh, to prepare for a siege on the city: in a notorious bloodbath that was execrated throughout the Arab world, Ma'arret an-Nu'man fell on 11 December 1098.

It is, then, extremely likely that some detachments, if not the entire expeditionary force of the Crusaders, found the site of Tell Mardikh particularly suitable as a temporary military camp for a few weeks before launching the attack on the southern city, by virtue of its particular structure, with the high ramparts that completely surrounded the place, forming a kind of ideal natural defence, and with the Acropolis that could serve as an excellent watchtower. To improve the natural defences of the site, it is plausible that they

Figure 13.7 Tell Mardikh, Area A, detail of a slab with Kufic inscription in praise of
Allah, limestone, 9th–10th century AD.

decided to bar access from one or more of the old city gates, and it is no
surprise that the materials they used for this purpose, complete with pious
inscriptions, were found by demolishing a sacred Islamic place nearby, something no Muslim would have done.

It is, then, highly probable that the army of Crusaders led by Raymond of
Saint Gilles, Robert of Flanders, and Bohemond of Antioch, in the autumn of
1098 camped inside the ancient walls of Tell Mardikh, while it organized the
siege of Ma'arret an-Nu'man and prepared to probe, by heading south, the
resistance of the Arab princes of inner Syria on the road that was to lead to
Jerusalem. And it is certainly significant that the first reliable written witness
of the singular and unexplained place-name which to this day still indicates
the vast field of ruins of the old city – Mardikh – appears in a chronicle of the
Crusades in that period.

Appendix

The Royal Palace of the Archives, Area G (Early Bronze IVA)

The extensive complex of the Royal Palace of the Archives (Area G) was identified in 1973 and gradually excavated in the following years: intensively between 1974 and 1990 and then in smaller, limited, and peripheral sectors over the following years, with further intensive work between 2002 and 2007 in the ceremonial, administrative, and storage regions. The palace included a very large complex of architectural structures which must have covered most of the Acropolis, probably built on the natural limestone outcrop of the original settlement above the superimpositions of previous settlements. The Royal Palace structures may well have extended over an area of at least 20,000 square metres (and probably more), whereas the area excavated to date comprises some 4,500 square metres and lies in the south-west region of the entire palace complex, where stood what was in all likelihood the only entrance to the palace.

The part we know of the Royal Palace of the mature Early Syrian Period can be divided into the following sectors: the Central Complex with the Monumental Gateway, which extended largely over the Acropolis and was by far the largest area; the Administrative Quarter with the Throne Room, the Court of Audience, the Northern Quarter, and the rooms housing the Royal Archives, which was basically a peripheral sector on the south-west slopes of the Acropolis; and the Southern Quarter, with the Hall of Painted Plaster, simply a small annex at the south-west foot of the Acropolis.

The Central Complex (Figure 14.1) was probably a series of structures the major cores of which would have been in the northern and central areas of the hill of the Acropolis. Only very peripheral parts have been excavated, on the south-western and southern slopes of the Acropolis, and on the western edge of the hill; the Monumental Gateway, a stairway some 22 m long, compensating for the 5 m difference in height between the Court of Audience and the western units on the Acropolis; the Kitchens of the Court of Audience, which opened onto the north side of the Monumental Gateway; the West Unit, the westernmost sector on the edge of the Acropolis; the North-West

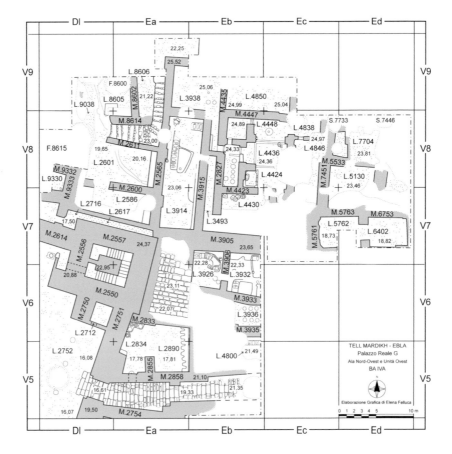

Figure 14.1 Ebla, Royal Palace G, schematic plan of the North-West Wing and of the West Unit of the Central Complex on the Acropolis, 24th century BC.

Wing, a small sector on the steep western slope of the Acropolis, north of the Court of Audience; and the South Unit, which was on the upper sector of the Acropolis's southern slope, north-east of the Southern Quarter.

The Monumental Gateway opened through the eastern wall of the Court of Audience north of the Administrative Quarter with which, however, it did not communicate. The 2.70 m-wide access led into a long west–east passageway, L.2753, slightly misaligned to the east, which led to the south-western area of the Central Complex, the various sectors of which, as yet unexplored and probably in a poor state of conservation given the superimposed constructions of Middle Bronze I and II, must, however, have risen to increasingly higher levels towards the north, as demonstrated by the successive terracing from south to north. The Court of Audience Kitchens, accessed through the only door opening into the north side of the Gateway, included a small vestibule,

L.2834, opening into a large room, L.2890, against the eastern wall of which were aligned more than eight fire-places, some of them still with their large shattered cooking pots inside. The West Unit was composed of a number of rooms on the terracing sloping from north to south, that had to be reached by means of a south–north ramp, which almost certainly was to the east of the area explored. The lower, southernmost rooms, L.3936 and L.3932, already had a 1.10 m difference in level, while the central ones such as the long room L.3914 were 1.70 m higher, and the upper rooms on the highest level, such as L.3938, were built on a further terrace, 1.50 m higher. All these rooms, covering a surface of some 250 square metres, were equipped with various fittings, benches, and small basins for the grinding of cereals. The North-West Wing, halfway down the slope of the hill, would seem to have included only two large rooms extending east–west, L.2586 and L.2601, on the floor of the first of which were found the first 42 tablets discovered in the building; the second produced various parts of precious carved and inlaid timber furniture; nothing similar was found anywhere else in the palace. The only access to these rooms was by means of a sharply angled staircase to the north, apparently only communicating with the areas on the top of the Acropolis near the West Unit, although the two rooms were situated against the northern wall of the huge Court of Audience, in its turn, however, somewhat lower down, at the same level as the Lower Town at the foot of the Acropolis. Only a 30 m extension of the South Unit in the Central Complex (Figure 14.3) has been excavated, on the east–west axis, in the upper sector of the southern slopes of the Acropolis, some 70 m away from the West Unit and some 25 m from the Southern Quarter, with eight rather irregular small rooms, all containing benches holding numerous jars and much smaller vases: to date no direct connection has been found with any other sector of the Royal Palace. All of these areas, from L.3518 to the east to L.3464 to the west, were adjacent with a thick east–west terracing wall, M.3470, and were placed at gradually higher levels from east to west, as if giving onto a northern staircase or ramp.

The best-preserved sector, more thoroughly explored with respect to its original extension, and consequently better known, is the complex including the Court of Audience, the Northern Quarter, the Ceremonial Staircase, and the Administrative Quarter, including the rooms of the Royal Archives (Figure 14.2). The Court of Audience was a large, open space, L.2752, with porches on at least two sides, the north and the east, which have been excavated and are partially preserved. The Court would have been some 42 m wide and with a possible length of no less than 60 m, though this can only be inferred. The columns, approximately 4 m apart, were fixed in the floor and rested on a limestone base sunk 0.50 m into the earth; two antae emerging from the tower of the Ceremonial Staircase mark the eastern point of juncture of the northern porch (L.2715) and the northern edge of the eastern one. An almost perfectly preserved rectangular dais most probably stood in the middle of the north side, to hold the throne, with steps only at the centre of the west and south sides. Before the

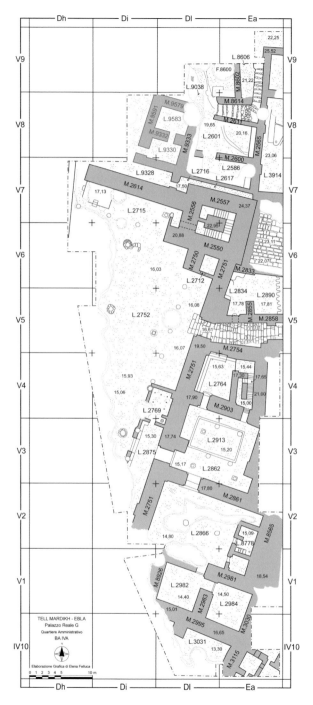

Figure 14.2 Ebla, Royal Palace G, schematic plan of the Administrative Quarter and of the Court of Audience on the west slope of the Acropolis, 24th century BC.

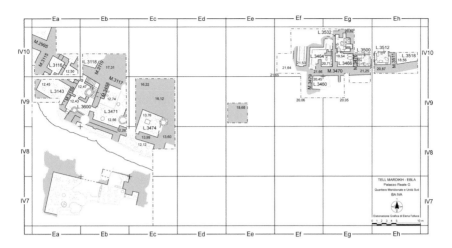

Figure 14.3 Ebla, Royal Palace G, schematic plan of the Southern Quarter with the Hall of Painted Plaster (Area FF), and the South Unit of the Central Complex on the south slope of the Acropolis, 24th century BC.

entrance to the Monumental Gateway was found a very fine round basalt well-curb, well-preserved and in place, rectangular on the inside; this would have decorated the mouth of a large cistern collecting the water conveyed in a wide channel which ran the whole length of the Gateway staircase, draining the rain water from the Acropolis. Four doors of different import-ance opened into the Court of Audience. The most significant was without doubt the Monumental Gateway, the public entrance to the Central Complex, which opened in the north sector of the eastern façade; some 18 m to the south, also on the eastern porch, was the remarkable entrance to the Administrative Quarter, while of no less importance was the door at the east end of the northern porch which led to the Ceremonial Staircase. On the other hand, near the west side of the royal dais, the entrance to the warehouses of the Northern Quarter, which opened behind the northern porch, was merely functional.

The Ceremonial Staircase was the first feature brought to light in the Royal Palace. This was enclosed in a high tower, 7.40 m of which are still standing, including walls M.2550, M.2556, M.2557, M.2751, and three of its perfectly preserved brick ramps (the fourth, which collapsed, was certainly suspended). All the steps of the ramps were decorated with wooden boards, inlaid with mother-of-pearl tesserae, forming stylized floral motifs: many of these were found in place. The lower door of the Ceremonial Staircase opened directly onto the short side of the northern porch of the Court, where the royal dais stood, while the upper door, obviously lost, must have led to a second floor, built above the Court Kitchens, giving access to the upper quarters of the Central Complex.

The Northern Quarter, extending to the north of the northern side of the Court of Audience, seems to have had its only access through the small door, opening immediately to the west of the royal dais, of the Court's northern porch; its rooms were all on the same level as the Court. It consisted in a long east–west room, L.9328, parallel to the north wall of the Court, M.2614; this first room then opened into a narrow corridor including rooms L.2716 and L.2617, the roof of which was the floor of room L.2586 of the North-West Wing of the Central Complex. These corridors were found full of pottery, often containing fragments of the sealings used on jars and caskets, with several impressions of cylinder seals. L.9328 then opened into a south–north oriented room, only partly excavated, leading into the large room L.9330 and the parallel L.9583. In the latter were found the well-preserved miniature statuettes of two queens, one seated and one standing, in wood, gold, silver, steatite, marble, and jasper, which must have belonged to a royal woman's standard.

The Administrative Quarter is a large, trapezoidal, and basic palace structure, extending for 44 m on the south–north axis and for 23 m on the east–west axis, between the eastern porch of the Court of Audience, built against the side of the 2.80 metre-wide M.2751, and the massive south–north terrace wall, M.8565, reached, as stated above, only through a minor, independent entrance in the eastern portico, to the south of the Monumental Gateway. Built at the level of the Lower Town at the foot of the Acropolis, against the terracing wall constructed to block the archaic levels of the older settlement on the hill, the Quarter was conceived according to a uniform project, and was an organic and compact building with high walls. Probably in a later phase a small, covered vestibule was added, including two rooms, obtained by connecting the wooden columns of the eastern porch of the Court of Audience with walls of the width of a single row of mud bricks. This extraordinarily important vestibule was accessed through an entrance paved with beautiful basalt slabs, with two steps decorated in mother-of-pearl floral motifs. It included a larger room, L.2875, with low benches against the west wall and the west stretch of the north wall, and a smaller room, L.2769, 5.30 m long and 3.50 m wide communicating with the first room. L.2769, with its west, north, and east walls covered with three wooden shelves, was the so-called Main Archive, since it stored the 15,500 inventory numbers of the Royal Archives cuneiform tablets (Figure 14.4). The Small Archive (Figure 14.5), L.2712, on the other hand, was a small room, created by building a wall only one brick thick, at the northern end of the same eastern porch: the cuneiform tablets stored there, broken into pieces corresponding to some 900 inventory numbers, were housed on two separate suspended shelves, clear traces of which remain on the scorched plaster of two of the walls.

The Administrative Quarter extended from the staircase of the Monumental Gateway to the north to the independent Southern Quarter to the south

Figure 14.4 Ebla, Royal Palace G, the room of the main Archive L.2769, with holes for the supports of the wooden shelves, from the west, 24th century BC.

Figure 14.5 Ebla, Royal Palace G, the room of the Small Archive L.2712, with the traces of the shelves, from the south-west, 24th century BC.

(Figure 14.2). The complex divided into rooms to the north and south of a small inner courtyard, L.2913, 10 m by 12 m, accessed directly from the outer vestibule of the eastern porch, and probably presenting porches with four columns like those of the Court of Audience, here supporting a covered gallery on all four sides. To the north of courtyard L.2913, in the west, was the so-called Trapezoid Archive, L.2764, with high benches on two of the walls and a small eastern storage room, and in the east a four-ramp staircase, leading to the second floor and the covered gallery of the courtyard. The structure of the southern sector was differently articulated, with more space allocated to very important functions and undoubtedly of considerable height, probably similar to that of the northern sector, although of one floor only. The south side of courtyard L.2913, where the porch L.2862 was situated, led to the largest room in the whole Royal Palace, L.2866, some 16 m wide by 10 m long, badly damaged only in the south-west corner. Three small rooms were added inside this large hall, by means of thin partition walls, one brick thick, to the south L.8495 and to the north L.8778 and L.8496, where a number of tablets were found covering accounts in the last months of the city's life. Two large columns on the east–west axis supported the roofing, with an intercolumniation of approximately 4.80/5.10 m; a door, slightly out of axis towards the east with respect to the central intercolumniation, opened on the south wall, M.2981, leading to two small, almost square rooms, L.2982 and L.2984, adjacent to each other on the south wall of the complex and without doors to the south. As in the northern porch of the Court of Audience, there was most probably a dais for the king's throne in the middle of the south wall of room L.2866: in this case, the position of the throne dais, of the two minor square rooms, and of the entrance to them in the Administrative Quarter is fully corresponding with that of the north porch of the Court of Audience. This similarity suggests that the two rooms situated behind the large hall were store-rooms, which is proved by the discovery of a large quantity of raw lapis lazuli in these rooms, particularly in that to the west, L.2982, with several fragments of inlaid panels and composite statuettes in limestone, lapis lazuli, steatite, and gold leaf. The large hall L.2866, with the two minor square rooms behind, seems without doubt to have been the Throne Room of the complex, with temporary store-rooms for the safekeeping of precious goods belonging to the palace administration.

In the area to the south of the Administrative Quarter the poor condition of the remains of the mature Early Syrian Period, caused by the superimposition of the Old Syrian Citadel's inner fortifications, makes it impossible to propose a plausible reconstruction for the remnants of peripheral sectors of the palace complex. This is particularly true of room L.3031, south of L.2982 and L.2984 but not communicating with them, making it a somewhat enigmatic annex, albeit monumental; the entrance was probably to the south or west, and thus independent of the Administrative Quarter.

To the east of the substantial south–north wall M.3115 rose the Southern Quarter, which, with an irregular succession of rather small rooms – L.3143,

L.3116, L.3600, the courtyard L.3471 and L.3474 – and by means of thin walls, seems to have formed, to the north, a group of minor rooms with galleries, very close to a massive east–west terracing wall, M.3117, with, further south, a number of wider, intermediate rooms, badly damaged by the superimposition of the inner fortification wall of the Old Syrian Citadel (M.3606), and lastly, further south, at least one large, enigmatic hall, L.8729 + 8613, badly preserved beneath the Old Syrian road which surrounded the Citadel. This peculiar hall was some 18 m on the east–west axis and 8.50 m from south to north (unless there had originally been a central partition wall, now completely removed), and was curiously arranged with three wide and deep niches in the eastern sector; here, in the western sector, were found numerous fragments of painted wall decoration, with various geometric motifs on white stucco, which must have fallen from a large, multi-recessed niche probably high on the west wall. This hall with three niches is what has been named the Hall of Painted Plaster.

The whole of Royal Palace G, in all its structures and outbuildings, from the sectors of the top of the Acropolis to the base of the small hill, was badly sacked and plundered at the time of the destruction which ended the life of Mardikh IIB1's great city, which was then set on fire; the very visible traces of this are everywhere. While there are indications that at least one important area, the Throne Room L.2866, was extensively excavated immediately after the fire, then rapidly covered over, there is no trace of any reuse or reconstruction of other parts of the destroyed palatine complex, which was seemingly abandoned beneath the massive walls which collapsed or were demolished during the sacking and the fire.

The Temple of the Rock, Area HH (Early Bronze IVA)

Occupying a topographically peripheral position in the mature Early Syrian urban pattern, a short distance from the south-east city gate, the Temple of the Rock (Area HH) is an imposing monument (Figure 14.6), excavated between 2004 and 2007. With the Red Temple, it is to date the only cult building identified as being from the Archives age, and the only one which it has been possible to excavate in its entirety. The reason for its name is two-fold. Not only was it built directly on the rock, which was possibly slightly raised in that area compared with the rest of the city, but inside both the cella and the vestibule the rock was never levelled out, thus incorporating, no doubt intentionally, cavities which must have had particular mythical, natural, or historical significance.

Situated with its entrance to the east, towards sunrise, the Temple of the Rock was a massive, imposing structure, with the typology of *in antis* façade and broad cella, 28 m long and some 21.50 m wide, its walls a consistent 6 m wide. The structure is simple and consists in a cella, L.9190, and vestibule, L.9495, of the same size – both are large rooms developed latitudinally, so wider (10 m) than they were long (8.30 m). Another peculiarity was the

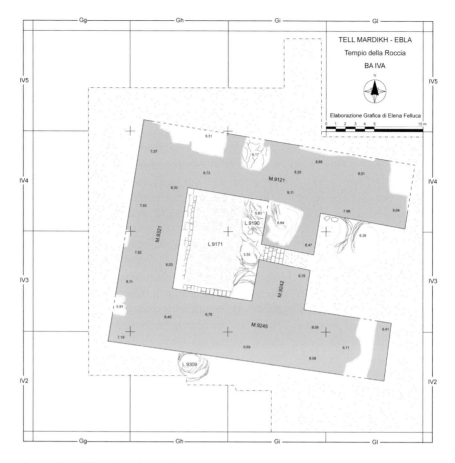

Figure 14.6 Ebla, Temple of the Rock (Temple HH), schematic plan of the mature
Early Syrian cult building, 24th century BC.

door connecting cella and vestibule, which was only 1.40 m wide but more
than 3.50 m in height, and opened in the middle of the dividing wall, a hefty
5.60 m wide. As regards structure, though the irregularities of the underlying
rock thwarted any uniformity of technical characteristics, the building had
stone foundations, mostly great basalt and limestone blocks of an average
height of some 0.80/1.20 m; the bricks used to raise the thick perimeter walls
were the rectangular type used in the mature Early Syrian Period; that is,
some 0.60 by 0.40 by 0.10 m. The flooring of the cella, which must have
been all but destroyed when the whole Mardikh IIB1 city was sacked, was
covered by a thin layer of gypsum plaster, applied to the only partially levelled rock: indeed, in the north-east corner a completely unlevelled section of
rock emerges. The structure of the stone foundation and the extraordinary
width of the perimeter walls, this last identical in both the side and back

walls, the opposite of normative practice in successive Old Syrian temples, all indicate that the temple had a considerable height, probably of some 15 m. Singularly, in the cella L.9190, which has been completely excavated, a large oval cavity opened in the rock, in the western part, against the back wall M.9321, near the edges of which were three wells, P.9719 to the west, P.9717 to the north, and P.9713 to the south, which most probably went down to the water-bearing stratum. There is no doubt that the three wells date back to the founding of the temple, nor that the cella was built there precisely on account of the wells, while the cavity might have been dug at the time of the destruction. After the ravaging destruction of the end of Early Bronze IVA, of which no traces remain in the building other than, curiously, in the door space between antecella and cella, the temple seems to have been meticulously cleared of all rubble and wreckage. At the beginning of Early Bronze IVB, the cella, in particular, was filled in with some 15 layers of mud bricks which formed a very effective sealing, possibly to protect it from further profanation. A number of other interventions – not precisely restoration but certainly containment strategies against structural collapse – probably belong to the same period: for example, the strange one-brick-thick layer of mud bricks around the south and west façades of the original structure and, to the east, masonry, again in mud bricks, added against the antae of the façade limiting the vestibule.

The location of the imposing remains of the monument of the mature Early Syrian city, which must have formed a small hillock some 4 m high, maintained all its sacrality for the inhabitants of the later cities. In a central and advanced phase of Early Bronze IVB, in fact, Temple HH4 (Figure 14.7) was built over the ruins of the south side of the vestibule of the older structure, a new considerable *in antis* building, with long cella L.9483, and a vestibule, L.9474, of some length, though shorter than the cella, similarly with its entrance facing the east. The temple is 17.30 m long and 10.90 m wide; the cella is 8.10 m long and 6.50 m wide, while the vestibule, unlike the Temple of the Rock, was only 5.20 m long but, like the cella, 6.50 m wide; the width of the perimeter walls, identical for all three, as in the Temple of the Rock, in opposition to the future norm in Old Syrian temples, was between 2.30 m and 2.10 m. The two low monolithic column bases in basalt, 1.10 m in diameter, probably reused in the classical Old Syrian Temple HH2, may well have been placed on the front of the late Early Syrian temple, at the entrance to the vestibule. Temple HH4, technically rather more unassuming than the Temple of the Rock, was badly destroyed and nowhere stands at more than 0.40 m. It had low stone foundations consisting of one row of small and medium-sized blocks, which collapsed at various points, and was built of irregular mud bricks mainly of the old 0.40 m by 0.60 m by 0.10 m format, although occasionally square and above all relatively thin at 5/7 cm.

Soon after Temple HH4 had been built, immediately to the north and in parallel with it, a second, identically oriented minor cult building was

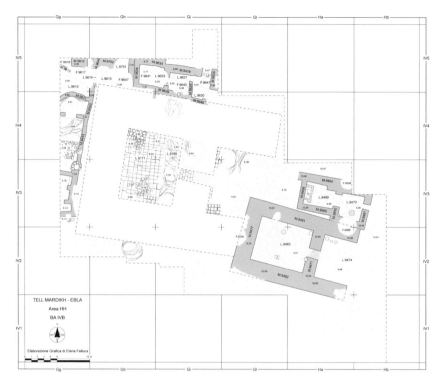

Figure 14.7 Ebla, Temples HH4 and HH5, schematic plan of the late Early Syrian cult
buildings, 23rd–21st century BC.

completed, Temple HH5. This was only 10.50 m long and 5.50 m wide, with a
longitudinal cella (L.9469) 4.50 m by 3.25 m, preceded by a shorter, irregular
vestibule (L.9470) – hardly definable as a temple *in antis*, since the vestibule
was closed off by a transversal wall, through which the entrance door opened.
A dais in mud bricks, seemingly once a low basin, stands at the centre of the
back wall of this small cella, in what appears more as a large votive chapel,
with an almost square vestibule, than an actual traditional temple. To the
same late Early Syrian phase of Temples HH4 and HH5, belong the very
scant and razed remains of rooms discovered to the north of the cult complex, and the majority of the pits dug at the top of the still emerging ruins of
the Temple of the Rock.

A large, tripartite Temple, HH3, possibly from the beginning of the archaic
Old Syrian Period, was erected over the almost totally razed Temple HH4,
again in the front, southern part of the large, oldest sanctuary, and similarly
facing east. This, in its turn, was destroyed, its materials removed and for the
most part lost. Over its ruins, during Middle Bronze II, was built Temple HH2,
the last cult building on the spot, belonging to the classical Old Syrian Period.

The Red Temple, Area D (Early Bronze IVA)

Built on the west side of the Acropolis, the Red Temple (Area D) overlooked the whole western Lower Town of the mature Early Syrian settlement, like the later Old Syrian Ishtar's Temple built exactly over its ruins during Middle Bronze I. It must have been founded in a central phase of Early Bronze IVA, as the structures of its front part overlie the razed ruins of the northern periphery of the West Unit of Royal Palace G's Central Complex, which had to be levelled to make room for part of the temple and a clearing in front of its façade. Partially identified in 1968, the Red Temple (Temple D2), so-defined on account of the intense, rather pure red clay of the mud bricks of its walls, was excavated completely in 2008, when it was possible to recover all the most significant planimetric and architectural elements east and west of Ishtar's Temple and in the cella, antecella, and vestibule of that building, which almost exactly over-laid the ruins of the older temple.

The entrance to the Red Temple (Figure 14.8), like that of the later Ishtar's Temple (Temple D) and indeed the majority of Ebla's Old Syrian temples, faced south. The construction, erected on foundations comprising two rows of medium-sized stones, was an isolated cult building, with an *in antis* façade, characterized by a slightly elongated cella, a rather deep vestibule, and the presence of two columns in the vestibule, forming a front porch, and four columns in the cella, dividing it into three small naves. The bases of the columns of the porch and the two front bases of the cella columns were formed from two large and approximately cylindrical blocks, which were slightly thicker in the centre. Being 1.20 m high and some 1.05/1.15 m in diameter, these were completely sunk into the floor, and were found in place, while the two other bases of the cella columns were discovered elsewhere, one reused in the masonry of the later Ishtar's Temple, the other lying close to the entrance to the sanctuary. The Red Temple was slightly wider and shorter than Ishtar's Temple above: some 24.20 m long and 17 m wide, with a consistent width of 3.80 m in its perimeter walls. Although it was only possible to ascertain the width of perimeter wall M.9902, in a very limited sample, given that the inner side of the eastern wall M.9900 is below Ishtar's Temple for the whole of its length, the four columns of the cella could only have been located at the same distance from the inner sides of those to the north and south, if the back wall too, equally completely concealed by the massive stone foundations of Ishtar's Temple, had had an identical width. The width of the central wall dividing vestibule and cella, M.9979, where it was possible to recover part of the communicating door between the two rooms, must have been about 3.50/3.60 m wide – slightly narrower than the perimeter walls, as in the contemporary Temple of the Rock. Unlike all Ebla's other Early and Old Syrian temples known to us, the four outside corners of the main structure of the Red Temple, both at the front, in the façade antae, and at the back, in the perimeter walls of the cella,

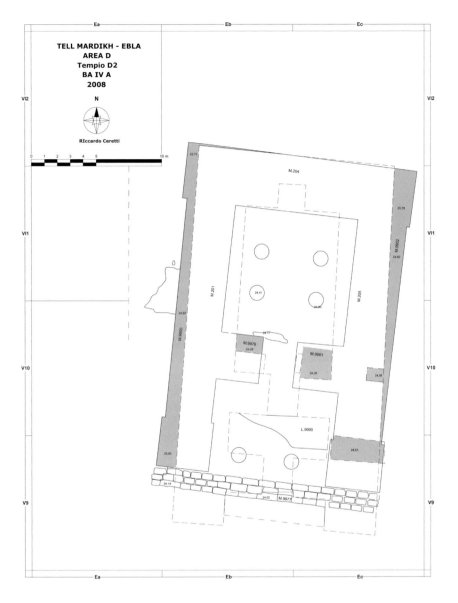

Figure 14.8 Ebla, Red Temple (Temple D2), schematic plan of the mature Early
   Syrian cult building related to the later Ishtar's Temple, 24th century BC.

presented a slight but regular and consistent structural projection of some
0.20/0.30 m in width, forming low, angular buttresses nearly of the same
size on each side. In all, then, the Red Temple included a front vestibule
with porch, L.9990, 6.70 m long by 9.40 m wide, and a four-columned cella,

L.9980, which was slightly longer (c. 10.20 m) than it was wide (c. 9.40 m). The short central nave of cella L.9980 was c. 3.40 m wide, while the two lateral naves had a width of approximately 2 m.

As already stated, the Red Temple must date from Early Bronze IVA, and it is possible that accounts in the Royal Archives, exceptionally mentioning a considerable amount of silver for Kura's Temple, recorded a large sum to complete the construction of the building. The floor of vestibule L.9990 rested on a ballast of medium-sized stones, mixed in with several ceramic fragments from the beginning of Early Bronze IVA, above all fragments of the typical storage jars in Royal Palace G, with triple-grooved rims, clearly from the razing of the West Unit of Royal Palace G's Central Complex. Almost no trace remains of the destruction of the mature Early Syrian temple, as its levelled ruins were covered over by the considerably more modest Early Bronze IVB temple, but there is no doubt as to its having been sacked and destroyed in the devastation at the end of Early Bronze IVA.

A new temple was built in the central area of the Red Temple ruins, in an indeterminable but probably initial phase of Early Bronze IVB: considerably smaller in size, it was also above all planimetrically and spatially very different from its mature Early Syrian predecessor. This sanctuary of the late Early Syrian Period, on the Acropolis, Temple D3 (Figure 14.9), had a broad and not long cella, and an antecella which was also wide but even shorter. The dimensions of the cella, c. 6.50 m in width and only 3 m in length, and those of the antecella, of the same width and only 2.50 m long, are known for certain, while the thickness of the perimeter walls can only be inferred (c. 2 m), based on the likelihood that, as in the Temple of the Rock and the successive Temple HH4, they would have been slightly thicker than the dividing wall of the cella and antecella, M.9914 + M.9916 (known to be c. 1.90 m).

Other, less probable, solutions can be proposed as regards Temple D3's plan, but the most plausible would seem to be that of an originally tripartite temple with vestibule, antecella, and cella, with *in antis* façade, axial entrances, and a latitudinally developed cella. According to this very feasible reconstruction of the late Early Syrian Temple D3, this must have been a modest construction, c. 13.50 m in length and c. 10.50 m in width.

Temple D3, with its elevation of light-brown bricks, considerably poorer than their reddish counterparts in the older Red Temple, and constructed on weak foundations of medium-sized stones, was almost certainly destroyed at the end of Early Bronze IVB, razed and filled in to make way for the robust stone foundations of Ishtar's Temple, built certainly no later than a central phase of Middle Bronze I.

The Archaic Palace, Area P (Early Bronze IVB)

This palace, founded in Early Bronze IVB, was discovered during soundings in 1993 of the Sector P North of the Lower Town, immediately to the north of the Northern Palace of the classical Old Syrian city, and systematically

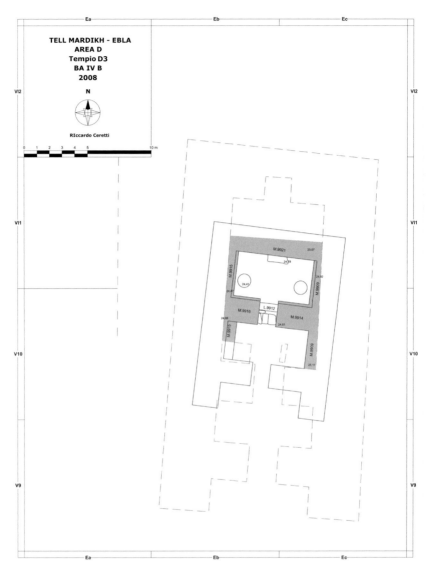

Figure 14.9 Ebla, Temple D3, schematic plan of the late Early Syrian cult building related to the later Ishtar's Temple, 23rd–21st century BC.

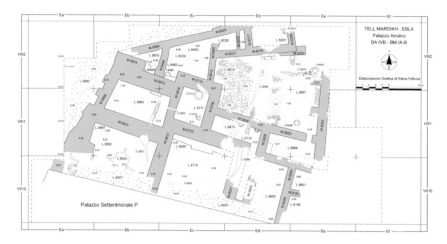

Figure 14.10 Ebla, Archaic Palace (Sector P North), schematic plan of the late Early
Syrian building with the archaic Old Syrian additions, 21st and 20th–
19th century BC.

explored in 1994–1996 (Figure 14.10). It was excavated over the whole of the
peripheral area not subsequently occupied by the Intermediate Palace from
late Middle Bronze I and by the Northern Palace itself, the latter relatively
well-preserved for most of its extension. The reason why the Intermediate
Palace, known only through very limited soundings, extends only over the
central and southern areas of the older Archaic Palace is almost certainly
because the northern area of the Archaic Palace was built in an area where the
many cavities of the underlying limestone layer made the ground too unstable
to afford adequate support for the foundations of the new archaic Old Syrian
Palace.

Of this no doubt strikingly monumental structure, with inner walls as thick
as 2.80 m, the excavations brought to light a peripheral northern area from
most probably the last years of the late Early Syrian Period; it is approximately 40 m in width on the east–west axis and just under 20 m in length
on the south–north axis. Although only the north-west wing was completed
according to the original plan, with two large parallel rooms, side by side,
c. 10 m in width, L.5893 and L.5892, the whole sector was clearly planned
on a symmetrical axis pivoting on a main central room, L.5715, with two
smaller rooms to the north, only one of which was actually built, L.5711,
and almost certainly two parallel rooms identical to those built to the west
which, however, were never accomplished. This original plan, in which, as in
the later buildings, the entrance was probably on the west side, had two pecu-
liarities: on the one hand, the plan was trapezoidal, predetermining a similar
conformation for the Northern Palace; on the other, the north façade, almost
certainly one of the side façades of the original complex, was characterized

by two smaller side buttresses and one bigger central buttress. The central room, L.5715, which proved impossible to excavate completely given the partial superimposition of the Northern Palace, was marked by several features including a narrow dais running along the whole northern wall, and the fact that its walls were very probably completely covered with wood, pointed to its having been the reception room for the complex.

The dating of phase I of the building to Early Bronze IVB is based on the finding exclusively of pottery from the end of the period, retrieved on the original floors of the long western rooms. However, the Archaic Palace was altered and refurbished in phases II–IV and perhaps for most of Middle Bronze I, or only for Middle Bronze IA, the changes to the original plan producing a less congruous and satisfactory result on both a technical and a planimetric level. In the early Mardikh IIIA phase, when the plan to complete the eastern sector was abandoned, a number of minor structures were built in exactly the same area, but based on a very different spatial articulation, which, however, respected the position of the eastern boundary wall, M.6033; this was extended northwards, beyond the original northern end, where additional walls increased the area of the building in an irregular fashion. The result of these additions on very different axes from those of the original Archaic Palace was to create a peculiar trapezoidal courtyard, L.6867, preceded by a paved area, L.5814, to the west, surrounded to the north, outside the original palace area, by new, irregular rooms such as L.6207 and L.6226, and to the south by long rectangular rooms, L.6873 and L.6868 lying inside the boundary walls of the first plan. A brick dais between two antae stood in this peculiar courtyard, against the eastern limit of the Palace, implying a ceremonial use for this part of the building at the beginning of the foundation of the archaic Old Syrian city, when the whole urban area was probably a vast building site. The Archaic Palace was abandoned perhaps at the end of Middle Bronze IA, possibly because it was no longer functional, and the Intermediate Palace was erected on its central-southern sector. On the razed ruins of the Intermediate Palace, in its turn, the Northern Palace was built, possibly in early Middle Bronze II.

It is very probable that in its initial phase the Archaic Palace was planned as a royal residence in the second Ebla, in the last years of the late Early Syrian Period, or as a place where the kings would formally receive. It was never possible to complete it. This last ceremonial function, however, was to remain unchanged in the royal buildings which succeeded the original in the following Old Syrian Period.

The Old Syrian city walls (Middle Bronze I)

The massive fortification of the third Ebla, built in the early years of the archaic Old Syrian Period, Middle Bronze IA, still impressively and visibly marks the extension of the archaeological site (Figure 14.11). Object of a series of soundings covering limited areas, the fortification was first studied

Figure 14.11 Ebla, aerial view of Tell Mardikh, with the line of the outer fortifications, and the central Acropolis; the north is at the bottom.

in 1964, also the first year of excavation, in a brief sounding on the southern stretch, close to the South-West Gate (Area A), and later on, in 1967, on the outside slope in the south-west sector. In 1969 a sounding was made in the inner slope in Area H, close to the summit of the southern stretch of the western rampart, while more extensive soundings in 1996 cut relatively deeply into the Area Z rampart. Important information also came from all the excavated sites of the large defence structures erected on the top, or on the sides of the steep slopes of the rampart, in Area V of the Western Fort, Area AA of the Northern Fort, Area DD of the North-West Gate, and Area EE of the East-North-East Fortress.

The archaic Old Syrian fortification is just under 3 kilometres long, and appears as an irregular oval, characterized by peculiar deviations, particularly in the two longest stretches, the eastern and western ramparts, and by a kind of flattened depression in correspondence with the South-West Gate, and a protrusion in the North-West Gate area. The fortification includes the ramparts, with an average base thickness of c. 45 m, in some stretches extending to 60 m, and was surrounded by a shallow outer moat which is still clearly visible although for the most part now filled up with earth. The bulk of the earthwork of the ramparts was without doubt contained, both within and without, by a retaining wall of generally large blocks, forming an almost vertical face. Its function on the curved outer face, where it was probably originally c. 4/5 m high, was clearly to make access to the rampart difficult if not impossible for assailants, and on the inside, to discourage private buildings and leave access for maintenance of the massive structure.

The rampart's inner structure probably varied technically in the different stretches of the fortification, but essentially, accumulated earth seems to have been used in two basic ways, according to whether it was earth dug from the countryside immediately surrounding the planned line of fortification, or debris collected when clearing and levelling the ruins of the late Early Syrian city from the last decades of the third millennium BC. Indeed, where, as in the southern stretch of the western rampart, the first case applied, the earth was placed in horizontal layers c. 0.50 m deep on average, alternating with clayey soil of intense red with whitish limestone rubble. Where soil from the ruins of the older city was used, as in the middle stretches of the western rampart and possibly everywhere on the southern rampart, the layers of these denser materials are always oblique and in blocks, with an incline which is the opposite to that of the exterior of the rampart.

The core of the ramparts on which were accumulated these layers of earth, variously positioned according to the different density and consistency of the materials used, was formed, probably everywhere, of the remains of a structure, preserved at different heights along the stretches of the city wall, built with the typically rectangular, large mud bricks of the Royal Archives age. This structure, preserved close to the surface near the north-west corner and at a greater depth in the middle of the western rampart, is without doubt the ancient city wall, more than 6 m thick, traditionally built in brick resting on a stone base from the mature Early Syrian city, which underwent considerable damage both from the destruction of the years around 2300 BC and the deterioration of the last three centuries of the third millennium BC, when the late Early Syrian city was considerably reduced in size.

To prevent weather damage, the top of the rampart had to be repeatedly covered in a layer of chalky plaster, probably daubed onto a thick base of mud and straw of the kind used in contemporary houses. It is the dissolving plaster which explains the crumbly, whitish layer still particularly visible in the higher parts of long sections of the ramparts, particularly in the eastern stretches.

One unresolved question is whether the top of the ramparts was accompanied in the entire length of the walls by a defensive wall, even of modest size. While we know that the continuous remains of the stone base of the defensive barrier of a communication trench or pathway are still clearly visible for long stretches on the outer top of the southern rampart, nothing is visible on the surface of its northern counterpart, and the sporadic rocks on the long eastern and western ramparts could be the remains of structures which have vanished on account of their extremely exposed location.

It is possible, though not yet documented with any certainty, that the irregular oval line of the rampart wall of the archaic Old Syrian city was determined completely by the line of the older city wall of stone and mud bricks of the mature Early Syrian settlement. Apparently, the irregularities in the later city's fortification seem to be closely connected to the rather peculiar technique and conformation of the ramparts. The misalignments, depressions, and protrusions with regard to the oval, along all stretches of the wall were functionally necessary to compensate for their conformation, allowing garrisons on the top of the walls to monitor all points on the outer foot of the ramparts, in the case of a siege, which the structure of the ramparts would otherwise have made impossible. On the basis of the same requirement were chosen the locations of the not infrequent major forts (Figure 14.12) and minor fortresses on the rampart top or slopes, at least those of the west and east, which with the strongly fortified structures of the city gates formed an integrated and highly effective defence system.

While of course completely separate at a topographic level, the inner wall of the Citadel was a different and essential integration in the overall defence system, offering further, extreme protection of the public buildings in the central Citadel of the Old Syrian city. This second wall exploited the slopes of the low hill produced by the superimposed layers of the older settlements, surrounding the Citadel with, at the base, a retaining scarp wall of limestone and basalt rocks, between 4 m and 5 m high; in the middle, the steep natural

Figure 14.12 Ebla, Northern Fort (Area AA), the structures at the top of the north-west rampart, from the south, 20th–17th century BC.

slope covered with clay plaster; and, at the top, a mud bricks scarp (3 m high), on which stood a thin wall of stones, on the edge of the Acropolis. A short, very ruined stretch of this stone wall, which certainly was the base of a mud brick structure, has been excavated on the eastern edge of the Citadel.

The imposing fortifications, inner and outer, of the classical Old Syrian city were, however, devastated during the conquest of the end of Middle Bronze IIB, and no trace is preserved of the ramparts lying orthogonally to the city rampart, which seem to have been the stratagem for attack on large cities in the eighteenth and seventeenth centuries BC, to obviate the obstacle of the imposing earthwork fortifications. It is not known whether the considerable and almost rectilinear rampart extending out into open countryside in parallel with a part of the east rampart is the ruin of an abandoned project to expand the city or a peculiar and exacting defence device (against counter-attacks from within the city) begun by the assailants in the years around 1600 BC.

The Old Syrian City Gates, Areas A, L, DD, BB (Middle Bronze I–II)

Four city gates were built at relatively regular intervals along the irregular oval circuit of the Middle Bronze IA ramparts; these certainly belong to the reconstruction plan of the third Ebla, at the beginning of the archaic Old Syrian period, but may even belong to the plan of the city of the Archives age. The best-preserved and probably most monumental in structure is the South-West Gate, also called Damascus Gate, in Area A, explored between 1964 and 1967, when the Tell Mardikh excavations started; in 2003 and 2004 further excavations and some restorations were made on the site, and also its outer structures were studied. The South-East Gate, or Steppe Gate, in Area L, received summary examination in 1972, and is certainly in very poor condition, while of the North-West Gate, or Aleppo Gate, in Area DD, only the defence features added to the east side were excavated in 1999–2001, without, however, uncovering any entrance structure into the city, due to the obstacles posed by the actual entrance to the archaeological site. Lastly, the North-East Gate, or Euphrates Gate, in Area BB, uncovered in 1997, is also badly damaged, preserved only in the foundations on the north side, the south side having been thoroughly pillaged for building materials. Probably all the Old Syrian Ebla's gates, with only slight uncertainty regarding the Steppe Gate, due to its state of deterioration, and the Aleppo Gate, still unexamined along the axis road, possessed the typical structure of Syro-Palestinian city gates in Middle Bronze I–II, with three pairs of buttresses with two intercalated and latitudinal rooms. In the archaic Old Syrian Ebla this was applied in particular monumental forms, strongly increased in length.

The spectacular Damascus Gate (Figure 14.13) actually had a double feature, the outer one having two pairs of buttresses and an intermediate room, L.853, and the inner one being classically structured with three pairs of buttresses and two intermediate rooms, L.41 and L.42, separated by a wide

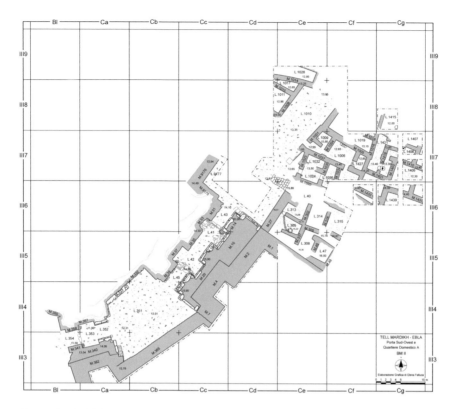

Figure 14.13 Ebla, Damascus Gate, schematic plan of the Old Syrian monument, 20th–17th century BC.

trapezoidal open courtyard, L.351. As the first feature was some 10.50 m in length and the second 21.50 m, while the courtyard with its oblique axis measured c. 16 m long, the whole complex was some 50 m long, and more than 55 m along the irregular eastern sides, determined by the imposing thickness of the ramparts, through which of course the city gate had to open. The whole east side of the Damascus Gate was lined with orthostats of large slabs of limestone for the recesses of the front wall, and of basalt for the fronts of the buttresses, c. 1.80 m high, still in place; on the contrary, the west side had no similar protection. This is possibly accounted for by different degrees of restraint needed to counter the static push of the superstructures: strong to the east, where stood the considerable mass of the eastern towers, and reduced to the west, where there is no trace of any such support device. At the same time, it cannot be excluded that the orthostats on the west side, buried in shallower ground and thus considerably more exposed than those on the east, have been gradually removed in centuries of spoliation of all the ruins slightly visible on the surface.

The very good state of preservation of the complex has allowed the locating of the two doors, one on the inner limit of the inner room L.41 and one on the outer limit of the outer room L.42, as attested by the deep door sockets, still in place, and the raised line of paving which functioned as a door-stop for the great wooden doors when closed. This indicates that, when at night or during an assault the city gates were closed, the shutters of the two outer doors were blocked from the inside, and those of the two inner doors were blocked from the outside, proving that they were closed by a garrison and high-ranking official present in the complex of rooms L.41 + L.44 + L.43, that they could not be opened, not only from the outside, but also from within the city, and were exclusively guarded by the soldiers stationed at the gate. While, as mentioned above, there are no traces of complementary fortifications on the west side, on the inside, all along the structure, walls M.2 and M.4, bordered to the north and south by walls M.1 and M.7, formed an imposing tower the core of which still stands, despite the loss of several blocks from its structure, as high as the top of the rampart itself: today a patrol wall-walk can still be seen, circling the rampart in correspondence with the gate, which probably continued for some way on the top of the south rampart. A similar tower protected the east side of the outer gate, in correspondence to wall M.362, while a stretch of some 30 metres at least of the outside rampart base east of the gate was protected by a revetment of large limestone blocks, which may have been present to the west too, where, however, it could have been removed because more exposed.

The Euphrates Gate (Figure 14.14) would have been less imposing in that its overall length with the three pairs of buttresses (of these, the front one, M.7027, and the central one, M.7025, are well-preserved) was c. 17 m, while the width of the rooms between the buttresses was c. 3.20 m. The technique was very similar to that of the Damascus Gate: although the whole south side has disappeared, including the foundations, on the north side the base blocks of the vanished orthostats of the facing wall are identical to those of the great South-West Gate. The fine slab paving of the Euphrates Gate covered a large channel which ran the whole of its length and carried waste water outside the city. The long straight terracing wall in continuation of the north side of the gate, M.7000, which extends eastwards outside the city for some 9.50 m, before disappearing completely, is what remains of the north boundary wall of the intermediate trapezoidal courtyard, L.7003, between the inner structure (still visible) and the outer one (now completely lost) of an overall plan which would have been similar to that of the Damascus Gate.

Aleppo Gate (Figure 14.15), with the Damascus Gate, was probably the most monumental of the Old Syrian city. It has not been excavated along its road axis given the presence of the modern entrance to the site. It too, however, certainly included three pairs of buttresses and two inner rooms and was similar in length to Damascus Gate. It is not certain, though, that there were an intermediate courtyard and the smaller, outer gate, extending towards the

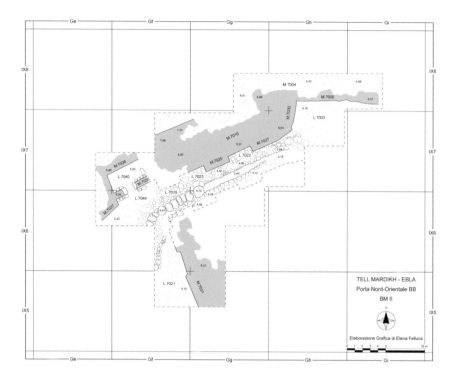

Figure 14.14 Ebla, Euphrates Gate (Area BB), schematic plan of the Old Syrian monument, 20th–17th century BC.

countryside, since, in comparison with the line of ramparts at this north gate, unlike its south-west counterpart, the main gate is located in correspondence to the outer slopes of the ramparts rather than, as in the Damascus Gate, the inner slopes: in other words, the classic layout of three pairs of buttresses in the Aleppo Gate was much more external than in the Damascus Gate, making the existence of an outer gate almost improbable, since it would have been actually outside the city.

The only part of the Aleppo Gate to have been uncovered so far is the powerful fortification on the east side of this entrance to the city, the remains of which rise up for c. 7 m and extend for more than 33 m. This is a large, semi-circular tower, M.7565, built near the top of the rampart, in correspondence to what must have been the innermost section of the gate, while at its base was the slope of the rampart itself, supported by successive terraces, M.7599, M.7681, and M.7684, progressively more advanced, which ended, further down, in a series of long buttresses, stretching towards the moat, which may be the ruins of casemates. In the easternmost sector of the outer terracing were at least two rooms, L.7578 and L.7574, located on the outer slope of the

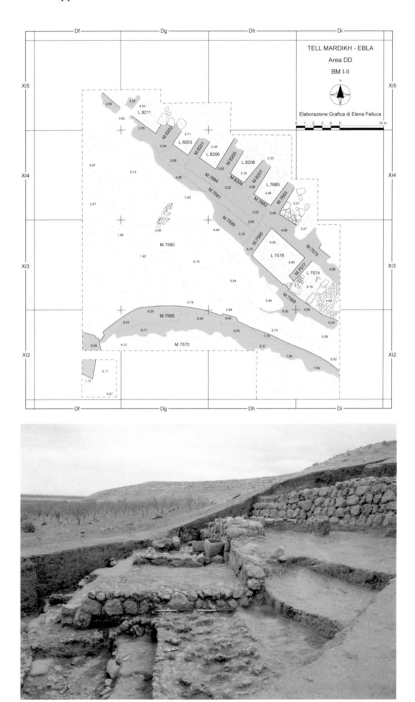

Figure 14.15, a & b Ebla, Aleppo Gate (Area DD), the massive semi-circular tower
and the advanced structures from the outside, schematic plan and
view from the west, 20th–17th century BC.

north rampart and containing a number of basins, possibly to provide water for animals in caravans which remained outside the city.

Although there are no certain clues as to their destruction, in part given the state of the architectural remains in areas particularly exposed to plundering, it is beyond doubt that all the city gates were set on fire during the final destruction of the classical Old Syrian city, c. 1600 BC. While there are no certain indications of salvaging and reuse for the other gates, probably around 1098, at the time of the First Crusade, in the Damascus Gate, a big structure of squared blocks was used to block access to what is now the ancient archaeological site, in order to use it as a fortified camp: the blocks, dating from the ninth–tenth century AD, bore Kufic inscriptions praising Allah, placed upside down in the structure.

The Western Fort, Area V (Middle Bronze II)

This is a rather massive defence complex of the classical Old Syrian city, excavated between 1995 and 1998, erected on the top of the western ramparts (Area V), and placed obliquely with respect to the axis of the imposing earthwork rampart, in such a way that its south-west end leant outwards with respect to the rampart itself, and the north-east end was almost at the level of the buildings of the Lower Town. It probably dates from Middle Bronze IIA, soon after 1800 BC, but was probably preceded by another, possibly lesser structure with a similar function, built during Middle Bronze IB, after the inner slope of the west rampart, possibly like that of the north, had been used as a cemetery for the populace during Middle Bronze IA, between c. 2000 and c. 1900 BC. The Western Fort is relatively well-preserved, considering that its altitude has exposed it to plundering and erosion throughout the centuries. The whole of the western perimeter wall has been lost on the outer slopes, and on the inside, part of the eastern wall too, while the southern part is almost complete, and stretches remain of the large northern perimeter structure. These gaps in the various sectors, however, in no way prevent an almost complete vision of the building both as regards its layout and its inner articulation.

The overall surface of the Western Fort (Figure 14.16) is c. 2,100 square metres, with an extension on the main south–north axis of more than 70 m and an original width which might have oscillated between 25 and 35 m, thus relatively elongated. Its entrance opened onto the central stretch of the eastern façade, looking towards the Lower Town, and it was divided into a series of independent units, pivoting on two successive courtyards of very different size, these also long and irregular. The lower, smaller courtyard, L.6378, stretched close to the east façade, and led into most of the wings of the complex's eastern sector, built like a central spine running through the middle section of the slope and for the most part used as store-houses. The upper, larger courtyard, L.6315 + L.6621 + L.6525, led to all the southern quarters, in particular along the long western edge on the top of the rampart.

Figure 14.16 Ebla, Western Fort (Area V), schematic plan of the classical Old Syrian complex, 18th–17th century BC.

The South-East Wing in the southern area, with rooms L.6423, L.6419, and L.6427, entered through a small staircase, was certainly a service sector devoted to food production (various grinding stones and mortars were found there), while the South-West Wing, built on the outside slope with sturdy terracing walls, was of two floors. The upper rooms probably served as look-out posts, and the lower as a sort of treasury for goods of some value, given that its entrance in vestibule L.6416 had jambs and a threshold made with large stone slabs. The East-South-East Wing in the central area, with monolithic stone basins and what appear to be fire-places in rooms L.6617, L.6634, and L.6308 in front of the small paved inner courtyard L.6306, was possibly used for metal-working, while the following Centre-East Wing, open onto the small lower courtyard through the small vestibule L.7121, unlike all the others, almost certainly housed store-rooms, and is particularly ruined in the southern, back area.

In this same central area, the opposite West Wing, similarly of two levels with typically palatine technical characteristics, was an important and certainly residential area looking out onto the countryside (Figure 14.18). One of the most extensive areas of the Fort, it was sub-divided into two parts, one to the south, with a central staircase, L.6320, and two large side rooms, L.6334 and L.6318, and the other to the north, with at least four small rooms with an independent entrance (L.6343). In the northern region, at least the two north and south units of the extensive North-East Wing were almost certainly used as store-rooms, and very probably also as shelters for the garrison soldiers. This wing was the only one in the whole Fort with at least three independent entrances into the small front eastern courtyard. One room, L.7113, with an independent entrance from the smaller courtyard, in the south unit, was a small, isolated room opening opposite the entrance to the whole fortified structure, and was very probably a chapel with cult functions. The North-West Wing (Figure 14.17), the most monumental of the complex, was a very regular and well-built rectangular structure, with the characteristic features of the fortresses forming part of the great forts of the ramparts, such as Fortress M to the east and Fortress AA in the Northern Fort, with a vestibule with orthostatic linings, L.6522, leading on one side into the staircase giving access to the upper floor, and on the other, to the first, L.6516, of the six rooms arranged in pairs in the northern sector. This wing would have had the double function of an arsenal for weapons, accumulated in the rooms accessed only from the terrace in that, as was the norm in Ebla fortresses, they were without doors, and would also have provided a high look-out tower for surveillance of the external foot of the west rampart in the long stretch northwards, towards the Northern Fort. This surveillance function was made feasible by the not inconsiderable misalignment of the northern stretch of the west rampart, immediately north of the Fort, allowing a good view over to the Northern Fort area. Naturally, the whole western sector of the North-West Wing, shored up by terracing walls which grew gradually higher as the rampart began to slope, was swept away into the countryside when the area

Figure 14.17 Ebla, Western Fort (Area V), the rooms in the massive tower-arsenal of the classical Old Syrian complex, from the south, 18th–17th century BC.

Figure 14.18 Ebla, Western Fort (Area V), the rooms in the residential quarter of the classical Old Syrian complex, from the north, 18th–17th century BC.

collapsed. While the larger, back upper courtyard was closed to the north and south, towards the outside slope of the rampart, between the West and the North-West Wings, a passage was left open, which was in correspondence with the communication walkway between the two courts, beginning at what must have been the only gate in the thick east wall, M.6534.

The Western Fort must have been taken and set on fire in the terrible destruction which put an end to the great classical Old Syrian city, towards 1600 BC. Witnesses to the battle for the fort are the well-preserved remains of two partly-burnt human bodies, probably members of the city garrison, found stretched on the ground before the tower of the North-West Wing. After the destruction, a number of rooms, particularly in the north sector, were used as very poor houses, at the beginning of Late Bronze I, certainly in the first decades of the sixteenth century BC, when limited and soon abandoned attempts were made to reconstruct the settlement.

The Northern Fort, Area AA (Middle Bronze II)

Following the complete exploration of the Western Fort, there was interest in discovering if the scattered remains that had just surfaced on the top of the ramparts were part of other fortified complexes linked in an integrated system of arsenals, forts, and towers that reinforced the defensive system of the ramparts. A sounding in 1996 identified a sector of the Northern Fort in Area AA, at the north-western edge of the ramparts. Extensive exploration of it between 1997 and 2002 still failed to wholly identify its limits. The Northern Fort, like the Western Fort and perhaps the smaller East-South-East and East-North-East Fortresses on the eastern rampart, must have been founded late in Middle Bronze IB or even in early Middle Bronze IIA, on the slopes used as a burial area in the archaic Old Syrian city, which had probably served previously only for less complex defensive structures. This impressive building, too, which was built where the northern edge of the western rampart begins to turn eastwards, was of striking size: at least 70 m from south-west to north-east and around 35 m from north-west to south-east. As the upper part of the fort was on the summit of the ramparts, it was seriously damaged, whereas the lower part being at the foot of them was difficult to reach, for the presence of later, albeit not very substantial, superimpositions.

Unlike the Western Fort, which largely extended across the top of the rampart, the Northern Fort (Figure 14.19) was completely built on the inner eastern slopes of the western rampart, so that its western limit, which is the only one certainly identified (M.6958 + M.6956), was on the very crest of the rampart itself, directly over the remains of a well-preserved section of the mud bricks town wall of the Early Syrian city of the Royal Archives (M.7357). Precisely because it was entirely built on the slopes of the rampart, in all its length, the individual units of the fort were separated by two high, thick terracing walls (Figure 14.20), still surviving to a height ranging from

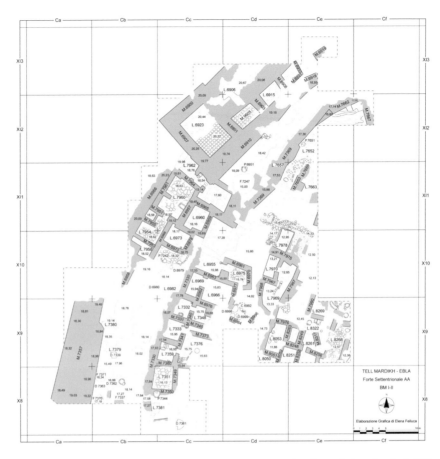

Figure 14.19 Ebla, Northern Fort (Area AA), schematic plan of the classical Old
Syrian complex, 18th–17th century BC.

4 m to 4.50 m, which ran from south-west to north-east and gave the various
quarters of the building levelled surfaces. These two walls were both more
or less parallel to the upper north-western city wall M.6958 + M.6956; the
middle one (the higher of the two terracing walls), M.7330 + M.7369, was
only about 8 m from it, while the lower one, M.7974 + M.7968, was a good
15 m from the middle one. In this way, the whole built-up area of the central
and southern sectors of the Northern Fort consisted of a long upper layer of
ground, slightly curved, about 8 m wide to the west at the foot of the town
wall M.6958; and a middle layer, curved in the same way, 15 m wide at the
centre, at the foot of the central terracing wall (M.7330 + M.7369), while a
third lower layer to the east, more or less at the height of the Lower Town, was
probably at the foot of the second terracing wall (M.7974 + M.7968), limited
to the east by the eastern wall of the fort, which has not yet been identified.

Figure 14.20 Ebla, Northern Fort (Area AA), the lower terracing north wall of the classical Old Syrian complex, from the east, 18th–17th century BC.

While the remains of the building in its south-western part are seriously ruined as they are so close to the surface, in the central area, the Central-West Wing, next to the western perimeter wall, consisted of communicating rooms, most of which were paved with slabs (L.7954 and L.7960), in two more or less parallel rows. In the middle layer, in the Central-South Wing, situated where the built-up area was twice that of the upper level at the foot of the central terrace, there was a series of more than seven units, perhaps dwellings, each one with two communicating rooms, like rooms L.6969 and L.6966 or L.7348 and L.7332, which could probably be reached from a path running eastwards on the edge of the second terraced wall. The South-East Wing, built almost at the level of the Lower Town, at the foot of the lower terrace, has been so little excavated that its layout is still unknown, but it, too, was probably sub-divided into small living units. To the north-west of the northern stretch of the upper terrace, M.7369, where there was an open space on the extreme north-west edge of the ramparts, the North-West Wing consisted of one big rectangular tower with three pairs of rooms, like L.6905 and L.6915 (the ones best preserved), which were reached from the terrace, which, in turn, was accessed from a staircase on the southern tip, L.6923. This tower was identical to those of the Western Fort and the East-South-East Fortress (Figure 14.21), which is perfectly preserved, and the East-North-East Fortress, which is in very poor condition (Figure 14.22).

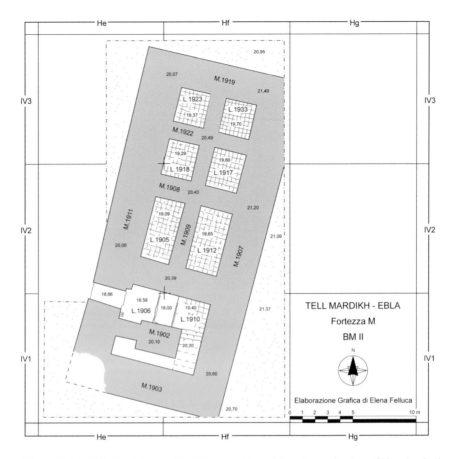

Figure 14.21 Ebla, East-South-East Fortress (Area M), schematic plan of the classical Old Syrian massive tower-arsenal, 18th–17th century BC.

The Northern Fort may have been the largest in the whole defensive system. It was certainly well garrisoned, perhaps, among other things, to protect the neighbouring North-West Gate, but was partially abandoned in the mature Old Syrian city's last period of crisis, because many rooms, particularly those of the Central-West Wing, were closed and sealed by a layer of mud bricks shortly before the destruction around 1600 BC.

Ishtar's Temple on the Citadel, Area D (Middle Bronze I–II)

Certainly the most important cult building in the Old Syrian Citadel, Ishtar's Temple was built along the western edge (Area D) of the fortified hill, which was the seat of political power in the first centuries of the second

Figure 14.22 Ebla, East-North-East Fortress (Area EE), human skeletons of persons killed during the siege in front of the Fortress, on top of the east rampart, from the north, 17th century BC.

millennium BC. It was certainly the sanctuary of Ishtar, the city goddess of the archaic and classical Old Syrian Ebla and the patron of kingship of the powerful city of inner Syria in the age of the Amorite Dynasties. This great sacred building, probably founded during the twentieth century BC in the years when Ebla must have been politically dominant in northern Syria, was brought to light in the early stages of the exploration of Tell Mardikh, in 1965 and 1966. It had a peculiar layout, compared to the other Eblaite religious buildings of the period, which usually had one cella only, but like them, it was completely independent of the adjacent buildings and without any additional rooms.

Clearly conceived as a larger version of the simple traditional scheme, Ishtar's Temple (Figure 14.23) had a tripartite longitudinal development, with an entrance with antae, without columns: the short vestibule L.213, the equally short antecella L.211, and the long cella L.202, though very different in length, were identical in breadth, 7.20 m. The building had been founded on a levelled strip of ground, a kind of mud bricks terrace, whose bricks were of the size typical for the mature Early Syrian period; thus, it clearly dated to Early Bronze IVA, and was actually no more than the levelled ruin of an important cult building beneath, dating from the city of the Archives age. It was around 30 m long on the south–north axis and a little less than 11.50 m wide on the east–west one; its sides consisted of two double foundation walls,

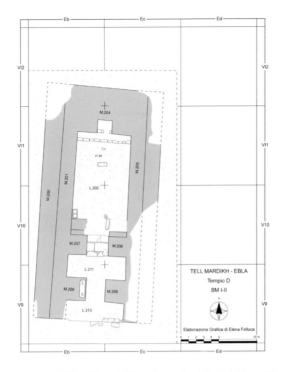

Figure 14.23 Ebla, Ishtar's Temple on the Citadel (Area D), schematic plan of the Old
Syrian cult building, 20th–17th century BC.

to the west M.200 outside and M.201 inside, and to the east M.205 inside and
M.210 outside, each about 2 m thick. However, only the two inner walls had
an elevation, which was thus only 2 m thick, while the outer ones were a base
for the heaps of stones thrown against the outer faces of the perimeter walls
in order to protect them; the back wall, M.204, as was usual in Old Syrian
religious architecture, was much thicker, reaching 4.90 m. Cella L.202 had
a marked longitudinal development, as was traditional in Old and Middle
Syrian architecture, 12.40 m long and 7.20 m wide, had a low bench against
the back north wall, little more than a simple step, onto which opened the
quite deep, almost square niche for the cult image.

Along with several remains of important basalt cult fittings, like a kind
of large round basin, with a central column-like support, in the south-west
corner of the cella, the limestone lustral double basin was still in place; it
was intact, with mythical and ritual depictions in relief on three of the sides.
Before the niche there were, also in place, a simple basalt offering table, with
two round holes, and two basalt standing stones, with rectangular section, one
still standing and intact, and the other one broken and lying on the floor. The
entrance to the cella, or less probably the entrance to the antecella, probably

featured jambs decorated with two big basalt carved images of lying lions, made up of three blocks: much of the rear block and part of the central one of one of the figures were found moved into the antecella. Probably, after the destruction of the classical Old Syrian city, Temple D, or part of it, was adapted to more modest functions of worship: the standing stones and the offering table may belong to this late phase of the Middle Syrian Period, when the sacred place might also have become an open-air sanctuary, which would explain the fact that the upper edges of the intact limestone cult basin were badly worn out.

In front of the main building was a large open space, that must have sloped gradually towards the south, with cult fittings, at least one of which, a big limestone round basin, was found in place, still quite well preserved. A short distance from the front of Temple D was a small shrine, about 5.10 m wide and little more than 4.60 m long, known as Shrine G3, with a broad cella, L.3939, and façade with antae, facing east, with stone foundations, and an adjacent room to the south in mud bricks, L.3816, with low benches along the walls. Both these rooms had functions connected with the liturgies of the sanctuary: remains of what were certainly royal votive statues were preserved in the small cella of the shrine, which was just 3.50 m wide and had a small axial niche on the western back wall, while clay livers, used for mantic purposes, have been found in the adjacent room. The base of Ishtar's Stele was embedded in one of the two outer corners of the small vestibule, while the other fragments of it were certainly scattered when the city was destroyed. They were found between the front of Temple D and the northern edge of the Acropolis: this was very probably not its original position, as two of the four relief faces would have been hidden from view.

Ishtar's Sacred Area in the Lower Town, Area P (Middle Bronze I–II)

Situated in the North-West Lower Town at the foot of the Old Syrian Citadel and immediately south of the southern façade of the Northern Palace (Area P), it was certainly the largest and most monumental cult area of the city in the early second millennium BC and was probably the public sanctuary of the popular goddess, while the Temple of Area D of the Acropolis was the royal dynastic sanctuary. The systematic exploration of Ishtar's Sacred Area in the Lower Town began in 1988, immediately after work was finished on the Northern Palace, to cast light on the topography between the palace and the presumed base of the inner fortification of the Old Syrian Citadel. This work in what was called Sector P Centre meant that as early as 1989, there was a complete idea of the plan of what seemed to be the largest temple of the Middle Bronze II city, called Temple P2. While work in the square in front of the temple continued, it was decided in 1990 to investigate the area immediately to the south-west, where not only sporadic large stone blocks appeared on the surface, but various clues also suggested that, strangely, there were also many large, almost uninterrupted lines of limestone blocks, close to the surface. In this way, as early as 1990, what was called Monument P3 was identified and its very peculiar form defined. It continued to be excavated in 1991 and 1992, when the investigations were extended west and east of Temple P2, to discover what other buildings might be present in what was clearly an extensive area of religious interest, and to acquire data on the chronology and layout of the whole area. Then, when in 2000 and 2001, restoration work began on Temple P2, after the restoration of Monument P3, inspection of the front of the west anta of Temple P2 brought to light a small single-cella building, P6, which had been seriously damaged near the surface of the tell, and might be a small temple of Iron III, built with poor technique, perhaps during one of the periods when the still imposing ruins of Temple P2 were being sacked.

The complex of Ishtar's Sacred Area in the Lower Town (Figure 14.24) includes the great Temple (P2), which was a traditional cult building with long cella and short vestibule, facing south, and the Cult Terrace of the Lions (P3), which was a massive structure of huge size, without an entrance, and consisting merely of a large inner courtyard facing east towards the open space L.5060, known as the Cisterns Square, stretching between the goddess's temple to the north, the terrace to the west, and the inner fortification of the Citadel to the south-east. To the north, between the back wall of Temple P2 and the southern wall of the Northern Palace, lay the east–west road L.4201, whereas a ring road probably ran at the foot of the Citadel, entering the Cisterns Square, and to the south, between the southern wall of the Cult Terrace of the Lions and the northern back wall of the Western Palace, there ran a large east–west road, L.5080, which must have reached the foot of the Citadel to the east. In the area immediately east of the northern sector of Temple P2 began the foundations of a building that is no longer retrievable, which extended eastwards and could have been store-houses of the Sacred Area, while in the open, apparently unbuilt space to the west, between the western side of the temple and the northern wall of the Cult Terrace of the Lions, provisional dilapidated structures have been found indicating that, when Old Syrian Ebla was destroyed, this part of the Lower Town was still a building site, certainly because Monument P3 was never completed.

Temple P2 is a large and imposing cult building (Figure 14.25), about 33.50 m long on the main south–north axis, and about 20 m wide. It consisted of a single cella, L.4304, with a classical longitudinal development of 20.50 m by 12.10 m. A broad, shallow niche of 6 m by 0.85 m opened at the centre of the northern wall M.4301; the front vestibule, L.4600, which, as usual, was more or less as wide as the cella, was only 2.50 m deep; while the walls of the building were particularly thick, the one at the back being about 7 m and the side ones about 5 m. These data mean that the building could have been even higher than 15 m; roofing the cella was certainly not easy, and therefore the inner space may have had four pairs of columns that could

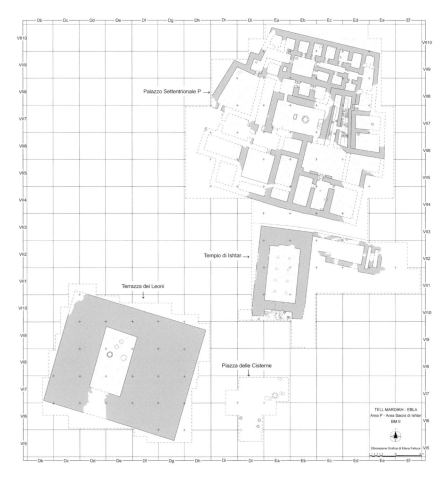

Figure 14.24 Ebla, Ishtar's Cult Area in the Lower Town (Area P), schematic plan of the Old Syrian cult complex, 20th–17th century BC.

have reduced the width of the room, creating a sort of partition in three naves, though this is obviously pure hypothesis. No traces of the original flooring have survived, as the building was thoroughly sacked of the foundation stones on several occasions, while the area of the cella was found filled with stones that were partly abandoned remains of those removed, as in the case of two fine, highly polished orthostats, which must originally have been linings for the foundations visible above ground. On the contrary, in vestibule L.4600, where most of the remains of the broken votive statuary were found, the preparation of the original flooring was kept in the north-east corner. In the eastern part of the vestibule, at some time between Iron III and the Persian Age, when there must have been serious sacking of building

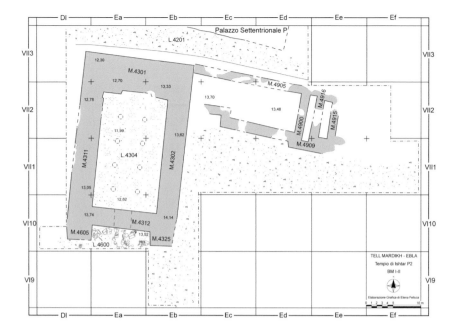

Figure 14.25 Ebla, Ishtar's Temple in the Lower Town (Temple P2), schematic plan of the archaic and classical Old Syrian building, 20th–17th century BC.

stones, a peculiar hiding-place was made to keep the only intact statue that has reached us. It was placed on a kind of bed of stones mainly taken from the fragments of two classical Old Syrian royal statues of a seated king and a standing queen. However, badly damaged but recognizable remains of some important furnishings, including two small fragments of a large carved basalt double basin of the usual early Old Syrian typology, have been found abandoned among the stones taken from the cella, whose flooring might have been laid over a stone platform, completely pillaged on the upper courses. A big female head in basalt, which was certainly part of a cult image, has been discovered in front of the eastern anta of the vestibule of the building, to which it certainly belonged. A large fragment of a statue of a walking lion, whose muzzle was hacked away at the time of the destruction of Mardikh IIIB, was discovered in the central area of the vestibule. It may well have belonged to an image of an apotropaic lion, originally placed at one of the jambs of the entrance to the cella.

The size of the Cult Terrace of the Lions (Figure 14.26) is imposing: the east–west axis is 52.50 m long, while the north–south axis is 42 m wide. The courtyard L.5050 is 23.20 m wide on the north–south axis and 12.40 m deep on the main east–west axis. The distance between the northern and southern limits of the courtyard, and the northern and southern façades of

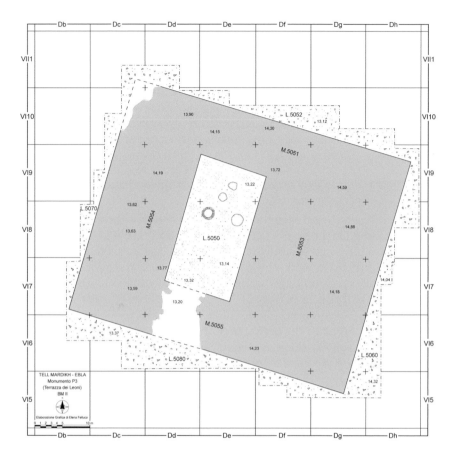

Figure 14.26 Ebla, Cult Terrace of the Lions (Monument P3), schematic plan of the classical Old Syrian cult building, 17th century BC.

the building are about 9.40 m, while the distance between the eastern front façade and the eastern limit of the courtyard is about 25 m, and only 15 m separate the western wall of the courtyard from the western façade of the whole building. The highest points of the Terrace that have been preserved are in two places of the inner courtyard, on the north side near the north-east corner and on the east side near the south-east corner: about 1.80/1.90 m. The walls of the building are extremely regular, as the whole construction used irregularly shaped blocks of limestone, that were, however, of the same height in each course: in effect, the lowest course of blocks that made up the walls of this spectacular building were about 0.70 m high, the second row about 0.60 m high, and the third, of which little has remained, about 0.50 m high. An unusual feature of the walls is the inclination of the outer faces of the building and of the inner walls of the courtyard. This inclination was obtained by rigorously respecting two principles: first, the blocks in the upper courses were constantly placed in such a way that their lower base was always set a few centimetres further back than the top of the blocks of the course beneath; second, though the blocks were irregular, they were cut so that the outer face of each block was slightly inclined and the top of the block itself slightly set back in relation to its base. The result of following these two principles was that the outer walls of the four outer façades and the walls of the courtyard are not vertical, but slightly and constantly tapered upwards, not unlike what we can see in the façades of the Egyptian funerary mastabas and in the terraces of the Mesopotamian ziggurats.

Various features show that the Cult Terrace of the Lions was still unfinished when Mardikh IIIB was destroyed. First, leaning all along the south outer façade, which was accurately built like the others, there was a layer of limestone crumble, in part concealing the façade itself, that also formed a sloping plane from the south-east corner to the centre of the wall. Second, the great courtyard L.5050, whose floor was identical to that of the exterior, had absolutely no furnishings, whether fixed or moveable, and was filled with re-employed soil rich in pottery of late Middle Bronze II, that showed no traces either of fire or destruction. Third, beneath this intentional filling, no trace has been found of the destruction of any furnishings, and the chemical analysis of the soil has shown no significant vegetable or organic traces that might suggest the presence of plants or animals. All this leads to the conclusion that work on the monument was continuing until shortly before it was destroyed, with the creation of a sloping plane to facilitate the placing higher up of the large limestone blocks; that, probably during the dangerous and perhaps prolonged siege, they decided to fill the monument to prevent it being profaned; that the inner courtyard was never furnished in any way, nor were there any plants or animals sacred to the goddess.

The area of the Cisterns Square must have been a fairly large urban space where there were various cisterns, but also the mouths of three *favissae* in which several votive objects and ritual vessels were thrown. Here were found two basalt statue bases with pairs of growling lions identical, though smaller, to the mutilated one referred to above which was found in a room of the Western Palace next to the one with the entrance to the Tomb of the Lord of the Goats and the so-called "Tomb of the Cisterns". Clearly the *favissae* were used for keeping minor votive objects, such as beads of the most varied materials, fragments of precious materials, clay figurines, usually of women, small objects in bronze such as snakes and bracelets, and even beautiful miniature figures such as a crouching lion in carnelian, all of them in various ways alluding to Ishtar's cult. The presence in front of the main façade of Temple P2 of two bases with lions for lost statues, that were probably of standing figures, suggests that, while the seated statues of kings and standing statues of queens that have been found in the vestibule of the temple were very probably royal votive images dedicated in the temple, the bases with lion figures belonged to a different typology of royal statue, probably commemorative rather than votive.

The Temples of Shapash/Shamash, Rashap, and Hadad (?), Areas N, B, HH (Middle Bronze I–II)

These cult places in the Lower Town were probably dedicated to the Sun-deity Shapash/Shamash, the god of the Underworld Rashap, and perhaps to the Storm-god Hadad, and were located respectively in the areas north and south-west of the foot of the Citadel, and to the extreme south-eastern outskirts of the city near the Steppe Gate. They were brought to light, again respectively, in 1972 in Area N, in 1965 in Area B, and in 2005 in Area HH. In the first two (Areas N and B), though the stone bases of the perimeter walls in mud bricks are fairly well preserved, their elevations are completely lost, as are the structures of the façades, and so any attempt to reconstruct them is conjectural and based on little more than comparison. By contrast, only the front walls of the third temple (Area HH) have been preserved, while the inner area, consisting of the cella, has been destroyed by the erosion of the tell, due to its relatively exposed position.

The entrance to Shapash/Shamash's Temple (Area N) faces east (Figure 14.27), and the building has the typical single-cella, longitudinal layout of the religious architecture in Old Syrian Ebla, with sturdy side walls (M.2393 and M.2502) 3 m thick, while the back wall, M.2501, is a little thicker: in the cella, L.2500, 7.50 m wide (its length is uncertain due to the loss of the front wall), a bench between 3.40 m and 2.80 m deep ran the whole length of the back wall, and cult images were probably placed on it. Against it were two large basalt slabs, perhaps for votive offerings, an irregular offering table, also in basalt, with a spout for cult liquid or the blood of sacrificial victims, and a limestone basin probably carved on four faces, of which only the rear half has been found in place (Figure 14.28). Two different door sockets are preserved, about 11.50 m away from the back wall, which were probably placed immediately inside the lost transversal wall, probably separating the vestibule, which has been lost as it was more or less on the surface, from cella L.2500, meaning that the cella was probably around 12 m long by 7.50 m wide. As was usual in the religious architecture of Ebla and other Old Syrian cities, the walls of the temple were surrounded by the empty space of a fairly wide road, and it is difficult to say if the rooms discovered mainly in the west and north belonged to a cult area or, more probably, were merely private houses surrounding the cult building.

Rashap's Temple (Area B) had a similar layout, though slightly smaller, overall 14.40 m by 10.50 m, but faced south (Figure 14.29) and featured orthostatic linings, largely pillaged, unlike Shapash/Shamash's Temple. This is the smallest cult building of Ebla: its side walls, M.191 and M.193, were 3 m thick, while the back wall, M.192, reached 4 m; the cella, L.190, was only

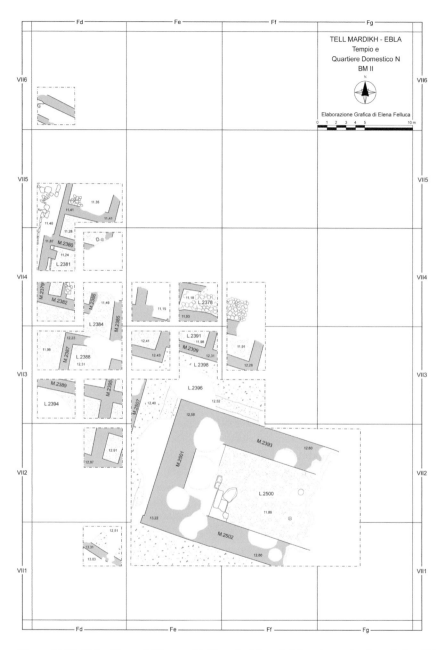

Figure 14.27 Ebla, Shapash/Shamash's Temple (Temple N), schematic plan of the Old
Syrian cult building, 18th–17th century BC.

Figure 14.28 Ebla, Shapash/Shamash's Temple (Temple N), the cult basin and the offering tables in place in the cella L.2500, from the east, 18th–17th century BC.

4.50 m wide and about 6.80 m deep, as, here too, as in the temple of Area N, about 6.30 m away from the back wall, there are two small door sockets, which indicate that, originally, there was a transversal wall, probably about 2 m thick, which was completely removed, and which was to separate the cella L.190 from the shallow vestibule. Quite a number of flat stones of the vestibule pavement are preserved, which formed two steps, where a small fragment was found of the lustral double basin in basalt retrieved before excavations began. Against the back wall of the cella, as in the temples of Areas D and N, was a low bench about 1.20 m deep, in which the mouth of quite a large cistern opened, in which have been found several fragments of another larger lustral double basin in basalt.

What we presume to have been Hadad's Temple (Temple HH2), which may have been built early in Middle Bronze II (Figure 14.30), over the imposing ruins of the Temple of the Rock of Early Bronze IVA in Area HH, was, unlike the other two, a classical tripartite temple, the only one of this kind in the Lower Town of Ebla, with vestibule, antecella, and cella, all of the same width, about 9.10 m, as was usual in this kind of cult building. Overall, this important monument must have been about 25 m long and was certainly 16 m wide, with the side walls, M.9200 and M.9235, 3.45 m thick, and the back wall certainly much thicker, probably about 6.50 m. As in the

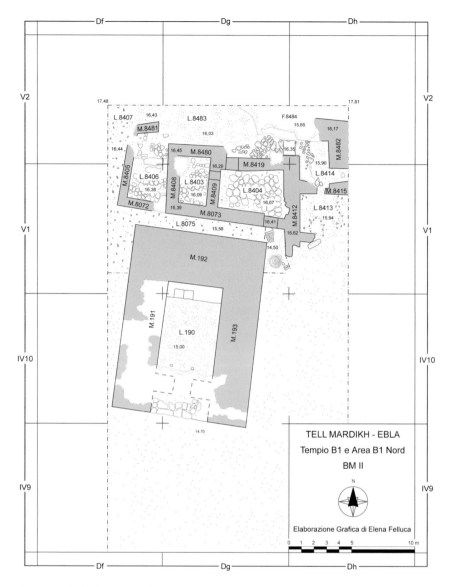

Figure 14.29 Ebla, Rashap's Temple (Temple B), schematic plan of the Old Syrian cult
building, 20th–17th century BC.

other tripartite temple of Ebla, Ishtar's Temple on the Citadel, the vestibule
L.9231 and the antecella L.9230 were much shallower: the former 2.50 m
and the latter 2.30 m. On the other hand, the cella is mostly lost, and only
its peculiar and unusual foundation is preserved, made of pressed limestone
crumble, for the west back wall. It was probably between 9.50 m and 10.50

Figure 14.30 Ebla, Hadad's Temple (?) (Temple HH2), schematic plan of the classical Old Syrian cult building, 18th–17th century BC.

m long, and thus of the long type (which had to be 10.50 m in length and 9.10 m wide). Temple HH3, another longitudinally tripartite temple, similar but smaller, built beneath Temple HH2, is almost completely lost. It must have been earlier than Temple HH2, dating from Middle Bronze I. The more recent of the two superimposed buildings probably featured two phases, during the second of which the vestibule had a flagstones flooring, forming a step to the outside.

All the Old Syrian temples of the third Ebla must have been destroyed in the terrible devastation that ended the city of Middle Bronze II, around 1600 BC, although there are very few traces of this fire, given the extremely exposed position of the ruins everywhere in the Lower Town. Only in Shapash/Shamash's Temple did the archaeological deposits include evident traces of the destruction.

The Sanctuary of the Deified Royal Ancestors, Area B
(Middle Bronze II)

Immediately south of Rashap's Temple (Area B), separated from it only by a small square, rose the slightly trapezoidal building, almost an irregular square of about 33 m per side, of the Sanctuary (B2) for the cult of the royal ancestors, probably built during Middle Bronze II, perhaps around 1800 BC, and destroyed in the final sack of the city towards 1600 BC. The building (Figure 14.31) was excavated in the years 1971–1972 and its central and eastern sectors are well preserved, but the south-west area is completely lost, due to the erosion of the Lower Town.

It faced towards the west, which, as the place where the sun set, was regarded as the region of the dead *par excellence*, and it had an irregular centric organization, with a large cult room in the central region and some very small or very elongated peripheral accessory cellas. The entrance to the sanctuary on the west side, mostly lost, must have consisted of a stairway sided by antae, which led into a front courtyard, L.2145, flanked to the north by the long room L.2137, which almost certainly had a lost symmetrical room to the south. This courtyard gave direct access to the almost square-shaped cult room, cella L.2124, which had low benches on three sides and a dais of mud bricks not far away from the south wall; the only room communicating with cella L.2124 was a secondary square cella to the north, L.2108, with a niche in a non-central position on the north side. The function of a rectangular room, L.2134, is uncertain: it had three thin pilasters on the south wall, south of the central cella, which may have been reached from the front courtyard. Access to the peripheral cellas was certainly through the long rectangular rooms, which lay alongside the entrance courtyard to the north and south. In fact, the north room, L.2137, led first to a long room of similar size and layout, and then to a small store-room, L.2120, which held various storage jars. On the other hand, the lost south room, on the other side of the building, led to the long cella, L.2161, to the south; to the small square cella, L.2140, in the south-east corner; to the main long cella, L.2113, to the east; and to the small store-room, L.2115. The complete lack of fitting in the central room of the north wing suggests it was not really a cella, but this part of the building was probably intended for preserving and preparing food for funerary rites, as there was a perfectly preserved bench with two grinding stones in place, in the north-east corner of L.2137. By contrast, the cellas, lying one after the other on the south and east sides, were certainly intended for cult purposes: the main one, L.2113, had a peculiar altar, with two stone antae and a brick in between, in the north-east corner, which was meant to contain a small, almost certainly bronze, image, and in the south-east corner two beautiful basalt offering tables, for what may have been blood sacrifices (Figure 14.32). Cella L.2124 also had the same altar with antae for a metallic statuette; while on the long south side of

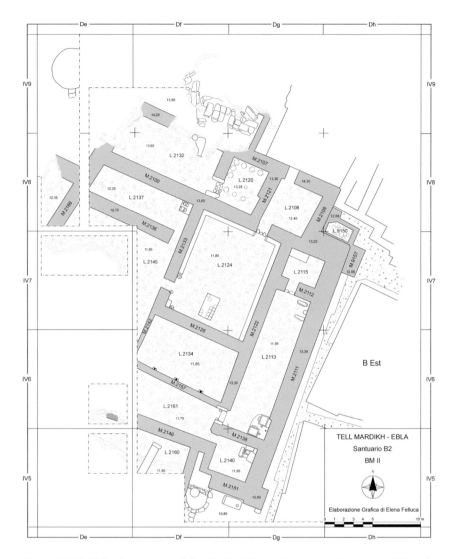

Figure 14.31 Ebla, Sanctuary of the Deified Royal Ancestors (Sanctuary B2), schematic plan of the Old Syrian cult building, 18th–17th century BC.

hall L.2161 was a limestone dais for some kind of furnishing. Clearly the whole complex had a cult function, and we must infer that the large central cella was the place for community rites and, in particular, banquets in honour of the deified royal ancestors, while individual deified dead kings were venerated in the perimeter cellas. The unusual layout of the building, which has made some suggest, against all evidence, that it was a palatine building, the benches and dais of the central main room, and the altars

Figure 14.32 Ebla, Sanctuary of the Deified Royal Ancestors (Sanctuary B2), the offering tables in the cella L.2113, from the west, 18th–17th century BC.

and offering tables in the small perimeter cellas can only be explained in relation to the cults of deified royal ancestors, common in the southern Mesopotamian milieus of the I Dynasty of Babylon and in the Middle Syrian one of Ugarit.

The Sanctuary of the Deified Royal Ancestors, which, together with Rashap's Temple and the Royal Tombs was a coherent whole, in some way connected, ideologically and perhaps functionally with the Western Palace, was sacked and destroyed at the end of Middle Bronze II in the disastrous destruction of the whole classical Old Syrian city around 1600 BC.

The Old Syrian Royal Palace, Area E (Middle Bronze II)

This palatine building, which was clearly the largest and most important in the early and classical Old Syrian city, was discovered when the northern edge of the Acropolis in Area E began to be inspected from 1968 onwards. Exploration of it was suspended in 1974 to concentrate on the mature Early Syrian Royal Palace (Area G) of the age of the Royal Archives. Work was resumed in 2008, though only systematically from 2009 onwards. Progress was slow due to the superimpositions on the Acropolis from Late Bronze I to the Persian Age. What has so far been retrieved are peripheral sectors of

Figure 14.33 Ebla, Royal Palace (Area E), schematic plan of the Old Syrian palace, 20th–17th century BC.

secondary importance to the north and north-west covering an area of c. 800 square metres.

Its original extent must have been much greater, as the whole complex was probably at least 130 m long on its south–north axis, and more than 100 m wide from west to east, making an estimated overall area of around 15,000 square metres. The northern façade of Royal Palace E looked onto the far edge of the Citadel (Figure 14.33): indeed, the northern perimeter wall was lost to the erosion of the edge of the Acropolis, while its western limit, which has not yet been identified with certainty, probably had a south–north layout, more or less parallel to the side of the great Temple of Ishtar, about 30 metres away, and a series of offsets which meant that it gradually advanced slightly to the south-west. So far, we have no information about the eastern perimeter wall. The whole structure of Royal Palace E must have been organized in quarters arranged on probably irregular terraces that descended gradually for almost the whole breadth of the complex, from north to south.

The building was probably conceived as a single complex, but only the North-West Wing has been recovered in its entirety. Our knowledge of three other sectors is very partial, including their area: the North Wing, at the north-east limit of the surface that has been excavated; the Centre-North Wing, in a central area immediately south of the two previous ones; and the West Wing, which seems to have taken up the western part of the building. The terraced walls of the North-West Wing leant against a kind of small hillock on the north-western outskirts of the Old Syrian Citadel. It included a rather large courtyard, L.156, sided to the north by three relatively small spaces (L.152, L.153, L.154), to the east by a large area divided into two rooms (L.759 and L.724) giving onto a small northern space, L.718, and to the south by a long space conventionally called the southern porch, L.1645. Though all these rooms had been almost entirely stripped of their original furnishings when they were found, the level of technical finishing in this sector was very high, with excellent concrete flooring and with the bases of the mud brick walls lined by very regular limestone and basalt orthostats. Similarly, all the thresholds and door jambs consisted of carefully worked and finished square slabs, often of basalt. The North Wing was immediately east of the North-West Wing and seems not to have communicated with it. It must have been quite large, though the extensive superimpositions, down to the Hellenistic Age, have made it impossible to bring to light more than part of a large room, L.761, with south–north axis, and two much smaller ones to the north. This sector of Royal Palace E, too, had concrete flooring and orthostatic facing of the bases. The Centre-North Wing, which is the only one that has so far been excavated in the crucial central sectors of the building, was immediately to the south of the porch L.1645, but significantly lower (between 1.50 and 2.10 m), helping to preserve it with its relatively striking elevations. This sector has still not been completely explored due to the later superimpositions, and its organization is still uncertain: it may have been very different from what replaced it in later periods. It is difficult to be sure of what the Centre-North Wing was like, as immediately after the destruction of the building, the better preserved walls of the original structure were re-employed for rather poor dwellings of Late Bronze I: at least six small, poorly built rooms were placed over and among the remains of the great monumental ruin of Royal Palace E. It is, in any case, certain that the south–north ramp was essential for communication between all the northern quarters, except for the North Wing, which was probably independent and may have had access from the east through a semi-peripheral system of circulation to the east, complementing the western one. In fact, this ramp gave access to the east, both to the porch L.1645 of the North-West Wing and to the Centre-North Wing by a door to L.748; and also, in the West Wing, to a series of terraces with rooms, such as L.463, and courtyards, such as L.745, which must have been situated against the western perimeter wall, which has still not been identified with certainty. The West Wing may have extended significantly southwards to an area that has not yet been excavated, but in the northern sectors at least, it seems to have included minor peripheral paved courtyards alternating with rooms whose layout is still uncertain. A sector of structures that probably belong to the extreme western area of Royal Palace E, with irregular terracing and rather small rooms, may indicate that it was put to different use, as in the Centre-North Wing. It seems to have had secondary access to what may have been the western perimeter buttressed wall, which gave onto the eastern side of Ishtar's Temple. It is more likely, however, that the secondary entrances date from Late Bronze I, when it was adapted and reused. The flooring of this extensive and complex building was very uneven, becoming noticeably lower moving from north to south, probably due to the ruins from the older Royal Palace G of the mature Early Syrian Period. As in other royal palaces of that period in the Lower Town, the centre of the building was probably intended for public and administrative functions and was in the central-southern part of the Centre-North Wing, while the main entrance to the building was certainly to the south or south-west, where the access ramp to the Citadel of the Old Syrian Period was located.

Like all the public buildings of the classical Old Syrian city, around 1600 BC, at the end of Middle Bronze II, Royal Palace E was sacked and set on fire. The structures of the building, particularly in the case of the mud brick walls, were best preserved when protected by the terracing that formed a sort of natural protection, as in the Centre-North Wing and the West Wing. It is certain that generally poor, partial and disorganized refurbishing and building work took place there, probably immediately after the destruction. These poor dwellings among the ruins probably housed those who had escaped the destruction, particularly in Late Bronze I. This temporary reoccupation may have continued into Late Bronze I and II, further damaging the remains of the original building that had survived the fire during the destruction around 1600 BC.

The Western Palace, Area Q (Middle Bronze I–II)

The largest palatine complex in the Lower Town was situated on a rocky rise which was probably a westward extension of the supposed limestone hillock that is now hidden by the superimposition of settlements of the Acropolis. The Western Palace (Area Q) was probably founded at some point in the archaic Old Syrian Period, and was identified in 1976 in a short southern sector of its eastern perimeter on the line and in the same direction as the presumed west wall of the Court of Audience of Royal Palace G of the mature Early Syrian Period, of which there is now no trace. Most of the building was brought to light during the excavations between 1978 and 1982, but work on this important Old Syrian complex was resumed in 2000 and 2001 to complete our understanding of a series of particular peripheral elements of the extended structure, particularly in the north-east and south-east sectors, while the final restoration of the building, completed in 2001–2002 was being prepared. In the central-eastern part of the Western Palace, in 1978 and 1979, three tombs of the Royal Necropolis were identified.

The Western Palace (Figure 14.34), which must have had an area of almost 7,500 square metres, was markedly long on the main south–north axis, which reached about 115 m, while east–west it ranged between 60 m and 70 m in width, because, though the west perimeter wall was straight and at right angles with the front south and back north walls, the western walls, for some reason, sometimes receded and sometimes included a quadrangular projection with four flights of stairs. The palace must date from a central part of the archaic Old Syrian Period, around 1900 BC, and must have been preceded by an older, smaller building, perhaps equally palatine, the remains of which have emerged in the western area; later on, in the classical Old Syrian Period, it was refurbished, as is clear mainly from the older flooring visible in some rooms. Later still, towards the end of the Old Syrian city, some doors were closed and the circulation inside the building changed, probably in relation to a general impoverishment of the city in the second half of the seventeenth century BC. The state of preservation of this large building varies considerably: it is very well preserved in the north and central parts, particularly towards the east, because here it was clearly protected from erosion by the overhanging slopes of the Acropolis, but the south-west front sector is completely lost, where the underlying rock emerges, and the south façade, as well as the whole central region, are razed to the lower inner courses of the foundations; part of the building, in the central area of the eastern sector, is obliterated by the massive and deep lower foundation of a not very large building, connected to a poor late Roman and Byzantine settlement, that must have reused much of the abundant stone of the foundations of the Old Syrian building. The pillage of the large amount of masonry of the foundations of the huge building, made easier in the west sectors because they were quite close to the surface, took place mainly in the later part of the Iron Age and then, perhaps extensively, in the late Roman and Byzantine Periods, when there was probably systematic sacking of the tombs of the underlying Royal Necropolis.

The architectural technique of this palatine building was certainly most sophisticated: the perimeter walls, which were 3.20 m thick, were decorated, as regards the outer faces, with beautiful limestone orthostats, which were 1.45 m high and generally between 3.15 m and 4.25 m long; some of these are still visible on the northern front of the north perimeter wall M.3136. The more important entrances, like that between L.3364 and L.2943, leading to the Audience Hall, have thresholds of highly polished basalt slabs and no less accurate basalt or limestone jambs; the whole central sector of the Audience Hall, L.3038, like its vestibule, also had regular limestone block foundations for the lining orthostats, which have now been completely lost. The mud brick elevations for at least one better preserved sector in the north-east region of

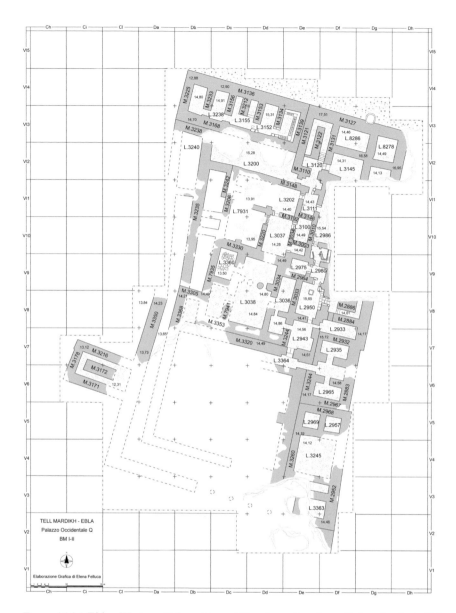

Figure 14.34 Ebla, Western Palace (Area Q), schematic plan of the classical Old
Syrian palace, 18th–17th century BC.

the palace, where rooms L.3146, L.8277, and L.8277 were situated, had mud bricks of deep red and light brown clay alternating, to form striking geometrical patterns on the walls, which is difficult to reconstruct as they might have appeared after the plastering, which was probably not of gypsum in these cases.

The front wall of the Western Palace, which dominated the South-West Lower Town, opened onto the top of a slightly rising road with short ramps, coming from the Damascus Gate. Its large basalt blocks were intended to form propylaea of some kind, but they are now completely lost. This southern façade probably had a porch, of which we can still see the round placements in the rock of at least two of the possible column bases. The front sector of the building, where there was probably a large courtyard, is now wholly lost. The central core of the building was the Audience Quarter, which had a tripartite latitudinal structure, with the Audience Hall, L.3038, divided into two parts by a small porch with two columns, flanked on both sides by two rooms, L.3306 and L.3360 to the west and L.3315 and L.3036 to the east, the southernmost of which acted as a side vestibule to the Audience Hall, which had no axial entrance. While the whole western sector of the palatine building is so poorly preserved that it is difficult to infer how circulation worked, and which were its functions, it is certain that the North-West Wing – which opened onto the north side of the rather large back rectangular courtyard, L.3200, with two long parallel rooms on each side of a central staircase with four ramps, L.3155 – must have been the area intended for food preparation. The easternmost of the four rooms, L.3136, which is rather well preserved, was furnished with a long horseshoe-shaped bench, on which were 16 basalt grindstones with their oblong pestles. The North-East Wing, which included four large rooms, L.3145, L.8286, L.8276, and L. 8278, was adjacent to a large, finely built long stairway with four ramps, L.3120 (Figure 14.35), and was very probably the residential quarter of the palace, which certainly also extended to the upper floor. One could move without interruption from the southern rooms flanking the eastern wing of the central quarter of the Audience Hall, to the northern vestibule, L.3149, of the great North-East Staircase, L.3120, passing through a smaller courtyard, L.2950, and a series of small rooms. It is certain, then, that while there may have been various small quarters to the east and west of the front courtyard, in the mainly lost southern sector of the palace, in the northern sector there was the Audience Quarter, with its two side wings in the centre, to the south, and, to the north, another central area consisting of several, rather large rooms, difficult to interpret as they have been seriously damaged. Around these two central cores there was a semi-peripheral path, which made it possible to move around the whole northern sector as far as the residential North-East Wing and the North-West Service Wing. Immediately north of the small side courtyard, L.2950, were the rooms beneath which were excavated the three tombs of the Royal Necropolis that

Figure 14.35 Ebla, Western Palace (Area Q), entrance to the North-East Staircase, from the south-east, 18th–17th century BC.

have so far been brought to light: they had been readapted in natural cavities of the rock. Another tomb, which has been completely sacked, could be reached through a steep staircase: it has been found north-west of the Audience Quarter. A striking characteristic of the Western Palace are the (at least) four staircases in the building, which make the existence of an upper floor in various parts of the building seem likely: in fact, besides the North-East Staircase, L.3120, of the residential North-East Wing and the smaller staircase, L.3155, in the North-West Service Wing, the remarkable projecting block in the west included a big staircase, L.3215 + L.3173, with four ramps, and at the far side from it, against the eastern perimeter wall, was another staircase, L.2952, also with four ramps, opening onto the western side of the small side courtyard L.2950.

Though it was seriously damaged by repeated sacking and frequent theft of stonework from the imposing foundations, the Western Palace (Figure 14.36) is by far the greatest public building of the Lower Town, and was a large royal palatine complex, certainly little smaller in size and monumental grandeur than Royal Palace E, which must have occupied much of the Old Syrian Citadel. The Western Palace was very probably planned as the crown prince's residence, and this was its function immediately before the fall of the city at the end of Middle Bronze II, when, like all the other palatine buildings of the period, it was sacked and set on fire in the terrible destruction that devastated the whole Old Syrian city around 1600 BC.

Figure 14.36 Ebla, Western Palace (Area Q), general view of the Old Syrian palace after the conservative restoration, from the north, 18th–17th century BC.

The Southern Palace, Area FF (Middle Bronze I–II)

The only public building of the classical Old Syrian Period so far identified at the foot of the Acropolis, in the southern region of the Lower Town is the Southern Palace (Area FF), identified in 2002 and excavated in 2003 and 2004 (Figure 14.37). With its back wall facing the inner wall of the Citadel, the structure of this sophisticated palatine building was originally more or less square, and its entrance was at the south-west corner, to which there may have been a street leading off the main radial road that started from the Damascus Gate. In its primitive form, the building, which must date from Middle Bronze I, probably extended for about 28 m on the east–west axis, and for about 33 m on the south–north axis, with an overall surface little less than 1,000 square metres; while refurbishing, rebuilding, and enlargements during

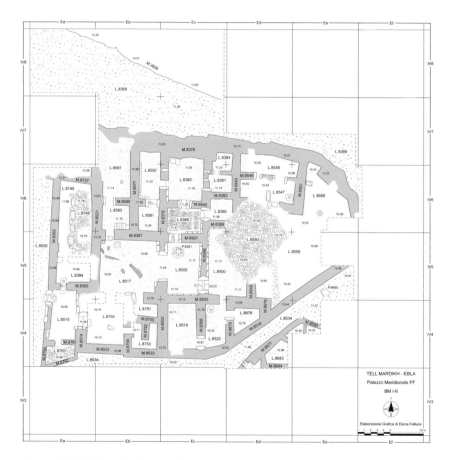

Figure 14.37 Ebla, Southern Palace (Area FF), schematic plan of the Old Syrian palace, 18th–17th century BC.

Middle Bronze II gave the building an elongated form, with an unusual triangular appendix to the east, giving a total of about 1,200 square metres, given that, at its point of maximum extension, the east–west axis was about 41 m long, while the south–north width remained unchanged. In the first and second phases, the annex of the Stables (150 square metres) was added to the building: this was a long structure with special functional features, built next to the western side of the building, with an independent entrance opening on the north side of a small square, whose eastern side was the entrance to the Southern Palace.

There are five main quarters in this compact and sophisticated palatine building, in which many of the bases of the walls have fine limestone orthostatic linings, and which is well preserved almost everywhere, sometimes with still fairly well- preserved walls in mud bricks. At the entrance, which opened onto the southern part of the west façade, partly concealed by the annex of the Stables, there was a small vestibule, L.8755, which led to the terrace, through a small stairway with four ramps, L.8753, as well as to the Audience Quarter of the building, which was an almost square large hall, L.8517, featuring the most carefully worked orthostats for the wall bases in the whole building. This was one of the two rooms of a typical Audience Quarter, and had in the back room, L.8505, situated east of the front one, the real Throne Room, which was small. This central area of the whole palace actually included three rooms, with two to the front on the west–east axis, L.8517 and L.8505, and one, still larger, at the back, L.8500, which was probably a large store-room for the two front rooms of the Audience Hall proper. In front of the public entrance to the large vestibule of the Audience Hall, to the north, was a second door giving onto two rooms one after the other, this time on the south–north axis, L.8583 and L.8591, which must have been store-rooms for the Audience Hall: in the second and larger one of this small quarter in the north-west, several impressions have been found in the floor of large storage jars arranged in two rows, along the west and east walls. The central Audience Quarter was located, very reasonably, between two other important palatine quarters, one to the north, which was larger, and must have been residential, and one to the south, which was certainly the Kitchen, given the presence of fire-places. The Central-Northern Quarter had a tripartite structure, with the main central body consisting of two rooms, L.8380 and L.8388; the lateral one, to the west, was formed of two rooms, L.8592 and L.8581; and the other lateral one, to the east, had three smaller rooms – L.8384, L.8381, and L.8390. The main room in this area was the central, residential one, L.8380, which originally had two wide entrances, later reduced, which led, east and west, to the side wings, and a central door to the south, which, through the small courtyard L.8388, paved with cobblestones, led directly to the Audience Hall L.8505, which was central to the whole system. In this way, this functionally basic hall could be reached both from the residential Central-Northern Quarter, and from the large store-room in the east (L.8500), communicating with the southern Kitchen Quarter, as well as from the west via an unusually large door that led to the large vestibule (L.8517) of the Audience Hall, through which those being received clearly entered. Thus the complex of vestibule and Audience Hall in the central area, which was the only one that communicated, even indirectly, with every sector of the building, had two entrances, one private and direct from the residential quarter, and the other public from the entrance area of the palace to the vestibule of the Audience Hall. The southern wing (Kitchen Quarter), which was clearly intended for food production, had a central room, L.8520, where there were fire-places, and two side rooms, one to the east, L.8676, almost triangular after the modifications to the building, and one to the west, L.8519, which must have been a store-room. Much of the large eastern part of the building of the last phase is the result of extensions which have made it an unusual trapezoidal area with a large open courtyard, L.8559. But it must originally have been a smaller back area, where there was, to the north, the North-East Quarter with only two east–west rooms (L.8547 and L.8548) to the south of the northern perimeter wall: they were probably part of the original plan, in which the building was more regular, and less extensive than it became in the final period, when L.8548 and L.8547 became longer.

The Southern Palace's functions were certainly closely connected to the Stables, consisting of just two rooms, very unusual in shape and furniture, which were set out on a south–north axis: the southern one, L.8394, which was a small vestibule, is now seriously damaged by a large pit that was probably caused by the underlying rock giving way, and the northern one, L.8748 + L.8749, which was the actual stable. It had a central set of five basins that were certainly mangers, separated by high monolithic pillars. This latter room to the east had a larger paved space, L.8748, where the animals could stand, and must have been intended for horses, while the narrower one to the west, L.8749, was clearly used by those working in the stables. The high technical quality of the buildings, as well as some significant, though rare, findings there, that show a clear connection with the palatine administration, and the close relation between building and Stables, suggest that the Southern Palace was an important public building of Ebla's central government.

The Royal Necropolis, Area Q (Middle Bronze I–II)

The Royal Necropolis, which used a series of natural cavities in the central sector of the Western Lower Town as funerary hypogea, was identified in Area Q in 1978, in the early excavations of the Western Palace. At least seven tombs were identified, mostly violated and sacked in ancient times, both under the flooring of the Western Palace itself, and to the south of it near Rashap's Temple (B1) and the Sanctuary of the Deified Royal Ancestors (B2). In 1978 and 1979, three important, communicating tombs were excavated entirely, beneath the central-eastern sector of the Western Palace: the so-called "Tomb of the Princess", the "Tomb of the Lord of the Goats", and the "Tomb of

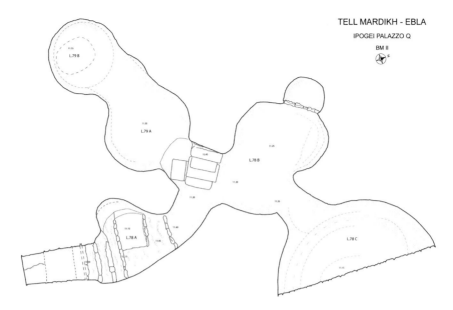

Figure 14.38 Ebla, hypogea of the Royal Tombs, schematic plan of the Tomb of the Princess (L.78A), the Tomb of the Lord of the Goats (L.78B–C), and the Tomb of the Cisterns (L.79A–B), 19th–17th century BC.

the Cisterns". Later, in 2002, during restoration work, another tomb, that had been completely sacked, was found in the central-western sector of the Western Palace, situated, like the others, in the area north of the Audience Hall L.3038.

Following a long-standing tradition in the Syro-Palestinian area of Middle Bronze I–II, the tombs of the Royal Necropolis (Figure 14.38) consisted of a hypogeum that was reached through a funerary shaft which led directly into the underground cavity; or through a shaft that reached the hypogeum via a stairway dug out of the rock, or built with stone slabs; or by means of a stairway that completely replaced the shaft. After burial, the funerary shaft was usually filled with stones, hidden from sight by flooring, and made essentially inaccessible, as in the case of the original shaft of the Tomb of the Lord of the Goats (L.2980), while the corridor or stairway could also be blocked by great slabs, as in the case of the Tomb of the Princess (L.2950). However, at least in one case, that of the Tomb of the Cisterns, which also communicated with the Tomb of the Lord of the Goats, access to the hypogea was through clearly visible slabs at the centre of a small room (L.2975) in the Western Palace. In many cases, however, the tombs of the Royal Necropolis were violated, mainly in three periods, distant in time from each other and in very different circumstances. In certain cases, like that of the Tomb of the Cisterns, the violation and sacking took place with the conquest and destruction of the city, around 1600 BC, precisely because the entrance was visible. Later, violations to plunder the hypogea happened sporadically during the Persian and Hellenistic Periods, the phase of Mardikh VIA–B, because certain sectors of the Lower Town had become visible. The most systematic and serious sacking took place, however, at the time of Mardikh VII, in the Byzantine Period, when there were excavations in the Western Palace, perhaps not only to obtain building materials for a small monastic settlement of stylites, but also to plunder the rich furnishings of the tombs that had now been discovered. Of the three tombs that were completely excavated, only the Tomb of the Princess was found untouched, though seriously damaged, particularly as regards the deposition, by the collapse of the stone vault and by strong infiltration of water, because it was originally separated from the Tomb of the Lord of the Goats by a mud brick wall. The Tomb of the Lord of the Goats and the Tomb of the Cisterns were violated, and violently and hastily plundered at the time of the destruction of the great city of Mardikh IIIB: the outraging and profanation of the bodies must have been quite deliberate, while it is certain that the sacking was hasty and careless, as quite a few objects, mainly hidden by the mud of the water infiltrations, were not removed, and some minor precious objects were lost on the stairway of the hypogeum and even in the entrance room to the tombs, whose sealing stones were found to have been moved and left half-open.

The oldest of the three tombs so far excavated, the Tomb of the Princess (Figure 14.39), who was probably buried between 1825 and 1775 BC, was

Figure 14.39 Ebla, Tomb of the Princess (Area Q), the *faïence* vase among jars of the Common Ware in Hypogeum L.78A, 19th–18th century BC.

fairly narrow, consisting of a single small hypogeum that was deliberately separated from the northern communicating cavities by a small mud brick wall which resisted for some time before water infiltrations destroyed it: however, it was still in place around 1600 BC when the conquerors of Mardikh IIIB penetrated from the entrance to the Tomb of the Cisterns as far as the hypogea of the Tomb of the Lord of the Goats. The royal personage who was buried in the Tomb of the Lord of the Goats was probably the Immeya whose name appears in a cuneiform inscription, carved on the rim of a fine silver bowl that was laid in the tomb. Whenever it was that he was interred (probably between 1750 and 1700 BC), he was given three cavities, which have been named Hypogea B1, B2, and C, all of which were north of the Tomb of the Princess. Hypogeum B1 was an approximately rectangular cave, that was shaped and extended to include the mouth of the funerary shaft that opened on its northern side and that was never opened: indeed, it was discovered during the excavations, completely blocked by thick layers of medium-size stones. Hypogeum B2 was a short corridor between Hypogeum B1 to the north and the large Hypogeum C to the east, into which some of the vases of the furniture in the Tomb of the Princess fell, when the dividing wall against which they were heaped gave way.

Hypogeum C was a large semi-circular cavity, created by a strong stone wall to block the whole eastern sector of a round cavity whose natural roof had probably collapsed (Figure 14.40). When the Lord of the Goats was buried, the west wall of the system of three hypogea was certainly in place, but it was removed (we do not know how voluntarily) when the entrance to the Tomb of the Cisterns was opened on that western wall. The tomb got its name from two communicating cisterns, whose mouths had been sealed with large slabs, and which opened immediately to the west of the Tomb of the Lord of the Goats. The entrance to the Tomb of the Cisterns, which is certainly the most recent of the three, was created by destroying the wall separating it from the Tomb of the Lord of the Goats: this entrance, which opened more or less at the centre of room L.2975, blocked by two large, highly visible limestone slabs, was opened by those who sacked the Western Palace and, in their flight, failed to close the entrance, allowing the materials, covered with ash from the destruction of Mardikh IIIB, to fall on the steps of the short entrance corridor to the two, now communicating, burials.

The Northern Palace, Area P (Middle Bronze II)

Situated north of the extended Ishtar's Sacred Area in the northern Lower Town, the Northern Palace, founded in the classical Old Syrian Period and occupying a surface area of around 3,500 square metres, was discovered during soundings carried out in 1986, and went on being explored systematically until 1989, with significant additions in 1994; some striking aspects of its structure were clarified, particularly in the damaged western sector of

Figure 14.40 Ebla, Tomb of the Lord of the Goats (Area Q), the hippopotamus ivory talisman in Hypogeum L.78C, 18th century BC.

the building, in 1999 and 2000 as part of the restoration work carried out in 2000. It was preceded by the Intermediate Palace of late Middle Bronze I, probably built around 1850 BC, whose well-preserved remains were identified in 1995 in some very limited soundings in some rooms of the north sector of the Northern Palace. On the other hand, this important later royal building may have been built in the decades between 1775 and 1750 BC, covering the central and southern quarters of the earlier Archaic Palace, which had been there since the last years of the late Early Syrian Period, not long before 2000 BC. Although the elevations are not strong, the northern and central parts of the Northern Palace are well preserved, as is the southern part, where a major east–west road, L.4201, separates it from Ishtar's Sacred Area; the peripheral south-east and south-west quarters are lost.

This important palatine building (Figure 14.41), whose peculiar trapez-oidal plan was actually determined by the pre-existing Archaic Palace, faced west, with its entrance in the centre of the unusually shaped west façade, which had a jutting central element, through which the entrance opened. Its main axis was west–east, extending perhaps more than 65 m, although the south–north axis was only slightly shorter at 63 m. Access to the building was gained from a longitudinal room sub-divided into two areas, a wide one at the front, L.4261, and a long one at the back, L.4198: this entrance had a main distributive function. In fact, the two side doors led, to the north, to the large

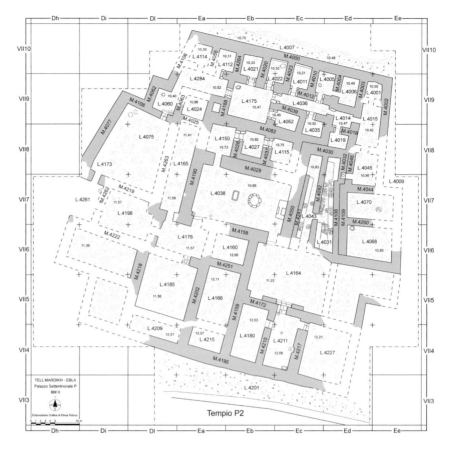

Figure 14.41 Ebla, Northern Palace (Area P), schematic plan of the classical Old
      Syrian palace, 18th–17th century BC.

northern service wing, and, to the south, to that part of the building set aside
for the sovereign's residential requirements; a third axial door, which opened
on the eastern side, led into a slightly smaller room, L.4176, which was the
vestibule to the topographically and functionally central core of the entire
building – the large Audience Hall, L.4038. As well as the large Audience
Hall, this sector included three small store-rooms, L.4150, L.4027, L.4115,
almost identical, in line on the north side, and three other rooms of varying
size on the south side, which were reached from the two doors to the Audience
Hall. In the central region of the building, behind the Audience Hall, to the
east, were two long irregular rooms, L.4031 and L.4043, with low benches, on
which rows of large storage jars for foodstuffs were still in place (Figure 14.42)
when they were excavated. Between these rooms and the largely lost eastern

Figure 14.42 Ebla, Northern Palace (Area P), storage jars in place in the store-room
L.4031, from the south-east, 18th–17th century BC.

perimeter wall, M.4002, there were two other rooms, oriented east–west, that
served as store-rooms or workshops. One of these, L.4070, contained many
ivories in the Egyptianizing style that must have decorated a valuable piece of
ceremonial furniture. On the front of the palatine building, before reaching
the extended northern service wing, there was a large room that must have
been a courtyard, L.4075, which led to the north-west corner, where there
were four small rooms, separated by a long and narrow fifth room, L.4284,
that certainly was an open-air communicating corridor.

This led to another small rectangular courtyard, L.4175, which, both directly and through the east–west corridor, L.4036, giving onto the eastern side,
led to all the small rooms in this area of the building, which were probably
designed for food preparation, given the presence there of moveable ovens.
While there was complete communication within the northern wing, the
southern area of the building was sub-divided into two separate sectors: the
south-western wing, which was next to the lost southern parts of the western
façade, and the south-eastern wing, which was to the south-east of the
Audience Hall. As we have said, the south-western wing was reached from the
vestibule, and it had at least six distinct rooms, which were certainly designed
for visitors – some of them must have been waiting rooms. The small room
L.4176, which may at first have led into the adjacent eastern room L.4160,
was a vestibule for the Audience Hall, L.4038, which was reached from an

entrance in the southern wall, M.4156, in the south-west corner, which was near the public part of the building; while on the same side of the room, towards the south-east corner, where the private sector was, there was a door for the king that was reached, within the south-east wing, through the larger courtyard L.4164. The south-east wing was conceived quite differently from the other quarters of the palace, and this courtyard led into three large parallel rooms with a north–south orientation, L.4180, L.4211, L.4227, which very probably formed the royal apartment: it was certainly the most private and protected wing in the building, communicating directly with the Audience Hall. This hall, L.4038, was a large rectangular room, 19.50 m long from west to east, along the same axis as the building, and 10.30 m wide. There was a (now badly damaged) dais on the eastern wall for the sovereign's throne, and, opposite it, a large round base set apart, 0.65 m high and 2.30 m across, lined by small orthostats, which must have held up a large basalt tripod, whose feet were worked in the round and carved, whose remains were found scattered around the base itself. On the same axis of the royal dais, between the round base and the western back wall, was a large, shallow basalt basin, which was found in place, but broken: like the tripod, it must have had a ceremonial function. Although large, the Audience Hall was originally covered: it was filled in by the burnt bricks of the collapsed perimeter walls, and under them by a thick mixture of burnt wooden beams and ashes. Access to it was from the south-west for those being received by the king, and from the south-east for the king himself and his officials, while the three smaller rooms along the north side must have been store-rooms for the highly-prized products exchanged between the king and his guests.

Like all the other royal public buildings of the classical Old Syrian city, the Northern Palace was sacked mercilessly in the years around 1600 BC, when the city was finally destroyed. Almost all the rooms that were preserved with their original deposit still bore visible traces of the flames at the moment of excavation.

The Western Residence, Area Z (Middle Bronze II)

In 1996 a survey began of the western rampart of the great outer fortification of the Old Syrian city, to check the structure and extent of this enormous outer wall. Excavation of Area Z continued until 2007, with interruptions for technical reasons, and is still incomplete. It led to the discovery, in an area of the western Lower Town close to the inner base of the rampart, of dwellings from Middle Bronze II, most of which were well preserved and tended to be more complex and extensive than other areas of private houses. Although, so far, no street has been found onto which the dwelling-places opened, it seems certain that in the northern part of this area there is a large sector of an unusually large private house that has been named the Western Residence. This unusual building is unlike the large royal or administrative buildings in the settlement of the Lower Town, which are all rigorously isolated, as it was

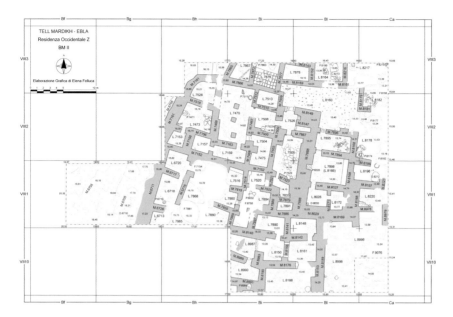

Figure 14.43 Ebla, Western Residence (Area Z), schematic plan of the classical Old Syrian building, 18th–17th century BC.

clearly part of an upper-class residential quarter, at least to the north and south. In extent and technique, it seems to fall between the public palaces and private houses.

Although it has not yet been completely explored, the Western Residence (Figure 14.43) seems to have had a front south–north unit (including at least rooms L.8178 and L.8198) that probably looked out on a road on the far western edge of the Lower Town, and must have allowed access to the large peripheral courtyard or square L.8160, immediately to the south, of houses that were not part of the Western Residence (including rooms L.7867, L.7876, L.7878, L.8164), with which it did not communicate. The south side of this northern courtyard led to three elongated parallel dwellings: the first two, to the east, with their entrances in L.7895 and L.7526; and the third, which shared with the second its entrance vestibule L.7526, followed by another vestibule, L.7508. Both of the first two units (the second of which is completely preserved) were developed along a south–north axis, while the third was more extensive and complex, built around a central core rather than developing longitudinally like the other two. The first, with its front vestibule L.7895, intermediate courtyard L.7896, and two rear rooms L.8028 and L.8172, had been conceived following a basic scheme common in the dwellings of Old Syrian Ebla; and the second seems to have been similar, with its vestibule L.7526 in the front sector, long courtyard L.7505, and, oddly, just one narrow room in the rear, L.7633. Nothing similar can be seen in the third and larger one, pivoting on the large central space L.7470, which was certainly a courtyard originally, but later was probably covered in part with the support of three columns whose quadrangular bases are still in place. This third and larger dwelling had its rooms arranged around the original central courtyard, its western side having the classical organization of vestibule to the front (L.7528), small intermediate courtyard (L.7473), and two rear rooms (L.7153 and L.7157, the latter communicating with a room on the south side, L.7159). Some significant findings in this sector, such as a jar with the dynastic seal of the son of king Indilimgur/Indilimma impressed on its shoulder, suggest that the Western Residence was the home of an important figure in the court of the sovereigns in the classical Old Syrian Period. Very probably, the original core of the Western Residence consisted only of the second and third areas described, which were effectively limited to the west by the base wall of the rampart, and featured a strikingly thick front boundary wall (M.7888) to the east. Only later did it extend eastwards, acquiring the spaces of the first dwelling described and a part of the building, so far not completely excavated, that was probably towards the front.

Like the partially excavated adjacent residences to the south, which seem to have had unusually large rooms, the Western Residence must have belonged to a socially high residential area in the city. Like the whole of the rest of the settlement, this sector too of the western Lower Town was strongly damaged by fire during the final destruction of Ebla at the end of Middle Bronze II, but there were greater attempts in early Late Bronze I to rebuild it than any of the other areas that have been discovered so far. Some quite thick walls that had been built over the ruins of the Residence were abandoned before completion, but, particularly in the area to the south, there were also rebuilding and reuse during Late Bronze I, which was also repeated during Late Bronze II, with again poorer structures.

Private houses quarter, Area B (Middle Bronze II)

The most extensive area of well-preserved Middle Bronze II private houses explored to date, in an area in the south-west Lower Town where excavations have taken place from the beginning of the exploration of Tell Mardikh, is located between the Sanctuary of the Deified Royal Ancestors (Sanctuary B2), to the west, the Southern Palace (Palace FF) to the east, and Rashap's Temple to the north-west: in all it covers some 1,300 square metres. Excavation on these private houses began in 1966 and continued over a number of years, but was only systematically reprised in 2002, completing the recovery of a wide sector between two south–north roads: road L.2110, to the west, flanking the eastern side of Sanctuary B2, and road L.9689, to the east, which flanks the western side of the Southern Palace, and is sub-divided into two larger blocks, to the north and south of an east–west diagonal road, L.8651. This area of

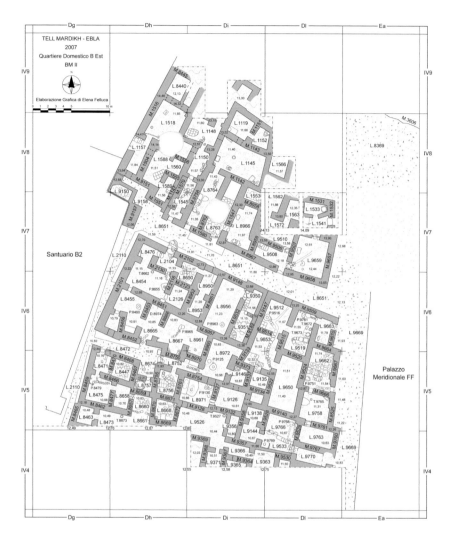

Figure 14.44 Ebla, private houses quarter in the south-west Lower Town (Area B East), schematic plan of the classical Old Syrian dwellings, 18th–17th century BC.

private housing (Figure 14.44), wedged between the Sanctuary in Area B and the Palace of Area FF, is the only one to extend to the south up to the circuit of inner fortifications around the Citadel, creating a short gap in the ring of public buildings, secular and religious, which form an irregular circle around the Citadel's base.

The houses of the relatively limited extension of the northern block, their entrance for the most part on the diagonal road L.8651, for the most part included a vestibule, a small courtyard, and two or more rooms on the side opposite the entrance. The last dwelling to the west is very well preserved with a number of lintels still in place over the doors; the elongated vestibule of the small elongated room L.1157 would seem to be the result of an extension which absorbed a smaller dwelling immediately to the west, most probably made up of the entrance, L.1589, a possible courtyard, L.1588, and at least one small side room, L.1560. After the extension, this larger housing unit consisted of an eastern wing opening onto the vestibule, formed by incorporating the adjacent small house, the original core centred on the courtyard, L.1518, and smaller rooms at the back, such as L.8440. This kind of dwelling was often considerably elongated, as in the case of the central unit which used the long vestibule L.8764 as entrance and had a rather large diagonal courtyard, L.1145, with two small rooms at the back, L.1119 and L.1152. In smaller units there appeared to be no vestibule, the first living area being a small elongated courtyard, L.8763, onto which opened one spacious side room, L.8966. In the far eastern block, on the other hand, the domestic units were larger and always had an entrance vestibule, L.9508, onto which a large room, L.9659, opened to the east, and to the north a relatively small diagonal courtyard, L.9510: at the back were a number of very small and differently collocated rooms, to both the north-west (L.1553 and L.1562) and the north-east (L.1563).

In the southern block, where entrances could be either on one of the three main roads or on a blind alley, L.8472, running west–east and with no function of circulation but only of distribution, there were much more extensive houses, once again often the result of enlargements of smaller units.

The most singular example is that of the largest house, at the north-western periphery of the southern block, apparently formed of two once independent units, one to the north, its entrance in the vestibule L.2104, opening onto the diagonal north road L.8651, and one to the south, opening onto the blind alley L.8472, similarly with its entrance in the vestibule, L.8665; the two units seem to have been separated originally by the east–west wall M.8451, into the eastern stretch of which a door would later have been cut to allow communication between the courtyard of the north unit, L.8454, and a side room in the south unit, L.8455. It is equally probable that the north unit was also the result of absorbing a smaller eastern unit, with its entrance in vestibule L.8950, given that its original door on to street L.8651 has clearly been bricked up, creating a lateral unit within the new, extended house. In all, this unusually large house had some ten rooms, a courtyard in a central area, L.8454, and a peripheral, south courtyard, L.8667; above all, and quite anomalously, it had retained two entrances, one main front entrance on the east–west road to the north, and a secondary one on the blind alley behind, to the south. The north-east area of the southern block seems to have housed small domestic units like the central building on the east–west diagonal road, comprising vestibule L.9350, the large lateral courtyard L.8956, and only one room, L.9351. Although seemingly adapted with some difficulty within the whole southern block, another small unit featured a characteristic structure, skilfully created from residual spaces: this house opened onto the eastern end of blind alley L.8472, with vestibule L.8752, diagonal court L.8972, and only one room at the back, L.9146. Equally peculiar, and almost certainly the result of successive, easily recognizable adaptations, is a relatively large house, the entrance of which stood on the north-east corner of the southern block on the main east street. This had a vestibule at the entrance, L.9663, court-yard L.9519, room L.9512, and probably a second inner courtyard, L.9653, followed by a small store-room, L.9135, and an unusually large living space, L.9650. While in some cases, however (for example, the house with vesti-bule L.9662), the arrangement of the rooms (here all adjacent to the façade looking onto the main south–north street L.9689) is totally anomalous, evin-cing extreme variety and flexibility in spatial solutions, others offer the trad-itional layout, with a deep, axial development, as in the south-east dwelling opening onto street L.9689. This had its entrance in vestibule L.9770, which was followed by courtyard L.9766 and ended, very typically, in the two back rooms, L.9144 and L.9138. Lastly, if the domestic unit with its entrance vesti-bule, L.8471, on the south side of the blind alley L.8472 was also considerably extended compared with the original plan, it is certain that one or two of the units in the central sector of the southern block would have had their entrance to the south of the limits of the excavated area, where there must have been a larger, east–west street which was probably the continuation to the west of street L.8534, flanking the south perimeter of the Southern Palace.

All the houses in Sector B East were set on fire in the destruction of the whole settlement which ended the life of the Middle Bronze II Old Syrian city; the tops of the mud brick walls of many of them lie not far beneath the present-day surface of the tell. The destruction would seem to have taken the city by surprise, given the various stored goods and domestic objects abandoned in the houses. Unlike, of course, the inevitable fate of the great royal buildings and possibly some of the cult structures, which were thoroughly plundered, the private houses were set on fire with no prior systematic looting.

Notes

Foreword

[pp. xxv–xxvi] As regards the Mesopotamian ideology, in particular the ancient Sumerian ideology, about the divine creation of cities, as foundations of civilization, depending from the primaeval foundation of the temple of the protecting deity of the city in the mythical time of origins, see now Matthiae (1994a). Within the frame of an attempt at reconstruction of several aspects of the Mesopotamian way of thinking as an organic and unitary system, the main texts are mentioned and partially translated, which refer to the mythical foundations and to the laments over the destructions of cities. These texts date from the end of the third to the first half of the second millennium BC. Also passages of the most important Assyrian inscriptions are taken into account, dealing with the building and reconstruction of the capitals of the empire between the ninth and the eighth century BC.

[pp. xxvi–xxvii] Otten (1984, pp. 50–60), presented the first information about the bilingual "Chant of Release": several large fragments of the poem were found by the German archaeological expedition at Boghazköy in the smaller temples of the Upper Town of the Hittite capital Hattusa between 1983 and 1985. The important elements about Ebla in the Hurrian–Hittite poem were immediately underlined in several contributions by the German philologists even before the publication of the final edition of the text (1996): see Otten (1988); Neu (1996b). The critical edition of all the fragments ascribed to this basic text of the Ancient Near East was published by Neu (1996a). S. de Martino (2000) provided an excellent overall analysis of this difficult text. P. Matthiae discussed for the first time at the Accademia Nazionale dei Lincei, on 8 November 2001 (unpublished lecture) the peculiar, and certainly unexpected, relations in important aspects of the poetic concept and of the narrative structure between this bilingual Hurrian–Hittite poem and the epic matter which was collected and re-elaborated in *The Iliad*.

1 From Tell Mardikh to Ebla: Archaeological exploration

[pp. 1–4] The history of the modern archaeological exploration of the regions where the pre-classical civilizations of the Ancient Orient flourished is complex, articulated, and tormented, due to the strong and repeated conditioning from international politics (sometimes direct) by the great Western powers, and from ideology and religion (frequently inter-related with the Arab–Israeli conflict): elements for a synthetic interpretation of this history may be found in Matthiae (2005); accurate analytical information about the development of excavations since the mid-nineteenth century until the Second World War, with special concern for, but not restricted to, Mesopotamia is provided by Parrot (1946); Moorey (1991) offers a balanced recent analysis of the archaeology based on the Bible, mainly concerning Palestine. The events of the excavations in Syria are described by Matthiae (1981a; 1989a). More recently Al-Maqdissi (2008) provided a commemoration of the outstanding figures of the Syrian archaeology of the past, pre-classical as well as classical.

[pp. 5–6] The British excavations at Tell Atshanah started in 1936, on behalf of the British Museum of London, and were led by Sir Leonard Woolley, who had just been made a baronet for his extraordinary accomplishments as excavator of Ur; on this site he had worked for 12 memorable campaigns between 1922 and 1934, and was so successful that Max Mallowan, his assistant at the time, and later on the excavator of Nimrud, stated: 'We will never see anything equal to this prodigy'. The great archaeologist of Ur decided to choose Tell Atshanah based on scientific reasons, related to his interest in the relations between the Levant and the Aegean, and on personal and human motivations, descending from his wish to conclude in a verdant Mediterranean region an unprecedented epoch of oriental archaeology, which had required of him a huge physical engagement in the desert regions of southern Mesopotamia. This second aim was summarized in the famous sentence by the charming and strong-willed Katherine Woolley: 'Leonard, next expedition on the sea shore!' The expedition went on until 1949, with interruptions due to the cut in grants, and, as an extremely bizarre consequence of Western politics, it started when the area under excavation was in Syria, and it was concluded when the area had been allotted to Turkey. The results were published in a successful volume (Woolley 1953) and in the succeeding final report, quite incomplete for several aspects, and rightly questioned for several unacceptable very high dates for the oldest levels (Woolley 1955).

The first, detailed revision of the chronology of Alalakh XVIII–VIII can be found in Hrouda (1957); a short study by Frankfort (1952) is seminal for his intuition of the continuity in the architectural tradition of Syria from Middle Bronze II to Iron Age II, based on the monumental architectural evidence of Alalakh in the second millennium BC.

More relevant, albeit partial, contributions on aspects of Syrian glyptics of the classical Old Syrian period, usually based on material of Alalakh VII, only partially published by Woolley, are Moortgat-Correns (1955); Porada (1957); Nagel and Strommenger (1958). Later on, the Alalakh glyptics were published in two exhaustive books by Collon (1975; 1982), where this rich material is completely available. More recently, Otto (2000) provided a satisfactory and systematic classification of the classical Old Syrian glyptics.

An attempt at revising, in an inclusive and unitary way, the reconstruction of the historical development of the artistic culture of Middle and Late Bronze Syria was made by Matthiae (1962), under the strong influence of Ranuccio Bianchi Bandinelli's innovatory teaching. These interpretations were presented for the first time (Matthiae 1975a), albeit in a very summary way, in an authoritative history of art of the Ancient Orient with a wide international collaboration.

[pp. 10–12] The triumph inscriptions of Sargon and Naram-Sin of Akkad mentioning Ebla were kept in faithful ancient copies of the Old Babylonian period, and can nowadays be found in reliable critical editions: Gelb and Kienast (1990, pp. 163–167, 253–264); Frayne (1993, pp. 27–29, 132–135). The close relation of Ebla with Urshum may be inferred from the inscription on Gudea of Lagash's Statue B, of the second half of the twenty-second century BC: Steible (1991, pp. 164–165); Edzard (2007, p. 33). Mentions of Urshum in the Old Hittite inscriptions of Hattusili I are listed by de Martino (2003). On the citation of Ebla in the geographical List inscribed on the seventh pylon of the celebrated Temple of Amun in Karnak, see Helck (1962, p. 147, No. 306); while for a historical evaluation of the military exploits of Thutmosis III against the kingdom of Mittani and in the Aleppo, Euphrates, and Balikh regions, see Redford (1992, pp. 157–160).

[pp. 10–12] On a swift, memorable journey from Jerusalem to Baghdad and finally Ur in 1926, a singular reversal of Abraham's presumed itinerary from Ur to Kharran and Jerusalem, William F. Albright (Albright, Dougherty 1926, p. 9), the uncontested master of American Biblical archaeology, paused on the acropolis of Tell Afis, correctly identified by him as the Aramaic centre of Hazrek, cited in the Old Testament and in the royal inscriptions of the Assyrian Empire as Khatarikka, a few kilometres north of Tell Mardikh, standing clear against the southern horizon. The village's inhabitants, he stated, mentioned two more large tells in the area: one they called Tell Tuqan, 15 km to the east which, however, Albright had too little time to visit; and another the name of which he did not catch or failed to understand. These were clearly Tell Mardikh, Tell Tuqan, and Tell Afis, the three large tells west of the marshes of Math, where Nahr Quweyq, Aleppo's river, comes to an end. These are also marked as the only ones larger than 25 hectares by van Liere (1963, p. 116). Albright's anonymous tell must have been Tell Mardikh, visible to him from a distance, but difficult to recognize for a scholar used to tells of more modest size and generally differently structured, as are those of Palestine. On the same journey he arrived at the Euphrates, investigated Tell Bi'a, the ancient Tuttul, near Raqqah, which he quite wrongly identified as Ebla, and then, further down the valley, Tell Hariri, which he was the first to identify, quite rightly, as a plausible candidate for Mari. Only a few years later, in 1933, a chance find at Tell Hariri prompted the French authorities to contact André Parrot of the Louvre, recently returned from the excavations at Telloh and at Larsa in Iraq, initiating the momentous and still ongoing exploration of Mari.

In 1963, in Aleppo, at the Hotel Baron, on his return from Tell Khuera, I met Anton Moortgat, leading master of the Germanic archaeological school of the Berlin Freie Universität, and asked for his opinion on Tell Mardikh. I had already decided to urge Rome University to file a request to excavate the site, and he replied enigmatically but prophetically: 'If Rome University should decide to ask for an excavation permit for Tell Mardikh, I don't believe they will regret it'.

In 1977, during a seminar at Yale University, Harald Ingholt, by then one of the major specialists on Syria under the Roman Empire, told me he remembered visiting Tell Mardikh shortly before 1937, when he was directing the Hamah excavations, and had been impressed by the size of the site and by the very close resemblance of surface ceramics with their own findings in Hamah from the older urban phases.

The double carved basalt basin, one of the essential elements behind Rome University's decision to systematically explore Tell Mardikh, had been found in the South-West Lower Town of the site in 1955 by functionaries of the Directorate General of Antiquities and Museums in Northern Syria, and had been placed in the temporary store-rooms of the Archaeological Museum in Aleppo, where, in 1962, I was able to access the immensely important collection while it awaited a more definitive location. Subhi Sawaf, the Aleppo functionary who (helped by Mardikh villagers) had found the piece (now in the National Museum in Damascus) had briefly announced the find (Sawaf 1963, pp. 38–39, fig. 18); he was the first representative of the Directorate General of Antiquities and Museums at the Tell Mardikh site throughout 1964, the first year of Italian excavations, and was convinced it belonged to the Aramaic Age, in the early first millennium BC. The date of Middle Bronze I was proposed by Matthiae (1965, pp. 71–80).

The find, as she told me many years later, had attracted the attention of J. Vorys Canby of Walters Art Gallery, Baltimore, in a visit to Aleppo shortly before 1960. In 1964 the inhabitants of the village of Mardikh were able to give me relatively precise directions to the flat clearing of the South-West Lower Town where they had located it: the result was the opening of excavation Area B that same year. When the site was temporarily extended in 1965, the second year of operations, a small angular fragment of the basin was indeed found (having clearly been lost when the basin was initially discovered) on the steps of what was then called Temple B, now identified as the Temple of Rashap: Matthiae (1966, pp. 130–32, pl. LIV 2).

[pp. 13–15] The policy behind the Tell Mardikh excavation has always been and still is based on a fundamental criterion which naturally emerges after considering the results of the single years against the extended period. A selection is made of historical issues of city planning, architectural reconstruction, and functional interpretation presented by the succession of large settlements on the site. These are then dealt with systematically and in chronological order in cycles of excavations, each lasting some years, until clarified in every possible aspect from a scrupulously organic analysis of the importance of the site in the different periods: Matthiae (1997a; 1997b, pp. 1–29).

The excellent results produced by the finding of Royal Palace G and the Early Bronze IVB State Archives met with great interest in international public opinion. Amply reported in the international press, not least *The Times* of London, they were also presented in a succinct overview by Matthiae (1977a) (but see particularly Matthiae 1977b). Academic opinion too was immediately positive: cf. that of an expert Assyriologist such as Veenhof (1977); the measured and authoritative considerations of one of the greatest experts of Akkadian language such as von Soden (1988); the significant appraisal of a distinguished scholar of Ancient Oriental languages like Diakonoff (1990); and that of a great Sumer specialist: Edzard (1993).

The double discovery of the Royal Palace G and the Royal Archives of Ebla similarly received prominent coverage in the more popular international press, although some confusion had been introduced by G. Pettinato's repeated and unfounded claims of linkage between the Ebla texts and Old Testament exegesis; this not only aroused the almost unhealthy interest of Anglo-Saxon, and particularly American, circles eager to imagine an illogical "Abraham's connection" in the ancient Early Syrian texts, but took the more concrete form of an aggressive, unjustified, and indecorous press campaign against the Syrian authorities who were absurdly accused of delaying publication of the texts on account of the putative Ebla–Bible links. For the many news items in the non-specialist press, see *Time–Life Books Nature/Science Annual 1978 Edition*, (Anonymous 1978, pp. 34–45) and La Fay, Stanfield, and Glanzman (1978), which quotes the now famous statement by the most prominent of Chicago's Assyriologists, the late Ignace J. Gelb: 'Italians at Ebla discovered a new culture, a new language, a new history'. On the frequently harsh and sometimes directly political polemics after the hasty and equivocal statements as to the contents of texts still largely unedited at the time and thus unavailable to the international scientific community, see P. Matthiae's trenchant reconstruction(2008a, pp. 223–227).

[pp. 15–18] The historical phases of Ebla were cohesively and exhaustively defined for the first time in 1977 in the first edition of an essay (Matthiae 1981a), which in this part remained substantially unaltered in the 1989 edition: Matthiae (1989a, pp. 36–65). Ebla's final destruction in late Middle Bronze II, at the end of the classical Old Syrian Period, in what is traditionally termed the Middle Chronology of the Ancient Orient, datable to c. 1600 BC, is placed within a wider historical perspective by Matthiae (2006a). Various attempts were made to reconstruct the devastated city, but were soon abandoned in a climate of radical crisis which was certainly demographic, economic, and social, but also possibly conditioned, if not actually determined, by a microclimatic crisis which may have been connected with the catastrophic eruption of Santorini in the Aegean Sea: Matthiae (2007b).

2 Ebla and early urbanization in Syria

[pp. 19–21] The historiographic problem of the forming of cities and states in western Asia and Egypt in the "First Urbanization" period of the second half of the fourth millennium BC is the object of a bibliography so extensive as to be beyond the range of even the most reduced of summaries here, but can be found in synthetic critical works more interested in the related question of the "Second Urbanization": Redman (1978); Nissen (1983); Lamberg-Karlowsky (1985, pp. 55–72; 1989); Diakonoff (1991); Frangipane (1996); Liverani (1998); Ramazzotti (1999); Postgate (2002); Trigger (2003); Butterlin (2003; 2009).

[pp. 21–23] On the link between the so-called colonies of Uruk on the Middle Euphrates and early forms of civilization in Upper Mesopotamia and Upper Syria, see Wattenmaker (1990) Stein and Rothman (1994); Stein (1999); Rothman (2001); and in particular, the essay by Schwartz (2001).

Informed and perceptive evaluations of the significant remains of Uruk in Upper Syria and their connections with the successive phenomena of regionalization and the subsequent blossoming of the "Second Urbanization" in Upper Syria and Upper Mesopotamia are advanced by G.M. Schwartz, in Akkermans and Schwartz (2003, pp. 181–232), where serviceable reference is also made to the urban development of Tell Brak-Nagar, Tell Leylan-Shekhna, and Tell Khuera.

[pp. 25–28] General considerations on the most ancient urban developments in Ebla may be found in Mazzoni (1991; 2000a; 2006).

On the discovery on the Ebla Acropolis of southern peripheral sections of what may have been a palatine building from Early Bronze III (building G2), see Matthiae (1987, pp. 136–138, figs 1–2; 2000a, pp. 573–576, figs 6–7).

A preliminary evaluation of the diffusion of settlements during Early Bronze I–III in the Orontes, Quweyq, and Sajur basins is given in Matthiae (1993a) while some considerations on ceramics of the period – their chronology, and their interconnections, all still valid despite the rapid progress in excavations and knowledge – can be found in Schwartz and Weiss (1992); a reliable general overview of the second urbanization in Syria is that of Akkermans and Schwartz (2003, pp. 233–287).

3 Ebla, Mari, Akkad: From city-states to empire

[p. 30] On the destructions of Ebla at the end of Early Bronze IVA, Early Bronze IVB, and Middle Bronze II, the historical context of the three events, and the archaeological documentation of Tell Mardikh, which very clearly endorses three considerably different situations, see Matthiae (2008–2009a, pp. 165–205).

[p. 30–32] On the kings of Ebla before the contemporary documentation of the Royal Archives, where however they are attested in royal lists in order of succession (one of these, Igrish-Khalab, the last sovereign cited, is the first to have had administrative documents conserved in the major Archive), and deified as royal ancestors and thus cult figures, as emerges from various rituals and economic texts, see: Archi (1986a; 1988a; 2001a); Fronzaroli (1988a); Bonechi (2001); and Stieglitz (2002a). It should be noted that in philological publications from the first years after the discovery of the Ebla

Royal Archives in 1975, now outdated since the names of the sovereigns of the Archives period only very rarely appear in the texts themselves under the regal title of *en*, both Ibrium and Ibbi-Zikir, at the time misread by some as Ibbi-Sipish, were both considered kings, but are now universally recognized as belonging to the supreme magistrature summarily defined as "vizierate"; data for the correct and definitive identification of the three sovereigns in the Royal Archives – Igrish-Khalab, Irkab-Damu, and Ishar-Damu – and their chronological order are collected in a number of articles in Archi (1988b); see also Biga and Pomponio (1987).

The reading and interpretation of SA.ZA[ki] is in Civil (1983). Although the Saza reading is less than certain, it now certainly seems to have designated the complex of palatine buildings housing the administrative and political power structures in several Sumerian cities, particularly Shuruppak. It would be perfectly feasible, then, if the same term were used by the Ebla chancery, linguistically and institutionally Sumerian, to indicate the complex of structures of the Tell Mardikh Acropolis which, though occupied for the most part by the buildings of Royal Palace G, also included other structures, at least one of which, the Red Temple, was sacred. The Saza identification problem is linked with the other much-discussed Sumerian term *é-siki*, literally the "House of Wool", but which, on the basis of the long-standing use of wool as the "gold standard", as it were, to establish the value of goods before silver was definitively adopted in the Royal Archives era, had taken on the meaning of "Treasury" and "Treasure" of the Royal Palace: Archi (1988c, pp. 50–52); this could concretely be the entire Administrative Quarter of Royal Palace G, or some part of it, where there have been consistent finds of mostly miniature works of art, precious stones, and above all considerable quantities of raw lapis lazuli. On the "Treasure" issue, see Matthiae (2008a, pp. 59–61), whose solutions are substantially the same as those of Archi (2005, p. 96); and lastly, on the recent important discovery of more than 20 kilos of unworked lapis lazuli in the warehouses to the south of the Throne Room of Royal Palace G see, in particular, Pinnock (2006a).

[pp. 32–34] Enna-Dagan of Mari's letter was initially published by Pettinato (1980a), with comments by Kienast (1980), while the official edition, reliably based on collations of the text, which radically alters the interpretation of the document is that by Edzard (1981a, pp. 89–97), on which see also Viganò (1988, pp. 227–246).

Sollberger (1980) presented the first critical edition of the Ebla–Abarsal treaty, defined as the most ancient diplomatic treaty in the history of humanity and which was later presented in a new, definitive edition by Fronzaroli (2003a, pp. 35–42). A historical-juridical appraisal of the text is to be found in Kienast (1988), while, after W.G. Lambert's (1987) critical observations, an updated and corrected edition, with considerably improved lines of interpretation was published by Edzard (1992). The ancient centre of Abarsal, a reading still controversial and difficult, has proved far from easy to locate on the ground, though it must have been in the area of the Middle Euphrates or Balikh, its left tributary; its initial identification as Assur, proposed by G. Pettinato and endorsed by B. Kienast, is completely untenable: Archi (1989a).

Useful but to be applied with caution are the contributions by Astour (1988a; 1988b) and Gordon (1992a). After A. Archi's first correct observations (1980a; 1981b), of considerable importance are the collections of quotations in the texts of the Royal Archives of a number of important cities in Upper Syria, the Valley of the Euphrates, Upper Mesopotamia, and Anatolia: Archi (1987a; 1988d; 1989a); Bonechi and Catagnoti (1990); Archi (1990a; 1990c; 1999a; 2008a). The identification of Armi/Armanum as Tell Bazi/Tell Banat was basically proposed by Otto (2006). Fundamental systematic collections of toponymy in the Ebla Royal Archives texts published to date are those of Archi, Piacentini, and Pomponio (1993) and Bonechi (1993).

The letter from a senior dignitary of Ebla under King Irkab-Damu to a correspondent in the town of Khamazi has recently been published with detailed philological apparatus in Fronzaroli (2003a, pp. 30–34). An Italian translation both of Enna-Dagan of Mari's letter regarding the Abarsal treaty and of the letter to Khamazi is given in Matthiae (2008a, pp. 237–238).

Ebla–Kish relations have received detailed study: see above all Archi (1981c; 1987b; 1987c); Moorey (1981); Gelb (1981). Not to be considered viable is Pomponio's hypothesis (1990), whereby the Kish repeatedly mentioned in the Ebla Archives texts is not the Kish of Akkad's kingdom but another homonymous city in Upper Mesopotamia (the existence of which is unsupported by any certain written testimony).

On relations with Nagar, present-day Tell Brak, much essential documentary evidence is included in the following studies: Archi (1998); Bonechi (1998); Catagnoti (1998); and Biga (1998).

[pp. 35–36] The Egyptian lamp in diorite with two of the names of Chefren's official titles and the alabaster cover with a *cartouche* listing various names of ceremonial titles from the early years of the rule of Pepy I have been recorded in their archaeological context by Matthiae (1978, pp. 229–231) and afterwards published by Scandone Matthiae (1979a; 1982; 1988); on the other stone-ware discovered in Royal Palace G, of certain pharaonic manufacture but lacking inscriptions of any kind, see Scandone Matthiae (1981).

Important for the chronology of Pepy I after the recent revisions of the chronology of Egypt of the pharaohs are the considerations of von Beckerath (1997); Kitchen (2000, pp. 39–52; 2007). R. Krauss's (2008) recent Low Chronology proposal would seem excessively "low" and insufficiently well-founded.

On the raw lapis lazuli in Royal Palace G: Pinnock (1986a; 1986b; 1987; and particularly 1985a and 1988). The particular value of lapis lazuli for the Mesopotamian mentality is illustrated by Winter (1999). More general consideration on Ebla's trade relations can be found in Pinnock (1985b; 1990; 1991); Klengel (1988); Archi (2003).

[pp. 36–38] For a historical overview of the states, kingdoms, or city states with which Ebla was linked, see Bonechi's interesting considerations (1990), while a preliminary framework of historical events during the Archives era is to be found in Archi (2006a). Astour (1992a) appears questionable and somewhat dated. Recent data on the military campaigns of Ibrium and Ibbi-Zikir in the later years of the period documented by the Royal Archives have been collated and studied by M.G. Biga, for access to which I am extremely grateful, while the same scholar is now concluding a complete and systematic account; Biga (2008) has also collated and presented a preliminary series of further, more exhaustive data. Ibbi-Zikir's important military campaign against Mari is reconstructed in Archi and Biga (2003) where, however, the proposed interpretation of Mari's responsibility for the fall of the first Ebla is unacceptable in that the important military victory seemingly celebrated in the seals issued by a king of Mari is with complete lack of evidence identified as that over Ebla. The seals are described in Beyer (2007).

[pp. 39–40] Immediately after the discovery of the Ebla Royal Archives and the initial excavations on Royal Palace G, I attributed the destruction of mature Early Syrian Ebla at the end of Early Bronze IVA to Naram-Sin of Akkad (c. 2250 BC): Matthiae (1976, pp. 205–215), although two of my publications in the following two years advanced the hypothesis that Sargon was the perpetrator: Matthiae (1977c, pp. 164–171) and, in particular, Matthiae (1978, pp. 229–36) in which, after the discovery of Pepy I's alabaster cover, the writer argued for the probable exclusion of any date earlier than Sargon, and still considering Naram-Sin as more plausible on the basis of the widely-accepted view that Sargon had subordinated but not destroyed Ebla, while his great nephew recalled the triumph over Armanum and Ebla, explicitly citing the destruction of Armanum and the name of his vanquished enemy, the king of Armanum (without however mentioning any king of Ebla, nor its destruction at his hands), and that the remains of Ebla's material and artistic culture could be contemporaneous with the early decades of the Akkad dynasty. On the basis of epigraphic considerations relating solely to the scribal tradition of Southern Mesopotamia but not to the actual scribal practices of contemporary Babylon, Pettinato (1980b, *passim*) argued for a much earlier date for the destruction, 'at the time of Fara'; that is, c. 2500 BC. Given the difficulty of attributing an absolute date to the material culture at the time of the destruction of Ebla, and considering that only 25 years separate the death of Sargon of Akkad from his nephew Naram-Sin's ascent to the throne, the reasons behind Sollberger's (1982) dating of the destruction to the Sargon years were his solid and authoritative palaeographic textual investigations. Sollberger excluded any possibility that Eblaite palaeography could be contemporaneous with Naram-Sin's, characterized by considerable innovation which is completely absent from the practices of the Ebla chancery, and roundly states that the palaeography of the texts was without doubt at some remove from Fara's era, in the years of Lugalzagesi of Uruk and Sargon of Akkad.

As this unfeasibly early date was gradually abandoned, that of Sargon of Akkad's period was accepted without dissent: Matthiae (1982a; 1989a, pp. 241–250; 1989b). The actual destroyer of the city remained problematic for some scholars however: Boese (1982); Michalowski (1985), and Geller (1987). Of little help towards a pondered solution were the bizarre and improbable theories of Astour (1992b), who considered the destruction 'random' and 'natural', occurring 'with certainty' shortly before Sargon and very shortly before Lugalzagesi and, against all archaeological evidence, regarding only the palace at Ebla and not the entire settlement.

That Mari fell at the hands of Sargon of Akkad a few years after Ebla (given that two sovereigns recorded in Mari's "Presargonic Palace" never appear in Ebla and seem to be the immediate successors of the king of Mari, attested apparently with certainty in the last years in the life of Ebla's Royal Palace G) is in no way an argument against Sargon's destruction of Mari: for a recent, systematic presentation of archaeological evidence regarding Mari, see Margueron (2004).

The hypothesis of a non-explicit mention of Sargon in one of the administrative texts of the Ebla Royal Archives was advanced by Sallaberger (2004).

4 The Royal Palace in the age of the Archives: Space and function

[p. 42–45] The explorations beneath the West Unit of the Central Complex of Royal Palace G documenting the existence of possibly palatine structures immediately preceding the age of the Archives in this area of the Acropolis are recorded in Matthiae (1993b, pp. 619–628).

A considerable amount of recent data regarding the historical reconstruction of the era of Akkad has been assembled and evaluated by Westenholz (1999), while the traditions surrounding the kings of Akkad have been analysed by Liverani (1993b).

Based on incontestable epigraphic and archaeological data and the historical and archaeological calculation that only a very short time can have elapsed between the arrival in Ebla of the unguent phial of a VI Egyptian Dynasty pharaoh and the destruction of Royal Palace G, the historical synchronism between Sargon of Akkad, Pepy I of Egypt, and Ishar-Damu of Ebla is of extraordinary value since it is the only pointer to a connection between Egypt, Mesopotamia, and Syria in the third millennium BC and thus the oldest time-line, based on sound evidence, linking with strong probability three major figures from three fundamental cultures of the late third millennium BC: Matthiae (1989b). Relations between Egypt of the Old Kingdom and the Syro-Palestinian area are now documented very precisely in Sowada (2009).

The (necessarily conjectural) attribution of the construction of Royal Palace G and the enormous labour of producing the strikingly monumental Administrative Quarter and Audience Hall to the reign of Igrish-Khalab, the most ancient sovereign to have texts preserved in the Royal Archives, is shared by Archi (1991).

On the fortification of Early Bronze IVA, initially, in 1996, identified as being to the south of the West Fort on the west rampart (Area V); and later, in 1998, within the Middle Bronze I rampart in the outer sector of the North

Fort (Area AA), see the data in Matthiae (1998, pp. 572–574; 2000a, pp. 580–581). On Building P4 at the north-east foot of the Acropolis, mainly explored between 1991 and 1997 and with an extension of up to 500 square metres although no completely accurate assessment of its perimeter walls is possible, of importance, besides the preliminary data in Matthiae (1993b, pp. 628–634; 1998, pp. 562–564), are the interpretations of Marchetti and Nigro (1995–1996). The non-palatine remains of mature Early Syrian Ebla are now concisely analysed by Matthiae (2008a, pp. 23–39).

[pp. 47–48] Royal Palace G was discovered in a sounding of 1973 on the west slope of the Acropolis which immediately produced an exceptionally elevated and well-preserved sector, the tower of the Ceremonial Stairway at the north-east corner of the Court of Audience. This led to the 1974 discovery of the rooms of the North-West Wing of the palace complex and in 1975, after a "full immersion" dig on this extraordinary site, to the discovery of the major archives: Matthiae (1989a, pp. 69–94; 2008a, pp. 41–77), supplemented in recent years, in view of the preservation work for the Archaeological Park, by important excavation which has brought to light the east sector of the Throne Room and a number of rooms in the North Sector and the South Annexe (to the south of the Throne Room): Matthiae (2004, pp. 306–318; 2006b, pp. 451–458); the considerable discoveries of 2007 and 2008 were presented on 29 May 2009 by P. Matthiae in a lecture at the Paris Académie des Inscriptions et Belles-Lettres: Matthiae (2009b).

[pp. 57–60] For a preliminary analysis of the architecture of Royal Palace G, see Matthiae (1982b). On the Royal Palace F, Tell Khuera, see Orthmann *et al.* (1995, pp. 121–125) and Akkermans and Schwartz (2003, pp. 259–260); on Palace B, Tuttul, see Strommenger and Kohlmeyer (2000, pp. 15–41).

[pp. 61–63] In 2002 and 2003 excavations were carried out in the Hall of Painted Plaster (Building FF2) in the seriously razed Area FF, immediately south of the Southern Quarter of Royal Palace G beyond the Old Syrian walls of the Citadel, in a particularly well-preserved part of the urban area, in the Southern Lower Town: Matthiae (2004, pp. 317–326). For an attempt to reconstruct the singular and indeed unique example of (possibly religious) Early Syrian Ebla architecture and a preliminary analysis of the painted elements, see Di Ludovico and Ramazzotti (2009).

The architecture of the Luwian and Aramaic principalities in Iron Age Syria, particularly from the viewpoint of continuity with the most ancient traditions, is analysed in Matthiae (1997c, pp. 114–119, 182–191). On the possible continuity and realizations of the Aramaic citadel of Hamat in Iron Age II, early first millennium BC, see Matthiae (2008b).

5 Early Syrian religion, the Red Temple, and the Temple of the Rock

[pp. 65–66] The total lack of data with which to construct a satisfactory idea of religion in ancient Syria in the age of Early Bronze archaic urbanization before the discovery of the Ebla Royal Archives emerges clearly from some of the authoritative studies of religion in the Syro-Palestinian area such as Albright (1968) and Gese, Höfner, and Rudolph (1979), while albeit with significant differences of interpretation organic overviews of Syrian religion at the time of Ebla are now given in the historical-religious syntheses by Haider, Hutter, and Kreuzer (1996); Nakhai (2001); Wright (2004, pp. 173–180); Biga and Capomacchia (2008, pp. 136–150), and not least, Mander (2005).

[pp. 66–70] There is now a considerable corpus of studies on individual aspects of religion in Archive-era Ebla, in particular analyses of the deities appearing in the economic texts of the Archives; these attempt to extract all possible elements illustrative of the divine characters of the deities in the many schematic quotations in the administrative texts, with some information forthcoming as to interesting ritual and cultural rituals only mentioned incidentally: Pomponio (1983); Xella (1986; 1988a); Lipiński (1987); Pardee (1988); Lambert (1989a); Archi (1992a; 1994; 1995; 1996a; 1997a); Loretz (1998), and Stieglitz (2002b). On continuity between the Ebla pantheon of the late third millennium BC and the so-termed Canaanite pantheon of the second millennium BC: Stieglitz (1990). Pomponio and Xella (1997) is extremely useful.

The unconvincing hypothesis that the enigmatic god Kura was an ancient Hurrian deity is advanced by Wilhelm (1992b), while the more recent thesis that Kura was a deity of the fields not unlike Dagan, still venerated in the first millennium BC, is proposed by Lawson Younger, Jr (2009). On the divine characteristics of Dagan and El, with whom Kura probably shares the principal aspects, see the still relevant essay by Pope (1955) and the recent comprehensive and informative study by Feliu (2003).

On Ishkhara the queen goddess, probably originating from Ebla itself: Archi (1993a; 2002b). Possible readings and interpretations of the difficult name of the god Idabal/Adabal are advanced by von Soden (1987) and particularly by Xella (1998); especially convincing, however, is the interpretation advanced by Fronzaroli (1997, pp. 288–289). Ishkhara is the object of a detailed monograph by Prechel (1996), which also takes into account the Eblaite documentation so far published, if undoubtedly incomplete compared with the abundance of citations of the goddess in the texts of the Royal Archives. On the different forms of the Storm-god in different areas of the Ancient Orient, and on the iconography of Hadad, particularly in the Syrian area, see Green (2003).

[pp. 72–73] The literary texts found in the Royal Archives of Ebla were published by Edzard (1984): after the community of scholars knew these texts, they were the object of many interpretations, and attempts at translation, as they are very difficult from the linguistic point of view. As concerns incantations, their very strong affinities with the contemporary late Early Dynastic Mesopotamian literary tradition were pointed out, as well as some analogies with ritual and literary practices of the later north-west Semitic world: Krebernik (1984); Fronzaroli (1988b; 2003b; 2003c); Gordon (1991; 1992b); Michalowski (1992); Civil and Rubio (1999).

For an important example of references to local Early Syrian myths in the texts of Eblaic incantations, see the study by Fronzaroli (1997), suggesting an extremely ancient attestation of the triumph of Hadad over the serpent in mythical times, known from Ugaritic poems: Caquot, Sznycer, and Herdner (1974, p. 239); Pardee (1997, p. 265); Wyatt (1998, p. 115). On the mythical combat between the Storm-God and the serpent, see also Fenton (1996); for a systematic survey of echoes of the Ugaritic myth in the Bible, see Day (1985).

Fronzaroli (1995b) evaluates the culture of the Ebla chancery scribes in relation to their Mesopotamian contemporaries. Sumerian myths in literary texts discovered at Ebla have been studied by Krebernik (1992) and by Lambert (1992), while on the hymn to the Sun-god Shamash discovered in the Great Archive of the Administrative Quarter, in Semitic, if not in the Eblaic language (TM.75.G.2421), considered the most ancient literary text in a Semitic language to have come down to us, see the analysis of Lambert (1989b): a translation is to be found in Matthiae (2008a, p. 252).

[pp. 74–77] The discovery of the Temple of the Rock in a 2004 sounding in the South-East Lower Town was announced by Matthiae (2006b; 2007a; 2008c). An account of the location of the temple as the principal and possibly primordial centre in Ebla dedicated to the god Kura is given in Matthiae (2008–2009b).

The data given in *De Dea Syra* on the Imperial Roman Period cella and cavity in Hierapolis can be found in Fusaro (2007, pp. 1816–1817).

The typically Mesopotamian concept of the patron god of Sumerian centres having chosen the place of his earthly residence at the origins of time, so that it was founded by him in mythical time and not by men in historical time is elucidated in Matthiae (1994a, pp. 7–38): the account of the mythical founding of the Eengurra Temple of the god Enki in the city of Eridu, erected on earth by the god himself on the model of his mythical residence of Apsu in the abyss is given in the hymn entitled "Enki's Journey to Nippur", a recent translation of which is in Black *et al.* (2004, pp. 330–333).

The formula in Ugarit mythical poems defining the residence of the god El 'at the source of the rivers, among the sources of the two abysses' is to be found in the so-called "Ba'al Cycle": Caquot, Sznycer, and Herdner (1974, pp. 121, 174, 204, 249); Wyatt (1998, pp. 52, 84, 99, 131).

The identification of El's Old Syrian iconography as a calque of its late Early Dynastic and Akkadic counterpart in the Mesopotamian world, Enki of Eridu, is in Amiet (1982, pp. 29–30). Further evidence has been adduced by Matthiae (1992a).

The passages from the Ebla "Ritual of Kingship" seemingly alluding to the Temple of Kura mentioned at the beginning of the ceremonies as the sacred spot where the solemnities started with the queen's entrance into the sanctuary are quoted in Fronzaroli (1998, pp. 3–4, 85–86).

The identification and discovery of all the most essential planimetric elements of the Red Temple in Area D of the Acropolis to emerge during the excavations of 2008 were expounded by P. Matthiae first at a presentation at the Louvre in Paris on 26 January 2009, and then in a lecture at the Académie des Inscriptions et Belles-Lettres, Paris, on 29 May 2009 (Matthiae 2009b), followed by a second, more specific presentation (unpublished) to the Accademia Nazionale dei Lincei on 11 June 2009, "Scavi ad Ebla, 2008: Il Tempio Rosso dell'Età degli Archivi".

[pp. 82–83] Before the discovery of the two mature Early Syrian temples in Ebla, the only cult buildings with antae in Syria had been found in Upper Mesopotamia, from the 'Kleiner Anten-Tempel', 'Nordtempel', and 'Aussenbau' in Tell Khuera to the 'Bau I' in Tell Halawa A and Temple III in Tell Qara Quzaq: Moortgat (1962, pp. 8–14; 1965, pp. 8–38); Orthmann and Meyer (1989, pp. 64–66); del Olmo Lete and Montero Fenollós (1998, pp. 297–300).

On the analogies between the two mature Early Syrian temples at Ebla and both the Early Bronze III sanctuaries in Palestine and most ancient examples of cult architecture in Upper Mesopotamia, see Sala (2008) and Werner (1994).

The Al-Rawda temples have been published by Castel and Awad (2006; 2007); Castel (2007).

[p. 83] On the Temple of Solomon, described in *I Kings*, see the very useful long history of modern studies in Busink (1970), while an excellent archaeological study of the much-debated issue remains that by Dever (1982). On the very critical views regarding the historical reality of Solomon and the monuments attributed to him in the Biblical tradition, see, from the many recent studies, Finkelstein (1996); Knoppers (1997), Van Seters (1997; 2009), and the balanced account by Hendel (2006). On the minutely detailed account of the Temple of Solomon in *I Kings* 6, see Matthiae (2002a), in which I underline new elements of Syrian influence deducible from the most recent discoveries of northern Syria, while Matthiae (1997d) emphasizes the complexity and variety of Palestinian architecture during the reign of Solomon.

From the vast bibliography on the enormous influence of the Biblical description of the Temple of Jerusalem on Western architecture, from the Middle Ages to the Renaissance and from the Baroque to the Enlightenment and beyond, particularly in North America in the nineteenth century, see at least Battisti (1960, pp. 79–86); Krinsky (1970, pp. 1–7); Gutman (1976); Morolli (1988; 1992–1993); Fagiolo (1996); Tuzi (2002); and Matthiae (2008d).

6 The State Archives: Economy, culture, and society

[pp. 84–85] The distribution of the cuneiform texts of the Archives in the different rooms of Royal Palace G according to both typology and filing arrangement – temporary, definitive, or random – is explained in detail in Matthiae (1986a), and Archi (1986b). On the arrangement of the tablets on the shelves of the Great Archive L.2769, possibly relevant as an indication of the precise time, much discussed, when the ancient scribes decided to turn them round 90° to assist reading, see Picchioni (1980) and the observations by

Archi (1988h). On the tablets found in the Southern Quarter, seemingly not belonging to the cores of archives in the Administrative Quarter, but which may belong to another, as yet undiscovered, administrative sector, see Archi (1993b). On the group of some 15 tablets discovered in the small areas created against the east wall of the Throne Room, see Matthiae (2006b, pp. 452–458).

For an appraisal of the value of the Ebla Royal Archives compared with the more relevant archaeological discoveries of ancient archives from the mid-nineteenth century to the present day, see Matthiae (2006b; 2008a); Pedersén (1998); Brosius (2003).

[pp. 90–93] The basis for the historical analyses of the economy of Early Syrian Ebla rests, of course, on the critical editions of the Archives, published by the Archaeological Mission of the Sapienza University of Rome, organized on the basis of systematic and continuous collations of the originals and cross-referenced revision by members of the Comitato Internazionale per lo Studio dei Testi di Ebla, part of the Mission itself: Edzard (1981b); Archi and Biga (1982); Biga and Milano (1984); Archi (1985; 1988c); Sollberger (1986); Milano (1990); Fronzaroli (2003a); Lahlouh and Catagnoti (2006); Pomponio (2008).

Of the many studies of Ebla's economy, the following are among those of primary interest and relevance; that is, based on the direct study of the texts or archaeological documentation: Milano (1980; 1984; 1987a; 1996; 2003); Edzard (1982); Pomponio (1982); Archi (1982a; 1984a; 1986c; 1987d; 1988e; 1988f; 1991; 1992a; 1993c; 1993d; 1993e; 1996b; 1999b; 1999c; 2003); Ascalone and Peyronel (2002; 2006); Peyronel (2004).

[p. 94] The language of the Royal Archives is of course among the elements most directly characterizing the culture of Ebla. Now generally defined only as Eblaic within academic circles, it is, however, an object of evaluation, debate, and interpretations which range (in very general terms) from considering it an eastern Semitic language, not least on account of its phonological, morphological, and syntactic characteristics, with marked western Semitic elements, mostly in lexis, to viewing it as a western Akkadian dialect. Among the many relevant analytic and/or more general studies of the issue, see: Cagni (1981; 1987); Fronzaroli (1979; 1982; 1984a; 1984b; 1984c; 1985a: 1987; 1990; 1991a; 1991b; 1992; 1994a; 1996; 2005); Parpola (1988); Kienast (1990); Hallo (1996); Krebernik (1996); Archi (2002a; 2006b); Tropper (2003); Huehnergard and Woods (2004); Edzard (2006); Huehnergard (2006); Rubio (2006).

[pp. 94–100] On the problems of institutional organization in Ebla, the social structure, and the chronology within the Ebla texts, all essential for a precise interpretation of the data in the Royal Archives texts, see: Archi (1982b; 1987c; 1996c; 1996d; 1997–1998; 1999d; 2002c; 2002d); Milano (1987b); Biga (1988; 1991; 1996; 1997; 1998; 2000; 2002; 2003a; 2003b; 2006); Michalowski (1988); Pomponio (1988); Tonietti (1988); Catagnoti (1989); Biga and Pomponio (1990; 1993); Hallo (1992); Pomponio (1993; 1997–1998).

On the question of royal titles in Early Dynastic Mesopotamia and the subsequent tradition, also in relation to the Ebla documentation, see Hallo (1957); Jacobsen (1957; 1991); Seibert (1969); Charvát (1982; 1988); Glassner

(1993); Schmandt-Besserat (1993); Steinkeller (1993; and particularly 1999); Pomponio (1994); Pitard (1997); Selz (1998).

[pp. 102–106] Ebla's lexical texts, of extraordinary value in terms not simply of Semitic philology and the enormous quantity of Semitic lemmas, frequently archaic, which they contain, but also of Sumerian philology, have been published by Pettinato (1981; 1982). Of the numerous studies on these basic texts, see: Krebernik (1982; 1983; 2006); Archi (1980b; 1981a; 1984b; 1987f; 1990b; 1992c); Fronzaroli (1984b; 1984c; 1994b; 1995a; 1996); Conti (1984; 1989; 1990; 1997; 2003); Krecher (1984); Baldacci (1994); Catagnoti (1997); Pasquali (1997; 2005a; 2005b); Sjöberg (1999; 2003a; 2003b; 2004); Bonechi (2000); Rositani (2001); and Civil (2008).

On the literary texts, both incantations and hymns, discovered in the Ebla Royal Archives, see the notes regarding pp. 72–73 above.

7 Artistic expressions and material culture in the mature Early Syrian Period

[pp. 111–114] An account of the first of numerous fragments and left-over inlay pieces, mainly limestone and shells, discovered in Royal Palace G is given in Dolce (1977; 1980). Many of the inlay pieces belonging to panels almost certainly in relief on wood and gold-leaf, with clothes in stone, are illustrated in Matthiae (1978, pp. 222–226, figs 10–16), while a wide selection is also given in Matthiae, Pinnock, and Scandone Matthiae (eds) (1995, pp. 301–314, 320–324, nos. 67–86, 99–105, 107–111).

The two heads of which only the splendidly wrought hair, in steatite, remains, are published by Matthiae (1980a), and are also discussed in Matthiae, Pinnock, and Scandone Matthiae (1995, pp. 298–299, 310, nos. 63–64, where on pp. 317–319, 322, 329, nos. 95–98, 106, 121, are published some of the more outstanding examples of the miniature statuary in the round; while pp. 325–328, nos. 114–120 illustrate various of the more significant examples of gold-leaf plating both from relief work and the miniature statues); a significant series of these was found when concluding excavations in the southern rooms of the Administrative Quarter: Matthiae (2004, pp. 310–317, figs. 8–17). For a stylistic evaluation of the fine miniature animal statuettes in the round, of no easy reconstruction, discovered in Royal Palace G, see Matthiae (1980b). A very rare possible evidence of the very damaged mature Early Syrian sculpture found outside Ebla, in the relatively nearby Atareb, has been published by Matthiae (1980c), while probably connected with it are the heads of unknown provenance published by Amiet (1984). Some preliminary but comprehensive evaluations of the figurative culture of Early Syrian Ebla are found in Matthiae (1989a, pp. 94–101); Dolce (1991; 1998; 2006; 2008); Mazzoni (2003).

On the inlay work of Early Dynastic Mesopotamia, see Dolce (1978); a historical-artistic overview of artistic production in pre-Sargonic Mesopotamia is given in Moortgat (1967, pp. 43–50).

[pp. 117–123] The large wall panel with open-work inlays on a wooden base made of long juxtaposed planks, initially named the "Ebla Standard", calqued on the Ur Standard, an item of inlaid furnishing typologically very different but of similar technique and subject, and on the so-termed Mari Standard, the images of which were also technically and iconographically very similar, was first published by Matthiae (1989c); numerous examples of inlay are found in Matthiae, Pinnock, and Scandone Matthiae (1995, pp. 274–279, 304–306, nos. 20–36). On the so-called Ur and Mari Standards: Woolley (1934, pls 91–100); Parrot (1956, pp. 134–155, pls LV–LVII), while a critical evaluation of the Kish inlay work is found in Moorey (1978, pp. 58–61). Critical reflections on the history of the celebrative monuments in the Mesopotamian late Early Dynastic world which were without doubt well-known in Ebla include those of Winter (1985; 1986); Dolce (2005); Nadali (2007); and Pinnock (2008).

On the typology of the Ebla royal tiara, a turban almost certainly made of wool, as it appears in the miniature statuary, the wooden inlay work, the glyptic friezes, and in the various texts, see Matthiae (1979a);Biga (1992); Pinnock (1992a); Dolce (2002); and Sallaberger (2009).

[pp. 123–124] The links between palatine arts and the literary genres of the texts are traced by Matthiae (1992b), while observations on the collocation of art works in the Administrative Quarter of Royal Palace G are to be found in Dolce (2007a).

A considerable range of inlay work from Royal Palace G is published in Matthiae (1984a, pls 37, 41–43; 1989a, pp. 105–111, pls 37–43). On palatine court glyptics, known almost exclusively from a not inconsiderable number of impressions on sealings, see, for now, Matthiae's considerations (1989a, pp. 101–105); the definitive study is underway.

On Mesopotamian glyptics contemporary to the Ebla productions, P. Amiet's study (1980) is still valid, while later important contributions of particular relevance to Mari are: Amiet (1963; 1985) and above all, Beyer (2007). On further contemporary glyptic production in the north-eastern area, see above all, though not exclusively, for Urkish and Nagar: Buccellati and Kelly-Buccellati (1996; 1998; 2002); Marchetti (1996; 1998); Matthews (1996); and Otto (2004).

Since 1976 I had opined – Matthiae (1976, p. 213) – that it was from an Eblaite conception that the famous universalistic Mesopotamian royal title of "king of the four regions (of the earth)", derived. This was assumed for the first time by Naram-Sin of Akkad – Hallo (1957, pp. 49–53) – in a relatively advanced phase of his reign and certainly after a number of his astonishing military feats, such as that of nine victories in one year and certainly before those over Armanum and Ebla, as J.-J. Glassner (1986, pp. 15–17) correctly maintains. At the time the hypothesis was based on the now rejected interpretation that the Ebla of Royal Palace G had been destroyed by Naram-Sin himself, but despite W.W. Hallo's reasonable reserves – Hallo (1980) – and while bearing in mind J.-J. Glassner's observations (1984), it still seems probable that the four-part division of the world originally derived from Ebla and the north-western Semitic area. In the Syro-Mesopotamian world, the image of the cylinder seal of an Ebla court dignitary with an Atlas, holding aloft the world represented as quadripartite, with two human and two leonine faces, is as far as I am aware unique (bar one exception) and has to mean, with plastic evidence, that the known world, not yet wholly civilized, has been partly so, as symbolized by the humans, the remaining half being still abandoned to the forces of chaos, as symbolized by the lions. The only, later, case of a possible representation of the world with the same four heads, probably documenting the persistence of a western tradition, is on a fine lapis lazuli cylinder, possibly reworked by Cypriot craftsmen around 1450 BC, discovered at Thebes in Boeotia and published in Porada (1981); Collon (1987, pp. 72–73, no. 317) recognizes the similarity between the representation of the Ebla seal and that exported to Boeotia. Since, as we now believe, Naram-Sin conquered not Ebla but Armanum, defeating its king who may have held the title of "king of Armanum and of Ebla", the idea of his chancery assuming for its king a title modelled on the idea of a four-part half-civilized, half-savage world is not to be connected with Sargon's conquest of Ebla some decades earlier, but with the absorption, through Sumerian-Akkadian culture, of a vision of that newly-subjected western world which had conceived such a resonant image of the known universe.

[pp. 136–137] On the discovery of the two composite statuettes of female figures, one standing and the other, smaller one, seated, see the preliminary announcement by Matthiae (2008e) and the detailed publication by the same author in Matthiae (2009a).

On the impressions of popular glyptic production, probably from rural or outlying districts, see the definitive account by Mazzoni (1992; 1993).

Relations with the contemporary Early Dynastic Mesopotamian world and evidence of differences between court and popular production also emerge in the manufacture of necklace beads, on which see the definitive account of Ebla material by Pinnock (1993;. see also 1983;1997).

[pp. 137–140] On ceramic production in Early Bronze IVA Ebla, see Mazzoni (1982; 1985; 1988; 1994; 1999; 2003). Some details of the chronology of ceramics between the end of Early Bronze III and archaic Early Bronze IVA are given in the excavation report (Matthiae 1993b), while for an overview of the development of ceramics production in northern Syria, see Mazzoni (2002).

8 The crisis in the Early Syrian world and the archaic Old Syrian renaissance

[pp. 142–147] Sound interpretations of Naram-Sin's inscription describing the seizing of Armanum are those of Foster (1982) and Buccellati (1993). The identification of Tell Bazi/Tell Banat with the Armi of the Ebla texts and the Armanum of Naram-Sin of Akkad's inscriptions is proposed, as stated above, by Otto (2006).

On the archaeological remains of the second, late Early Syrian Ebla see, in addition to P. Matthiae's general considerations in Matthiae (1989a): Matthiae (1998, pp. 564–568; 2000a, pp. 580–581; 2006c; 2007a).

General considerations on late Early Syrian Ebla, some of them debatable, are given in Dolce (1999; 2001; 2007b).

On the temples of Tell Halawa A, Tell Khuera, and Tell Qara Quzaq: Orthmann and Meyer (1989, pp. 64–66; figs 34–36, pl. 10); Orthmann (1990a; 1990b); and del Olmo Lete and Montero Fenollós (1998, pp. 297–300, fig. 3). The structure of the Early Bronze IVA and IVB temple recently excavated at Tell Qarqur is still difficult to evaluate: see Dornemann (2008a; 2008b).

[pp. 148–153] On the ceramics of the late Early Syrian Period of Early Bronze IVB see, as regards Ebla, data supplied by Matthiae (1989a, pp. 125–132, fig. 25), and, in general, the appraisals of Schwartz and Weiss (1992, pp. 240–243) and of Akkermans and Schwartz (2003, pp. 277–287). New data regarding the identification of at least four distinguishable phases of ceramics from the stratification of Area HH in Ebla in relation to Temples HH4 and HH5 are presented concisely in Matthiae (2007a, pp. 507–512, figs 25–27). The chronological sequence of Hamah J5-1 is still apparently reliable, although results of an excavation in the 1930s were published by Fugmann (1958, pp. 62–85).

The very fragmentary inscription of Shu-Sin of Ur in which Ebla (the name only partly preserved but reconstructable beyond any doubt) is mentioned beside Mari and Tuttul in a context which soon afterwards also mentions the Upper Sea, after the geographically incongruous Urkish and Mukish, already studied by Kärki (1987, pp. 130–131), and by Heimpel (1987, p. 79), was recently published by Frayne (1997, pp. 300–301, no. 2). It should be noted that in this type of triumphal inscription, handed down in Old Babylonian copies on tablets and originally written on statues or original steles found in a sanctuary of Sumer, mainly Nippur, it is rare for the name of the cities mentioned not to refer to centres conquered by the author of the votive inscription. The mention of personages from Ebla in a text by Ishbi-Erra of Isin, together with people from Mari, is cited in Pettinato (1976, p. 10). The putative mention of a 'Tower of Ebla' in the year-name No. 27 of Sumula-El of the First Dynasty of Babylon, already considered highly dubious, has rightly been dismissed as unfounded in the recent critical edition of the year-names of the Dynasty concerned by Horsnell (1999, p. 57).

9   From Ebla to Yamkhad: The territorial states of the Amorite Age

[pp. 156–161] On the sharp break in the development of the material culture, not least ceramics, between Early Bronze IVB and Middle Bronze I, see Schwartz and Weiss (1992); Mazzoni (2002); and Akkermans and Schwartz (2003, pp. 282–287). Some far from secondary aspects of continuity in artistic culture, on the other hand, have been rightly noted by Pinnock (2004).

Within the time-line of the very early years of the second millennium BC in the Near East, characterized by the emergence of Amorite principalities at least in Babylon (though perhaps not only there, as the still scant evidence of Ebla would indicate), as delineated by Liverani (1988, pp. 317–350), evidence of ongoing updating in skills is presented systematically by Charpin (2004). In the re-emergence of urban culture in Syria in early Middle Bronze I, it is presumed that Ebla and possibly other minor centres as yet unidentified played a prime political, economic, and cultural role analogous to that of Isin and Larsa in the archaic Old Babylonian world, both in Syria and in Babylon, under the guidance of authoritative Amorite princes. In a hypothetical and still very general reconstruction of this kind, Ebla would have been the political protagonist of the entire archaic Old Syrian Period, as were the two ancient Babylonian cities, centres of new Amorite kingdoms some time later, rivalling other centres such as Uruk, Eshnunna, and First Dynasty Babylon itself during the so-called archaic Old Babylonian Period. In southern Mesopotamia it was Hammurabi of Babylon who put a stop to this in the same decades and in apparently parallel but considerably destructive ways; in northern Syria probably more peaceable action was taken by Yarim-Lim I of Aleppo, an older contemporary and ally of Hammurabi, and probably his equal in political stature. For a critical presentation of the historical data on Syria of the Old Syrian Period, especially the reign of Yamkhad/Aleppo, see Klengel (1965, pp. 102–202), now updated and re-elaborated in the authoritative synthesis of Klengel (1992a, pp. 39–83).

Ibbit-Lim king of Ebla's inscription has been published by Matthiae (1970, pp. 55–71); Pettinato (1970, pp. 73–76); Matthiae and Pettinato (1972); Lambert (1981). The most convincing edition on account of a series of substantial re-readings and reinterpretations is that of Gelb (1984). The thesis whereby Ibbit-Lim of Ebla may have been responsible for electing Ishtar as patron goddess of the great Old Syrian city in early Middle Bronze I is formulated by Matthiae (2003, pp. 381–402).

On the term "Meki", sometimes taken as a relatively common dynastic personal name given to sovereigns not just in Ebla but in the Amorite Age in Syria too, though generally interpreted as the royal title in the principates of Upper Syria and Upper Mesopotamia, at least from Middle Bronze I, see Owen and Veenker (1987); Tonietti (1997); Scandone Matthiae (1997a); Kühne (1998); and Rainey (2006). Further proof in favour of Meki as a royal title is the fact that in Mari royal correspondence the title also belongs to kings in Upper Mesopotamia: Charpin and Ziegler (1997, pp. 243–248).

While the rare archaic Old Syrian evidence of Ebla in the texts from Kanish, present-day Kültepe in Central Anatolia and location of the most important Old Assyrian commercial emporium of Cappadocia, is analysed by Bilgiç (1992), the seal impressions mentioning Ebla kings discovered in the Kültepe commercial archives have been collected by Teissier (1994, pp. 177, 233).

[pp. 162–163] The relatively scant data on the political rise of Aleppo at the time of Yarim-Lim I of Aleppo and the consequent constitution of the muscular rule of Yamkhad, like that on the dynastic marriage between Ebla and Alalakh, are discussed by Klengel (1992a, pp. 44–64). For a study of the kings of Middle Bronze I–II Ebla, known via both finds there and external sources, see Matthiae (1984a, pp. 124–125) and more recently, Bonechi (1997, pp. 33–38). On Immeya, in all probablility the "Lord of the Goats" of the homonymous tomb in the Ebla Royal Necropolis, see Archi and Matthiae (1979).

Information regarding pharaoh Hotepibra's mace, discovered in the Tomb of the Lord of the Goats, very probably the burial of the Ebla king Immeya, is to be found in Scandone Matthiae (1979b; 1988; 1997b). Hotepibra Harnejheryotef was very probably of Asian origin, his name appearing with the appellatives *Aamu* or *Sa Aamu*, in Middle Egyptian meaning "Asiatic" and "Son of the Asiatic"; on this, see von Beckerath (1964, pp. 39–40, 231–232), who has doubts regarding this interpretation which, however, is far more probable than that of "Peasant" favoured by Posener (1957, pp. 145–163): the "Asiatic" interpretation is rightly preferred by Vernus (1982, pp. 129–135) and Bietak (1994, p. 116). Ryholt's hypothesis (1997, pp. 213–214), identifying Hotepibra with Sehotepibra II of the Turin King List does not modify the interpretation of the mace sent to Ebla since the chronological collocation of the pharaoh in question in the official Egyptian dynastic lists remains unchanged in the first decades of the XIII Dynasty of Egypt, while the same author's opinion (1997, p. 338) that the mace presents 'roughly executed' hieroglyphics is completely unfounded: although some had worked loose and been remounted by Ebla goldsmiths with no knowledge of hieroglyphics (one sign, for example, *hotep*, is upside-down and another, a phonetic complement, *p*, is missing), these are among the finest examples of classical Middle Egyptian hieroglyphic writing of definitely pharaonic production: Kitchen (2000).

The seal of Maratewari (exact reading uncertain), son of Indilimgur, which should probably be read Indilimma, of exceptional dimensions (7.5 cm high) and stylistic quality, and which appears in different sealings on jars found in connection with both the Western Palace and what has been called the Western Residence at the foot of the west rampart, has been published by Matthiae (1969; 2000a, pp. 605–608, figs 31–32) and Matthiae, Pinnock, and Scandone Matthiae (1995, n. 242, pp. 395, 405). Matthiae The dynastic character of the Maratewari seal is recognized by Collon (1987, p. 128, fig. 545).

[pp. 164–167] For an overview of the great Old Hittite sovereigns' expeditions in Upper Syria, see now Klengel (1992a, pp. 80–83; 1999), while the texts of the Hattusa Royal Archives regarding the exploits of Hattusili I and Mursili I against Yamkhad and its allies are to be found in Kempinski (1983) and de Martino (2003).

The bilingual Hurrian-Hittite poem of the "Chant of Release" discovered at Boghazköy (see Chapter 12, pp. xxx–xxx) and published in an excellent critical edition by Neu (1996a), must have been composed in the eastern Hurrian milieu of the important cultural centre of Kumme (on which see Wilhelm 1994); or in the western milieu of the otherwise unknown Igagallish, as observed by both the editor of the text and, with new arguments, by Wilhelm (1992a). The hypothesis that the Hittite translation of the poem was commissioned at the time of the minor king Tudhaliya I in relation to his aim to emulate the endeavours of Mursili I in Syria (Klengel 1999, p. 114) is that of de Martino (2000, pp. 297–298). It should be added that the attribution is all the more plausible if one holds that the Hittite Mursili I and Pizikarra of Nineveh were allies in a memorable military exploit which ultimately brought about the destruction of both Aleppo and Ebla. See too S. de Martino's observations (1999); Richter (2005); Archi (2007, particularly pp. 188–191). For an overview of the events in the Middle Hittite era, see the considerations of Freu (1995). Lastly, on the god Teshub of Kumme, see Trémouille (2000).

The historical reconstruction of events surrounding the fall of Ebla at the end of Middle Bronze II on the basis of the historical-mythical account in the "Chant of Release" is given in considerable detail in Matthiae (2006a; 2007b).

Any consideration of the political situation in the reign of Hattusili I, who probably died a violent death during serious internal riots (Pecchioli Daddi 1992, pp. 11–19), should take into account the following facts: in the "Annals" of the sovereign concerned it is mentioned that while he was waging sundry wars in western Anatolia his kingdom was attacked by the Hurrians, provoking a general revolt in which only Hattusa remained faithful to the king (de Martino 2003, pp. 36–38): on the occasion of the victorious assault on Urshum on the part of Hattusili I himself, a Hurrian king, called the 'son of the Storm-god' (which could allude to Teshub of Kumme) is mentioned as an ally of Urshum, as observed by Beckman (1995); when attacked by Hattusili I, the king of the city of Ilanzura, on the Upper Tigris, requested the help of the 'kings of the Hurrian peoples' (Soysal 1988; de Martino 2002); lastly and above all, a letter exists, the discoverer of which is unknown, in which Hattusili I urgently asked a Hurrian king, Tunip-Teshub of Tikunana, in Upper Mesopotamia, to join forces and support his struggle against the Upper Syrian city of Khakhkhum, allied with Aleppo: Salvini (1990).

On the issue of the illegitimate detention of Purra and the Igagallish notables at Ebla, cause of the god Teshub's rage and object of the last requests of the great god of Kumme, see the interpretations of Wilhelm (1997), and of Bachvarova (2005). The location of Igagallish to the north of Urshum is rightly proposed by Astour (1988b, p. 142). The unsustainable hypothesis that the destruction of Ebla recounted in the poem is that of the second Ebla, c. 2000 BC, rather than that of c. 1600 BC, as maintained by Astour (2002, pp. 141–164) is discussed in Matthiae (2008–2009a), who also adduces a series of topographical differences between late Middle Bronze II Ebla and the Ebla of 2000 BC.

On the complex question of the historical reconstruction of the great Old Hittite kings' repeated attacks on the kingdom of Yamkhad, initially inconclusive but ending with Mursili I's enormous victory, it is plausible that in this last battle, Aleppo sought to ally itself with Samsuditana of Babylon, possibly in virtue of a traditional and now centuries-old alliance, as conjectured by Klengel (1990, pp. 183–195; 1992b, pp. 341–353).

The thesis proposed here, that the fall of Aleppo, Ebla, and Babylon was the consequence of a decisive alliance between Hittites, Hurrians (of the east), and Kassites, is in part in line with the reconstruction of an alliance between Mursili I and the Khana Kassites against the Hurrians, advanced for the first time by Landsberger (1954), and later accepted by, among others, Garelli (1969, pp. 142–143, 307). This would go some way towards explaining the bold raid of the Hittite king against Babylon, but above all his lightening success and equally sudden retreat, leaving Babylon in the hands of the Kassites. The possible hypothesis offered by the new documentation recorded here, illustrated in more detail by Matthiae (2007b, pp. 22–32), is obviously more comprehensive: the alliance proposed by first Hattusili I and then Mursili I was certainly more extensive than B. Landsberger imagined, and would necessarily have been more flexible. Although the historical texts of the two great Old Hittite kings speak generically of Hurrians, the historical situation behind this ethnic designation is complex, and, as against Landsberger's hypothesis quoted above, Hurrian kings such as Pizikarra of Nineveh and probably Tunip-Teshub of Tikunana must have gone over to the Hittites, thereby altering the balance which had hitherto allowed Aleppo, Ebla, and Babylon to maintain their prestige and power.

10 Town planning and architecture in the Old Syrian city

[pp. 168–170] If there is no doubt that the perimeter of the archaic Old Syrian city was conditioned by the course of the walls of the ancient Early Bronze IVA fortifications, discovered in different states of preservation both at the northern extremity of the central part of the western rampart and seemingly faithfully followed as the base for the substantial archaic Middle Bronze I rampart, probably without variations or at most with some small modifications of direction, what sharply distinguishes the mature Early Syrian city from its archaic and classical Old Syrian counterpart is the division between the Upper Town or central Citadel and the circular Lower Town, separated by a continuous boundary wall – the internal fortress of the Middle Bronze I–II city – which certainly did not exist in the city of the Royal Archives age: Matthiae (2008a, pp. 23–39). The reason for isolating the Citadel of the archaic Old Syrian city, containing the main royal residence, the seat of central administration, and the dynastic temple(s) from the rest of the urban area probably lay in a specific conception of city planning in the Syria of the Amorite Period possibly shared in part by contemporary Babylon: Battini (1998). It is possible but as yet unproven that the examples of the putatively circular city of Mari from the late Early Dynastic I Period and the various important Upper Mesopotamian "Kranzhügel" settlements from at least the middle of the third millennium BC, from Tell Khuera to Tell Beydar, ancient Nabada, possibly dependent on Nagar, with the citadel–lower town division, had some influence on urban layout in Old Syrian Ebla: Margueron (2004, pp. 83–122); Meyer and Hempelmann (2006); Meyer (2007). In an as yet unpublished lecture given at the Akademie der Wissenschaften, Vienna, in November 2006 entitled "Ebla and the Asiatic Towns during the Middle Kingdom: Elements for a Comparison", when speaking of the Syro-Palestinian urban foundations of the Middle Bronze I–II Period I maintained that first, notwithstanding various forms of historical and natural conditioning, the planning of the period often produced original cities reprising without pedantically imitating previous models of the archaic urbanization of Early Bronze III and IVA, using the prevalent ellipsoidal and trapezoidal morphology and a not uncommon separation of citadel and lower town: second, that the period saw the consolidation of the ideological and applied model of the organic city containing all the functional social components of the urban structure, while omitting areas characterized exclusively by a single function – administrative, sacred, or crafts production – and third, that from both a monumental and topographical viewpoint, the central element in the Syro-Palestinian city is undoubtedly the palace, often if not always adjacent to a dynastic temple; while in Mesopotamia, both in Babylonia, from Isin to Larsa, and in Assyria, in Assur, the opposite seems continually to be the case: the sanctuary of Gula, at Isin, or of Shamash at Larsa is the central feature of the city, and the palace only secondary, despite the political importance of the two cities. On the discussion of the construction of the great fortified walls of Mesopotamia's urban centres in the early years of the Isin, Larsa, and Babylon I dynasties, see: Sigrist (1988, p. 14 [Ishbi-Erra, year 12]; 1990, pp. 9–10 [Gungunum, year 21]).

Among the three separate sectors of the archaic Old Syrian city of Middle Bronze I, the prominence of the Citadel, clearly surmounting the rest of the settlement, must have depended on two intentionally combined factors: on the one hand, the fact that, as demonstrated in the remains of the archaic Early Syrian Early Bronze III city, described in Chapter 2, by the middle of the third millennium, the site of the Acropolis probably already emerged very visibly above the surrounding plain on account of the underlying ruins of ancient settlements, possibly from the mid- fourth millennium BC, which would have been completely absent from even limited areas of the future Old Syrian Lower Town; on the other hand, it is certain that the dilapidated ruins of the structures of Royal Palace G, not least the Central Complex, like other ruins of contemporary buildings such as those, clearly documented, of the Red Temple, must have further raised the height of the Acropolis hill, creating a considerable misalignment even compared with the monumental buildings of the Lower Town such as the Western Palace, situated on a high natural rocky formation although lacking any substructure of older layers of settlements. On the urban structure and architectural scale of Old Syrian Ebla, see Pinnock (2002), while the account given by Matthiae (1991) requires updating in the light of more recent discoveries such as those of the Southern Palace and the completed excavation of the extensive adjacent area of private dwellings in Area B of the Middle Bronze II South-West Lower Town. The continuity in building typologies between the mature Early Syrian centre of the age of the Royal Archives and the re-founded archaic Old Syrian city is clearly visible not only in the fortified city wall, but with demonstrable certainty in at least some of the traditional cult places such as the Temple of the Rock and the Red Temple; in all likelihood it is also demonstrable in the Temples of Ishtar and of Shapash/Shamash respectively, in excavation Areas P and N in the Lower Town, and with certainty in Middle Bronze I–II Royal Palace E, built above the ruins of sectors of the ancient Royal Palace G, and in the Northern Palace, built above the Archaic Palace and the Intermediate Palace (Area P), while the Western Palace (Area Q) and Southern Palace (Area FF) would seem to be new foundations from the Middle Bronze I period (though probably not at the beginning). Interesting topographical results of the last great settlement are emerging from the 2002 geo-physical survey of the entire urban area of Tell Mardikh: Ramazzotti (2008).

[pp. 171–175] The entire fortifications system of Old Syrian Ebla is illustrated in detail by Matthiae (2001a). On the fortifications of the Citadel, the upper sections of which were brought to light in the 1988 soundings in an eastern sector of the Acropolis (Area R) and in the lower sectors, particularly in the south-western sector, of the hill (Areas G and FF), where today more than 30 metres of the massive stone revetment are exposed, see Matthiae (1990a, pp. 414–417). An exhaustive comparative study of the archaeological documentation on the fortifications of Syria and Palestine in Middle Bronze I–II, in which Ebla is treated in great detail, is to be found in Burke's updated monograph (2008). Brilliant but unacceptable, on the other hand, is the recent interpretation by Finkelstein (1992), and of Bunimovitz (1992), according to whom the great rampart structures of the early second millennium BC in Syria-Palestina have no defensive function whatsoever, but are manifestations of political power, governmental prestige, and social organization. The hypothesis is roundly contradicted by the variations in trajectory of the ramparts, not least those in Ebla, clearly mapped to allow control from the summit of 250/300-metre stretches of the base of the ramparts, the weak point in their convex structure: Matthiae (1998, pp. 574–579) (the function was assigned to the rectangular tower denominated as the North-West Wing, which was also a weapons arsenal). On the other hand, the various but eloquent expressions found in contemporary letters of kings of Upper Mesopotamia from the Old Babylonian Period conserved in Mari's Royal Archives graphically illustrate the difficulty of breaching the enormous ramparts of the period, even for a large and organized assault troop; the commonest strategy was to construct 'a rampart as high as the rampart' of the city attacked, the only hope of penetrating otherwise near-unassailable urban centres: Dossin (1950, pp. 28–29) (a letter from Shamshi-Addu I to his son Yasmakh-Addu, co-regent of Mari, which speaks of the conquest on the part of his other son, Ishme-Dagan, co-regent of Assur, of the city of Nilimmar by precisely this method, when the earth of the rampart erected by the besieging troops had reached the same height as the rampart of the besieged city); more in general, Durand (2008–2010, Vol. II, pp. 294–299).

[pp. 176–178] After indications in Matthiae's report (1998, pp. 564–568, fig. 5), the Archaic Palace was the object of preliminary study identifying the different phases of construction: Matthiae (2006c). Of particular interest, given its clear connection with the initially frenetic reconstruction of the city, is the seemingly anomalous presence of a trapezoidal courtyard in the north sector of the unfinished Early Bronze IVB construction, readapted at the beginning of Middle Bronze I, and of a dais with side antae placed against the new eastern perimeter wall, which would have been an excellent vantage point from which to coordinate the complex work of reconstructing the city.

The particulars of structure and layout of the Ebla described in the "Chant of Release" are compared in some detail with the archaeological reality of the excavated Old Syrian Ebla by, in particular, Matthiae (2007b). As regards the identification of the terms for 'upper city', 'lower city', and 'hearth' in V. Haas and I. Wegner's study (1995) of the bilingual nature of the "Chant of Release", the 'hearth', apparently incongruous if read as a fixed domestic feature, is most probably a place of burning, a fire, of public interest in producing smoke signals which are well-documented in letters in the Mari Royal Archives as an efficient means of long-distance communication: Durand (2008–2010, Vol. II, pp. 303–304). Remains of such a site of burning were indeed found on the summit of the walls of the Northern Fort of Ebla, and it is very likely that more would have been built on the Citadel in extreme defence of the most delicate and protected part of the city: Matthiae (1998, pp. 580–583, fig. 16 [L.6906]). A site of burning with the same function may well have existed in the Western Fort too: Peyronel (2000).

On Ebla's city walls, see: Matthiae (1989a, pp. 143–147 [Damascus Gate]; 2000a, pp. 593–600; 2002b, pp. 553–558 [Aleppo Gate]; 1998, pp. 584–588 [Euphrates Gate]). For a historical evaluation of the city gates of Middle Bronze I–II, besides Gregori (1986), Herzog (1986) is still informative.

[pp. 180–184] On the major Western and Northern Forts on the western ramparts and the minor East-South-East Fortress on the eastern ramparts, which seem objectively to have been less well equipped, see: Matthiae (1984a, pl. 89; 1989a, pp. 147–149; 1998, pp. 574–584; 2000a, pp. 580–593; 2002b, pp. 547–553; Peyronel (2000; 2007).

In Matthiae (2001a), on the basis of documentation available to date was advanced the hypothesis that the four Ebla ramparts were differently organized at their summit for reasons which as yet totally escape us: the western rampart had at least three extensive, well-equipped forts with multifunctional structures, from the residence of the garrison commander to barracks for soldiers and even workshops; the eastern rampart had a number of compact and very simple fortresses: virtually rectangular towers which doubled up as watch-towers and arsenals for weapons; the southern rampart, on the basis of clear surface traces, might have had a continuous curtain wall around its entire summit, defending a sort of walkway, while of the northern rampart, astonishingly, not a trace remains, not even the bases of architectural remains, arguing for its having been devoid of any kind of superstructure.

As to the possibility that the integrated defence system of the Ebla ramparts was repeated in other important contemporary cities in the Palestinian area, while it is very likely that something similar existed in the centre of Hazor in northern Palestine, as yet unendorsed by excavations (Yadin 1972, pp. 51–57), a rectangular-towered fortress of the Ebla type is known only at Gezer: Kempinski (1992).

[p. 185–193] A detailed account of Royal Palace E in the Citadel, identified in a 1966 sounding in the far north area of the Acropolis although exploration was halted in 1974 and resumed only in 2009, is given in Matthiae (1989a, pp. 160–162). Since buildings in the Lower Town of Ebla were explored in a long series of excavations, given here are only references to accounts providing elements essential for an understanding of these fundamental public buildings in the Old Syrian city. On the Western Palace (Area Q), the first to be explored from 1978 onwards: Matthiae (1980d; 1982c, pp. 303–315; 1982d; 1983, pp. 532–542; 1984b; 1989a, pp. 162–171; 2002b, pp. 558–565). On the Northern Palace (Area P), where excavations began in 1986: Matthiae (1987, pp. 152–160; 1989a, pp. 171–175; 1990a, pp. 405–410). On the Southern Palace, discovered in 2002: Matthiae (2004).

[pp. 194–198] The tracing of a specific and repeated layout in the audience halls of the Old Syrian royal palaces is the work of Matthiae (1990b). I have outlined the possible Mesopotamian origins of this spatial conception in the monuments of the III Ur Dynasty at the centre of political power: Matthiae (2002c); of relevance on this point is the analysis of possible Ur–Ebla cultural relations presented by Pinnock (2006b). Probable analogies between the palatine architecture of Ebla and that of Middle Bronze II Palestine have been drawn by Nigro (1994a, pp. 29–118; 1994b). An important update with the evidence of the resumed excavation of Tilmen Hüyük, an important centre at the foot of the Amanus in the political sphere of Yamkhad is Marchetti (2006). The substantial differences between palatine Old Syrian architecture and its contemporary counterpart in Anatolia and Mesopotamia can be verified in two essential works: Naumann (1971, pp. 411–430) and Margueron (1982, pp. 573–582).

On the royal palace of Tuttul (which is very similar to the so-called *Shakkanakku* palace in Mari), and that of Qatna from the Old Syrian Period, see Akkermans and Schwartz (2003, pp. 286–287); Novák and Pfälzner (2000; 2001; 2002; 2003); Novák (2004;2006).

[pp. 199–200] The first information on the temples of the Old Syrian city began to emerge in the second season of excavations in 1965, when both the Temple of Ishtar on the Citadel (Area D) and that of Rashap in the South-West Lower Town (Area B) were identified, while the Temple of Shapash/Shamash in the North Lower Town (Area N) was explored in 1972: Matthiae (1975b; 1989a, pp. 148–155). The other Old Syrian temples excavated to date – the Temple of Ishtar in the North-West Lower Town (Area P) and the Temple possibly of Hadad in the South-East Lower Town (Area HH) – were excavated respectively in 1988–1990 and 2005–2006, with more limited later soundings; on the Temple of Ishtar in the Lower Town, see the following note, while the Temple in Area HH was presented by Matthiae (2006b, pp. 479–492;

2007a, pp. 512–525). A number of minor, non-templar, classical Old Syrian places of worship in Ebla were identified by Matthiae (2006d). The problem of assigning the different deities to their respective temples has been systematically approached by Matthiae (1986b). Useful for a comparison with other cult places in Syria are the considerations of Margueron (1984), the inventory by Werner (1994), and the synthesis by Akkermans and Schwartz (2003). On the extraordinary discovery of the monumental Temple of Hadad on the Citadel of Aleppo, the basic architectural structures of which are attributed by the excavators to Middle Bronze II, principally on the basis of striking technical analogies with the major Ebla monuments, although deeper soundings have thrown up evidence of a preceding cult building, almost certainly from Early Bronze IVA–B, see the publications by Kohlmeyer (2000) and by Gonnella, Khayyata, and Kohlmeyer (2005).

[pp. 203–206] On the cult complex of the Temple of Ishtar (Temple P2) in the North-West Lower Town (Sector P Centre) and the Cult Terrace of the Lions (Monument P3) giving respectively, from north and west onto the Square of the Cisterns, at the centre of the Cult Area of Ishtar, the most relevant data are to be found in Matthiae (1990a, pp. 410–414; 1990c, and above all, 1993b). Important materials recovered in three different *favissae*, all opening into the Square of the Cisterns, where various pots and small votive objects of unascertainable cult usage were found, have been published by Marchetti and Nigro (1997; 1999); a third contribution by the same authors entitled "A Third *Favissa* in the Sacred Area of Ishtar and the Transition from Middle Bronze II to Late Bronze I at Ebla" was presented in Paris at the 3rd International Congress on the Archaeology of the Ancient Near East, April 2002. The hypothesis that a very specific cult building among the great sanctuaries in archaic Old Syrian Syria dedicated to the cult of Ishtar – built to accommodate the lions sacred to the goddess, like that of Monument P3 in Ebla, still unique in pre-classical Syrian architecture – was represented on a number of rare cylinder seals in a style in some aspects comparable with the artistic culture of contemporary Ebla has been advanced by Matthiae (1994b), while possible Early Syrian antecedents have been suggested in texts from the Royal Archives by Bonechi (1992).

On the issue of the possible relation between monuments like the Cult Terrace of the Lions in Old Syrian Ebla and at least some of the so-called "high places" of the Bible, fundamental data is provided in Vaughan (1974, particularly pp. 29–36, 55). The famous libel on the great Syrian goddess by Lucian (or probably Pseudo-Lucian) of Samosata, is important in relation to the interpretation given here because it both testifies to the presence of lions and eagles in the great Roman sanctuaries in Syria and states that among the simulacra of Hera and Zeus – that is, Atargatis and Hadad – in the famous Temple of Hierapolis, present-day Membij, was to be found the enigmatic and contentious *semeion*, sometimes erroneously considered to be the image of a god-son of the putative Hierapolitan triad (Clemen 1938, p. 241), but now generally interpreted as a very ancient simulacrum or cult standard conserved and venerated in the ancient sanctuary to the Syrian goddess during the Roman Empire: Attridge and Oden (1976, pp. 44–45). The thesis maintaining that the Hierapolis *semeion* was an ancient divine simulacrum was authoritatively argued by Caquot (1955, p. 66) and accepted almost definitively, with further arguments adduced, by Oden, Jr (1989). On the other hand, H. Seyrig's evocative suggestion (Seyrig 1960) that the Hierapolitan *semeion* described in the *De Dea Syra* is simply a standard present in several Old Syrian seals, both archaic and classical, from the antique market, with two superimposed heads, possibly of gods, supported by a crouching lion, appears to me as both fascinating and well-founded, not least because the first new cylinder bearing the symbol and found during an excavation was found in 1992, in one of the *favissae* of the Cult Area of Ishtar at Ebla (Matthiae 1993b, p. 659, fig. 25). Successive excavations in Ebla uncovered two further cylinder seals with the representation of the presumed Hieropolitan *semeion,* implying that the symbol, probably present in the Temple of Ishtar in the Lower Town, was particularly venerated in the city. Two main deductions can be made from the above. On the one hand, if Seyrig's brilliant hypothesis is well-founded, then the Hierapolitan *semeion* may well have been simply a long-standing cult object in Ebla reproduced not infrequently on many cylinder seals now known to us and connected above all with the figurative culture of archaic Old Syrian Ebla. On the other hand, this was probably transferred, possibly at the start of Middle Bronze II and for reasons difficult to specify but undoubtedly connected with Yamkhad's consolidation of power, to the sanctuary at Membij which in pre-classical times preceded the sanctuary from the Imperial Roman period: Matthiae (1993b, pp. 658–660).

[pp. 207–208] A functional identification of the individual sectors of Sanctuary B2 in the South-East Lower Town of Old Syrian Ebla (on which see Matthiae 1989a, pp. 155–156) and the consequent interpretation of the specific religious meaning of this typologically unique cult building from Middle Bronze II are advanced in Matthiae (1990d). On the bronze figurines of deified kings which may have been placed on the brick of the small altars in the peripheral cellas of Sanctuary B2, see the two studies by Negbi (1976) and Seeden (1980). The Sanctuary of the Deified Royal Ancestors in Ebla is the first archaeological evidence of the cult of dead and deified kings in the Syro-Palestinian world: of the considerable literature on this cult, it is worth citing at least Caquot (1960); de Moor (1976); Dietrich, Loretz, and Sanmartín (1976); L'Heureux (1979); Matthiae (1979b); Pope (1981); Levine and de Tarragon (1984); del Olmo Lete (1986; 2008); Xella (1988b); Pardee (1996).

[p. 209] For observations on Ebla's importance in the creation and continuation of architectural traditions in Syria down to the end of the Iron Age, see Matthiae (1995a), while I provide a detailed historical analysis of architectural culture in the Old Syrian Period and of contemporary Old Babylonian, Old Assyrian, and Old Hittite cultures in Mesopotamia and Anatolia in Matthiae (2000b).

11 Old Syrian artistic culture: Originality and continuity

[pp. 211–212] On the titles "Sun of Nagar" and "Star of Ebla", see Matthews and Eidem (1993) and Archi (2001b). Mention of Ishtar *Eblaitu* is found in ritual texts from the Middle Assyrian Temple of Assur published by Frankena (1953, pp. 8–12, 92); Van Driel (1969, p. 65).

An updated list of year-names of the Isin and Larsa Dynasties is to be found in Sigrist (1988; 1990). A critical edition of the year-names of the First Dynasty of Babylon has been published by Horsnell (1999).

[pp. 212–222] All the most important remains of votive statues of kings, queens, and possibly priests discovered in the temples of Ebla have been published by Matthiae (1992c; 1996b; 2006e). An account of Old Syrian statuary comparable with that of Ebla and produced in environments, topographical and general, very close to Ebla itself has been published by Mazzoni (1980) and by Hempelmann (2003). Of considerable importance and artistry are the headless statue of a seated king of Qatna, probably from the classical Old Syrian Period, and the two very fine complete statues of kings recently discovered in the Royal Tomb of Qatna, almost certainly dating from the large city's early Middle Syrian Period: Morandi Bonacossi (2006); Al-Maqdissi *et al.* (2003); Pfälzner (2009). For a comparison between Ebla statuary and contemporary plastic production in Mesopotamia, see Spycket (1981); Matthiae (2000b); Braun-Holzinger (2007).

Both the theme of communication between kings and gods in the Mesopotamian world through votive statues which "speak" to the transcendental world, confirming the truth of divine inspiration and recording exploits achieved and their positive outcome, as warranty of the transparency, truthfulness, and efficacy of the king's social, religious, and military undertakings in the internal and external relations of the cities of Babylon, and the references to statuary in Old Babylonian "year-names" are treated in a preliminary study by Matthiae (1994a, pp. 47–49) and will be the object of a specific study by the same author now under preparation. The major groups of statuary of the pharaohs of the Middle Kingdom are the subject of long-established studies such as those by Evers (1929); Schäfer (1936); Aldred (1950); Wolf (1957, pp. 316–318); and Vandier (1958, pp. 173–179). The Stele of Hadad, only an important central fragment of which remains, and which is the most ancient figurative document with the iconography of this great god of Aleppo, well known from a series of classical Old Syrian cylinder seals, often beautifully made, from the best, mostly royal, workshops in the larger urban centres of inland Upper Syria, has been published by Matthiae (1993c). Lastly, for extensive figurative documentation of the great Storm-god, whose most important centre of worship was the spectacular Sanctuary on the Citadel of Aleppo, but who was venerated in a multitude of centres in Upper Syria and in many other often famous sanctuaries, see Schwemer (2001) and Green (2003). An unfortunately small fragment of a stele, published by Matthiae (2002b, pp. 568–569, fig. 32), shows a royal figure standing still and concentrated before a divinity, almost identical to the famous Stele of Hammurabi: evidence of enormous importance, and comparable in style and period to an important, more complete Old Syrian fragment from Karkemish which also depicts a royal figure, included in Matthiae (1975a, pp. 468–469, 484, pl. 414b). For other Karkemish sculptures which have been dated considerably later but are probably to be attributed to the classical Old Syrian Period on the basis of the comparison with works from Ebla, see Di Paolo (2006).

As regards the large statues of standing kings, erect on a base of two roaring lions flanking a central image of a seated monarch, the most significant example, found in a small area adjacent to that containing the entrance of the Tomb of the Lord of the Goats is found in Matthiae (2000c), while two more important bases of similar statues with roaring lions, the one complete, the other fragmentary and with the extremity of the lower part of the standing figure idiosyncratically shod, have been published by Matthiae (1998, pp. 568–572, figs 7–9). The corresponding bases of statues of deified royal ancestors from the Neo-Syrian Period from Karkemish, present-day Jerablus, and Samal, present-day Zincirli, have been published by Woolley (1914, pl. B1b); Woolley and Barnett (1952, pp. 192, 243, pls B53ab–54a); von Luschan (1911, figs 261–268); and Orthmann (1970, pp. 509, 545 [Karkemish F/17, pl. 32abd; Zincirli E/1, pl. 62cde]). The tradition of relief and Neo-Syrian funerary statues has been analysed by Bonatz (2000).

The well-preserved basalt head of a female figure, somewhat larger than life-size, found near the eastern anta of the Temple of Ishtar in Area P of the North-West Lower Town has been published by Matthiae (2001b, pp. 272–281). On the technique of applying gold or silver leaf to stone or wooden sculptures, important epigraphic accounts exist in texts from the Ebla Royal Archives of the mature Early Syrian Period: see Archi (1988g, n. 77; 1990b); and Fronzaroli (1996).

[pp. 222–228] The carved basins of the Temple of Rashap in the Lower Town and of Ishtar on the Citadel are described in Matthiae (1965; 1966; 1984a, pls 58–62); and Matthiae, Pinnock, and Scandone Matthiae (1995, nos 290–291, pp. 421–422). Fundamental to the dating of the basins to within a few decades between late Middle Bronze I and early Middle Bronze II were comparisons of antiquarian and iconographic elements clearly shared between the basins at the sanctuaries of Old Syrian Ebla and the archaic Old Syrian seals on the tablets of the Old Assyrian merchants of Cappadocia: Teissier (1994) – comparisons endorsed by the discovery in front of Temple P2 of the Sacred Area of Ishtar in the Lower Town of a large fragment of a splendid and superbly-crafted circular offering table in basalt, with a bull's hooves tripod support, depicted both on the temple basins in Ebla and in the cult scenes of seals impressed on the tablets of Kanish II: Matthiae (1994c); Matthiae, Pinnock, and Scandone Matthiae (1995, no. 469, p. 504). On the complex and controversial subject of sacred marriage in the Mesopotamian world, a sound illustration of the issue can be found in the work by Lapinkivi (2004).

[pp. 229–237] The ivory talisman of the "Lord of the Goats" has been published in preliminary form in a number of studies including Matthiae, Pinnock, and Scandone Matthiae (1995, no. 470, pp. 505, 529). On the ivory of the offering bearer with the gazelle and that with the figure of a king probably to be reconstructed in a specular composition on one side of a stylized palmette, see respectively, Matthiae (1995b, pp. 677–680, fig. 21); and Matthiae (1987, pp. 158–160) and Matthiae, Pinnock, and Scandone Matthiae (1995, no. 382, pp. 463, 477).

The mirror-like duplicate image of kingship, often present in classic Old Syrian cylinder seals and certainly dependent from the Egyptian representations of the pharaohs who faced one another as kings of Upper and Lower Egypt could be at the origin of the duplicate representation of the Neo-Assyrian sovereign in the North-West Palace of Ashurnasirpal II at Nimrud in the first half of the ninth century BC: Matthiae (1989d). The theme of the Egyptianizing subjects in the Old Syrian glyptic has been handled by two overall studies, useful for material collection more than critical evaluations: Eder (1995) and Teissier (1996).

The Egyptianizing ivories of the Northern Palace, discovered in a back room of the palace, almost certainly a store-room or possibly restoration workshop were communicated to the British Academy, then published by Matthiae (1989c, pp. 25–56), and by G. Scandone Matthiae (1990; 1991a; 1991b; 2002; 2006). On the variously styled Ebla ivories in the context of the figurative culture of the Old Syrian Period, see Matthiae (2000b, pp. 169–217).

[pp. 238–242] The Stele of Ishtar was published by Matthiae (1986c), and Matthiae, Pinnock, and Scandone Matthiae (1995, no. 236, pp. 390–391, 403). On the origins of the austere iconography of the great goddess on the stele of the Temple of Ishtar on the Citadel, see Matthiae (1989e), while the fact that the somewhat licentious iconography of the goddess was familiar in Ebla is documented in the minimal remains of the basin originally standing in the Temple of Ishtar in the North-West Lower Town analysed in Matthiae (1996c). The image also appears in the Syrian-style seal impressions on the Cappadocia tablets of Kanish II: Teissier (1994, pp. 177–179, 233–234). A partly comparable stele found reused at Hamah in a level of the early first millennium BC, also providing possible data for the reconstruction of the lost upper register of the Stele of Ishtar at Ebla, has been studied by Pinnock (1992b).

[pp. 243–249] As mentioned in the notes to Chapter 9 above (pp. xxx–xxx), the seal of the last Old Syrian crown prince, son of king Indilimma and possibly named Maratewari, was published by Matthiae (1969; 1984a, pl. 87), and Matthiae, Pinnock, and Scandone Matthiae (1995, no. 242, pp. 395, 405), where the seal of the probable palace prefect of the same years also appears: Matthiae, Pinnock, and Scandone Matthiae (1995, no. 243, p. 496); and Matthiae (1984a, pl. 88). Originally considered some few decades older, according to the most recent developments in the dating of Old Syrian glyptic, these splendid seals are undoubtedly from between 1650 and 1600 BC: Otto (2000).

On the other classes of Old Syrian seals in Ebla, on cylinders which may be from Ebla workshops, and on Eblaite iconographic problems, see Mazzoni (1975; 1979; 1986); Baffi Guardata (1979); Pinnock (1996; 2000a; 2000b; 2003; 2006c).

On the issue as to whether the Ebla palace workshops of the classical Old Syrian Period were part of the seemingly parallel currents of profound change taking place in Mesopotamia and Egypt between the nineteenth and eighteenth centuries BC and influencing the major carving traditions of the Ancient Near East, see, regarding the Mesopotamian world, Schlossman (1978–1979; 1981–1982); and, for the Egyptian world, Wildung (1984) and Assmann (1990).

The basin of the Temple of Shapash/Shamash (Temple N) in the North Lower Town was published in preliminary fashion by Matthiae (1984a, pls 61–62), while the same author proposed the interpretation of the rare representation of the long back face with functionaries embracing and raising a hand to their mouths, as if alluding to a pact or alliance: Matthiae (1986b); and the most plausible time-line for the various Ebla basins extant, entire, or fragmentary: Matthiae (2006e, pp. 434–438). The Obelisk of Ishtar, extraordinarily similar in type to the Stele of Ishtar, with which it shares both the equal-sized register division and the framing of the single figural spaces, together with some few but central subjects of its composite structure, was published for the journal *Académie des Inscriptions et Belles-Lettres. Comptes Rendus*, 2011 (see Bibliographical update). The subject of the acrobat mounted on the bull, which in all probability appeared on one of the incomplete registers of the Ebla obelisk, has been analysed in detail in the publication of the celebrated paintings of Tell ed-Dab'a in the Egyptian Delta, the location of the Hyksos capital Avaris: Bietak, Marinatos, and Palivou (2007). The subject was generally considered typically Aegean in Syria's figurative culture, but had so far not appeared on any Asian monument and was known only from a number of cylinder seals of apparently Aegean influence, while the Ishtar Obelisk obviously evinces no element, either iconic or stylistic, with any Cretan connection: Collon (1994).

12 Old Syrian material culture: Characteristics and development

[pp. 252–258] On Middle Bronze I–II ceramics in Ebla, see, among the various publications, Pinnock (1981; 2007); Nigro (1996; 2000; 2002a; 2002b; 2007).

For an accurate chronological classification of coroplastic art in Ebla, the following studies should be considered essential: Marchetti (2001; 2007).

Different kinds of bronze weapons and utensils from Middle Bronze I–II Ebla have been the objects of analytical studies: de Maigret (1976–1977); Pinnock (1979; 2000c); Matthiae (1980e); Mazzoni (2000b);Rossoni (2007). A number of bronze utensils, arms, and ornaments of the Old Syrian Period in Ebla have been published in Matthiae, Pinnock, and Scandone Matthiae (1995, pp. 422–440). On weapons of the same period in the Syrian area, see the extremely useful and detailed study by Philip (1989).

[pp. 259–275] On the discovery of the Royal Tombs in the necropolis below the Western Palace, see the numerous accounts and communications in: Matthiae (1979b; 1979c; 1980f; 1980g; 1980h; 1981b; 1982d; 1982e; 1982f; 1984b).

A concise but exhaustive account of the typologies of jewels from the tombs is given in Matthiae (1981c), to which the chronological observations of Nigro should now be added: Nigro (2008, pp. 159–175). In general, for an overview of the Ebla jewels and their place in the contemporary production of the Ancient Orient, see the specific study by Negbi (1970), usefully supplemented by Maxwell-Hyslop (1971).

On *faïence* and North Syrian painted ceramics in Ebla, see the studies by Mazzoni (1987) and by Matthiae (1989f).

For an important and extensive account of late Middle Bronze II ceramics from contexts sealed by the fire at the end of the classical Old Syrian Period, see Pinnock (2005).

13 From Ebla to Tell Mardikh: Decline of a great urban centre

[pp. 277–279] On Ebla's final destruction c. 1600 BC and successive unsuccessful attempts at reconstruction, see Matthiae's considerations (2008–2009a). Of considerable relevance to the crisis in the settlements in the Ebla area at the end of the Old Syrian Period and the westward retreat of settlements at the beginning of Late Bronze I, are the observations made during a survey along the course of the River Quweyq, between Aleppo and the Ebla area in the heart of inland Syria: Matthers (1981).

A still valid collection of sources and detailed analyses regarding the history of northern Syria in the second millennium BC, not least after the waves of destruction caused by the military campaigns of Hattusili I and Mursili I, is given in Klengel (1965–1970). For a more recent, updated synthesis and critical evaluation of the complex events in central-northern Syria with the alternating ascendancy of Mittani, Egyptians, and Hittites after the destruction of the kingdom of Yamkhad and that of Ebla in the late Old Syrian Period, particularly in the Nukhashshe area, see Klengel (1992a, pp. 82–99). On the recent finding of a sealing impressed with the seal of an Imperial Hittite functionary at Tell Mardikh, Late Bronze II, see Archi (2008b). Among considerations of the many complex problems of chronology, both absolute and relative, regarding correlations between the doings of Hattusili I and Mursili I and the rise of the rule of Mittani, the thesis whereby Mittani basically filled the gap left by Yamkhad is advanced by de Martino (2004), while there is increasing consensus in favour of the idea that the core of Mittani's rule predates the fall of Aleppo and Babylon at the hands of Mursili I by one or two generations: Van Koppen (2004); Novák (2007). The list of Asiatic cities conquered by Thutmosis III of the Temple of Karnak is published by Helck (1962, pp. 146–150).

[pp. 280–282] While it is impossible even to cite the very extensive bibliography regarding the dire crisis affecting many urban centres in the eastern Mediterranean at the end of Late Bronze II, when the name of Ebla seems to vanish definitively from ancient texts, some recent dialectical studies offering a critical evaluation of a series of in-context aspects of the crisis are: Ward and Sharp Joukowsky (1992); Drews (1993); Oren (2000); Sherratt (2003); Mazar (2005); Feldman (2006); Pedrazzi (2007); Venturi (2007); Mountfort Monroe (2009); Bachhuber and Gareth Roberts (2009). On the events of Iron I–III in Upper Syria, particularly with reference to the country of La'ash, the city of Hazrek/Khatarikka, and the dominion of Hamat under king Zakkur, see the overview clearly delineated by Liverani (1988, pp. 629–666), but also some of the syntheses of the Luwian and Aramaean world: Hawkins (1982); Sader (1987); Ponchia (1991); Jasink (1995); Dion (1997); Klengel (2000); Lipiński (2000); Schniedewind (2002); Novák (2005); Lawson Younger, Jr (2007). For a historical interpretation of the periodization of the Iron Age, see Mazzoni (2000c).

[pp. 283–288] On the Persian Residence and the Achaemenid and Hellenistic evidence at Tell Mardikh, see Mazzoni (1984; 1990), and the more general studies by Sartre (1989); Elayi (1990); Mazzoni (1991–1992); and Lund (1993).

On the experience of the oriental monasticism of the stylites in inland northern Syria, see Peña, Castellana, and Fernandez (1975).

Fundamental considerations on the itineraries followed by the Crusaders remain those of Dussaud (1927), and the historical framework provided by Cahen (1940), while on the military events of the First Crusade see the classic syntheses of Runciman (1951–1954) and Setton (1969–1977).

Bibliography

Akkermans, P.M.M.G., Schwartz, G.M. (2003) *The Archaeology of Syria: From Complex Hunter-Gatherers to Early Urban Societies (ca. 16,000–300 BC)*. Cambridge: Cambridge University Press.

Albright, W.F. (1968) *Yahweh and the Gods of Canaan: A Historical Analysis of Two Contrasting Faiths (Jordan Lectures 1965)*. London: The Athlone Press.

Albright, W.F., Dougherty, R.P. (1926) 'From Jerusalem to Baghdad down the Euphrates' in *Bulletin of the American Schools of Oriental Research*, 21: 1–21.

Al-Maqdissi, M. (2008) *Pionniers et protagonistes de l'archéologie syrienne 1860–1960: D'Ernest Renan à Sélim Abdulhak*. Damascus: Ministry of Culture (Documents d'Archéologie Syrienne XIV).

Al-Maqdissi, M., Dohmann-Pfälzner, H., Pfälzner, P., Suleiman, A. (2003) 'Das königliche Hypogäeum von Qatna: Bericht über die syrisch-deutsche Ausgrabungen im November-Dezember 2002', in *Mitteilungen der Deutschen Orient-Gesellschaft*, 135: 189–218.

Alberti, M.A., Ascalone, E., Peyronel, L. (eds) (2006) *Proceedings of the International Colloquium: Weights in Context: Bronze Age Weighing Systems of the Eastern Mediterranean*. Rome: Quasar.

Aldred, C. (1950) *Middle Kingdom Art in Ancient Egypt, 2300–1590 B.C.* London: Tiranti.

Amiet, P. (1963) 'La glyptique syrienne archaïque: Notes sur la diffusion de la civilisation mésopotamienne en Syrie du nord', in *Syria*, 60: 57–72.

Amiet, P. (1980) *Glyptique mésopotamienne archaïque*. 2nd Edition. Paris: CNRS.

Amiet, P. (1982) 'Jalons pour une interprétation du répertoire des sceaux-cylindres syriens du IIe millénaire', in *Akkadica*, 28: 19–40.

Amiet, P. (1984) 'Antiquités syriennes du Louvre', in *Studi Eblaiti*, 7: 139–144.

Amiet, P. (1985) 'La glyptique de Mari: État de la question', in *M.A.R.I.*, 4: 475–485.

Anonymous (1978) 'The Lost Empire of Ebla', in *Nature/Science Annual*. Washington, DC: *Time/Life* Books: 34–45.

Archi. A. (1980a) 'Notes on Eblaite Geography', in *Studi Eblaiti*, 2: 41–47.

Archi, A. (1980b) 'Les textes bilingues d'Ébla', in *Studi Eblaiti*, 2: 81–89.

Archi, A. (1981a) 'La "Lista dei nomi e professioni" ad Ebla', in *Studi Eblaiti*, 4: 177–204.

Archi, A. (1981b) 'Notes on Eblaite Geography II', in *Studi Eblaiti*, 4: 1–17.

Archi, A. (1981c) 'Kish nei testi di Ebla', in *Studi Eblaiti*, 4: 77–87.

Archi, A. (1982a) 'Wovon lebte man in Ebla?', in *Archiv für Orientforschung*, 19: 173–188.

398 *Bibliography*

Archi, A. (1982b) 'About the Organization of the Eblaite State', in *Studi Eblaiti*, 5: 201–220.

Archi, A. (1984a) 'Allevamento e distribuzione del bestiame ad Ebla', in *Studi Eblaiti*, 7: 45–81.

Archi, A. (1984b) 'The "Names and Professions List": More Fragments from Ebla', in *Revue d'Assyriologie*, 78: 171–174.

Archi, A. (1985) *Archivi Reali di Ebla, Testi*, I: *Testi amministrativi: assegnazioni di tessuti (Archivio L.2769)*. Rome: University of Rome.

Archi, A. (1986a) 'Die ersten zehn Könige von Ebla', in *Zeitschrift für Assyriologie*, 77: 213–217.

Archi, A. (1986b) 'The Archives of Ebla', in K.R. Veenhof (ed.), *Cuneiform Archives and Libraries: Papers Read at the 30e Rencontre Assyriologique Internationale, Leiden, 4–8 July 1983*. Leiden/Istanbul: Nederlands Historisch-Archaeologisch Instituut (Uitgaven van het Nederlands Historisch-Archaeologisch Instituut te Istanbul LVII): 72–86.

Archi, A. (1986c) 'Berechnungen von Zuwendungen an Personengruppen in Ebla', in *Altorientalische Forschungen*, 13: 191–205.

Archi, A. (1987a) 'Ugarit dans les textes d'Ébla', in *Revue d'Assyriologie*, 81: 185–186.

Archi, A. (1987b) 'More on Ebla and Kish', *Eblaitica*, 1: 125–159.

Archi, A. (1987c) 'Les titres de en et de lugal à Ébla et les cadeaux pour le roi de Kish', in *M.A.R.I.*, 5: 37–52.

Archi, A. (1987d) 'Reflections on the System of Weights from Ebla', in *Eblaitica*, 1: 47–89.

Archi, A. (1987e) 'Gifts for a Princess', in *Eblaitica*, 1: 115–124.

Archi, A. (1987f) 'The "Sign-List" from Ebla', in *Eblaitica*, 1: 91–113.

Archi, A. (1988a) 'Cult of the Ancestors and Tutelary God at Ebla', in Y. L. Arbeitman (ed.), *Fucus: Semitic/Afrasian Gathering in Memory of A. Ehrman*. Amsterdam/Philadelphia, PA: John Benjamins (Amsterdam Studies in the Theory and History of Linguistic Science LVIII): 103–112.

Archi, A. (ed.) (1988b) *Archivi Reali di Ebla, Studi*, I: *Eblaite Personal Names and Semitic Name-Giving. Papers of a Symposium Held in Rome July 15–17, 1985*. Rome: University of Rome.

Archi, A. (1988c) *Archivi Reali di Ebla, Testi*, VII: *Testi amministrativi: registrazioni di metalli e tessuti (L.2769)*. Rome: University of Rome.

Archi, A. (1988d) 'Harran in the III Millennium B.C.' in *Ugarit-Forschungen*, 20: 1–8.

Archi, A. (1988e) 'Zur Organisation der Arbeit in Ebla', in H. Waetzoldt, H. Hauptmann (eds) 1988: 131–138.

Archi, A. (1988f) 'Prices, Workers' Wages and Maintenance at Ebla', in *Altorientalische Forschungen*, 15: 24–29.

Archi, A. (1988g) 'Minima eblaitica 6: igi-dub = ba-nu-ú: lame, feuille pour le visage, visage', in *N.A.B.U.*, nr 77.

Archi, A. (1988h) 'Position of the Tablets of Ebla', in *Orientalia*, 57: 67–69.

Archi, A. (1989a) 'La ville d'Abarsal', in M. Lebeau, Ph. Talon (eds) 1989: 15–19.

Archi, A. (1989b) '"Ga-ne-iš/šu" in the Ebla Texts', in K. Emre, B. Hrouda, M. Mellink, N. Özgüç (eds) 1989: 11–14.

Archi, A. (1990a) 'Tuttul-sur-Balikh à l'âge d'Ébla', in Ö. Tunca (ed.) 1990: 197–207.

Archi, A. (1990b) 'Données épigraphiques éblaïtes et production artistique', in *Revue d'Assyriologie*, 84: 101–105.

Archi, A (1990c) 'Imar au IIIe millénaire d'après les Archives d'Ébla' in *M.A.R.I.*, 6: 21–38.

Archi, A. (1991) 'Ebla: La formazione di uno Stato del III millennio a.c.', in *La Parola del Passato*, 46: 195–219.

Archi, A. (1992a) 'Substrate: Some Remarks on the Foundation of the West Hurrian Pantheon', in H. Otten, E. Akurgal, H. Ertem, A. Süel (eds), *Hittite and Other Anatolian and Near Eastern Studies in Honour of Sedat Alp*. Ankara: Türk Tarih Kurumu: 7–14.

Archi, A. (1992b) 'The City of Ebla and the Organization of Its Rural Territory', in *Altorientalische Forschungen*, 19: 24–28.

Archi, A. (1992c) 'Transmission of the Mesopotamian Lexical and Literary Texts', in P. Fronzaroli (ed.) 1992: 1–29.

Archi, A. (1993a) 'Divinités sémitiques et divinités de substrat: Le cas d'Išḫara et d'Ištar à Ébla', in *M.A.R.I.*, 7: 71–78.

Archi, A. (1993b) *Five Tablets from the Southern Wing of Palace G – Ebla*. Malibu, CA: Undena (Syro-Mesopotamian Studies V/2).

Archi, A. (1993c) 'Fifteen Years of Studies in Ebla: A Summary', in *Orientalistische Literaturzeitung*, 88: 461–471.

Archi, A. (1993d) 'Trade and Administrative Practice: The Case of Ebla', in *Altorientalische Forschungen*, 20: 43–58.

Archi, A. (1993e) 'Bronze Alloys in Ebla', in M. Frangipane, H. Hauptmann, M. Liverani, P. Matthiae, M.J. Mellink (eds) 1993: 615–625.

Archi, A. (1994) 'Studies in the Pantheon of Ebla', in *Orientalia*, 63: 249–256.

Archi, A. (1995) 'La religione e il culto nel Periodo Protosiriano', in P. Matthiae, F. Pinnock, G. Scandone Matthiae (eds) 1995: 13–39.

Archi, A. (1996a) 'Il in the Personal Names', in *Orientalistische Literaturzeitung*, 91: 133–151.

Archi, A. (1996b) 'Les comptes rendus annuels des métaux (CAM)', in *Amurru*, 1: 73–99.

Archi, A. (1996c) 'Chronologie relative des textes d'Ébla', in *Amurru*, 1: 11–28.

Archi, A. (1996d) 'Les femmes du roi Irkab-Damu', in *Amurru*, 1: 101–124.

Archi, A. (1997a) 'Studies in the Ebla Pantheon II', in *Orientalia*, 66: 414–425.

Archi, A. (1997b), 'Enfants et nourrices à Ébla', in *Ktéma*, 22: 35–44.

Archi, A. (1997–1998) 'Procedures in Publishing the Ebla Texts', in *Archiv für Orientforschung*, 44–45: 108–114.

Archi, A. (1998) 'The Regional State of Nagar According to the Texts of Ebla', in *Subartu*, 4/2: 1–16.

Archi, A. (1999a) 'Aleppo in the Ebla Texts', in *Annales Archéologiques Arabes Syriennes*, 43: 131–136.

Archi, A. (1999b) 'Cereals at Ebla', in *Archiv Orientální*, 67: 503–518.

Archi, A. (1999c) 'The Steward and His Jar', in *Iraq*, 61: 147–158.

Archi, A. (1999d) 'The "Lords", "lugal-lugal" of Ebla: A Prosopographic Study', in *Vicino Oriente*, 12: 19–58.

Archi, A. (2001a) 'The King-List of Ebla', in T. Abusch *et al.* (eds), *Historiography in the Cuneiform World: Proceedings of the XLVe Rencontre Assyriologique Internationale*. Bethesda, MD: CDL Press: 1–13.

Archi, A. (2001b) 'Star of Ebla, Megi', in *N.A.B.U.*, nr 1: 14.

Archi, A. (2002a) 'Prepositions at Ebla', in *Eblaitica*, 4: 1–21.

Archi, A. (2002b) 'Formation of the West Hurrian Pantheon: The Case of Išḫara', in K.A. Yener, H.A. Hoffner, Jr (eds), *Recent Developments in Hittite Archaeology and History: Papers in Memory of Hans G. Güterbock*. Winona Lake, IN: Eisenbrauns: 21–33.

Archi, A. (2002c) 'Jewels for the Ladies of Ebla', in *Zeitschrift für Assyriologie*, 92: 161–199.

Archi, A. (2002d) 'The Role of Women in the Society of Ebla', in S. Parpola, R.M. Whiting (eds) *Sex and Gender in the Ancient Near East: Proceedings of the 47ᵉ Rencontre Assyriologie Internationale, Helsinki, July 2nd–6th, 2001*. Winona Lake, IN: Eisenbrauns: 1–9.

Archi, A. (2003) 'Commercio e politica: Deduzioni dagli Archivi di Ebla (ca. 2400–2350 a.C.)', in C. Zaccagnini (ed.), *Mercanti e politica nel mondo antico*. Rome: L'Erma di Bretschneider: 41–54.

Archi, A. (2005) 'The Head of Kura – The Head of Adabal', in *Journal of Near Eastern Studies*, 52.

Archi, A. (2006a) 'Ebla e la Siria del III millenio a.C.', in A. Barbero (ed.), *Storia d'Europa e del Mediterraneo: Il Mondo antico*, I. Rome: Salerno: 655–682.

Archi, A. (2006b) 'Eblaite: Its Geographic and Historical Context', in G. Deutscher, N.J.C. Kouwenberg (eds) 2006: 96–110.

Archi, A. (2007) 'Transmission of Recitative Literature by the Hittites', in *Altorientalische Forschungen*, 34: 185–203.

Archi, A. (2008a) 'Ḫaššu/Ḫaššuwan and Uršum/Uršaum from the Point of View of Ebla', in T. Tarhan, A. Tibet (eds) 2008: 87–102.

Archi, A. (2008b) 'A Hittite Official at Ebla', in *Orientalia*, 77: 397–400.

Archi, A., Biga, M.G. (1982) *Archivi Reali di Ebla, Testi, III: Testi amministrativi di vario contenuto (Archivio L.2769: TM.75.G.3000–4101)*. Rome: University of Rome.

Archi, A., Biga, M.G. (2003) 'A Victory over Mari and the Fall of Ebla', in *Journal of Cuneiform Studies*, 55: 1–44.

Archi, A., Matthiae, P. (1979) 'Una coppa d'argento con iscrizione cuneiforme dalla "Tomba del Signore dei Capridi"', in *Studi Eblaiti*, I: 191–193.

Archi, A., Piacentini, P., Pomponio, F. (eds) (1993) *Archivi Reali di Ebla, Studi, II: I nomi di luogo dei testi di Ebla (ARET I-IV, VII-X e altri documenti editi e inediti)*. Rome: University of Rome.

Ascalone, E., Peyronel, L. (2002) 'Early Bronze IVA Weights at Tell Mardikh-Ebla: Archaeological Association and Contexts', in M.A. Alberti, E. Ascalone, L. Peyronel (eds) 2006: 49–70.

Ascalone, E., Peyronel, L. (2006) *Materiali e Studi Archeologici di Ebla, VII: I pesi da bilancia del Bronzo Antico e del Bronzo Medio*. Rome: University of Rome.

Assmann, J. (1990) 'Ikonologie der Identität: Vier Stilkategorien der Altägyptischen Bildniskunst', in M. Kraatz, J. Meyer zur Cappellen, D. Seckel (eds), *Das Bildnis in der Kunst des Orients*. Stuttgart: Franz Steiner (Abhandlungen für die Kunde des Morgenlanes L/1): 17–42.

Astour, M. (1988a) 'Toponimy and Ethnohistory of Northern Syria: A Preliminary Survey', in *Journal of the American Oriental Society*, 108: 345–355.

Astour, M. (1988b) 'The Geographical and Political Structure of the Ebla Empire', in H. Waetzoldt, H. Hauptmann (eds) 1988: 139–158.

Astour, M. (1992a) 'An Outline of the History of Ebla (Part 1)', in *Eblaitica*, 3: 3–82.

Astour, M. (1992b) 'The Date of the Destruction of Palace G at Ebla', in M.W. Chavalas, J.L. Hayes (eds) 1992: 23–40.

Astour, M. (2002) 'A Reconstruction of the History of Ebla (Part 2)', in *Eblaitica*, 4: 57–195.

Attridge, H.W., Oden, R.A. (1976) *The Syrian Goddess ("De Syria Dea") Attributed to Lucian.* Missoula, MT: Scholars Press (Texts and Translations IX).

Bachhuber, Ch., Gareth Roberts, R. (2009) *Forces of Transformation: The End of the Bronze Age in the Mediterranean.* Oxford: Oxbow (Banea Monographs I).

Bachvarova, M.B. (2005) 'Relations between God and Man in the Hurro-Hittite "Song of Release"', in *Journal of the American Oriental Society*, 125: 45–58.

Baffi, F., Dolce, R., Mazzoni, S., Pinnock, F. (eds) (2006) *Ina kibrāt erbetti: Studi di Archeologia Orientale dedicati a Paolo Matthiae.* Rome: University of Rome.

Baffi Guardata, F. (1979) 'Su un'impronta di sigillo paleosiriano tardo dal Santuario B2', in *Studi Eblaiti*, 1: 97–114.

Baldacci, M. (1994) 'Some Eblaite Bird Names and Biblical Hebrew', in *Die Welt des Orients*, 25: 57–65.

Battini. L. (1998) 'Opposition entre acropole et ville basse comme critère de définition de la ville mésopotamienne', in *Akkadica*, 108: 5–29.

Battisti, E. (1960) *Rinascimento e Barocco.* Turin: Einaudi.

Beckman, G. (1995) 'The Siege of Uršu Text (CTH 7) and Old Hittite Chronology', in *Journal of Cuneiform Studies*, 47: 23–34.

Beyer, D. (2007) 'Les sceaux de Mari au IIIe millénaire: Observations sur la documentation ancienne et les données nouvelles des Villes I et II', in *Akh Purattim*, 1: 231–260.

Bietak, M. (ed.) (1994) *Pharaonen und Fremden: Dynastien im Dunkel. Sonderausstellung des Historischen Museums der Stadt Wien, 8. 9.–23. 10. 1994.* Vienna: Vienna Museum.

Bietak, M. (ed.) (2000) *The Synchronisation of Civilizations in the Eastern Mediterranean in the Second Millennium BC: Proceedings of an International Symposium at Schloss Haindorf, 15th–17th November 1996 and at the Austrian Academy, Vienna 11th–12th of May 1998.* Vienna: Österreichische Akademie der Wissenschaften (Contributions to the Chronology of the Eastern Mediterranean I).

Bietak, M., Czerny, E. (eds) (2007) *The Synchronisation of Civilisations in the Eastern Mediterranean in the Second Millennium B.C.,* III: *Proceedings of the SCIEM 2000 – 2nd Euro-Conference Vienna, 28th of May–1st of June 2003.* Vienna: Österreichische Akademie der Wissenschaften (Contributions to the Chronology of the Eastern Mediterranean IX).

Bietak, M., Marinatos, N., Palivou, C. (2007) *Taureador Scenes in Tell al-Da'a (Avaris) and Knossos.* Vienna: Österreichische Akademie der Wissenschaften (Untersuchungen der Zweigstelle Kairo des Österreichischen Archäologischen Institutes XXVII).

Biga, M.G. (1988) 'Frauen in der Wirtschaft von Ebla', in H. Waetzoldt, H. Hauptmann (eds) 1988: 159–177.

Biga, M.G. (1991) 'Le donne alla corte di Ebla', in *La Parola del Passato*, 46: 295–303.

Biga, M.G. (1992) 'Les vêtements neufs de l'empereur', in *N.A.B.U.*, nr 19.

Biga, M.G. (1996) 'Prosopographie et datation relative des textes d'Ébla', in *Amurru*, 1: 29–124.

Biga, M.G. (1997) 'Enfants et nourrices à Ébla', in *Ktéma*, 22: 35–44.

402   *Bibliography*

Biga, M.G. (1998) 'The Marriage of Eblaite Princess Tagriš-Damu with a Son of Nagar's King', in *Subartu*, 4/2: 17–22.

Biga, M.G. (2000) 'Wet-Nurses at Ebla: A Prosopographic Study', in *Vicino Oriente*, 12: 59–88.

Biga, M.G. (2002) 'Les foires d'après les Archives d'Ébla', in *Florilegium Marianum*, 6: 277–288.

Biga, M.G. (2003a) 'The Reconstruction of a Relative Chronology for the Ebla Texts', in *Orientalia*, 72: 345–367.

Biga, M.G. (2003b) 'Feste e fiere a Ebla', in C. Zaccagnini (ed.), *Mercanti e politica nel mondo antico*. Rome: L'Erma di Bretschneider: 55–68.

Biga, M.G. (2006) 'Operatori cultuali a Ebla', in *Studi Epigrafici e Linguistici*, 23: 17–37.

Biga, M.G. (2008) 'Au-delà des frontières: Guerre et diplomatie à Ébla', in *Orientalia*, 77: 289–334.

Biga, M.G., Capomacchia, A.M.G. (2008) *Il politeismo vicino-orientale*. Rome: Poligrafico dello Stato: 136–150.

Biga, M.G., Milano. L. (1984) *Archivi Reali di Ebla, Testi*, IV: *Testi amministrativi: assegnazioni di tessuti (Archivio L.2769)*. Rome: University of Rome.

Biga, M.G., Pomponio, F. (1987) 'Iš'ar-Damu, roi d'Ébla', in *N.A.B.U.*, nr 106.

Biga, M.G., Pomponio, F. (1990) 'Elements for a Chronological Division of the Administrative Documents of Ebla', in *Journal of Cuneiform Studies*, 42: 179–201.

Biga, M.G., Pomponio, F. (1993) 'Critères de rédaction comptable et chronologie relative des textes d'Ébla', in *M.A.R.I.*, 7: 107–128.

Bilgiç, E. (1992) 'Ebla in Cappadocian Inscriptions', in H. Otten, E. Akurgal, H. Ertem, A. Süel (eds), *Hittite and Other Anatolian and Near Eastern Studies in Honour of Sedat Alp*. Ankara: Türk Tarih Kurumu: 61–66.

Black, J., Cunningham, G., Robson, E., Zólyomi, G. (2004) *The Literature of Ancient Sumer*. Oxford: Oxford University Press.

Boese, J. (1982) 'Zur absoluten Chronologie der Akkad-Zeit', in *Wiener Zeitschrift für die Kunde des Morgenlandes*, 74: 4–53.

Bonatz, D. (2000) *Das syro-hethitische Grabdenkmal: Untersuchungen zur Entstehung einer neuen Bildgattung in der Eisenzeit im nordsyrisch-südostanatolischen Raum*. Mainz: Von Zabern.

Bonechi, M. (1990) 'I "regni" dei testi degli Archivi di Ebla', in *Aula Orientalis*, 8: 151–174.

Bonechi, M. (1992) 'A propos de la terrasse cultuelle à Ébla', in *N.A.B.U.*, nr 128.

Bonechi, M. (1993) *Répertoire Géographique des Textes Cunéiformes*, XXII/1: *I nomi geografici dei testi di Ebla*. Wiesbaden: Harrassowitz (Beihefte zum Tübinger Atlas des Vorderen Orients B 7/12).

Bonechi, M. (1997) 'II Millennium Ebla Kings', in *Revue d'Assyriologie*, 41: 33–38.

Bonechi, M. (1998) 'Remarks on the III Millennium Geographical Names of the Syrian Upper Mesopotamia', in *Subartu*, 4/2: 219–241.

Bonechi, M. (2000) 'Noms d'oiseaux à Ébla: Les rapaces', in Topoi, Supplement II: 251–281.

Bonechi, M. (2001) 'The Dynastic Past of the Rulers of Ebla', in *Ugarit-Forschungen*, 33: 53–64.

Bonechi, M., Catagnoti, A. (1990) '"Ḫa-zu/su-wa-an" nei testi di Ebla', in *N.A.B.U.*, nr 30.

Braun-Holzinger, E. (2007) *Das Herrscherbild in Mesopotamien und Elam: Spätes 4. bis frühes 2. Jt. v. Chr.* Münster: Ugarit-Verlag (Alter Orient und Altes Testament CCCXLII).

Brosius, M. (ed.) (2003) *Ancient Archives and Archival Traditions: Concepts of Record-Keeping in the Ancient World*. Oxford: Oxford University Press.

Buccellati, G. (1993) 'Through a Tablet Darkly: A Reconstruction of Old Akkadian Monuments Described in Old Babylonian Copies', in M.E. Cohen, D.C. Snell, D.B. Weisberg (eds), *The Tablet and the Scroll: Near Eastern Studies in Honor of W.W. Hallo*. Bethesda, MD: CDL Press: 58–71.

Buccellati, G., Kelly-Buccellati, M. (1996) 'The Seals of the King of Urkesh: Evidence from the Western Wing of the Royal Storehouse AK', in *Wiener Zeitschrift für die Kunde des Morgenlandes*, 86 (Volume in Honour of H. Hirsch): 65–100.

Buccellati, G., Kelly-Buccellati, M. (1998) 'The Courtiers of the Queen of Urkesh: Glyptic Evidence from the Western Wing of Storehouse AK', in *Subartu*, 4/2: 195–216.

Buccellati, G., Kelly-Buccellati, M. (2002) 'Tur'am-Agade, Daughter of Naram-Sin, at Urkesh', in L. al Gailani-Werr, J. Curtis, H. Martin, A. McMahon, J. Oates, J. Reade (eds) 2002: 11–31.

Bunimovitz, S. (1992) 'Middle Bronze Age Fortifications in Palestine as a Social Phenomenon', in *Tel Aviv*, 19: 221–234.

Burke, A.A. (2008) *"Walled up to Heaven": The Evolution of Middle Bronze Age Fortification Strategies in the Levant*. Winona Lake, IN: Eisenbrauns (Harvard Semitic Museum Publications).

Busink, Th.A. (1970) *Der Tempel von Jerusalem von Salomo bis Herodes*, I: *Der Tempel Salomos*. Leiden: Brill.

Butterlin, P. (2003) *Les temps proto-urbains de Mésopotamie: Contacts et acculturation à l'époque d'Uruk au Moyen-Orient*. Paris: CNRS Éditions.

Butterlin, P. (ed.) (2009) *À propos de Tepe Gawra.: Le monde proto-urbain de Mésopotamie*. Turnhout: Brepols (*Subartu* 23).

Cagni, L. (ed.) (1981) *La lingua di Ebla: Atti del Convegno internazionale (Napoli, 21–23 aprile 1980)*. Naples: Istituto Universitario Orientale (Dipartimento di Studi Asiatici, Series Minor XIV).

Cagni, L. (ed.) (1984) *Il bilinguismo a Ebla: Atti del Convegno Internazionale (Napoli, 19–21 aprile 1982)*. Naples: Istituto Universitario Orientale (Dipartimento di Studi Asiatici, Series Minor XXII).

Cagni, L. (ed.) (1987) *Ebla 1975–1985: Dieci anni di studi linguistici e filologici. Atti del Convegno internazionale (Napoli, 9–11 ottobre 1985)*. Naples: Istituto Universitario Orientale (Dipartimento di Studi Asiatici, Series Minor XXVII).

Cahen, C. (1940) *La Syrie du Nord à l'époque des Croisades*. Paris: Geuthner.

Caquot, A. (1955) 'Note sur le *séméion* et les inscriptions de Hatra', in *Syria*, 32: 59–69.

Caquot, A. (1960) 'Les Rephaim ougaritiques', in *Syria*, 37: 75–90.

Caquot, A., Sznycer, M., Herdner, M. (1974) *Textes ougaritiques*, I: *Mythes et légendes*. Paris: Éditions du Cerf.

Castel, C. (2007) 'Stratégie de subsistance et modes d'occupation de l'espace dans la micro-région d'Al-Rawda au Bronze ancien final (Shamiyeh)', in D. Morandi Bonaccossi (ed.), *Studi archeologici su Qatna*, I: *Urban and Natural Landscapes of an Ancient Syrian Capital. Settlement and Environment at Tell Mishrifeh/Qatna and in Central Western Syria* (Proceedings of the International Conference Held at Udine 9–11 December 2004): Udine: Forum: 283–294.

Castel, C., Awad, N. (2006) 'Quatrième Mission archéologique franco-syrienne dans la micro-Région d'Al-Rawda (Syrie intérieure): La campagne de 2005', in *Orient-Express*, 1: 7–14.

Castel, C., Awad, N. (2007) 'Cinquième Mission archéologique franco-syrienne dans la micro-Région d'Al-Rawda (Syrie intérieure): La campagne de 2006', in *Orient-Express*, 1–2: 26–32.

Catagnoti, A. (1989) 'I NE.DI nei testi amministrativi degli Archivi di Ebla', in *Miscellanea Eblaitica*, 2: 148–201.

Catagnoti, A. (1997) 'Sul lessico dei giuramenti a Ebla: Nam-kud', in *Miscellanea Eblaitica*, 4: 111–137.

Catagnoti, A. (1998) 'The IIIrd Millennium Personal Names from the Ḫabur Triangle in the Ebla, Brak and Mozan Texts', in *Subartu*, 4/2: 41–66.

Charpin, D. (2004) 'Histoire politique du Proche-Orient amorite (2002–1595)', in D. Charpin, D.O. Edzard, M. Stol (eds), *Mesopotamien: Die altbabylonische Zeit*. Fribourg/Göttingen: Academic Press/Vandenhoeck & Ruprecht (Orbis Biblicus et Orientalis CLX/4): 23–440.

Charpin, D., Ziegler, N. (1997) 'Mékum, roi d'Apišal', in *M.A.R.I.*, 8: 243–248.

Charvát, P. (1982) 'Early Ur: War Chiefs and Kings of Early Dynastic III', in *Altorientalische Forschungen*, 9: 43–50.

Charvát, P. (1988) 'The Origins of Sumerian States: A Modest Proposal', in P. Vavroušek, V. Souček (eds), *Papers on the Ancient Near East Presented at the International Conference of Socialist Countries (Prague, Sept. 30–Oct. 3, 1986)*. Prague: Univerzita Karlova: 101–132.

Chavalas, M.W., Hayes, J.L. (eds) (1992) *New Horizons in the Study of Ancient Syria*. Malibu, CA: Undena (Bibliotheca Mesopotamica XXV).

Civil, M. (1983) 'The Sign LAK 384', in *Orientalia*, 52: 233–240.

Civil, M. (2008) *Archivi Reali di Ebla, Studi IV: The Early Dynastic Practical Vocabulary A (Archaic ḪAR-ra A)*. Rome: University of Rome.

Civil, M., Rubio, G. (1999) 'An Ebla Incantation against Insomnia and the Semiticization of Sumerian', in *Orientalia*, 68: 254–266.

Clemen, C. (1938) *Lukian's Schrift über die Syrische Göttin*. Leipzig: Hinrichs'sche Buchhandlung (Der Alte Orient XXXVII/3–4).

Collon, D. (1975) *The Seal Impressions of Tell Atchana/Alalakh*. Neukirchen/Vluyn: Butzon & Bercker (Alter Orient und Altes Testament XXVII).

Collon, D. (1982) *The Alalakh Cylinder Seals: A New Catalogue of the Actual Seals Excavated by Sir Leonard Woolley at Tell Atchana*. Oxford: British Archaeological Reports (BAR International Series CXXXII).

Collon, D. (1987) *First Impressions: Cylinder Seals in the Ancient Near East*. London: British Museum Publications.

Collon, D. (1994) 'Bull Leaping in Syria', in *Ägypten und Levant*, 4: 81–88.

Conti, G. (1984) 'Arcaismi in eblaita', in P. Fronzaroli (ed.) 1984a: 159–187.

Conti, G. (1989) 'Osservazioni sulla sezione KA della lista lessicale bilingue eblaita', in *Miscellanea Eblaitica*, 2: 45–78.

Conti, G. (1990) *Il sillabario della quarta fonte della lista lessicale bilingue eblaita*. Florence: University of Florence (Quaderni di Semitistica XVII).

Conti, G. (1997) 'Carri ed equipaggi nei testi di Ebla', in *Miscellanea Eblaitica*, 4: 23–71.

Conti, G. (2003) 'Il Pennsylvania Sumerian Dictionary e il sumerico di Ebla', in P. Marrassini (ed.) 2003: 116–133.

Day, J. (1985) *God's Conflict with the Dragon and the Sea: Echoes of a Canaanite Myth in the Old Testament*. Cambridge: Cambridge University Press.

de Maigret, A. (1976–1977) 'Due punte di lancia da Tell Mardikh-Ebla', in *Rivista degli Studi Orientali*, 50: 31–41.

de Martino, S. (1999) 'Problemi di traduzione per antichi scribi ittiti: La redazione bilingue del "Canto della liberazione"', in *Hethitica*, 14: 7–18.

de Martino, S. (2000) 'Il "Canto della liberazione", composizione letteraria bilingue hurrico-ittita sulla distruzione di Ebla', in *La Parola del Passato*, 55: 296–320.

de Martino, S. (2002) 'The Military Exploits of the Hittite King Ḫattušili I in Lands Situated between the Upper Euphrates and the Upper Tigris', in P. Taracha (ed.), *Silva Anatolica: Anatolian Studies Presented to M. Popko*. Warsaw: Agade: 77–85.

de Martino, S. (2003) *Annali e "Res Gestae" antico hittiti*. Pavia: Italian University Press (Studia Mediterranea XII).

de Martino, S. (2004) 'A Tentative Chronology of the Kingdom of Mittani from Its Rise to the Reign of Tušratta', in H. Hunger, R. Pruszinsky (eds), *Mesopotamian Dark Ages Revisited: Proceedings of an International Conference of SCIEM 2000 (Vienna, 8th–9th November 2002)*. Vienna: Österreichische Akademie der Wissenschaften (Contributions to the Chronology of the Eastern Mediterranean VI): 35–42.

de Moor, J.C. (1976) 'Rapiuma-Rephaim', in *Zeitschrift für Alttestamentliche Wissenschaft*, 88: 323–345.

del Olmo Lete, G. (1986) 'Liturgia funeraria de los reyes de Ugarit (KTU 1.106)', in *Studi Epigrafici e Linguistici*, 3: 55–71.

del Olmo Lete, G. (2008) 'Mythologie et religion de la Syrie au IIème millénaire av. J.C. (1500–1200)', in G. del Olmo Lete (ed.), *Mythologie et religion des Sémites occidentaux*, II: *Émar, Ougarit, Israël, Phénicie, Aram, Arabie*. Leuven: Peeters (Orientalia Lovaniensia Analecta CXLIII): 25–164.

del Olmo Lete, G., Montero Fenollós, J.L. (1998) 'Du temple à l'entrepôt: Un exemple de transformation de l'espace urbain à Tell Qara Quzaq en Syrie du nord', in M. Fortin, O. Aurenche (eds), *Espace naturel, espace habité en Syrie du Nord (10ᵉ–2ᵉ millénaire av. J.-C.: Actes du Colloque tenu à l'Université Laval (Québec) du 5 au 7 mai 1997*. Québec/Lyon: Canadian Society for Mesopotamian Studies/Maison de l'Orient Méditerranéen: 295–304.

Deutscher, G., Kouwenberg, N.J.C. (eds) (2006) *The Akkadian Language in Its Semitic Context*. Leiden: Brill.

Dever, W.G. (1982) 'Monumental Architecture in Ancient Israel in the Period of the United Monarchy', in T. Ishida (ed.), *Studies in the Period of David and Solomon and Other Essays: Papers Read at the International Symposium for Biblical Studies, Tokyo, 5–7 December 1979*. Winona Lake, IN: Eisenbrauns: 269–306.

Diakonoff, I.M. (1990) 'The Importance of Ebla for History and Linguistics', in *Eblaitica*, 2: 3–29.

Diakonoff, I.M. (ed.) (1991) *Early Antiquity*. Chicago, IL: Chicago University Press.

Dietrich, M., Loretz, O., Sanmartín, J. (1976) 'Die ugaritischen Totengeister *RPU(M)* und die biblischen Rephaim', in *Ugarit-Forschungen*, 8: 45–52.

Di Ludovico, A., Ramazzotti, M. (2009) 'A Grammar of Ancient Geometric Paintings: The Decorative System of an EB IVA Painted Wall Decoration in the "Building FF2" at Tell Mardikh-Ebla', in *Orientalia*, 78: 335–349.

Dion, P.-E. (1997) *Les Araméens à l'Âge du Fer: Histoire politique et structure sociale*. Paris: Gabalda.

Di Paolo (2006) 'The Relief Art of Northern Syria in the Middle Bronze Age: The Alsdorf Stele and Some Sculptures from Karkemish', in F. Baffi, R. Dolce, S.

Mazzoni, F. Pinnock (eds), *Ina kibrāt erbetti: Studi di Archeologia Orientale dedicati a Paolo Matthiae*. Rome: University of Rome: 139–172.

Dolce, R. (1977) 'Nuovi frammenti di intarsi protosiriani da Tell Mardikh-Ebla', in *Oriens Antiquus*, 16: 1–21.

Dolce, R. (1978) *Gli intarsi mesopotamici dell'Epoca Protodinastica*. Rome: University of Rome (Serie Archeologica XXIII).

Dolce, R. (1980) 'Gli intarsi figurativi protosiriani del Palazzo Reale G', in *Studi Eblaiti*, 2: 105–128.

Dolce, R. (1991) 'La produzione artistica e il palazzo di Ebla nella cultura urbana della Siria del III millennio', in *La Parola del Passato*, 46: 237–269.

Dolce, R. (1998) 'The Palatial Ebla Culture in the Context of North Mesopotamian and North Syrian Main Powers', in *Subartu*, 4/2: 67–81.

Dolce, R. (1999) 'The "Second Ebla": A View on EB IVB City', in *Isimu*, 2: 293–304.

Dolce, R. (2001) 'Ebla after the "Fall"': Some Preliminary Considerations on the EB IVB City', in *Damaszener Mitteilungen*, 13 (Festschrift A. Abu Assaf): 11–28.

Dolce, R. (2002) '"Royal" Hairdresses and Turbans at the Court of Ebla: Two Marks of Royalty Compared', in M.G. Amadasi Guzzo, M. Liverani, P. Matthiae (eds), *Da Pyrgi a Mozia: Studi sull'archeologia del Mediterraneo in memoria di Antonia Ciasca*. Rome: University of Rome (Vicino Oriente. Quaderni 3/1): 201–211.

Dolce, R. (2005) 'Narrare gli eventi bellici: Cronaca e storia di alcuni conflitti eccellenti nella rappresentazione visiva della Mesopotamia e della Siria preclassiche', in F. Pecchioli Daddi, M.C. Guidotti (eds), *Narrare gli eventi: Atti del Convegno degli egittologi e degli orientalisti in margine alla mostra "La Battaglia di Qadesh"*. Rome: CNR (Studia Asiana III): 149–161.

Dolce, R. (2006) 'Ebla and Akkad: Clues of an Early Meeting. Another Look at the Artistic Culture of Palace G', in F. Baffi, R. Dolce, S. Mazzoni, F. Pinnock (eds) 2006: 173–206.

Dolce, R. (2007a) 'Committenza, circolazione e tesaurizzazione di manufatti preziosi ad Ebla protodinastica: Una questione aperta', in D. Bredi, L. Capezzone, W. Dahmash, L. Rostagno (eds), *Scritti in onore di B. Scarcia Amoretti*, II. Rome: Quasar: 545–576.

Dolce, R. (2007b) 'Du Bronze Ancien IVB au Bronze Moyen I à Ébla: Limites et problèmes pour une définition chronologique relative pendant la période de la ville protosyrienne récente', in P. Matthiae, F. Pinnock, L. Nigro, L. Peyronel (eds) 2007: 171–194.

Dolce, R. (2008) 'Ebla before the Achievement of Palace G Culture: Some Preliminary Evaluations', in H. Kühne, M. Czichon, F. Janoscha Kreppner (eds) 2008, II: 65–80.

Dornemann, R.H. (2008a) 'The 2004 Season of Excavations at Tell Qarqur', in *Studia Orontica*, 1: 91–100.

Dornemann, R.H. (2008b) 'The 2005 Season of Excavations at Tell Qarqur', in *Studia Orontica*, 1: 101–121.

Dossin, G. (1950) *Archives Royales de Mari*, I: *Correspondance de Šamši-Addu*. Paris. Imprimerie Nationale.

Drews, R. (1993) *The End of the Bronze Age: Changes in Warfare and the Catastrophe ca. 1200 B.C.* Princeton, NJ: Princeton University Press.

Durand, J.-M. (2008–2010) *Documents épistolaires du Palais de Mari,* I-III. Paris: Les Éditions du Cerf (Littératures anciennes du Proche-Orient XVI–XVIII).

Dussaud, R. (1927) *Topographie historique de la Syrie antique et médiévale*. Paris. Geuthner (Bibliothèque Archéologique et Historique IV).

Eder, Ch. (1995) *Die ägyptischen Motive in der Glyptik des östlichen Mittelmeerraumes zu Anfang des 2. Jts. v. Chr.* Leuven: Peeters (Orientalia Lovaniensa Analecta LXXI).

Edzard, D.O. (1981a) 'Neue Erwägungen zum Brief des Enna-Dagan von Mari (TM.75.G.2367)', in *Studi Eblaiti*, 4: 89–97.

Edzard, D.O. (1981b) *Archivi Reali di Ebla, Testi*, II: *Verwaltungstexte verschiedenen Inhalts (Aus dem Archiv L.2769)*. Rome: University of Rome.

Edzard, D.O. (1982) 'Neue Erwägungen zur Typologie der Verwaltungstexte von Ebla', in *Studi Eblaiti*, 5: 33–38.

Edzard, D.O. (1984) *Archivi Reali di Ebla, Testi*, V: *Hymnen, Beschwörungen und Verwandtes (Aus dem Archiv L.2769)*. Rome: University of Rome.

Edzard, D.O. (1992) 'Der Vertrag von Ebla mit A-bar-QA', in P. Fronzaroli (ed.) 1992: 187–217.

Edzard, D.O. (1993) 'Ébla ou la grande surprise de l'histoire du Proche-Orient ancien', in *Akkadica*, 88: 18–29.

Edzard, D.O. (2006) 'Das Ebla-Akkadische als Teil des akkadischer Dialektcontinuums', in G. Deutscher, N.J.C. Kouwenberg (eds) 2006: 76–83.

Edzard, D.O. (2007) *The Royal Inscriptions of Mesopotamia: Early Periods*, III/1, *Gudea and His Dynasty*. Toronto, ON/Buffalo, NY/London: University of Toronto Press.

Ehrich, R.W. (ed.) (1992) *Chronologies in Old World Archaeology*. Chicago, IL/London: University of Chicago Press.

Elayi, J. (1990) *Économie des cités phéniciennes sous l'Empire perse*. Naples. Istituto Universitario Orientale.

Evers, H.G. (1929) *Staat aus dem Stein: Denkmäler, Geschichte und Bedeutung der ägyptischen Plastik während des Mittleren Reiches*, I-II. Munich: F. Bruckmann.

Fagiolo, M. (1996) 'Il modello originario delle facciate a torre del Barocco ibleo: La facciata cinquecentesca della Cattedrale di Siracusa e il suo significato', in *Annali del Barocco in Sicilia*, 3: 42–58.

Feldman, M.H. (2006) *Diplomacy by Design: Luxury Arts and 'International Style' in the Ancient Near East, 1400–1200 B.C.* Chicago, IL/London: Chicago University Press.

Feliu, L. (2003) *The God Dagan in Bronze Age Syria*. Leiden/Boston, MA: Brill (Culture and History of the Ancient Near East XIX).

Fenton, T. (1996) 'Baal au foudre: Of Snakes and Mountains: Myth and Message', in N. Wyatt, W.G.E. Watson, J.B. Lloyd (eds), *Ugarit: Religion and Culture: Proceedings of the International Colloquium on Ugarit, Religion and Culture, Edinburgh, July 1994. Essays Presented in Honour of Professor John C.L. Gibson.* Münster: Ugarit-Verlag (Ugaritisch-Biblische Literatur XIII): 49–64.

Finkelstein, I. (1992) 'Middle Bronze Age Fortifications: A Reflection of Social Organization and Political Formations', in *Tel Aviv*, 19: 201–220.

Finkelstein, I. (1996) 'The Archaeology of the United Monarchy: An Alternative View', in *Levant*, 28: 177–187.

Foster, B.J. (1982) 'The Siege of Armanum', in *Journal of the Ancient Near Eastern Society*, 14: 27–36.

Frangipane, M. (1996) *La nascita dello Stato nel Vicino Oriente: Dai lignaggi alla burocrazia nella Grande Mesopotamia*. Rome/Bari: Laterza.

Frangipane, M., Hauptmann, H., Liverani, M., Matthiae, P., Mellink, M.J. (eds) (1993) *Between the Rivers and over the Mountains: Archaeologica Anatolica et Mesopotamica Alba Palmieri dedicata*. Rome: University of Rome.

Frankena, R. (1953) *"Tākultu": De sakrale maaltijd in het Assyrische ritueel*. Leiden: Nederlands Historisch-Archaeologische Instituut.

Frankfort, H. (1952) 'The Origin of the "bît ḫilāni"', in *Iraq*, 14: 120–131.

Frayne, D. (1993) *The Royal Inscriptions of Mesopotamia, Early Periods*, II: *Sargonic and Gutian Periods (2334–2113 BC)*. Toronto, ON/Buffalo, NY/London: University of Toronto Press.

Frayne, D. (1997) *The Royal Inscriptions of Mesopotamia, Early Periods*, III/2: *Ur III Period (2112–2004 BC)*. Toronto, ON/Buffalo, NY/London: University of Toronto Press.

Freu, J. (1995) 'De l'ancien Royaume au Nouvel Empire: Les temps obscures de la monarchie hittite', in O. Carruba, M. Giorgieri, C. Mora (eds), *Atti del II Congresso Internazionale di Hittitologia, Pavia, 28 giugno–2 luglio 1993*. Pavia: Italian University Press: 130–150.

Fronzaroli, P. (1979) 'Problemi di fonetica eblaita', in *Studi Eblaiti*, 1: 65–89.

Fronzaroli, P. (1982) 'Per una valutazione della morfologia eblaita', in *Studi Eblaiti*, 5: 93–120.

Fronzaroli, P. (ed.) (1984a) *Studies on the Language of Ebla*. Florence: University of Florence (Quaderni di Semitistica XIII).

Fronzaroli, P. (1984b) 'Materiali per il lessico eblaita', in *Studi Eblaiti*, 7: 145–190.

Fronzaroli, P. (1984c) 'The Eblaic Lexikon: Problems and Appraisal', in P. Fronzaroli (ed.) 1984a: 117–157.

Fronzaroli, P. (1985a) 'Per una valutazione della morfologia eblaita', in *Studi Eblaiti*, 5: 93–120.

Fronzaroli, P. (1985b) 'L'avverbio eblaita *ba*', in *Studi Epigrafici e Linguistici*, 2: 25–35.

Fronzaroli, P. (1987) 'Le pronom déterminatif relatif à Ébla', in *M.A.R.I.*, 5: 267–274.

Fronzaroli, P. (1988a) 'Il culto dei re defunti in ARET 3, 178', *in Miscellanea Eblaitica*, 1: 1–33.

Fronzaroli, P. (1988b) 'Tre scongiuri eblaiti (ARET 5. 1–3)', in *Vicino Oriente*, 7: 1–23.

Fronzaroli, P. (1990) 'Forms of the Dual in the Texts of Ebla', in *Maarav*, 5–6: 111–125.

Fronzaroli, P. (1991a) 'Niveaux de langue dans les graphies éblaïtes', in A.S. Kaye (ed.), *Studies in Honor of W. Leslau*. Wiesbaden: Harrassowitz: 462–474.

Fronzaroli, P. (1991b) 'Lingua e testo negli archivi di Ebla', in *La Parola del Passato*, 46: 220–236.

Fronzaroli, P. (ed.) (1992) *Literature and Literary Language at Ebla*. Florence: University of Florence (Quaderni di Semitistica XVIII).

Fronzaroli, P. (1994a) 'Eblaic and the Semitic Languages', in L. Del Lungo Camiciotti, F. Granucci, M.P. Marchese, R. Stefanelli (eds), *Studi in onore di C.A. Mastrelli: Scriti di allievi e amici fiorentini*. Padua: Unipress (Quaderni del Dipartimento di Linguistica, Studi I): 89–94.

Fronzaroli, P. (1994b) 'Osservazioni sul lessico delle bevande dei testi di Ebla', in L. Milano (ed.), *Drinking in Ancient Societies: History and Culture of Drinks in the Ancient Near East. Papers of the Symposium Held in Rome, May 17–19, 1990*. Padua: Sargon (History of the Ancient Near East, Studies VI): 121–127.

Fronzaroli, P. (1994c) 'Notes sur la syntaxe éblaïte', in *Amurru*, I: 125–134.

Fronzaroli, P. (1995a) 'Fonti di lessico nei testi di Ebla', in *Studi Epigrafici e Linguistici*, 12: 51–64.

Fronzaroli, P. (1995b) 'La lingua e la cultura letteraria di Ebla nel Periodo Protosiriano', in P. Matthiae, F. Pinnock, G. Scandone Matthiae (eds) 1995: 156–163.

Fronzaroli, P. (1996) 'À propos de quelques mots éblaïtes d'orfèvrerie', in Ö. Tunca, D. Deheselle (eds), *Tablettes et images aux Pays de Sumer et d'Akkad: Mélanges offerts à M. H. Limet*. Liège: Alpha (Association pour la promotion de l'Histoire et de l'Archéologie Orientales, Mémoires I): 51–68.

Fronzaroli, P. (1997) 'Les combats de Hadda dans les textes d'Ébla', in *M.A.R.I.*, 8: 283–290.

Fronzaroli, P. (1998) *Archivi Reali di Ebla, Testi*, XI: *Testi rituali della regalità (Archivio L.2769)*. Rome: University of Rome.

Fronzaroli, P. (2003a) *Archivi Reali di Ebla, Testi*, XIII: *Testi di cancelleria: i rapporti con le città (L.2769)*. Rome: University of Rome.

Fronzaroli, P. (2003b) 'The Hail Incantation (ARET 5, 4)', in Selz (ed.) 2003: 89–107.

Fronzaroli, P. (2003c) 'L'incantation des deux haches (TM.75.G.2302)', in J. Lentin, A. Lonnet (eds), *Mélanges D. Cohen: Études sur les langues, les dialectes, les littératures*. Paris: Maisonneuve & Larose: 25–64.

Fronzaroli, P. (2005) 'Structures linguistiques et histoire des langues au IIIe millénaire av. J.-C.', in P. Fronzaroli, P. Marrassini (eds) 2005: 155–167.

Fronzaroli, P., Marrassini, P. (eds) (2005) *Proceedings of the 10th Meeting of Chamito-Semitic (Afroasiatic) Linguistics, Florence, 18–20 April 2001*. Florence: University of Florence.

Fugmann, E. (1958) *Hama: Fouilles et recherches de la Fondation Carlsberg, 1931–1938*, II/1: *L'architecture des périodes pré-hellénistiques*. Copenhagen: National Museum (Nationalmuseets Skrifter, Større Beretninger IV).

Fusaro, D. (2007) *Luciano di Samosata: Tutti gli scritti*. Milan: Bompiani.

Gailani-Werr, L. al, Curtis, J., Martin, H., McMahon, A., Oates, J., Reade, J. (eds) (2002) *Of Pots and Plans: Papers in the Archaeology and History of Mesopotamia and Syria Presented to D. Oates in Honour of His 75th Birthday*. London: Nabu Publications.

Garelli, P. (1969) *Le Proche-Orient asiatique des origines aux invasions des Peuples de la Mer*. Paris: Presses Universitaires de France (Nouvelle Clio II).

Gelb, I.J. (1981) 'Ebla and the Kish Civilization', in L. Cagni (ed.) 1981: 9–73.

Gelb, I.J. (1984) 'The Inscription of Jibbit-Lim, King of Ebla', in *Studia Orientalia*, 55: 213–229.

Gelb, I.J., Kienast, B. (1990) *Die altakkadischen Königsinschriften des dritten Jahrtausends v. Chr*. Stuttgart: Franz Steiner (Freiburger Orientalische Studien VII).

Geller, M.J. (1987) 'The *Lugal* of Mari at Ebla and the Sumerian King List', in *Eblaitica*, 1: 140–145.

Gese, H., Höfner, M., Rudolph, K. (1979) *Die Religionen Altsyriens, Altarabiens und der Mandäer*. Stuttgart/Berlin/Cologne/Mainz: Kohlhammer.

Glassner, J.-J. (1984) 'La division quinaire de la terre', in *Akkadica*, 40: 17–34.

Glassner, J.-J. (1986) *La chute d'Agadé: L'évènement et sa mémoire*. Berlin: Reimer (Berliner Beiträge zum Vorderen Orient V).

Glassner, J.-J. (1993) 'Le roi prêtre en Mésopotamie au milieu du 3e millénaire: Mythe ou réalité?', in *Studia Orientalia*, 70: 9–19.

Gonnella, J., Khayyata, W., Kohlmeyer, K. (2005) *Die Zitadelle von Aleppo und der Tempel des Wettergottes: Neue Forschungen und Entwicklungen*. Münster: Rhema.

Gordon, C.H. (1991) 'The Ebla Incantations and Their Affinities with Northwest Semitic Magic', in *Maarav*, 7: 117–129.

Gordon, C.H. (1992a) 'The Geographical Horizons of Ebla', in M.W. Chavalas, J.L. Hayes (eds) 1992: 64–68.

Gordon, C.H. (1992b) 'The Ebla Exorcism', in *Eblaitica*, 3: 105–126.

Green, A.R.W. (2003) *The Storm-God in the Ancient Near East*. Winona Lake, IN: Eisenbrauns (Biblical and Judaic Studies from the University of California, San Diego VIII).

Gregori, B. (1986) '"Three-Entrance" City-Gates of the Middle Bronze Age in Syria and Palestine', in *Levant*, 17, 83–102.

Gutman, J. (ed.) (1976) *The Temple of Solomon: Archaeological Fact and Medieval Tradition in Christian, Islamic and Jewish Art*. Missoula, MT: American Schools of Oriental Research.

Haas, V., Wegner, I. (1995) 'Stadtverfluchungen in den Texten von Boghazköy sowie die hurrische Terminologie für "Oberstadt", "Unterstadt" und "Herd"', in U. Finkbeiner, R. Dittmann, H. Hauptmann (eds), *Beiträge zur Kulturgeschichte Vorderasiens: Festschrift für R.M. Boehmer*. Mainz: Von Zabern: 187–195.

Haider, P., Hutter, M., Kreuzer, S. (1996) *Religionsgeschichte Syriens: Von der Frühzeit bis zur Gegenwart*. Stuttgart/Cologne/Berlin/Mainz: Kohlhammer.

Hallo, W.W. (1957) *Early Mesopotamian Royal Titles: A Philological and Historical Analysis*. New Haven, CT: American Oriental Society.

Hallo, W.W. (1980) 'Royal Titles from the Mesopotamian Periphery', in *Anatolian Studies*, 30: 189–195.

Hallo, W.W. (1992) 'Ebrium at Ebla', in *Eblaitica*, 3: 139–150.

Hallo, W.W. (1996) 'Bilingualism and the Beginning of Translation', in M-V. Fox, V.A. Hurovitz, A.M. Hurvitz, M.L. Klein, B.J. Schwartz, N. Shupak (eds), *Texts, Temples and Traditions: A Tribute to M. Haran*. Winona Lake, IN: Eisenbrauns: 345–357.

Hawkins, J. (1982) 'The Neo-Hittite States in Syria and Anatolia', in J. Boardman, I.E.S. Edwards, N.G.L. Hammond, E. Sollberger (eds), *The Cambridge Ancient History*, III/1. 2nd Edition. Cambridge: Cambridge University Press: 372–441.

Heimpel, W. (1987) 'Das Untere Meer', in *Zeitschrift für Assyriologie*, 77: 22–91.

Helck, W. (1962) *Die Beziehungen Ägyptens zu Vorderasien im 3. und 2. Jahrtausend v. Chr.* Wiesbaden: Harrassowitz (Ägyptologische Abhandlungen V).

Hempelmann, R. (2003) 'Zur Datierung von drei Statuen aus Taftanaz', in R. Dittmann, Ch. Eder, B. Jacobs (eds), *Altertumswissenschaften in Dialog: Festschrift für Wolfram Nagel zur Vollendung seines 80. Lebensjahres*. Münster: Ugarit-Verlag (Alter Orient und Altes Testament 306): 291–299.

Hendel, R. (2006) 'The Archaeology of Memory: King Solomon, Chronology, and Biblical Representation', in S. Gitin, J.E. Wright, J.P. Dessel (eds), *Confronting the Past: Archaeological and Historical Essays on Ancient Israel in Honor of William G. Dever*. Winona Lake, IN: Eisenbrauns: 219–230.

Herzog, Z. (1986) *Das Stadttor in Israel und in der Nachbarländern*. Mainz: Von Zabern.

Horsnell, M.J.A. (1999) *The Year-Names of the First Dynasty of Babylon*, II: *The Year-Names Reconstructed and Critically Annotated in Light of Their Exemplars*. Toronto, ON: McMaster University Press.

Hrouda, B. (1957) *Die bemalte Keramik des zweiten Jahrtausends in Nordmesopotamien und Nordsyrien*. Berlin: Gebr. Mann.

Huehnergard, J. (2006) 'Proto-Semitic and Proto-Akkadian', in G. Deutscher, N.J.C. Kouwenberg (eds) 2006: 1–18.

Huehnergard, J., Woods, Ch. (2004) 'Akkadian and Eblaite', in R.D. Woodard (ed.), *The Cambridge Encyclopedia of the World's Ancient Languages*. Cambridge: Cambridge University Press: 138–159.

Jacobsen, Th. (1957) 'Early Political Development in Mesopotamia', in *Zeitschrift für Assyriologie*, 52: 91–140.

Jacobsen, Th. (1991) 'The Term Ensi', in *Aula Orientalis*, 9: 113–121.

Jasink, A.M. (1995) *Gli Stati neo-hittiti: Analisi delle fonti scritte e sintesi storica*. Padua: Sargon (History of the Ancient Near East/Studies IV).

Kärki, I. (1987) *Die Königsinschriften der dritten Dynastie von Ur*. Helsinki: Finnish Oriental Society (Studia Orientalia LVIII).

Kelly-Buccellati, M. (ed.) (1986) *Insight through Images: Studies in Honor of Edith Porada*. Malibu, CA: Undena (Bibliotheca Mesopotamica XXI).

Kempinski, A. (1983) *Syrien und Palästina (Kanaan) in der letzten Phase der Mittelbronze IIB-Zeit (1650–1570 v. Chr.)*. Wiesbaden: Harrassowitz (Ägypten und Altes Testament XLII).

Kempinski, A. (1992) 'Middle and Late Bronze Age Fortifications', in A. Kempinski, R. Reich (eds), *The Architecture of Ancient Israel: From the Prehistoric to the Persian Periods. In Memory of I. Dunayevsky*. Jerusalem: Israel Exploration Society: 127–142.

Kienast, B. (1980) 'Der Feldzugbericht des Ennadagan im literarihistorischer Sicht', in *Oriens Antiquus*, 19: 247–261.

Kienast, B. (1990) 'Zwölf Jahre Ebla: Versuch einer Bestandsaufnahme', in *Eblaitica*, 2: 31–77.

Kienast, B. (1988) 'Der Vertrag Ebla-Assur in rechthistorischer Sicht', in H. Waetzoldt, H. Hauptmann (eds) 1988: 231–243.

Kitchen, K.A. (2000) 'Regnal and Genealogical Data of Ancient Egypt (Absolute Chronology I): The Historical Chronology of Ancient Egypt: A Current Assessment', in M. Bietak (ed.) 2000: 39–52.

Kitchen, K.A. (2007) 'Egyptian and Related Chronologies: Look, No Sciences, No Pots', in M. Bietak, E Czerny (eds) 2007: 163–171.

Klengel, H. (1965) *Geschichte Syriens im 2. Jahrtausend v.u.Z.: Teil I – Nordsyrien*. Berlin: Akademie Verlag.

Klengel, H. (1965–1970) *Geschichte Syriens im 2. Jahrtausend v.u.Z.*, I-III. Berlin: Akademie Verlag.

Klengel, H. (1988) 'Ebla im Fernhandel des 3. Jahrtausends', in H. Waetzoldt, H. Hauptmann (eds) 1988: 245–251.

Klengel, H. (1990) 'Halab-Mari-Babylon: Aspekte syrisch-mesopotamischer Beziehungen in altbabylonischer Zeit', in Ö. Tunca (ed.) 1990: 183–195.

Klengel, H. (1992a) *Syria 3000 to 300 B.C.: A Handbook of Political History*. Berlin: Akademie Verlag.

Klengel, H. (1992b) 'Die Hethiter und Syrien: Aspekte einer Auseinandersetzung', in H. Otten, E. Akurgal, H. Ertem, A. Süel (eds), *Hittite and Other Anatolian and Near Eastern Studies in Honour of Sedat Alp*. Ankara: Türk Tarih Kurumu: 341–353.

Klengel, H. (1999) *Geschichte des Hethitischen Reiches*. Leiden/Boston, MA/ Cologne: Brill (Handbuch der Orientalistik I/34).

Klengel, H. (2000) 'The "Crisis Years" and the New Political System in Early Iron Age Syria: Introductory Remarks', in G. Bunnens (ed.), *Essays on Syria in the Iron Age*. Louvain/Paris/Sterling, VA: Peeters (Ancient Near Eastern Studies VII): 21–30.

Knoppers, G.N. (1997) 'The Vanishing Solomon: The Disappearance of the United Monarchy from Recent Histories of Ancient Israel', in *Journal of Biblical Literature*, 116: 19–44.

Kohlmeyer, K. (2000) *Der Tempel des Wettergottes von Aleppo*. Münster: Rhema.

Krauss, R. (2008) 'Ein Versuch zur Chronologie des späten Alten Reiches im Anschluss an die Monddaten im Neferirkare-Archiv', in *Orientalia*, 77: 377–385.

Krebernik, M. (1982/1983) 'Zu Syllabar und Orthographie der lexikalischen Texte aus Ebla', in *Zeitschrift für Assyriologie*, 72: 178–236, 73: 1–47.

Krebernik, M. (1984) *Die Beschwörungen aus Fara und Ebla*. Hildesheim: Olms.

Krebernik, M. (1992) 'Mesopotamian Myths at Ebla: ARET 5, 6 and ARET 5, 7', in P. Fronzaroli (ed.) 1992: 63–159.

Krebernik, M. (1996) 'The Linguistic Classification of Eblaite', in J.S. Cooper, G.M. Schwartz (eds), *The Study of the Ancient Near East in the Twenty-First Century: The William F. Albright Centennial*. Winona Lake, IN: Eisenbrauns: 233–249.

Krebernik, M. (2006) 'Some Questions Concerning Word Formation in Akkadian', in G. Deutscher, N.J.C. Kouwenberg (eds) 2006: 84–95.

Krecher, J. (1984) 'Sumerische und nichtsumerische Schicht in der Schriftkultur von Ebla', in L. Cagni (ed.) 1984: 139–166.

Krinsky, C. (1970) 'Representations of the Temple of Jerusalem before 1500', in *Journal of Warburg and Courtauld Institutes*, 33: 1–7.

Kühne, C. (1998) 'Meki, Megum und Mekum/Mekim', in S. Izre'el, I. Singer, R. Zadok (eds), *Past Links: Studies in the Languages and Cultures of the Ancient Near East. Festschrift A. Rainey* (Israel Oriental Studies XVIII). Winona Lake, IN: Eisenbrauns: 311–322.

Kühne, H., Czichon, M., Janoscha Kreppner, F. (eds) (2008) *Proceedings of the 4th International Congress of the Archaeology of the Ancient Near East, Berlin 29 March–3 April 2004*, I–III. Wiesbaden: Harrassowitz.

La Fay, H., Stanfield, J.L., Glanzman, L.S. (1978) 'Ebla: The Splendor of an Unknown Empire', in *National Geographic*, 154: 730–759.

Lahlouh, M., Catagnoti, A. (2006) *Archivi Reali di Ebla, Testi*, XII: *Testi amministrativi di vario contenuto (Archivio L.2769)*. Rome: University of Rome.

Lamberg-Karlowsky, C.C. (1985) 'The "Long Durée" of the Ancient Near East', in J.-L. Huot, M. Yon, Y. Calvet (eds), *De l'Indus aux Balkans: Recueil à la mémoire de Jean Deshayes*. Paris: Éditions Recherche sur les Civilisations: 55–72.

Lamberg-Karlowsky, C.C. (ed.) (1989) *Archaeological Thought in America*. Cambridge: Cambridge University Press.

Lambert, W.G. (1981) 'The Statue Inscription of Ibbit-Lim of Ebla', in *Revue d'Assyriologie*, 75: 95–101.

Lambert, W.G. (1987) 'The Treaty of Ebla', in L. Cagni (ed.) 1987: 353–364.

Lambert, W.G. (1989a) 'A Further Note on the Eblaite God NidaKUL', in *Revue d'Assyriologie*, 83: 96.

Lambert, W.G. (1989b) 'Notes on a Work of the Most Ancient Semitic Literature', in *Journal of Cuneiform Studies*, 41: 1–33.

Lambert, W.G. (1992) 'The Language of ARET V, 6 and 7', in P. Fronzaroli (ed.) 1992: 41–62.

Landsberger, B. (1954) 'Assyrische Königslisten und "Dunkles Zeitalter"', in *Journal of Cuneiform Studies*, 8: 31–45, 106–133.

Lapinkivi, P. (2004) *The Sumerian Sacred Marriage in the Light of Comparative Evidence*. Helsinki: University of Helsinki (State Archives of Assyria Studies XV).

Lawson Younger, Jr, K. (2007) 'The Late Bronze Age/Iron Age Transition and the Origin of the Arameans', in K. Lawson Younger, Jr (ed.), *Ugarit at Seventy-Five*. Winona Lake, IN: Eisenbrauns: 131–174.

Lawson Younger, Jr, K. (2009) 'The Deity Kur(r)a in the First Millennium B.C.', in *Journal of the Ancient Near Eastern Religions*, 9: 1–23.

Lebeau, M., Talon, Ph. (eds) (1989) *Reflets des deux fleuves: Volume de mélanges offerts à André Finet*. Leuven: Peeters (*Akkadica*, Supplementum VI).

Levine, B.A, de Tarragon, J.-M. (1984) 'Dead Kings and Rephaim of the Ugaritic Dynasty', in *Journal of the American Oriental Society*, 104: 649–659.

L'Heureux, E. (1979) *Rank among the Canaanite Gods: El, Ba'al, and the Repha'im.* Ann Arbor, MI: Scholar Press (Harvard Semitic Monographs XXI).

Lipiński, E. (1987) 'Le dieu Damu: Les pharyngales fricatives en fin de syllabe fermé', in L. Cagni (ed.) 1987: 91–99.

Lipiński, E. (2000) *The Arameans: Their Ancient History, Culture, Religion.* Leuven: Peeters (Orientalia Lovaniensia Analecta C).

Liverani, M. (1988) *Antico Oriente: Storia, società, economia.* Rome/Bari: Laterza.

Liverani, M. (ed.) (1993a) *Akkad: The First World Empire: Structure, Ideology, Tradition.* Padua: Sargon (History of the Ancient Near East. Studies V).

Liverani, M. (1993b) 'Model and Actualization: The Kings of Akkad in the Historical Tradition', in M. Liverani (ed.) 1993a: 41–68.

Liverani, M. (1998) *Uruk: La prima città.* Rome/Bari: Laterza.

Loretz, D. (1998) 'Eblaitisch *Larugatu* = ugaritisch *lrgt*: Traditionen der Yarih-Verherung in Ugarit', in *Ugarit-Forschungen*, 30: 489–496.

Lund, J. (1993) 'The Archaeological Evidence for the Transition from the Persian Period to the Hellenistic Age in North-Western Syria', in *Transeuphratène*, 6: 27–45.

Maeir, A.M., de Miroschedji, P. (eds) (2006) *"I Will Speak the Riddles of Ancient Times": Archaeological and Historical Studies in Honor of Amihai Mazar*, I–II. Winona Lake, IN: Eisenbrauns.

Mander, P. (2005) *La religione di Ebla.* Rome: Carocci (Le Religioni del Vicino Oriente Antico I).

Marchetti, N. (1996) 'The Ninevite 5 Glyptik of the Khabur Region and the Chronology of the Piedmont Style Motives', in *Baghdader Mitteilungen*, 17: 81–115.

Marchetti, N. (1998) 'The Mature Early Syrian Glyptic from the Khabur Region', in *Subartu*, 4/2: 115–153.

Marchetti, N. (2001) *Materiali e Studi Archeologici di Ebla*, V: *La coroplastica eblaita e siriana nel Bronzo Medio. Campagne 1964–1980*, I-II. Rome: University of Rome.

Marchetti, N. (2006) 'Middle Bronze Age Public Architecture at Tilmen Hüyük and the Architectural Tradition of Old Syrian Palaces', in F. Baffi, R. Dolce, S. Mazzoni, F. Pinnock (eds) 2006: 275–309.

Marchetti, N. (2007) 'Chronology and Stratification of Middle Bronze Age Clay Figurines in Syria and Northern Palestine', in P. Matthiae, F. Pinnock, L. Nigro, L. Peyronel (eds) 2007: 247–283.

Marchetti, N., Nigro, L. (1995–1996) 'Handicraft Production, Secondary Food Transformation and Storage in the Public Building P4 at EBA Ebla', in *Berytus*, 42: 9–36.

Marchetti, N., Nigro, L. (1997) 'Cultic Activities in the Sacred Area of Ishtar during the Old Syrian Period: The Favissae F.5238 and F.5327', in *Journal of Cuneiform Studies*, 49: 1–44.

Marchetti, N., Nigro, L. (1999) 'The Favissa F.5238 in the Sacred Area of Ishtar and the Transition from Middle Bronze I to the Middle Bronze II at Ebla', in K. Van Lerberghe, G. Voet (eds), *Languages and Cultures in Contact at the Crossroads of Civilizations in the Syro-Mesopotamian Realm: Actes de la 42e Rencontre Assyriologique Internationale, Leuven, 3–7 juillet 1995*. Leuven: Peeters (Orientalia Lovaniensia Analecta XCVI): 245–287.

Margueron, J.-Cl. (1982) *Recherches sur les palais mésopotamiens de l'Âge du Bronze* I–II. Paris: Geuthner (Bibliothèque archéologique et Historique CVII).

Margueron, J.-Cl. (1984) 'À propos des temples de Syrie du Nord', in M. Philonenko, M. Simon (eds), *Sanctuaires et clergés*. Paris: Geuthner (Études d'Histoire des Religions IV): 11–38.

Margueron, J.-Cl. (2004) *Mari: Métropole de l'Euphrate au IIIe et au début du IIe millénaire av. J.C.* Paris: Picard.

Marrassini, P. (ed.) (2003) *Semitic and Assyriological Studies Presented to Pelio Fronzaroli*. Wiesbaden: Harrassowitz.

Marro, C., Hauptmann, H. (eds) (2000) *Chronologie des pays de Caucase et de l'Euphrate aux IVe-IIIe millénaires*. Paris: Institut Français d'Études Anatoliennes (Varia Anatolica X).

Matthers, J. (ed.) (1981) *The River Qoueiq, Northern Syria, and Its Catchment: Studies Arising from the Tell Rifa'at Survey 1977–1979*. Oxford: British Archaeological Reports (B.A.R. International Series XCVIII).

Matthews, D.M. (1996) *The Early Glyptic of Tell Brak: Cylinder Seals of Third Millennium Syria*. Fribourg/Göttingen: University Press/Vandenhoeck & Ruprecht (Orbis Biblicus et Orientalis, Series Archaelogica XV).

Matthews, D., Eidem, J. (1993) 'Tell Brak and Nagar', in *Iraq*, 55: 201–207.

Matthiae, P. (1962) *Ars Syra: Contributi alla storia dell'arte della Siria durante il Bronzo Medio e Tardo*. Rome: University of Rome (Serie Archeologica IV).

Matthiae, P. (1965) 'Le sculture in basalto', in P. Matthiae (ed.), *Missione Archeologica Italiana in Siria: Rapporto preliminare della campagna 1964*. Rome: University of Rome: 61–80.

Matthiae, P. (1966) 'Le sculture in pietra', in P. Matthiae (ed.), *Missione Archeologica Italiana in Siria: Rapporto preliminare della campagna 1965 [Tell Mardikh]*. Rome: University of Rome: 103–142.

Matthiae, P. (1969) 'Empreintes d'un cylindre paléosyrien de Tell Mardikh', in *Syria*, 46: 1–43.

Matthiae, P. (1970) 'Mission archéologique de l'Université de Rome à Tell Mardikh: Rapport préliminaire sur la quatrième et cinquième campagnes, 1967 et 1968', in *Annales Archéologiques Arabes Syriennes*, 20: 55–72.

Matthiae, P. (1975a) 'Syrische Kunst', in W. Orthmann (ed.), *Propyläen Kunstgeschichte*, XIV: *Der Alte Orient*. Berlin: Propyläen Verlag: 466–493.

Matthiae, P. (1975b) 'Unité et développement du temple dans la Syrie du Bronze Moyen', in *Le temple et le culte: Compte Rendu de la vingtième Rencontre Assyriologique Internationale, Leiden, 3–7 Juillet 1972*. Leiden: Nederlands Historisch-Archaeologisch Instituut te Istanbul: 43–72.

Matthiae, P. (1976) 'Ébla à l'époque d'Akkad: Archéologie et histoire', in *Académie des Inscriptions et Belles-Lettres. Comptes Rendus*: 190–215.

Matthiae, P. (1977a) 'Ebla: Tell Mardikh Discoveries', in *Unesco Courier*, 30: 6–12.

Matthiae, P. (1977b) 'La scoperta del Palazzo Reale G e degli Archivi di Stato di Ebla (c. 2400–2350 a.C.)', in *La Parola del Passato*, 31: 233–266.

Matthiae, P. (1977c) 'Le Palais Royal protosyrien d'Ébla: Nouvelles recherches archéologiques à Ébla 1976', in *Académie des Inscriptions et Belles-Lettres. Comptes Rendus*: 148–174.

Matthiae, P. (1978) 'Recherches archéologiques à Ébla, 1977: Le Quartier Administratif du Palais Royal G', in *Académie des Inscriptions et Belles-Lettres. Comptes Rendus*: 204–236.

Matthiae, P. (1979a) 'Appunti di iconografia eblaita, I: Il turbante regale (?) eblaita di Mardikh IIB1', in *Studi Eblaiti*, 1: 17–32.

Matthiae, P. (1979b) 'Princely Cemetery and Ancestors Cult at Ebla during Middle Bronze II: A Proposal of Interpretation', in *Ugarit-Forschungen*, 11 (Festschrift C.F.A. Schaeffer): 563–569.

Matthiae, P. (1979c) 'Scavi a Tell Mardikh-Ebla, 1978', in *Studi Eblaiti*, 1: 129–184.

Matthiae, P. (1980a) 'Some Fragments of Early Syrian Sculpture from the Royal Palace G of Tell Mardikh-Ebla', in *Journal of Near Eastern Studies*, 39: 249–273.

Matthiae, P. (1980b) 'About the Style of a Miniature Animal Sculpture from the Royal Palace G of Ebla', in *Studi Eblaiti*, 3: 99–120.

Matthiae, P. (1980c) 'Appunti di iconografia eblaita, II: La testa di Atareb', in *Studi Eblaiti*, 2: 41–47.

Matthiae, P. (1980d), 'Fouilles à Tell Mardikh-Ébla, 1978: Le Bâtiment Q et la nécropole princière du Bronze Moyen', in *Akkadica*, 17: 1–52.

Matthiae, P. (1980e) 'Sulle asce fenestrate del "Signore dei Capridi"', in *Studi Eblaiti*, 3: 53–62.

Matthiae, P. (1980f) 'Two Princely Tombs at Tell Mardikh-Ebla', in *Archaeology*, 33: 8–17.

Matthiae, P. (1980g) 'Campagne de fouilles à Ébla en 1979: Les tombes princières et le palais de la Ville basse à l'époque amorrhéenne', in *Académie des Inscriptions et Belles-Lettres. Comptes Rendus*: 94–118.

Matthiae, P. (1980h) 'L'area cemeteriale principesca nella Città Bassa di Ebla amorrea', in *La Parola del Passato*, 35: 212–231.

Matthiae, P. (1981a) *Ebla: An Empire Rediscovered*. New York: Doubleday (English translation by Christopher Holme of *Ebla: Un impero ritrovato* [1977]. Turin: Einaudi).

Matthiae, P. (1981b) 'A Hypothesis on the Princely Burial Area of Middle Bronze II at Ebla', in *Archív Orientální*, 49: 55–65.

Matthiae, P. (1981c) 'Osservazioni sui gioielli delle tombe principesche di Mardikh IIB', in *Studi Eblaiti*, 4: 205–225 (English translation in Matthiae 2013: 127–140).

Matthiae, P. (1982a) 'The Problem of the Relations between Ebla and Mesopotamia in the Time of the Royal Palace of Mardikh IIB1 (ca. 2400–2350 B.C.)', in H.J. Nissen, J. Renger (eds) 1982: 111–123.

Matthiae, P. (1982b) 'Il Palazzo Reale G di Ebla e la tradizione architettonica protosiriana', in *Studi Eblaiti*, 5: 75–92.

Matthiae, P. (1982c) 'Fouilles de 1981 à Tell Mardikh-Ébla et à Tell Touqan: Nouvelles lumières sur l'architecture paléosyrienne du Bronze Moyen I-II', in *Académie des Inscriptions et Belles-Lettres. Comptes Rendus*: 299–331.

Matthiae, P. (1982d) 'The Western Palace of the Lower Town of Ebla: A New Administrative Building of Middle Bronze I-II', in *Archiv für Orientforschung, Beiheft*, 19: 121–129.

Matthiae, P. (1982e) 'Die Fürstengräber des Palastes Q at Ebla', in *Antike Welt*, 13: 2–14.

Matthiae, P. (1982f) 'Fouilles à Tell Mardikh-Ébla: Le Palais Occidental de l'époque amorrhéenne', in *Akkadica*, 28: 41–87.

Matthiae, P. (1982g) 'A New Palatial Building and the Princely Tombs of Middle Bronze II at Ebla', in H. Klengel (ed.), *Gesellschaft und Kultur im Alten Vorderasien*. Berlin: Akademie Verlag (Schriften zur Geschichte und Kultur des Alten Orients XV): 187–194.

416   *Bibliography*

Matthiae, P. (1983) 'Fouilles à Tell-Mardikh-Ébla en 1982: Nouvelles recherches sur l'architecture palatine d'Ébla', in *Académie des Inscriptions et Belles-Lettres. Comptes Rendus*: 530–554.

Matthiae, P. (1984a) *I tesori di Ebla* (Haskell Lectures 1981, Oberlin College, Oberlin, Ohio). Rome/Bari: Laterza.

Matthiae, P. (1984b) 'New Discoveries at Ebla: The Excavation of the Western Palace and the Royal Necropolis of the Amorite Period', in *Biblical Archaeologist*, 47: 18–32.

Matthiae, P. (1986a) 'The Archives of the Royal Palace G of Ebla: Distribution and Arrangement of the Tablets according to the Archaeological Evidence', in K.R. Veenhof (ed.), *Cuneiform Archives and Libraries: Papers Read at the 30e Rencontre Assyriologique Internationale, Leiden, 4–8 July 1983*. Leiden/Istanbul: Nederlands Historisch-Archaeologisch Instituut (Uitgaven van het Nederlands Historisch-Archaeologisch Instituut te Istanbul LVII): 53–71.

Matthiae, P. (1986b) 'Sull'identità degli dèi titolari dei templi paleosiriani di Ebla', in *Contributi e Materiali di Archeologia Orientale*, 1: 335–362. (English translation in Matthiae 2013: 301–322).

Matthiae, P. (1986c) 'Una stele paleosiriana arcaica da Ebla e la cultura figurativa della Siria attorno al 1800 a.C.', in *Scienze dell'Antichità*, 1: 447–495 (English translation in Matthiae 2013: 517–555).

Matthiae, P. (1987) 'Les dernières découvertes d'Ébla en 1983–1986', in *Académie des Inscriptions et Belles-Lettres. Comptes Rendus*: 135–161.

Matthiae, P. (1989a) *Ebla, un impero ritrovato: Dai primi scavi alle ultime scoperte*, 2nd Revised Edition. Turin: Einaudi.

Matthiae, P. (1989b) 'The Destruction of Ebla Royal Palace: Interconnections between Syria, Mesopotamia and Egypt in the Late EB IVA', in P. Åström (ed.), *High, Middle or Low? Acts of an International Colloquium on Absolute Chronology Held at the University of Gothenburg 20th–22nd August 1987*, III. Gothenburg: Åström: 163–169.

Matthiae, P. (1989c) 'Masterpieces of Early and Old Syrian Art: Discoveries of the 1988 Ebla Excavations in a Historical Perspective', in *Proceedings of the British Academy*, 75: 25–56.

Matthiae, P. (1989d) 'Old Syrian Ancestors of Some Neo-Assyrian Figurative Symbols of Kingship', in L. De Meyer, E. Haerinck (eds), *Archaeologia Iranica et Orientalis: Miscellanea in Honorem L. Vanden Berghe*. Leuven: Peeters: 367–391.

Matthiae, P. (1989e) 'Le temple et le taureau: Origine et continuité de l'iconographie de la grande déesse à Ébla', in M. Lebeau, Ph. Talon (eds), *Reflets des deux fleuves: Volume de mélanges offerts à André Finet*. Leuven: Peeters (Akkadica, Supplementum VI): 127–135.

Matthiae, P. (1989f) 'Jugs of the North Syrian/Cilician and Levantine Painted Wares from the Middle Bronze II Royal Tombs at Ebla', in K. Emre, B. Hrouda, M. Mellink, N. Özgüç (eds), *Anatolia and the Ancient Near East: Studies in Honor of Tahsin Özgüç*, Ankara: Türk Tarih Kurumu: 303–313.

Matthiae, P. (1990a) 'Nouvelles fouilles à Ébla en 1987–1989', in *Académie des Inscriptions et Belles-Lettres. Comptes Rendus*: 384–431.

Matthiae, P. (1990b) 'The Reception Suites of the Old Syrian Palaces', in Ö. Tunca (ed.), *De la Babylonie à la Syrie, en passant par Mari: Mélanges offerts à M. J.-R. Kupper à l'occasion de son 70e anniversaire*. Liège: University of Liège: 209–228.

Matthiae, P. (1990c) 'A New Monumental Temple of Middle Bronze II at Ebla and the Unity of the Architectural Tradition of Syria-Palestine', in *Annales Archéologiques Arabes Syriennes*, 40: 111–121.

Matthiae, P. (1990d) 'A Class of Old Syrian Bronze Statuettes and the Sanctuary B2 at Ebla', in P. Matthiae, M. van Loon, H. Weiss (eds), *Resurrecting the Past: A Joint Tribute to Adnan Bounni*. Leiden: Nederlands Historisch-Archaeologisch Instituut te Istanbul: 345–362.

Matthiae, P. (1991) 'Architettura e urbanistica di Ebla paleosiriana', in *La Parola del Passato*, 46: 304–371 (English translation in Matthiae 2013: 259–284).

Matthiae, P. (1992a) 'Some Notes on the Old Syrian Iconography of the God Yam', in D.J.W. Meijer (ed.), *Natural Phenomena: Their Meaning, Depiction and Description in the Ancient Near East*. Amsterdam: Royal Netherlands Academy of Arts and Sciences: 169–192.

Matthiae, P. (1992b) 'Figurative Themes and Literary Texts', in P. Fronzaroli (ed.) 1992: 219–241.

Matthiae, P. (1992c) 'High Old Syrian Royal Statuary from Ebla', in B. Hrouda, S. Kroll, P.Z. Spanos. (eds), *Von Uruk nach Tuttul: Eine Festschrift für Eva Strommenger*. Munich: Profil Verlag (Münchener Vorderasiatische Studien XII): 111–128.

Matthiae, P. (1993a) 'On this Side of the Euphrates: A Note on the Urban Origins in Inner Syria', in M. Frangipane, H. Hauptmann, M. Liverani, P. Matthiae, M.J. Mellink (eds) 1993: 523–530.

Matthiae, P. (1993b) 'L'aire Sacrée d'Ishtar à Ébla: Résultats des fouilles de 1990–1992', in *Académie des Inscriptions et Belles-Lettres. Comptes Rendus*: 613–662.

Matthiae, P. (1993c) 'A Stele Fragment of Hadad from Ebla', in M.J. Mellink, E. Porada, T. Özgüç (eds) 1993: 389–397.

Matthiae, P. (1994a) *Il sovrano e l'opera: Arte e potere nella Mesopotamia antica*. Rome/Bari: Laterza.

Matthiae, P. (1994b) 'The Lions of the Great Goddess of Ebla: A Hypothesis about Some Archaic Old Syrian Cylinders', in H. Gasche, M. Tanret, C. Janssen, A. Degraeve (eds), *Cinquante-deux réflexions sur le Proche-Orient ancien offertes en hommage à L. De Meyer*. Leuven: Peeters (Mesopotamian History and Environment, Occasional Publications II): 329–338.

Matthiae, P. (1994c) 'Old Syrian Basalt Furniture from Ebla Palaces and Temples', in P. Calmeyer, K. Hecker, L. Jacob-Tost, C.B.F. Walker (eds), *Beiträge zur Altorientalischen Archäologie und Altertumskunde: Festschrift für Barthel Hrouda zum 65. Geburtstag*. Wiesbaden: Harrassowitz: 167–177.

Matthiae, P. (1995a) 'Ebla e la tradizione architettonica della Siria nell'Età del Bronzo', in P. Matthiae, F. Pinnock, G. Scandone Matthiae (eds) (1995): 226–235.

Matthiae, P. (1995b) 'Fouilles à Ébla en 1993–1994: Les palais de la Ville basse', in *Académie des Inscriptions et Belles-Lettres. Comptes Rendus*: 651–681.

Matthiae, P. (ed.) (1996a) 'Gli Archivi dell'Oriente antico', in *Archivi e Cultura*, 29.

Matthiae, P. (1996b) 'Nouveaux témoignages de sculpture paléosyrienne du grand sanctuaire d'Ishtar à Ébla', in H. Gasche, B. Hrouda (eds), *Collectanea Orientalia: Histoire, art de l'espace et industrie de la terre. Études offertes à A. Spycket*. Neuchâtel, Paris: Recherches et Publications (Civilisations du Proche-Orient, Série I. Archéologie et Environnement III): 199–204.

Matthiae, P. (1996c) 'Due frammenti di un nuovo bacino scolpito dal Tempio P2 di Ebla', in *Studi Miscellanei*, 30 (Studi in memoria di Lucia Guerrini): 3–12.

Matthiae, P. (1997a) 'Ebla and Syria in the Middle Bronze Age', in E.D. Oren (ed.), *The Hyksos: New Historical and Archaeological Perspectives*. Philadelphia, PA: University of Pennsylvania (University Museum Monographs XCV): 379–414.

Matthiae, P. (1997b) 'Vingt ans de fouilles et de découvertes: La renaissance d'Ébla amorrhéenne', in *Akkadica*, 101: 1–29.

Matthiae, P. (1997c) *La Storia dell'Arte dell'Oriente Antico: I primi imperi e i principati del Ferro, 1600–700 a.C.* Milan: Electa.

Matthiae, P. (1997d) 'Some Notes about Solomon's Palace and Ramesside Architectural Culture', in *L'impero ramesside: Convegno Internazionale in onore di Sergio Donadoni*. Rome: University of Rome (Vicino Oriente, Quaderni I): 117–130.

Matthiae, P. (1998) 'Les fortifications d'Ébla paléosyrienne: Fouilles à Tell Mardikh (1995–1997)', in *Académie des Inscriptions et Belles-Lettres. Comptes Rendus*: 557–588.

Matthiae, P. (2000a) 'Nouvelles fouilles à Ébla (1998–1999): Forts et palais de l'enceinte urbaine', in *Académie des Inscriptions et Belles-Lettres. Comptes Rendus*: 567–610.

Matthiae, P. (2000b) *La Storia dell'Arte dell'Oriente antico: Gli stati territoriali, 2100–1600 a.C.* Milan: Electa.

Matthiae, P. (2000c) 'A Statue Base from the Western Palace of Ebla and the Continuity of the Old Syrian Artistic Tradition', in R. Dittmann, B. Hrouda, U. Löw, P. Matthiae, R. Mayer-Opificius, S. Thürwächter (eds), *Variatio delectat: Iran und der West. Gedenkschrift für P. Calmeyer*. Münster: Ugarit-Verlag (Alter Orient und Altes Testament CCLXXII 2): 385–402.

Matthiae, P. (2001a) 'A Preliminary Note on the MB I-II Fortifications System at Ebla', in *Damaszener Mitteilungen*, 13 (Festschrift A. Abu Assaf): 29–51.

Matthiae, P. (2001b) 'The Face of Ishtar of Ebla', in J.-W. Meyer, M. Novák, A. Pruß (eds), *Beiträge zur Vorderasiatischen Archäologie, W. Orthmann gewidmet*. Frankfurt am Main: Johann Wolfgang Goethe University: 272–281.

Matthiae, P. (2002a) 'Una nota sul Tempio di Salomone e la cultura architettonica neosiriana', in *Da Pyrgi a Mozia: Studi sull'archeologia del Mediterraneo in memoria di A. Ciasca*, I. Rome: University of Rome (Vicino Oriente, Quaderni III): 339–344.

Matthiae, P. (2002b) 'Fouilles et restaurations à Ébla en 2000–2001: Le Palais Occidental, la Résidence Occidentale et l'urbanisme de la ville paléosyrienne', in *Académie des Inscriptions et Belles-Lettres. Comptes Rendus*: 531–574.

Matthiae, P. (2002c) 'About the Formation of Old Syrian Architectural Tradition', in L. al Gailani-Werr, J. Curtis, H. Martin, A. McMahon, J. Oates, J. Reade (eds), *Of Pots and Plans: Papers on the Archaeology and History of Mesopotamia and Syria presented to David Oates in Honour of His 75th Birthday*. London: Nabu Publications: 191–209.

Matthiae, P. (2003) 'Ishtar of Ebla and Hadad of Aleppo: Notes on Terminology, Politics and Religion of Old Syrian Ebla', in P. Marrassini (ed.) 2003: 381–402.

Matthiae, P. (2004) 'Le Palais méridional dans la Ville basse d'Ébla paléosyrienne: Fouilles à Tell Mardikh (2002–2003)', in *Académie des Inscriptions et Belles-Lettres. Comptes Rendus*: 301–346.

Matthiae, P. (2005) *Prima lezione di archeologia orientale*. Rome/Bari: Laterza.

Matthiae, P. (2006a) 'Archaeology of a Destruction: The End of MB II Ebla in the Light of Myth and History', in E. Czerny, I. Heim, H. Hunger, D. Melman, A. Schwab (eds), *Timelines: Studies in Honour of Manfred Bietak*, III. Leuven: Peeters (Orientalia Analecta Lovaniensia CXLIX, 3): 39–51.

Matthiae, P. (2006b) 'Un grand temple de l'époque des Archives dans l'Ébla protosyrienne: Fouilles à Tell Mardikh 2004–2005', in *Académie des Inscriptions et Belles-Lettres. Comptes Rendus*: 447–493.

Matthiae, P. (2006c) 'The Archaic Palace at Ebla: A Royal Building between Early Bronze Age IVB and Middle Bronze Age I', in S. Gitin, J.E. Wright, J.P. Dessel (eds), *Confronting the Past: Archaeological and Historical Essays on Ancient Israel in Honor of William G. Dever*. Winona Lake, IN: Eisenbrauns: 85–103.

Matthiae, P. (2006d) 'Middle Bronze II Minor Cult Places at Ebla?', in A.M. Maeir, P. de Miroschedji (eds) 2006: 217–233.

Matthiae, P. (2006e) 'Old Syrian Statuary and Carved Basins from Ebla: New Documents and Interpretations', in P. Butterlin, M. Lebeau, J.-Y. Monchambert, J.L. Montero Fenollós, B. Muller (eds), *Les espaces syro-mésopotamiens: Dimensions de l'expérience humaine au Proche-Orient ancien. Volume d'hommage offert à Jean-Claude Margueron* (*Subartu* 17): 423–438.

Matthiae, P. (2007a) 'Nouvelles fouilles à Ébla en 2006: Le Temple du Rocher et ses successeurs protosyriens et paléosyriens', in *Académie des Inscriptions et Belles-Lettres. Comptes Rendus*: 481–525.

Matthiae, P. (2007b) 'The Destruction of Old Syrian Ebla at the End of Middle Bronze II: New Historical Data', in P. Matthiae, F. Pinnock, L. Nigro, L. Peyronel (eds) 2007: 5–32.

Matthiae, P. (2008a) *Gli Archivi Reali di Ebla: La scoperta, i testi, il significato*. Milan: Mondadori/Sapienza.

Matthiae, P. (2008b) 'Une note sur l'architecture araméenne de Hama et le problème de ses origines', in D. Bonatz, R.M. Czichon, F. Janoscha Kreppner (eds), *Fundstellen: Gesammelte Schriften zur Archäologie und Geschichte Altvoderasiens ad honorem Hartmut Kühne*. Wiesbaden: Harrassowitz: 207–213.

Matthiae, P. (2008c) 'The Temple of the Rock of Early Bronze IVA-B at Ebla: Structure, Chronology, Continuity', in J-M. Córdoba, M. Molist, M.C. Pérez, I. Rubio, S. Martinez (eds), *Proceedings of the 5th International Congress on the Archaeology of the Ancient Near East, Madrid, April 3–8 2006*. Madrid: Autonomous University of Madrid: 547–570.

Matthiae, P. (2008d) 'Il Tempio di Gerusalemme: La suggestione infinita di una rovina scomparsa', in M. Barbanera (ed.), *Relitti riletti: Metamorfosi delle rovine e identità culturale*. Turin: Bollati Boringhieri: 416–430.

Matthiae, P. (2008e) 'Temples and Queens at Ebla: Recent Discoveries in a Syrian Metropolis between Mesopotamia, Egypt and Levant', in *Interconnections in the Eastern Mediterranean: Lebanon in the Bronze and Iron Ages. Proceedings of the International Symposium, Beirut 2008* (BAAL, Hors-Série VI): 117–139.

Matthiae, P. (2008–2009a) 'Crisis and Collapse: Similarity and Diversity in the Three Destructions of Ebla from EB IVA to MB II', in *Scienze dell'Antichità*, 15–16: 165–205.

Matthiae, P. (2008–2009b) 'Il Tempio della Roccia ad Ebla: La residenza mitica del dio Kura e la fondazione della città protosiriana', in *Scienze dell'Antichità*, 15–16: 451–494.

Matthiae, P. (2009a) 'The Standard of the *maliktum* of Ebla in the Royal Archives Period', in *Zeitschrift für Assyriologie*, 99: 270–311.

Matthiae, P. (2009b) 'Temples et reines de l'Ébla protosyrienne: Résultats des fouilles à Tell Mardikh en 2007 et 2008', in *Académie des Inscriptions et Belles-Lettres. Comptes Rendus*: 747–792.

Matthiae, P. (2013) *Studies on the Archaeology of Ebla 1980–2010* (Edited by F. Pinnock). Wiesbaden: Harrassowitz.

Matthiae, P., Enea, A., Peyronel, L., Pinnock, F. (eds) (2000) *Proceedings of the First International Congress on the Archaeology of the Ancient Near East, Rome, May 18th–23rd 1998,* I–II. Rome: University of Rome.

Matthiae, P., Pettinato, G. (1972) *Il torso di Ibbit-Lim, re di Ebla.* Rome: Institute for the Study of the Near East, University of Rome.

Matthiae, P., Pinnock, F., Nigro, L., Peyronel, L. (eds) (2007) *Proceedings of the International Colloquium "From Relative Chronology to Absolute Chronology: The Second Millennium B.C. in Syria-Palestine" (Rome 29th November–1st December 2001).* Rome: Accademia Nazionale dei Lincei.

Matthiae, P., Pinnock, F., Scandone Matthiae, G. (eds) (1995) *Ebla: Alle origini della civiltà urbana. Trenta anni di scavi in Siria dell'Università di Roma "La Sapienza". Roma, Palazzo Venezia, 18 marzo–30 giugno 1995.* Milan: Electa.

Matthiae, P., van Loon, M., Weiss, H. (eds) (1990) *Resurrecting the Past: A Joint Tribute to A. Bounni.* Istanbul: Nederlands Historisch-Archaeologisch Instituut (Uitgaven van het Nederlands Historisch-Archaeologisch Instituut te Istanbul LXVII).

Maxwell-Hyslop, K.R. (1971) *Western Asiatic Jewellery c. 3000–612 B.C.* London: Methuen & Co.

Mazar, A. (2005) 'The Debate over the Chronology of the Iron Age in the Southern Levant: Its History, the Current Situation, and a Suggested Resolution', in T.E. Levy, T. Higham (eds), *The Bible and Radiocarbon Dating: Archaeology, Text and Science.* London: Oakville: 15–30.

Mazzoni, S. (1975) 'Tell Mardikh e una classe siro-anatolica di sigilli del periodo di Larsa', in *Annali dell'Istituto Universitario Orientale di Napoli,* 35: 32–43.

Mazzoni, S. (1979) 'A proposito di un sigillo in stile lineare-corsivo di Mardikh IIIB', in *Studi Eblaiti,* 1: 49–64.

Mazzoni, S. (1980) 'Una statua reale paleosiriana del Cleveland Museum', in *Studi Eblaiti,* 3: 79–98.

Mazzoni, S. (1982) 'La produzione ceramica del Palazzo Reale G di Ebla e la sua posizione storica nell'orizzonte ceramico siro-mesopotamico del III millennio a.C.', in *Studi Eblaiti,* 5: 77–92.

Mazzoni, S. (1984) 'L'insediamento persiano-ellenistico di Tell Mardikh', in *Studi Eblaiti,* 7: 87–132.

Mazzoni. S. (1985) 'Elements of the Ceramic Culture of Early Syrian Ebla in Comparison with Syro-Palestinian EB IV', in *Bulletin of the American Schools of Oriental Research,* 107: 1–18.

Mazzoni, S. (1986) 'Continuity and Development in the Syrian and the Cypriote Common Glyptic Styles', in M. Kelly-Buccellati (ed.) 1986: 171–182.

Mazzoni, S. (1987) 'Faience in Ebla during Middle Bronze II', in M. Binson, I.C. Freestone (eds), *Early Vitreous Materials.* London, British Museum (British Museum Occasional Papers LVI): 65–77.

Mazzoni, S. (1988) 'Economic Features of the Pottery Equipment of Palace G', in H. Waetzoldt, H. Hauptmann (eds) 1988: 81–105.

Mazzoni, S. (1990) 'La période perse à Tell Mardikh et dans sa région dans le cadre de l'Âge du Fer en Syrie', in *Transeuphratène,* 2: 187–199.

Mazzoni, S. (1991) 'Ebla e la formazione della cultura urbana in Siria', in *La Parola del Passato,* 46: 163–194.

Mazzoni, S. (1991–1992) 'Lo sviluppo degli insediamenti in Siria in età persiana', in *Egitto e Vicino Oriente*, 14–15: 55–72.

Mazzoni, S. (1992) *Materiali e Studi Archeologici di Ebla*, I: *Le impronte su giare eblaite e siriane nel Bronzo Antico*. Rome: University of Rome.

Mazzoni, S. (1993) 'Cylinder Seals Impressions on Jars at Ebla: New Evidence', in M.J. Mellink, E. Porada, T. Özgüç (eds) 1993: 399–414.

Mazzoni, S. (1994) 'Drinking Vessels in Syria: Ebla and the Early Bronze Age', in L. Milano (ed.), *Drinking in Ancient Societies: History and Culture of Drinks in the Ancient Near East. Papers of the Symposium Held in Rome, May 17–19, 1990.* Padua: Sargon (History of the Ancient Near East: Studies 6): 245–276.

Mazzoni, S. (1999) 'Pots, People and Cultural Borders in Syria', in L. Milano, S. de Martino, F.M. Fales, G.B. Lanfranchi (eds), *Landscapes, Territories, Frontiers and Horizons in the Ancient Near East: Papers presented to the XLIV Rencontre Assyriologique Internationale*. Padua: Sargon: 139–152.

Mazzoni, S. (2000a) 'From the Late Chalcolithic to Early Bronze I in North-West Syria. Anatolian Contact and Regional Perspective', in C. Marro, H. Hauptmann (eds) 2000: 97–109.

Mazzoni, S. (2000b) 'Handled Pans from Ebla and the Evidence of Anatolian Connections', in R. Dittmann, B. Hrouda, U. Löw, P. Matthiae, R. Mayer-Opificius, S. Thürwächter (eds), *Variatio delectat: Iran und der West. Gedenkschrift für P. Calmeyer*. Münster: Ugarit-Verlag (Alter Orient und Altes Testament CCLXXII 2): 403–427.

Mazzoni, S. (2000c) 'Syria and the Periodization of the Iron Age: A Cross-Cultural Perspective', in G. Bunnens (ed.), *Essays on Syria in the Iron Age*. Louvain/Paris/Sterling, VA: Peeters (Ancient Near Eastern Studies VII): 31–59.

Mazzoni, S. (2002) 'The Ancient Bronze Age Pottery Tradition in North-Western Central Syria', in M. Al-Maqdissi, V. Matoïan, Ch. Nicolle (eds), *Céramique de l'Âge du Bronze en Syrie*, I: *La Syrie du Sud et la Vallée de l'Oronte*. Beirut: Institut Français d'Archéologie du Proche-Orient (Bibliothèque Archéologique et Historique CLXI): 69–96.

Mazzoni, S. (2003) 'Ebla Craft and Power in an Emergent State of Third Millennium B.C. Syria', in *Journal of Mediterranean Archaeology*, 16: 173–191.

Mazzoni, S. (2006) 'Syria and Emergence of Cultural Complexity', in F. Baffi, R. Dolce, S. Mazzoni, F. Pinnock (eds) 2006: 321–347.

Mellink. M.J., Porada, E., Özgüç, T. (eds) (1993) *Aspects of Art and Archaeology: Anatolia and Its Neighbors. Studies in Honor of N. Özgüç*. Ankara: Türk Tarih Kurumu.

Meyer, J.-W. (2007) 'Town Planning in 3rd Millennium Tell Chuera', in J. Bretschneider, J. Driessen, K. Van Lerberghe (eds), *Power and Architecture: Monumental Public Architecture in the Bronze Age Near East and Aegean. Proceedings of the International Conference on the 21st and 22th of November 2002.* Leuven/Paris/Dudley, MA: Peeters (Orientalia Lovaniensia Analecta CLVI): 129–142.

Meyer, J.-W., Hempelmann, R. (2006) 'Bemerkungen zu Mari aus der Sicht von Tell Chuera: Ein Beitrag zur Geschichte der ersten Hälfte des 3. Jts. V. Chr.', in *Altorientalische Forschungen*, 33: 22–41.

Meyer, J.-W., Sommerfeld, W. (eds) (2004) *2000 v. Chr. Politische, wirtschaftliche und kulturelle Entwicklung einer Jahrtausendwende. 3: Internationales Colloquium der Deutschen Orient-Gesellschaft, 4. –7. April 2000 in Frankfurt/Main und Marburg/Lahn*. Saarbrücken: Saarbrücker Druckerei und Verlag.

Michalowski, P. (1985) 'Third Millennium Contacts: Observations on the Relationships between Mari and Ebla', in *Journal of the American Oriental Society*, 105: 293–298.

Michalowski, P. (1988) 'Thoughts about Ibrium', in H. Waetzoldt, H. Hauptmann (eds) 1988: 267–277

Michalowski, P. (1992) 'The Early Mesopotamian Incantation Tradition', in P. Fronzaroli (ed.) 1992: 305–326.

Milano, L. (1980) 'Due rendiconti di metalli da Ebla', in *Studi Eblaiti*, 3: 1–21.

Milano, L. (1984) 'Distribuzione di bestiame minuto ad Ebla: Criteri contabili e implicazioni economiche', in P. Fronzaroli (ed.) 1984a: 205–223.

Milano, L. (1987a) 'Barley for Rations and Barley for Sowing (ARET II, 51 and Related Matters)', in *Acta Sumerologica*, 9: 177–201.

Milano, L. (1987b) 'Food Rations at Ebla', in *M.A.R.I.*, 5: 519–550.

Milano, L. (1990) *Archivi Reali di Ebla, Testi*, IX: *Testi amministrativi: assegnazioni di prodotti alimentari (Archivio L.2712 – Parte I)*. Rome. University of Rome.

Milano, L. (1996) 'Ebla: Gestion des terres et gestion des ressources alimentaires', in *Amurru*, 1: 135–171.

Milano, L. (2003) 'Les affaires de Monsieur Gida-na'im', in P. Marrassini (ed.) 2003: 411–429.

Moorey, P.R.S. (1978) *Kish Excavations 1923–1933*. Oxford: Clarendon Press.

Moorey, P.R.S. (1981) 'Abu Salabikh, Kish, Mari and Ebla: Mid-Third Millennium Archaeological Connections', in *American Journal of Archaeology*, 85: 447–448.

Moorey, P.R.S. (1991) *A Century of Biblical Archaeology*. Cambridge: Lutterworth Press.

Moortgat, A. (1962) *Tell Chuera in Nordost Syrien: Vorläufiger Bericht über die dritte Grabungskampagne 1960*. Cologne/Opladen: Westdeutscher Verlag.

Moortgat, A. (1965) *Tell Chuera in Nordost Syrien: Vorläufiger Bericht über die vierte Grabungskampagne 1963*. Cologne/Opladen: Westdeutscher Verlag.

Moortgat, A. (1967) *Die Kunst des Alten Mesopotamien: Die klassische Kunst Vorderasiens*. Cologne: DuMont Schauberg.

Moortgat-Correns, U. (1955) 'Neue Anhaltspunkte zur zeitlichen Ordnung syrischer Glyptik', in *Zeitschrift für Assyriologie*, 51: 88–101.

Morandi Bonacossi, D. (2006) 'New Royal Statue from Tell Mishrifeh/Qatna', in E. Czerny, I. Heim, H. Hunger, D. Melman, A. Schwab (eds), *Timelines: Studies in Honour of Manfred Bietak*, III. Leuven: Peeters (Orientalia Analecta Lovaniensia CXLIX, 3): 53–62.

Morolli, G. (1988) 'Salomone versus Vitruvio', in C. Cresti (ed.), *Massoneria e Architettura: Convegno di Firenze 1988*. Foggia: Bastogi: 271–302.

Morolli, G. (1992–1993) 'L'ordine degli ordini: La colonna salomonica e l'origine biblica degli ordini architettonici classici', in *Quasar*, 8–9: 38–53.

Mountfort Monroe, Ch. (2009) *Scales of Fate: Trade, Tradition, and Transformation in the Eastern Mediterranean ca. 1350–1175 B.C.* Münster: Ugarit-Verlag (Alter Orient und Altes Testament CCCLVII).

Nadali, D. (2007) 'Monuments of War, War of Monuments: Some Considerations on Commemorative War in the Third Millennium B.C.', in *Orientalia*, 76: 236–267.

Nagel, W., Strommenger, E. (1958) 'Alalaḫ und Siegelkunst', in *Journal of Cuneiform Studies*, 12: 109–123.

Nakhai, B.A. (2001) *Archaeology and the Religion of Canaan and Israel*. Boston, MA: American Schools of Oriental Research (American Schools of Oriental Research Books VII).

Naumann, R. (1971) *Architektur Kleinasiens von ihren Anfängen bis zum Ende der hellenistischen Zeit*. 2nd Edition. Tübingen: Wasmuth.

Negbi, O. (1970) *The Hoards of Goldwork from Tell el-'Ajjul*. Lund: Bloms (Studies in Mediterranean Archaeology XXV).

Negbi, O. (1976) *Canaanite Gods in Metal: An Archaeological Study of Ancient Syro-Palestinian Figurines*. Tel Aviv: Tel Aviv University (Publications of the Institute of Archaeology VI).

Neu, E. (1996a) *Das hurritische Epos der Freilassung*, I: *Untersuchungen zu einem hurritisch-hethitischen Textensemble aus Ḫattuša*. Wiesbaden: Harrassowitz (Studien zu den Boghazköy-Texten XXXII).

Neu, E. (1996b) 'La bilingue hurro-hittite de Hattusha: Contenu et sens', in *Amurru*, 1: 189–196.

Nigro, L. (1994a) *Ricerche sull'architettura palaziale della Palestina nelle Età del Bronzo e del Ferro: Contesto archeologico e sviluppo storico*. Rome: University of Rome (Contributi e Materiali di Archeologia Orientale V).

Nigro, L. (1994b) 'Palace 5019 of Megiddo: Its Eblaic Counterparts and the Unity of the Architectural Tradition of Syria-Palestine', in *Orient-Express*: 51–52.

Nigro, L. (1996) 'Ebla and the Ceramic Provinces of Northern Syria in the Middle Bronze Age: Relationships and Interconnections with the Pottery Horizon of Upper Mesopotamia', in *Subartu*, 4/2: 271–304.

Nigro, L. (2000) 'Coordinating MB Pottery Horizon of Syria and Palestine', in P. Matthiae, A. Enea, L. Peyronel, F. Pinnock (eds) 2000, II: 1187–1210.

Nigro, L. (2002a) 'The MB Pottery Horizon of Tell Mardikh/Ancient Ebla in a Chronological Perspective', in M. Bietak (ed.), *The Middle Bronze Age in the Levant: Proceedings of an International Conference on MB IIA Ceramic Material, Vienna, 24th–26th of January 2001*. Vienna: Österreichische Akademie der Wissenschaften: 297–328.

Nigro, L. (2002b) 'The Middle Bronze Age Pottery Horizon of Northern Syria on the Basis of the Stratified Assemblages of Tell Mardikh and Hama', in M. Al-Maqdissi, V. Matoïan, Ch. Nicolle (eds), *Céramique de l'Âge du Bronze en Syrie*, I: *La Syrie du Sud et la Vallée de l'Oronte*. Beirut: Institut Français d'Archéologie du Proche-Orient (Bibliothèque Archéologique et Historique CLXI): 97–125.

Nigro, L. (2007) 'Towards a Unified Chronology of Syria and Palestine: The Beginning of the Middle Bronze Age', in P. Matthiae, F. Pinnock, L. Nigro, L. Peyronel. (eds) (2007): 365–390.

Nigro, L. (2008) 'The Eighteenth Century BC Princes of Byblos and Ebla and the Chronology of the Middle Bronze Age', in *Interconnections in the Eastern Mediterranean: Lebanon in the Bronze and Iron Ages. Proceedings of the International Symposium, Beirut 2008* (BAAL, Hors-Série VI): 159–175.

Nissen, H.J. (1983) *Grundzüge einer Geschichte der Frühzeit des Vorderen Orients*. Darmstadt: Wissenschaftliche Buchgesellschaft.

Nissen, H.J., Renger, J. (eds) (1982) *Mesopotamien und seine Nachbarn: Politische und kulturelle Wechselbeziehungen im alten Vorderasien vom 4. bis 1. Jahrtausend v. Chr. XXV Rencontre Assyriologique Internationale, 3. bis 7. July 1978*. Berlin: Dietrich Reiner (Berliner Beiträge zum Vorderen Orient I).

Novák, M. (2004) 'The Chronology of the Royal Palace of Qatna', in *Ägypten und Levante*, 14: 229–318.

Novák, M. (2005) 'Aramaeans and Luwians: Processes of an Acculturation', in W. Van Soldt, R. Kalvelagen, D. Katz (eds), *Ethnicity in Ancient Mesopotamia: Papers*

Read at the 48th Rencontre Assyriologique Internationale, Leiden 1–4 July 2002.
Leiden: Nederlands Instituut voor het Nabije Oosten (Uitgaven van het Nederlands
Instituut voor het Nabije Oosten te Leiden CII): 252–266.

Novák, M. (2006) 'Fundamentierungstechniken im Palast von Qatna', in E. Czerny,
I. Heim, H. Hunger, D. Melman, A. Schwab (eds), *Timelines: Studies in Honour
of Manfred Bietak*, III. Leuven: Peeters: 63–71 (Orientalia Analecta Lovaniensia
CXLIX, 3).

Novák, M. (2007) 'Mittani Empire and the Question of Absolute Chronology: Some
Archaeological Considerations', in M. Bietak, E Czerny (eds) 2007: 389–401.

Novák, M., Pfälzner, P. (2000) 'Ausgrabungen in Tall Mišrife/Qatna 1999: Vorbericht
der deutschen Komponente des internationalen Projektes', in *Mitteilungen der
Deutschen Orient-Gesellschaft*, 132: 253–296.

Novák, M., Pfälzner, P. (2001) 'Ausgrabungen in Tall Mišrife/Qatna 2000: Vorbericht
der deutschen Komponente des internationalen Projektes', in *Mitteilungen der
Deutschen Orient-Gesellschaft*, 133: 157–198.

Novák, M., Pfälzner, P. (2002) 'Ausgrabungen in Tall Mišrife/Qatna 2001: Vorbericht
der deutschen Komponente des internationalen Projektes', in *Mitteilungen der
Deutschen Orient-Gesellschaft*, 134: 207–246.

Novák, M., Pfälzner, P. (2003) 'Ausgrabungen in bronzezeitlichen Palast von Tall
Mišrife/Qatna 2002: Vorbericht der deutschen Komponente des internationalen
Projektes', in *Mitteilungen der Deutschen Orient-Gesellschaft*, 135: 131–165.

Oden, R.A., Jr (1989) *Studies in Lucian's "De Syria Dea"*. Boston, MA: Scholar Press
(Harvard Semitic Monographs XV).

Oren, E.D. (ed.) (2000) *The Sea Peoples and Their World: A Reassessment*. Philadelphia,
PA: University of Pennsylvania (University Museum Monographs CVIII).

Orthmann, W. (1970) *Untersuchungen zur späthethitischen Kunst*. Bonn: Habelt.

Orthmann, W. (1990a) 'L'architecture religieuse de Tell Chuera', in *Akkadica*, 69:
1–18.

Orthmann. W. (1990b) 'Zu den monumentalen Steinbauten von Tell Chuera', in P.
Matthiae, M. van Loon, H. Weiss (eds) 1990: 240–259.

Orthmann, W., Meyer, J.-W. (1989) 'Die Ausgrabungen in den Planquadraten L und
M', in W. Orthmann (ed.), *Halawa 1980 bis 1986: Vorläufiger Bericht über 4.-9.
Grabungskampagne*. Bonn: Habelt (Saarbrücker Beiträge zur Altertumskunde
LII): 63–84.

Orthmann, W., Hempelmann, R., Klein, H., Kühne, H., Novák, M., Pruß, A. *et al.*
(eds) (1995) *Ausgrabungen in Tell Chuera in Nord-Ost Syrien*, I: *Vorbericht über die
Grabungskampagnen 1986 bis 1992*. Saarbrücken: Saarbrücker Druckerei und Verlag
(Vorderasiatische Forschungen der Max Freiherr von Oppenheim-Stiftung 2).

Otten, H. (1984) 'Blick in die altorientalischeGeisteswelt: Neufund einer hethitischen
Tempelbibliothek', in *Jahrbuch der Akademie der Wissenschaften in Göttingen*:
50–60.

Otten, H. (1988) 'Ebla in der hurritisch-hethitischen Bilingue aus Boghazköy', in H.
Waetzoldt, H. Hauptmann (eds) 1988: 291–292.

Otto, A. (2000) *Die Entstehung und Entwicklung der Klassisch-Syrischen Glyptik*.
Berlin: De Gruyter (Untersuchungen zur Assyriologie und Vorderasiatischen
Archäologie VIII).

Otto, A. (2004) *Tall Bi'a/Tuttul*, IV: *Siegel und Siegelabrollungen*. Saarbrücken:
Saarbrücker Druckerei und Verlag.

Otto, A. (2006) 'Archaeological Perspectives on the Localization of Naram-Sin's
Armanum', in *Journal of Cuneiform Studies*, 58: 1–26.

Owen, D., Veenker, R. (1987) 'MeGum, the First Ur III Ensi of Ebla', in L. Cagni (ed.) 1987: 263–291.

Pardee, D. (1988) 'An Evaluation of the Proper Names from Ebla from a West-Semitic Perspective: Pantheon Distribution According to Genre', in A. Archi (ed.) 1988b: 119–151.

Pardee, D. (1996) '"Marzihu", "Kispu", and the Ugaritic Funerary Cult: A Minimalist View', in N. Wyatt, W.G.E. Watson, J.B. Lloyd (eds), *Ugarit, Religion and Culture: Proceedings of the International Colloquium, Edinburgh, July 1994. Essays Presented in Honour of Professor John C.L. Gibson.* Münster: Ugarit-Verlag (Ugaritisch-Biblische Literatur II): 273–287.

Pardee, D. (1997) 'West Semitic Canonical Compositions', in W.W. Hallo (ed.), *The Context of Scripture*, I: *Canonical Compositions of the Biblical World.* Leiden: Brill.

Parpola, S. (1988) 'Proto-Assyrian', in H. Waetzoldt, H. Hauptmann (eds) 1988: 293–298.

Parrot, A. (1946) *Archéologie mésopotamienne*, I: *Les étapes.* Paris: Albin Michel.

Parrot, A. (1956) *Mission Archéologique de Mari*, I: *Le Temple d'Ishtar.* Paris: Geuthner (Bibliothèque Archéologique et Historique LXV).

Pasquali, J. (1997) 'La terminologia semitica dei tessili nei testi di Ebla', in *Miscellanea Eblaitica*, 4: 217–270.

Pasquali, J. (2005a) *Il lessico dell'artigianato nei testi di Ebla.* Florence: University of Florence (Quaderni di Semitistica XXIII).

Pasquali, J. (2005b) 'Innovazione e continuità nel lessico dell'artigianato nella Siria del III milennio a.C.', in P. Fronzaroli, P. Marrassini (eds) 2005: 267–299.

Pecchioli Daddi, F. (1992) 'Note di storia politica antico-ittita', in *Studi Epigrafici e Linguistici*, 9: 11–19.

Pedersén, O. (1998) *Archives and Libraries in the Ancient Near East, 1500–300 B.C.* Bethesda, MD: CDL Press.

Pedrazzi, T. (2007) *Le giare da conservazione e trasporto del Levante: Uno studio archeologico dell'economia tra Bronzo Tardo II e Ferro I (ca. 1400–900 a.C.).* Pisa: Edizioni Ets.

Peña, I., Castellana, P., Fernandez, R. (1975) *Les stylites syriens.* Milan: Franciscan Printing Press (Publications du Studium Biblicum Franciscanum. Collectio Minor XVI).

Pettinato, G. (1970) 'Inscription de Ibbit-Lim, roi d'Ebla', in *Annales Archéologiques Arabes Syriennes*, 20: 73–76.

Pettinato, G. (1976) 'Ibla (Ebla)', *Reallexikon der Assyriologie*, V.

Pettinato, G. (1980a) 'Bollettino militare della campagna di Ebla contro la città di Mari', in *Oriens Antiquus*, 19: 231–245.

Pettinato, G. (1980b) *Ebla: Un impero inciso nell'argilla.* Milan: Mondadori.

Pettinato, G. (1981) *Testi lessicali monolingui della Biblioteca L.2769.* Naples: Istituto Universitario Orientale (Materiali Epigrafici di Ebla III).

Pettinato, G. (1982) *Testi lessicali bilingui della Biblioteca L.2769.* Naples: Istituto Universitario Orientale (Materiali Epigrafici di Ebla IV).

Peyronel, L. (2000) 'The Middle Bronze II Fortress V at Tell Mardikh-Ebla (Syria): Preliminary Analysis of Architectural Contexts and Archaeological Materials', in P. Matthiae, A. Enea, L. Peyronel, F. Pinnock (eds) 2000, II: 1353–1377.

Peyronel, L. (2004) *Materiali e Studi Archeologici di Ebla*, IV: *Gli strumenti di tessitura dall'Età del Bronzo all'Epoca Persiana.* Rome: University of Rome.

Peyronel, L. (2007) 'Late Old Syrian Fortifications and Middle Syrian Re-Occupation on the Western Rampart at Tell Mardikh-Ebla', in M. Bietak, E Czerny (eds) 2007: 83–102.

Pfälzner, P. (2009) 'Meisterwerke der Plastik: Die Ahnenstatuen aus dem Hypogäum', in M. Al-Maqdissi, D. Morandi Bonacossi, P. Pfälzner (eds), *Schätze des Alten Syrien: Die Entdeckung des Königreichs Qatna. Grosse Landesausstellung 17 Oktober 2009 bis 14 März 2010*. Stuttgart: Konrad Theiss: 204–207.

Philip, G. (1989) *Metal Weapons of the Early and Middle Bronze Ages in Syria-Palestine*, I-II. Oxford: British Archaeological Reports (B.A.R. International Series DXXVI).

Picchioni, S. (1980) 'La direzione della scrittura cuneiforme e gli archivi di Tell Mardikh/Ebla', in *Orientalia*, 49: 225–251.

Pinnock, F. (1979) 'Nota sui "sonagli" della "Tomba del Signore dei Capridi"', in *Studi Eblaiti*, 1: 185–193.

Pinnock, F. (1981) 'Caratteri della produzione ceramica eblaita del Bronzo Medio II', in *Studi Eblaiti*, 4: 61–75.

Pinnock, F. (1983) 'Coppe protosiriane in pietra dal Palazzo Reale G', in *Studi Eblaiti*, 6: 61–75.

Pinnock, F. (1985a) 'A proposito del commercio del lapislazzuli tra Mari ed Ebla nel III millennio a.C.', in *Studi Eblaiti*, 8: 21–34.

Pinnock, F. (1985b) 'About the Trade of Early Syrian Ebla', in *M.A.R.I.*, 4: 85–92.

Pinnock, F (1986a) 'Il lapislazzuli nel Palazzo Reale G di Ebla', in *Studi Eblaiti*, 9: 103–138.

Pinnock , F. (1986b) 'The Lapis Lazuli Trade in the Third Millennium B.C. and the Evidence of the Royal Palace G of Ebla', in M. Kelly-Buccellati (ed.) 1986: 221–228.

Pinnock, F. (1987) 'The Lapis Lazuli in the Royal Palace of Ebla', in *Studies in the History and Archaeology of Palestine: Proceedings of the First International Symposium on the Antiquities of Palestine*, I. Aleppo: Aleppo University Press: 65–71.

Pinnock, F. (1988) 'Observations on the Trade of Lapis Lazuli in the 3rd Millennium B.C.', in H. Waetzoldt, H. Hauptmann (eds) 1988: 107–110.

Pinnock, F. (1990) 'Patterns of Trade at Ebla in the Third Millennium B.C.', in *Annales Archéologiques Arabes Syriennes*, 40: 39–49.

Pinnock, F. (1991) 'Considerazioni sul sistema commerciale di Ebla protosiriana (ca. 2350–2300 a.C.)', in *La Parola del Passato*, 46: 270–284.

Pinnock, F. (1992a) 'Le turban royal éblaïte', in *N.A.B.U.*, nr 15–16.

Pinnock, F. (1992b) 'Una riconsiderazione della stele di Hama 6B599', in *Contributi e Materiali di Archeologia Orientale*, 4: 101–121.

Pinnock, F. (1993) *Materiali e Studi Archeologici di Ebla*, II: *Le perle del Palazzo Reale G*. Rome: University of Rome.

Pinnock, F. (1996) 'Su alcuni sigilli paleosiriani di probabile produzione eblaita', in *Contributi e Materiali di Archeologia Orientale*, 6: 171–180.

Pinnock, F. (1997) 'Tipologia di un pugnale rituale del III millennio a.C.', in *Contributi e Materiali di Archeologia Orientale*, 7: 463–493.

Pinnock, F. (2000a) 'The Doves of the Goddess: Elements of Ishtar's Cult in Middle Bronze Ebla', in *Levant*, 32: 127–134.

Pinnock, F. (2000b) 'Some Thoughts about the Transmission of Iconographies between North Syria and Cappadocia, End of the Third – Beginning of the Second Millennium B.C.', in P. Matthiae, A. Enea, L. Peyronel, F. Pinnock (eds) 2000, II: 1397–1416.

Pinnock, F. (2000c) 'The Relations between North-Syria and Iran in the Second Millennium B.C.: A Contribution from Ebla Metalworking', in R. Dittmann, B. Hrouda, U. Löw, P. Matthiae, R. Mayer-Opificius, S. Thürwächter (eds), *Variatio delectat: Iran und der West. Gedenkschrift für P. Calmeyer.* Münster: Ugarit-Verlag (Alter Orient und Altes Testament CCLXXII, 2): 593–606.

Pinnock, F. (2002) 'The Urban Landscape of Old Syrian Ebla', in *Journal of Cuneiform Studies*, 53: 13–34.

Pinnock, F (2003) 'Osservazioni sulla glittica di Alalakh', in *Contributi e Materiali di Archeologia Orientale*, 9: 203–222.

Pinnock, F. (2004) 'Change and Continuity of Art in Syria Viewed from Ebla', in J.-W. Meyer, W. Sommerfeld (eds) 2004: 87–118.

Pinnock, F. (2005) *Materiali e Studi Archeologici di Ebla*, VI: *La ceramica del Palazzo Settentrionale del Bronzo Medio II*. Rome: University of Rome.

Pinnock, F. (2006a) 'The Raw Lapis Lazuli in the Royal Palace G of Ebla: New Evidence from Annexes of the Throne Room', in M.A. Alberti, E. Ascalone, L. Peyronel (eds) 2006: 347–357.

Pinnock, F. (2006b) 'Ebla and Ur: Relations, Exchanges and Contacts between Two Great Capitals of the Ancient Near East', in *Iraq*, 48: 85–97.

Pinnock, F. (2006c) 'Paying Homage to the King: Protocol and Ritual in Old Syrian Art', in F. Baffi, R. Dolce, S. Mazzoni, F. Pinnock (eds) 2006: 487–509.

Pinnock, F. (2007) 'Middle Bronze Ceramic Horizon at Ebla: Typology and Chronology', in P. Matthiae, F. Pinnock, L. Nigro, L. Peyronel (eds) 2007: 457–472.

Pinnock, F. (2008) 'The Stele of Halawa: A Reappraisal', in D. Bonatz, R.M. Czichon, F. Janoscha Kreppner (eds), *Fundstellen: Gesammelte Schriften zur Archäologie und Geschichte Altvoderasiens ad honorem Hartmut Kühne*. Wiesbaden: Harrassowitz: 71–77.

Pitard, W.T. (1997) 'The Meaning of EN at Ebla', in G.D. Young, M.W. Chavalas, R.E. Averbeck, K.L. Danti (eds), *Crossing Boundaries and Linking Horizons: Studies in Honor of M.C. Astour*. Bethesda, MD: CDL Press: 399–416.

Pomponio, F. (1982) 'Note su alcuni termini dei testi amministrativi di Ebla', in *Vicino Oriente*, 5: 203–215.

Pomponio, F. (1983) 'I nomi divini nei testi di Ebla', in *Ugarit-Forschungen*, 15: 141–156.

Pomponio, F. (1988) 'Gli ugula nell'amministrazione di Ebla', in H. Waetzoldt, H. Hauptmann (eds) 1988: 317–323.

Pomponio, F. (1990) 'Exit Kish dagli orizzonti di Ebla', in *Mesopotamia*, 25: 175–184.

Pomponio, F. (1993) 'Ebrium e il matrimonio dell' "En" di Ebla', in *Archiv für Orientforschung*, 40–41: 39–45.

Pomponio, F. (1994) 'Re di Uruk, "re di Kish"', in *Rivista degli Studi Orientali*, 68: 1–14.

Pomponio, F. (1997–1998) 'I rendiconti annuali di uscite di argento e le offerte alle divinità nella documentazione di Ebla', in *Archiv für Orientforschung*, 44–45: 101–107.

Pomponio, F. (2008) *Archivi Reali di Ebla, Testi*, XV/1–2: *Testi amministrativi: assegnazioni mensili di tessuti: periodo di Arrugum (Archivio L.2769)*. Rome: University of Rome.

Pomponio, F, Xella, P. (1997) *Les dieux d'Ébla: Étude analytique des divinités éblaïtes à l'époque des Archives Royales du IIIe millénaire*. Münster: Ugarit-Verlag (Alter Orient und Altes Testament CCXLV).

Ponchia, S. (1991) *L'Assiria e gli Stati transeufratici nella prima metà dell'VIII secolo a.C.* Padua: Sargon (History of the Ancient Near East/Studies IVbis).

Pope, M.H. (1955) *El in the Ugaritic Texts*. Leiden: Brill (Vetus Testamentum, Supplement 2).

Pope, M.H. (1981) 'The Cult of the Dead at Ugarit', in D. Young (ed.), *Ugarit in Retrospect: Fifty Years of Ugarit and Ugaritic*. Winona Lake, IN: Eisenbrauns: 159–179.

Porada. E. (1957) 'Syrian Seal Impressions on Tablets Dated in the Time of Hammurabi and Samsuiluna', in *Journal of Near Eastern Studies*, 16: 192–197.

Porada, E. (1981) 'The Cylinder Seals Found at Thebes in Boeotia', in *Archiv für Orientforschung*, 28: 1–78.

Posener, G. (1957) 'Les Asiatiques en Égypte sous la XIIᵉ et XIIIᵉ dynasties', in *Syria*, 34: 145–163.

Postgate, J.N. (ed.) (2002) *Artefacts of Complexity: Tracking the Uruk in the Near East*. London: British School of Archaeology in Iraq.

Prechel, D. (1996) *Die Göttin Išḫara: Ein Beitrag zur altorientalischen Religionsgeschichte*. Münster: Ugarit-Verlag (Abhandlungen zur Literatur Alt-Syriens-Palästinas und Mesopotamiens XI).

Rainey, A.F. (2006) 'Sinouhe's World', in A.M. Maeir, P. de Miroschedji (eds) 2006: 277–299.

Ramazzotti, M. (1999) *La Bassa Mesopotamia come laboratorio storico: Le Reti Neurali Artificiali come strumento di ausilio alle ricerche di archeologia territoriale*. Rome: University of Rome (Contributi e Materiali di Archeologia Orientale VIII).

Ramazzotti, M. (2008) 'An Integrated Analysis for the Urban Settlement Reconstruction: The Topographical, Mathematical and Geophysical Frame of Tell Mardikh – Ancient Ebla', in H. Kühne, M. Czichon, F. Janoscha Kreppner (eds) 2008: 191–206.

Redford, D.B. (1992) *Egypt, Canaan, and Israel in Ancient Times*. Princeton, NJ: Princeton University Press.

Redman, Ch.J. (1978) *The Rise of Civilization: From Early Farmers to Urban Society in the Ancient Near East*. San Francisco, CA: Freeman and Company.

Richter, T. (2005) 'Hurriter und Hurritisch in bronzezeitlichen Syrien', in D. Prechel (ed.), *Motivation und Mechanismen des Kulturkontaktes in den Späten Bronzezeit*. Florence: University of Florence (Eothen XIII): 145–178.

Rositani, A. (2001) 'I tessili della documentazione eblaita come elementi per la datazione interna', in *Aula Orientalis*, 9: 261–270.

Rossoni, G. (2007) 'Production d'armes dans la Syrie intérieure au Bronze Moyen: Deux exemples de haches en bronze d'Ébla', in P. Matthiae, F. Pinnock, L. Nigro, L. Peyronel (eds) 2007: 499–509.

Rothman, M.S. (ed.) (2001) *Uruk Mesopotamia and Its Neighbors*. Santa Fe, NM: School of American Research.

Rubio, G. (2006) 'Eblaite, Akkadian and Proto-Semitic', in G. Deutscher, N.J.C. Kouwenberg (eds) 2006: 110–139.

Runciman, S. (1951–1954) *History of the Crusades*, I–III. Cambridge: Cambridge University Press.

Ryholt, K.S.B. (1997) *The Political Situation in Egypt during the Second Intermediate Period c.1800–1530 B.C.* Copenhagen: Carsten Niebuhr Institute (Carsten Niebuhr Institute Publications XX).

Sader, H. (1987) *Les États araméens de Syrie depuis leur fondation jusqu'à leur transformation en provinces assyriennes*. Beirut: Franz Steiner (Beiruter Texte und Studien XXVI).

Sala, M. (2008) *L'architettura sacra della Palestina nell'età del Bronzo Antico I-III: Contesto archeologico, analisi architettonica, sviluppo storico*. Rome: University of Rome (Contributi e Materiali di Archeologia Orientale XIII).

Sallaberger, W. (2004) 'Relative Chronologie von der späten Frühdynastischen bis zur Altbabylonische Zeit', in J.-W. Meyer, W. Sommerfeld (eds) 2004: 15–43.

Sallaberger, W. (2009) 'Von der Wollration zum Ehrenkleid: Textilien als Prestigegüter am Hof von Ebla', in B. Hildebrandt, C. Veir (eds), *Der Weg der Dinge: Güte im Prestigediskurs*. Munich: Herbert Utz Verlag: 241–278.

Sallaberger, W., Westenholz, A. (eds) (1999) *Mesopotamien: Akkade-Zeit und Ur III-Zeit*. Fribourg/Göttingen: Academic Press/Vandenhoeck & Ruprecht.

Salvini, M. (1990) 'Una lettera di Ḫattušili I relativa alla spedizione contro Ḫaḫḫum', in *Studi Micenei ed Egeo-Anatolici*, 34: 61–80.

Sartre, M. (1989) 'La Syrie sous la domination achéménide', in J.-M- Dentzer, W. Orthmann (eds), *Archéologie et Histoire de la Syrie*, II: *Les périodes hellénistique, romaine et byzantine*. Saarbrücken: Saarland University: 9–18.

Sawaf, S. (1963) *Alep, son histoire, sa citadelle, son musée et ses monuments*. Aleppo: Service des Antiquités.

Scandone Matthiae, G. (1979a) 'Vasi iscritti di Chefren e Pepi I nel Palazzo Reale G di Ebla', in *Studi Eblaiti*, 1: 33–43.

Scandone Matthiae, G. (1979b) 'Un oggetto faraonico della XIII dinastia dalla "Tomba del Signore dei Capridi"', in *Studi Eblaiti*, 1: 119–128.

Scandone Matthiae, G. (1981) 'I vasi egiziani in pietra del Palazzo Reale G', in *Studi Eblaiti*, 4: 99–127.

Scandone Matthiae, G. (1982) 'Inscriptions royales égyptiennes de l'Ancien Empire à Ébla', in H.J. Nissen, J. Renger (eds) 1982: 125–130.

Scandone Matthiae, G. (1988) 'Les relations entre Ébla et l'Égypte au IIIe et au IIe millénaire av. J.Chr.', in H. Waetzoldt, H. Hauptmann (eds) 1988: 67–73.

Scandone Matthiae, G. (1990) 'Egyptianizing Ivory Inlays from Palace P at Ebla', in *Annales Archéologiques Arabes Syriennes*, 40: 146–160.

Scandone Matthiae, G. (1991a) 'Gli intarsi egittizzanti del Palazzo Settentrionale di Ebla', in *Scienze dell'Antichità*, 5: 423–439.

Scandone Matthiae, G. (1991b) 'Una testa paleosiriana in avorio con corona *atef*', in *La Parola del Passato*, 46: 382–393.

Scandone Matthiae, G. (1997a) 'Méki/Mékum (d'Ébla) dans l'"Histoire de Sinouhé" ?', in *M.A.R.I.*, 8: 249–250.

Scandone Matthiae, G. (1997b) 'The Relations between Ebla and Egypt', in E.D. Oren (ed.), *The Hyksos: New Historical and Archaeological Perspectives*. Philadelphia, PA: University of Pennsylvania (University Museum Monographs XCV): 415–417.

Scandone Matthiae, G. (2002) *Materiali e Studi Archeologici di Ebla*, III: *Gli avori egittizzanti dal Palazzo Settentrionale*. Rome: University of Rome.

Scandone Matthiae (2006) 'Nuovi frammenti di avori egittizzanti da Ebla', in E. Czerny, I. Heim, H. Hunger, D. Melman, A. Schwab (eds), *Timelines: Studies in Honour of Manfred Bietak,* III. Leuven: Peeters (Orientalia Analecta Lovaniensia CXLIX, 3): 81–86.

Schäfer, H. (1936) *Das ägyptische Bildnis*. Glückstadt: Augustin (Leipziger Ägyptologische Studien V).

Schlossman, B.L. (1978–1979) 'Portraiture in Mesopotamia in the Late Third and Early Second Millennium B.C.: Part I, The Late Third Millennium', in *Archiv für Orientforschung*, 26: 56–77.

Schlossman, B.L. (1981–1982) 'Portraiture in Mesopotamia in the Late Third and Early Second Millennium B.C.: Part II, The Early Second Millennium', in *Archiv für Orientforschung*, 28: 143–170.

Schmandt-Besserat, D. (1993) 'Images of Enship', in M. Frangipane, H. Hauptmann, M. Liverani, P. Matthiae, M.J. Mellink (eds) 1993: 201–219.

Schniedewind, W. (2002) 'The Rise of Aramean States', in M.W. Chavalas, K. Lawson Younger, Jr (eds), *Mesopotamia and the Bible: Comparative Explorations*. Sheffield/ Grand Rapids, MI: Sheffield Academic Press/ Baker (Journal for the Study of the Old Testament, Supplement CCCXLI): 276–287.

Schwartz, G.M. (2001) 'Syria and Uruk Expansion', in M.S. Rothman (ed.) 2001: 233–264.

Schwartz, G.M., Weiss, H. (1992) 'Syria, ca. 10,000–2000 B.C.', in R.W. Ehrich (ed.) 1992: 232–243.

Schwemer, D. (2001) *Die Wettergottgestalten Mesopotamiens und Nordsyriens im Zeitalter der Keilschriftkulturen: Materialien und Studien nach den schriftlichen Quellen*. Wiesbaden: Harrassowitz.

Seeden, H. (1980) *The Standing Armed Figurines in the Levant*. Munich: Beck (Prähistorische Bronzefunde I/1).

Seibert, I. (1969) *Hirt – Herde – König: Zur Herausbildung des Königtums in Mesopotamien*. Berlin: de Gruyter.

Selz, G.J. (1998) 'Über mesopotamische Herrschaftskonzepte: Zu den Ursprüngen mesopotamischer Herrscherideologie im 3. Jahrtausend', in M. Dietrich, O, Loretz (eds), *"Dubsar anta-men": Studien zur Altorientalistik. Festschrift für W.H.Ph. Römer*. Münster: Ugarit-Verlag (Alter Orient und Altes Testament CCLIII): 281–344.

Selz, G.J. (ed.) (2003) *Festshrift für B. Kienast zu seinem 70. Geburtstage*. Münster: Ugarit-Verlag (Alter Orient und Altes Testament CCLXXIV).

Setton, K.M. (ed.) (1969–1977) *A History of the Crusades*, I-IV. Madison, WI/ London: Wisconsin University Press.

Seyrig, H. (1960) 'Antiquités syriennes, 78: Les dieux de Hiérapolis', in *Syria*, 37: 233–240.

Sherratt, S. (2003) 'The Mediterranean Economy: "Globalization" at the End of the Second Millennium B.C.', in W.G. Dever, S. Gitin (eds), *Symbiosis, Symbolism and the Power of the Past: Canaan, Ancient Israel, and Their Neighbors from the Late Bronze Age to Roman Palestine. Proceedings of the Centennial Symposium of the W.F. Albright Institute of Archaeological Research and ASOR, Jerusalem, May 29– 31, 2000*. Winona Lake, IN: Eisenbrauns: 37–62.

Sigrist, M. (1988) *Isin Year Names*. Berrien Springs, MI: Andrews University Press (Institute of Archaeology Publications, Assyriological Studies II).

Sigrist, M. (1990) *Larsa Year Names*. Berrien Springs, MI: Andrews University Press (Institute of Archaeology Publications, Assyriological Studies III).

Sjöberg, Å.W. (1999) 'Notes on Selected Entries from the Ebla Vocabulary $eš_2$- bar-kin_5 (II)', in M. Böck, E. Cancik-Kirschbaum, T. Richter (eds), *Munuscula Mesopotamica: Festschrift für J. Renger*. Münster: Ugarit-Verlag (Alter Orient und Altes Testament CCLXVII): 513–552.

Sjöberg, Å.W. (2003a) 'Notes on Selected Entries from the Ebla Vocabulary $eš_2$-bar-kin5 (I)', in G.J. Selz (ed.) 2003: 527–568.

Sjöberg, Å.W. (2003b) 'Notes on Selected Entries from the Ebla Vocabulary $eš_2$-bar-kin_5 (IV)', in W. Sallaberger, K. Volk, A. Zgoll (eds), *Literatur, Politik und Recht in Mesopotamien: Festschrift für C. Wilcke*. Wiesbaden: Harrassowitz (Orientalia Biblica et Christiana XIV): 251–266.

Sjöberg, Å.W. (2004) 'Notes on Selected Entries from the Ebla Vocabulary eš₂-bar-kin₅ (III)', in H. Waetzoldt (ed.), *Von Sumer nach Ebla und zurück: Festschrift für G. Pettinato*. Heidelberg: Heidelberger Orientverlag (Heidelberger Studien zum Alten Orient IX): 257–283.

Sollberger, E. (1980) 'The So-Called Treaty between Ebla and "Ashur"', in *Studi Eblaiti*, 3: 129–155.

Sollberger, E. (1982) 'Notes sur la paléographie des textes d'Ébla', in *Studi Eblaiti*, 5: 221–227.

Sollberger, E. (1986) *Archivi Reali di Ebla, Testi*, VIII: *Administrative Texts Chiefly Concerning Textiles (L.2752)*. Rome: University of Rome.

Sowada, K.N. (2009) *Egypt in the Eastern Mediterranean during the Old Kingdom: An Archaeological Perspective*. Fribourg/Göttingen: Academic Press/Vandenhoeck & Ruprecht (Orbis Biblicus et Orientalis CCXXXVII).

Soysal, O. (1988) 'Einige Überlegungen zu KBo III 60', in *Vicino Oriente*, 7: 107–128.

Spycket, A. (1981) *La statuaire du Proche-Orient ancien*. Leiden/Cologne: Brill (Handbuch der Orientalistik, VII. Abteilung, Kunst und Archäologie, I. 2, B/2).

Steible, H. (1991) *Die neusumerischen Bau- und Weihinschriften*, I: *Inschriften der II. Dynastie von Lagaš*. Stuttgart: Franz Steiner (Freiburger Altorientalische Studien IX 1).

Stein, G. (1999) *Rethinking World-Systems: Diasporas, Colonies and Interaction in Uruk Mesopotamia*. Tucson, AZ: University of Arizona Press.

Stein, G., Rothman, M.S. (eds) (1994) *Chiefdoms and Early States in the Near East*. Madison, WI: Prehistory Press.

Steinkeller, P. (1993) 'Early Political Development in Mesopotamia and the Origin of the Sargonic Empire', in M. Liverani (ed.) 1993a: 107–129.

Steinkeller, P. (1999) 'On Rulers, Priests and Sacred Marriage: Tracing the Evolution of Early Sumerian Kingship', in K. Watanabe (ed.), *Priests and Officials in the Ancient Near East: Papers of the Second Colloquium on the Ancient Near East – The City and Its Life, Held at the Middle East Centre in Japan (Mitaka, Tokyo), March 22–24, 1996*. Heidelberg: Universitätsverlag C. Winter: 103–136.

Stieglitz, R.R. (1990) 'Ebla and the Gods of Canaan', in *Eblaitica*, 2: 79–89.

Stieglitz, R.R. (2002a) 'Deified Kings of Ebla', in *Eblaitica*, 4: 215–22.

Stieglitz, R.R. (2002b) 'Divine Pairs in the Ebla Pantheon', in *Eblaitica*, 4: 209–214.

Strommenger, E., Kohlmeyer, K. (2000) *Tall Bi'a/Tuttul – III: Die Schichten des 3. Jahrtausends v. Chr. im Zentralhügel E*. Saarbrücken: Saarbrücker Druckerei und Verlag.

Tarhan, T., Tibet, A. (eds) (2008) *Muhibbe Darga Armagani*. Ankara: Türk Tarih Kurumu.

Teissier, B. (1994) *Sealing and Seals on Texts from Kültepe "kārum" Level 2*. Leiden: Nederlands Historisch-Archaeologisch Instituut (Uitgaven van het Nederlands Historisch-Archaeologisch Instituut te Istanbul LXX).

Teissier, B. (1996) *Egyptian Iconography on Syro-Palestinian Seals of the Middle Bronze Age*. Fribourg/Göttingen: University Press/Vandenhoeck & Ruprecht (Orbis Biblicus et Orientalis. Series Archaeologica XI).

Tonietti, M.V. (1988) 'La figura del "NAR" nei testi di Ebla: Ipotesi per una cronologia delle liste di nomi presenti nei testi economici', in *Miscellanea Eblaitica*, 1: 79–119.

Tonietti, M.V. (1997) 'Le cas de Mékim: Continuité ou innovation dans la tradition éblaïte entre IIIᵉ et IIᵉ millénaire?', in *M.A.R.I.*, 8: 225–242.

Trémouille, M.-C. (2000) 'La religione dei Hurriti', in *La Parola del Passato*, 55: 114–170.

Trigger, B.G. (2003) *Understanding Early Civilizations: A Comparative Study*. Cambridge: Cambridge University Press.

Tropper, J. (2003) 'Eblaitisch und die Klassifikation der Semitischen Sprachen', in G.J. Selz (ed.) 2003: 647–657.

Tunca, Ö. (ed.) (1990) *De la Babylonie à la Syrie, en passant par Mari: Mélanges offerts à M. Jean-Robert Kupper à l'occasion de son 70ᵉ anniversaire*. Liège: Université de Liège.

Tuzi, E. (2002) *Le Colonne e il Tempio di Salomone: La storia, la leggenda, la fortuna*. Rome: Gangemi.

Vandier, J. (1958) *Manuel d'archéologie égyptienne*, III: *Les grandes époques: la statuaire*. Paris: Albin Michel.

Van Driel, G. (1969) *The Cult of Aššur*. Leiden: Bar Gorcum & Co.

Van Liere, W.J. (1963) 'Capitals and Citadels of Bronze-Iron Age in Their Relationships to Land and Water', in *Annales Archéologiques Syriennes*, 13: 107–122.

Van Koppen, F. (2004) 'The Geography of the Slave Trade and of Northern Mesopotamia in the Late Old Babylonian Period', in H. Hunger, R. Pruszinsky (eds), *Mesopotamian Dark Ages Revisited: Proceedings of an International Conference of SCIEM 2000 (Vienna, 8th–9th November 2002)*. Vienna: Österreichische Akademie der Wissenschaften (Contributions to the Chronology of the Eastern Mediterranean VI): 9–33.

Van Seters, J. (1997) 'Solomon's Temple: Fact and Ideology in Biblical and Near Eastern Historiography', in *Catholic Biblical Quarterly*, 50: 45–57.

Van Seters, J. (2009) *The Biblical Saga of King David*. Winona Lake, IN: Eisenbrauns.

Vaughan, P.H. (1974) *The Meaning of "bamā" in the Old Testament: A Study of Etymological, Textual, and Archaeological Evidence*. Cambridge: Cambridge University Press (The Society for Old Testament Study, Monograph Series III).

Veenhof, K.R. (1977) 'Ebla-Tell Mardikh', in *Phoenix*, 23: 7–25.

Venturi, F. (2007) *La Siria nell'età delle trasformazioni (XIII-X secolo a.C.): Nuovi contributi dagli scavi di Tell Afis*. Bologna: University of Bologna (Studi e testi orientali VIII, Serie archeologica I).

Vernus, P. (1982) 'La stèle du roi Sekhemsankhtaouyre Neferhotep Iykhernofret et la domination hyksos en Égypte (stèle Caire JE59635)', in *Annales du Service des Antiquités du Caire*, 68: 129–135.

Viganò, L. (1988) 'Enna-Dagan's Letter to the en of Ebla', in *Liber Annuus*, 38: 227–246.

von Beckerath, J. (1964) *Untersuchungen zur politischen Geschichte der Zweiten Zwischenzeit in Ägypten*. Glückstadt: J.J. Augustin (Ägyptologische Forschungen XXIII).

von Beckerath, J. (1997) *Chronologie des pharaonischen Ägypten*. Mainz: Von Zabern (Münchener Ägyptologische Studien XLVI).

von Luschan, F. (1911) *Ausgrabungen in Sendschirli*, IV. Berlin: Speman.

von Soden, W. (1987) 'Itab/pal und Damu: Götter in den Kulten und in den theophoren Namen nach den Ebla-Texten', in L. Cagni (ed.) 1987: 75–90.

von Soden, W. (1988) 'Ebla, die früheste Schriftkultur Syriens', in H. Waetzoldt, H. Hauptmann (eds) 1988: 325–332.

Waetzoldt, H., Hauptmann, H. (eds) (1988) *Wirtschaft und Gesellschaft von Ebla: Akten der Internationalen Tagung Heidelberg 4.–7. November 1986*. Heidelberg: Heidelberger Orientverlag (Heidelberger Studien zum Alten Testament II).

Ward, W.A., Sharp Joukovsky, M. (eds) (1992) *The Crisis Years: The 12th Century B.C. from Beyond the Danube to the Tigris*. Dubuqe, IA: Kendall Hunt.

Wattenmaker, P. (1990) *Household and State in Upper Mesopotamia: Specialized Economy and the Social Uses of Goods in an Early Complex Society*. Washington, DC: Smithsonian Institution Press.

Werner, P. (1994) *Die Entwicklung der Sakralarchitektur in Nordsyrien und Südostanatolien vom Neolithikum bis in das I. Jt. v. Chr.* Munich/Vienna: Profil Verlag (Münchener Vorderasiatische Studien V).

Westenholz, A. (1999) 'The Old Akkadian Period: History and Culture', in W. Sallaberger, A. Westenholz (eds) 1999: 15–117.

Wildung, D. (1984) *Sesostris und Amenemhet: Ägypten im Mittleren Reich*. Munich: Hirmer.

Wilhelm, G. (1992a) 'Hurritische Lexikographie und Grammatik: Die hurritisch-hethitische Bilingue aus Boghazköy', in *Orientalia*, 61: 122–141.

Wilhelm, G. (1992b) 'Zum eblaitischen Gott Kura', in *Vicino Oriente*, 8: 179–188.

Wilhelm, G. (1994) 'Kumme und *Kummar: Zur hurritischen Ortsnamenbildung', in P. Calmeyer, K. Hecker, L. Jacob-Tost, C.B.F. Walker (eds), *Beiträge zur Altorientalischen Archäologie und Altertumskunde: Festschrift für B. Hrouda*. Wiesbaden: Harrassowitz: 315–319.

Wilhelm, G. (1997) 'Die Könige von Ebla nach der hurritisch-hethitischen Serie "Freilassung"', in *Altorientalische Forschungen*, 24 (Festschrift für H. Klengel): 277–293.

Winter, I.J. (1985) 'After the Battle Is Over: The Stele of Vultures and the Beginning of Historical Narrative in the Art of the Ancient Near East', in H.L. Kessler, M. Shreve Simpson (eds), *Pictorial Narrative in Antiquity and the Middle Ages* (Studies in the History of Arts 16): 11–32.

Winter, I.J. (1986) 'Eannatum and the "King of Kish"? Another Look at the Stele of the Vultures and "Cartouches" in Early Sumerian Art', in *Zeitschrift für Assyriologie*, 76: 105–112.

Winter, I.J. (1999) 'The Aesthetic Value of Lapis Lazuli in Mesopotamia', in A. Caubet (ed.), *Cornaline et pierres précieuses: La Méditerranée de l'Antiquité à l'Islam. Actes du Colloque Musée du Louvre 1995*. Paris: Musée du Louvre: 43–57.

Wolf, W. (1957) *Die Kunst Ägyptens: Gestalt und Geschichte*. Stuttgart: Kohlhammer.

Woolley, C.L (1914) *Carchemish: Report on the Excavations at Djerabis*, I: *Introductory*. London: British Museum.

Woolley, C.L. (1934) *Ur Excavations*, II: *The Royal Cemetery. A Report of the Predynastic and Sargonic Graves Excavated between 1926 and 1931*. London/ Philadelphia, PA: Oxford University Press.

Woolley, C.L. (1953) *A Forgotten Kingdom, Being a Record of the Results Obtained from the Excavation of Two Mounds, Atchana and Al Mina, in the Turkish Hatay*. Harmondsworth: Penguin Books.

Woolley, C.L. (1955) *Alalakh: An Account of the Excavations at Tell Atchana in the Hatay, 1937–1949*. Oxford: Society of Antiquaries (Reports of the Research Committee of the Society of Antiquaries of London XVIII).

Woolley, C.L., Barnett, R.D. (1952) *Carchemish: Report on the Excavations at Djerabis*, III: *The Excavations in the Inner Town*. London: British Museum.

Wright, D.P. (2004) 'Syria and Canaan', in S.J. Johnston (ed.), *Religions of the Ancient World: A Guide*. Cambridge, MA: Harvard University Press: 173–180.

Xella, P. (1986) ' "Le grand froid": Le dieu "Baradu madu" à Ébla', in *Ugarit-Forschungen*, 17: 141–156.

Xella, P. (1988a) 'Tradition und Innovation: Bemerkungen zum Pantheon von Ebla', in H. Waetzoldt, H. Hauptmann (eds) 1988: 349–358.

Xella, P. (1988b) ' "I figli del re e le figlie del re": Culto dinastico e tradizioni amorree nei rituali ugaritici', in *Studi Epigrafici e Linguistici*, 5: 219–225.

Xella, P. (1998) 'The Eblaite God Nidabal', in M. Dietrich, I. Kottsieper (eds), *"Und Moses schrieb dieses Lied auf": Studien zum Alten Testament und Alten Orient. Festschrift für O. Loretz*. Münster: Ugarit-Verlag (Alter Orient und Altes Testament CCL): 883–895.

Yadin, Y. (1972) *Hazor: The Head of All Those Kingdoms*. London: Oxford University Press.

Bibliographical update

The following titles have appeared after 2010. They are not cited in the chapter endnotes, and are presented in chronological order as a necessary complement.

Nigro, L. (2009) *Materiali e Studi Archeologici di Ebla*, VIII: *I corredi vascolari delle Tombe Reali di Ebla e la cronologia ceramica della Siria interna nel Bronzo Medio*. Rome: University of Rome.

Catagnoti, A., Fronzaroli, P. (2010) *Archivi Reali di Ebla, Testi*, XVI: *Testi di cancelleria: Il re e I funzionari*, I *(Archivio L.2769)*. Rome: University of Rome.

Matthiae, P. (2010) 'Early Syrian Palatial Architecture: Some Thoughts about Its Unity', in J. Becker, R. Hempelmann, E. Rehm (eds), *Kulturlandschaft Syrien: Zentrum und Peripherie. Festschrift für Jan-Waalke Meyer*. Münster: Ugarit-Verlag (Alter Orient und Altes Testament CCCLXXI): 349–358.

Matthiae, P. (2010) 'The Seal of Ushra-Samu, Official of Ebla, and Ishkhara's Iconography', in S.C. Melville, A.L. Slotsky (eds), *Opening the Tablet Box: Near Eastern Studies in Honor of Benjamin Foster*. Leiden/New York: Brill (Culture and History of the Ancient Near East XLII): 271–290.

Matthiae, P. (2011) 'The Gods and Rapi'uma of Yamkhad: An Interpretation of a Rare Old Syrian Cylinder Seal', in B.S. Düring, A. Wossink, P.M.M.G. Akkermans (eds), *Correlates of Complexity: Essays in Archaeology and Assyriology Dedicated to Diederik J.H. Meijer in Honour of His 65th Birthday*. Leiden: Netherlands Instituut voor het Nabije Oosten (Netherlands Instituut voor het Nabije Oosten Uitgaven van het Nederlands Instituut voor het Nabije Oosten te Leiden CXVI): 161–175.

Matthiae, P. (2011) 'Fouilles à Tell Mardikh-Ébla en 2009–2010: Les débuts de l'exploration de la Citadelle paléosyrienne', in *Académie des Inscriptions et Belles-Lettres. Comptes Rendus*: 735–773.

Pinnock, F. (2011) *Materiali e Studi Archeologici di Ebla*, IX: *Le giarette con decorazione applicata del Bronzo Medio II*. Rome: University of Rome.

Archi, A. (2012) 'Cult of the Ancestors and Funerary Practices at Ebla', in P. Pfälzner, H. Niehr, E. Pernicka, A. Wissing (eds), *(Re-)Constructing Funerary Rituals in the Ancient Near East: Proceedings of the First International Symposium of the Tübingen Post-Doctorate School "Symbols of the Dead" in May 2009*. Wiesbaden: Harrassowitz (Qatna Studien Supplementa I): 1–33.

Biga, M.G., Roccati, A. (2012) 'Tra Egitto e Siria nel III millennio a.C.', in *Atti dell'Accademia delle Scienze di Torino: Classe di Scienze Morali, Storiche e Filologiche*, 146: 17–42.

Catagnoti, A. (2012) *La grammatica della lingua di Ebla*. Florence: University of Florence (Quaderni di Semitistica XXIX).

Matthiae, P. (2012) 'L'archéologie du culte: Les ancêtres royaux dans la documentation archéologique d'Ébla et les témoignages textuels d'Ougarit', in *Académie des Inscriptions et Belles-Lettres. Comptes Rendus*: 951–992.

Peyronel, L. (2012) 'Resources Exploitation and Handicraft Activities at Tell Mardikh-Ebla (Syria) during the Early and Middle Bronze Ages', in R. Matthews, J. Curtis (eds), *Proceedings of the 7th International Congress of the Archaeology of the Ancient Near East, 12 April–16 April 2010, British Museum and UCL, London*, III. Wiesbaden: Harrassowitz: 475–496.

Pinnock, F. (2012) 'Colours and Light in the Royal Palace G of Early Syrian Ebla', in R. Matthews, J. Curtis (eds), *Proceedings of the 7th International Congress of the Archaeology of the Ancient Near East, 12 April–16 April 2010, British Museum and UCL, London*, II. Wiesbaden: Harrassowitz: 271–286.

Pinnock, F. (2012) 'Some Gublite Artifacts Possibly Made at Ebla', in *Syria*, 89: 85–100.

Biga, M.G., Charpin, D., Durand, J.-M. (eds) (2012–2013) *Recueil d'études historiques, philologiques et épigraphiques en l'honneur de Paolo Matthiae.* (*Revue d'Assyriologie*, 106–107). Paris: Presses Universitaires de France.

Archi, A. (2013) 'Ritualization at Ebla', in *Journal of Ancient Near Eastern Religions*, 13: 212–237.

Matthiae, P. (2013) *Studies on the Archaeology of Ebla 1980–2010* (Edited by F. Pinnock). Wiesbaden: Harrassowitz.

Matthiae, P., Marchetti, N. (eds) (2013) *Ebla and Its Landscape: Early State Formation in the Ancient Near East*. Walnut Creek, CA: Left Coast Press.

Orthmann, W., Matthiae, P., Al-Maqdissi, P. (eds) (2013) *Archéologie et Histoire de la Syrie*, I: *La Syrie de l'époque néolithique à l'âge du Fer*. Wiesbaden: Harrassowitz (Schriften zur vorderasiatischen Archäologie X).

Archi, A. (2014) 'La situation géopolitique de la Syrie avant l'expansion d'Akkad', in P. Butterlin, J.-C. Margueron, B. Muller, M. Al-Maqdissi, D. Beyer, A. Cavigneaux (eds), *Mari ni Est, ni Ouest: Actes du colloque tenu les 20–22 octobre 2010 à Damas, Syrie* (*Syria*, Supplément 2): 161–171.

Archi, A. (2014) 'Who Led the Army of Ebla? Administrative Documents vs. Commemorative Texts', in H. Neumann, R. Dittmann, S. Paulus, G. Neumann, A. Schuster-Brandis (eds), *Krieg und Frieden im Alten Vorderasien: 52e Rencontre Assyriologique Internationale, Münster, 17.–21. July 2006.* Münster: Ugarit-Verlag (Alter Orient und Altes Testament CDI): 19–25.

Biga, M.G. (2014) 'The Marriage of an Eblaite Princess with the King of Dulu', in S. Gaspa, A. Greco, D. Morandi Bonacossi, S. Ponchia, R. Rollinger (eds), *From Source to History: Studies on Ancient Near Eastern Worlds and Beyond. Dedicated to Giovanni Battista Lanfranchi on the Occasion of His 65th Birthday on June 23, 2014*. Münster: Ugarit-Verlag (Alter Orient und Altes Testament CDXII): 73–79.

Matthiae, P. (2014) 'Materia epica preomerica nell'Anatolia hittita: Il *Canto della liberazione* e la conquista di Ebla', in P. Canettieri, A. Punzi (eds), *Dai pochi ai molti: Studi in onore di Roberto Antonelli*, II. Rome: Viella: 1075–1090.

Matthiae, P. (2014) 'Notes et études éblaïtes, I: Le *séméion* de Hiérapolis dans l'Ébla paléosyrienne', in *Revue d'Assyriologie*, 108: 95–122.

Matthiae, P. (2014) 'Temples et palais d'Ébla protosyrienne et le problème de l'unité architecturale de la Syrie au Dynastique Archaïque final', in P. Butterlin, J.-C. Margueron, B. Muller, M. Al-Maqdissi, D. Beyer, A. Cavigneaux (eds), *Mari, ni*

Est, ni Ouest: Actes du colloque tenu les 20–22 octobre 2010 à Damas, Syrie (*Syria*, Supplément 2): 483–516.

Peyronel, L., Vacca, A., Wachter-Sarkady, C. (2014) 'Food and Drink Preparation at Ebla, Syria: New Data from the Royal Palace G (c.2450–2300 B.C.)', in *Food & History*, 12: 3–38.

Pinnock, F. (2014) 'Ancestors' Cult and Female Roles in Early and Old Syrian Syria', in *Cult and Ritual on the Levantine Coast and Its Impact on the Eastern Mediterranean Realm: Proceedings of the International Symposium, Beirut 2012*. Beirut: Ministère de la Culture (BAAL, Hors-Série X): 135–156.

D'Andrea, M., Vacca, A. (2015) 'The Northern and Southern Levant during the Late Early Bronze Age: A Reappraisal of the "Syrian Connection"', in *Studia Eblaitica*, 1: 43–73.

Matthiae, P. (2015) 'Cult Architecture between Early Bronze IVA and Middle Bronze I: Continuity and Innovation in the Formative Phase of a Great Tradition: An Evaluation', in *Studia Eblaitica*, 1: 75–108.

Peyronel, L. (2015) 'The "Outer Town" of Ebla during the Old Syrian Period: A Preliminary Analysis of the Off-Site Survey 2010', in *Studia Eblaitica*, 1: 131–164.

Pinnock, F. (2015) 'From Ebla to Guzana: The Image of Power in Syria between the Bronze and Iron Age', in *Studia Eblaitica*, 1: 109–129.

Pinnock, F. (2015) 'The King's Standard from Ebla Palace G', in *Journal of Cuneiform Studies*, 67: 3–22.

Polcaro, A. (2015) 'The Bone Talisman and the Ideology of Ancestors in Old Syrian Ebla: Tradition and Innovation in the Royal Funerary Ritual Iconography', in *Studia Eblaitica*, 1: 169–204.

Vacca, A. (2015) 'Before the Royal Palace: The Stratigraphy and Pottery Sequence of the West Unit of the Central Complex: The Building G5', in *Studia Eblaitica*, 1: 1–32.

Archi, A. (2016) 'Ebla and Mari in Years 2381/2380–2360 BC', in J. Patrier, Ph. Quenet, P. Butterlin (eds), *Mille et une empreintes: Un Alsacien en Orient. Mélanges en l'honneur du 65ᵉ anniversaire de Dominique Beyer*. Turnhout: Brepols (*Subartu* 36): 1–16.

Archi, A. (2016) 'Egypt or Iran in the Ebla Texts?', in *Orientalia*, 85: 1–49.

D'Andrea, M. (2016) 'New Data from Old Excavations: Preliminary Study of the EB IVB Pottery from Area H at Tell Mardikh-Ebla, Syria', in O. Kaelin, H.-P. Mathys (eds), *Proceedings of the 9th International Congress on the Archaeology of the Ancient Near East, 8–14 June 2014, Basel*, III. Wiesbaden: Harrassowitz: 199–215.

Matthiae, P., D'Andrea, M. (eds) (2016) *L'archeologia del sacro e l'archeologia del culto: Ebla e la Siria dall'Età del Bronzo all'Età del Ferro, Roma 8–11 ottobre 2013*. Rome: Accademia Nazionale dei Lincei (Atti dei Convegni Lincei CCCIV).

Peyronel, L. (2016) 'From Ebla to Ugarit: Lead Ingots in the Levant and Anatolia during the Bronze Age', in *Studia Eblaitica*, 2: 103–118.

Peyronel, L. (2016) 'Tablets, Sealings and Weights at Ebla: Administrative and Economic Procedures at the Beginning of the Archaic State in Syria', in *Archéo-Nil*, 26: 49–66.

Pinnock, F. (2016) 'Royal Images and Kingship Rituals in Early Syrian Ebla: A Multi-Faceted Strategy of Territorial Control in EB IVA North Inner Syria', in *Zeitschrift für Orient-Archäologie*, 9: 98–116.

Archi, A. (2017) 'How Ebla Has Changed Our Perception of the Ancient Near East in the Third Millennium B.C.', in *Ash-Sharq*, 1: 187–192.

Archi, A. (2017) 'The Two Calendars of Ebla', in *Orientalia*, 86: 181–201.

Matthiae, P. (2017) 'The Victory Panel of Early Syrian Ebla in Its Historical Context: Finding, Structure, Dating', in *Studia Eblaitica*, 3: 33–83.

Mazzoni, S. (2017) 'Seal Impressions on Jars: Images, Storage and Food' in A.M. Jasink, J. Weingarten, S. Ferrara (eds), *Non-Scribal Communication Media in the Bronze Age Aegean and Surrounding Areas*. Florence: Firenze University Press: 185–206.

Scarpa, E. (2017) *The City of Ebla: A Complete Bibliography of Its Archaeological and Textual Remains*. Venice: Edizioni Ca' Foscari.

Matthiae, P., Abdulkerim, M., Pinnock, F., Alkhalid, M. (eds) (2017) *Studies on the Archaeology of Ebla after 50 Years of Discoveries* (= *Annales Archéologiques Arabes Syriennes*, 57–58 [2014–2015]). Damascus: Ministère de la Culture.

Archi, A. (2018). *Archivi Reali di Ebla, Testi*, XX: *Administrative Texts: Allotments Texts: Allotments of Clothing for the Palace Personnel (Archive L.2769)*. Wiesbaden: Harrassowitz.

Marchetti, N., Vacca, A. (2018) 'Building Complexity: Layers from Initial EB IVA2 in Area P South at Ebla', in A. Vacca, S. Pizzimenti, M.G. Micale (eds), *A Oriente del Delta: Scritti sull'Egitto e il Vicino Oriente in onore di Gabriella Scandone Matthiae*. Rome: University of Rome (Contributi e Materiali di Archeologia Orientale XVIII): 317–358.

Matthiae, P. (2018) 'Doni faraonici alla corte di Ebla nell'Antico Regno: Una riflessione sul contesto storico', in A. Vacca, S. Pizzimenti, M.G. Micale (eds), *A Oriente del Delta: Scritti sull'Egitto e il Vicino Oriente in onore di Gabriella Scandone Matthiae*. Rome: University of Rome (Contributi e Materiali di Archeologia Orientale XVIII): 347–366.

Matthiae, P. (2018) 'The Old Syrian Temple N's Carved Basin and the Relation between Aleppo and Ebla', in *Studia Eblaitica*, 4: 109–137.

Matthiae, P., Pinnock, F., D'Andrea, M. (eds) (2018) *Ebla and Beyond: Ancient Near Eastern Studies after Fifty Years of Discoveries at Tell Mardikh. Proceedings of the International Congress Held in Rome, 15th–17th December 2014*. Wiesbaden: Harrassowitz.

Pinnock, F. (2018) 'Building Up a History of Art of the Ancient Near East: The Case of Ebla and the Third-Millennium B.C.E. Court Ladies', in S. Svärd, A. Garcia-Ventura (eds), *Studying Gender in the Ancient Near East*. Philadelphia, PA: Eisenbrauns: 353–371.

Pinnock, F. (2018) 'A New Dress for the *Maliktum*: Attires and Functions of Court Ladies at Ebla in the Early and Old Syrian Periods', in *Studia Eblaitica*, 4: 59–108.

Pinnock, F. (2018) 'Polymaterism in Early Syrian Ebla', in S. Di Paolo (ed.), *Composite Artefacts in the Ancient Near East: Exhibiting an Imaginative Materiality, Showing a Genealogical Nature*. Oxford: Archaeopress (Ancient Near Eastern Archaeology III): 73–84.

Archi, A. (2019) '"Palace" of Ebla: An Emic Approach', in D. Wircke (ed.), *Der Palast im antiken und islamischen Orient: 9. Internationales Colloquium der Deutschen Orient-Gesellschaft, 30 März–1 April 2016, Frankfurt am Main*. Wiesbaden: Harrassowitz: 1–33.

D'Andrea, M. (2019) 'The EB-MB Transition at Ebla: A State-of-the-Art Overview in the Light of the 2004–2008 Discoveries at Tell Mardikh-Ebla', in M. D'Andrea, M.G. Micale, D. Nadali, S. Pizzimenti, A. Vacca (eds), *Pearls of the Past: Studies on*

Near Eastern Art and Archaeology in Honour of Frances Pinnock. Münster: Zaphon (Marru VIII): 263–293.

Matthiae, P. (2019) 'A Problem of Iconology: A Note on the Banquets of the Old Syrian Basins of Ebla', in M. D'Andrea, M.G. Micale, D. Nadali, S. Pizzimenti, A. Vacca (eds), *Pearls of the Past: Studies on Near Eastern Art and Archaeology in Honour of Frances Pinnock*. Münster: Zaphon (Marru VIII): 571–600.

Matthiae, P. (2019) 'The Architectural Culture of the Middle Bronze Palaces of Ebla in a Historical Perspective', in M. Bietak, P. Matthiae, S. Prell (eds), *Ancient Egyptian and Ancient Near Eastern Palaces*, II: *Proceedings of a Workshop Held at the 10th ICAANE in Vienna, 25–26 April 2016*. Wiesbaden: Harrassowitz (Contributions to the Archaeology of Egypt, Nubia and the Levant, CAENL 8): 81–98.

Samir, I. (2019) *Archivi Reali di Ebla, Testi*, XIX: *Wirtschaftstexte: Monatliche Buchführung über Textilien in Ibriums Amtszeit*. Wiesbaden: Harrassowitz.

Vacca, A. (2019) 'Some Reflections about the *Chora* of Ebla during the EB III and IVA1 Periods', in M. D'Andrea, M., M.G. Micale, D. Nadali, S. Pizzimenti, A. Vacca (eds), *Pearls of the Past: Studies on Near Eastern Art and Archaeology in Honour of Frances Pinnock*. Münster: Zaphon (Marru VIII): 869–898.

Index

Entries in *italics* denote figures.